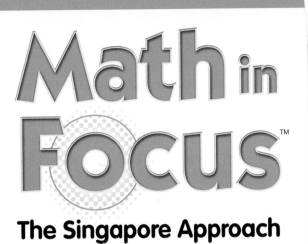

The Singapore Approach

Teacher's Edition

2A

Consultant and Author
Dr. Fong Ho Kheong

Authors
Chelvi Ramakrishnan and Michelle Choo

U.S. Consultants
Dr. Richard Bisk, Andy Clark
and Patsy F. Kanter

© 2009 Marshall Cavendish International (Singapore) Private Limited

Published by Marshall Cavendish Education
An imprint of Marshall Cavendish International (Singapore) Private Limited
A member of Times Publishing Limited

Marshall Cavendish International (Singapore) Private Limited
Times Centre, 1 New Industrial Road
Singapore 536196
Tel: +65 6411 0820
Fax: +65 6266 3677
E-mail: fps@sg.marshallcavendish.com
Website: www.marshallcavendish.com/education

Distributed by
Great Source
A division of Houghton Mifflin Harcourt Publishing Company
181 Ballardvale Street
P.O. Box 7050
Wilmington, MA 01887-7050
Tel: 1-800-289-4490
Website: www.greatsource.com

First published 2009
Reprinted 2010 (twice)

Math in Focus™ is a trademark of Times Publishing Limited.

Great Source® is a registered trademark of Houghton Mifflin Harcourt Publishing Company.

Math in Focus™ Grade 2 Teacher's Edition Book A
ISBN 978-0-669-01318-4

Printed in China
3 4 5 6 7 8   1897   16 15 14 13 12 11 10
4500259897   B C D E

Program Overview

Your Teacher's Edition is key to the successful implementation of any mathematics program. The next few pages will help you understand and appreciate the unique attributes of the **Math in Focus** *program.*

You will learn how your students will gain depth of understanding, fluency with skills, and confidence in problem solving. You will learn how to use the Workbook in conjunction with the Student Book, how to prepare students for formal assessments, and how to remediate and enrich to meet all your students' needs.

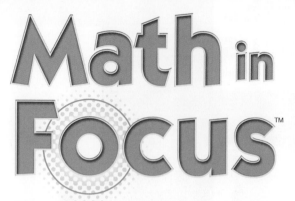

Math in Focus: The Singapore Approach *is an elementary mathematics program for Kindergarten through Grade 5 created specifically to address the recommendations for instructional materials agreed upon by national and international panels of mathematics education specialists.*

Meeting the Needs of U.S. Classrooms...

Top performing countries have gained ground on and now surpass the U.S. in mathematics education, as shown by the Trends in International Math and Science Study (TIMSS)[1]. Efforts to reverse this trend have led to a large body of solid research. Analysis of the research base has led the National Council of Teachers of Mathematics (NCTM)[2], the National Math Advisory Panel[3], the American Institutes for Research[4], and the National Research Council[5] to make several undisputed key recommendations.

1. Above all, a focused, coherent curriculum, without significant repitition year after year

2. An equal emphasis on conceptual understanding, and fluency with skills

3. Use of concrete and pictorial representations

4. Multi-step and non-routine problem-solving

...by Drawing on Success in Singapore

Singapore students have been top performers in the TIMSS assessment since 1995. Their success can be largely attributed to the mathematics curriculum revision implemented by the Singapore Ministry of Education[6] in the 1980s.

Key requirements of their instructional materials as described that parallel the recommendations of U.S. specialists are:

- **Precise framework** of concepts and skills (specifics of what to exclude as well as what to include provides hierarchy and linkage)

- **Skills and concepts** taught in depth to allow for mastery (consolidation of concepts and skills)

- **Use of a concrete to visual to abstract development** of concepts using model drawings to connect visual representation to problem solving

- **Emphasis on problem solving** considered central to all mathematics study

---

Footnotes

1. Gonzales, Patrick, Juan Carlos Guzmán, Lisette Partelow, Erin Pahlke, Leslie Jocelyn, David Kastberg, and Trevor Williams. *Highlights From the Trends in International Mathematics and Science Study:* TIMSS 2003. U.S. Department of Education, National Center for Education Statistics, 2004.

2. National Council of Teachers of Mathematics. *Curriculum Focal Points for Prekindergarten through Grade 8 Mathematics,* 2006.

3. National Mathematics Advisory Panel. *Foundations for Success.* U.S. Department of Education, 2008.

4. American Institutes for Research® *What the United States Can Learn from Singapore's World-Class Mathematics System.* U. S. Department of Education Policy and Program Studies Services, 2005.

5. National Research Council. *Adding It Up: Helping Children Learn Mathematics.* Washington, DC, National Academy Press, 2001.

6. Ministry of Education, Singapore. *Mathematics Syllabus: Primary,* 2007.

Math in Focus is the Solution

Math in Focus retains the world-class Singaporean pedagogy, methodology and instructional materials while adopting the Singaporean mathematics standards to correspond to the NCTM Focal Points of the United States.

● A Focused, Coherent Syllabus

Answering the call for a "focused, coherent progression of mathematics learning, with an emphasis on proficiency with key topics," *Math in Focus* authors created a strategic, articulated sequence of topics to be developed in depth to allow true mastery. (*see* Scope and Sequence Introduction, p. T24)

● Integrated Concepts and Skills

Math in Focus helps students build a solid conceptual understanding through use of manipulative materials and visual models. Computational skills develop from this conceptual understanding and are reinforced through practice. As skills fluency increases, understanding is reinforced in turn. (*see* Learning and Consolidating Skills and Concepts, p. T8–T11)

● Concrete to Pictorial to Abstract

The *Math in Focus: The Singapore Approach* series consistently employs the Concrete ▶ Pictorial ▶ Abstract pedagogy. Clear and engaging visuals that present concepts and model solutions allow all students regardless of language skills to focus on the math lesson.

Market research for *Math in Focus* included multiple rounds of research including focus group testing and discussions with experienced educators. Regional and national studies ensured that the student books and teacher support meet the current needs of students and teachers across the U.S.

For more details, visit www.greatsource.com/mathinfocus

● Extensive Problem Solving

The creators of *Math in Focus: The Singapore Approach* believe not only that all children can learn math but that they can also enjoy math. Students learn to use model drawings to visualize and solve problems through mathematical reasoning and critical thinking. (*see* Applying Concepts and Skills, pp. T12–T13)

National and International Research Recommendations

▶ Focus and Depth

National Council of Teachers of Mathematics

"A curriculum is more than a collection of activities: it must be coherent, focused on important mathematics, and well articulated across the grades."

—*Curriculum Focal Points for Prekindergarten through Grade 8 Mathematics*, 2006.

Math in Focus

addresses fewer topics in greater depth at each level.

- Knowledge is built carefully and thoroughly with both *multi-page* lessons and *multi-day* lessons.

- Time is built into the program to develop understanding with *hands-on activities* with manipulatives as well as *extensive skills practice*.

Grade 1, Chapter 3, Lesson 1

▶ Interlocking Concepts and Skills

National Math Advisory Panel

"Use should be made of what is clearly known from rigorous research about how children learn, especially by recognizing the mutually-reinforcing benefits of conceptual understanding, procedural fluency, and automatic (i.e., quick and effortless) recall of facts."

—*Foundations for Success*, 2008.

Math in Focus

develops concepts and skills in tandem.

- Manipulatives and visual representations provide a conceptual backbone.

- *Skills are connected to concepts* through visual representations.

- Extensive problem solving *merges conceptual understanding with computational skills*.

the *WHY*
Concept Building
Skill Building
the *HOW*

▶ Clear Visuals and Use of Models

National Research Council

"Opportunities should involve connecting symbolic representations and operations with physical or pictorial representations, as well as translating between various symbolic representations."

—*Adding It Up: Helping Children Learn Mathematics*, 2001.

Math in Focus
uses clear and engaging visuals that present concepts and model solutions.

- *Minimal text* and simple, direct visuals allow all students regardless of language skills to focus on the math lesson.

- The use of *model drawings* offer a visual representation of word problems, leading to symbolic solutions of rich and complex problems.

- Consistent use of the *concrete–pictorial–abstract pedagogy* repeatedly "models" the model-drawing problem-solving strategy.

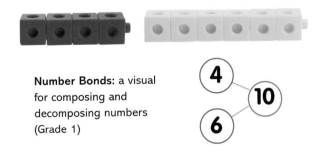

Number Bonds: a visual for composing and decomposing numbers (Grade 1)

▶ Emphasis on Problem Solving

Singapore Ministry of Education

"Mathematical problem solving is central to mathematics learning. It involves the acquisition and application of mathematics concepts and skills in a wide range of situations, including non-routine, open-ended, and real-world problems."

—*Mathematics Syllabus: Primary*, 2006.

Math in Focus
uses a scaffolded approach to solving word problems, focusing on model drawing to build success and confidence.

- The visual representation of word problems leads to symbolic solutions of *rich and complex problems*.

- Students draw on prior knowledge as well as recently acquired concepts and skills as they combine *problem-solving strategies with critical thinking skills*.

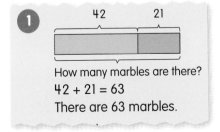

Bar Model: a visual representation of a word problem (Grade 2)

Instructional Pathway
Learning, Consolidating and Applying Grades 1–5

Math in Focus *Student Books and Workbooks follow an instructional pathway of:*

- *learning* concepts and skills through visual lessons and teacher instruction
- *consolidating* concepts and skills through practice, activities, and math journals, and
- *applying* concepts and skills with extensive problem-solving practice and challenges

Learning Concepts and Skills
Understanding the **How** *and the* **Why**

Each lesson in the Student Book is introduced with a **Learn** *element. Mathematical concepts are presented in a straightforward visual format, with specific and structured learning tasks.*

Scaffolded, coherent instruction promotes deep math understanding for all students with:

- clearly explained thought processes
- carefully selected visuals
- minimal text
- focus on both the *how* and the *why*

Building a Solid Foundation at Each Level

Concrete

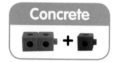

Manipulatives are used to explain abstract mathematical concepts.

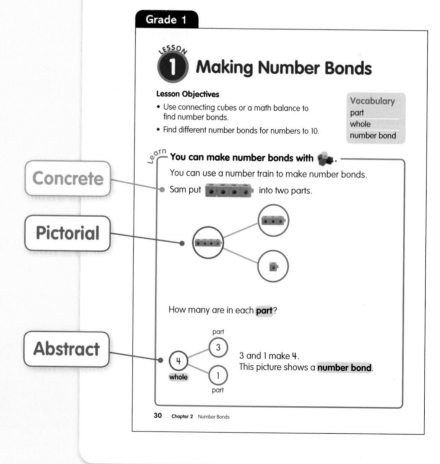

> " Increase the number, variety, and overall use of pictorial representations directly tied to concepts in textbooks. "

— National Math Advisory Panel

Within each lesson, from chapter to chapter, and from year to year, instruction follows the concrete to pictorial to abstract sequence.

Pictorial

Pictures, models, and diagrams are used to present examples with solutions.

Abstract

$$2 + 1 = 3$$

Only numerals, mathematical notation, and symbols are used once students are familiar with the abstract representation.

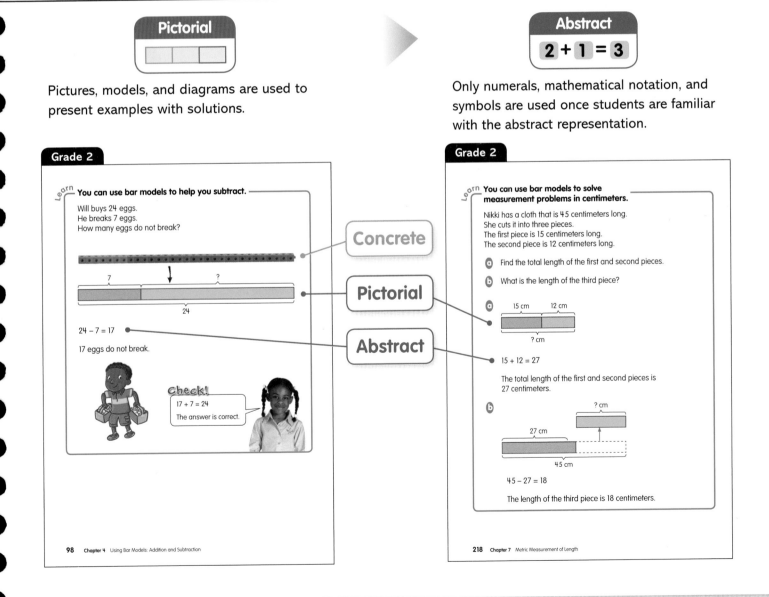

Grade 2

Learn **You can use bar models to help you subtract.**

Will buys 24 eggs.
He breaks 7 eggs.
How many eggs do not break?

Concrete

7   ↓   ?

24

Pictorial

$24 - 7 = 17$

Abstract

17 eggs do not break.

Check!
$17 + 7 = 24$
The answer is correct.

98   Chapter 4 Using Bar Models: Addition and Subtraction

Grade 2

Learn **You can use bar models to solve measurement problems in centimeters.**

Nikki has a cloth that is 45 centimeters long.
She cuts it into three pieces.
The first piece is 15 centimeters long.
The second piece is 12 centimeters long.

ⓐ Find the total length of the first and second pieces.

ⓑ What is the length of the third piece?

ⓐ   15 cm   12 cm

? cm

$15 + 12 = 27$

The total length of the first and second pieces is 27 centimeters.

ⓑ   ? cm

27 cm

45 cm

$45 - 27 = 18$

The length of the third piece is 18 centimeters.

218   Chapter 7 Metric Measurement of Length

Consolidating Concepts and Skills
for Deep Math Understanding

Extensive Practice

Each **Learn** element of the lesson is followed by opportunities to develop deeper understanding through these features:

- carefully crafted skills practice in the lesson using Guided Practice and Let's Practice

- real-world problems

- independent practice in the Workbook

- additional practice problems in the Extra Practice Book

> **Guided Practice** allows students to check their understanding while working with some guidance.

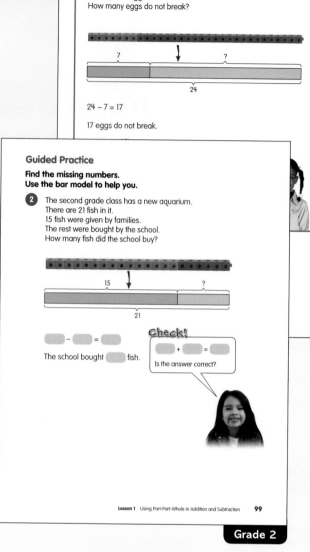

> ### Let's Practice
> consolidates learning and checks all prerequisite skills needed before students work independently in the Workbook.

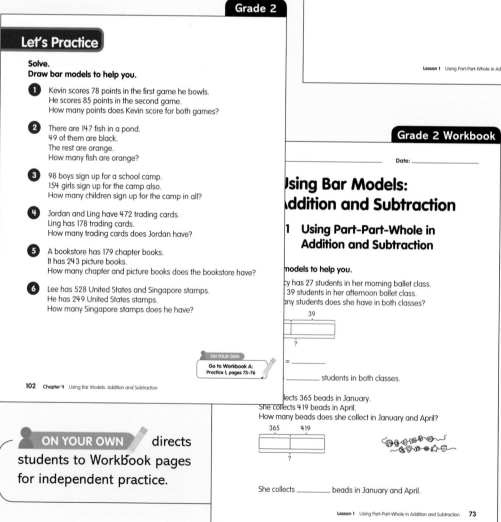

> **ON YOUR OWN** directs students to Workbook pages for independent practice.

Hands-On Work in Pairs and Small Groups

Students develop concepts and explore connections as they practice skills and reasoning processes.

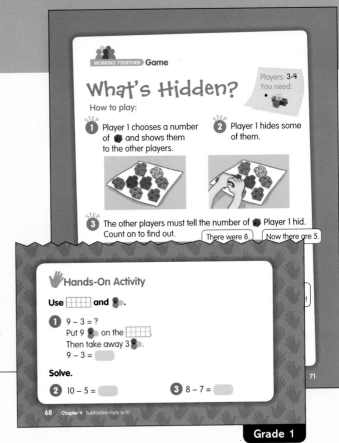

> **Hands-On Activity** and **Game** reinforce skills, concepts, and problem-solving strategies in small group or partner settings.

> **Let's Explore!** provides opportunities for students to carry out investigative activities and to discuss alternate solutions to open-ended questions.

Communication and Reflection

Students communicate with each other, discuss their thinking, and reflect on the math they are practicing.

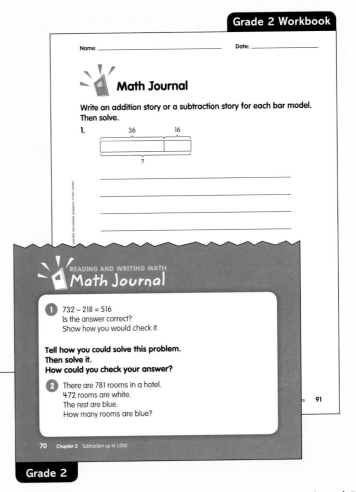

> **Math Journal** offers opportunities for students to reflect on mathematical learning.

Applying Concepts and Skills
Builds Real-World Problem Solvers

Frequent Exposure

Math in Focus: The Singapore Approach embeds problem solving throughout a lesson.

Learn elements use models to explain computation concepts. Students become accustomed to seeing and using visual models to form mental images of mathematical ideas.

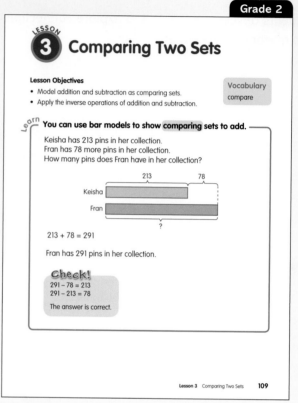

Frequent Practice

Practice pages in the Workbook include both computation and problem-solving sections.

• Each set of problems encompasses previous skills and concepts.

• Word problems progress in complexity from 1-step to 2-step to multi-step.

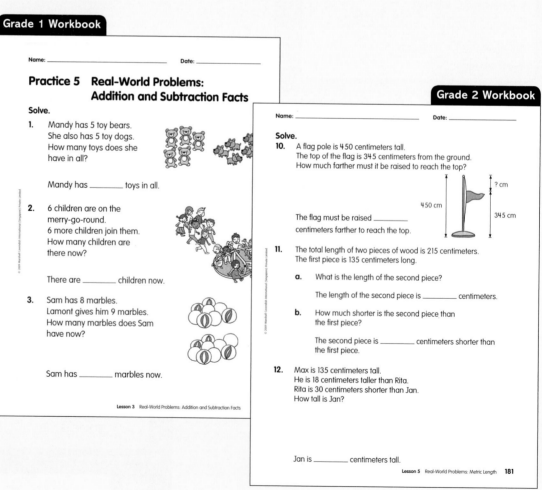

Model-Drawing Strategies

Using bar models as a problem-solving tool is taught explicitly in Grades 2–5. Students become familiar with this systematic way to translate complex word problems into mathematical equations, and avoid the common issue with not knowing where to start.

Model Drawing

- helps children solve simple and complex word problems
- develops algebraic thinking
- follows the introduction of operational skills
- helps visualize the part-whole structure of the problem
- develops operational sense
- fosters proportional reasoning

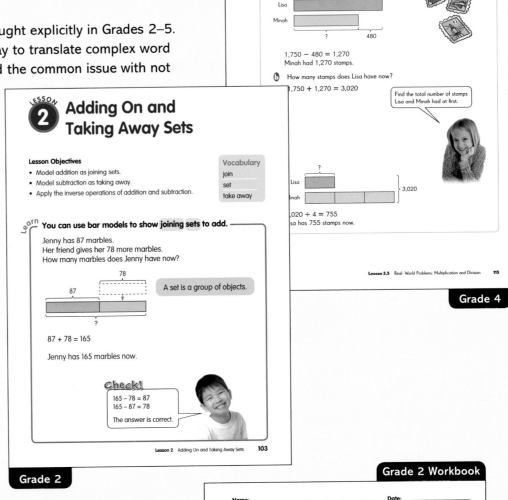

Challenging Problems

Each *Math in Focus* chapter concludes with **Put on Your Thinking Cap!** which challenges students to solve non-routine questions.

These problems ask children to draw on *deep prior knowledge* as well as recently acquired concepts, combining problem-solving strategies with *critical thinking skills*.

Critical thinking skills students develop with *Math in Focus* include:

- classifying
- comparing
- sequencing
- analyzing parts and whole
- identifying patterns and relationships
- induction (from specific to general)
- deduction (from general to specific)
- spatial visualization

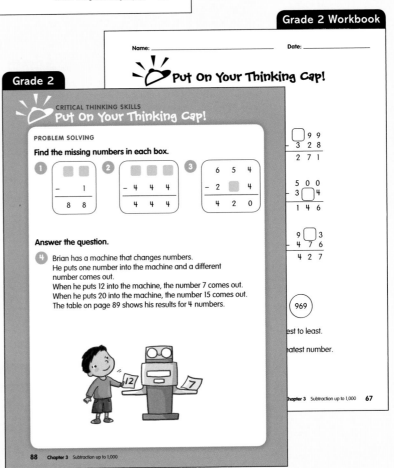

Extensive Teacher Support

Step-by-Step Support
and Embedded Professional Development

Math in Focus *Teacher's Editions provide comprehensive lesson plans with pacing suggestions, step-by-step instructional support, and embedded professional development including math background discussions and classroom management tips.*

> **Math Background** clearly outlines the mathematical significance of key concepts.

> **Skills Trace** shows concepts and skills learned in the previous level that this chapter is based on, as well as concepts and skills in the following level that this chapter will lead to.

CHAPTER 4

Chapter Overview

Subtraction Facts to 10

Math Background

Children have learned the part-whole concept and addition of numbers to 10. These two concepts are related to subtraction skills and concepts.

In this chapter, children will learn different methods of subtraction, the most basic of which is the taking-away strategy. The addition concept is the inverse of subtraction, and one of the ways to subtract involves counting on. Other strategies are counting on, counting back, and using number bonds.

All the subtraction strategies can be taught using the part-whole concept. If you know one part and the whole amount, and need to know the other part, you use subtraction. The subtraction strategy that builds and reinforces this concept most effectively involves the use of number bonds, which relate parts with the whole, and relate addition with subtraction.

As is found in addition, there is an Identity Property of Subtraction. This property states that zero subtracted from any number is equal to that number. Another property of subtraction states that any number subtracted from itself equals zero.

This chapter also requires children to use problem-solving skills to solve simple real-world word problems that involve subtraction. Children solve problems by writing subtraction sentences from number bonds.

Cross-Curricular Connections

Reading/Language Arts Read aloud *Subtraction Action* by Loreen Leedy (Holiday House, © 2002) about Miss Prime and her students' subtraction adventures at the fair. As a class, brainstorm subtraction story ideas. Choose one of them to be the setting for your own illustrated class book about subtraction.

Skills Trace

Grade K	Represent subtraction stories with small whole numbers. (Chap. 18)
Grade 1	Subtract 2-digit numbers up to 100. (Chap. 4, 8, 13, 14 and 17)
Grade 2	Subtract 3-digit numbers up to 1000. (Chap. 3, 4, and 10)

**EVERY DAY COUNTS®
Calendar Math**

The October activities provide...

Preview of geometric patterns and attributes of rectangles (skills and concepts taught at depth in Chapter 5)

Review of number patterns (Chapter 1) and length comparisons using *longer*, *shorter*, and the *same length as* (Kindergarten skill)

Practice of sums and differences involving the number 6 (see Lessons 1 and 2 of this chapter) and writing addition and subtraction sentences (see Lessons 3 and 4)

> **Every Day Counts®** is an interactive bulletin board companion piece for grades K–5 to encourage classroom discussion through all the strands.

> **Cross-Curricular Connections** provide suggestions for tying the chapter topics to other parts of the student's day.

> **Each chapter** begins with a day of guiding children to recall prior knowledge and a quick check to assess children's readiness to proceed.

✔ Quick Check

Count on to find the missing numbers in the pattern.

1 2, 3, 4, ⬡5⬡, ⬡6⬡, ⬡7⬡, 8

2 5, 6, ⬡7⬡, 8, ⬡9⬡, ⬡10⬡

Complete the number bond.

3

Student Book A p. 66

Recall Prior Knowledge

Counting

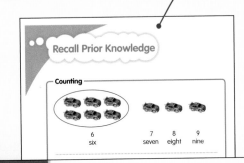

6	7	8	9
six	seven	eight	nine

Chapter Introduction

CHAPTER
4 Subtraction Facts to 10

Lesson 1 Ways to Subtract
Lesson 2 Making Subtraction Stories
Lesson 3 Real-World Problems: Subtraction
Lesson 4 Making Fact Families

Chapter 4
Vocabulary

take away	to get rid of or remove something	Lesson 1
subtract	to take away, remove, or compare	Lesson 1
minus (−)	the symbol used to show how many things to subtract	Lesson 1
subtraction sentence	a number sentence that represents taking away	Lesson 1
less than	4 is less than 5	Lesson 1
subtraction story	a word problem that is solved using a subtraction sentence	Lesson 2
fact family	NEED DEFINITION	Lesson 4

> Definitions of key chapter **Vocabulary** for easy reference.

> **Big Idea** previews what the chapter will teach and how it will be presented.

CHAPTER
4 Subtraction Facts to 10

Lesson 1 Ways to Subtract
Lesson 2 Making Subtraction Stories
Lesson 3 Real-World Problems: Subtraction
Lesson 4 Making Fact Families

 Subtraction can be used to find how many are left.

64

Student Book A p. 64

💡 Big Idea (page 64)

Basic subtraction facts are the main focus of this chapter.

- Children use strategies, such as the take-away concept, number bonds, counting on and counting back to identify and learn these facts.
- They write subtraction sentences to represent familiar situations, and begin to see the inverse relationship between addition and subtraction by using number bonds.

Chapter Opener (page 64)

The pictures illustrate the taking-away concept in subtraction using the number bond 2-3-5. This is similar to work children did in kindergarten. In this chapter subtraction will be extended to numbers up to 10 and will include writing number bonds and number sentences for number stories.

- Using the pictures in the Chapter Opener, have children describe what is happening. Be sure they recognize that the story is presented from left to right.
- **Ask:** How many stickers did the boy start with? How many stickers did he drop? How many does he have left?
- Explain to children that finding how many are left is called subtracting, and that they will learn many ways of subtracting in this chapter.

(e 66)

...ic tool to assess children's level
...fore they progress to this chapter.
...ounting skills taught in Chapter 1.
...he part-whole concept of number

Assessment

For additional assessment of children's prior knowledge and chapter readiness, use the Chapter 4 Pretest on pages 00–00 of **Assessments**.

Extensive Teacher Support

For Deep Understanding

Math in Focus: The Singapore Approach is designed for deep understanding through:

- multi-page lessons
- multi-day lessons
- support for learners
- support for teachers

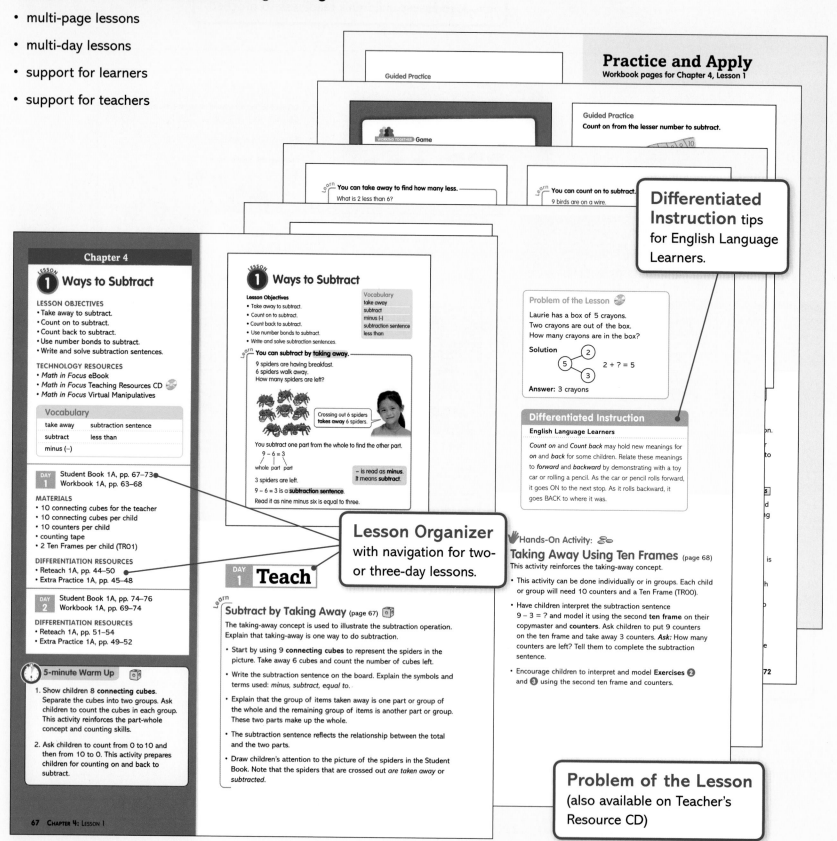

Practice and Apply
Workbook pages for Chapter 4, Lesson 1

Guided Practice

Guided Practice
Count on from the lesser number to subtract.

Guided Practice

WORKING TOGETHER Game

Learn **You can take away to find how many less.**
What is 2 less than 6?

Learn **You can count on to subtract.**
9 birds are on a wire.

Differentiated Instruction tips for English Language Learners.

Chapter 4

1 Ways to Subtract

LESSON OBJECTIVES
- Take away to subtract.
- Count on to subtract.
- Count back to subtract.
- Use number bonds to subtract.
- Write and solve subtraction sentences.

TECHNOLOGY RESOURCES
- *Math in Focus* eBook
- *Math in Focus* Teaching Resources CD
- *Math in Focus* Virtual Manipulatives

Vocabulary

take away	subtraction sentence
subtract	less than
minus (−)	

DAY 1 Student Book 1A, pp. 67–73
Workbook 1A, pp. 63–68

MATERIALS
- 10 connecting cubes for the teacher
- 10 connecting cubes per child
- 10 counters per child
- counting tape
- 2 Ten Frames per child (TR01)

DIFFERENTIATION RESOURCES
- Reteach 1A, pp. 44–50
- Extra Practice 1A, pp. 45–48

DAY 2 Student Book 1A, pp. 74–76
Workbook 1A, pp. 69–74

DIFFERENTIATION RESOURCES
- Reteach 1A, pp. 51–54
- Extra Practice 1A, pp. 49–52

5-minute Warm Up

1. Show children 8 **connecting cubes**. Separate the cubes into two groups. Ask children to count the cubes in each group. This activity reinforces the part-whole concept and counting skills.

2. Ask children to count from 0 to 10 and then from 10 to 0. This activity prepares children for counting on and back to subtract.

1 Ways to Subtract

Lesson Objectives
- Take away to subtract.
- Count on to subtract.
- Count back to subtract.
- Use number bonds to subtract.
- Write and solve subtraction sentences.

Vocabulary
take away
subtract
minus (−)
subtraction sentence
less than

Learn **You can subtract by taking away.**
9 spiders are having breakfast.
6 spiders walk away.
How many spiders are left?

Crossing out 6 spiders **takes away** 6 spiders.

You subtract one part from the whole to find the other part.
9 − 6 = 3
whole part part

3 spiders are left.

9 − 6 = 3 is a **subtraction sentence**.
Read it as nine minus six is equal to three.

− is read as **minus**. It means **subtract**.

DAY 1 Teach

Lesson Organizer with navigation for two- or three-day lessons.

Learn **Subtract by Taking Away** (page 67)
The taking-away concept is used to illustrate the subtraction operation. Explain that taking-away is one way to do subtraction.

- Start by using 9 **connecting cubes** to represent the spiders in the picture. Take away 6 cubes and count the number of cubes left.

- Write the subtraction sentence on the board. Explain the symbols and terms used: *minus, subtract, equal to.*

- Explain that the group of items taken away is one part or group of the whole and the remaining group of items is another part or group. These two parts make up the whole.

- The subtraction sentence reflects the relationship between the total and the two parts.

- Draw children's attention to the picture of the spiders in the Student Book. Note that the spiders that are crossed out *are taken away* or *subtracted*.

Problem of the Lesson

Laurie has a box of 5 crayons.
Two crayons are out of the box.
How many crayons are in the box?

Solution
5 ⟨ 2 / 3 ⟩   2 + ? = 5

Answer: 3 crayons

Differentiated Instruction

English Language Learners

Count on and *Count back* may hold new meanings for *on* and *back* for some children. Relate these meanings to *forward* and *backward* by demonstrating with a toy car or rolling a pencil. As the car or pencil rolls forward, it goes ON to the next stop. As it rolls backward, it goes BACK to where it was.

Hands-On Activity:
Taking Away Using Ten Frames (page 68)
This activity reinforces the taking-away concept.

- This activity can be done individually or in groups. Each child or group will need 10 counters and a Ten Frame (TR00).

- Have children interpret the subtraction sentence 9 − 3 = ? and model it using the second **ten frame** on their copymaster and **counters**. Ask children to put 9 counters on the ten frame and take away 3 counters. **Ask:** How many counters are left? Tell them to complete the subtraction sentence.

- Encourage children to interpret and model **Exercises 2** and **3** using the second ten frame and counters.

Problem of the Lesson
(also available on Teacher's Resource CD)

Practice and Apply
Workbook pages provide independent practice with the day's concepts and skills.

Common Error alerts help teachers identify and correct likely misconceptions.

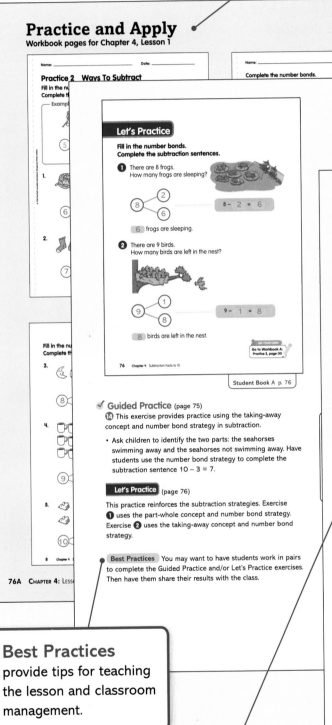

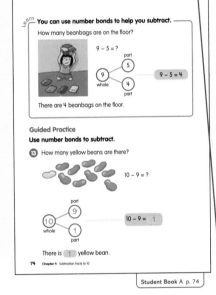

Best Practices provide tips for teaching the lesson and classroom management.

Day Two of Lesson 1 continues to develop the same topic.

Guided Practice provides ongoing assessment.

Core Components

The direct correlation of **Student Books** and **Workbooks** provides the full program of learning, consolidating and practicing. Student Books and Workbooks are designed to work together. The Student Books focus on learning, classroom teaching, and discussion. The Workbook problems are assigned for individual work.

Student Book

Workbook

Teacher's Edition

Student Book

Workbook

Teacher's Edition

Differentiation Resources

English Language Learners

The clear drawings and visual aspect of *Math in Focus: The Singapore Approach* means the entire program is inherently accessible to English language learners. Additionally, the *Math in Focus* Teacher's Edition provides lesson-specific suggestions for facilitating instruction for English language learners.

For Struggling Learners

Reteach pages provide more exposure to concepts for those students who need more time to master new skills or concepts. Additionally, the *Math in Focus* Teacher's Edition provides tips for helping struggling students at point of use.

For On-Level Students

Extra Practice pages correlate directly to the Workbook practices. Here again, Put on Your Thinking Cap! questions provide more practice on both non-routine and strategy-based questions.

School-to-Home Connections

includes newsletters in English and Spanish to promote family involvement with chapter vocabulary, concepts and Math activity suggestions.

For Advanced Students

Enrichment exercises of varying complexity provide advanced students opportunities to extend the concepts, skills, and strategies they have learned in the Student Book and Workbook.

The *Math in Focus* **Kindergarten** program has a unique instructional pathway with special Kindergarten components. For more information visit www.greatsource.com/mathinfocus

Assessment Opportunities

Assessment opportunities in *Math in Focus* offer a complete picture of student progress. The Student Book, the Workbook, the Assessments Book and the Teacher's Edition all work in concert to provide both short-term and long-term assessment options.

Prior Knowledge

- **Recall Prior Knowledge** in the Student Book: At the start of each chapter, students review related prior knowledge, then try Quick Check questions to ensure they are ready for the new chapter.

- **Pre-Test** in the Assessments Book: A paper and pencil pretest is also available for a more formal diagnostic assessment.

Ongoing Diagnostic

- **Guided Practice** in the Student Book: After each Learn element students work out Guided Practice examples with either peer or teacher input. Tips in the Teacher's Edition help in assessing student understanding.

- **Common Errors** in the Teacher's Edition. Common Error alerts help teachers recognize and correct potential misconceptions before students practice on their own.

Formal Assessment

- **Chapter Review/Test** in the Workbook: This can be used as either review exercises or formal assessment.

- **Chapter Assessment** (Test Prep) in the Assessments Book: This can be used as an alternate chapter test.

- **Cumulative and Mid-Year Assessments** in the Workbook: These Assessments provide opportunities for consolidation of concepts and skills from small chunks of chapters.

- **Benchmark Tests** in the Assessments Book: Midway through each book, these assessments provide further test-prep practice combined with the opportunity to consolidate concepts and skills acquired over a period of time.

- **Mid-Year and End-of-Year Tests** in the Assessments Book: These end-of book assessments in test-prep format provide cumulative assessment for each book.

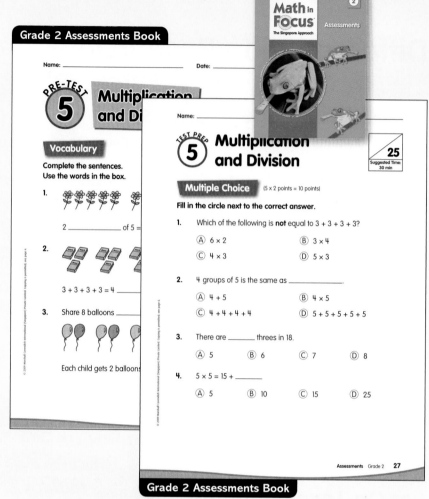

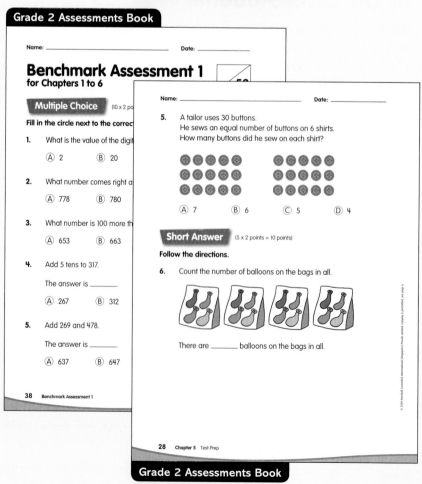

Classroom Manipulatives Kit for Grade 2

Manipulative use plays a key role in the concrete-pictorial-abstract learning sequence. The following materials are included in the Grade 2 Math in Focus Classroom Manipulatives Kit.

Grade 2 Manipulatives Kit	Suggested Alternatives
Attribute blocks	Laminated construction paper cutouts
Base-ten blocks	Grid-paper cutouts
Blank number cubes with stickers	Number cards, spinners
Coin and bill combination set	Real coins and construction-paper bills
Connecting cubes	Paper clips
Counters	Coins, beans, or paper clips
Craft sticks	Marker sets, unused pencils
Demonstration clock	Cardboard clock face with hands fastened with brad
Dual scale ruler	Classroom inch rulers, centimeter rulers
Dual-dial platform scale	Kitchen scale (grams and ounces), bathroom scale (kilograms and pounds)
Geometric solids	Cans, boxes, balls, or shapes made from modeling clay
Measuring pitchers	Kitchen measuring cups
Measuring tape	String and meter stick / yardstick
Number cubes	Number cards, spinners
Ten-sided dice	Number cards, spinners
Transparent spinners	Number cards

Technology Resources

Convenient, practical, technology-based resources available online and on CD-ROMs to facilitate class instruction and discussions.

Online eBooks (Student Book, Workbook, and Teacher's Edition pages) for convenient access or use with projection technology

Online Assessment Generator to create customized tests and practice sets

Math in Focus
Virtual Manipulatives CD-ROM for use with interactive whiteboard technology or other projection technology

Teacher Resources CD-ROM with Problem of the Lessons, Reteach, Extra Practice, Enrichment, Assessments, School-to-Home Connections and additional blackline masters in printable pdf format

 Online Resources
Visit www.greatsource.com/mathinfocus for more information.

Program Authors and Consultants

Program Authors Grades 1–5

Dr. Fong Ho Kheong

Dr. Fong Ho Kheong is an Associate Professor and the Head of Math and Science Department of the Emirates College for Advanced Education in Abu Dhabi, United Arab Emirates. He was involved in training Mathematics teachers in the National Institute of Education, Nanyang Technological University, Singapore, for 25 years. He is the Founding President of the Association of the Mathematics Educators, Singapore.

Dr. Fong specializes in teaching both high-ability children and children who have problems in mathematics. His research work includes diagnosing children with mathematical difficulties, teaching thinking to solve mathematical problems, and applying psychological theories for the teaching and learning of mathematics. His experience in curriculum development has led him to innovate the use of the model-drawing approach to tackle challenging problems. He is the consultant and principal author of Marshall Cavendish's *My Pals are Here!* math series, which is currently being used by 80% of the primary schools in Singapore.

Chelvi Ramakrishnan

Chelvi Ramakrishnan has been teaching for 25 years and has authored primary mathematics books since 1997.

Bernice Lau Pui Wah

Bernice Lau Pui Wah has been teaching for 36 years in primary and secondary schools. She has authored primary mathematics books since 1997.

Michelle Choo

Michelle Choo has been teaching in Singapore for 20 years, including 5 years in the Gifted Education Program. She has been writing primary mathematics books for the past 12 years and also conducts math review classes and workshops on the use of problem-solving skills and strategies.

Gan Kee Soon

Gan Kee Soon has been an Inspector of Schools, a Principal of a secondary school and a Lecturer at the National Institute of Education, Nanyang Technological University, Singapore. There, for 22 years, he trained and supervised primary mathematics teachers.

Kindergarten Program Author

Dr. Pamela Sharpe

Dr. Pamela Sharpe has been involved in training teachers in both Singapore and the United Kingdom for 38 years and has also played a major role in setting up early childhood programs in Singapore. She was formerly an associate professor at the National Institute of Education, Nanyang Technological University, Singapore. She is currently a part time lecturer there, as well as a consultant for early childhood programs and early childhood intervention programs.

Dr. Sharpe specializes in teaching both high-ability children and children who have problems in mathematics at the preschool level. Her research work includes studying the adjustment patterns of children in transition from preschool to primary school, as well as identifying and assessing preschool children with special needs. Dr. Sharpe has also been deeply involved in the development of the preschool mathematics curriculum in Singapore.

U.S. Consultants

Andy Clark

Andy Clark was the Math Coordinator for Portland Public Schools in Portland, Oregon, where he was previously an elementary and middle school teacher. Andy is coauthor of *Every Day Counts® Calendar Math, Every Day Counts® Algebra Readiness, Partner Games,* and *Summer Success®: Math* published by Great Source Education Group.

Patsy F. Kanter

Patsy F. Kanter is an author, teacher, and math consultant. Until 1997, Patsy was the Lower School Math Coordinator and Assistant Principal at Isidore Newman School in New Orleans, Louisiana, for 13 years where she developed and implemented a hands-on activity-based math program. Patsy is the senior author of numerous supplemental math programs including *Afterschool Achievers: Math Club K-5, Summer Success®: Math K-8,* co-author of *Every Day Counts® Calendar Math Grades K-6,* and *Every Day Counts® Partner Games* K-6, published by Great Source Education Group.

Dr. Richard Bisk

Dr. Richard Bisk is a professor in the Mathmatics Department at Worcester State College in Massachusetts. For over thirty years, he has taught a wide array of mathematics courses and has focused on improving the mathematical understanding of teachers. He has provided professional development using the Singapore Math materials since 2000.

Teacher Reviewers

Judy Chambers, Educational Consultant
Fayetteville, GA

Carolyn Goodnight, Grade 4 Teacher
Helen Carr Castello Elementary School
Elk Grove, CA

Shelly Gufert, Grade 5 Special Education
PS/MS 95X
Bronx, NY

Karin Hanson, Math Curriculum Chair
St. Robert School
Shorewood, WI

Diane Popp, Middle School Teacher
St. Rita of Cascia School
Dayton, OH

Lorianne Rotz, Assistant Principal
St. Margaret Mary Catholic School
Winter Park, FL

Roslyn Rowley-Penk, Lead Science Teacher
Maplewood Heights Elementary
Renton, WA

Elizabeth Sher, Curriculum Coordinator
Gwyneed-Mercy Academy Elementary
Spring House, PA

Nadine Solomon, Elementary Math &
Science Specialist
City of Arlington
Arlington, MA

Kathryn Tobon, Curriculum Program
Specialist
Broward County
Broward Country, FL

Jeanette Valore, Grade 4 Math and
Science Teacher
St. Anthony of Padua Catholic School
The Woodlands, TX

Melissa Walsh, Elementary Math Coach
Baldwin-Whitehall School District
Pittsburgh, PA

Key Differences
and Distinguishing Characteristics

Articulated Sequence

Math in Focus answers the call for a coherent sequence of topics giving students time to master foundational topics, so that little repetition is required the next year. Thus, each grade level covers fewer topics but in more depth, and you will not find all topics in every grade level.

- **"Missing topics"** When a topic appears to be "missing," you can be assured that it is found in either an earlier or later grade level. For example you will find calendar concepts in grades K and 1, but not repeated in grade 2.

- **More advanced** As a result of not repeating topics year after year, students who use *Math in Focus* will advance faster than students in other programs. As a result, you may find topics that seem to be "too advanced." However, you will find your students easily able to handle the challenge as long as they have had the appropriate preliminary instruction.

Preparation for Algebra

Math in Focus answers the call to prepare students for Algebra. As recommended by the National Math Panel, the *Math in Focus* sequence of topics emphasizes:

- **Number sense, basic facts, and computation** An early understanding of composition and decomposition of numbers is developed in tandem with mastery of basic facts and computation algorithms in Grades K–2.

- **Fractions and proportional reasoning** Significant time is allocated for in-depth work with fractions in Grades 3–5.

- **Problem-solving** Challenging problem-solving is built into each chapter in every grade level.

Developmental Continuum

Kindergarten	Grades 1–2	Grades 3–5

View the complete K–5 Scope and Sequence at **www.greatsource.com/mathinfocus**

Foundational concepts through songs, rhymes, hands-on activities

- counting
- sorting
- number sense

Concept and skill development through hands-on instruction and practice

- basic facts
- place value
- mental math
- geometry concepts

Emphasis on problem-solving, skill consolidation, and a deep understanding in preparation for algebra

- fractions
- decimals
- ratios
- model drawing
- expressions, equations, and inequalities

	Grade 1	Grade 2	Grade 3
Number and Operations			
Sets and Numbers	Use concrete and pictorial models to create a set with a given number of objects. (Up to 100) Group objects and numbers up to 100 in tens and ones. Use cardinal numbers up to 100 and ordinal numbers up to 10th.	Use concrete and pictorial models to create a set with a given number of objects. (Up to 1,000) Group objects and numbers up to 1,000 into hundreds, tens, and ones. Group objects into equal sized groups.	
Number Representation	Use number bonds to represent number combinations. Represent numbers to 100 on a number line.	Use place-value models to create equivalent representations of numbers. Represent numbers to 1,000 on a number line.	Represent numbers to 10,000 in different equivalent forms.
Count	Count to 100. Count by 1s, 2s, 5s, and 10s forward and backward to 100.	Count to 1,000. Count by multiples of ones, tens, and hundreds.	Count to 10,000. Count by hundreds and thousands.
Compare and Order	Compare and order whole numbers to 100. Compare and order using the terms *same, more, fewer, greater than, less than, equal to, greatest, least*.	Compare and order whole numbers to 1,000. Use <, >, = to compare whole numbers.	Compare and order whole numbers to 10,000.
Place Value	Use place value models and place-value charts to represent numbers to 100. Express numbers to 100 in standard and word forms.	Use base-ten models and place-value charts to represent numbers to 1,000. Express numbers to 1,000 in terms of place value. Compose and decompose multi-digit numbers (including expanded form).	Use place-value models to read, write, and represent numbers to 10,000.

Number and Operations (continued)	Grade 1	Grade 2	Grade 3
Fraction Concepts		Connect geometric concepts with unit fractions halves, thirds, fourths.	Understand the meanings and uses of fractions including fraction of a set.
		Understand the relationship between a fraction and a whole.	Understand that the size of a fractional part is relative to the size of the whole.
		Compare and order halves, thirds, fourths using bar models.	Compare fractions using models and number lines.
			Identify equivalent fractions through the use of models, multiplication, division and number lines.
			Add and subtract like fractions.
Decimal Concepts		Use the dollar sign and decimal point.	Use the dollar sign and decimal point in money amounts.
Money	Identify and relate coin values (penny, nickel, dime, quarter).	Identify $1, $5, $10, $20 bills.	Add and subtract money.
	Count and make coin combinations.	Count and make combinations of coins and bills. Compare money amounts.	Solve real-world problems involving addition and subtraction of money.
Whole Number Computation: Addition and Subtraction	Model addition and subtraction situations.	Model addition and subtraction with place value.	Model regrouping in addition and subtraction with place value.
	Use models, numbers, and symbols for addition and subtraction facts to 20.	Recall addition and subtraction facts.	Add and subtract whole numbers to 10,000.
	Use the order, grouping, and zero properties to develop addition and subtraction fact strategies.	Use different methods to develop fluency in adding and subtracting multi-digit numbers.	
	Add and subtract up to 2-digit numbers with and without regrouping.	Add and subtract whole numbers to 1,000.	
Whole Number Computation: Addition and Subtraction Real-World Problems	Formulate addition and subtraction stories.	Solve multi-digit addition and subtraction problems using a bar model.	Solve addition and subtraction problems with greater numbers using a bar model.
	Solve addition and subtraction problems using basic facts.		

	Grade 1	Grade 2	Grade 3
Number and Operations (continued)			
Whole Number Computation: Multiplication and Division Concepts	Count by 2s, 5s, and 10s. Adding the same number to multiply. Represent sharing equally and making equal groups.	Multiply and divide with 2, 3, 4, 5, and 10. Represent multiplication as repeated addition. Represent division as repeated subtraction. Use the ×, ÷, and = symbols to represent multiplication and division situations.	Multiply and divide with 6, 7, 8, and 9. Represent multiplication in different ways. Represent division in different ways.
Whole Number Computation: Multiplication and Division Algorithms			Multiply ones, tens, and hundreds with and without regrouping. Use addition and multiplication properties to multiply. Divide tens and ones with and without regrouping, no remainder.
Whole Number Computation: Multiplication and Division Real-World Problems		Use bar models to represent multiplication and division situations. Solve multiplication and division fact problems.	Use bar models to represent multiplication and division situations. Solve one and two-step multiplication and division problems.
Fraction Computation		Add and subtract like fractions. (halves, thirds, fourths)	Add and subtract like fractions.
Decimal Computation	Add and subtract money.	Solve addition and subtraction money problems.	Add and subtract money amounts.
Estimation and Mental Math	Use mental math strategies to add and subtract. Estimate quantity by using referents.	Use mental math strategies to add and subtract. Round to the nearest ten to estimate sums and differences.	Use mental math strategies to add subtract, multiply, and divide. Use front-end estimation and rounding to estimate sums and differences.

Table of Contents

Book **A**

CHAPTER 1 Numbers to 1,000

Recall Prior Knowledge and Quick Check
Number bonds • Counting • Counting on from a given number • Using objects
to show numbers • Using base-ten blocks to show numbers and place value
• Comparing numbers • Making number patterns

1 Counting [2 DAY Lesson]

Learn Use base-ten blocks to show numbers • Use base-ten blocks to count on by ones
• Use base-ten blocks to count on by tens • Use base-ten blocks to count on by hundreds

Let's Practice and Practice and Apply Workbook A: Practice 1

2 Place Value [2 DAY Lesson]

Learn Use base-ten blocks and a place-value chart to show a number • Write numbers in
word form, standard form, and expanded form

Game Show the Number!

Let's Practice and Practice and Apply Workbook A: Practice 2

3 Comparing Numbers [2 DAY Lesson]

Learn Use base-ten blocks to compare numbers

Game Roll and Show!

Let's Practice and Practice and Apply Workbook A: Practice 3

Look for **Assessment Opportunities**

Student Book A and Student Book B	**Workbook A and Workbook B**
• Quick Check at the beginning of every chapter to assess chapter readiness	• Chapter Review/Test in every chapter to review or test chapter material
• Guided Practice after every example or two to assess readiness to continue lesson	• Cumulative Reviews eight times during the year
	• Mid-Year and End-of-Year Reviews to assess test readiness

CHAPTER 2 Addition up to 1,000

1 Addition Without Regrouping 38

    Learn Add using base-ten blocks and a place-value chart

    Let's Practice and **Practice and Apply** Workbook A: Practice 1 and 2 .... **40–41**

2 Addition with Regrouping in Ones 42

    Learn Add using base-ten blocks and a place-value chart to regroup ones

    Game Make a Hundred!

    Let's Practice and **Practice and Apply** Workbook A: Practice 3 and 4 .... **44–45**

Look for **Practice** and **Problem Solving**

Student Book A and Student Book B	**Workbook A and Workbook B**
• **Let's Practice** in every lesson	• **Independent Practice** for every lesson
• *Put on Your Thinking Cap!* in every chapter	• *Put on Your Thinking Cap!* in every chapter

CHAPTER
3 Subtraction up to 1,000

CHAPTER 4 Using Bar Models: Addition and Subtraction

CHAPTER

5 Multiplication and Division

1 How to Multiply 2 DAY Lesson **127**

2 How to Divide 2 DAY Lesson **134**

3 Real-World Problems: Multiplication and Division **142**

CHAPTER 7 Metric Measurement of Length

CHAPTER

8 Mass

Comparing weights of objects on a balance • Finding weights of objects in non-standard units • Adding and subtracting without regrouping • Adding and subtracting with regrouping

1 Measuring in Kilograms

Learn Compare mass using kilograms • The mass of an object can be equal to 1 kilogram • The mass of an object can be less than 1 kilogram • The mass of an object can be more than 1 kilogram • Use a balance scale to find the mass of objects • Subtract to find the mass of an object

Hands-On Activity Guess and measure the mass of objects

Let's Practice and **Practice and Apply** Workbook A: Practice 1

2 Comparing Mass in Kilograms

Learn Compare masses in kilograms

Let's Practice and **Practice and Apply** Workbook A: Practice 2

3 Measuring in Grams

Learn Use smaller units to measure the mass of lighter objects • Use the measuring scale to measure the mass of objects less than 1 kilogram

Hands-On Activity Use a measuring scale to find mass

Let's Practice and **Practice and Apply** Workbook A: Practice 3

4 Comparing Mass in Grams

Learn Compare masses in grams • Subtract to find the difference in mass

Hands-On Activities Guess, measure, and compare masses of objects • Subtract to find the difference in mass

Let's Practice and **Practice and Apply** Workbook A: Practice 4

CHAPTER

9

Volume

CHAPTER 10 Mental Math and Estimation

1 Meaning of Sum 6

    Learn Meaning of sum

2 Mental Addition [2 DAY Lesson] 8

    Learn Add ones to a 2-digit number mentally using the 'add 10 then subtract the extra ones'
    strategy • Add ones to a 3-digit number mentally using the 'add the ones' strategy •
    Add ones to a 3-digit number mentally using the 'add 10 then subtract the extra ones'
    strategy • Add tens to a 3-digit number mentally using the 'add the tens' strategy •
    Add tens to a 3-digit number mentally using the 'add 100 then subtract the extra tens'
    strategy • Add hundreds to a 3-digit number mentally using the 'add the hundreds' strategy

    Game Add Mentally!

    Let's Explore! Different ways of adding numbers mentally

Look for Assessment Opportunities

Student Book A and Student Book B	Workbook A and Workbook B
• **Quick Check** at the beginning of every chapter to assess chapter readiness	• **Chapter Review/Test** in every chapter to review or test chapter material
• **Guided Practice** after every example or two to assess readiness to continue lesson	• **Cumulative Reviews** eight times during the year
	• **Mid-Year** and **End-of-Year Reviews** to assess test readiness

Look for **Practice** and **Problem Solving**

Student Book A and Student Book B	**Workbook A and Workbook B**
• **Let's Practice** in every lesson	• **Independent Practice** for every lesson
• Put on Your Thinking Cap! in every chapter	• Put on Your Thinking Cap! where applicable

CHAPTER 11 Money

1 Coins and Bills 〔3 DAY〕 Lesson 46

Learn Bills have different values • Exchange bills • Combine bills to show a given amount • Exchange a one-dollar bill for coins • Count the coins • Put bills and coins together to find out how much money there is in all • Write an amount of money in different ways • Exchange cents for dollars • Exchange dollars for cents

Let's Explore! Change pennies for other coins • Ways to show amount of money

Hands-On Activity Count amounts of money

2 Comparing Amounts of Money 62

Learn Use dollars and cents tables to compare amounts of money

3 Real-World Problems: Money 66

Learn Use bar models to solve real-world problems

Fractions

1 Understanding Fractions 75

Learn Make equal parts in many ways • Use fractions to describe equal parts of a whole • Name fractional parts • Use model drawings to show a whole in different ways

Hands-On Activity Show equal parts of a whole • Draw models to show equal parts of a whole

2 Comparing Fractions 83

Learn Use models to compare fractions • Use identical models to compare $\frac{1}{2}, \frac{1}{3}, \frac{1}{4}$, and arrange them in order

Hands-On Activity Use paper strips to compare and order fractions

3 Adding and Subtracting Like Fractions 90

Learn Fractions can name more than one equal part of a whole • Use fraction models to add like fractions • Use fraction models to subtract like fractions

Game Fix and Win!

CHAPTER 13 Customary Measurement of Length

1 Measuring in Feet 103

Learn Use a ruler to measure length and height

Hands-On Activity Guess the lengths of objects in the classroom and measure using a ruler

2 Comparing Lengths in Feet 107

Learn Compare lengths or heights in feet

Hands-On Activity Use a ruler to compare lengths of objects on the playground

3 Measuring in Inches 111

Learn Use inches to measure the length of shorter objects • Use a ruler to measure height and length of objects to the nearest inch • Measure objects using a different start point

4 Comparing Lengths in Inches 118

Learn Measure in inches to compare the lengths of objects

Hands-On Activity Compare lengths of objects in inches

5 Real-World Problems: Customary Length 122

Learn Use bar models to solve measurement problems

CHAPTER
14

Time

1 The Minute Hand 133

2 Reading and Writing Time. 137

3 Using A.M. and P.M. 142

4 Elapsed Time 150

CHAPTER
(15) Multiplication Tables of 3 and 4

CHAPTER 16 Using Bar Models: Multiplication and Division

CHAPTER 17 Picture Graphs

CHAPTER 18 Lines and Surfaces

CHAPTER 19 Shapes and Patterns

1 Plane Shapes [3 DAY] Lesson **271**

> **Learn** Get to know more plane shapes • Combine and separate plane shapes • Make figures by combining different shapes • Separate the plane shapes that make up a figure • Use dot grid paper to draw plane figures • Use square grid paper to draw plane figures
>
> **Hands-On Activities** Make a list of things that have plane shapes • Trace, cut, and combine shapes to form other bigger shapes • Use cut-outs to make figures • Draw lines to show the different shapes in a figure
>
> **Let's Practice** and **Practice and Apply** Workbook B: Practice 1 . . . .**284–285**

2 Solid Shapes **287**

> **Learn** Build models with solid shapes
>
> **Hands-On Activity** Use solids to make models
>
> **Let's Practice** and **Practice and Apply** Workbook B: Practice 2 . . . . **291**

3 Making Patterns [2 DAY] Lesson **292**

> **Learn** Make repeating patterns with plane shapes • Make repeating patterns with plane shapes that change in more than one way • Make repeating patterns with solid shapes • Make repeating patterns with solid shapes that change in more than one way
>
> **Hands-On Activity** Make a pattern mobile
>
> **Let's Practice** and **Practice and Apply** Workbook B: Practice 3 . . . .**300–301**
>
> Put on Your Thinking Cap! Problem Solving. **303**
>
> **Practice and Apply** Workbook B: Challenging Practice **303**

Chapter Wrap Up **304–305**
  Workbook B: Chapter Review/Test **305A**
Assessments Book Test Prep 19 . . . . **305B**
Workbook B: Cumulative Review for Chapters 18 and 19. . . . . **305C**
Workbook B: End-of-Year Review. **305D**
Assessments Book End-of-Year Test **305G**

Glossary (Book B) **306–309**

Teacher Resources

Chapter Overview

Numbers to 1,000

Math Background

In Grade 1, children learned to read, write, count, and compare up to 100. In this chapter, children will extend their concept of numbers, and learn how to count, read, and write up to 1,000. Base-ten blocks, place-value charts, and number lines are used to develop the association between the physical representation of the number, the number symbol, and the number word. At this stage, children are still shown concrete representations to help them better understand the concept of numbers.

The concept of place value of ones and tens is reinforced and children are now taught the *hundreds* place value. Children are expected to be able to identify a number and place it according to the value of its digits in terms of ones, tens, and hundreds. Children are also expected to be able to identify numbers in both numerals and words, for example, given the number 538, children should be able to read, recognize, and write it as *five hundred thirty-eight* in words. This is a fundamental skill which children may need later on in life for everyday activities such as writing a check.

Children are encouraged to compare and verbally describe more than two numbers in a set using the terms *least* and *greatest*. The ability to compare will also enable children to grasp the increasing or decreasing order of numbers and hence complete number patterns. This skill will help children in understanding other topics that they will learn later in this book such as *length*, *weight,* and *volume*, when they have to compare different units of measure.

Cross-Curricular Connections

Reading/Language Arts Have children work in pairs to create and solve riddles. For example, *I am 2 groups of hundreds, 3 groups of tens, and 6 groups of ones. What number am I?* (Answer: 236)

Physical Education Draw a chalk number line from 235 to 255 on the ground. Invite children to hop or skip to a number as you say it aloud. For example, *say:* 253. Guide children to locate and hop to 253. For variation, *say:* one number before 242. Guide children to find and skip to 241, and so on.

Skills Trace

Grade 1	Count and compare numbers to 100. (Chaps. 1, 7, 12, and 16)
Grade 2	Count and compare numbers to 1,000. (Chap. 1)
Grade 3	Count and compare numbers to 10,000. (Chap. 1)

EVERY DAY COUNTS®
Calendar Math
The August activities provide...

Review of one-to-one correspondence and reading and writing numerals (Grade 1)

Preview of using place-value models and adding with regrouping (Chapter 2)

Practice of relating number words and numerals to quantities (Lesson 1 in this chapter) and comparing and ordering numbers (Lessons 3 and 4 in this chapter)

Differentiation Resources

Differentiation for Special Populations

	English Language Learners	Struggling Reteach 2A	On Level Extra Practice 2A	Advanced Enrichment 2A
Lesson 1	p. 9	pp. 1–8	pp. 1–4	Enrichment pages can be used to challenge advanced children.
Lesson 2	p. 12	pp. 9–14	pp. 5–10	
Lesson 3	p. 21	pp. 15–20	pp. 11–14	
Lesson 4	p. 27	pp. 21–24	pp. 15–17	

Additional Support

For English Language Learners

Select activities that reinforce the chapter vocabulary and the connections among these words, such as having children

• create a Word Wall that includes terms, definitions, and examples

• show concrete and/or pictorial examples and have children use vocabulary terms to identify them

• ask yes/no questions using comparison vocabulary terms, for example: Is 431 greater than 341?

• discuss the Chapter Wrap Up, encouraging children to use the chapter vocabulary

For Struggling Learners

Select activities that go back to the appropriate stage of the Concrete-Pictorial-Abstract spectrum, such as having children

• use base-ten models to represent numbers through 1,000

• draw pictures of base-ten models to represent and compare numbers

• count on orally between two numbers, for example count on from 56 to 68 or from 478 to 500

• create, share, and describe simple number patterns

See also pages 13–14

For Advanced Learners

See suggestions on pages 21 and 22–23.

Assessment and Remediation

Chapter 1 Assessment

Prior Knowledge

	Resource	Page numbers
Quick Check	Student Book 2A	pp. 4–5
Pre-Test	Assessments 2	pp. 1–3

Ongoing Diagnostic

	Resource	Page numbers
Guided Practice	Student Book 2A	pp. 7, 8, 9, 12–14, 21, 25, 27
Common Error	Teacher's Edition 2A	pp. 10, 30–31
Best Practices	Teacher's Edition 2A	pp. 19–20, 27

Formal Evaluation

	Resource	Page numbers
Chapter Review/Test	Workbook 2A	pp. 21–24
Chapter 1 Test Prep	Assessments 2	pp. 4–6

Remediation Options

Problems with these items...   Can be remediated with...

Objective	Review/Test Items Workbook 2A pp. 21–24	Chapter Assessment Items Assessments 2 pp. 4–6	Reteach Reteach 2A	Student Book Student Book 2A
Use chapter vocabulary correctly.	1	Not assessed	In context as needed	pp. 6, 11, 18, 24
Use base-ten blocks to recognize, read, and write numbers to 1,000.	2		pp. 1–3, 5–7	Lesson 1
Count on by 1s, 10s, and 100s to 1,000.	13	3–4	pp. 1, 5–7	Lesson 1
Use base-ten blocks and a place-value chart to read, write, and represent numbers to 1,000.	5–6	1, 7	pp. 9, 10, 13, 14	Lesson 2
Read and write numbers to 1,000 in standard form, expanded form, and word form.	3–4	2, 6	pp. 9–14	Lesson 2
Use base-ten blocks to compare numbers.			pp. 16–19	Lesson 3
Compare numbers using the terms **greater than** and **less than**.	7	9	pp. 15–20	Lesson 3
Compare numbers using symbols > and <.	8–9	8	pp. 16–19	Lesson 3
Order three-digit numbers.	10	10	pp. 21–24	Lesson 4
Identify the greatest number and the least number.	10, 12	5	pp. 21, 22	Lesson 4
Identify number patterns.	11	11–12	pp. 21, 23, 24	Lesson 4

Chapter Planning Guide

1 Numbers to 1,000

Lesson	Pacing	Instructional Objectives	Vocabulary
Chapter Opener pp. 1–5 Recall Prior Knowledge Quick Check	*1 day	💡**Big Idea** Count and compare numbers to 1,000.	
Lesson 1, pp. 6–10 Counting	2 days	• Use base-ten blocks to recognize, read, and write numbers to 1,000. • Count on by 1s, 10s, and 100s to 1,000.	• hundred • hundreds • thousand
Lesson 2, pp. 11–17 Place Value	2 days	• Use base-ten blocks and a place-value chart to read, write, and represent numbers to 1,000. • Read and write numbers to 1,000 in standard form, expanded form, and word form.	• standard form • expanded form • word form
Lesson 3, pp. 18–23 Comparing Numbers	2 days	• Use base-ten blocks to compare numbers. • Compare numbers using the terms **greater than** and **less than**. • Compare numbers using symbols > and <.	• greater than (>) • less than (<)
Lesson 4, pp. 24–31 Order and Pattern	2 days	• Order three-digit numbers. • Identify the greatest number and the least number. • Identify number patterns.	• greatest • least • more than • less than

*Assume that 1 day is a 45–55 minute period.

Resources	Materials	NCTM Focal Points	NCTM Process Standards
Student Book 2A, pp. 1–5 **Assessments 2,** pp. 1–3			
Student Book 2A, pp. 6–10 **Workbook 2A,** pp. 1–6 **Extra Practice 2A,** pp. 1–4 **Reteach 2A,** pp. 1–8	• 1 set of base-ten blocks	***Number and Operations*** Develop an understanding of the base-ten numeration system and place-value concepts and count in units and multiples of hundreds, tens, and ones.	Connections Representation
Student Book 2A, pp. 11–17 **Workbook 2A,** pp. 7–12 **Extra Practice 2A,** pp. 5–10 **Reteach 2A,** pp. 9–14	• 1 set of base-ten blocks (optional) • 1 Place-Value Mat (TR01) • 1 Place-Value Chart (TR03) per pair • 1 Base-Ten Cut-Outs (TR03) per group (optional) • Index cards (optional)	***Number and Operations*** Use place value and properties of operations to create equivalent representations of given numbers and understand multi-digit numbers in terms of place value.	Communication Connections Representation
Student Book 2A, pp. 18–23 **Workbook 2A,** pp. 13–14 **Extra Practice 2A,** pp. 11–14 **Reteach 2A,** pp. 15–20	• 1 set of base-ten blocks • 1 number cube per group • 1 ten-sided die per group • 1 Place-Value Chart (TR03) per child.	***Number and Operations*** Develop an understanding of the base-ten numeration system and place-value concepts and compare and order numbers.	Communication Representation
Student Book 2A, pp. 24–31 **Workbook 2A,** pp. 15–18 **Extra Practice 2A,** pp. 15–17 **Reteach 2A,** pp. 21–24	• 1 ten-sided die per group • 1 Number Line (TR02) per child • 1 Place-Value Chart (TR03) per child • 1 Number Chart (TR04) per child	***Number and Operations*** Count in units and multiples of hundreds, tens, and ones and compare and order numbers. ***Algebra*** Use number patterns.	Problem Solving Reasoning/Proof Communication

3 Comparing Numbers

LESSON OBJECTIVES
- Use base-ten blocks to compare numbers.
- Compare numbers using the terms **greater than** and **less than**.
- Compare numbers using symbols > and <.

TECHNOLOGY RESOURCES
- *Math in Focus* eBooks
- *Math in Focus* Teacher Resources CD
- *Math in Focus* Virtual Manipulatives

Vocabulary
greater than (>)

less than (<)

DAY 1   Student Book 2A, pp. 18–21

MATERIALS
- 1 set of base-ten blocks
- 1 number cube per group
- 1 ten-sided die per group
- 1 Place-Value Chart (TR02) per child

DAY 2   Student Book 2A, pp. 22–23
Workbook 2A, pp. 13–14

DIFFERENTIATION RESOURCES
- Reteach 2A, pp. 15–20
- Extra Practice 2A, pp. 11–14

 5-minute Warm Up

Place children in groups of four. Provide each group with a set of **base-ten blocks** (12 unit cubes and 12 ten-rods) and **Place-Value Charts** (TR02). Ask children to produce two numbers per group by tossing the **number cube** twice to obtain the digits for a two-digit number. Compare the numbers using the base-ten blocks and Place-Value Charts. Deduce the greater and lesser number. Repeat the steps two or three times.

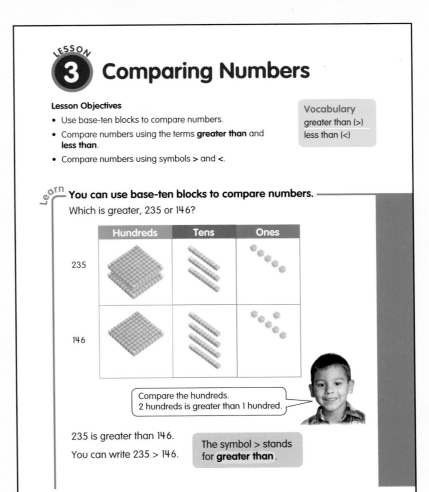

Student Book A p. 18

DAY 1 # Teach

Use Base-Ten Blocks to Compare Numbers
(pages 18 to 20)

Children learned in the previous lessons to represent numbers to 1,000 using base-ten blocks and a place-value chart. In this lesson, children go on to compare these numbers.

- Draw a place-value chart on the board and write 235 and 146 on it. Help children recall that one method of comparing numbers is to look at the digits in the greatest place value, i.e. hundreds place.

- Introduce the symbol > for *greater than*. Lead children to see that 2 hundreds is greater than (>) 1 hundred, and hence 235 > 146.

- Repeat the above steps to compare 372 and 345, looking at the digits in the hundreds place. Because the digits are the same, move on to compare the digits in the tens place.

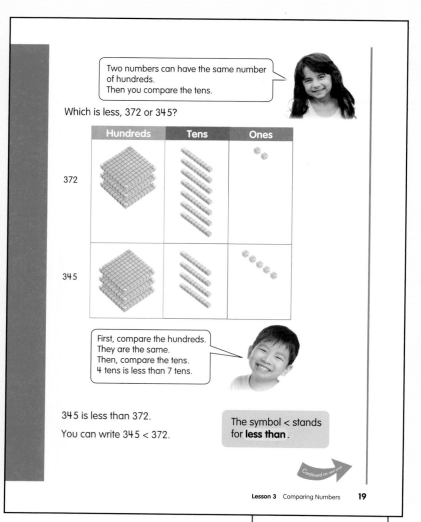

Two numbers can have the same number of hundreds.
Then you compare the tens.

Which is less, 372 or 345?

Hundreds	Tens	Ones
372		
345		

First, compare the hundreds.
They are the same.
Then, compare the tens.
4 tens is less than 7 tens.

345 is less than 372.
You can write 345 < 372.

The symbol < stands for **less than**.

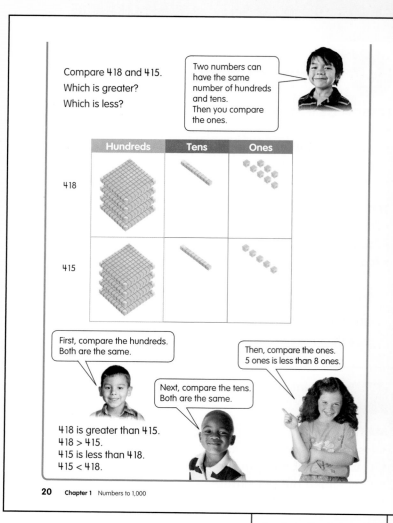

Compare 418 and 415.
Which is greater?
Which is less?

Two numbers can have the same number of hundreds and tens.
Then you compare the ones.

Hundreds	Tens	Ones
418		
415		

First, compare the hundreds.
Both are the same.

Next, compare the tens.
Both are the same.

Then, compare the ones.
5 ones is less than 8 ones.

418 is greater than 415.
418 > 415.
415 is less than 418.
415 < 418.

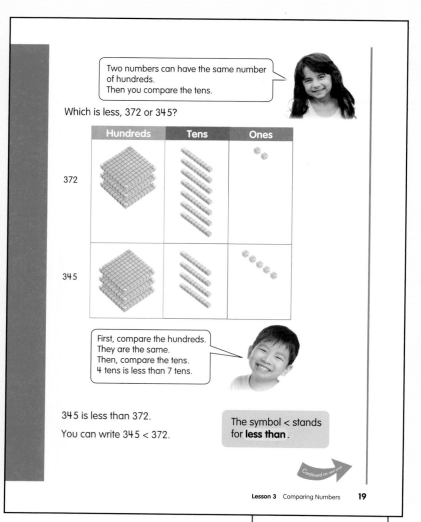

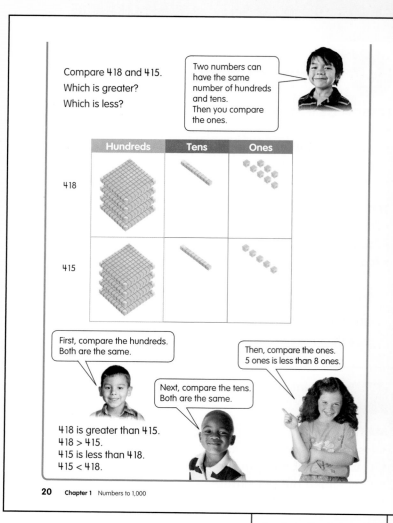

Continued on next page

Lesson 3 Comparing Numbers **19**

20 **Chapter 1** Numbers to 1,000

Student Book A p. 19

Student Book A p. 20

Learn

- Introduce the symbol < for *less than*. Lead children to see that 4 tens is less than (<) 7 tens, and hence 345 < 372.

- Repeat the above steps to compare 418 and 415, looking at the digits in the hundreds, tens, and then the ones place.

- Lead children to see that 8 ones is greater than (>) 5 ones, hence 418 > 415.

- Conversely, 5 ones is less than (<) 8 ones, and hence 415 < 418.

Best Practices Check that children know how to identify which number is greater by looking at the places of the numbers in multi-digit numbers. Remind children to compare the hundreds, then the tens, and then the ones.

Guided Practice

Answer with greater than or less than.

1

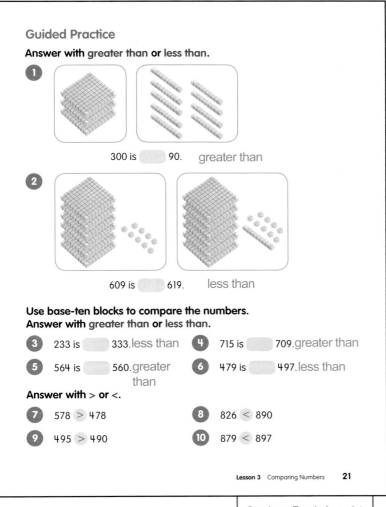

300 is [____] 90.   greater than

2

609 is [____] 619.   less than

Use base-ten blocks to compare the numbers.
Answer with greater than or less than.

3 233 is [____] 333. less than   **4** 715 is [____] 709. greater than

5 564 is [____] 560. greater than   **6** 479 is [____] 497. less than

Answer with > or <.

7 578 [>] 478   **8** 826 [<] 890

9 495 [>] 490   **10** 879 [<] 897

Student Book A p. 21

(a) Amir has 290 stamps. Cindy has 285 stamps. Who has more stamps?

(b) Henri has a greater number of stamps than Amir. Could Henri have 250, 289, or 300 stamps? Explain your answer.

Solution:

(a) 290 > 285, so Amir has more stamps than Cindy.

(b) Henri has more stamps than Amir.
    250 < 290 and 289 < 290, but 300 > 290, so Henri could have 300 stamps.

Answer:

(a) Amir has more stamps.

(b) Henri could have 300 stamps.

Differentiated Instruction

English Language Learners

Have children practice saying the phrases *greater than* and *less than*. Guide children to point to the side of the symbol that represents greater than when they say *greater than*. Repeat this procedure for the *less than* side of the symbol.

Check for Understanding

Guided Practice (page 21)

1 to **10** These provide practice in comparing numbers by comparing their digits in the hundreds, tens, and ones places using **base-ten blocks** and place-value charts. The exercises also provide practice for children to use and familiarize themselves with the terms and symbols *greater than* (>) and *less than* (<).

For Advanced Learners You may want to have children explain their answers to Exercises **1** to **10** by saying how much greater than or less than the numbers on the left side are than the numbers on the right side.

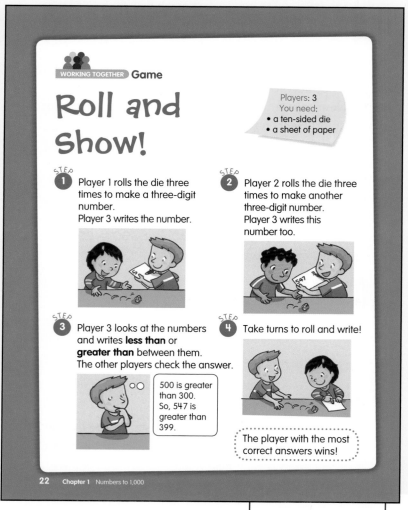

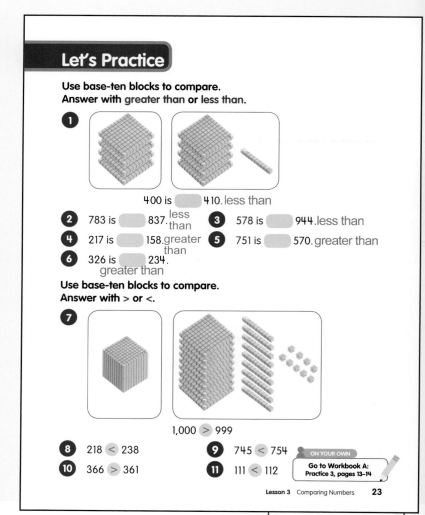

Student Book A p. 22

Student Book A p. 23

DAY 2 Teach

See the Lesson Organizer on page 18 for Day 2 resources.

WORKING TOGETHER Game:
Roll and Show! (page 22)

This game reinforces the concept of comparing numbers by looking at the digits in the hundreds, tens, and ones places using the appropriate terms and symbols.

- Have children work in groups of three. Number them as Player 1, Player 2, and Player 3.

- Have Player 1 roll the **ten-sided die** three times to make a three-digit number. Have Player 2 do the same.

- Player 3 writes down both numbers on a sheet of paper and compares them using appropriate symbols and terms.

- Children take turns to roll and write.

For Advanced Learners You may wish to ask children to roll the die again to get three more numbers. Then have children arrange the numbers in ascending or descending order.

Let's Practice (page 23)

This practice reinforces the skill of comparing numbers by looking at the digits in the hundreds, tens, and ones places using the appropriate terms and symbols. Exercises **1** to **6** require children to compare numbers using the terms *greater than* and *less than*. Exercises **7** to **11** require children to compare using the symbols > and <.

Common Error Some children have difficulty remembering how to write the *greater than* and *less than* symbols. Tell children to put two dots by the greater number and one dot by the number that is less. Have children connect the dots to make the symbol.

ON YOUR OWN

Children practice comparing numbers using the appropriate terms and symbols in Practice 3, pages 13 and 14 of **Workbook 2A**. These pages (with the answers) are shown on page 23A.

Differentiation Options Depending on children's success with the Workbook pages, use these materials as needed.
Struggling: Reteach 2A, pp. 15–20
On Level: Extra Practice 2A, pp. 11–14

Practice and Apply
Workbook pages for Chapter 1, Lesson 3

Name: _____   Date: _____

Practice 3   Comparing Numbers
Write *greater than* or *less than* in the blanks.

Example

256 is _greater than_ 246.

First compare the hundreds.
If the hundreds are the same, compare the tens.
If the tens are the same, compare the ones.

1.
118 is ___less than___ 181.

2.
595 is ___less than___ 959.

Compare.
Write > or < in the ◯.

Example

555 (>) 550

Lesson 3 Comparing Numbers **13**

Workbook A p. 13

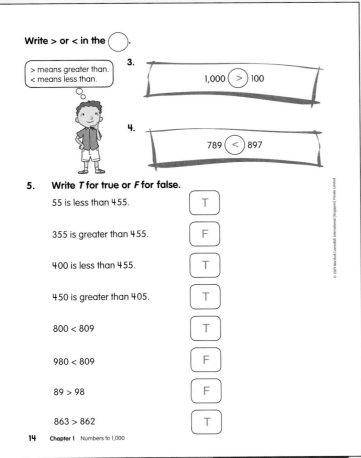

Write > or < in the ◯.

> means greater than.
< means less than.

3.
1,000 (>) 100

4.
789 (<) 897

5.   **Write *T* for true or *F* for false.**

55 is less than 455.   [T]

355 is greater than 455.   [F]

400 is less than 455.   [T]

450 is greater than 405.   [T]

800 < 809   [T]

980 < 809   [F]

89 > 98   [F]

863 > 862   [T]

14   **Chapter 1** Numbers to 1,000

Workbook A p. 14

Notes

LESSON 4 Order and Pattern

LESSON OBJECTIVES
• Order three-digit numbers.
• Identify the greatest number and the least number.
• Identify number patterns.

TECHNOLOGY RESOURCES
• *Math in Focus* eBooks
• *Math in Focus* Teacher Resources CD
• *Math in Focus* Virtual Manipulatives

Vocabulary

greatest	least	more than
less than		

DAY 1 Student Book 2A, pp. 24–28

MATERIALS
• 1 ten-sided die per group
• 1 Number Line (TR04) per child
• 1 Place-Value Charts (TR02) per child
• 1 Number Chart (TR05) per child

DAY 2 Student Book 2A, pp. 29–31
Workbook 2A, pp. 15–18

DIFFERENTIATION RESOURCES
• Reteach 2A, pp. 21–24
• Extra Practice 2A, pp. 15–17

5-minute Warm Up

Place children in equal groups. Provide each group with their own set of **Number Lines** (TR04). Pick a random two-digit number from 10 to 99. Have each group form number patterns of 1, 2, 5, and 10 using the number picked by filling in the five subsequent numbers and five preceding numbers.

E.g. 47

42	43	44	45	46	47
48	49	50	51	52	

LESSON 4 Order and Pattern

Lesson Objectives
• Order three-digit numbers.
• Identify the greatest number and the least number.
• Identify number patterns.

Vocabulary
greatest
least
more than
less than

Learn — You can use place-value charts to order numbers. —

Order 489, 236, and 701 from least to greatest.

	Hundreds	Tens	Ones
489	4	8	9
236	2	3	6
701	7	0	1

Compare the hundreds. 701 is greater than 489. 701 is greater than 236.

701 is the **greatest**.

236 is the **least**.

From least to greatest, the numbers are:

236 , 489 , 701
least

489 is greater than 236.

Student Book A p. 24

DAY 1 # Teach

Learn
Use Place-Value Charts to Order Numbers
(page 24)

Children learned earlier in this chapter to use base-ten blocks and place-value charts to represent and compare two 3-digit numbers.

• Copy the place-value chart on the board. Help children recall how to compare the numbers by starting with comparing the digits in the hundreds place.

• Introduce the new terms *greatest* and *least*.

• Have children identify the numbers which are the greatest and the least.

• Lead children to deduce the order of the numbers, from least to greatest.

Guided Practice

Find the missing numbers.

1 Identify the greatest and least number.
Then, order 459, 574, and 558 from greatest to least.

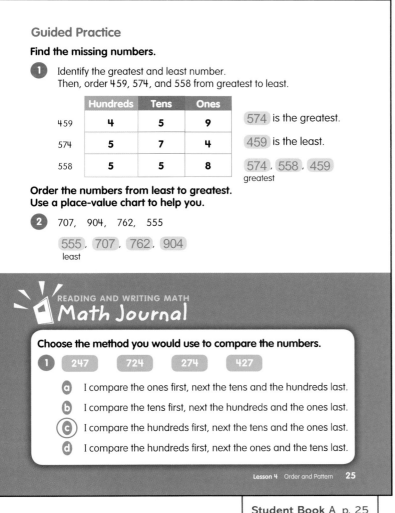

	Hundreds	Tens	Ones
459	4	5	9
574	5	7	4
558	5	5	8

574 is the greatest.

459 is the least.

574 , 558 , 459
greatest

**Order the numbers from least to greatest.
Use a place-value chart to help you.**

2 707, 904, 762, 555

555 , 707 , 762 , 904
least

READING AND WRITING MATH
Math Journal

Choose the method you would use to compare the numbers.

1 247 724 274 427

ⓐ I compare the ones first, next the tens and the hundreds last.

ⓑ I compare the tens first, next the hundreds and the ones last.

ⓒ I compare the hundreds first, next the tens and the ones last.

ⓓ I compare the hundreds first, next the ones and the tens last.

Lesson 4 Order and Pattern **25**

Student Book A p. 25

---

2 Are the numbers ordered from greatest to least? No.
Explain why or why not. Answers vary.
Use a place-value chart to help you.

724 247 274 427

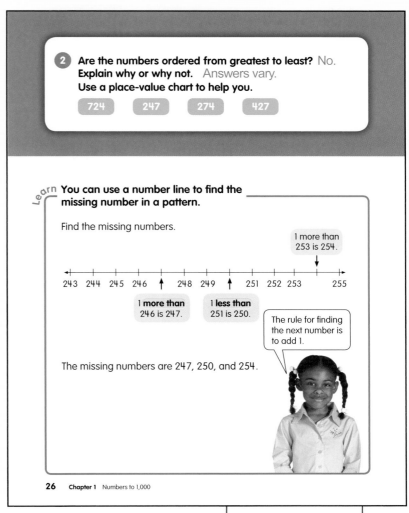

Learn You can use a number line to find the missing number in a pattern.

Find the missing numbers.

1 more than 253 is 254.

243 244 245 246 ↑ 248 249 ↑ 251 252 253 255

1 more than 246 is 247.

1 less than 251 is 250.

The rule for finding the next number is to add 1.

The missing numbers are 247, 250, and 254.

26 Chapter 1 Numbers to 1,000

Student Book A p. 26

Check for Understanding
Guided Practice (page 25)

1 and **2** These provide further practice in comparing numbers using the concepts taught in Lesson 3. They also provide further practice in identifying the least and greatest numbers and ordering the numbers. Provide children with a **Place-Value Chart** (TRO2) to help them order the numbers in Exercise **2**.

READING AND WRITING MATH
Math Journal (pages 25 and 26)

This section allows children to reflect on their observations and understanding of the concepts taught in Lessons 3 and 4.

In Exercise **1**, children are asked to recall the method of comparing numbers by first comparing the digits in the hundreds place, then tens, and ones places.

In Exercise **2**, children are asked to recall and apply the concept of comparing and ordering numbers using the terms greatest and least. Encourage children to use **Place-Value Charts** (TRO2) in comparing.

Learn
Use a Number Line to Find the Missing Number in a Pattern (page 26)

A number line is useful in illustrating the terms *1 more than* and *1 less than*.

• With reference to the number line, show children that the number 247 to the right of 246 is 1 more.

• Similarly show children that the number 250 to the left of 251 is 1 less.

• Familiarize children with this pattern and deduce that two places right of a number is 2 more and two places left of a number is 2 less. Increase the number of places right or left of a number and ask the children to identify the number.

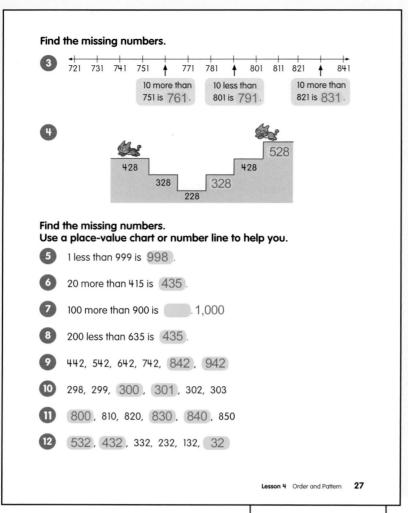

Find the missing numbers.

3 721 731 741 751 ↑ 771 781 ↑ 801 811 821 ↑ 841

10 more than 751 is **761**.

10 less than 801 is **791**.

10 more than 821 is **831**.

4

528
428   428
  328   328
     228

Find the missing numbers.
Use a place-value chart or number line to help you.

5 1 less than 999 is **998**.

6 20 more than 415 is **435**.

7 100 more than 900 is ____ . 1,000

8 200 less than 635 is **435**.

9 442, 542, 642, 742, **842**, **942**

10 298, 299, **300**, **301**, 302, 303

11 **800**, 810, 820, **830**, **840**, 850

12 **532**, **432**, 332, 232, 132, **32**

Lesson 4 Order and Pattern **27**

Student Book A p. 27

Problem of the Lesson

What is the missing number in each pattern?
1. 122, 124, 126, _____, 130, 132
2. 420, 400, 380, _____, 340, 320
3. 300, 350, 400, _____, 500, 550

Answer:
1. 128
2. 360
3. 450

Differentiated Instruction

English Language Learners

Have children practice the vocabulary *more than* and *less than*. Ask children to locate a number on the number line. Guide them to move to the left to find a number *less than* using the mnemonic *left for less*, and to move to the right for a number that is *more than*.

✓Guided Practice (page 27)

3 and **9** to **12** These exercises provide practice in counting on and counting back on a number line to identify the number more than or less than the highlighted number.

4 This exercise shows steps, which is an improvisation of the number line. Ensure children are able to apply the properties of the number line accordingly.

5 to **8** These help reinforce the concepts of *more than* and *less than*. Use a **Number Line** (TRO4) to help children if necessary.

Best Practices For Exercises **9** to **12**, you may want to have children work together to first identify the pattern rules. Then invite children to use the rules and complete the patterns on the board. In Exercises **11** and **12**, note whether children can work backward to fill in the starting numbers.

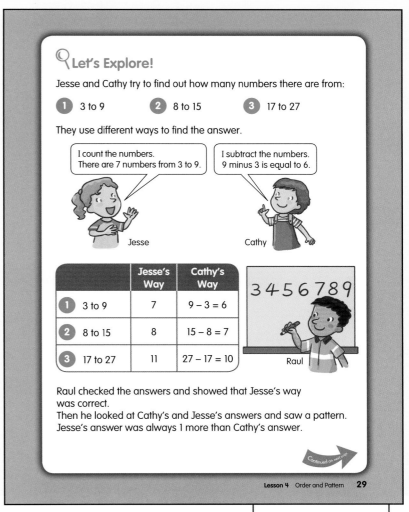

 **Game:**

Roll and Count! (page 28)

This game reinforces the concept of *more than* and *less than*.

- Arrange children in groups of five or six.

- Have them take turns to roll the **ten-sided die** three times to make three-digit numbers and stop when everyone has obtained a three-digit number. If a number greater than 900 is obtained, roll the die three times again to obtain a new number.

- Children fill in the **Number Chart** (TR05). The child with all correct answers in the shortest time wins.

Let's Explore!

Number Patterns (pages 29 and 30)

This activity helps children to see and count the total number of numbers within a given range of numbers.

- Have children work in groups and prompt the children to come up with their own methods of finding how many numbers are in a given range in Exercises **1** to **3**.

- Compare the answers provided by children and check their answers by writing out the range of numbers provided.

- Discuss why some children got it wrong. Help them correct or improve on their given methods.

- Then have children complete Exercises **4** to **6** and check them in Exercise **7** by counting.

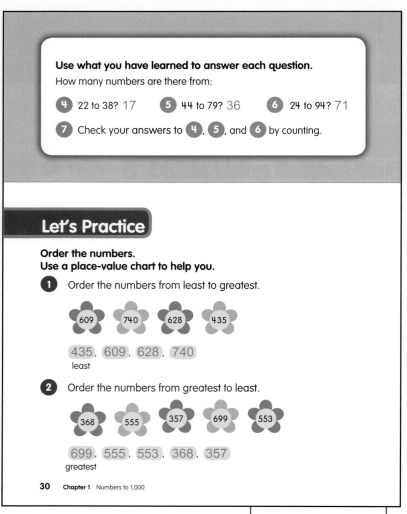

Use what you have learned to answer each question.
How many numbers are there from:

4 22 to 38? 17   **5** 44 to 79? 36   **6** 24 to 94? 71

7 Check your answers to **4** , **5** , and **6** by counting.

Let's Practice

Order the numbers.
Use a place-value chart to help you.

1 Order the numbers from least to greatest.

609   740   628   435

435, 609, 628, 740
least

2 Order the numbers from greatest to least.

368   555   357   699   553

699, 555, 553, 368, 357
greatest

Find the missing numbers.
Use a place-value chart or number line to help you.

3 1 more than 293 is 294 .   **4** 10 more than 528 is 538 .

5 100 more than 190 is 290 .   **6** 20 more than 425 is 445 .

7 100 more than 762 is 862 .   **8** 200 more than 204 is 404 .

Find the missing numbers.
Use a place-value chart or number line to help you.

9 1 less than 717 is 716 .   **10** 5 less than 685 is 680 .

11 10 less than 480 is 470 .   **12** 30 less than 257 is 227 .

13 100 less than 921 is 821 .   **14** 200 less than 635 is 435 .

Complete the number patterns.
Use place-value charts or number lines if you need to.

15 203, 204 , 205, 206, 207, 208 , 209, 210 , 211 .

16 648, 658, 668 , 678, 688 , 698 , 708 , 718

17 721, 621, 521 , 421 , 321, 221 , 121 , 21

18 342, 341 , 340 , 339 , 338, 337, 336

ON YOUR OWN
Go to Workbook A:
Practice 4, pages 15–18

Let's Practice (pages 30 and 31)

This practice reinforces the skills in ordering numbers, identifying numbers more than and less than a given number and completing number patterns. Exercises **1** and **2** involve the ordering of numbers.

Common Error Some children might be confused ordering numbers with some of the same digits, such as 555 and 553. Suggest that children cross out digits starting from the hundreds place that are the same, so they can focus on the digits that are different to determine which number should be written next.

Exercises **3** to **14** deal with the concepts of *more than* and *less than*, while Exercises **15** to **18** provide practice in completing number patterns. Have children give the rule for completing each pattern. These practices should be used together with **Place-Value Charts** (TRO2) and **Number Lines** (TRO4) where necessary.

ON YOUR OWN

Children practice counting in Practice 4, pages 15 to 18 of **Workbook 2A**. These pages (with the answers) are shown on page 31A.

Differentiation Options Depending on children's success with the Workbook pages, use these materials as needed.
Struggling: Reteach 2A, pp. 21–24
On Level: Extra Practice 2A, pp. 15–17

Practice and Apply
Workbook pages for Chapter 1, Lesson 4

Name: _____ Date: _____

Practice 4   Order and Pattern
Order the numbers.
Use the place-value chart to help you.

1.

	Hundreds	Tens	Ones
214	2	1	4
457	4	5	7
590	5	9	0

_214_ , _457_ , _590_
least

2.

	Hundreds	Tens	Ones
810	8	1	0
794	7	9	4
823	8	2	3

_823_ , _810_ , _794_
greatest

3.

	Hundreds	Tens	Ones
361	3	6	1
348	3	4	8
607	6	0	7

_348_ , _361_ , _607_
least

Lesson 4   Order and Pattern   **15**

Name: _____ Date: _____

What is the missing number?

12.
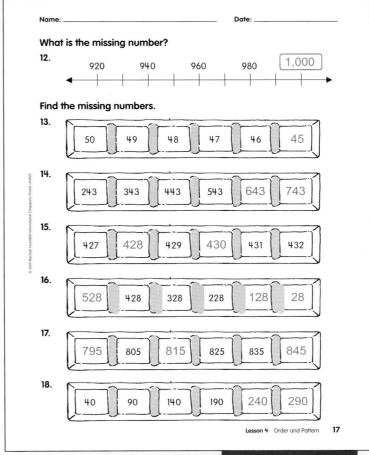
920   940   960   980   [1,000]

Find the missing numbers.

13.   50 49 48 47 46 45

14.   243 343 443 543 643 743

15.   427 428 429 430 431 432

16.   528 428 328 228 128 28

17.   795 805 815 825 835 845

18.   40 90 140 190 240 290

Lesson 4   Order and Pattern   **17**

---

4.   Order the numbers
     from least to greatest.

 34   47   73   77

5.   Order the numbers
     from greatest to least.

 653   563   536   356

Find the missing numbers.

6.   1 more than 205 is _206_.

7.   _555_ is 2 less than 557.

8.   10 more than 235 is _245_.

9.   10 less than 455 is _445_.

10. 100 less than 347 is _247_.

11. _345_ is 200 more than 145.

16   Chapter 1   Numbers to 1,000

Math Journal

Count on or count back.

1.
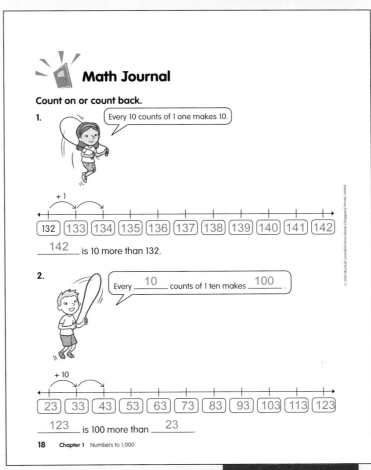

Every 10 counts of 1 one makes 10.

+ 1

[132] [133] [134] [135] [136] [137] [138] [139] [140] [141] [142]

_142_ is 10 more than 132.

2.

Every ____10____ counts of 1 ten makes ____100____.

+ 10

[23] [33] [43] [53] [63] [73] [83] [93] [103] [113] [123]

_123_ is 100 more than ____23____.

18   Chapter 1   Numbers to 1,000

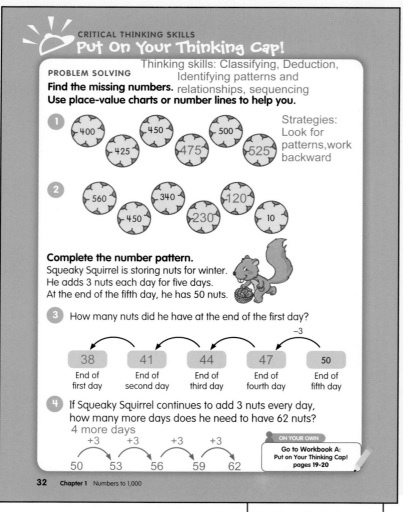

CRITICAL THINKING SKILLS
Put On Your Thinking Cap!

PROBLEM SOLVING

Thinking skills: Classifying, Deduction, Identifying patterns and relationships, sequencing

Find the missing numbers.
Use place-value charts or number lines to help you.

1. 400 425 450 475 500 525

Strategies:
Look for patterns, work backward

2. 560 450 340 230 120 10

Complete the number pattern.
Squeaky Squirrel is storing nuts for winter.
He adds 3 nuts each day for five days.
At the end of the fifth day, he has 50 nuts.

3. How many nuts did he have at the end of the first day?

38	41	44	47	50
End of first day	End of second day	End of third day	End of fourth day	End of fifth day

−3

4. If Squeaky Squirrel continues to add 3 nuts every day, how many more days does he need to have 62 nuts?
4 more days

+3 +3 +3 +3
50 53 56 59 62

ON YOUR OWN
Go to Workbook A:
Put on Your Thinking Cap!
pages 19-20

Student Book A p. 32

CRITICAL THINKING AND PROBLEM SOLVING
Put on Your Thinking Cap! (page 32)

This problem solving exercise involves identifying and completing number patterns. Exercises 1 and 2 involve identifying the more complex number patterns involving differences of 25 and 110 respectively. Exercises 3 and 4 involve simpler patterns of *3 more* using a different approach to the questions. Guide the children in identifying these complex patterns and answering these non-routine questions using place-value charts and number lines if necessary.

ON YOUR OWN

Because all children should be challenged, have all children try the Challenging Practice and Problem Solving pages in **Workbook 2A**, pages 19 and 20. These pages (with the answers) are shown on page 32A.

Differentiation Options Depending on children's success with the Workbook pages, use these materials as needed.
On Level: Extra Practice 2A, p. 18
Advanced: Enrichment 2A, pp. 1–10

Thinking Skills

- Classifying
- Deduction
- Identifying patterns and relationships
- Sequencing

Problem Solving Strategies

- Look for patterns
- Work backward

Practice and Apply
Workbook pages for Put on Your Thinking Cap!

Name: _____ **Date:** _____

Put On Your Thinking Cap!
Challenging Practice

Answer the question.

Sunny Snake has swallowed some eggs.
The eggs have numbers that follow a pattern.
Find the missing numbers.

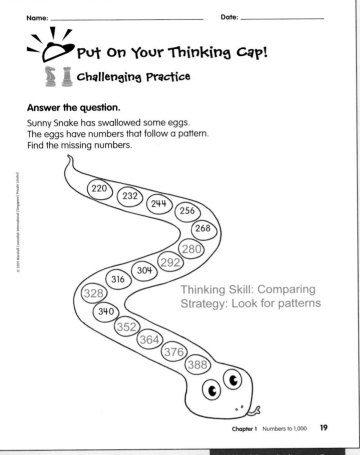

Thinking Skill: Comparing
Strategy: Look for patterns

Chapter 1 Numbers to 1,000 **19**

Put On Your Thinking Cap!
Problem Solving

Answer the question.

Sally and Hans started counting at the same time.
Sally counted on by tens from 300.
Hans counted back by hundreds.
After six counts, they had reached the same number.
What number did Hans start counting from?

> Draw a diagram or act it out.

Sally

	+10	+10	+10	+10	+10	+10
start	①	②	③	④	⑤	⑥
300	310	320	330	340	350	360

Hans

	+100	+100	+100	+100	+100	+100
start	①	②	③	④	⑤	⑥
960	860	760	660	560	460	360

He started counting from 960.

Thinking Skills: Identifying patterns and relationships, Sequencing
Strategies: Act it out, Use a diagram/model, Work backward

20 Chapter 1 Numbers to 1,000

Notes

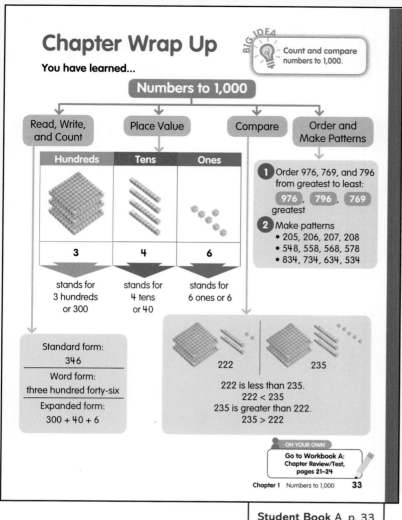

Student Book A p. 33

Chapter Wrap Up (page 33)

Review reading and writing by having children read the standard form or word form at random from a display on the board or from cards. Have children write the value of each digit given at random. Give any three-digit number and ask children to write its standard, word, and expanded form. Have children compare and order numbers. Have children write the missing numbers in a number pattern/line. As you work through the examples, encourage children to use the chapter vocabulary:

- hundred
- hundreds
- thousand
- standard form
- word form
- expanded form

- greater than (>)
- less than (<)
- greatest
- least
- more than
- less than

ON YOUR OWN

Have children review the vocabulary, concepts, and skills from Chapter 1 with the Chapter Review/Test in **Workbook 2A**, pages 21 to 24. These pages (with the answers) are shown on page 33A.

Assessment

Use the Chapter 1 Test Prep on pages 4 to 6 of **Assessments 2** to assess how well children have learned the material of this chapter. This assessment is appropriate for reporting results to adults at home and administrators. This test is shown on page 33B.

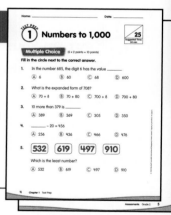

Assessments 2 pp. 4–6

Workbook pages for Chapter Review/Test

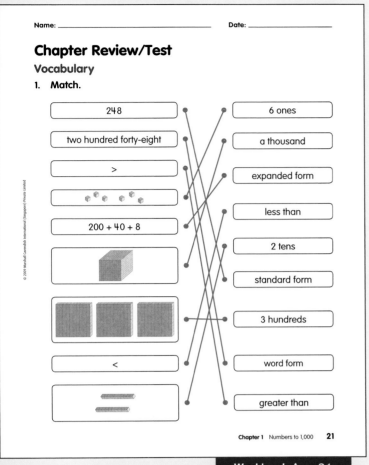

Name: _____ **Date:** _____

Chapter Review/Test
Vocabulary

1. Match.

248	6 ones
two hundred forty-eight	a thousand
>	expanded form
(cubes)	less than
200 + 40 + 8	2 tens
(rod)	standard form
(flats)	3 hundreds
<	word form
(tens rods)	greater than

Chapter 1 Numbers to 1,000   **21**

Workbook A p. 21

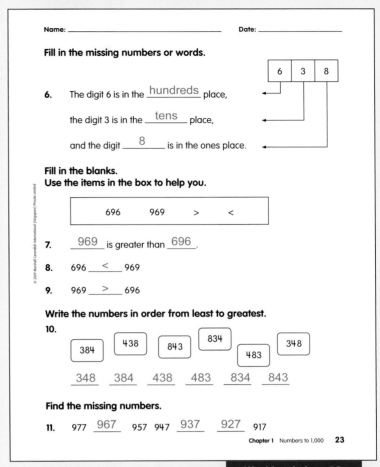

Name: _____ **Date:** _____

Fill in the missing numbers or words.

6	3	8

6. The digit 6 is in the __hundreds__ place,

the digit 3 is in the __tens__ place,

and the digit __8__ is in the ones place.

Fill in the blanks.
Use the items in the box to help you.

696	969	>	<

7. __969__ is greater than __696__.

8. 696 __<__ 969

9. 969 __>__ 696

Write the numbers in order from least to greatest.

10.

384   438   843   834   483   348

__348__   __384__   __438__   __483__   __834__   __843__

Find the missing numbers.

11. 977 __967__ 957 947 __937__ __927__ 917

Chapter 1 Numbers to 1,000   **23**

Workbook A p. 23

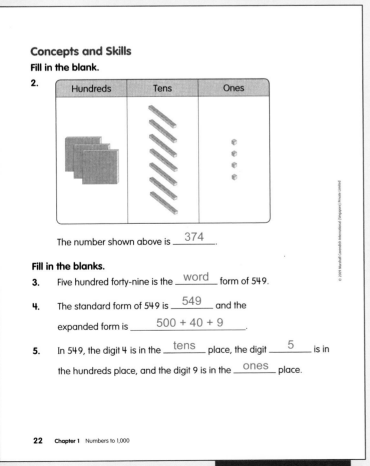

Concepts and Skills
Fill in the blank.

2.

Hundreds	Tens	Ones
(3 flats)	(7 rods)	(4 ones)

The number shown above is __374__.

Fill in the blanks.

3. Five hundred forty-nine is the __word__ form of 549.

4. The standard form of 549 is __549__ and the

expanded form is __500 + 40 + 9__.

5. In 549, the digit 4 is in the __tens__ place, the digit __5__ is in

the hundreds place, and the digit 9 is in the __ones__ place.

22   Chapter 1 Numbers to 1,000

Workbook A p. 22

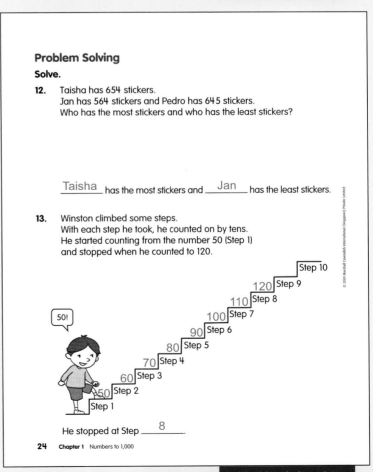

Problem Solving
Solve.

12. Taisha has 654 stickers.
Jan has 564 stickers and Pedro has 645 stickers.
Who has the most stickers and who has the least stickers?

__Taisha__ has the most stickers and __Jan__ has the least stickers.

13. Winston climbed some steps.
With each step he took, he counted on by tens.
He started counting from the number 50 (Step 1)
and stopped when he counted to 120.

Step 10
120 Step 9
110 Step 8
100 Step 7
90 Step 6
80 Step 5
70 Step 4
60 Step 3
50 Step 2
Step 1

50!

He stopped at Step __8__.

24   Chapter 1 Numbers to 1,000

Workbook A p. 24

Assessments Book pages for Chapter 1 Test Prep
Answer key appears in Assessments Book.

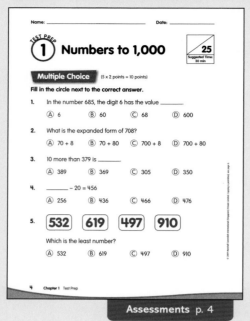

Assessments p. 4

Name: _____ Date: _____

Short Answer (5 x 2 points = 10 points)

Follow the directions.

6. Write the number in word form.

   | 712 〉

7. Fill in the missing number.

   In 239, the digit _____ is in the tens place.

8. Write > or < in the ◯.

   553 ◯ 355

9. Write *greater than* or *less than* in the blank.

   300 is _____ 163.

10. Write the numbers in order from least to greatest.

    [657] [756] [675] [567]

    least _____ _____ _____ _____

Assessments p. 5

Name: _____ Date: _____

Extended Response (Question 11: 2 points, Question 12: 3 points)

Complete the number pattern.

Melvin is getting ready for a swimming race.
Every day, he swims 5 more meters than the day before.
On the fifth day, he swims 50 meters.

11. How many meters did Melvin swim on the first day?

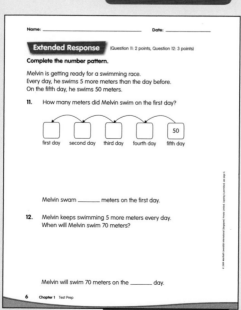

Melvin swam _____ meters on the first day.

12. Melvin keeps swimming 5 more meters every day.
    When will Melvin swim 70 meters?

Melvin will swim 70 meters on the _____ day.

6   Chapter 1 Test Prep

Assessments p. 6

CHAPTER 2

Chapter Overview

Addition up to 1,000

Math Background

Children have learned addition up to 100 in Grade 1, when they were taught the basic addition algorithm of adding from right to left (from the ones place to the tens place). Children have been introduced to the Commutative Property of Addition ($a + b = b + a$), the Associative Property of Addition ($a + b + c = [a + b] + c = a + [b + c]$) where a, b, and c are whole numbers, and the Identity Property in Addition: $n + 0 = 0 + n = n$, where n is any number. Children were taught how to compose and decompose numbers through place value and number bonds. Children have also been taught to apply place value in addition with and without regrouping in numbers up to 100.

In this chapter, children apply these concepts to 3-digit numbers. They are taught multiple regroupings by using base-ten blocks and a place-value chart as concrete representations, allowing them to visualize addition with regrouping in the ones and tens places. For example, in the equation $125 + 237 = \_\_\_$, the sum of digits in the ones place equals 12 ones. Children are led to deduce that 12 ones can be regrouped as 1 ten and 2 ones. Therefore the sum of digits in the tens place would be $1 + 2 + 3 = 6$. The same strategy is applied in regrouping in the tens place and regrouping in the ones and tens places.

Cross-Curricular Connections

Reading/Language Arts Read aloud *Mission: Addition* by Loreen Leedy (Holiday House, © 1999) about Miss Prime, her students, and story problems. As a class, brainstorm addition story ideas. Design and produce your own illustrated class book about addition.

Drama Have children work in small groups to produce a short play about a teacher teaching place value and addition with regrouping. One child can be the teacher and other children the students. Encourage them to use base-ten blocks and place-value charts as props.

Skills Trace

Grade 1	Add one- and two-digit numbers, with and without regrouping to 100. (Chaps. 3, 8, 13, 14, and 17)
Grade 2	Add three-digit numbers with and without regrouping to 1,000. (Chaps. 2, 4, and 10)
Grade 3	Use multiple strategies in addition up to 10,000 (with multiple regroupings) to solve real-world problems. (Chaps. 2, 3, and 5)

EVERY DAY COUNTS®
Calendar Math

The September activities provide...

Review of relating number words and numerals to quantities, counting on, and comparing and ordering numbers (Chapter 1)

Preview of regrouping to subtract and modeling of subtraction with objects (Chapter 3)

Practice of regrouping to add, addition strategies, and using place-value models (Lessons 2, 3, and 4 in this chapter)

Differentiation Resources

Differentiation for Special Populations

	English Language Learners	Struggling Reteach 2A	On Level Extra Practice 2A	Advanced Enrichment 2A
Lesson 1	p. 39	pp. 25–36	pp. 19–20	Enrichment pages can be used to challenge advanced children.
Lesson 2	p. 43	pp. 37–42	pp. 21–22	
Lesson 3	p. 47	pp. 43–46	pp. 23–24	
Lesson 4	p. 50	pp. 47–50	pp. 25–26	

Additional Support

For English Language Learners

Select activities that reinforce the chapter vocabulary and the connections among these words, such as having children

- add terms, definitions, and examples to the Word Wall
- act out vocabulary terms
- draw pictures to illustrate each term
- discuss the Chapter Wrap Up, encouraging children to use the chapter vocabulary

For Struggling Learners

Select activities that go back to the appropriate stage of the Concrete-Pictorial-Abstract spectrum, such as having children

- act out addition stories within the chapter
- use manipulatives to model addition with and without regrouping
- tell and solve addition number stories
- create addition stories for given addition sentences

See also pages 43 and 47

If necessary, review

- Chapter 1 (Numbers to 1,000).

For Advanced Learners

See suggestions on page 51–52.

Assessment and Remediation

Chapter 2 Assessment

Prior Knowledge		
	Resource	**Page numbers**
Quick Check	Student Book 2A	p. 37
Pre-Test	Assessments 2	pp. 7–8
Ongoing Diagnostic		
Guided Practice	Student Book 2A	pp. 39, 40–41, 43, 47–48, 51
Common Error	Teacher's Edition 2A	pp. 40–41, 44–45, 48
Formal Evaluation		
Chapter Review/Test	Workbook 2A	pp. 45–48
Chapter 2 Test Prep	Assessments 2	pp. 9–11

Problems with these items...   Can be remediated with...

Remediation Options

	Review/Test Items	Chapter Assessment Items	Reteach	Student Book
Objective	**Workbook 2A pp. 45-48**	**Assessments 2 pp. 9–11**	**Reteach 2A**	**Student Book 2A**
Use chapter vocabulary correctly.	1	Not assessed	In context as needed	pp. 38, 42
Add up to three-digit numbers without regrouping.	2, 3	1, 6	pp. 26–36	Lesson 1
Add up to three-digit numbers with regrouping in ones.	2, 4	2, 7	pp. 38–41	Lesson 2
Add up to three-digit numbers with regrouping in tens.		3, 8	pp. 43–46	Lesson 3
Add up to three-digit numbers with regrouping in ones and tens.	2, 5	4, 5, 9, 11	pp. 47–50	Lesson 4
Solve real-world addition problems.	3–6	10, 11, 12	pp. 29, 32, 35, 36, 41, 46, 50	Lessons 1, 2, 3, and 4

Chapter Planning Guide

CHAPTER 2 Addition up to 1,000

Lesson	Pacing	Instructional Objectives	Vocabulary
Chapter Opener pp. 34–37 Recall Prior Knowledge Quick Check	*1 day	💡**Big Idea** Three-digit numbers can be added with and without regrouping.	
Lesson 1, pp. 38–41 Addition Without Regrouping	1 day	• Use base-ten blocks to add numbers without regrouping. • Add up to three-digit numbers without regrouping. • Solve real-world addition problems	• add • place-value chart
Lesson 2, pp. 42–45 Addition with Regrouping in Ones	1 day	• Use base-ten blocks to add numbers with regrouping. • Add up to three-digit numbers with regrouping. • Solve real-world addition problems.	• regroup
Lesson 3, pp. 46–48 Addition with Regrouping in Tens	1 day	• Use base-ten blocks to add numbers with regrouping. • Add up to three-digit numbers with regrouping. • Solve real-world addition problems.	
Lesson 4, pp. 49–54 Addition with Regrouping in Ones and Tens	1 day	• Use base-ten blocks to add numbers with regrouping. • Add three-digit numbers with regrouping. • Solve real-world addition problems.	

*Assume that 1 day is a 45–55 minute period.

Resources	Materials	NCTM Focal Points	NCTM Process Standards
Student Book 2A, pp. 34–37 **Assessments 2,** pp. 7–8			
Student Book 2A, pp. 38–41 **Workbook 2A, pp.** 25–30 **Extra Practice 2A,** pp. 19–20 **Reteach 2A,** pp. 25–36	• 1 set of base-ten blocks	***Number and Operations and Algebra*** Use efficient, accurate, and generalizable methods to add and subtract multi-digit whole numbers. Apply understanding of addition and subtraction models.	Problem Solving Representation
Student Book 2A, pp. 42–45 **Workbook 2A,** pp. 31–34 **Extra Practice 2A,** pp. 21–22 **Reteach 2A,** pp. 37–42	• 1 set of base-ten blocks • 2 ten-sided dice per group • 1 Place-Value Mat (TRO1) per group	***Number and Operations*** Add and subtract to solve a variety of problems. ***Number and Operations and Algebra*** Compose and decompose multi-digit numbers. Apply understanding of addition and subtraction models.	Problem Solving Communication Representation
Student Book 2A, pp. 46–48 **Workbook 2A,** pp. 35–38 **Extra Practice 2A,** pp. 23–24 **Reteach 2A,** pp. 43–46	• 1 set of base-ten blocks • 1 Place-Value Chart (TRO2) per child (optional) • 2 index cards per pair (optional)	***Number and Operations and Algebra*** Develop fluency with efficient procedures for adding and subtracting whole numbers. Apply understanding of addition and subtraction models.	Problem Solving Representation
Student Book 2A, pp. 49–54 **Workbook 2A,** pp. 39–42 **Extra Practice 2A,** pp. 25–26 **Reteach 2A,** pp. 47–50	• 1 set of base-ten blocks • 1 Place-Value Mat (TRO1) per group • 1 Place-Value Chart (TRO2) per child (optional) • 3 sets of Number Cards (TRO6) per group	***Number and Operations*** Add and subtract to solve a variety of problems. ***Number and Operations and Algebra*** Use efficient, accurate, and generalizable methods to add and subtract multi-digit whole numbers.	Problem Solving Reasoning/Proof Communication Representation

Lesson	Pacing	Instructional Objectives	Vocabulary
Problem Solving p. 54 Put on Your Thinking Cap!	$\frac{1}{2}$ day	**Thinking Skill** • Deduction **Problem Solving Strategy** • Work backward	
Chapter Wrap Up p. 55	$\frac{1}{2}$ day	• Reinforce and consolidate chapter skills and concepts.	
Chapter Assessment	1 day		

*Assume that 1 day is a 45–55 minute period.

Resources	Materials	NCTM Focal Points	NCTM Process Standards
Student Book 2A, p. 54 **Workbook 2A**, pp. 43–44 **Extra Practice 2A**, pp. 27–28 **Enrichment 2A**, pp. 11–20		***Number and Operations and Algebra*** Add and subtract multi-digit whole numbers to solve non-routine problems.	Problem Solving Reasoning/Proof
Student Book 2A, p. 55 **Workbook 2A**, pp. 45–48			
Assessments 2, pp. 9–11			

Technology Resources for easy classroom management
- *Math in Focus* eBooks
- *Math in Focus* Teacher Resources CD
- *Math in Focus* Virtual Manipulatives
- Online Assessment Generator

Chapter Introduction

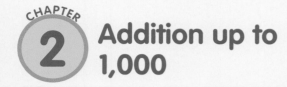

CHAPTER 2 Addition up to 1,000

Chapter 2 Vocabulary

add	put together two or more parts to make a whole	Lesson 1
place-value chart		Lesson 1

Hundreds	Tens	Ones
2	3	1

regroup	change 10 ones to 1 ten or 1 ten to 10 ones change 10 tens to 1 hundred or 1 hundred to 10 tens	Lesson 2

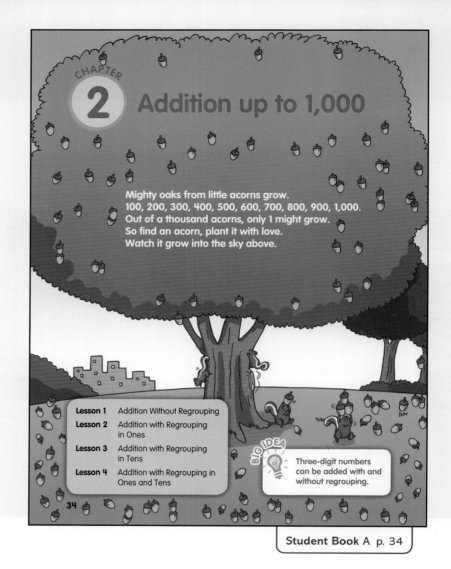

Student Book A p. 34

Big Idea (page 34)

Addition up to three-digit numbers with and without regrouping is the main focus of this chapter.

- Children use the regrouping concept to learn addition up to 1,000.

- They learn addition with regrouping in ones, tens, and hundreds.

Chapter Opener (page 34)

The picture illustrates a huge oak tree and many little acorns, some still on the tree and others scattered on the ground. Used together with the poem, the picture gives the idea that 1,000 is a large number containing 10 hundreds.

- Show children the picture and the poem.

- Read the poem aloud and have children read each sentence after you.

- Read the second line again, writing the numbers on the board, one below another in a vertical column.

- *Ask:* How many hundreds are in 1,000? (10)

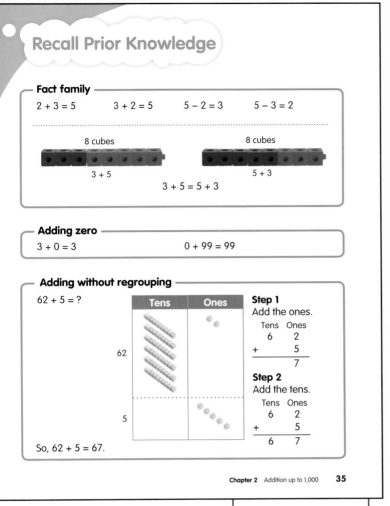

Fact family

$2 + 3 = 5$ $3 + 2 = 5$ $5 - 2 = 3$ $5 - 3 = 2$

8 cubes   8 cubes

$3 + 5$ $5 + 3$

$3 + 5 = 5 + 3$

Adding zero

$3 + 0 = 3$ $0 + 99 = 99$

Adding without regrouping

$62 + 5 = ?$

Tens	Ones

Step 1
Add the ones.

Tens Ones
6   2
+   5
7

Step 2
Add the tens.

Tens Ones
6   2
+   5
6   7

So, $62 + 5 = 67$.

Student Book A p. 35

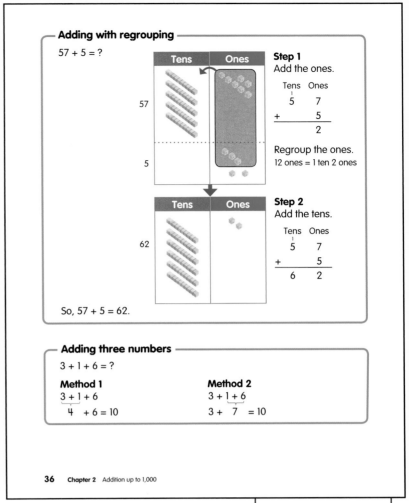

Adding with regrouping

$57 + 5 = ?$

Tens	Ones

Step 1
Add the ones.

Tens Ones
5   7
+   5
2

Regroup the ones.
12 ones = 1 ten 2 ones

Tens	Ones

Step 2
Add the tens.

Tens Ones
5   7
+   5
6   2

So, $57 + 5 = 62$.

Adding three numbers

$3 + 1 + 6 = ?$

Method 1
$3 + 1 + 6$
$4 + 6 = 10$

Method 2
$3 + 1 + 6$
$3 + 7 = 10$

Student Book A p. 36

Recall Prior Knowledge (pages 35 to 37)

Fact Family 🎲

Children learned to show the inverse relationship between addition and subtraction using fact families in Grade 1.

• Show children the number sentence $2 + 3 = 5$.

• Have children identify the other possible number sentences using the same three numbers. Use concrete representations such as **connecting cubes** if required.

• Help children recall the Commutative Property of Addition with the related addition sentences $3 + 5 = 5 + 3$.

Adding Zero

Children learned the zero concept in Grade 1.

• Show the two number sentences.

• Have children recall the Identity Property in Addition: $n + 0 = 0 + n = n$ for any number n.

Adding Without Regrouping

Children learned addition up to 100 without regrouping in Grade 1.

• Show children the problem $62 + 5 = ?$.

• Help children recall the strategy for adding numbers: Add from right to left (first add ones then the tens).

Adding with Regrouping

Children learned addition up to 100 with regrouping in Grade 1.

• Show children the problem $57 + 5 = ?$. Lead children to see that the strategy of adding without regrouping does not work here.

• Have children recall the regrouping concept: 1 ten = 10 ones.

• Lead children to deduce that 5 tens and 12 ones = 6 tens and 2 ones.

Adding Three Numbers

Children learned the Associative Property of Addition in Grade 1.

• Show children the number sentence $3 + 1 + 6 = 10$.

• Explain to children the possible methods of solving this number sentence.

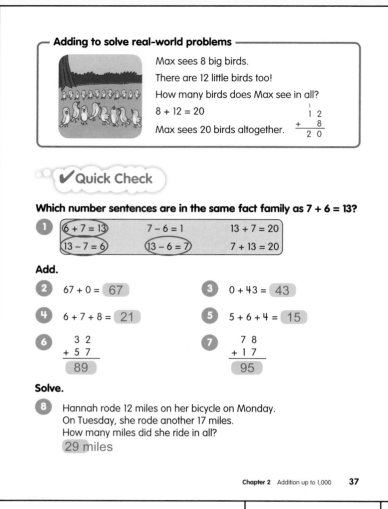

Student Book A p. 37

Adding to Solve Real-World Problems

Children learned how to apply addition to real-world problems in Grade 1.

- Show children the picture and the story.

- Relate the addition sentence to the story.

- Encourage children to check the answer by counting the birds in the picture.

✔Quick Check (page 37)

Use this section as a diagnostic tool to assess children's level of prerequisite knowledge before they progress to this chapter.

Exercise ❶ assesses their understanding of fact families.

Exercises ❷ and ❸ assess their understanding of the zero concept.

Exercises ❹ and ❺ assess their ability to add without regrouping.

Exercises ❻ and ❼ assess their ability to add with regrouping using vertical form.

Exercise ❽ assesses their ability to solve real-world addition problems.

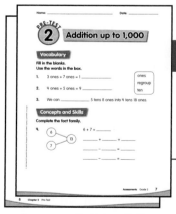

Assessments 2 pp. 7–8

Assessment

For additional assessment of children's prior knowledge and chapter readiness, use the Chapter 2 Pre-Test on pages 7 and 8 of **Assessments 2**.

LESSON 1 Addition Without Regrouping

LESSON OBJECTIVES
- Use base-ten blocks to add numbers without regrouping.
- Add up to three-digit numbers without regrouping.
- Solve real-world addition problems.

TECHNOLOGY RESOURCES
- *Math in Focus* eBooks
- *Math in Focus* Teacher Resources CD
- *Math in Focus* Virtual Manipulatives

Vocabulary

add	place-value chart

DAY 1   Student Book 2A, pp. 38–41
Workbook 2A, pp. 25–30

MATERIALS
- 1 set of base-ten blocks

DIFFERENTIATION RESOURCES
- Reteach 2A, pp. 25–36
- Extra Practice 2A, pp. 19–20

5-minute Warm Up

Place children in pairs. Have each pair write a 2-digit number and a 1-digit number. They are to show how the digits of the 1-digit number are aligned to the 2-digit number before adding. This activity ensures that children are able to align the digits correctly according to place value.

LESSON 1 Addition Without Regrouping

Lesson Objectives
- Use base-ten blocks to add numbers without regrouping.
- Add up to three-digit numbers without regrouping.
- Solve real-world addition problems.

Vocabulary
add
place-value chart

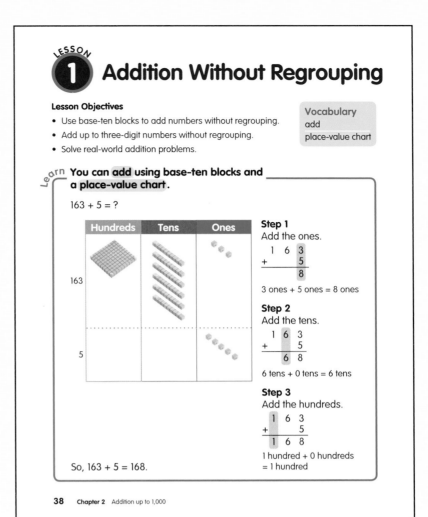

Student Book A p. 38

DAY 1 **Teach**

Add Using Base-Ten Blocks and a Place-Value Chart (page 38)

Children learned to use base-ten blocks and place-value charts to add numbers to 100 without regrouping in Grade 1. This Learn section introduces children to the addition of ones involving 3-digit numbers.

- Draw a place-value chart on the board and write the numbers 163 and 5 in the appropriate places on the chart.

- Ask some children to show the value of each digit in both numbers by holding up the correct number of **base-ten blocks**. Ask children to add the blocks in each place value column.

- Help children recall the strategy of adding numbers from right to left. Show and explain to children how to present their answer in both vertical and horizontal forms. Ensure children align all the ones, tens, and hundreds digits correctly.

You can add using base-ten blocks and a place-value chart.

271 + 27 = ?

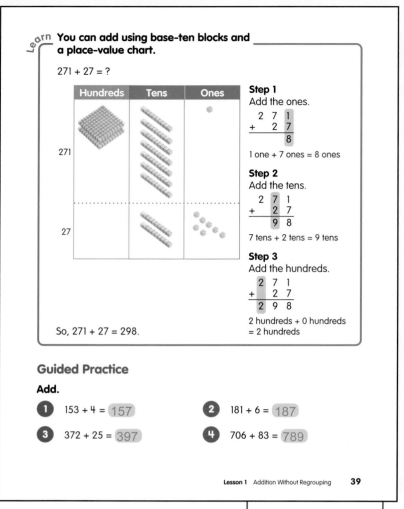

Hundreds	Tens	Ones

271

27

So, 271 + 27 = 298.

Step 1
Add the ones.

```
  2 7 1
+   2 7
      8
```

1 one + 7 ones = 8 ones

Step 2
Add the tens.

```
  2 7 1
+   2 7
    9 8
```

7 tens + 2 tens = 9 tens

Step 3
Add the hundreds.

```
  2 7 1
+   2 7
  2 9 8
```

2 hundreds + 0 hundreds
= 2 hundreds

Guided Practice

Add.

1 153 + 4 = 157

2 181 + 6 = 187

3 372 + 25 = 397

4 706 + 83 = 789

Lesson 1 Addition Without Regrouping **39**

Student Book A p. 39

Add Using Base-Ten Blocks and a Place-Value Chart (page 39)

This Learn section introduces children to the addition of tens and ones involving 3-digit numbers.

- Draw a place-value chart on the board and write the numbers 271 and 27 in the appropriate places on the chart.

- Ask some children to show the value of each digit in both numbers by holding up the correct number of **base-ten blocks**. Ask them to add the blocks in each place-value column.

- Help children recall the strategy of adding numbers from right to left. Show and explain to children how to present their answer in both vertical and horizontal forms. Ensure children align all the ones, tens, and hundreds digits correctly.

Check for Understanding
✓Guided Practice (page 39)

1 to **4** These exercises reinforce the strategy of addition without regrouping. Provide pairs of children with **base-ten blocks** and a **Place-Value Chart (TRO2)** if required.

Problem of the Lesson

Andrew has 242 marbles. Ben has 111 more marbles than Andrew. How many marbles do they have in all?

Solution:
242 + 111 = 353
Benny has 353 marbles.

```
  353    +    242   = 595
(Benny)     (Andrew)
```

Answer: They have 595 marbles in all.

Differentiated Instruction

English Language Learners

Have children design and create their own place-value workmat. Have them label the chart with the words: *hundreds*, *tens*, and *ones*. They may wish to draw or cut out pictures of base-ten blocks to represent the hundreds, tens, and ones to glue on their chart.

Best Practices You may want to use a copy of a **Place-Value Chart (TRO2)** to help children vertically align the numbers. Use a green marker to highlight the ones column of the chart. Use the mnemonic *green means go/start*. Children will know to begin adding at the green line.

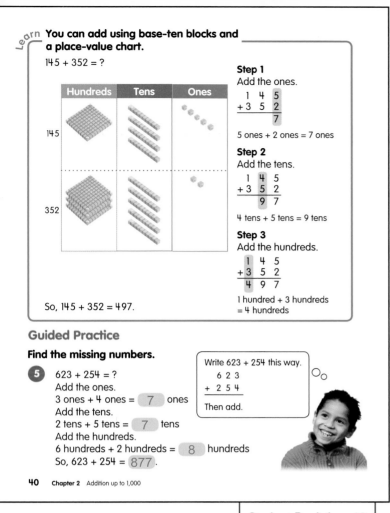

Learn · You can add using base-ten blocks and a place-value chart.

145 + 352 = ?

Hundreds	Tens	Ones
145		
352		

Step 1
Add the ones.

```
  1 4 5
+ 3 5 2
      7
```

5 ones + 2 ones = 7 ones

Step 2
Add the tens.

```
  1 4 5
+ 3 5 2
    9 7
```

4 tens + 5 tens = 9 tens

Step 3
Add the hundreds.

```
  1 4 5
+ 3 5 2
  4 9 7
```

1 hundred + 3 hundreds
= 4 hundreds

So, 145 + 352 = 497.

Guided Practice

Find the missing numbers.

5 623 + 254 = ?
Add the ones.
3 ones + 4 ones = ⬤ **7** ⬤ ones
Add the tens.
2 tens + 5 tens = ⬤ **7** ⬤ tens
Add the hundreds.
6 hundreds + 2 hundreds = ⬤ **8** ⬤ hundreds
So, 623 + 254 = **877** .

Write 623 + 254 this way.
```
  6 2 3
+ 2 5 4
```
Then add.

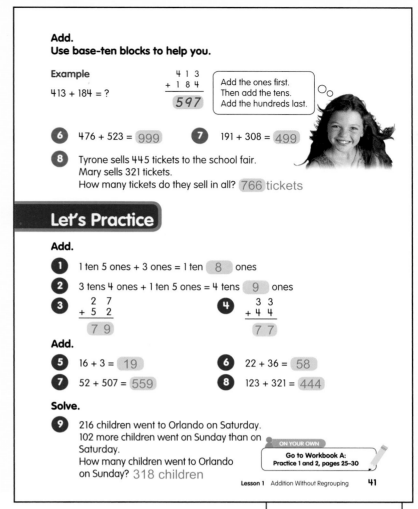

Add.
Use base-ten blocks to help you.

Example

413 + 184 = ?

```
  4 1 3
+ 1 8 4
  5 9 7
```

Add the ones first.
Then add the tens.
Add the hundreds last.

6 476 + 523 = **999**   **7** 191 + 308 = **499**

8 Tyrone sells 445 tickets to the school fair.
Mary sells 321 tickets.
How many tickets do they sell in all? **766** tickets

Let's Practice

Add.

1 1 ten 5 ones + 3 ones = 1 ten **8** ones

2 3 tens 4 ones + 1 ten 5 ones = 4 tens **9** ones

3
```
  2 7
+ 5 2
  7 9
```

4
```
  3 3
+ 4 4
  7 7
```

Add.

5 16 + 3 = **19**   **6** 22 + 36 = **58**

7 52 + 507 = **559**   **8** 123 + 321 = **444**

Solve.

9 216 children went to Orlando on Saturday.
102 more children went on Sunday than on Saturday.
How many children went to Orlando on Sunday? **318 children**

ON YOUR OWN
Go to Workbook A:
Practice 1 and 2, pages 25–30

Add Using Base-Ten Blocks and a Place-Value Chart (page 40)

This Learn section introduces children to the addition of two 3-digit numbers.

- Draw a place-value chart on the board and write the numbers 145 and 352 in the appropriate places on the chart.

- Ask some children to show the value of each digit in both numbers by holding up the correct number of **base-ten blocks**. Ask them to add the blocks in each place-value column.

- Help children recall the strategy of adding numbers from right to left. Show and explain to children how to present their answer in both vertical and horizontal forms.

Guided Practice (pages 40 and 41)

5 This exercise leads children through the strategy of addition by using place values, reinforcing their understanding of place-value concepts in addition.

6 and **7** These exercises provide further practice with less guidance. **8** This exercise requires children to solve an addition word problem. Help children recognize the 'part-whole' concept in addition used in the problem.

Let's Practice (page 41)

This practice reinforces the skills of addition without regrouping. Exercises **1** and **2** require children to apply their understanding of place-value concepts in addition. Exercises **3** to **8** provide practice to reinforce the addition strategies and presentation in both vertical and horizontal forms. Exercise **9** provides practice for children to work on a problem by relating the word problem to addition of numbers.

Common Error Some children may not line up the numbers correctly when adding a two- and a three-digit number. Tell children their numbers should align on the right side in the ones column.

ON YOUR OWN

Children practice addition without regrouping in Practice 1 and 2, pages 25 to 30 of **Workbook 2A**. These pages (with the answers) are shown on pages 41A and 41B.

Differentiation Options Depending on children's success with the Workbook pages, use these materials as needed.
Struggling: Reteach 2A, pp. 25–36
On Level: Extra Practice 2A, pp. 19–20

Practice and Apply
Workbook pages for Chapter 2, Lesson 1

Name: _____ Date: _____

(2) CHAPTER Addition up to 1,000

Practice 1   Addition Without Regrouping
Add.

1. 232 + 645 = ?

Add the ones.
2 ones + 5 ones = ___7___ ones

Add the tens.
3 tens + 4 tens = ___7___ tens

Add the hundreds.
2 hundreds + 6 hundreds = ___8___ hundreds

232 + 645 = ___877___

```
  2 3 2
+ 6 4 5
  ___7
```
Write 232 + 645 this way. Then add.

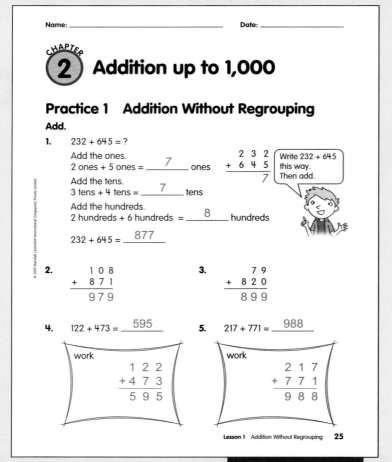

2.
```
  1 0 8
+   8 7 1
  9 7 9
```

3.
```
    7 9
+ 8 2 0
  8 9 9
```

4. 122 + 473 = ___595___

work
```
  1 2 2
+ 4 7 3
  5 9 5
```

5. 217 + 771 = ___988___

work
```
  2 1 7
+ 7 7 1
  9 8 8
```

Add.

6. Three friends have some addition cards.
Some answers will win prizes.
Help them add to find their prizes.

I win the _bears_

```
  3 4 8      3          1 3 2
+ 2 5 1    + 2 5 1    +   3 6
  5 9 9      2 5 4      1 6 8
```

I win the _book_

```
    1 7      5 5 2      3 1 3
+ 2 4 0    + 3 4 6    + 3 2 0
  2 5 7      8 9 8      6 3 3
```

I win the _hat_

```
  7 6 5      5 4 3      6 5 1
+ 2 3 4    + 3 3 3    +   3 3
  9 9 9      8 7 6      6 8 4
```

bears	ball	book	hat	toy car
168	989	633	876	252

Name: _____ Date: _____

Practice 2   Addition Without Regrouping
Solve.

Example

A bakery sells 567 bagels on Monday.
It sells 412 bagels on Tuesday.
How many bagels does the bakery sell on both days?

567 + 412 = 979

```
  5 6 7
+ 4 1 2
  9 7 9
```

The bakery sells ___979___ bagels on both days.

1. There are 623 steps in Castle A.
There are 245 more steps in Castle B than in Castle A.
How many steps are there in Castle B?

623 + 245 = 868

There are ___868___ steps in Castle B.

Solve.

2. Chef Lila baked 271 muffins on Saturday.
She baked another 308 muffins on Sunday.
How many muffins did Chef Lila bake in all?

271 + 308 = 579

Chef Lila baked ___579___ muffins in all.

3. The Jones family drive 106 miles on Monday.
On Tuesday they drive another 252 miles.
How many miles do they drive altogether?

106 + 252 = 358

They drive ___358___ miles altogether.

Lesson 1   Addition Without Regrouping   25

Workbook A p. 25

Workbook A p. 27

26   Chapter 2   Addition up to 1,000

Workbook A p. 26

Lesson 1   Addition Without Regrouping   27

28   Chapter 2   Addition up to 1,000

Workbook A p. 28

41A   CHAPTER 2: LESSON 1

Name: _____ **Date:** _____

4. Allen is training for a skipping contest.
   He skips 373 times in the morning.
   He skips 324 times in the evening.
   How many times does Allen skip altogether?

   373 + 324 = 697

   Allen skips ____697____ times altogether.

5. Ladonna sold 210 tickets yesterday.
   She sells 365 more tickets today than yesterday.
   How many tickets does Ladonna sell today?

   210 + 365 = 575

   Ladonna sells ____575____ tickets today.

Workbook A p. 29

Solve.

6. Anna scores 93 points in a computer game.
   Lee scores 106 points in a computer game.
   How many points do they score altogether?

   93 + 106 = 199

   They score ____199____ points altogether.

7. Greenwood School has 322 students.
   Seaview Preschool has 75 students.
   How many students do the schools have in all?

   322 + 75 = 397

   The schools have ____397____ students in all.

Workbook A p. 30

Notes

Chapter 2

LESSON
2 Addition with Regrouping in Ones

LESSON OBJECTIVES

- Use base-ten blocks to add numbers with regrouping.
- Add up to three-digit numbers with regrouping.
- Solve real-world addition problems.

TECHNOLOGY RESOURCES

- *Math in Focus* eBooks
- *Math in Focus* Teacher Resources CD
- *Math in Focus* Virtual Manipulatives

Vocabulary

regroup

DAY 1 Student Book 2A, pp. 42–45
Workbook 2A, pp. 31–34

MATERIALS

- 1 set of base-ten blocks
- 2 ten-sided dice per group
- 1 Place-Value Mat (TR01) per group

DIFFERENTIATION RESOURCES

- Reteach 2A, pp. 37–42
- Extra Practice 2A, pp. 21–22

5-minute Warm Up

- Provide children with a pair of 2-digit numbers, where the digit in the ones place of both numbers is greater than 5. For example, 19 and 38.

- Draw a place-value chart and write the numbers 19 and 38 in the appropriate places on the chart.

- Ask children to add the ones. Then write: 9 ones + 8 ones = 17 ones

- Remind children that 10 ones = 1 ten.

- Regroup the ones. 17 ones = 1 ten 7 ones.

- Ask children to add the tens. 1 ten + 1 ten + 3 tens = 5 tens

- Write 19 + 38 = 57.

- Repeat with a different pair of 2-digit numbers Ensure the sum is less than 100.

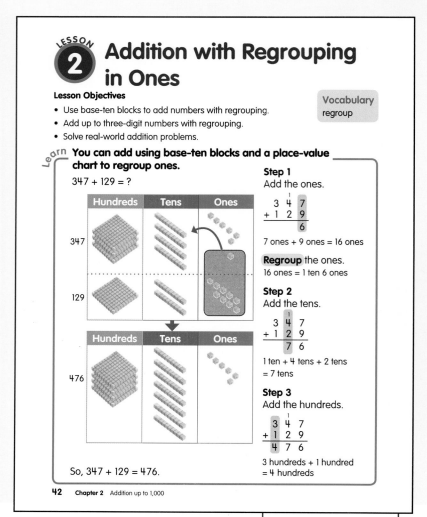

Student Book A p. 42

DAY 1 **Teach**

Add Using Base-Ten Blocks and a Place-Value Chart to Regroup Ones (page 42)

Children learned to use base-ten blocks and place-value charts to add numbers to 100 with regrouping in Grade 1. This Learn section introduces children to the addition of two 3-digit numbers with regrouping of ones.

- Draw a place-value chart on the board and write the numbers 347 and 129 in the appropriate places on the chart.

- Ask some children to show the value of each digit in both numbers by holding up the correct number of **base-ten blocks**.

- Help children recall the strategy of adding numbers from right to left. *Say:* Add the ones. Have the two children holding the unit cubes combine and count their unit cubes together. *Say:* 7 ones + 9 ones = 16 ones.

- *Say:* Let's regroup the ones. Lead children to recall 10 ones = 1 ten. 16 ones = 1 ten + 6 ones. Have one of the children holding the unit cubes return to his or her seat after giving 10 unit cubes to a child with the ten-rods. Exchange the 10 unit cubes for a ten-rod.

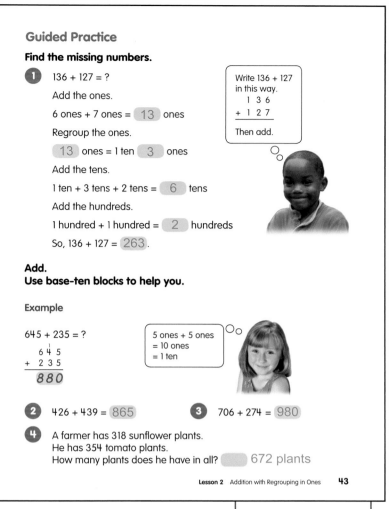

Guided Practice

Find the missing numbers.

1 136 + 127 = ?

Add the ones.

6 ones + 7 ones = ⬚ 13 ⬚ ones

Regroup the ones.

⬚ 13 ⬚ ones = 1 ten ⬚ 3 ⬚ ones

Add the tens.

1 ten + 3 tens + 2 tens = ⬚ 6 ⬚ tens

Add the hundreds.

1 hundred + 1 hundred = ⬚ 2 ⬚ hundreds

So, 136 + 127 = ⬚ 263 ⬚.

> Write 136 + 127
> in this way.
> 1 3 6
> + 1 2 7
>
> Then add.

Add.
Use base-ten blocks to help you.

Example

645 + 235 = ?

```
    1
  6 4 5
+ 2 3 5
-------
  8 8 0
```

> 5 ones + 5 ones
> = 10 ones
> = 1 ten

2 426 + 439 = ⬚ 865 ⬚

3 706 + 274 = ⬚ 980 ⬚

4 A farmer has 318 sunflower plants.
He has 354 tomato plants.
How many plants does he have in all? ⬚ 672 plants

Lesson 2   Addition with Regrouping in Ones   **43**

Student Book A p. 43

Problem of the Lesson

Amanda has 416 stamps. Sam gives her 38 stamps. Use place value to find the number of stamps Amanda has after that.

Solution:
416 = 4 hundreds 1 ten 6 ones
38 = 3 tens 8 ones
416 + 38:

```
        4 hundreds  1 ten    6 ones
    +                3 tens  8 ones
        ---------------------------
    = 4 hundreds  4 tens  14 ones
    = 4 hundreds  5 tens   4 ones
    = 454
```

Answer:
Amanda has 454 stamps

Differentiated Instruction

English Language Learners

Write the word *regroup* on the board. Say it aloud and have children repeat the word. Circle the word *group* in the word *regroup*. Explain that when you regroup you make new groups. Demonstrate regrouping straws, **craft sticks**, and **base-ten blocks** as you say *regroup*.

- Have children add the tens and hundreds.

- *Say:* The answer is four hundred seventy-six.
  347 + 129 = 476.

For Struggling Learners You may want to have children review basic regrouping facts such as 8 + 5 = 13 and 9 + 6 = 15 before assigning the exercises.

Check for Understanding
✓ **Guided Practice** (page 43)

1 to **3** This exercise reinforces the addition strategy involving regrouping in ones. Recap for children the steps involved in addition with regrouping:

1. Add the ones.
2. Regroup the ones to tens.
3. Add the tens.
4. Add the hundreds.

4 This exercise provides further practice in solving a real-world problem involving addition of three-digit numbers.

Best Practices Have children work in small groups. Use base-ten blocks and a **Place-Value Mat** (TR01) and practice physically combining the ones into a ten. *Say:* Show me 6 + 7. Have children take 6 unit cubes and add 7 unit cubes to the mat. Group the 13 blocks into 1 ten and 3 ones. Repeat this procedure with other numbers greater than 10.

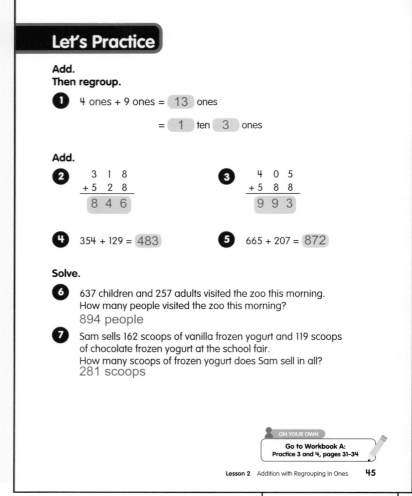

 WORKING TOGETHER Game:

Make a Hundred! (page 44)

This game reinforces the concept of regrouping ones in addition. You may use **Base-Ten Cut-Outs** (TR03) instead of base-ten blocks.

- Have children work in groups of three or four. One child will act as the banker. This child receives 20 unit cubes and 9 ten-rods for each player, and 1 hundred-square for the group.

- Children are to take turns to roll the two **ten-sided dice**. They should add the numbers shown on the two dice.

- Children should exchange 10 unit cubes for a ten-rod from the banker.

- Continue the game until one child gets 10 ten-rods to make a hundred-square. This child is the winner.

Let's Practice (page 45)

These exercises provide children with more practice in addition with regrouping in ones. Exercises **1** to **5** check children's understanding of regrouping ones in addition. Exercises **6** and **7** require children to apply the strategies in solving real-world addition problems.

Common Error Some children may not regroup. Remind children that each place value should only have one digit.

👤 **ON YOUR OWN**

Children practice addition with regrouping in ones in Practice 3 and 4, pages 31 to 34 of **Workbook 2A**. These pages (with the answers) are shown on page 45A.

Differentiation Options Depending on children's success with the Workbook pages, use these materials as needed.
Struggling: Reteach 2A, pp. 37–42
On Level: Extra Practice 2A, pp. 21–22

Practice and Apply
Workbook pages for Chapter 2, Lesson 2

Name: _____ **Date:** _____

Practice 3 Addition with Regrouping in Ones
Add and regroup the ones.

1. 778 + 119 = ?

Add and regroup the ones.

8 ones + 9 ones = __17__ ones

= __1__ ten __7__ ones

Add the tens.
1 ten + 7 tens + 1 ten = __9__ tens

Add the hundreds.
7 hundreds + 1 hundred = __8__ hundreds

778 + 119 = __897__

```
    1
  7 7 8
+ 1 1 9
-------
  8 9 7
```

Write 778 + 119 this way. Then add.

2.
```
  5 6 8
+ 1 2 3
-------
  6 9 1
```

3.
```
  6 3 8
+ 1 5 5
-------
  7 9 3
```

4. 576 + 207 = __783__

5. 631 + 329 = __960__

```
work
      1
  5 7 6
+ 2 0 7
-------
  7 8 3
```

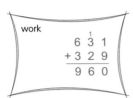

```
work
      1
  6 3 1
+ 3 2 9
-------
  9 6 0
```

Add.
An example is shown.

6.

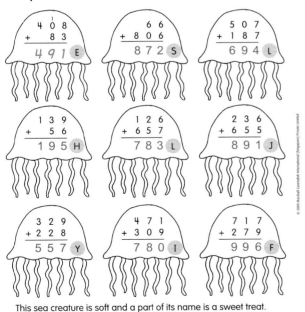

```
    1
  4 0 8
+   8 3
-------
  4 9 1  E
```
```
  6 6
+ 8 0 6
-------
  8 7 2  S
```
```
  5 0 7
+ 1 8 7
-------
  6 9 4  L
```
```
  1 3 9
+   5 6
-------
  1 9 5  H
```
```
  1 2 6
+ 6 5 7
-------
  7 8 3  L
```
```
  2 3 6
+ 6 5 5
-------
  8 9 1  J
```
```
  3 2 9
+ 2 2 8
-------
  5 5 7  Y
```
```
  4 7 1
+ 3 0 9
-------
  7 8 0  I
```
```
  7 1 7
+ 2 7 9
-------
  9 9 6  F
```

This sea creature is soft and a part of its name is a sweet treat.
What is this creature?
Write the letters that match the numbers.

J   E   L   L   Y   F   I   S   H
891 491 783 694 557 996 780 872 195

Name: _____ **Date:** _____

Practice 4 Addition with Regrouping in Ones
Solve.

1. Chef Andrew makes 447 chicken sandwiches.
He makes 46 turkey sandwiches.
How many sandwiches does Chef Andrew make in all?

447 + 46 = 493

Chef Andrew makes __493__ sandwiches in all.

2. At a school fair, 209 cups of cider are sold in the morning.
179 cups of cider are sold in the afternoon.
How many cups of cider are sold?

209 + 179 = 388

__388__ cups of cider are sold.

3. Julian uses 454 tiles to cover the floor of one bedroom.
He uses 307 tiles for another bedroom.
How many tiles does he use for both rooms?

454 + 307 = 761

He uses __761__ tiles for both rooms.

Solve.

4. Mr. Souza has 182 stamps.
His brother gives him another 209 stamps.
How many stamps does Mr. Souza have altogether?

182 + 209 = 391

Mr. Souza has __391__ stamps altogether.

5. Dena decorates a patio with a string of 354 party lights.
Eric has a string of lights that has 27 more lights than
Dena's string of lights.
How many lights does Eric's string of lights have?

354 + 27 = 381

Eric's string of lights has __381__ lights.

6. Lucy ties 136 red ribbons for the parade.
She ties 59 more yellow ribbons than red ribbons.
How many yellow ribbons does Lucy tie?

136 + 59 = 195

Lucy ties __195__ yellow ribbons.

Chapter 2

LESSON 3 Addition with Regrouping in Tens

LESSON OBJECTIVES
- Use base-ten blocks to add numbers with regrouping.
- Add up to three-digit numbers with regrouping.
- Solve real-world addition problems.

TECHNOLOGY RESOURCES
- *Math in Focus* eBooks
- *Math in Focus* Teacher Resources CD
- *Math in Focus* Virtual Manipulatives

| DAY 1 | Student Book 2A, pp. 46–48 |
| | Workbook 2A, pp. 35–38 |

MATERIALS
- 1 set of base-ten blocks
- 1 Place-Value Chart (TR02) per child (optional)
- 2 index cards per pair (optional)

DIFFERENTIATION RESOURCES
- Reteach 2A, pp. 43–46
- Extra Practice 2A, pp. 23–24

5-minute Warm Up

- Ask children to think of 2 two-digit numbers greater than 60. Randomly select two numbers suggested by children.

- Have children add the two numbers. For example, 67 + 72 = 139. Show children 139 = 100 + 30 + 9. Highlight that 100 = 10 tens, and therefore 130 = 13 tens = 1 hundred and 3 tens.

- This prepares children for addition with regrouping in tens.

LESSON 3 Addition with Regrouping in Tens

Lesson Objectives
- Use base-ten blocks to add numbers with regrouping.
- Add up to three-digit numbers with regrouping.
- Solve real-world addition problems.

Learn **You can add using base-ten blocks and a place-value chart to regroup tens.**

182 + 93 = ?

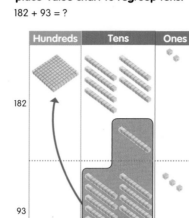

Step 1
Add the ones.

```
   1 8 2
 +   9 3
       5
```

2 ones + 3 ones = 5 ones

Step 2
Add the tens.

```
   1
   1 8 2
 +   9 3
     7 5
```

8 tens + 9 tens = 17 tens

Regroup the tens.

17 tens = 1 hundred 7 tens

46 Chapter 2 Addition up to 1,000

Student Book A p. 46

Teach

Learn

Add Using Base-Ten Blocks and a Place-Value Chart to Regroup Tens (pages 46 and 47)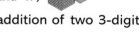

This Learn section introduces children to the addition of two 3-digit numbers with regrouping of tens.

- Draw a place-value chart on the board and write the numbers 182 and 93 in the appropriate places on the chart.

- Ask some children to show the value of their digit in one of the numbers by holding up the correct number of **base-ten blocks**.

- Help children recall the strategy of adding numbers from right to left. *Ask:* What do we get when we add the ones? (2 ones + 3 ones = 5 ones.) Collect these blocks as the children return to their places.

- *Say:* Now add the tens. Have the children holding the ten-rods combine and count their cubes together. *Say:* 8 tens + 9 tens = 17 tens.

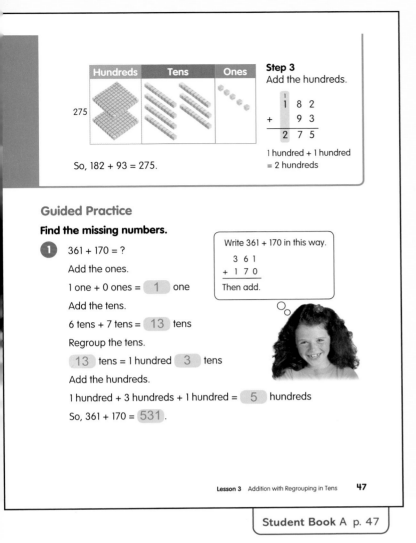

Step 3
Add the hundreds.

$$
\begin{array}{r}
\overset{\scriptstyle 1}{1}\ 8\ 2 \\
+\quad\ \ 9\ 3 \\
\hline
2\ 7\ 5
\end{array}
$$

1 hundred + 1 hundred
= 2 hundreds

So, 182 + 93 = 275.

Guided Practice

Find the missing numbers.

1 361 + 170 = ?

Add the ones.

1 one + 0 ones = [1] one

Add the tens.

6 tens + 7 tens = [13] tens

Regroup the tens.

[13] tens = 1 hundred [3] tens

Add the hundreds.

1 hundred + 3 hundreds + 1 hundred = [5] hundreds

So, 361 + 170 = [531].

> Write 361 + 170 in this way.
>
> $$
> \begin{array}{r}
> 3\ 6\ 1 \\
> +\ 1\ 7\ 0 \\
> \end{array}
> $$
>
> Then add.

Student Book A p. 47

Problem of the Lesson

Ask children to explain why the following solutions are incorrect.

(a)
$$
\begin{array}{r}
2\ 7\ 9 \\
+\ 1\ 8\ 0 \\
\hline
3\ 5\ 9
\end{array}
$$

(b)
$$
\begin{array}{r}
6\ 2\ 7 \\
+\ 1\ 4\ 6 \\
\hline
7\ 6\ 1
\end{array}
$$

(c)
$$
\begin{array}{r}
3\ 1\ 5 \\
+\ 2\ 4\ 8 \\
\hline
5\ 5\ 3
\end{array}
$$

Answer:

(a) The tens should be regrouped to add one more hundred, so the answer should read 459.

(b) The sum of the ones is 13, and the ones should be regrouped to add one more ten, so the answer should read 773.

(c) The ones should be regrouped to add one more ten, so the answer should read 563.

Differentiated Instruction

English Language Learners

Have children work in pairs. Give each pair two index cards. Have them write *regrouping* on one card and *no regrouping* on the other card. Have partners take turns writing three-digit addition problems and the other partner determining if the problem requires regrouping or no regrouping.

• *Say*: Let's regroup the tens. Lead children to recall 10 tens = 1 hundred. 17 tens = 1 hundred + 7 tens. Have one of the children holding the ten-rods return to his or her seat after giving 10 ten-rods to the child with the hundred-square. Exchange the 10 ten-rods for a hundred-square.

• *Say*: Now add the hundreds: 1 hundred + 1 hundred = 2 hundreds. The answer is two hundred seventy-five. 182 + 93 = 275

Check for Understanding
Guided Practice (pages 47 and 48)

1 to **3** These exercises reinforce the addition strategy involving regrouping in tens. Recap for children the steps involved in addition with regrouping:

1. Add the ones.
2. Add the tens.
3. Regroup the tens.
4. Add the hundreds.

For Struggling Learners You may want to give children a copy of a **Place-Value Chart** (TR02) to help them vertically align the hundreds, tens, and ones in these exercises.

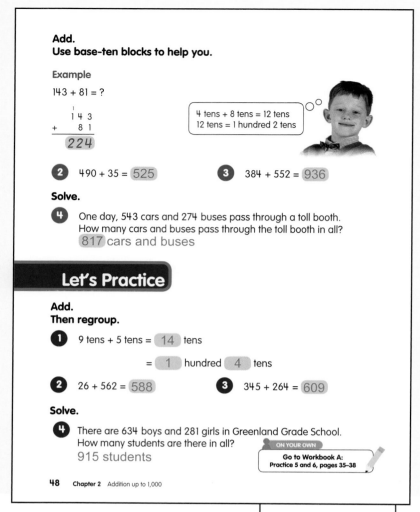

Add.
Use base-ten blocks to help you.

Example

143 + 81 = ?

```
    1
  1 4 3
+   8 1
-------
  2 2 4
```

4 tens + 8 tens = 12 tens
12 tens = 1 hundred 2 tens

2   490 + 35 = 525   **3**   384 + 552 = 936

Solve.

4   One day, 543 cars and 274 buses pass through a toll booth.
How many cars and buses pass through the toll booth in all?
817 cars and buses

Let's Practice

Add.
Then regroup.

1   9 tens + 5 tens = 14 tens

             = 1 hundred 4 tens

2   26 + 562 = 588   **3**   345 + 264 = 609

Solve.

4   There are 634 boys and 281 girls in Greenland Grade School.
How many students are there in all?
915 students

ON YOUR OWN
Go to Workbook A:
Practice 5 and 6, pages 35–38

48   **Chapter 2**   Addition up to 1,000

Student Book A p. 48

---

4 This exercise provides further practice in solving a real-world addition problem.

Let's Practice (page 48)

These exercises provide children with more practice in addition with regrouping in tens in numbers up to 1,000. Exercises **1** to **3** check children's understanding of regrouping tens in addition. Exercise **4** requires children to apply the strategies in solving real-world addition problems.

Common Error Some children may regroup when it is not necessary. Remind children that the only time they regroup is when a ten or hundred is made.

Best Practices You may want to allow children who understood regrouping ones to work on their own. You can review regrouping using **base-ten blocks** and **Place-Value Mats** (TR01) with smaller groups of children who had difficulty with the previous lesson.

ON YOUR OWN

Children practice addition with regrouping in tens in Practice 5 and 6, pages 35 to 38 of **Workbook 2A**. These pages (with the answers) are shown on page 48A.

Differentiation Options Depending on children's success with the Workbook pages, use these materials as needed.
Struggling: Reteach 2A, pp. 43–46
On Level: Extra Practice 2A, pp. 23–24

Practice and Apply
Workbook pages for Chapter 2, Lesson 3

Name: _____ Date: _____

Practice 5   Addition with Regrouping in Tens

Add and regroup the tens.

1. 534 + 283 = ?

Add the ones.

4 ones + 3 ones = ___7___ ones

Add and regroup the tens.

3 tens + 8 tens = ___11___ tens

= ___1___ hundred ___1___ ten

Add the hundreds.

1 hundred + 5 hundreds + 2 hundreds = ___8___ hundreds

534 + 283 = ___817___

> Write 534 + 283
> this way.
>   5 3 4
> + 2 8 3
> Then add.

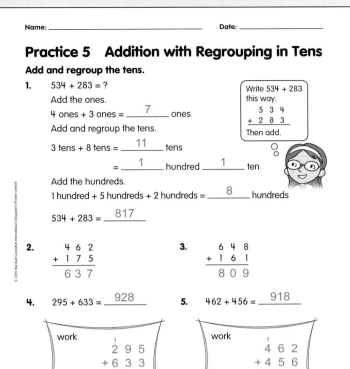

2.
```
  4 6 2
+ 1 7 5
  6 3 7
```

3.
```
  6 4 8
+ 1 6 1
  8 0 9
```

4. 295 + 633 = ___928___

5. 462 + 456 = ___918___

work
```
  1
  2 9 5
+ 6 3 3
  9 2 8
```

work
```
    1
  4 6 2
+ 4 5 6
  9 1 8
```

Add.

6.

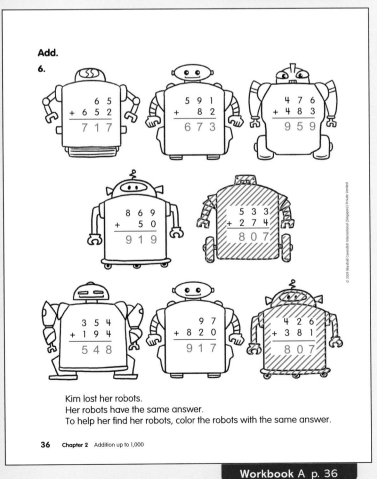

```
  6 5
+ 6 5 2
  7 1 7
```
```
  5 9 1
+   8 2
  6 7 3
```
```
  4 7 6
+ 4 8 3
  9 5 9
```
```
  8 6 9
+   5 0
  9 1 9
```
```
  5 3 3
+ 2 7 4
  8 0 7
```
```
  3 5 4
+ 1 9 4
  5 4 8
```
```
    9 7
+ 8 2 0
  9 1 7
```
```
  4 2 6
+ 3 8 1
  8 0 7
```

Kim lost her robots.
Her robots have the same answer.
To help her find her robots, color the robots with the same answer.

Name: _____ Date: _____

Practice 6   Addition with Regrouping in Tens

Solve.

1. Farmer Black has 374 chickens and 383 ducks on his farm.
How many ducks and chickens does he have in all?

374 + 383 = 757

He has ___757___ ducks and chickens in all.

2. Maria has 381 baseball cards.
She has 492 football cards.
How many cards does she have in all?

381 + 492 = 873

She has ___873___ cards in all.

3. Peter collects 280 stamps.
Then his brother gives him another 163 stamps.
How many stamps does Peter have now?

280 + 163 = 443

Peter has ___443___ stamps now.

Solve.

4. Kirk has painted 460 bricks.
He has 262 bricks left to paint.
How many bricks does Kirk have to paint in all?

460 + 262 = 722

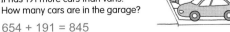

Kirk has to paint ___722___ bricks in all.

5. Leroy has 299 model airplanes.
Keisha gives him another 120 model airplanes.
How many model airplanes does Leroy have now?

299 + 120 = 419

Leroy has ___419___ model airplanes now.

6. A parking garage has 654 vans.
It has 191 more cars than vans.
How many cars are in the garage?

654 + 191 = 845

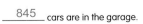

___845___ cars are in the garage.

Addition with Regrouping in Ones and Tens

LESSON 4

LESSON OBJECTIVES
- Use base-ten blocks to add numbers with regrouping.
- Add three-digit numbers with regrouping.
- Solve real-world addition problems.

TECHNOLOGY RESOURCES
- *Math in Focus* eBooks
- *Math in Focus* Teacher Resources CD
- *Math in Focus* Virtual Manipulatives

DAY 1 Student Book 2A, pp. 49–54
Workbook 2A, pp. 39–42

MATERIALS
- 1 set of base-ten blocks
- 1 Place-Value Mat (TRO1) per group
- 3 sets of Number Cards (TRO6) per group
- 1 Place-Value Chart (TRO2) per child (optional)

DIFFERENTIATION RESOURCES
- Reteach 2A, pp. 47–50
- Extra Practice 2A, pp. 25–26

5-minute Warm Up

- Randomly provide children with a 3-digit number, for example 373.

- Have children fill in the blanks in the following:
  373 = 373 ones = <u>3</u> hundreds 73 ones
  = <u>37</u> tens 3 ones
  = <u>3</u> hundreds <u>7</u> tens <u>3</u> ones.

Addition with Regrouping in Ones and Tens

LESSON 4

Lesson Objectives
- Use base-ten blocks to add numbers with regrouping.
- Add three-digit numbers with regrouping.
- Solve real-world addition problems.

Learn **You can add using base-ten blocks and a place-value chart to regroup ones and tens.**

278 + 386 = ?

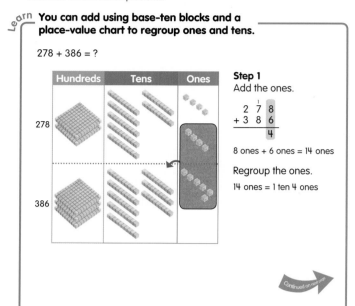

Step 1
Add the ones.

$$\begin{array}{r} 2\ 7\ \overset{1}{8} \\ +\ 3\ 8\ 6 \\ \hline 4 \end{array}$$

8 ones + 6 ones = 14 ones

Regroup the ones.

14 ones = 1 ten 4 ones

Continued on next page

Student Book A p. 49

DAY 1 # Teach

Learn

Add Using Base-Ten Blocks and a Place-Value Chart to Regroup Ones and Tens (pages 49 and 50)

This Learn section introduces children to the addition of two 3-digit numbers with regrouping of ones and tens.

- Draw a place-value chart on the board and write the numbers 278 and 386 in the appropriate places on the chart.

- Ask some children to show the value of their digit in one of the numbers by holding up the correct number of **base-ten blocks**.

- You may want to group the children and have them use base-ten blocks and **Place-Value Mats** (TRO1) to follow along at their desks.

- Help children recall the strategy of adding numbers from right to left. *Say:* Add the ones. 8 ones + 6 ones = 14 ones. *Say:* Let's regroup the ones. 14 ones = 1 ten + 4 ones. Have one of the children holding the unit cubes give 10 unit cubes to a child with the ten-rods. Exchange the 10 unit cubes for a ten-rod.

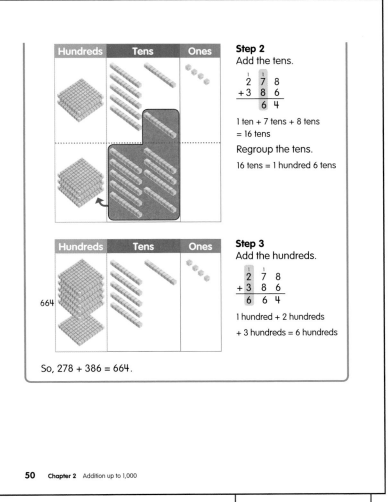

Step 2
Add the tens.

$$\begin{array}{r} {\scriptstyle 1 \ 1} \\ 2\ 7\ 8 \\ +\ 3\ 8\ 6 \\ \hline 6\ 4 \end{array}$$

1 ten + 7 tens + 8 tens
= 16 tens

Regroup the tens.

16 tens = 1 hundred 6 tens

Step 3
Add the hundreds.

$$\begin{array}{r} {\scriptstyle 1 \ 1} \\ 2\ 7\ 8 \\ +\ 3\ 8\ 6 \\ \hline 6\ 6\ 4 \end{array}$$

1 hundred + 2 hundreds
+ 3 hundreds = 6 hundreds

So, 278 + 386 = 664.

Student Book A p. 50

- *Say:* Now add the tens. 1 ten + 7 tens + 8 tens = 16 tens. Regroup the tens. 16 tens = 1 hundred 6 tens. Have one of the children holding the ten-rods give 10 ten-rods to a child with the hundred-squares. Exchange the 10 ten-rods for a hundred-square.

- *Say:* Now add the hundreds. 1 hundred + 2 hundreds + 3 hundreds = 6 hundreds. You get six hundred sixty-four. 278 + 386 = 664.

Problem of the Lesson

Complete this number sentence.
369 + 247 = ?
Show your answer using place value.

Solution:
369 = 3 hundreds 6 tens 9 ones
247 = 2 hundreds 4 tens 7 ones

369 + 247:

$$\begin{array}{ll} & 3\text{ hundreds}\quad 6\text{ tens } 9\text{ ones} \\ + & 2\text{ hundreds}\quad 4\text{ tens } 7\text{ ones} \\ \hline & 5\text{ hundreds } 10\text{ tens } 16\text{ ones} \end{array}$$

= 5 hundreds 11 tens 6 ones
= 6 hundreds   1 ten 6 ones
= 616

Answer: 616

Differentiated Instruction

English Language Learners

Children may be unsure where to begin when adding. When reading, they read left to right; to solve these math problems, they work right to left. Have children work with a partner and practice moving their finger from right to left on math problems.

Best Practices   Allow children who understand regrouping to complete the Guided Practice on their own and then play the game. Provide **Place-Value Charts** (TR02) for children who continually have trouble with alignment.

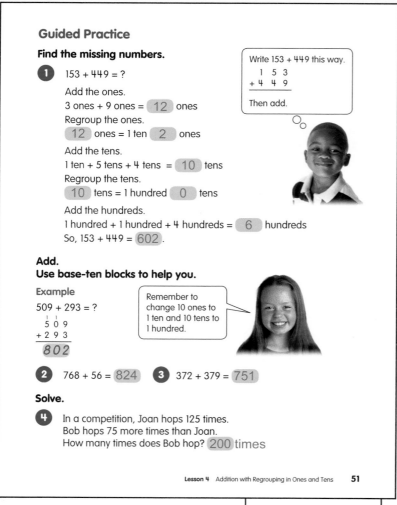

Guided Practice

Find the missing numbers.

1 153 + 449 = ?

Write 153 + 449 this way.

$$\begin{array}{r} 1\ 5\ 3 \\ +\ 4\ 4\ 9 \\ \hline \end{array}$$

Then add.

Add the ones.

3 ones + 9 ones = ⬚12⬚ ones

Regroup the ones.

⬚12⬚ ones = 1 ten ⬚2⬚ ones

Add the tens.

1 ten + 5 tens + 4 tens = ⬚10⬚ tens

Regroup the tens.

⬚10⬚ tens = 1 hundred ⬚0⬚ tens

Add the hundreds.

1 hundred + 1 hundred + 4 hundreds = ⬚6⬚ hundreds

So, 153 + 449 = ⬚602⬚.

Add.
Use base-ten blocks to help you.

Example

509 + 293 = ?

Remember to change 10 ones to 1 ten and 10 tens to 1 hundred.

$$\begin{array}{r} \overset{1\ \ 1}{5\ 0\ 9} \\ +\ 2\ 9\ 3 \\ \hline 8\ 0\ 2 \end{array}$$

2 768 + 56 = ⬚824⬚   **3** 372 + 379 = ⬚751⬚

Solve.

4 In a competition, Joan hops 125 times. Bob hops 75 more times than Joan. How many times does Bob hop? ⬚200⬚ times

Student Book A p. 51

WORKING TOGETHER Game

Go For The Greatest!

Players: 2–4
You need:
• three sets of number cards from 0 to 9
• pencil and paper

STEP 1 Shuffle the cards. Each player picks six cards.

STEP 2 Use the six cards to make as many three-digit numbers as possible. Write them down.

STEP 3 Add any 2 three-digit numbers. (Hint: Pick the numbers that will give the greatest answer.) If the hundreds digits add up to more than 9, choose another number.

The player with the greatest answer wins the game!

Student Book A p. 52

Check for Understanding
✓ Guided Practice (page 51)

1 to **3** These exercises reinforce the addition strategy involving regrouping in ones and tens. Recap for children the steps involved in addition with regrouping:

1. Add the ones.
2. Regroup the ones.
3. Add the tens.
4. Regroup the tens.
5. Add the hundreds.

4 This exercise provides practice in solving a real-world addition problem.

WORKING TOGETHER Game:
Go for the Greatest! (page 52)

This game reinforces the concept of addition with regrouping.

• Arrange children in groups of two to four. Distribute the sets of **Number Cards** (TR06).

• Read and explain to children the steps on the Student Book page.

• Have children repeat the activity as often as time allows.

For Advanced Learners Have children repeat the activity but try for the smallest possible sums.

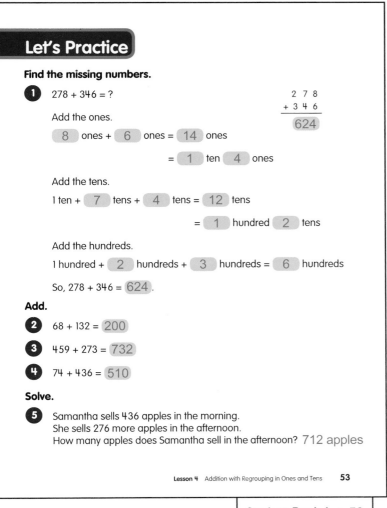

Student Book A p. 53

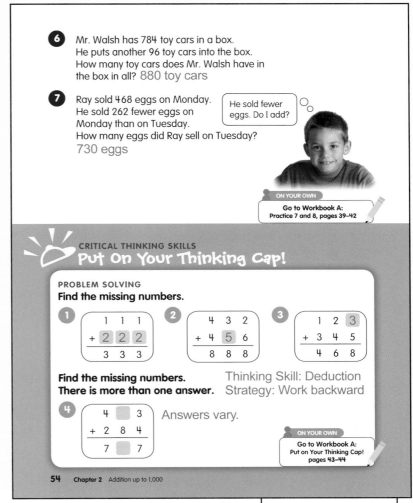

Student Book A p. 54

Let's Practice (pages 53 and 54)

Exercises ❶ to ❹ provide practice in addition with regrouping ones and tens. Exercises ❺ to ❼ provide practice in solving real-world problems involving addition of three-digit numbers.

ON YOUR OWN

Children practice addition with regrouping in ones and tens in Practice 7 and 8, pages 39 to 42 of **Workbook 2A**. These pages (with the answers) are shown on page 54A.

Differentiation Options Depending on children's success with the Workbook pages, use these materials as needed.
Struggling: Reteach 2A, pp. 47–50
On Level: Extra Practice 2A, pp. 25–26

CRITICAL THINKING AND PROBLEM SOLVING
Put on Your Thinking Cap! (page 54)

This problem solving exercise involves addition with or without regrouping. Children work individually or in groups to answer the questions and to present the solutions to the class.

For Exercises ❶ to ❸, ask children to think of a possible number to fill each blank, e.g. 1 + ? = 3. (2); 3 + ? = 8 (5); ? + 5 = 8 (3).

For Exercise ❹, ask children to think of possible pairs of answers, but lead them to see that the tens have been regrouped in the hundreds place. Encourage children to share the different methods of solving the problem.

Thinking Skill
• Deduction

Problem Solving Strategy
• Work backward

ON YOUR OWN

Because all children should be challenged, have all children try the Challenging Practice and Problem Solving pages in **Workbook 2A**, pages 43 and 44. These pages (with the answers) are shown on page 54B.

Differentiation Options Depending on children's success with the Workbook pages, use these materials as needed.
On Level: Extra Practice 2A, pp. 27–28
Advanced: Enrichment 2A, pp. 11–20

Practice and Apply
Workbook pages for Chapter 2, Lesson 4

Practice 7   Addition with Regrouping in Ones and Tens

Add and regroup.

1. 488 + 123 = ?

   Add and regroup the ones.
   8 ones + 3 ones

   = _____11_____ ones

   = _____1_____ ten _____1_____ one

   Add and regroup the tens.
   1 ten + 8 tens + 2 tens = _____11_____ tens

   = _____1_____ hundred _____1_____ ten

   Add the hundreds.
   1 hundred + 4 hundreds + 1 hundred = _____6_____ hundreds

   488 + 123 = _____611_____

   > Write 488 + 123 this way.
   >   4 8 8
   > + 1 2 3
   > Then add.

   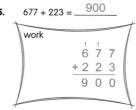

2.   5 9 5
   + 1 2 7
   _____
     7 2 2

3.   2 8 7
   + 5 3 4
   _____
     8 2 1

4. 789 + 121 = _____910_____

   work
     1 1
     7 8 9
   + 1 2 1
   _____
     9 1 0

5. 677 + 223 = _____900_____

   work
     1 1
     6 7 7
   + 2 2 3
   _____
     9 0 0

Workbook A p. 39

Whose toys are these?
Add.
Then match the owner to the toy.

6.

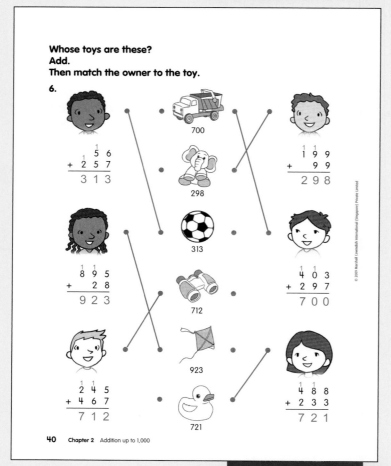

Workbook A p. 40

Name: _____   Date: _____

Practice 8   Addition with Regrouping in Ones and Tens

Solve.

1. On Wednesday, 487 people visit the zoo.
   On Thursday, 135 more people visit the zoo than on Wednesday.
   How many people visit the zoo on Thursday?

   487 + 135 = 622

   _____622_____ people visit the zoo on Thursday.

2. After selling 694 books, Mr. Brown has 276 books left.
   How many books did he have at first?

   694 + 276 = 970

   He had _____970_____ books at first.

3. A toy company gives away 777 toys in a contest.
   There are 177 toys left.
   How many toys are there at first?

   777 + 177 = 954

   There are _____954_____ toys at first.

Workbook A p. 41

Solve.

4. There are 167 dolls in a toy store.
   The owner buys 533 more dolls.
   How many dolls are there now?

   167 + 533 = 700

   There are _____700_____ dolls now.

5. Sunshine Camp has 324 boys.
   There are 379 girls.
   How many campers are at Sunshine Camp?

   324 + 379 = 703

   There are _____703_____ campers at Sunshine Camp.

6. Luke has 548 coins in his collection.
   Luke has 276 fewer coins than Sam.
   How many coins does Sam have?

   548 + 276 = 824

   Sam has _____824_____ coins in his collection.

Workbook A p. 42

Practice and Apply

Workbook pages for Put on Your Thinking Cap!

 **Put On Your Thinking Cap!**

 Challenging Practice

Write the missing numbers.

1.
```
    5 3 ③
  + 1 4 1
  ───────
    6 7 4
```

2.
```
    ⑥ 4 5
  + 2 3 4
  ───────
    8 7 9
```

3.
```
    7 ⓪ 8
  + 2 9 1
  ───────
    9 9 9
```

4.
```
      1
    4 2 6
  + 3 ③ 5
  ───────
    7 6 1
```

5.
```
    1 1
    3 ③ 7
  + 5 9 5
  ───────
    9 3 2
```

6.
```
    1 1
    6 5 3
  + 2 ⑧ 9
  ───────
    9 4 2
```

Do these.

7.

(455) (544) (554) (545) (454)

a. Order the numbers from greatest to least.

554   545   544   455   454

b. Add 100 to the least number.
Show your work.
```
      1 0 0
    + 4 5 4
    ───────
      5 5 4
```
100 + 454 = 554

 **Put On Your Thinking Cap!**

Problem Solving

Make two 3-digit numbers from the numbers below.
Use each number only once.
What are the two 3-digit numbers that give the greatest
answer when you add them?

 [3] [5] [2] [4] [1] [0]

Thinking skills: Classifying, Comparing,
Identifying patterns and relationships
Strategies: Guess and check, Make a list

Answers vary. Sample:

  5 3 0 + 4 2 1 = 9 5 1

Notes

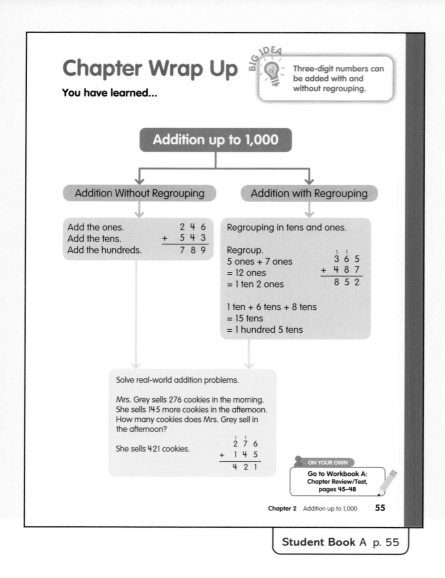

Student Book A p. 55

Chapter Wrap Up (page 55)

Use the examples on page 55 to review addition with and without regrouping. As you work through the examples, encourage children to use the chapter vocabulary:

- add
- place-value chart
- regroup

ON YOUR OWN

Have children review the vocabulary, concepts and skills from Chapter 2 with the Chapter Review/Test in **Workbook 2A**, pages 45 to 48. These pages (with the answers) are shown on page 55A.

Assessment

Use the Chapter 2 Test Prep on pages 9 to 11 of **Assessments 2** to assess how well children have learned the material of this chapter. This assessment is appropriate for reporting results to adults at home and administrators. This test is shown on page 55B.

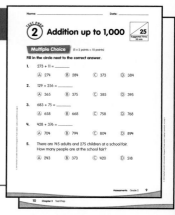

Assessments 2 pp. 9–11

Workbook pages for Chapter Review/Test

Chapter Review/Test

Vocabulary

Fill in the blanks with words from the box.
The words may be used more than once.

1.

ones	tens	hundreds	regroup	hundred

Step 1
Add the ___ones___.
2 ones + 8 ones = 10 ones
___Regroup___ the ones.
10 ones = 1 ten 0 ones

Step 2
Add the ___tens___.
1 ten + 6 tens + 6 tens = 13 tens
___Regroup___ the tens.
13 tens = 1 ___hundred___ 3 ___tens___

Step 3
Add the ___hundreds___.
1 hundred + 4 hundreds + 2 hundreds
= 7 hundreds

462 + 268 = 730

Workbook A p. 45

Concepts and Skills

Add.
Then match the problems with the same answer.

2.

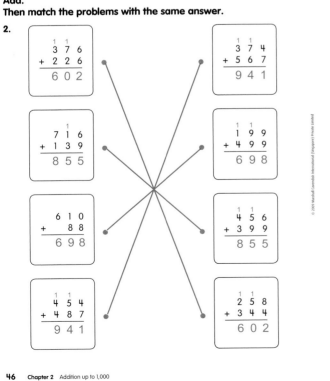

Workbook A p. 46

Name: _____   Date: _____

Problem Solving

Solve.

3. Mr. Thomas drives 173 miles on Monday.
   On Tuesday, he drives 216 miles.
   How many miles does he drive in all?

   173 + 216 = 389

   He drives ___389___ miles in all.

4. A carpenter has 362 pieces of lumber.
   He needs another 228 pieces of lumber to build a bridge.
   How many pieces of lumber does he need to build the bridge?

   362 + 228 = 590

   He needs ___590___ pieces of lumber to build the bridge.

Workbook A p. 47

Solve.

5. A movie theater sells 294 tickets to the first show.
   It sells 457 tickets to the second show.
   How many tickets does it sell in all?

   294 + 457 = 751

   It sells ___751___ tickets in all.

6. Shantel has 546 stickers in her collection.
   She has 278 fewer stickers than Sherice.
   How many stickers does Sherice have in her collection?

   546 + 278 = 824

   Sherice has ___824___ stickers in her collection.

Workbook A p. 48

Assessments Book pages for Chapter 2 Test Prep
Answer key appears in Assessments Book.

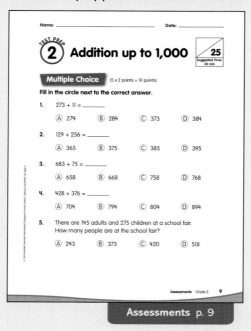

Name: _____ Date: _____

TEST PREP
(2) Addition up to 1,000   25   Suggested Time: 30 min

Multiple Choice   (5 x 2 points = 10 points)

Fill in the circle next to the correct answer.

1. 273 + 11 = _____
    Ⓐ 274   Ⓑ 284   Ⓒ 373   Ⓓ 384

2. 129 + 256 = _____
    Ⓐ 365   Ⓑ 375   Ⓒ 385   Ⓓ 395

3. 683 + 75 = _____
    Ⓐ 658   Ⓑ 668   Ⓒ 758   Ⓓ 768

4. 428 + 376 = _____
    Ⓐ 704   Ⓑ 794   Ⓒ 804   Ⓓ 894

5. There are 145 adults and 275 children at a school fair.
    How many people are at the school fair?
    Ⓐ 243   Ⓑ 373   Ⓒ 420   Ⓓ 518

Assessments Grade 2   9

Assessments p. 9

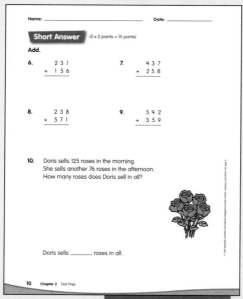

Name: _____ Date: _____

Short Answer   (5 x 2 points = 10 points)

Add.

6.   2 3 1   7.   4 3 7
    + 1 5 6   + 2 5 8

8.   2 3 8   9.   5 4 2
    + 5 7 1   + 3 5 9

10. Doris sells 125 roses in the morning.
     She sells another 76 roses in the afternoon.
     How many roses does Doris sell in all?

     Doris sells _____ roses in all.

10   Chapter 2   Test Prep

Assessments p. 10

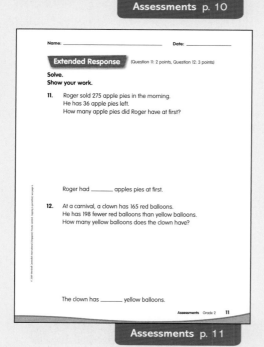

Name: _____ Date: _____

Extended Response   (Question 11: 2 points, Question 12: 3 points)

Solve.
Show your work.

11. Roger sold 275 apple pies in the morning.
     He has 36 apple pies left.
     How many apple pies did Roger have at first?

     Roger had _____ apples pies at first.

12. At a carnival, a clown has 165 red balloons.
     He has 198 fewer red balloons than yellow balloons.
     How many yellow balloons does the clown have?

     The clown has _____ yellow balloons.

Assessments Grade 2   11

Assessments p. 11

CHAPTER 3

Chapter Overview

Subtraction up to 1,000

Math Background

Children have learned subtraction up to 100 in Grade 1, when they were taught the basic subtraction algorithm of subtracting from right to left. Children have also been taught to apply their knowledge of number bonds and place value to decompose and compose numbers in regrouping to find sums and differences.

In this chapter, children will learn two types of multi-digit subtraction: basic subtraction without regrouping and subtraction with regrouping. Children are taught subtraction with regrouping using base-ten blocks and place-value charts as concrete representations, aiding children in visualizing the regrouping of tens as ones, hundreds as tens and hundreds as tens and ones. For example, in the evaluation of 242 − 128 = _____, children are led to deduce that 4 tens and 2 ones in 242 can be regrouped as 3 tens and 12 ones. The same strategy is applied in regrouping in the hundreds and tens places and regrouping in the hundreds, tens, and ones places. Children are also reminded that addition and subtraction are inverse operations so addition can be used to check subtraction.

Another method of subtraction taught in this chapter is subtraction across zeros. In this particular situation, regrouping is done in the hundreds first, followed by tens and ones. For example, in the evaluation of 200 − 76 = _____, 200 is regrouped as 1 hundred and 10 tens and this is further regrouped as 1 hundred, 9 tens, and 10 ones.

Cross-Curricular Connections

Reading/Language Arts Read aloud *Subtraction Action* by Loreen Leedy (Holiday House, © 2002) about Miss Prime and her students using subtraction problems as they get ready for their school fair.

Social Studies Display information on the Great Lakes.

Great Lakes Facts

	Lake Erie	Lake Huron	Lake Michigan	Lake Ontario	Lake Superior
Length	241 miles	206 miles	307 miles	193 miles	350 miles
Width	57 miles	183 miles	118 miles	53 miles	160 miles

Skills Trace

Grade 1	Subtract one- and two-digit numbers with and without regrouping. (Chaps. 4, 8, 13, 14, and 17)
Grade 2	Subtract three-digit numbers with and without regrouping. (Chaps. 3, 4, and 10)
Grade 3	Use multiple strategies in subtraction up to 10,000 (with multiple regroupings) to solve real-world problems. (Chaps. 2, 3, and 5)

EVERY DAY COUNTS®
Calendar Math

The October activities provide...

Review of regrouping to add and using place-value models (Chapter 2)

Preview of part and whole relationships and continuing number patterns (Chapter 4)

Practice of regrouping to subtract, modeling of subtraction with objects, and relating addition and subtraction (Lessons 2, 3, 4, and 5 in this chapter)

Differentiation Resources

Differentiation for Special Populations

	English Language Learners	Struggling Reteach 2A	On Level Extra Practice 2A	Advanced Enrichment 2A
Lesson 1	p. 62	pp. 51–62	pp. 29–30	Enrichment pages can be used to challenge advanced children.
Lesson 2	p. 68	pp. 63–68	pp. 31–32	
Lesson 3	p. 75	pp. 69–72	pp. 33–34	
Lesson 4	p. 81	pp. 73–76	pp. 35–36	
Lesson 5	p. 85	pp. 77–80	pp. 37–38	

Additional Support

For English Language Learners

Select activities that reinforce the chapter vocabulary and the connections among these words, such as having children

- add terms, definitions, and examples to the Word Wall
- act out vocabulary terms
- draw pictures to illustrate differences between addition and subtraction
- discuss the Chapter Wrap Up, encouraging children to use the chapter vocabulary

For Struggling Learners

Select activities that go back to the appropriate stage of the Concrete-Pictorial-Abstract spectrum, such as having children

- act out subtraction stories in the chapter
- use manipulatives to model subtraction with and without regrouping
- tell and solve subtraction number stories
- create subtraction number stories for given addition number sentences

See also page 82–83

If necessary, review

- Chapter 1 (Numbers to 1,000)
- Chapter 2 (Addition to 1,000).

For Advanced Learners

See suggestions on page 88.

Assessment and Remediation

Chapter 3 Assessment

Prior Knowledge		
	Resource	**Page numbers**
Quick Check	Student Book 2A	pp. 59–60
Pre-Test	Assessments 2	pp. 12–13
Ongoing Diagnostic		
Guided Practice	Student Book 2A	pp. 63, 64, 69–70, 74–75, 81–82, 86–87
Common Error	Teacher's Edition 2A	pp. 76–77
Formal Evaluation		
Chapter Review/Test	Workbook 2A	pp. 69–72
Chapter 3 Test Prep	Assessments 2	pp. 14–16

Problems with these items...   **Can be remediated with...**

Remediation Options

	Review/Test Items	Chapter Assessment Items	Reteach	Student Book
Objective	**Workbook 2A pp. 69–72**	**Assessments 2 pp. 14–16**	**Reteach 2A**	**Student Book 2A**
Use chapter vocabulary correctly.	1	Not assessed	In context as needed	p. 61
Subtract from three-digit numbers without regrouping.	2	2, 6, 8	pp. 52–61	Lesson 1
Subtract from three-digit numbers with regrouping in tens and ones.	2	1, 7	pp. 64–67	Lesson 2
Subtract from three-digit numbers with regrouping in hundreds and tens.	2	8, 11	pp. 69–72	Lesson 3
Subtract from three-digit numbers with regrouping in hundreds, tens, and ones.	2–5	3, 4, 9, 10, 12	pp. 73–76	Lesson 4
Subtract from three-digit numbers with zeros.	2, 6	5	pp. 77–80	Lesson 5
Apply the inverse operations of addition and subtraction.	1, 3–6	1, 3	pp. 52–61, 64–67, 69–75, 79, 80	Lessons 1, 2, 3, 4, and 5
Solve real-world subtraction problems.	3–6	10, 11, 12	pp. 55, 58, 61, 67, 72, 76, 80	Lessons 1, 2, 3, 4, and 5

Chapter Planning Guide

CHAPTER 3 Subtraction up to 1,000

Lesson	Pacing	Instructional Objectives	Vocabulary
Chapter Opener pp. 56–60 Recall Prior Knowledge Quick Check	*1 day	💡**Big Idea** Subtract up to three-digit numbers with and without regrouping	
Lesson 1, pp. 61–66 Subtraction Without Regrouping	1 day	• Use base-ten blocks to subtract numbers without regrouping. • Subtract from three-digit numbers without regrouping. • Apply the inverse operations of addition and subtraction. • Solve real-world subtraction problems.	• subtract
Lesson 2, pp. 67–71 Subtraction with Regrouping in Tens and Ones	1 day	• Use base-ten blocks to subtract with regrouping. • Subtract from three-digit numbers with regrouping. • Apply the inverse operations of addition and subtraction. • Solve real-world subtraction problems.	
Lesson 3, pp. 72–77 Subtraction with Regrouping in Hundreds and Tens	1 day	• Use base-ten blocks to subtract with regrouping. • Subtract from a three-digit number with regrouping. • Apply the inverse operations of addition and subtraction. • Solve real-world subtraction problems.	
Lesson 4, pp. 78–83 Subtraction with Regrouping in Hundreds, Tens, and Ones	1 day	• Use base-ten blocks to subtract with regrouping. • Subtract from a three-digit number with regrouping. • Apply the inverse operations of addition and subtraction. • Solve real-world subtraction problems.	

*Assume that 1 day is a 45–55 minute period.

Resources	Materials	NCTM Focal Points	NCTM Process Standards
Student Book 2A, pp. 56–60 **Assessments 2,** pp. 12–13			
Student Book 2A, pp. 61–66 **Workbook 2A,** pp. 49–52 **Extra Practice 2A,** pp. 29–30 **Reteach 2A,** pp. 51–62	• 1 set of base-ten blocks • Place-Value Mats (TRO1) as needed • Index cards (optional)	***Number and Operations and Algebra*** Apply relationships and properties of number. Use efficient, accurate, and generalizable methods to add and subtract multi-digit whole numbers.	Problem Solving Reasoning/Proof Communication Connections Representation
Student Book 2A, pp. 67–71 **Workbook 2A,** pp. 53–56 **Extra Practice 2A,** pp. 31–32 **Reteach 2A,** pp. 63–68	• 1 set of base-ten blocks • 1 Place-Value Mat (TRO1) per group (optional)	***Number and Operations*** Add and subtract to solve a variety of problems. ***Number and Operations and Algebra*** Compose and decompose multi-digit numbers. Apply understanding of models of addition and subtraction.	Problem Solving Reasoning/Proof Communication Connections Representation
Student Book 2A, pp. 72–77 **Workbook 2A,** pp. 57–60 **Extra Practice 2A,** pp. 33–34 **Reteach 2A,** pp. 69–72	• 1 set of base-ten blocks • 2 ten-sided dice per group • 1 Place-Value Mat (TRO1) per group (optional)	***Number and Operations and Algebra*** Develop fluency with efficient procedures for adding and subtracting whole numbers. Apply understanding of models of addition and subtraction.	Problem Solving Communication Connections Representation
Student Book 2A, pp. 78–83 **Workbook 2A,** pp. 61–64 **Extra Practice 2A,** pp. 35–36 **Reteach 2A,** pp. 73–76	• 1 set of base-ten blocks • 1 Place-Value Mat (TRO1) per group • 1 Place-Value Chart (TRO2) per child (optional)	***Number and Operations and Algebra*** Add and subtract to solve a variety of problems. Use efficient, accurate and generalizable methods to add and subtract multi-digit whole numbers.	Problem Solving Connections Representation

Chapter Planning Guide

Lesson	Pacing	Instructional Objectives	Vocabulary
Lesson 5, pp. 84–87 Subtraction Across Zeros	1 day	• Use base-ten blocks to subtract with regrouping. • Subtract from a three-digit number with regrouping. • Apply the inverse operations of addition and subtraction. • Solve real-world subtraction problems.	
Problem Solving, pp. 88–89 Put on Your Thinking Cap!	$\frac{1}{2}$ day	**Thinking Skills** • Deduction • Identifying patterns and relationships **Problem Solving Strategies** • Work backward • Use a diagram/model	
Chapter Wrap Up pp. 90–91	$\frac{1}{2}$ day	• Reinforce and consolidate chapter skills and concepts.	
Chapter Assessment	1 day		

*Assume that 1 day is a 45–55 minute period.

Resources	Materials	NCTM Focal Points	NCTM Process Standards
Student Book 2A, pp. 84–87 **Workbook 2A,** pp. 65–66 **Extra Practice 2A,** pp. 37–38 **Reteach 2A,** pp. 77–80	• 1 set of base-ten blocks • 1 Place-Value Mat (TR01) per group (optional) • 2 index cards per pair (optional)	***Number and Operations and Algebra*** Add and subtract to solve a variety of problems. Use efficient, accurate, and generalizable methods to add and subtract multi-digit whole numbers.	Problem Solving Reasoning/Proof Connections Representation
Student Book 2A, pp. 88–89 **Workbook 2A,** pp. 67–68 **Extra Practice 2A,** pp. 39–40 **Enrichment 2A,** pp. 21–30		***Number and Operations and Algebra*** Add and subtract multi-digit whole numbers to solve non-routine problems.	Problem Solving Reasoning/Proof
Student Book 2A, pp. 90–91 **Workbook 2A,** pp. 69–72			
Assessments 2, pp. 14–16			

Technology Resources for easy classroom management
- *Math in Focus* eBooks
- *Math in Focus* Teacher Resources CD
- *Math in Focus* Virtual Manipulatives
- Online Assessment Generator

Chapter Introduction

Chapter 3
Vocabulary

| subtract | take away one part from the whole to find the other part | Lesson 1 |

Student Book A p. 56

Big Idea (page 56)

Subtraction up to 3-digit numbers with and without regrouping is the main focus of this chapter.

- Children use the regrouping concept to subtract from numbers up to 1,000.

- They learn subtraction with regrouping in the tens and ones, hundreds and tens, and hundreds, tens, and ones.

- They learn subtraction with regrouping across zeros.

Chapter Opener (page 56)

The picture illustrates a bug with many legs hopping around. Used together with the poem, it provides a starting point for talking about subtraction from 1,000.

- Show children the picture and the poem. Read the poem aloud and have children read each sentence after you. Have children read the poem again as a class or in groups.

- *Ask:* How many legs does the bug have left now? (999)

- Give another version of the last verse:
  '*Hop around, hop around/Have you seen the missing mate of the missing leg of mine?/If it can't be found,/I shall have to hop around/ On my other _____ !*

- Ask children to fill in the last words (nine hundred ninety eight).

Encourage children to use the count-back strategy to find the answer.

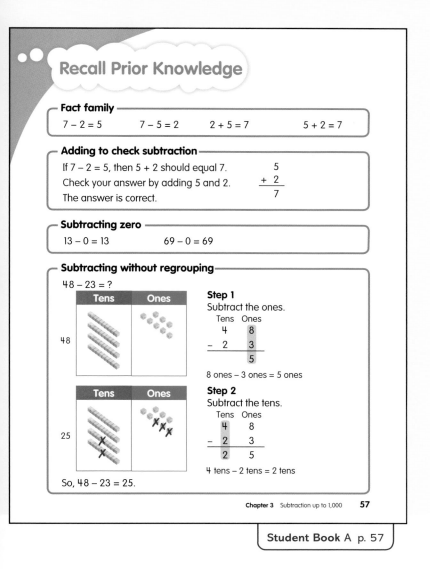

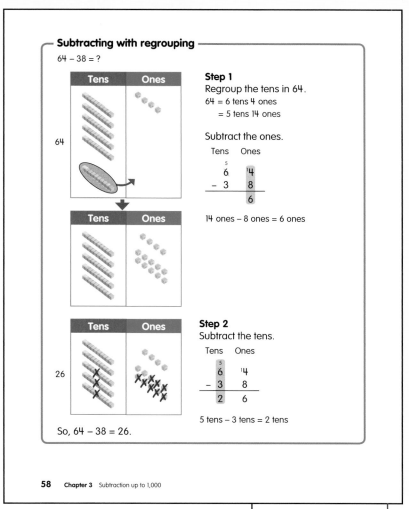

Recall Prior Knowledge (pages 57 to 59)

Fact Family

Children learned to write fact families in Grade 1.

• Show children the number sentence 7 − 2 = 5.

• Have children identify the other possible number sentences using the same three numbers.

• Help children to see that all four number sentences represent the number bond 7–2-5.

Adding to Check Subtraction

Children learned to show the inverse relationship between addition and subtraction up to 20.

• Show children the number sentence 7 − 2 = 5.

• Have children check the above number sentence with the related addition sentence 5 + 2 = 7.

• Help children to deduce that the earlier number sentence is correct.

Subtracting Zero

Children learned the zero concept in Grade 1.

• Show the two number sentences. Help children recall the Identity Property taught in Grade 1, $n − 0 = n$ for any number n.

Subtracting Without Regrouping

Children learned subtraction up to 100 without regrouping in Grade 1.

• Show children the number sentence. Help children recall the strategy for subtracting numbers: Subtract from right to left (first subtract the ones, then the tens).

Subtracting with Regrouping

Children learned subtraction up to 100 with regrouping in Grade 1. This example may need more review than the others.

• Show children the number sentence.

• Have children recall the regrouping concept: 1 ten = 10 ones.

• Lead children to deduce that 6 tens and 4 ones = 5 tens and 14 ones.

• Explain that the example illustrates the taking-away method of subtraction.

Student Book A p. 59

There are 12 horses in all.
8 horses are white.
How many horses are brown?

12 – 8 = 4

4 horses are brown.

Solve.

1. Find a subtraction sentence that belongs to the same fact family as 14 + 5 = 19. 19 – 5 = 14

2. Find the addition sentence that will help you check if 56 – 3 = 53 is correct. 53 + 3 = 56

Chapter 3 Subtraction up to 1,000 **59**

Student Book A p. 60

Subtract.

3. 33 – 0 = 33

4. 87 – 0 = 87

Subtract.

5. 25 – 13 = 12

6. 37 – 6 = 31

Regroup the tens and ones.
You can use base-ten blocks to help you.

7. 32 = 3 tens 2 ones
   = 2 tens 12 ones

Subtract.
You can use base-ten blocks to help you.

8. 4 2
   – 3 3
   ____
     9

9. 6 7
   – 2 9
   ____
    3 8

Solve.

10. Jackie buys 24 eggs.
    She drops the bag of eggs and 17 eggs break.
    How many eggs are left?
    7 eggs

check!
 1 7
+   7
____
 2 4

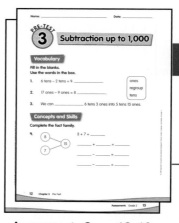

60 Chapter 3 Subtraction up to 1,000

Subtracting to Solve Real-World Problems

Children learned how to apply subtraction to real-world examples in Grade 1.

- Show children the picture and the story.

- Help children to apply the part–whole concept to solve the problem. Point out that regrouping is necessary.

- Have children check their answers by counting the brown horses in the picture.

✔Quick Check (pages 59 and 60)

- Use this section as a diagnostic tool to assess children's level of prerequisite knowledge before they progress to this chapter.

- Exercises **1** and **2** assess children's understanding of fact families.

- Exercises **3** and **4** assess children's understanding of the Identity Property of subtraction.

- Exercises **5** and **6** assess the skill of subtracting without regrouping.

- Exercises **7** to **9** assess the skill of subtracting with regrouping. Provide **base-ten blocks** to help children if necessary.

- Exercise **10** assesses children's ability to solve real-world subtraction problems.

Assessments 2 pp. 12–13

Assessment

For additional assessment of children's prior knowledge and chapter readiness, use the Chapter 3 Pre-Test on pages 12 and 13 of **Assessments 2**.

1 LESSON Subtraction Without Regrouping

LESSON OBJECTIVES

- Use base-ten blocks to subtract numbers without regrouping.
- Subtract from three-digit numbers without regrouping.
- Apply the inverse operations of addition and subtraction.
- Solve real-world subtraction problems.

TECHNOLOGY RESOURCES

- *Math in Focus* eBooks
- *Math in Focus* Teacher Resources CD
- *Math in Focus* Virtual Manipulatives

Vocabulary

subtract

| DAY 1 | Student Book 2A, pp. 61–66 |
| | Workbook 2A, pp. 49–52 |

MATERIALS

- 1 set of base-ten blocks
- Place-Value Mats (TR01) as needed
- Index cards (optional)

DIFFERENTIATION RESOURCES

- Reteach 2A, pp. 51–62
- Extra Practice 2A, pp. 29–30

5-minute Warm Up

Have children choose a 1-digit number. Subtract it from 39 by first breaking 39 into a group of 30 and a group of 9. Repeat the activity with other numbers. This activity prepares children for subtraction without regrouping up to 1,000.

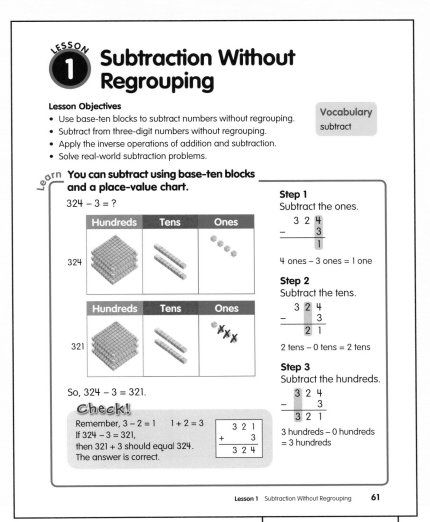

Student Book A p. 61

| DAY 1 | **Teach** |

Learn Subtract Using Base-Ten Blocks and a Place-Value Chart (page 61)

Children learned to use base-ten blocks and place-value charts to subtract numbers up to 100 without regrouping in Grade 1. This Learn section introduces children to the subtraction of ones from 3-digit numbers.

- Draw a place-value chart on the board and write the number 324 in the appropriate places on the chart.

- Ask three children to show the value of their digit in 324 by holding up the correct number of **base-ten blocks**. Ask the child holding the unit cubes to give you 3 cubes, counting aloud. Explain that you are *taking away* 3 from the number. *Ask:* How many are left? (321)

- Help children recall the strategy of subtracting numbers from right to left. Show and explain to children how to write the problems in both vertical and horizontal forms. Ensure children align the ones digits correctly.

- Ask children to check their work by working backward and adding the difference to the subtrahend.

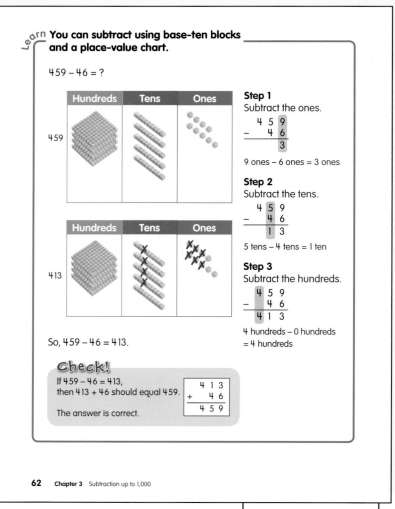

Learn You can subtract using base-ten blocks and a place-value chart.

459 − 46 = ?

Hundreds	Tens	Ones

459

Step 1
Subtract the ones.

```
  4 5 9
−   4 6
      3
```

9 ones − 6 ones = 3 ones

Step 2
Subtract the tens.

```
  4 5 9
−   4 6
    1 3
```

5 tens − 4 tens = 1 ten

Hundreds	Tens	Ones

413

Step 3
Subtract the hundreds.

```
  4 5 9
−   4 6
  4 1 3
```

4 hundreds − 0 hundreds
= 4 hundreds

So, 459 − 46 = 413.

Check!
If 459 − 46 = 413,
then 413 + 46 should equal 459.

The answer is correct.

```
  4 1 3
+   4 6
  4 5 9
```

62   Chapter 3 Subtraction up to 1,000

Student Book A p. 62

Problem of the Lesson

Charlie has 476 bottle caps. David has 44 fewer bottle caps. If David gives away 221 bottle caps, how many bottle caps will he have left?

Solution:
476 − 44 = 432
432 − 221 = 211

Answer:
David will have 211 bottle caps left.

Differentiated Instruction

English Language Learners

Review vocabulary *add* and *subtract*. Have children work in pairs. Write *add* and *subtract* on index cards. Have one partner demonstrate adding or subtracting with base-ten blocks. The other partner observes the operation and says add or subtract and points to the corresponding index card. Partners switch roles and repeat.

Learn

Subtract Using Base-Ten Blocks and a Place-Value Chart (page 62)

This Learn section introduces children to subtraction of 2-digit numbers from 3-digit numbers.

- Draw a place-value chart on the board and write the number 459 in the appropriate places on the chart.

- Ask three children to show the value of their digit in 459 by holding up the correct number of **base-ten blocks**. Write the subtraction sentence: 459 − 46 = ? on the board. Ask the child holding the unit cubes to give you 6 cubes, counting aloud. Then take 4 tens from the child with the ten-rods. *Ask:* How many are left? (413)

- Help children recall the strategy of subtracting numbers from right to left. Show and explain to children how to write the problems in both vertical and horizontal forms. Ensure children align the digits correctly.

- Ask children to check their answers by working backward and adding the difference to the subtrahend.

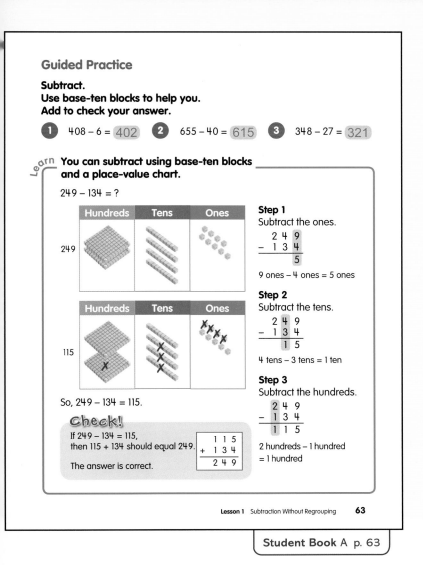

Guided Practice

Subtract.
Use base-ten blocks to help you.
Add to check your answer.

1 $408 - 6 =$ `402`   **2** $655 - 40 =$ `615`   **3** $348 - 27 =$ `321`

Learn You can subtract using base-ten blocks and a place-value chart.

$249 - 134 = ?$

Hundreds	Tens	Ones
249		

Step 1
Subtract the ones.

$$\begin{array}{r} 2\ 4\ 9 \\ -\ 1\ 3\ 4 \\ \hline 5 \end{array}$$

9 ones − 4 ones = 5 ones

Hundreds	Tens	Ones
115		

Step 2
Subtract the tens.

$$\begin{array}{r} 2\ 4\ 9 \\ -\ 1\ 3\ 4 \\ \hline 1\ 5 \end{array}$$

4 tens − 3 tens = 1 ten

Step 3
Subtract the hundreds.

$$\begin{array}{r} 2\ 4\ 9 \\ -\ 1\ 3\ 4 \\ \hline 1\ 1\ 5 \end{array}$$

2 hundreds − 1 hundred = 1 hundred

So, $249 - 134 = 115$.

Check!
If $249 - 134 = 115$,
then $115 + 134$ should equal 249.

$$\begin{array}{r} 1\ 1\ 5 \\ +\ 1\ 3\ 4 \\ \hline 2\ 4\ 9 \end{array}$$

The answer is correct.

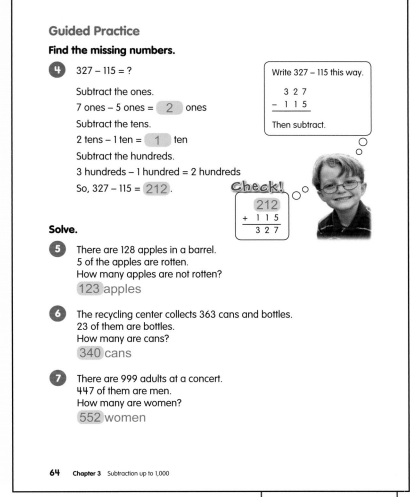

Guided Practice

Find the missing numbers.

4 $327 - 115 = ?$

Subtract the ones.
7 ones − 5 ones = `2` ones
Subtract the tens.
2 tens − 1 ten = `1` ten
Subtract the hundreds.
3 hundreds − 1 hundred = 2 hundreds
So, $327 - 115 =$ `212`.

Write 327 − 115 this way.

$$\begin{array}{r} 3\ 2\ 7 \\ -\ 1\ 1\ 5 \end{array}$$

Then subtract.

Check!

$$\begin{array}{r} 2\ 1\ 2 \\ +\ 1\ 1\ 5 \\ \hline 3\ 2\ 7 \end{array}$$

Solve.

5 There are 128 apples in a barrel.
5 of the apples are rotten.
How many apples are not rotten?
`123` apples

6 The recycling center collects 363 cans and bottles.
23 of them are bottles.
How many are cans?
`340` cans

7 There are 999 adults at a concert.
447 of them are men.
How many are women?
`552` women

Check for Understanding

Guided Practice (page 63)

1 to **3** These exercises reinforce the skill of subtracting 1- and 2-digit numbers from 3-digit numbers without regrouping. Provide children with **base-ten blocks** and **Place-Value Mats** (TRO1) if necessary. Have children work backward and add the difference to the subtrahend to check answers.

Subtract Using Base-Ten Blocks and a Place-Value Chart (page 63)

This Learn section introduces children to the subtraction of 3-digit numbers.

- Draw a place-value chart on the board and write the number 249 in the appropriate places on the chart.

- Ask three children to show the value of their digit in 249 by holding up the correct number of **base-ten blocks**. Write the subtraction sentence: $249 - 134 = ?$ on the board. Ask another volunteer to take away the required number of cubes from each child holding the base-ten blocks. *Ask:* How many are left? (115)

- Help children recall the strategy of subtracting numbers from right to left. Show and explain to children how to write the problems in both vertical and horizontal forms. Ensure children align the digits correctly.

- Ask children to check their answers by working backward and adding the difference to the subtrahend.

Best Practices You may want to teach this lesson as two mini-lessons. The first lesson will focus on just subtracting. Then go back and focus on adding to check your answers.

✓ Guided Practice (page 64)

4 This exercise reinforces children's understanding of place-value concepts in subtraction.

5 to **7** These exercises provide practice for children to apply subtraction strategies in solving real-world problems. Help children understand that the 'part-whole' concept in subtraction is applied in solving these problems.

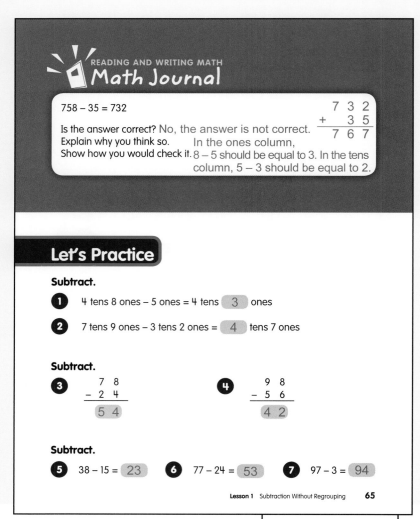

Student Book A p. 65

Subtract.
Use base-ten blocks to help you.

Example

$398 - 253 = \boxed{145}$

$$\begin{array}{r} 3\ 9\ 8 \\ -\ 2\ 5\ 3 \\ \hline \boxed{1\ 4\ 5} \end{array}$$

Subtract the ones first. Then subtract the tens. Remember to subtract the hundreds last.

8 $564 - 321 = \boxed{243}$

9 $683 - 532 = \boxed{151}$

10 $475 - 54 = \boxed{421}$

Solve.
Show how to check your answer.

Add to check your answer.

11 There are 687 boxes of cereal at a store. 324 of them have toys inside. How many cereal boxes do not have toys inside?
363

12 Ramon has 798 trading cards. He gives 265 of them to his sister. How many trading cards does he have left?
533

ON YOUR OWN

Go to Workbook A:
Practice 1 and 2, pages 49–52

66   Chapter 3   Subtraction up to 1,000

Student Book A p. 66

READING AND WRITING MATH
Math Journal (page 65)

This section allows children to reflect on their observations and understanding of the inverse operations of addition and subtraction. Have children present their work in vertical form. Lead children to see that the correct answer is 723 and to check it by using addition.

Let's Practice (pages 65 and 66)

This provides children with more practice in subtraction up to 1,000 without regrouping.

Exercises **1** and **2** require children to apply their understanding of place-value concepts in subtraction.

Exercises **3** to **10** require children to apply subtraction strategies and presentation in both vertical and horizontal forms.

Exercises **11** and **12** require children to solve real-world problems involving subtraction.

Common Error   Some children may begin subtracting the hundreds first, instead of the ones. Circling the ones in green will remind children to begin subtracting these numbers first.

ON YOUR OWN

Children practice subtraction without regrouping in Practice 1 and 2, pages 49 to 52 of **Workbook 2A**. These pages (with the answers) are shown on page 66A.

Differentiation Options   Depending on children's success with the Workbook pages, use these materials as needed.
Struggling: Reteach 2A, pp. 51–62
On Level: Extra Practice 2A, pp. 29–30

Practice and Apply
Workbook pages for Chapter 3, Lesson 1

Name: _____ Date: _____

 CHAPTER 3 Subtraction up to 1,000

Practice 1 Subtraction Without Regrouping

Subtract.

1. $432 - 221 = ?$

   Subtract the ones.

   2 ones – 1 one = ____1____ one

   Subtract the tens.

   3 tens – 2 tens = ____1____ ten

   Subtract the hundreds.

   4 hundreds – 2 hundreds = ____2____ hundreds

   $432 - 221 = $ ___211___

   Use addition to check your answer.

   > Write 432 – 221 this way.
   >
   >   4 3 2
   > – 2 2 1
   >
   > Then subtract.

   $$\begin{array}{r} 2\;1\;1 \\ +\;2\;2\;1 \\ \hline 4\;3\;2 \end{array}$$

2. $\begin{array}{r} 6\;8\;5 \\ -\;\;\;7\;1 \\ \hline 6\;1\;4 \end{array}$

3. $\begin{array}{r} 5\;6\;6 \\ -\;4\;1\;3 \\ \hline 1\;5\;3 \end{array}$

4. $\begin{array}{r} 7\;9\;7 \\ -\;5\;2\;7 \\ \hline 2\;7\;0 \end{array}$

5. $999 - 693 = $ ___306___

   work $\begin{array}{r} 9\;9\;9 \\ -\;6\;9\;3 \\ \hline 3\;0\;6 \end{array}$

6. $864 - 354 = $ ___510___

   work $\begin{array}{r} 8\;6\;4 \\ -\;3\;5\;4 \\ \hline 5\;1\;0 \end{array}$

Workbook A p. 49

Subtract.

Example

$572 - 262 = ?$

$$\begin{array}{r} 5\;7\;2 \\ -\;2\;6\;2 \\ \hline 3\;1\;0 \end{array}$$

7. $395 - 184 = ?$

   $\begin{array}{r} 3\;9\;5 \\ -\;1\;8\;4 \\ \hline 2\;1\;1 \end{array}$

8. $457 - 352 = ?$

   $\begin{array}{r} 4\;5\;7 \\ -\;3\;5\;2 \\ \hline 1\;0\;5 \end{array}$

9. $668 - 420 = ?$

   $\begin{array}{r} 6\;6\;8 \\ -\;4\;2\;0 \\ \hline 2\;4\;8 \end{array}$

10. $597 - 523 = ?$

    $\begin{array}{r} 5\;9\;7 \\ -\;5\;2\;3 \\ \hline 7\;4 \end{array}$

11. $135 - 22 = ?$

    $\begin{array}{r} 1\;3\;5 \\ -\;\;\;2\;2 \\ \hline 1\;1\;3 \end{array}$

12. $768 - 420 = ?$

    $\begin{array}{r} 7\;6\;8 \\ -\;4\;2\;0 \\ \hline 3\;4\;8 \end{array}$

Look for the answers in the puzzle and circle them.
They can only be in the direction ↓, → or ↘.
Your answers may overlap.

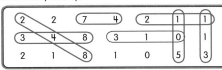

Workbook A p. 50

Name: _____ Date: _____

Practice 2 Subtraction Without Regrouping

Solve.
Show how to check your answer.

Example

Mr. Ong's orchard has 175 trees.
152 trees grow fruit.
How many trees do not grow fruit?

$175 - 152 = 23$

$\begin{array}{r} 1\;7\;5 \\ -\;1\;5\;2 \\ \hline 2\;3 \end{array}$

___23___ trees do not grow fruit.

1. Gina has 436 beads.
   She uses 123 beads to make a necklace.
   How many beads does she have left?

   $436 - 123 = 313$

   She has ___313___ beads left.

2. David's book has 345 pages.
   He reads 231 pages of the book.
   How many pages does he have left to read?

   $345 - 231 = 114$

   He has ___114___ pages left to read.

Workbook A p. 51

Solve.
Show how to check your answer.

3. The lunchroom has 498 chairs.
   The janitor removes 211 chairs.
   How many chairs are left in the lunchroom?

   $498 - 211 = 287$

   ___287___ chairs are left in the lunchroom.

4. Last year, Kennedy School recycled 745 plastic bottles.
   This year, the school recycled 133 fewer plastic bottles than last year.
   How many plastic bottles did the school recycle this year?

   $745 - 133 = 612$

   Kennedy School recycled ___612___ plastic bottles this year.

5. A pilot made 347 flights last year.
   He made 124 fewer flights this year than last year.
   How many flights did the pilot make this year?

   $347 - 124 = 223$

   The pilot made ___223___ flights this year.

Workbook A p. 52

LESSON 2 Subtraction with Regrouping in Tens and Ones

LESSON OBJECTIVES
- Use base-ten blocks to subtract with regrouping.
- Subtract from three-digit numbers with regrouping.
- Apply the inverse operations of addition and subtraction.
- Solve real-world subtraction problems.

TECHNOLOGY RESOURCES
- *Math in Focus* eBooks
- *Math in Focus* Teacher Resources CD
- *Math in Focus* Virtual Manipulatives

DAY 1 Student Book 2A, pp. 67–71
Workbook 2A, pp. 53–56

MATERIALS
- 1 set of base-ten blocks
- 1 Place-Value Mat (TRO1) per group (optional)

DIFFERENTIATION RESOURCES
- Reteach 2A, pp. 63–68
- Extra Practice 2A, pp. 31–32

5-minute Warm Up

- Write any 2-digit number on the board. Have children fill in the blanks as follows:

  _____ tens _____ ones = _____ ones.

- Repeat the above exercise three to four times. This exercise prepares children for regrouping in tens and ones.

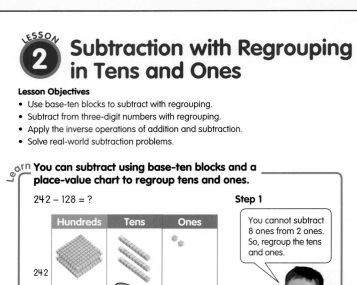

LESSON 2 Subtraction with Regrouping in Tens and Ones

Lesson Objectives
- Use base-ten blocks to subtract with regrouping.
- Subtract from three-digit numbers with regrouping.
- Apply the inverse operations of addition and subtraction.
- Solve real-world subtraction problems.

Learn You can subtract using base-ten blocks and a place-value chart to regroup tens and ones.

$242 - 128 = ?$

Step 1

You cannot subtract 8 ones from 2 ones. So, regroup the tens and ones.

Subtract the ones. Regroup the tens and ones in 242.

$$\begin{array}{r} 2\ \overset{3}{\cancel{4}}\ {}^{1}2 \\ -\ 1\ 2\ 8 \\ \hline \end{array}$$

4 tens 2 ones
= 3 tens 12 ones

Continued on next page

Lesson 2 Subtraction with Regrouping in Tens and Ones **67**

Student Book A p. 67

DAY 1 # Teach

Subtract Using Base-Ten Blocks and a Place-Value Chart to Regroup Tens and Ones

(pages 67 and 68)

Children learned to subtract numbers up to 100 with regrouping in tens and ones in Grade 1. This Learn section introduces children to the subtraction of 3-digit numbers up to 1,000 with regrouping in tens and ones.

- Draw a place-value chart on the board and write the number 242 in the appropriate places on the chart.

- Ask three children to show the value of their digit in 242 by holding up the correct number of **base-ten blocks**. Write the subtraction sentence: $242 - 128 = ?$ on the board.

- *Say:* Since 2 ones is less than 8 ones, regroup 1 ten for 10 ones to make 12 ones. Demonstrate this using the base-ten blocks being held by the children.

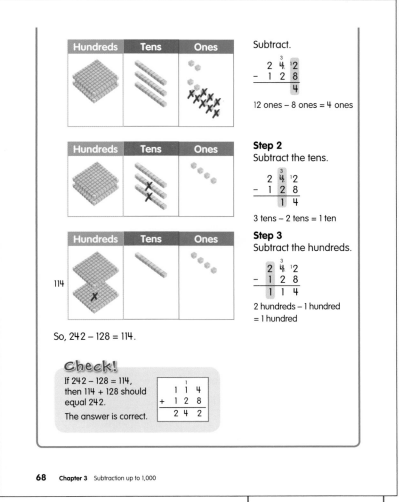

Subtract.

$$\begin{array}{r} 2\ \overset{3}{4}\ {}^{1}2 \\ -\ 1\ 2\ 8 \\ \hline 4 \end{array}$$

12 ones − 8 ones = 4 ones

Step 2
Subtract the tens.

$$\begin{array}{r} 2\ \overset{3}{4}\ {}^{1}2 \\ -\ 1\ 2\ 8 \\ \hline 1\ 4 \end{array}$$

3 tens − 2 tens = 1 ten

Step 3
Subtract the hundreds.

$$\begin{array}{r} 2\ \overset{3}{4}\ {}^{1}2 \\ -\ 1\ 2\ 8 \\ \hline 1\ 1\ 4 \end{array}$$

2 hundreds − 1 hundred
= 1 hundred

So, 242 − 128 = 114.

Check!
If 242 − 128 = 114,
then 114 + 128 should
equal 242.
The answer is correct.

$$\begin{array}{r} \overset{1}{1}\ 1\ 4 \\ +\ 1\ 2\ 8 \\ \hline 2\ 4\ 2 \end{array}$$

Student Book A p. 68

- Write this problem in vertical form on the board and show each subsequent step after the demonstration with base-ten blocks. Ensure that children align the digits correctly.

- Ask another child to take away 8 unit cubes, 2 ten-rods, and 1 hundred-square to show subtraction of 128. *Ask:* How many are left? (114)

- Ask children to check their answers by working backward and adding the difference to the subtrahend.

Problem of the Lesson

Is the following correct? Explain your answer.

$$\begin{array}{r} 7\ 3\ 2 \\ -\ 2\ 4\ 1 \\ \hline 5\ 1\ 1 \end{array}$$

Answer: Not correct. Subtraction of digits in the tens place is wrong. The correct answer is 491 instead of 511, since 491 + 241 = 732.

Differentiated Instruction

English Language Learners

Have children work in small groups to review place value vocabulary: *hundreds, tens,* and *ones.* Invite them to use base-ten blocks or to draw pictures to represent the hundreds, tens, and ones.

Best Practices Place children in small groups. Use **base-ten blocks** and **Place-Value Mats** (TRO1) and practice physically breaking apart a ten-rod into ten unit cubes. *Say:* Show me 12 − 9. Have children take 1 ten-rod and 2 unit cubes and regroup them as 12 unit cubes to demonstrate subtracting 9. Repeat with other subtraction problems that require regrouping.

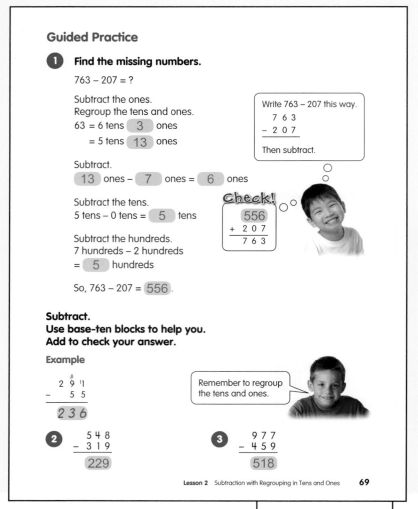

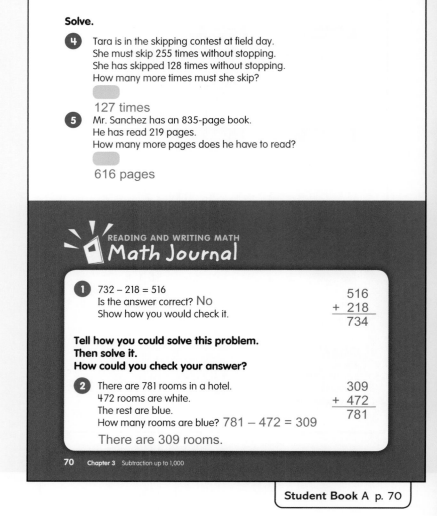

Student Book A p. 69

Student Book A p. 70

Check for Understanding

✓ **Guided Practice** (pages 69 and 70)

1 to **3** These exercises reinforce subtraction and regrouping strategies. Help children recall the steps involved in subtraction with regrouping:

1. Regroup the tens to ones.
2. Subtract the ones.
3. Subtract the tens.
4. Subtract the hundreds.

4 and **5** These exercises allow children to apply the subtraction and regrouping strategies in solving real-world subtraction problems.

READING AND WRITING MATH

Math Journal (page 70)

This section allows children to reflect on their observations and understanding of the subtraction and regrouping strategies. Have children present their work in vertical form.

For Exercise **1**, lead children to see that the correct answer should be 514 and that the error was made by subtracting 2 from 8 instead of regrouping the tens into ones before subtracting. Ask children to work backward and add, using the difference to check the answer.

For Exercise **2**, ask children to explain each step they used to find the difference.

Let's Practice

Regroup the tens and ones.
Use base-ten blocks to help you.

1 142 = 1 hundred 4 tens 2 ones

= 1 hundred 3 tens 12 ones

2 570 = 5 hundreds 7 tens 0 ones

= 5 hundreds 6 tens 10 ones

3 612 = 6 hundreds 1 ten 2 ones

= 6 hundreds 0 tens 12 ones

Subtract.
Use base-ten blocks to help you.

4
```
   8 8 0
 − 6 5 6
   2 2 4
```

5
```
   9 9 2
 − 8 7 9
   1 1 3
```

 Add to check your answer.

6
```
   7 8 3
 −   6 9
   7 1 4
```

7
```
   4 1 6
 − 3 0 7
   1 0 9
```

Solve.
Show how to check your answer.

8 A castle tower has 283 steps.
Jake climbs 77 steps.
How many more steps must he climb to reach the top? 206 steps

9 Movie Theater A has 407 seats.
Movie Theater B has 673 seats.
How many more seats does Movie
Theater B have than Movie Theater A?
266 seats

ON YOUR OWN
Go to Workbook A:
Practice 3 and 4, pages 53–56

Lesson 2 Subtraction with Regrouping in Tens and Ones **71**

Student Book A p. 71

Let's Practice (page 71)

These exercises provide children with more practice in subtraction with regrouping tens to ones in numbers up to 1,000.

Exercises **1** to **3** require children to regroup tens into ones.

Exercises **4** to **7** require children to apply their understanding of regrouping concepts in subtraction in vertical form.

Exercises **8** and **9** require children to apply the strategies in solving real-world problems. Remind children to add to check their answers.

Common Error Some children will see regrouping as adding and continue to add throughout the problem. Circle the operation symbol and remind children that they are subtracting. Tell children that when regrouping, they are not adding. Rather, they are rearranging the numbers, that is, writing the numbers in a different form.

ON YOUR OWN

Children practice subtraction without regrouping in Practice 3 and 4, pages 53 to 56 of **Workbook 2A.** These pages (with the answers) are shown on page 71A.

Differentiation Options Depending on children's success with the Workbook pages, use these materials as needed.
Struggling: Reteach 2A, pp. 63–68
On Level: Extra Practice 2A, pp. 31–32

Practice and Apply
Workbook pages for Chapter 3, Lesson 2

Name: _____   Date: _____

Practice 3   Subtraction with Regrouping in Tens and Ones

Regroup the tens and ones. Then subtract.

> Write 242 – 117 this way.
> 2 4 2
> – 1 1 7
> Then subtract.

1. 242 – 117 = ?

    242 – 117

    = 2 hundreds 4 tens 2 ones – 1 hundred 1 ten 7 ones

    = 2 hundreds 3 tens __12__ ones – 1 hundred 1 ten 7 ones

    = __1__ hundred __2__ tens __5__ ones

    = __125__

    242 – 117 = __125__

    Use addition to check your answer.

    ⬭(1 2 5)
    + 1 1 7
    ———
    2 4 2

2. 6 6 1
    – 2 4 6
    ———
    4 1 5

3. 7 4 3
    – 5 2 9
    ———
    2 1 4

4. 861 – 312 = __549__

    work
    8 6 1
    – 3 1 2
    ———
    5 4 9

5. 987 – 739 = __248__

    work
    9 8 7
    – 7 3 9
    ———
    2 4 8

Workbook A p. 53

---

6. **Subtract and match.**
    The first one is done for you.

    3 5 4
    – 2 3 5
    ———
    1 1 9

    4 8 0
    – 1 6 8
    ———
    3 1 2

    5 5 5
    – 2 4 6
    ———
    3 0 9

    3 5 7
    – 1 3 9
    ———
    2 1 8

    218
    309
    312
    119

Workbook A p. 54

Name: _____   Date: _____

Practice 4   Subtraction with Regrouping in Tens and Ones

Solve.
Show how to check your answer.

1. Calvin counts 264 red toy cars at a toy shop.
    David counts 58 fewer blue toy cars than Calvin.
    How many cars does David count?

    264 – 58 = 206

    David counts __206__ cars.

2. A library has 985 books.
    547 of them are borrowed.
    How many books are left?

    985 – 547 = 438

    __438__ books are left.

3. During one week, 231 animals were brought to an animal shelter.
    112 of them were adopted.
    How many animals are still at the animal shelter?

    231 – 112 = 119

    __119__ animals are still at the animal shelter.

Workbook A p. 55

Solve.
Show how to check your answer.

4. 464 cars are parked in a parking lot.
    There are 345 fewer trucks than cars in the lot.
    How many trucks are in the parking lot?

    464 – 345 = 119

    __119__ trucks are in the parking lot.

5. King Elementary School has 961 students.
    555 of the students are girls.
    How many students are boys?

    961 – 555 = 406

    __406__ students are boys.

6. Cally makes 628 Chinese dumplings for the fair.
    She fries 309 of the Chinese dumplings and steams the rest.
    How many Chinese dumplings does Cally steam?

    628 – 309 = 319

    Cally steams __319__ Chinese dumplings.

Workbook A p. 56

Subtraction with Regrouping in Hundreds and Tens

LESSON OBJECTIVES
- Use base-ten blocks to subtract with regrouping.
- Subtract from a three-digit number with regrouping.
- Apply the inverse operations of addition and subtraction.
- Solve real-world subtraction problems.

TECHNOLOGY RESOURCES
- *Math in Focus* eBooks
- *Math in Focus* Teacher Resources CD
- *Math in Focus* Virtual Manipulatives

DAY 1 Student Book 2A, pp. 72–77
Workbook 2A, pp. 57–60

MATERIALS
- 1 set of base-ten blocks
- 2 ten-sided dice per group
- 1 Place-Value Mat (TR01) per group (optional)

DIFFERENTIATION RESOURCES
- Reteach 2A, pp. 69–72
- Extra Practice 2A, pp. 33–34

 5-minute Warm Up

Place children in groups of four. Have each group say a 1-digit number greater than 1.

Subtract this number from 41.

Repeat the steps as often as necessary.

This prepares children for regrouping of hundreds and tens.

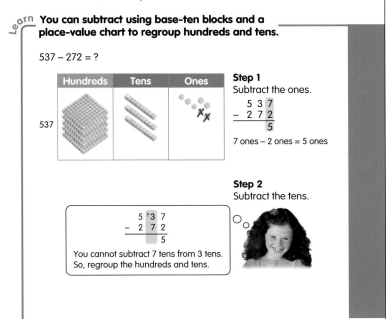

3 Subtraction with Regrouping in Hundreds and Tens

Lesson Objectives
- Use base-ten blocks to subtract with regrouping.
- Subtract from a three-digit number with regrouping.
- Apply the inverse operations of addition and subtraction.
- Solve real-world subtraction problems.

Learn **You can subtract using base-ten blocks and a place-value chart to regroup hundreds and tens.**

$537 - 272 = ?$

Hundreds	Tens	Ones

537

Step 1
Subtract the ones.

$$\begin{array}{r} 5\ 3\ 7 \\ -\ 2\ 7\ 2 \\ \hline 5 \end{array}$$

7 ones − 2 ones = 5 ones

Step 2
Subtract the tens.

$$\begin{array}{r} 5\ ?3\ 7 \\ -\ 2\ 7\ 2 \\ \hline 5 \end{array}$$

You cannot subtract 7 tens from 3 tens. So, regroup the hundreds and tens.

72 **Chapter 3** Subtraction up to 1,000

Student Book A p. 72

DAY 1 # Teach

Learn

Subtract Using Base-Ten Blocks and a Place-Value Chart to Regroup Hundreds and Tens (pages 72 to 74)

Children learned to subtract numbers up to 100 with regrouping of tens in Grade 1. This Learn section introduces children to the subtraction of 3-digit numbers up to 1,000 with regrouping of hundreds and tens.

- Draw a place-value chart on the board and write the number 537 in the appropriate places on the chart.

- Ask three children to show the value of their digit in 537 by holding up the correct number of **base-ten blocks**. Write the subtraction sentence: $537 - 272 = ?$ on the board.

- Have another child take away 2 unit cubes from the child holding the ones.

- *Say:* Since 3 tens is less than 7 tens, regroup 1 hundred for 10 tens to make 13 tens. Demonstrate this using the base-ten blocks held by the children.

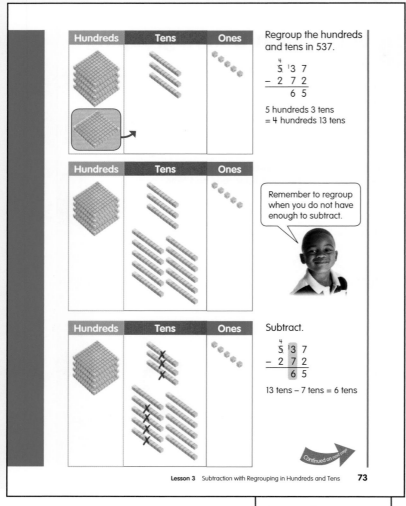

Regroup the hundreds and tens in 537.

$$\begin{array}{r} {}^{4}\!\!\not{5}\,{}^{1}\!3\;7 \\ -\;2\;7\;2 \\ \hline 6\;5 \end{array}$$

5 hundreds 3 tens
= 4 hundreds 13 tens

Remember to regroup when you do not have enough to subtract.

Subtract.

$$\begin{array}{r} {}^{4}\!\!\not{5}\,{}^{1}\!3\;7 \\ -\;2\;7\;2 \\ \hline 6\;5 \end{array}$$

13 tens – 7 tens = 6 tens

Continued on next page

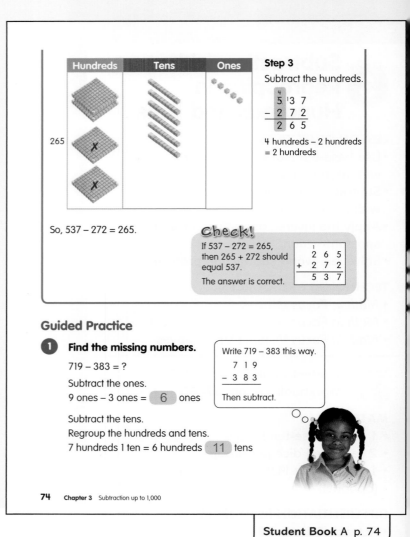

Step 3
Subtract the hundreds.

$$\begin{array}{r} {}^{4}\!\!\not{5}\,{}^{1}\!3\;7 \\ -\;2\;7\;2 \\ \hline 2\;6\;5 \end{array}$$

4 hundreds – 2 hundreds
= 2 hundreds

265

So, 537 – 272 = 265.

Check!
If 537 – 272 = 265,
then 265 + 272 should
equal 537.
The answer is correct.

$$\begin{array}{r} 2\;6\;5 \\ +\;2\;7\;2 \\ \hline 5\;3\;7 \end{array}$$

Guided Practice

1 **Find the missing numbers.**

719 – 383 = ?

Subtract the ones.

9 ones – 3 ones = 6 ones

Subtract the tens.
Regroup the hundreds and tens.
7 hundreds 1 ten = 6 hundreds 11 tens

Write 719 – 383 this way.

$$\begin{array}{r} 7\;1\;9 \\ -\;3\;8\;3 \end{array}$$

Then subtract.

- Write this problem in vertical form on the board and show each subsequent step after the demonstration with base-ten blocks. Ensure that children align the digits correctly.

- Ask another child to take away 7 ten-rods and 2 hundred-squares to show subtraction of 270. *Ask:* How many are left? (265)

- Ask children to check their answer by working backward and adding the difference to the subtrahend.

Best Practices Have children who understand regrouping complete pages 74 and 75 independently and then play the game. You can review regrouping using base-ten blocks and **Place-Value Mats** (TR01) with a smaller group of children who had difficulty with the previous lesson. Remind children who repeatedly have trouble with alignment to use the Place-Value Mats.

Subtract.

11 tens – 8 tens = 3 tens

Subtract the hundreds.

6 hundreds – 3 hundreds = 3 hundreds.

So, 719 – 383 = 336.

Check!

```
    336
  + 383
    719
```

Subtract.
Use base-ten blocks to help you.

② 647
  – 267
  ___
  380

③ 915
  – 824
  ___
  91

④ 336
  – 154
  ___
  182

Solve.

⑤ Aisha has 235 stickers.
Pedro has 153 fewer stickers than Aisha.
How many stickers does Pedro have? 82 stickers

⑥ A baker made 306 rolls in the morning.
256 rolls are sold during the day.
How many rolls are left? 50 rolls

Lesson 3 Subtraction with Regrouping in Hundreds and Tens **75**

Student Book A p. 75

Suppose you have to regroup the hundreds and tens to solve these problems.

(a) 7 3 2
   – 2 ▢ 1

(b) 9 4 7
   – 1 ▢ 3

(c) 3 1 6
   – 2 ▢ 5

What possible digits can be placed in the boxes? Then subtract to find the answer.

Answers: (a) 4, 5, 6, 7, 8, 9; Answers vary.
(b) 5, 6, 7, 8, 9; Answers vary.
(c) 2, 3, 4, 5, 6, 7, 8, 9; Answers vary.

Differentiated Instruction

English Language Learners

Write *regroup* on the board. Underline *re-*. Explain that the prefix *re-* means to do something again. *Regroup* means to group again. Provide examples of other words that begin with the prefix *re-*. For example: *reread* means to *read again*. Repeat this procedure for other words that begin with *re-*.

Check for Understanding

Guided Practice (pages 74 and 75)

① to ④ These exercises reinforce the subtraction strategy involving regrouping of hundreds and tens. Help children recall the steps involved in subtraction with regrouping:

1. Subtract the ones.
2. To subtract the tens, first regroup the hundreds and tens. Then subtract.
3. Subtract the hundreds.

⑤ and ⑥ These exercises provide practice in solving real-world subtraction problems involving regrouping of hundreds and tens.

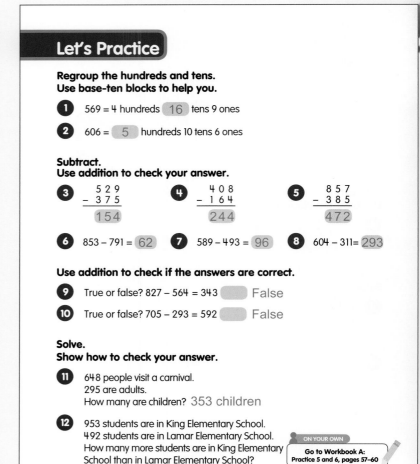

 **WORKING TOGETHER** **Game:**

Break a Hundred! (page 76)

This game reinforces the concept of regrouping hundreds and tens.

- Place children in groups of three or four. One child acts as the banker. This child receives 30 unit cubes, 30 ten-rods and 3 hundred-squares.

- Each child, except the banker, gets a hundred-square from the banker.

- Children exchange the hundred-square for 9 ten-rods and 10 unit cubes from the banker on their first turn.

- Children take turns tossing two **ten-sided dice** and doing the following: Add the numbers on the dice. If the numbers are 2 and 1, the sum is 3. Take away 3 ones. When necessary, the player has to trade 1 ten-rod for 10 unit cubes before giving the required number away.

- Each child takes a turn to 'give away' his or her cubes. The first child to give away all his or her ten-rods and unit cubes is the winner!

Let's Practice (page 77)

These exercises provide children with more practice in subtraction with regrouping hundreds and tens in numbers up to 1,000. Exercises **1** and **2** require children to regroup hundreds and tens. Exercises **3** to **10** require children to apply their understanding of regrouping concepts in subtraction and using addition to check their answers. Exercises **11** and **12** require children to apply the strategies in solving real-world problems.

Common Error Check for those children who make errors in subtraction because they do not remember their basic facts. Practice with flash cards to help them master the facts. Children may also benefit from a fact sheet taped to their desk.

ON YOUR OWN

Children practice subtraction with regrouping in hundreds and tens in Practice 5 and 6, pages 57 to 60 of **Workbook 2A**. These pages (with the answers) are shown on page 77A.

Differentiation Options Depending on children's success with the Workbook pages, use these materials as needed.
Struggling: Reteach 2A, pp. 69–72
On Level: Extra Practice 2A, pp. 33–34

Practice and Apply
Workbook pages for Chapter 3, Lesson 3

Name: _____   Date: _____

Practice 5   Subtraction with Regrouping in Hundreds and Tens

Regroup the hundreds and tens.
Then subtract.

> Write 335 – 142 this way.
> ```
>   3 3 5
> – 1 4 2
> ```
> Then subtract.

1.   335 – 142 = ?

335 – 142

= 3 hundreds 3 tens 5 ones – 1 hundred
4 tens 2 ones

= 2 hundreds __13__ tens 5 ones
– 1 hundred 4 tens 2 ones

= __1__ hundred __9__ tens __3__ ones

= __193__

335 – 142 = __193__

Use addition to check your answer.

```
 (1 9 3)
+ 1 4 2
 3 3 5
```

2.
```
  6 6 9
– 2 8 1
  3 8 8
```

3.
```
  7 1 4
– 3 6 3
  3 5 1
```

4.   765 – 695 = __70__

```
work    6 1
       7̶ 6 5
     – 6 9 5
         7 0
```

5.   908 – 568 = __340__

```
work    8 1
       9̶ 0 8
     – 5 6 8
       3 4 0
```

Workbook A p. 57

Name: _____   Date: _____

Practice 6   Subtraction with Regrouping in Hundreds and Tens

Solve.
Show how to check your answer.

1.   A store has 519 model airplanes.
It sells 228 model airplanes.
How many model airplanes are left?

519 – 228 = 291

There are __291__ model airplanes left.

2.   A florist sells 755 roses in the morning.
She sells 191 roses in the afternoon.
How many fewer roses does she sell in the afternoon?

755 – 191 = 564

She sells __564__ fewer roses in the afternoon.

3.   478 babies were born in August and September.
190 babies were born in August.
How many babies were born in September?

478 – 190 = 288

__288__ babies were born in September.

Workbook A p. 59

Subtract.

6.

```
  3 4 8
– 2 8 2
    6 6
```

```
  4 0 9
– 1 2 8
  2 8 1
```

```
  2 3 9
–   6 7
  1 7 2
```

```
  4 1 3
– 3 6 1
    5 2
```

```
  5 5 5
– 1 9 5
  3 6 0
```

```
  6 3 8
– 3 5 6
  2 8 2
```

```
  8 1 9
–   9 9
  7 2 0
```

```
  7 1 9
– 5 2 5
  1 9 4
```

Workbook A p. 58

Solve.
Show how to check your answer.

4.   Washington Elementary School has 883 students.
693 of the students go to the school baseball game.
How many students do not go to the game?

883 – 693 = 190

__190__ students do not go to the game.

5.   366 beads are in a box.
195 of the beads are green.
How many of the beads are not green?

366 – 195 = 171

__171__ of the beads are not green.

6.   Mario has 534 kites at his shop.
He sells 452 of the kites in a week.
How many kites does Mario have left?

534 – 452 = 82

Mario has __82__ kites left.

Workbook A p. 60

Subtraction with Regrouping in Hundreds, Tens, and Ones

LESSON OBJECTIVES
- Use base-ten blocks to subtract with regrouping.
- Subtract from a three-digit number with regrouping.
- Apply the inverse operations of addition and subtraction.
- Solve real-world subtraction problems.

TECHNOLOGY RESOURCES
- *Math in Focus* eBooks
- *Math in Focus* Teacher Resources CD
- *Math in Focus* Virtual Manipulatives

DAY 1 Student Book 2A, pp. 78–83
Workbook 2A, pp. 61–64

MATERIALS
- 1 set of base-ten blocks
- 1 Place-Value Mat (TR01) per group
- 1 Place-Value Chart (TR02) per child (optional)

DIFFERENTIATION RESOURCES
- Reteach 2A, pp. 73–76
- Extra Practice 2A, pp. 35–36

 5-minute Warm Up

Write any 3-digit number on the board. Have children fill in the blanks as follows:

234 = <u>2</u> hundreds <u>3</u> tens <u>4</u> ones
     = <u>1</u> hundred <u>13</u> tens <u>4</u> ones.
      (Recall that this is regrouping in hundreds and tens.)
     = <u>1</u> hundred <u>12</u> tens <u>14</u> ones.
      (Recall that this is regrouping in tens and ones.)

 Subtraction with Regrouping in Hundreds, Tens, and Ones

Lesson Objectives
- Use base-ten blocks to subtract with regrouping.
- Subtract from a three-digit number with regrouping.
- Apply the inverse operations of addition and subtraction.
- Solve real-world subtraction problems.

Learn You can subtract using base-ten blocks and a place-value chart to regroup hundreds, tens, and ones.

432 – 178 = ?

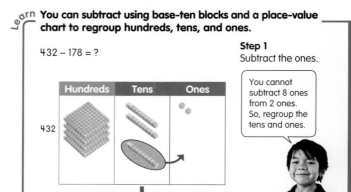

Step 1
Subtract the ones.

You cannot subtract 8 ones from 2 ones. So, regroup the tens and ones.

Regroup the tens and ones in 432.

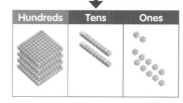

3 tens 2 ones
= 2 tens 12 ones

78 **Chapter 3** Subtraction up to 1,000

Student Book A p. 78

DAY 1 # Teach

Learn

Subtract Using Base-Ten Blocks and a Place-Value Chart to Regroup Hundreds, Tens, and Ones (pages 78 to 80)

This Learn section introduces children to the subtraction of 3-digit numbers up to 1,000 with regrouping of hundreds, tens, and ones.

- Draw a place-value chart on the board and write the number 432 in the appropriate places on the chart.

- Ask three children to show the value of their digit in 432 by holding up the correct number of **base-ten blocks**. Write the subtraction sentence: 432 – 178 = ? on the board.

- *Say:* Since 2 ones is less than 8 ones, regroup 1 ten as 10 ones to make 12 ones. Demonstrate this using the base-ten blocks being held by the children. You may want to group the children and have them use base-ten blocks and **Place-Value Mats** (TR01) to follow along at their desks.

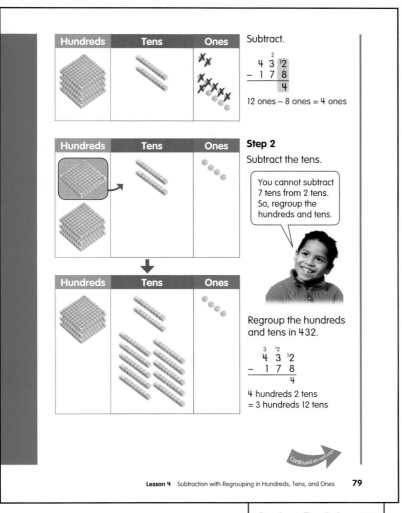

Subtract.

$$\begin{array}{r} 4\ 3\ ^{1}2 \\ -\ 1\ 7\ 8 \\ \hline 4 \end{array}$$

12 ones − 8 ones = 4 ones

Step 2

Subtract the tens.

You cannot subtract 7 tens from 2 tens. So, regroup the hundreds and tens.

Regroup the hundreds and tens in 432.

$$\begin{array}{r} 3\ \ ^{1}2 \\ 4\ 3\ 2 \\ -\ 1\ 7\ 8 \\ \hline 4 \end{array}$$

4 hundreds 2 tens
= 3 hundreds 12 tens

Continued on next page

Lesson 4 Subtraction with Regrouping in Hundreds, Tens, and Ones **79**

Student Book A p. 79

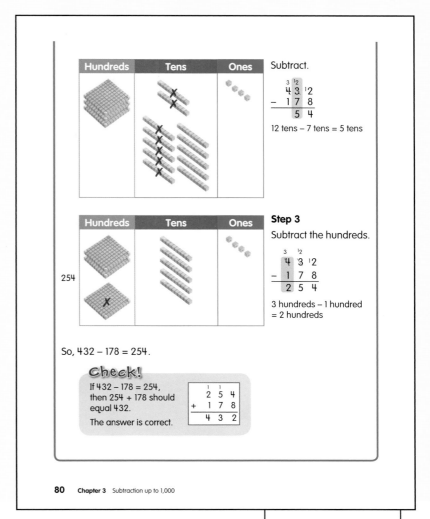

Subtract.

$$\begin{array}{r} 3\ ^{1}2 \\ 4\ 3\ 2 \\ -\ 1\ 7\ 8 \\ \hline 5\ 4 \end{array}$$

12 tens − 7 tens = 5 tens

Step 3

Subtract the hundreds.

254

$$\begin{array}{r} 3\ \ ^{1}2 \\ 4\ 3\ 2 \\ -\ 1\ 7\ 8 \\ \hline 2\ 5\ 4 \end{array}$$

3 hundreds − 1 hundred
= 2 hundreds

So, 432 − 178 = 254.

Check!

If 432 − 178 = 254,
then 254 + 178 should
equal 432.

The answer is correct.

$$\begin{array}{r} ^{1}\ ^{1} \\ 2\ 5\ 4 \\ +\ 1\ 7\ 8 \\ \hline 4\ 3\ 2 \end{array}$$

80 Chapter 3 Subtraction up to 1,000

Student Book A p. 80

- Write this problem in vertical form on the board and show each subsequent step after the demonstration with base-ten blocks. Ensure that children align the digits correctly.

- Ask another child to take away 8 unit cubes to show subtraction of 8.

- *Say:* Since 2 tens is less than 7 tens, regroup 1 hundred for 10 tens to make 12 tens. Demonstrate this using the base-ten blocks being held by the children.

- Ask another child to take away 7 ten-rods and 1 hundred-square to show subtraction of 170. *Ask:* How many are left? (254)

- Ask children to check their answer by working backward and adding the difference to the subtrahend.

Best Practices You may want to use copies of **Place-Value Charts** (TRO2) to help children vertically align the numbers in this lesson. Highlight the right side of the chart with a green marker to help children find the ones column so they know where to begin.

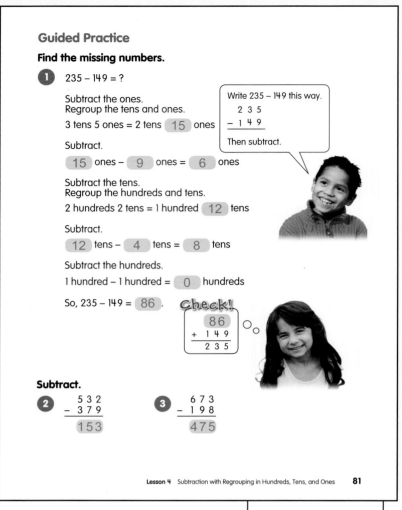

Guided Practice

Find the missing numbers.

1 235 − 149 = ?

Subtract the ones.
Regroup the tens and ones.
3 tens 5 ones = 2 tens 〔15〕 ones

Write 235 − 149 this way.

```
  2 3 5
− 1 4 9
```

Then subtract.

Subtract.
〔15〕 ones − 〔9〕 ones = 〔6〕 ones

Subtract the tens.
Regroup the hundreds and tens.
2 hundreds 2 tens = 1 hundred 〔12〕 tens

Subtract.
〔12〕 tens − 〔4〕 tens = 〔8〕 tens

Subtract the hundreds.
1 hundred − 1 hundred = 〔0〕 hundreds

So, 235 − 149 = 〔86〕.   *Check!*

```
    86
+ 1 4 9
  2 3 5
```

Subtract.

2
```
  5 3 2
− 3 7 9
  1 5 3
```

3
```
  6 7 3
− 1 9 8
  4 7 5
```

Lesson 4   Subtraction with Regrouping in Hundreds, Tens, and Ones   **81**

Student Book A p. 81

Suppose you have to regroup the hundreds and tens to solve these problems.

What possible digits can be placed in the boxes? Subtract to find the answer.

(a)
```
  5 6 2
− 3 ▪ ▪
```

(b)
```
  9 4 7
− 1 ▪ ▪
```

Answer: (a) 7, 8, 9 (tens), 3, 4, 5, 6, 7, 8, 9
   (ones); Answers vary.
   (b) 5, 6, 7, 8, 9 (tens), 8, 9 (ones);
      Answers vary.

Differentiated Instruction

English Language Learners

Many different words and phrases can be used to express subtraction. Discuss some of the words/phrases that are found in this lesson, for example, *how many fewer, how many are not.* Display a list of phrases that signify subtraction.

Check for Understanding
✔**Guided Practice** (pages 81 and 82)

1 to **3** These exercises reinforce the subtraction strategy involving regrouping of hundreds, tens, and ones. Help children recall the steps involved in subtraction with regrouping:

1. Regroup the tens and ones.
2. Subtract the ones.
3. Regroup the hundreds and tens.
4. Subtract the tens.
5. Subtract the hundreds.

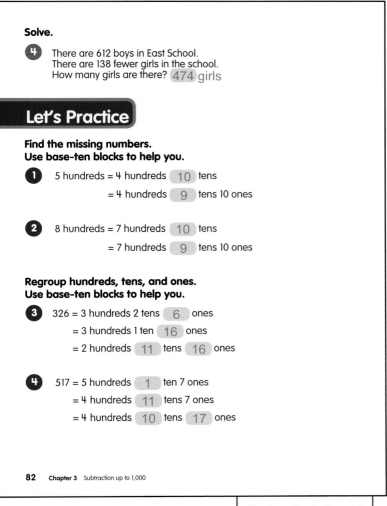

Solve.

4 There are 612 boys in East School.
There are 138 fewer girls in the school.
How many girls are there? 474 girls

Let's Practice

Find the missing numbers.
Use base-ten blocks to help you.

1 5 hundreds = 4 hundreds 10 tens
= 4 hundreds 9 tens 10 ones

2 8 hundreds = 7 hundreds 10 tens
= 7 hundreds 9 tens 10 ones

Regroup hundreds, tens, and ones.
Use base-ten blocks to help you.

3 326 = 3 hundreds 2 tens 6 ones
= 3 hundreds 1 ten 16 ones
= 2 hundreds 11 tens 16 ones

4 517 = 5 hundreds 1 ten 7 ones
= 4 hundreds 11 tens 7 ones
= 4 hundreds 10 tens 17 ones

82   Chapter 3   Subtraction up to 1,000

Student Book A p. 82

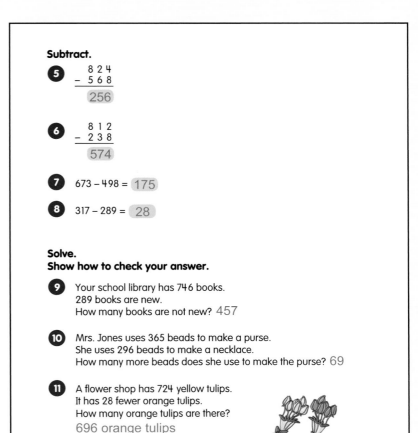

Subtract.

5
```
  8 2 4
- 5 6 8
-------
  2 5 6
```

6
```
  8 1 2
- 2 3 8
-------
  5 7 4
```

7 673 − 498 = 175

8 317 − 289 = 28

Solve.
Show how to check your answer.

9 Your school library has 746 books.
289 books are new.
How many books are not new? 457

10 Mrs. Jones uses 365 beads to make a purse.
She uses 296 beads to make a necklace.
How many more beads does she use to make the purse? 69

11 A flower shop has 724 yellow tulips.
It has 28 fewer orange tulips.
How many orange tulips are there?
696 orange tulips

ON YOUR OWN
Go to Workbook A:
Practice 7 and 8, pages 61–64

Lesson 4   Subtraction with Regrouping in Hundreds, Tens, and Ones   83

Student Book A p. 83

---

4 This exercise provides additional practice in solving real-world subtraction problems involving regrouping of hundreds, tens, and ones.

For Struggling Learners You may want to tell children they can use base-ten blocks to help them decide ahead of time how many times they need to regroup. Tell children to model each problem to decide if there are enough ones and enough tens to subtract. Based on the blocks, they would write a 0, 1, or 2 by each problem to show how many times they will need to regroup to complete the subtraction.

Let's Practice (pages 82 and 83)

Exercises **1** to **4** require children to regroup hundreds, tens, and ones. These exercises provide children with more practice in subtraction with regrouping hundreds, tens, and ones in numbers up to 1,000.

- Subtract the ones.

- Regroup the hundreds and tens.

Exercises **5** to **8** require children to apply their understanding of regrouping concepts in subtraction using the vertical form.

Exercises **9** to **11** require children to apply the strategies in solving real-world problems, and to use addition to check their answers.

Common Error Some children may have difficulty recording each regrouping correctly. Drawing dotted lines between each place value will help children visualize each place.

ON YOUR OWN

Children practice subtraction with regrouping in hundreds, tens, and ones in Practice 7 and 8, pages 61 to 64 of **Workbook 2A**. These pages (with the answers) are shown on page 83A.

Differentiation Options Depending on children's success with the Workbook pages, use these materials as needed.
Struggling: Reteach 2A, pp. 73–76
On Level: Extra Practice 2A, pp. 35–36

Practice and Apply
Workbook pages for Chapter 3, Lesson 4

Name: _____   Date: _____

Practice 7   Subtraction with Regrouping in Hundreds, Tens, and Ones

Regroup.
Then subtract.

1.   241 – 173 = ?

Write 241 – 173 this way.
  2 4 1
– 1 7 3

Then subtract.

241 – 173

= 2 hundreds 4 tens 1 one – 1 hundred 7 tens 3 ones

= 2 hundreds ___3___ tens 11 ones – 1 hundred 7 tens 3 ones

= ___1___ hundred 13 tens 11 ones – 1 hundred 7 tens 3 ones

= ___0___ hundreds ___6___ tens ___8___ ones

= ___68___

241 – 173 = ___68___

Use addition to check your answer.

  6 8
+ 1 7 3
  2 4 1

2.   4 7 8
     – 1 9 9
      2 7 9

3.   5 5 5
     – 4 5 7
        9 8

4.   924 – 886 = ___38___

work   8 1 11
       9 2 4
     –   8 8 6
          3 8

5.   818 – 669 = ___149___

work   7 10 1
       8 1 8
     –   6 6 9
         1 4 9

Workbook A p. 61

Help Daryl ride past these rocks to reach the shore.
Subtract and write the correct answer on each rock.

6.

  9 8 8
– 7 9 9
  1 8 9

  4 8 3
– 2 9 7
  1 8 6

  2 1 2
– 1 2 3
     8 9

  6 3 4
– 1 9 6
  4 3 8

  4 4 6
– 2 6 8
  1 7 8

  6 6 1
– 3 7 4
  2 8 7

  5 3 5
– 4 6 8
     6 7

  7 8 4
– 5 9 6
  1 8 8

  1 3 6
–   9 9
     3 7

  8 8 3
– 1 9 8
  6 8 5

Workbook A p. 62

Name: _____   Date: _____

Practice 8   Subtraction with Regrouping in Hundreds, Tens, and Ones

Solve.
Show how to check your answer.

1.   817 children will march in the Thanksgiving Day Parade.
359 of the children are girls.
How many are boys?

817 – 359 = 458

___458___ are boys.

2.   There are 605 children at a swimming pool.
There are 278 girls.
How many are boys?

605 – 278 = 327

___327___ are boys.

3.   A sandwich shop sells 456 ham sandwiches.
It sells 298 fewer cheese sandwiches than ham sandwiches.
How many cheese sandwiches does it sell?

456 – 298 = 158

It sells ___158___ cheese sandwiches.

Workbook A p. 63

Solve.
Show how to check your answer.

4.   Hal drove 853 miles this year on his vacation.
This was 154 more miles than he drove last year.
How many miles did Hal drive on vacation last year?

853 – 154 = 699

Hal drove ___699___ miles on vacation last year.

5.   Mrs. Ruiz makes 381 glasses of apple juice for a school fair.
She sells 192 glasses.
How many glasses of apple juice does Mrs. Ruiz have left?

381 – 192 = 189

Mrs. Ruiz has ___189___ glasses of apple juice left.

6.   Tracey has 982 stickers.
She has 496 stickers more than Zach.
How many stickers does Zach have?

982 – 496 = 486

Zach has ___486___ stickers.

Workbook A p. 64

LESSON 5 Subtraction Across Zeros

LESSON OBJECTIVES
- Use base-ten blocks to subtract with regrouping.
- Subtract from a three-digit number with regrouping.
- Apply the inverse operations of addition and subtraction.
- Solve real-world subtraction problems.

TECHNOLOGY RESOURCES
- *Math in Focus* eBooks
- *Math in Focus* Teacher Resources CD
- *Math in Focus* Virtual Manipulatives

DAY 1 Student Book 2A, pp. 84–87
Workbook 2A, pp. 65–66

MATERIALS
- 1 set of base-ten blocks
- 1 Place-Value Mat (TR01) per group (optional)
- 2 index cards per pair (optional)

DIFFERENTIATION RESOURCES
- Reteach 2A, pp. 77–80
- Extra Practice 2A, pp. 37–38

5-minute Warm Up

Place children in groups of four. Provide each group with its own set of **base-ten blocks** and place-value charts. Have children practice regrouping by exchanging blocks and filling in the missing blanks in the following:

200 = (2) hundreds
= 1 hundred (10) tens
= 1 hundred (9) tens (10) ones

On the board, write

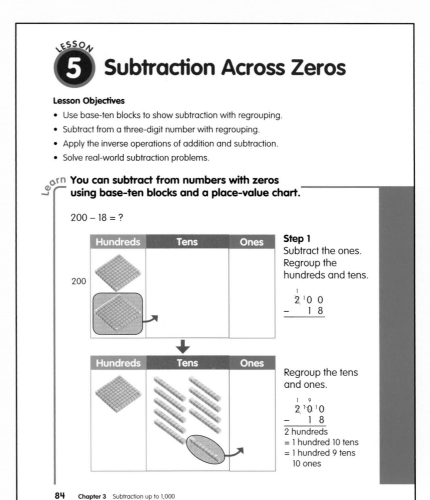

LESSON 5 Subtraction Across Zeros

Lesson Objectives
- Use base-ten blocks to show subtraction with regrouping.
- Subtract from a three-digit number with regrouping.
- Apply the inverse operations of addition and subtraction.
- Solve real-world subtraction problems.

Learn You can subtract from numbers with zeros using base-ten blocks and a place-value chart.

200 − 18 = ?

Hundreds	Tens	Ones

Step 1
Subtract the ones.
Regroup the hundreds and tens.

$$\begin{array}{r} {\overset{1}{2}}^{1}0\,0 \\ -\ \ 1\,8 \end{array}$$

Hundreds	Tens	Ones

Regroup the tens and ones.

$$\begin{array}{r} {\overset{1}{2}}\,{\overset{9}{\cancel{1}}}^{1}0\,{}^{1}0 \\ -\ \ 1\,8 \end{array}$$

2 hundreds
= 1 hundred 10 tens
= 1 hundred 9 tens 10 ones

84 **Chapter 3** Subtraction up to 1,000

Student Book A p. 84

DAY 1 # Teach

Learn

Subtract from Numbers with Zeros Using Base-Ten Blocks and a Place-Value Chart

(pages 84 and 85)

This Learn section introduces children to subtraction from 3-digit numbers with zeros up to 1,000 with regrouping.

- Draw a place-value chart on the board and write the number 200 in the appropriate places on the chart.

- Ask a child to show the number in the hundreds place by holding up 2 hundred-squares. Write the subtraction sentence: 200 − 18 = ? on the board.

- *Say:* Since there are 0 ones and 0 tens, regroup 1 hundred for 10 tens and one of the tens to make 10 ones. Ask some children to model the regrouping using **base-ten blocks.**

- Lead children to recall 10 tens = 1 hundred and 10 ones = 1 ten.

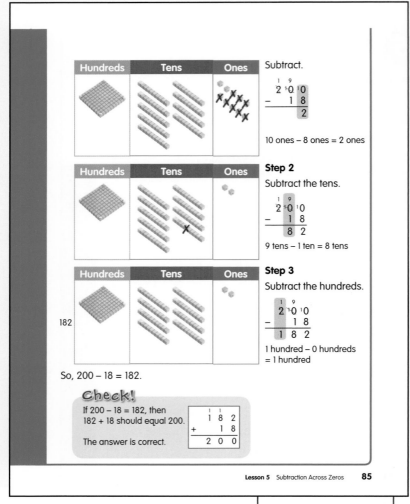

Subtract.

$$\begin{array}{r} {}^{1}{}^{9} \\ 2{}^{1}0{}^{1}0 \\ -18 \\ \hline 2 \end{array}$$

10 ones – 8 ones = 2 ones

Step 2

Subtract the tens.

$$\begin{array}{r} {}^{1}{}^{9} \\ 2{}^{1}0{}^{1}0 \\ -18 \\ \hline 82 \end{array}$$

9 tens – 1 ten = 8 tens

Step 3

Subtract the hundreds.

$$\begin{array}{r} {}^{1}{}^{9} \\ 2{}^{1}0{}^{1}0 \\ -18 \\ \hline 182 \end{array}$$

1 hundred – 0 hundreds
= 1 hundred

182

So, 200 – 18 = 182.

Check!

If 200 – 18 = 182, then
182 + 18 should equal 200.

The answer is correct.

$$\begin{array}{r} {}^{1}{}^{1} \\ 182 \\ +18 \\ \hline 200 \end{array}$$

Student Book A p. 85

Problem of the Lesson

Solve:

(a) 300 – 87 = _____
(b) 600 – 478 = _____

Answers: (a) 213
(b) 122

Differentiated Instruction

English Language Learners

Have children work with a partner. Give each pair two index cards labeled *regrouping* and *no regrouping*. Have one partner write a 3-digit subtraction problem and the other partner determine if the problem requires regrouping or no regrouping, then place the corresponding index card on the problem. Partners switch roles and repeat.

- Write this problem in vertical form on the board and show each subsequent step after the demonstration with base-ten blocks. Ensure that children align the digits correctly.

- Ask another child to take away 8 unit cubes and 1 ten-rod to show subtraction of 18.

- *Ask:* How many are left? (182)

- Ask children to check their answer by working backward and adding the difference to the subtrahend.

Best Practices You may want to use **base-ten blocks** and **Place-Value Mats** (TRO1) to teach this lesson. Using Place-Value Mats will show the children that, even though a place is currently empty, once the base-ten blocks have been regrouped, it will be filled.

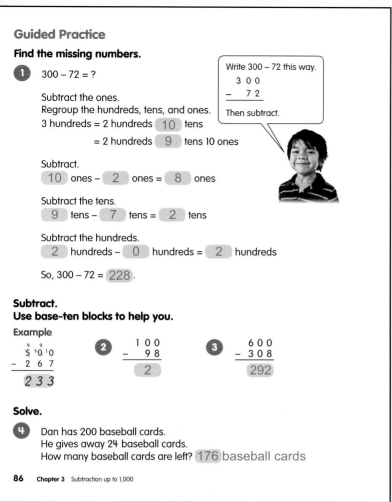

Guided Practice

Find the missing numbers.

1 300 − 72 = ?

Write 300 − 72 this way.
3 0 0
−   7 2
Then subtract.

Subtract the ones.
Regroup the hundreds, tens, and ones.
3 hundreds = 2 hundreds [10] tens

= 2 hundreds [9] tens 10 ones

Subtract.
[10] ones − [2] ones = [8] ones

Subtract the tens.
[9] tens − [7] tens = [2] tens

Subtract the hundreds.
[2] hundreds − [0] hundreds = [2] hundreds

So, 300 − 72 = [228].

Subtract.
Use base-ten blocks to help you.

Example
$\begin{array}{r} 4\ 9 \\ \cancel5\ \cancel{10}\ \cancel{10} \\ -\ 2\ 6\ 7 \\ \hline 2\ 3\ 3 \end{array}$

2
1 0 0
−   9 8
[2]

3
6 0 0
− 3 0 8
[292]

Solve.

4 Dan has 200 baseball cards.
He gives away 24 baseball cards.
How many baseball cards are left? [176] baseball cards

86   Chapter 3   Subtraction up to 1,000

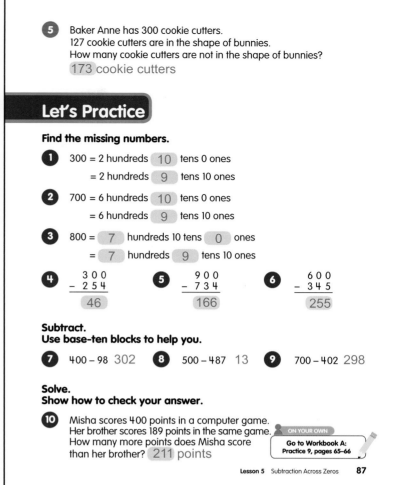

5 Baker Anne has 300 cookie cutters.
127 cookie cutters are in the shape of bunnies.
How many cookie cutters are not in the shape of bunnies?
[173] cookie cutters

Let's Practice

Find the missing numbers.

1 300 = 2 hundreds [10] tens 0 ones
= 2 hundreds [9] tens 10 ones

2 700 = 6 hundreds [10] tens 0 ones
= 6 hundreds [9] tens 10 ones

3 800 = [7] hundreds 10 tens [0] ones
= [7] hundreds [9] tens 10 ones

4
3 0 0
− 2 5 4
[46]

5
9 0 0
− 7 3 4
[166]

6
6 0 0
− 3 4 5
[255]

Subtract.
Use base-ten blocks to help you.

7 400 − 98 [302]   **8** 500 − 487 [13]   **9** 700 − 402 [298]

Solve.
Show how to check your answer.

10 Misha scores 400 points in a computer game.
Her brother scores 189 points in the same game.
How many more points does Misha score
than her brother? [211] points

ON YOUR OWN
Go to Workbook A:
Practice 9, pages 65–66

Lesson 5   Subtraction Across Zeros   87

Check for Understanding
Guided Practice (pages 86 and 87)

1 to **3** These exercises reinforce the subtraction strategy involving subtraction from 3-digit numbers with zeros and regrouping of hundreds and tens. Help children recall the steps involved in subtraction across zeros:

1. Regroup the hundreds to tens and tens to ones.
2. Subtract the ones.
3. Subtract the tens.
4. Subtract the hundreds.

4 and **5** These exercises provide practice in solving real-world subtraction problems involving numbers with zeros and regrouping of hundreds and tens.

Let's Practice (page 87)

These exercises provide children with more practice in subtraction from numbers with zeros up to 1,000.

Exercises **1** to **3** require children to regroup hundreds and tens.

Exercises **4** to **6** require children to apply their understanding of regrouping concepts in subtraction using vertical form.

Exercises **7** to **9** require children to subtract from numbers with zeros. If necessary, children can use **base-ten blocks**.

Exercise **10** requires children to apply the strategies in solving real-world problems, and check their answers.

Common Error Some children may have difficulty in determining if regrouping is necessary. Teach this poem to help them decide.

More on top? No need to stop!
More on the floor? Go next door.
Get one ten. That's ten ones more.

ON YOUR OWN

Children practice subtraction from numbers with zeros by regrouping hundreds to ones in Practice 9, pages 65 and 66 of **Workbook 2A**. These pages (with the answers) are shown on page 88.

Differentiation Options Depending on children's success with the Workbook pages, use these materials as needed.
Struggling: Reteach 2A, pp. 77–80
On Level: Extra Practice 2A, pp. 37–38

Practice and Apply
Workbook pages for Chapter 3, Lesson 5

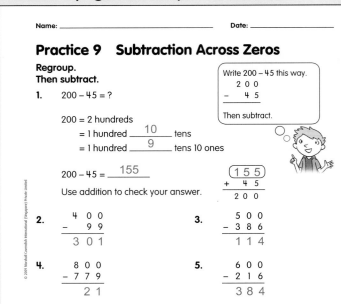

Name: _____ Date: _____

Practice 9   Subtraction Across Zeros

Regroup.
Then subtract.

> Write 200 – 45 this way.
>   2 0 0
> –   4 5
> Then subtract.

1.   200 – 45 = ?

200 = 2 hundreds
    = 1 hundred ___10___ tens
    = 1 hundred ___9___ tens 10 ones

200 – 45 = ___155___

Use addition to check your answer.

    1 5 5
  +   4 5
    2 0 0

2.   4 0 0
      –   9 9
        3 0 1

3.   5 0 0
      – 3 8 6
        1 1 4

4.   8 0 0
      – 7 7 9
          2 1

5.   6 0 0
      – 2 1 6
        3 8 4

6.   900 – 789 = ___111___

7.   700 – 423 = ___277___

work
      8 9
    9 0 0
  – 7 8 9
    1 1 1

work
      6 9
    7 0 0
  – 4 2 3
    2 7 7

Workbook A p. 65

Solve.
Show how to check your answer.

8.   700 children enter an art contest.
     98 of them win a prize.
     How many children do not win a prize?

     700 – 98 = 602

     ___602___ children do not win a prize.

9.   The library needs to order 600 books.
     It has ordered 263 books.
     How many more books does
     the library still need to order?

     600 – 263 = 337

     The library still needs to order ___337___ more books.

10. 500 adults are at a concert.
     291 of them are women.
     How many men are at the concert?

     500 – 291 = 209

     There are ___209___ men at the concert.

Workbook A p. 66

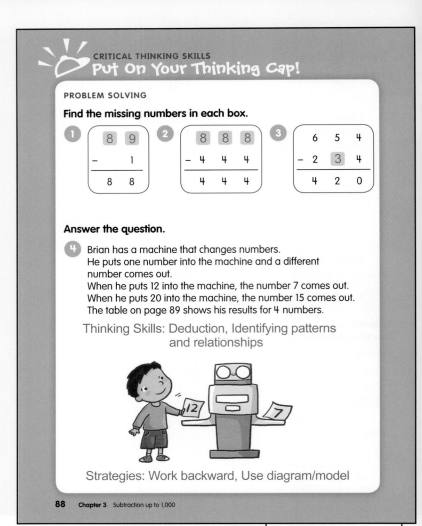

CRITICAL THINKING SKILLS
Put On Your Thinking Cap!

PROBLEM SOLVING

Find the missing numbers in each box.

1
    8 9
  –   1
    8 8

2
    8 8 8
  – 4 4 4
    4 4 4

3
    6 5 4
  – 2 3 4
    4 2 0

Answer the question.

4 Brian has a machine that changes numbers.
He puts one number into the machine and a different
number comes out.
When he puts 12 into the machine, the number 7 comes out.
When he puts 20 into the machine, the number 15 comes out.
The table on page 89 shows his results for 4 numbers.

Thinking Skills: Deduction, Identifying patterns
and relationships

Strategies: Work backward, Use diagram/model

Student Book A p. 88

CRITICAL THINKING AND PROBLEM SOLVING
Put on Your Thinking Cap!
(pages 88 and 89)

Exercises **1** to **3** involve working backward to either add or subtract without regrouping to work out the answer. Children work individually or in groups to answer the questions and to present the solutions to the class. If necessary, help children see that they can work backward to solve the problem.

Example:
This is the same as 444 + 444 = ___.

For Exercise **4**, explain the question using the example on page 89, and help children find the answer by counting on using the number line on the page. Draw a number line on the board from 5 to 20. Guide children to find the rule, subtract 5 from the number put in. Lead them to subtract 5 from 100 using the regrouping strategies taught in this chapter. Lead children to apply the inverse relationship between addition and subtraction to find the last answer.

For Advanced Learners You may want to give children index cards to make up their own addition/subtraction number-machine tables to share with the class. Ask children to exchange tables with classmates to find the missing rules and numbers.

Write the rule the machine uses to change the numbers. Then, find the two missing numbers.

Use the example below to help you.

Number in	Number out
12	7
20	15
49	44
82	77
100	95
205	200

Rule: −5 to the number put in.

Example

Number in	Number out
4	6
7	9
10	12
19	21

6 is 2 more than 4, 9 is 2 more than 7, 12 is 2 more than 10. So, the rule is to add 2 to the number put in.

Rule: + 2 to the number put in.

ON YOUR OWN
Go to Workbook A: Put on Your Thinking Cap! pages 67–68

Chapter 3 Subtraction up to 1,000   **89**

Student Book A p. 89

Thinking Skills

- Deduction
- Identifying patterns and relationships

Problem Solving Strategies

- Work backward
- Use a diagram/model

ON YOUR OWN

Because all children should be challenged, have all children try the Challenging Practice and Problem Solving pages in **Workbook 2A**, pages 67 and 68. These pages (with the answers) are shown on the right.

Differentiation Options Depending on children's success with the Workbook pages, use these materials as needed.
On Level: Extra Practice 2A, pp. 39–40
Advanced: Enrichment 2A, pp. 21–30

Practice and Apply
Workbook pages for Put on Your Thinking Cap!

Name: _____   Date: _____

Put On Your Thinking Cap!
Challenging Practice

Write the missing numbers.

1.
```
  2 [7] 4
−  1  2  3
─────────
  1  5  1
```

2.
```
 [5] 9  9
−  3  2  8
─────────
   2  7  1
```

3.
```
  8  1  6
−  6 [2] 5
─────────
  1  9  1
```

4.
```
  5  0  0
−  3 [5] 4
─────────
  1  4  6
```

5.
```
  7  0 [0]
−  2  5  1
─────────
  4  4  9
```

6.
```
  9 [0] 3
−  4  7  6
─────────
  4  2  7
```

Solve.

7. 966   699   996   696   969

   a. Write the numbers in order from greatest to least.
      996, 969, 966, 699, 696
   b. Subtract the least number from the greatest number.
      Show your work. 996 − 696 = 300
      Thinking skills: Comparing, Deduction
      Strategies: Guess and check, Solve part of the problem, Work backward

   Chapter 3 Subtraction up to 1,000   **67**

Workbook A p. 67

Put On Your Thinking Cap!
Problem Solving

Fill in the blanks with the numbers below.

0   2   3   6   8

```
  6 [0] 8
− [3] 9 [2]
─────────
  2  1  6
```

Thinking skills: Comparing, Deduction, Identifying patterns and relationships
Strategies: Guess and check, Make a list

68   Chapter 3 Subtraction up to 1,000

Workbook A p. 68

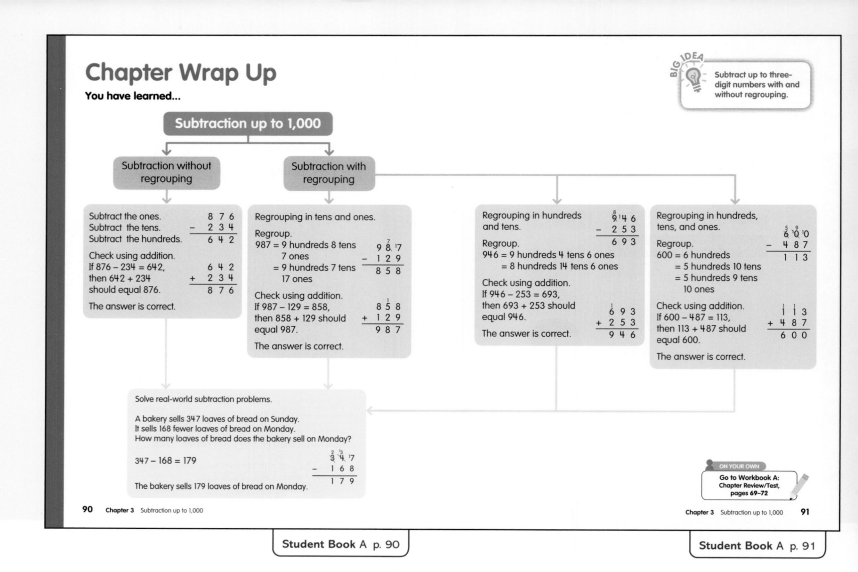

Chapter Wrap Up

You have learned...

BIG IDEA: Subtract up to three-digit numbers with and without regrouping.

Subtraction up to 1,000

Subtraction without regrouping

Subtract the ones.
Subtract the tens.
Subtract the hundreds.

```
  8 7 6
- 2 3 4
  6 4 2
```

Check using addition.
If 876 − 234 = 642,
then 642 + 234
should equal 876.

```
  6 4 2
+ 2 3 4
  8 7 6
```

The answer is correct.

Subtraction with regrouping

Regrouping in tens and ones.

Regroup.
987 = 9 hundreds 8 tens 7 ones
   = 9 hundreds 7 tens 17 ones

```
  9 8⁷ ¹7
-   1 2 9
    8 5 8
```

Check using addition.
If 987 − 129 = 858,
then 858 + 129 should
equal 987.

```
  8 ⁵8
+ 1 2 9
  9 8 7
```

The answer is correct.

Regrouping in hundreds and tens.

```
  ⁸9 ¹4 6
-   2 5 3
    6 9 3
```

Regroup.
946 = 9 hundreds 4 tens 6 ones
   = 8 hundreds 14 tens 6 ones

Check using addition.
If 946 − 253 = 693,
then 693 + 253 should
equal 946.

```
  6 ¹9 3
+ 2 5 3
  9 4 6
```

The answer is correct.

Regrouping in hundreds, tens, and ones.

```
  ⁵6 ¹0 ¹0
-   4 8 7
      1 1 3
```

Regroup.
600 = 6 hundreds
   = 5 hundreds 10 tens
   = 5 hundreds 9 tens 10 ones

Check using addition.
If 600 − 487 = 113,
then 113 + 487 should
equal 600.

```
  ¹1 ¹1 3
+ 4 8 7
  6 0 0
```

The answer is correct.

Solve real-world subtraction problems.

A bakery sells 347 loaves of bread on Sunday.
It sells 168 fewer loaves of bread on Monday.
How many loaves of bread does the bakery sell on Monday?

347 − 168 = 179

```
  ²3 ³4 ¹7
-   1 6 8
    1 7 9
```

The bakery sells 179 loaves of bread on Monday.

ON YOUR OWN
Go to Workbook A:
Chapter Review/Test,
pages 69–72

Student Book A p. 90

Student Book A p. 91

Chapter Wrap Up (pages 90 and 91)

Use the examples on pages 90 and 91 to review subtraction with and without regrouping. As you work through the examples, encourage children to use the chapter vocabulary:
• subtract

ON YOUR OWN

Have children review the vocabulary, concepts and skills from Chapter 3 with the Chapter Review/Test in **Workbook 2A**, pages 69 to 72. These pages (with the answers) are shown on page 91A.

Assessment

Use the Chapter 3 Test Prep on pages 14 to 16 of **Assessments 2** to assess how well children have learned the material of this chapter. This assessment is appropriate for reporting results to adults at home and administrators. This test is shown on page 91B.

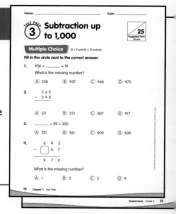

Assessments 2 pp. 14–16

Workbook pages for Chapter Review/Test

Chapter Review/Test
Vocabulary

1. Fill in the blanks with words from the box.
   The words may be used more than once.

   (ones   tens   hundreds   regroup   addition)

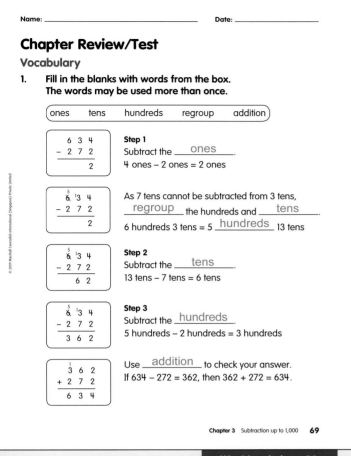

| 6 3 4 |
| − 2 7 2 |
| 2 |

Step 1
Subtract the ___ones___.
4 ones − 2 ones = 2 ones

| 5 13 4 |
| − 2 7 2 |
| 2 |

As 7 tens cannot be subtracted from 3 tens,
___regroup___ the hundreds and ___tens___.
6 hundreds 3 tens = 5 ___hundreds___ 13 tens

| 5 13 4 |
| − 2 7 2 |
| 6 2 |

Step 2
Subtract the ___tens___.
13 tens − 7 tens = 6 tens

| 5 13 4 |
| − 2 7 2 |
| 3 6 2 |

Step 3
Subtract the ___hundreds___.
5 hundreds − 2 hundreds = 3 hundreds

| 1 |
| 3 6 2 |
| + 2 7 2 |
| 6 3 4 |

Use ___addition___ to check your answer.
If 634 − 272 = 362, then 362 + 272 = 634.

Workbook A p. 69

Concepts and Skills

Subtract.
Then match those with the same answer.

2.

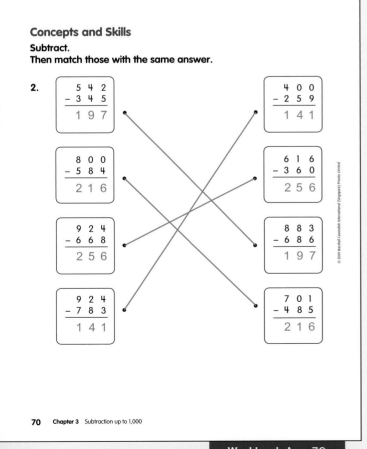

| 5 4 2 |
| − 3 4 5 |
| 1 9 7 |

| 4 0 0 |
| − 2 5 9 |
| 1 4 1 |

| 8 0 0 |
| − 5 8 4 |
| 2 1 6 |

| 6 1 6 |
| − 3 6 0 |
| 2 5 6 |

| 9 2 4 |
| − 6 6 8 |
| 2 5 6 |

| 8 8 3 |
| − 6 8 6 |
| 1 9 7 |

| 9 2 4 |
| − 7 8 3 |
| 1 4 1 |

| 7 0 1 |
| − 4 8 5 |
| 2 1 6 |

Workbook A p. 70

Problem Solving
Solve.
Show how to check your answer.

3. A supermarket has 412 bottles of apple juice.
   123 bottles of apple juice are sold.
   How many bottles of apple juice are left?

   412 − 123 = 289

   ___289___ bottles of apple juice are left.

4. Mr. Smith made 207 sandwiches.
   18 sandwiches are tuna.
   How many sandwiches are not tuna?

   207 − 18 = 189

   ___189___ sandwiches are not tuna.

Workbook A p. 71

---

5. The Morgans drive 864 miles in the first week of their vacation.
   They drive 178 fewer miles in the second week.
   How many miles do they drive in the second week?

   864 − 178 = 686

   They drive ___686___ miles in the second week.

6. The Health Food Store has 600 jars of strawberry jam.
   It has 167 more jars of strawberry jam than blueberry jam.
   How many jars of blueberry jam does the store have?

   600 − 167 = 433

   The store has ___433___ jars of blueberry jam.

Workbook A p. 72

Assessments Book pages for Chapter 3 Test Prep

Answer key appears in Assessments Book.

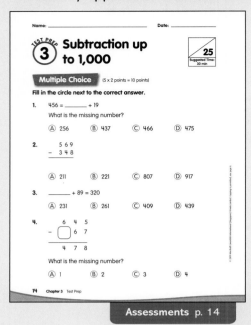

Name: _____   Date: _____

TEST PREP 3 Subtraction up to 1,000

25 Suggested Time: 30 min

Multiple Choice (5 × 2 points = 10 points)

Fill in the circle next to the correct answer.

1. 456 = _____ + 19

   What is the missing number?

   Ⓐ 256   Ⓑ 437   Ⓒ 466   Ⓓ 475

2.   5 6 9
   − 3 4 8

   Ⓐ 211   Ⓑ 221   Ⓒ 807   Ⓓ 917

3. _____ + 89 = 320

   Ⓐ 231   Ⓑ 261   Ⓒ 409   Ⓓ 439

4.   6 4 5
   − ☐ 6 7
   ‾‾‾‾‾‾‾‾‾‾
     4 7 8

   What is the missing number?

   Ⓐ 1   Ⓑ 2   Ⓒ 3   Ⓓ 4

14   Chapter 3   Test Prep

Assessments p. 14

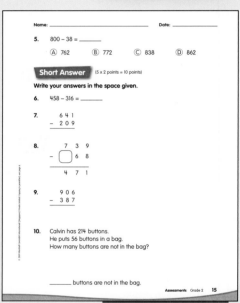

Name: _____   Date: _____

5. 800 − 38 = _____

   Ⓐ 762   Ⓑ 772   Ⓒ 838   Ⓓ 862

Short Answer (5 × 2 points = 10 points)

Write your answers in the space given.

6. 458 − 316 = _____

7.   6 4 1
   − 2 0 9

8.   7 3 9
   − ☐ 6 8
   ‾‾‾‾‾‾‾‾‾‾
     4 7 1

9.   9 0 6
   − 3 8 7

10. Calvin has 214 buttons.
    He puts 56 buttons in a bag.
    How many buttons are not in the bag?

    _____ buttons are not in the bag.

    Assessments   Grade 2   **15**

Assessments p. 15

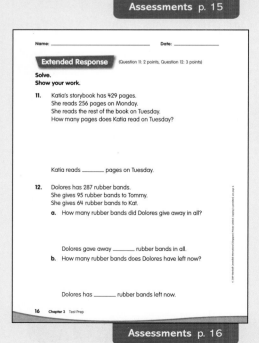

Name: _____   Date: _____

Extended Response (Question 11: 2 points, Question 12: 3 points)

Solve.
Show your work.

11. Katia's storybook has 429 pages.
    She reads 256 pages on Monday.
    She reads the rest of the book on Tuesday.
    How many pages does Katia read on Tuesday?

    Katia reads _____ pages on Tuesday.

12. Dolores has 287 rubber bands.
    She gives 95 rubber bands to Tommy.
    She gives 64 rubber bands to Kat.
    a. How many rubber bands did Dolores give away in all?

    Dolores gave away _____ rubber bands in all.
    b. How many rubber bands does Dolores have left now?

    Dolores has _____ rubber bands left now.

16   Chapter 3   Test Prep

Assessments p. 16

Chapter Overview

Using Bar Models: Addition and Subtraction

Math Background

Children added and subtracted numbers up to 1,000 in Chapters 2 and 3 and applied the concepts and strategies used in these operations to solve real-world problems.

In this chapter, children will learn strategies such as adding on and taking away sets represented by bar models to solve addition and subtraction problems. They also learn to compare two models to solve more complex addition and subtraction problems. A combination of all these strategies is used in solving two-step real-world problems.

The part-part-whole concept illustrated in bar models teaches children to represent values on a single bar model by dividing the model into parts. Because it is not feasible to represent large numbers with concrete models such as base-ten blocks, bar models provide a useful pictorial representation of sets as parts making up a whole. Children label the bars with words as well as numbers, so they can use bar models to illustrate a problem, indicating on the model the known and unknown parts or the whole. Comparing sets using bar models helps children to see clearly whether to add or subtract to solve a given problem, incorporating the part-part whole concept as well as the concepts of *more than* and *fewer than*.

The importance of bar models to the Singapore approach cannot be over-emphasized. This model is used consistently from Grade 2 up, and becomes a bedrock for proportional reasoning and algebraic thinking in later grades. It works as well for part-whole relationships and comparisons in Grade 2 as it does for fraction operations and proportions in Grade 5 and is a major factor in the Singapore success story. Extra time spent on this chapter will go far in helping your students relate the words in a real-world problem to the number sentence needed to solve it.

Cross-Curricular Connections

Reading/Language Arts Read aloud ***Quack and Count*** by Keith Baker (Harcourt, © 1999) about a family of lively ducks and the many ways they add up to seven.

Art Give each child some modeling clay. Have children divide the clay into three pieces and then roll two of the pieces into different lengths. Have children compare the two lengths of clay. Which is longer? How much? With the third piece of clay, children can make a part that when added to the shorter piece, will equal the length of the longer piece.

Skills Trace

Grade 1	Solve addition and subtraction problems of one- and two-digit numbers with and without regrouping. (Chaps. 3, 4, 8, 13, 14, and 17)
Grade 2	Solve multi-digit addition and subtraction problems, including real-world problems, by using a bar model. (Chaps. 2, 3, and 4)
Grade 3	Solve addition and subtraction problems, including real-world problems, with greater numbers by using a bar model. (Chap. 5)

EVERY DAY COUNTS®
Calendar Math

The October activities provide...

Review of comparing numbers, looking for patterns, and grouping and counting by ones (Chapter 1)

Preview of classifying geometric figures (Chapter 19)

Practice of part and whole relationships (Lesson 1 in this chapter) and adding/subtracting double digits (Lessons 2 to 4 in this chapter)

Differentiation Resources

Differentiation for Special Populations

	English Language Learners	Struggling Reteach 2A	On Level Extra Practice 2A	Advanced Enrichment 2A
Lesson 1	p. 97	pp. 81–86	pp. 41–42	Enrichment pages can be used to challenge advanced children.
Lesson 2	p. 104	pp. 87–90	pp. 43–46	
Lesson 3	p. 110	pp. 91–94	pp. 47–48	
Lesson 4	p. 116	pp. 95–98	pp. 49–52	

Additional Support

For English Language Learners

Select activities that reinforce the chapter vocabulary and the connections among these words, such as having children

- add terms, definitions, and examples to the Word Wall
- use children's own language to describe meaning of each term
- use manipulatives to act out terms
- discuss the Chapter Wrap Up, encouraging children to use the chapter vocabulary

For Struggling Learners

Select activities that go back to the appropriate stage of the Concrete-Pictorial-Abstract spectrum, such as having children

- take turns acting out different meanings for addition and subtraction
- use manipulatives to model different methods of addition and subtraction
- tell how to use each method to solve given verbal problems
- create addition and subtraction stories for each method learned

See also page 108

If necessary, review

- Chapter 2 (Addition up to 1,000)
- Chapter 3 (Subtraction up to 1,000).

For Advanced Learners

See suggestions on page 100–101.

Assessment and Remediation

Chapter 4 Assessment

Prior Knowledge		
	Resource	**Page numbers**
Quick Check	Student Book 2A	p. 95
Pre-Test	Assessments 2	pp. 17–18
Ongoing Diagnostic		
Guided Practice	Student Book 2A	pp. 97, 99, 101, 104, 106, 107, 110, 111–112, 113, 116–120
Common Error	Teacher's Edition 2A	pp. 102, 113–114
Formal Evaluation		
Chapter Review/Test	Workbook 2A	pp. 95–98
Chapter 4 Test Prep	Assessments 2	pp. 19–24
Cumulative Review for Chapters 1 to 4	Workbook 2A	pp. 99–106

Problems with these items...   **Can be remediated with...**

Remediation Options

Objective	Review/Test Items Workbook 2A pp. 95–98	Chapter Assessment Items Assessments 2 pp. 19–24	Reteach Reteach 2A	Student Book Student Book 2A
Use chapter vocabulary correctly.	1, 2, 3	Not assessed	In context as needed	pp. 103, 109
Use bar models to solve addition and subtraction problems.	4, 5	1–10	pp. 81–86	Lesson 1
Model addition as joining sets.	9	1, 3, 6	pp. 87–88	Lesson 2
Model subtraction as taking away.		2, 4, 5, 7, 9	pp. 89–90	Lesson 2
Model addition and subtraction as comparing sets.	6–11	8, 10	pp. 91–94	Lesson 3
Use bar models to solve two-step addition and subtraction problems.	8–11	11, 12	pp. 95–98	Lesson 4
Apply the inverse operations of addition and subtraction.		1–12	pp. 82–98	Lessons 1, 2, 3, and 4

CHAPTER 4 Using Bar Models: Addition and Subtraction

Lesson	Pacing	Instructional Objectives	Vocabulary
Chapter Opener pp. 92–95 Recall Prior Knowledge Quick Check	*1 day	**Big Idea** Addition and subtraction can be shown with bar models.	
Lesson 1, pp. 96–102 Using Part-Part–Whole in Addition and Subtraction	2 days	• Use bar models to solve addition and subtraction problems. • Apply the inverse operations of addition and subtraction.	
Lesson 2, pp. 103–108 Adding On and Taking Away Sets	2 days	• Model addition as joining sets. • Model subtraction as taking away. • Apply the inverse operations of addition and subtraction.	• join • set • take away
Lesson 3, pp. 109–114 Comparing Two Sets	2 days	• Model addition and subtraction as comparing sets. • Apply the inverse operations of addition and subtraction.	• compare
Lesson 4, pp. 115–121 Real-World Problems: Two-Step Problems	1 day	• Use bar models to solve two-step addition and subtraction problems. • Apply the inverse operations of addition and subtraction.	

*Assume that 1 day is a 45–55 minute period.

Resources	Materials	NCTM Focal Points	NCTM Process Standards
Student Book 2A, pp. 92–95 **Assessments 2**, pp. 17–18			
Student Book 2A, pp. 96–102 **Workbook 2A**, pp. 73–76 **Extra Practice 2A**, pp. 41–42 **Reteach 2A**, pp. 81–86	• 30 connecting cubes per group • 3 paper bags	***Number and Operations and Algebra*** Demonstrate understanding of models of addition and subtraction. Develop fluency with efficient procedures for adding and subtracting whole numbers.	Problem Solving Communication Connections Representation
Student Book 2A, pp. 103–108 **Workbook 2A**, pp. 77–80 **Extra Practice 2A**, pp. 43–46 **Reteach 2A**, pp. 87–90	• 1 set of Paper Strips (TR07) • 1 paper bag • scissors • 1 set of counters (optional) • 1 blank transparency (optional)	***Number and Operations*** Apply understanding of models of addition and subtraction. Develop fluency with efficient procedures for adding and subtracting whole numbers.	Problem Solving Communication Connections Representation
Student Book 2A, pp. 109–114 **Workbook 2A**, pp. 81–84 **Extra Practice 2A**, pp. 47–48 **Reteach 2A**, pp. 91–94	• 1 set of Paper Strips (TR07) • scissors • 1 index card • 2 pieces of construction paper (optional) • 1 set of counters (optional)	***Number and Operations and Algebra*** Develop fluency with efficient procedures for adding and subtracting whole numbers. Understand why procedures work. Use them to solve problems.	Problem Solving Communication Connections Representation
Student Book 2A, pp. 115–121 **Workbook 2A**, pp. 85–92 **Extra Practice 2A**, pp. 49–52 **Reteach 2A**, pp. 95–98		***Number and Operations*** Add and subtract to solve a variety of problems. ***Number and Operations and Algebra*** Apply understanding of models of addition and subtraction. Develop fluency with efficient procedures for adding and subtracting whole numbers.	Problem Solving Reasoning/Proof Connections Representation

Chapter Planning Guide

Lesson	Pacing	Instructional Objectives	Vocabulary
Problem Solving, p. 121 Put on Your Thinking Cap!	$\frac{1}{2}$ day	**Thinking Skills** • Analyzing parts and whole • Comparing **Problem Solving Strategies** • Act it out • Use a diagram/model • Use before-and-after concept	
Chapter Wrap Up pp. 122–123	$\frac{1}{2}$ day	• Reinforce and consolidate chapter skills and concepts.	
Chapter Assessment	1 day		
Review			

*Assume that 1 day is a 45–55 minute period.

Resources	Materials	NCTM Focal Points	NCTM Process Standards
Student Book 2A, p. 121 **Workbook 2A**, pp. 93–94 **Extra Practice 2A**, pp. 53–54 **Enrichment 2A**, pp. 31–37		***Number and Operations and Algebra*** Add and subtract multi-digit whole numbers to solve non-routine problems.	Problem Solving Reasoning/Proof
Student Book 2A, pp. 122–123 **Workbook 2A**, pp. 95–98			
Assessments 2, pp. 19–24			
Workbook 2A, pp. 99–106			

Technology Resources for easy classroom management
- *Math in Focus* eBooks
- *Math in Focus* Teacher Resources CD
- Online Assessment Generator

Chapter Introduction

CHAPTER 4 Using Bar Models: Addition and Subtraction

Chapter 4 Vocabulary

join	bring together two or more sets	Lesson 2
set	a collection of items	Lesson 2
take away	remove one part from the whole	Lesson 2
compare	find out which of two sets has more or fewer things	Lesson 3

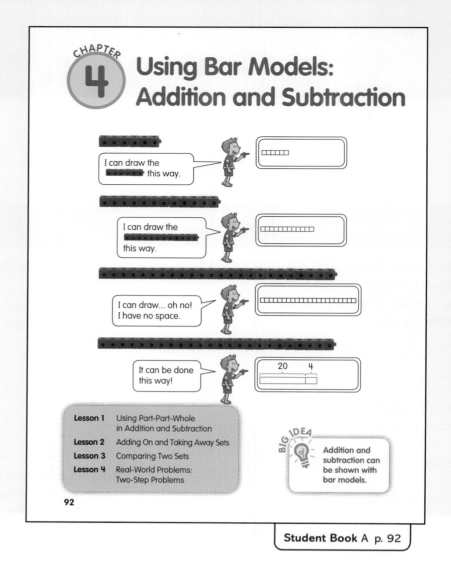

Student Book A p. 92

Big Idea (page 92)

Adding and subtracting using bar models is the main focus of this chapter.

- Children apply the part-part-whole concept in addition and subtraction.

- Children use strategies such as adding on and taking away sets represented by bar models to add and subtract.

- Children compare two sets using bar models.

- Children apply strategies to solve real-world, two-step problems.

Chapter Opener (page 92)

The picture illustrates a boy who draws models to represent the number of cubes.

- Direct children's attention to the picture.

- Help children see the link between the unit cube representation and the bar models by having a volunteer use red and blue **connecting cubes** to model the first number train.

- Have children count the number of red and blue connecting cubes in the model and picture. Draw the corresponding model on the board.

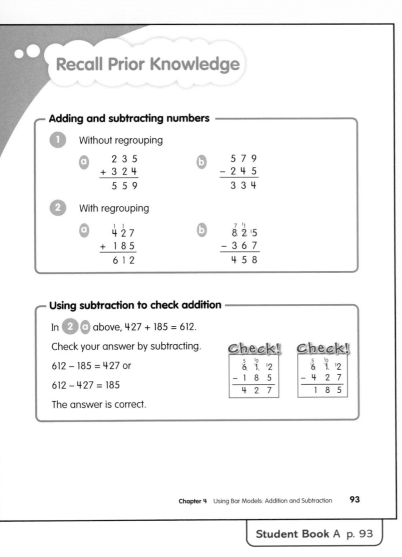

Recall Prior Knowledge

Adding and subtracting numbers

1 Without regrouping

a
```
  2 3 5
+ 3 2 4
-------
  5 5 9
```

b
```
  5 7 9
- 2 4 5
-------
  3 3 4
```

2 With regrouping

a
```
  ¹ ¹
  4 2 7
+ 1 8 5
-------
  6 1 2
```

b
```
    ⁷ ¹¹
  8 2 ⁵
- 3 6 7
-------
  4 5 8
```

Using subtraction to check addition

In **2 a** above, 427 + 185 = 612.

Check your answer by subtracting.

612 − 185 = 427 or

612 − 427 = 185

The answer is correct.

Check!
```
  ⁵ ¹⁰
  6 ¹ ¹2
- 1 8 5
-------
  4 2 7
```

Check!
```
  ⁵ ¹⁰
  6 ¹ ¹2
- 4 2 7
-------
  1 8 5
```

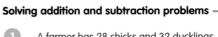

Solving addition and subtraction problems

1 A farmer has 28 chicks and 32 ducklings.
How many chicks and ducklings does he have in all?

28 + 32 = 60

The farmer has 60 chicks and ducklings in all.

2 Our teacher has 50 pens and pencils.
28 of them are pens.
How many pencils are there?

50 − 28 = 22

There are 22 pencils.

3 Jim has 56 pennies in his piggy bank.
His mother puts 17 more pennies into the bank.
How many pennies does he have now?

56 + 17 = 73

He has 73 pennies now.

4 Mr. Armstrong bakes 92 muffins.
He sells 38 of them.
How many muffins does he have left?

92 − 38 = 54

He has 54 muffins left.

- Repeat with the second and third number trains.

- *Ask:* Why is the boy unable to draw 24 units on the model? (He has no space.) Point out to children that the boy in the picture has to fit his model within the box.

- Explain that the boy has drawn a bar model to represent the sets of blue and red cubes. Draw the bar model on the board and point out to children where the numbers 24 and 4 should be written.

Recall Prior Knowledge (pages 93 and 94)

Adding and Subtracting Numbers

Children have learned to add and subtract 3-digit numbers with and without regrouping in Chapters 2 and 3.

- Write the problems on the board and ask some children to solve them. Have other children check their answers against those in the Student Book.

- Exercise **2** helps children recall the regrouping method in both addition and subtraction.

Using Subtraction to Check Addition

Children learned the inverse relationship between addition and subtraction in Grade 1.

- Write on the board the addition sentence 427 + 185 = 612.

- Ask some children to write the two related subtraction sentences 612 − 185 = 427 and 612 − 427 = 185.

- Ask other children to complete these subtraction problems on the board to check if the answer 612 is correct.

Solving Addition and Subtraction Problems

Children learned to apply addition and subtraction strategies to solve one-step real-world problems in Grade 1.

- Ask some children to solve each of the exercises on the board in vertical form.

- Have other children check their answers with those in the Student Book.

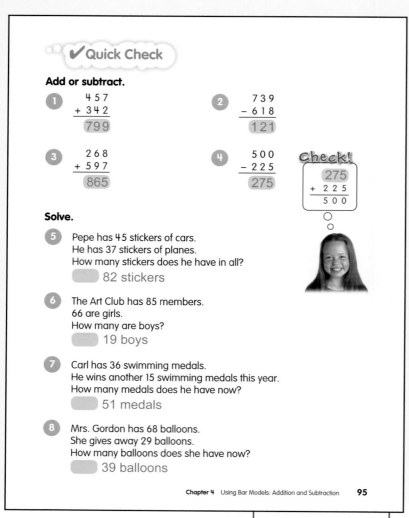

Quick Check

Add or subtract.

1.
$$\begin{array}{r} 457 \\ + 342 \\ \hline 799 \end{array}$$

2.
$$\begin{array}{r} 739 \\ - 618 \\ \hline 121 \end{array}$$

3.
$$\begin{array}{r} 268 \\ + 597 \\ \hline 865 \end{array}$$

4.
$$\begin{array}{r} 500 \\ - 225 \\ \hline 275 \end{array}$$

Check!
$$\begin{array}{r} 275 \\ + 225 \\ \hline 500 \end{array}$$

Solve.

5. Pepe has 45 stickers of cars.
He has 37 stickers of planes.
How many stickers does he have in all?

    82 stickers

6. The Art Club has 85 members.
66 are girls.
How many are boys?

    19 boys

7. Carl has 36 swimming medals.
He wins another 15 swimming medals this year.
How many medals does he have now?

    51 medals

8. Mrs. Gordon has 68 balloons.
She gives away 29 balloons.
How many balloons does she have now?

    39 balloons

Chapter 4 Using Bar Models: Addition and Subtraction **95**

Student Book A p. 95

✔Quick Check (page 95)

Use this section as a diagnostic tool to assess children's level of prerequisite knowledge before they progress to this chapter.

Exercises ❶ to ❹ assess adding and subtracting with and without regrouping.

Exercises ❺ to ❽ assess children's ability to apply the strategies taught to solve one-step real-world problems.

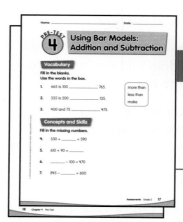

Assessments 2 pp. 17–18

Assessment

For additional assessment of children's prior knowledge and chapter readiness, use the Chapter 4 Pre-Test on pages 17 and 18 of **Assessments 2**.

LESSON 1 Using Part-Part-Whole in Addition and Subtraction

LESSON OBJECTIVES
- Use bar models to solve addition and subtraction problems.
- Apply the inverse operations of addition and subtraction.

TECHNOLOGY RESOURCES
- *Math in Focus* eBooks
- *Math in Focus* Teacher Resources CD

DAY 1 Student Book 2A, pp. 96–99

MATERIALS
- 30 connecting cubes per group
- 3 paper bags

DAY 2 Student Book 2A, pp. 100–102
Workbook 2A, pp. 73–76

DIFFERENTIATION RESOURCES
- Reteach 2A, pp. 81–86
- Extra Practice 2A, pp. 41–42

5-minute Warm Up

- Ask a child to make a number train combining two number trains made of **connecting cubes** of different colors (not more than 10 of each color).

- Ask another child to count the number of **connecting cubes** of each color. Then draw a model on the board showing the number of units. Provide pens of two colors for this activity.

- Have the other children check if the number of units in the model matches the number of cubes.

- Repeat the activity with another pair of children.

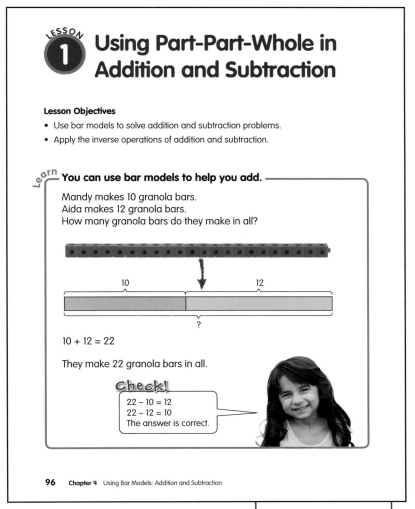

Student Book A p. 96

DAY 1 # Teach

^{Learn}
Use Bar Models to Add (page 96)

Bar models are used to illustrate the part-part-whole concept in addition. Explain that in this Learn section, pictorial models are used to find the whole from two or more parts.

- Use **connecting cubes** to represent the 10 and 12 granola bars made by Mandy and Aida respectively.

- Lead children to think of a pictorial model they can use to show what they see.

- Introduce the part-part-whole model by showing two bars to represent 10 and 12 (with the shorter bar representing 10 and the longer one representing 12). Show children that the two parts in the model form the whole.

- Label the bars clearly to show the given information and the unknown. Show children how to draw the braces ⌐ and ⌐ .

- Write the addition sentence 10 + 12 = 22 on the board. Relate the addition sentence to the bar model. Have children check the answer using subtraction.

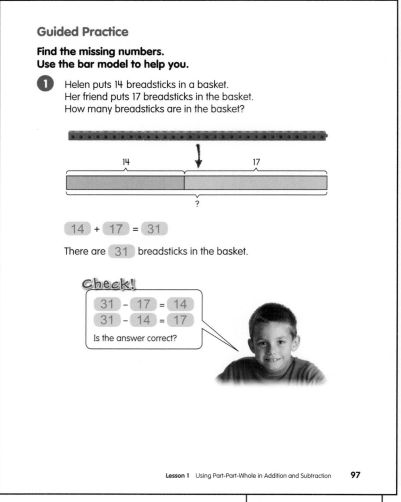

Guided Practice

Find the missing numbers.
Use the bar model to help you.

1 Helen puts 14 breadsticks in a basket.
Her friend puts 17 breadsticks in the basket.
How many breadsticks are in the basket?

14   17

?

14 + 17 = 31

There are 31 breadsticks in the basket.

Check!

31 − 17 = 14
31 − 14 = 17

Is the answer correct?

Lesson 1   Using Part-Part-Whole in Addition and Subtraction   **97**

Student Book A p. 97

Student Book A p. 97

Problem of the Lesson

Jerry and Kenneth bought 64 erasers in all. Jerry bought 18 erasers. How many erasers did Kenneth buy? Draw a bar model to represent the erasers. Then solve the problem.

Solution:

18   ?

64

64 − 18 = 46

Answer:
Kenneth bought 46 erasers.

Differentiated Instruction

English Language Learners

Work in small groups. The first child writes two 2-digit numbers. The second child writes an addition problem with a missing part. The third child tells a story problem using the numbers while the fourth child solves the problem. Exchange roles and repeat.

Check for Understanding
✓ Guided Practice (page 97)

1 This exercise provides practice in using bar models to help in addition. It also encourages children to write a number sentence for a problem and include an answer statement.

• Ask a child to draw the bar model on the board.

• Ask some children to provide the missing numbers in the number sentence and answer statement.

• Have children work backward and subtract to check the answer.

Best Practices   Divide children into small groups. Give each group several **connecting cubes** in two colors. Have groups put cubes together to model each problem. To generalize each concrete model, draw bar models on the board.

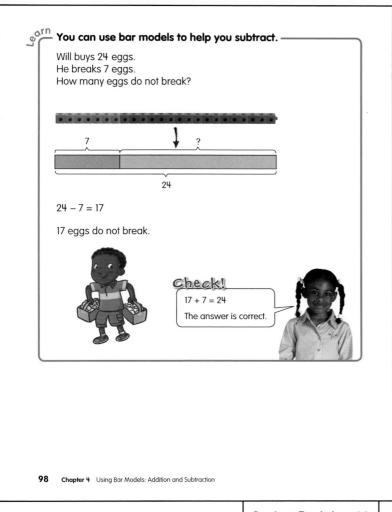

Learn **You can use bar models to help you subtract.**

Will buys 24 eggs.
He breaks 7 eggs.
How many eggs do not break?

24 – 7 = 17

17 eggs do not break.

Check!
17 + 7 = 24
The answer is correct.

Student Book A p. 98

Guided Practice

Find the missing numbers.
Use the bar model to help you.

2 The second grade class has a new aquarium.
There are 21 fish in it.
15 fish were given by families.
The rest were bought by the school.
How many fish did the school buy?

21 – 15 = 6

The school bought 6 fish.

Check!
15 + 6 = 21
Is the answer correct?

Student Book A p. 99

Use Bar Models to Subtract (page 98)

Bar models are used to illustrate the part-part-whole concept in subtraction. Explain that in this Learn section, models are used to find part of a whole.

- Use **connecting cubes** to represent the 24 eggs, using 7 cubes of one color to represent the 7 broken eggs.

- Introduce the part-part-whole model by first drawing a long bar to represent 24 eggs. Explain that this makes the *whole*.

- Divide the bar into two unequal bars, with the shorter bar representing 7 and the longer representing the rest. Point out to children that these are *parts* that combine to form the *whole*.

- Label the bars clearly to show the given information and the unknown. Show children how to draw the braces.

- Write the subtraction sentence on the board: 24 – 7 = ? and ask children to complete it with the correct answer.

- Remind children to check their answer using addition.

✔Guided Practice (page 99)

2 This exercise provides practice in using bar models to help in subtraction. It also encourages children to write a number sentence for a problem and include an answer statement.

- Ask a child to draw the bar model on the board.

- Ask some children to provide the missing numbers in the number sentence and answer statement.

- Remind children to work backward and subtract to check the answer.

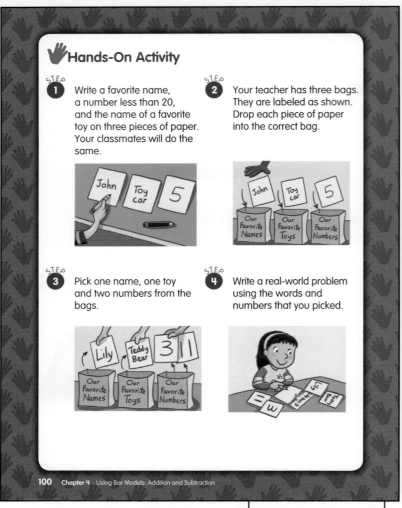

Hands-On Activity

STEP 1 Write a favorite name, a number less than 20, and the name of a favorite toy on three pieces of paper. Your classmates will do the same.

STEP 2 Your teacher has three bags. They are labeled as shown. Drop each piece of paper into the correct bag.

STEP 3 Pick one name, one toy and two numbers from the bags.

STEP 4 Write a real-world problem using the words and numbers that you picked.

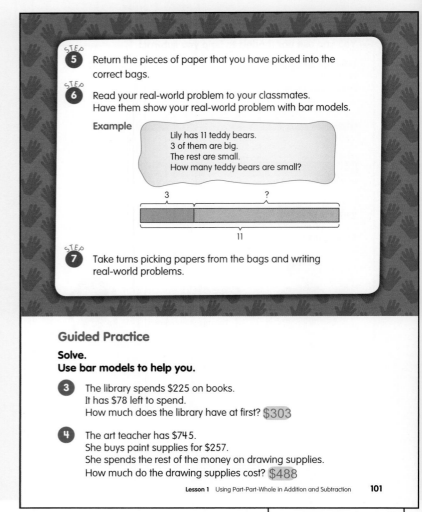

STEP 5 Return the pieces of paper that you have picked into the correct bags.

STEP 6 Read your real-world problem to your classmates. Have them show your real-world problem with bar models.

Example

> Lily has 11 teddy bears.
> 3 of them are big.
> The rest are small.
> How many teddy bears are small?

STEP 7 Take turns picking papers from the bags and writing real-world problems.

Guided Practice

Solve.
Use bar models to help you.

3 The library spends $225 on books.
It has $78 left to spend.
How much does the library have at first? $303

4 The art teacher has $745.
She buys paint supplies for $257.
She spends the rest of the money on drawing supplies.
How much do the drawing supplies cost? $488

Student Book A p. 100

Student Book A p. 101

  **Teach** See the Lesson Organizer on page 96 for Day 2 resources.

Hands-On Activity:
Write Real-World Problems and Draw Bar Models (pages 100 and 101)

This whole-class activity lets children write their own real-world problems and show them using part-part-whole bar models.

- Label three paper bags as follows:

  Our Favorite Names

  Our Favorite Toys

  Our Favorite Numbers

- Have each child write his or her favorite name, toy, and number (less than 20) on separate pieces of paper and place them into the respective bags.

- Have one child draw a piece of paper from each bag while the other children use the information on the paper to make up a real-world problem involving addition or subtraction.

- Ask children to draw a bar model to help them solve their problem.

- Repeat the activity by having another child pick three new pieces of paper from the bags.

For Advanced Learners Have children draw a model using a bar divided into three sections and three numbers. Ask them to formulate a word problem based on their model.

✔ Guided Practice (page 101)

3 and **4** These exercises provide practice in using bar models to help add and subtract. Encourage children to write the number sentences, and use bar models to help them solve the problems.

Let's Practice

Solve.
Draw bar models to help you.

1 Kevin scores 78 points in the first game he bowls.
He scores 85 points in the second game.
How many points does Kevin score for both games? 163 points

2 There are 147 fish in a pond.
49 of them are black.
The rest are orange.
How many fish are orange? 98 fish

3 98 boys sign up for a school camp.
154 girls sign up for the camp also.
How many children sign up for the camp in all? 252 children

4 Jordan and Ling have 472 trading cards.
Ling has 178 trading cards.
How many trading cards does Jordan have? 294 trading cards

5 A bookstore has 179 chapter books.
It has 243 picture books.
How many chapter and picture books does the bookstore have?
422 books

6 Lee has 528 United States and Singapore stamps.
He has 249 United States stamps.
How many Singapore stamps does he have?
279 Singapore stamps

See Additional Answers

ON YOUR OWN
Go to Workbook A:
Practice 1, pages 73–76

Student Book A p. 102

 (page 102)

These exercises reinforce applying bar models and the part-part-whole concept to solve addition and subtraction problems. Exercises **1**, **3**, and **5** require children to use bar models to solve addition problems, while Exercises **2**, **4**, and **6** require children to use bar models to help them solve subtraction problems. See Additional Answers, page T64.

Common Error Some children may choose the wrong operation. Discuss how terms in the problems can help children determine whether to add or subtract. For example, *how many in all* and *for both* indicate addition, while phrases like *the rest* indicate subtraction.

ON YOUR OWN

Children practice addition and subtraction using bar models in Practice 1, pages 73 to 76 of **Workbook 2A**. These pages (with the answers) are shown on page 102A.

Differentiation Options Depending on children's success with the Workbook pages, use these materials as needed.
Struggling: Reteach 2A, pp. 81–86
On Level: Extra Practice 2A, pp. 41–42

Practice and Apply
Workbook pages for Chapter 4, Lesson 1

Name: _____ Date: _____

CHAPTER 4 Using Bar Models: Addition and Subtraction

Practice 1 Using Part-Part-Whole in Addition and Subtraction

Solve.
Use the bar models to help you.

1. Miss Lucy has 27 students in her morning ballet class.
She has 39 students in her afternoon ballet class.
How many students does she have in both classes?

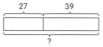

27 + 39 = ___66___

She has ___66___ students in both classes.

2. Rani collects 365 beads in January.
She collects 419 beads in April.
How many beads does she collect in January and April?

365 + 419 = 784

She collects ___784___ beads in January and April.

Lesson 1 Using Part-Part-Whole in Addition and Subtraction **73**

Workbook A p. 73

Name: _____ Date: _____

Solve.
Use the bar models to help you.

5. There are 278 people at a camp.
26 of them are teachers and the rest are children.
How many children are there?

278 − 26 = ___252___

There are ___252___ children.

6. Mr. Wilson packs 431 files in two boxes.
He packs 216 files in the first box.
How many files does he pack in the second box?

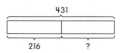

431 − 216 = 215

He packs ___215___ files in the second box.

Lesson 1 Using Part-Part-Whole in Addition and Subtraction **75**

Workbook A p. 75

Solve.
Draw bar models to help you.

3. Mr. Jackson drove 427 miles last week.
This week, he drove 215 miles.
How many miles did he drive in the two weeks?

427 + 215 = 642

He drove ___642___ miles in the two weeks.

4. 143 men and 62 women go to a concert.
How many adults go to the concert?

143 + 62 = 205

___205___ adults are at the concert.

74 Chapter 4 Using Bar Models: Addition and Subtraction

Workbook A p. 74

Solve.
Draw bar models to help you.

7. A letter carrier delivers 999 letters in two days.
The carrier delivers 306 letters on Monday and
the rest of the letters on Tuesday.
How many letters does the carrier deliver on Tuesday?

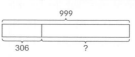

999 − 306 = 693

The carrier delivers ___693___ letters on Tuesday.

8. A factory makes 674 toys in two days.
325 toys are made on the first day.
How many toys does the factory make on the second day?

674 − 325 = 349

The factory makes ___349___ toys on the second day.

76 Chapter 4 Using Bar Models: Addition and Subtraction

Workbook A p. 76

LESSON 2 Adding On and Taking Away Sets

LESSON OBJECTIVES
- Model addition as joining sets.
- Model subtraction as taking away.
- Apply the inverse operations of addition and subtraction.

TECHNOLOGY RESOURCES
- *Math in Focus* eBooks
- *Math in Focus* Teacher Resources CD
- *Math in Focus* Virtual Manipulatives

Vocabulary
join

set

take away

DAY 1 Student Book 2A, pp. 103–105

MATERIALS
- 1 set of Paper Strips (TR07)
- 1 paper bag
- scissors
- 1 set of counters (optional)
- 1 blank transparency (optional)

DAY 2 Student Book 2A, pp. 106–108
Workbook 2A, pp. 77–80

DIFFERENTIATION RESOURCES
- Reteach 2A, pp. 87–90
- Extra Practice 2A, pp. 43–46

5-minute Warm Up

- Ask a child to name any number from 1 to 20 and have him or her draw a bar model to represent it on the board.
- Ask another child to name another number from 1 to 20, and have him or her draw a bar adjacent to the first bar. Ensure that the relative lengths of the bars match the relative magnitude of the two numbers.
- Have a third child write the addition sentence for the model.
- Repeat with another set of children and numbers.

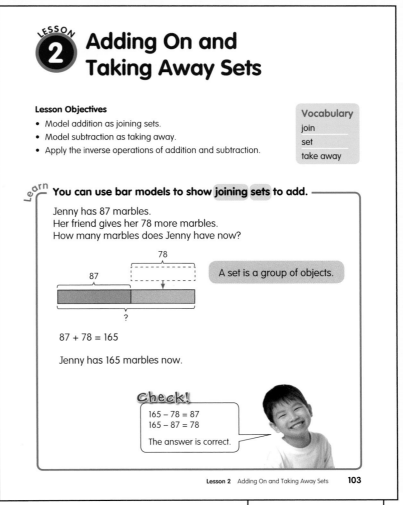

LESSON 2 Adding On and Taking Away Sets

Lesson Objectives
- Model addition as joining sets.
- Model subtraction as taking away.
- Apply the inverse operations of addition and subtraction.

Vocabulary
join
set
take away

Learn You can use bar models to show joining sets to add.

Jenny has 87 marbles.
Her friend gives her 78 more marbles.
How many marbles does Jenny have now?

78

87

A set is a group of objects.

?

87 + 78 = 165

Jenny has 165 marbles now.

Check!

165 − 78 = 87
165 − 87 = 78

The answer is correct.

Lesson 2 Adding On and Taking Away Sets **103**

Student Book A p. 103

DAY 1 # Teach

Learn
Use Bar Models to Show Joining Sets to Add
(page 103)

Bar models are used to represent the 'adding on' or 'joining sets' concept in addition.

Prepare **Paper Strips** (TR07) of different lengths so that they may be affixed to the board.

- As you read the problem in the Student Book, show and paste a strip of a suitable length on the board to represent each part of the problem. Keep the strips separate. For each strip, *say:* This represents a set of 87 or 78 marbles.

- Ask children how the strips can be used to show the total number of marbles Jenny has. Guide them to see that the second strip representing 78 marbles has to be added on to the first. Show this by joining the second strip to the first.

- Have children add to solve the problem.

- Help children recall that they should subtract to check the answer.

Guided Practice

Solve.
Use bar models to help you.

1 Carlos has 9 stickers.
His cousin gives him 3 stickers.
His sister buys him another 5 stickers.
How many stickers does Carlos have in all?

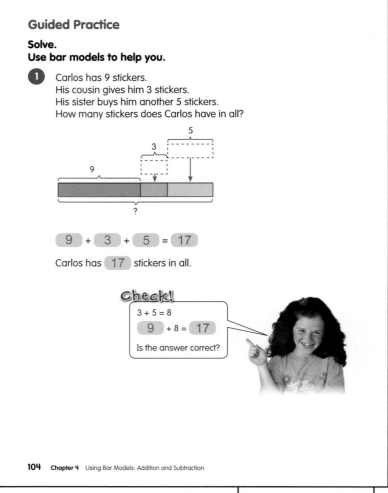

9 + 3 + 5 = 17

Carlos has 17 stickers in all.

Check!

3 + 5 = 8

9 + 8 = 17

Is the answer correct?

Student Book A p. 104

Problem of the Lesson

Look at these bar models. Write a real-world problem based on each model and solve it.

(a)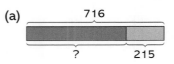

(b)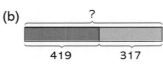

Solution: Answers vary. Examples:

(a) A parking lot has 716 cars. 215 of them stay all day and the others are there for a shorter time. How many cars are there for a shorter time?
716 − 215 = 501
501 cars are there for a shorter time.

(b) There are 419 girls and 317 boys in a school. How many students are there in all?
419 + 317 = 736
There are 736 students in all.

Answer: (a) 501   (b) 736

Check for Understanding
✓ **Guided Practice** (page 104)

1 This exercise provides practice in joining one or more parts to another to add.

• Give three children one **Paper Strip** (TR07) of appropriate length each.

• Have each child affix the given strip on the board as you read each sentence in the problem.

• Guide children to understand that each strip is added on to join the others in forming the whole.

• Have children complete the number sentence on the board to solve the problem. Encourage them to work backward and subtract to check the answer.

Differentiated Instruction

English Language Learners

Use **counters** to make sets. Say the word *set* as you point to the set of counters. Demonstrate *joining* sets and *taking away* from sets as you say the vocabulary terms. Have children repeat the words as you demonstrate.

Student Book A p. 105

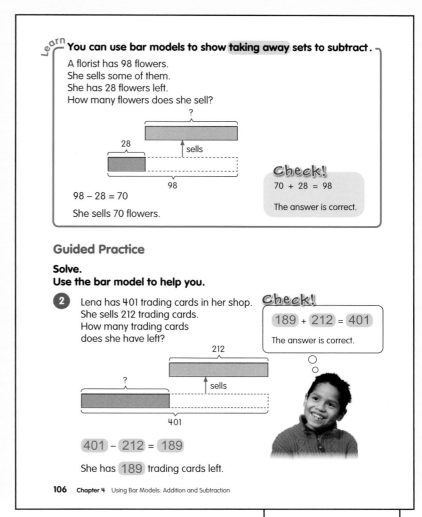

Student Book A p. 106

Hands-On Activity:
Write Real-World Problems and Draw Bar Models (page 105)

This activity lets children write their own real-world problems and show them using 'adding-on' bar models.

- Place various small items in a 'surprise' bag. Have a volunteer pick an item from within and show it to the class.

- Ask the child to say the names of three friends and three numbers less than 20.

- Model the activity by writing an 'adding-on' number story with the selected item, names, and numbers on the board. Have children show the problem using a bar model.

- Repeat this, asking another child to pick an item and write a story.

DAY 2 See the Lesson Organizer on page 103 for Day 2 resources.

Teach

Use Bar Models to Show Taking Away Sets to Subtract (page 106)

Bar models are used to represent the 'taking away sets' concept in subtraction.

- Prepare **Paper Strips** (TR07) of different lengths so that they may be affixed to the board.

- As you read the problem in the Student Book, show and affix a paper strip to the board to represent each part of the problem. Begin with a long strip to represent 98 flowers. Using scissors, cut off a small piece of the strip. *Say:* This represents the 28 flowers she has left. Move the longer strip (the flowers she sells) away from the shorter strip, as shown in the Student Book. *Say:* This represents the flowers she sells.

- Remind children that subtraction involves taking away a set or part from the whole. Have children create a subtraction sentence to solve the problem.

- Ask children to add to check the answer.

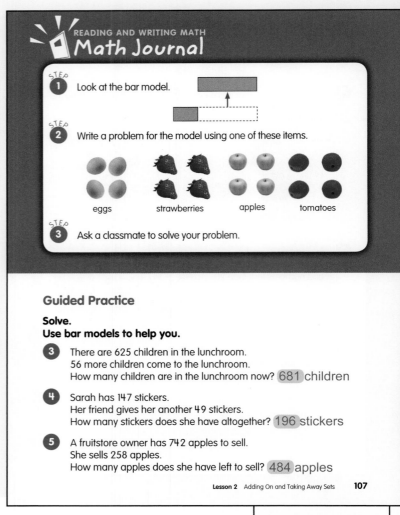

READING AND WRITING MATH
Math Journal

STEP 1 Look at the bar model.

STEP 2 Write a problem for the model using one of these items.

eggs   strawberries   apples   tomatoes

STEP 3 Ask a classmate to solve your problem.

Guided Practice

Solve.
Use bar models to help you.

3 There are 625 children in the lunchroom.
56 more children come to the lunchroom.
How many children are in the lunchroom now? 681 children

4 Sarah has 147 stickers.
Her friend gives her another 49 stickers.
How many stickers does she have altogether? 196 stickers

5 A fruitstore owner has 742 apples to sell.
She sells 258 apples.
How many apples does she have left to sell? 484 apples

Lesson 2 Adding On and Taking Away Sets **107**

Student Book A p. 107

✔ Guided Practice (page 106)

2 This exercise provides practice in taking away sets to subtract. It also encourages children to write the number sentences and complete the answer statement. Have children solve the problem using the bar model. Encourage children to work backward and add to check their answer.

READING AND WRITING MATH
Math Journal (page 107)

This section allows children to reflect on their understanding of the taking away strategy in subtraction using a bar model.

- Have children work in pairs. One child looks at the model given and makes up a problem based on the model using one of the items shown. Have the other child solve the problem.

- Encourage children to write more than one number story using the given items.

✔ Guided Practice (page 107)

3 and **4** These exercises reinforce the strategy of joining sets in addition. Have children solve the problems using bar models. Encourage children to work backward and subtract to check their answers.

5 This exercise reinforces the strategy of taking away sets in subtraction. Have children solve the problem using a bar model. Encourage children to work backward and add to check their answer.

Let's Practice

Solve.
Use bar models to help you.

1 The art teacher has 138 markers in a box.
She adds 55 markers to the box.
How many markers does she have in all? 193 markers

2 Adams Elementary School enrolled 785 children in September.
During the year, 156 children left the school.
How many children were enrolled at the end of the year? 629 children

3 There are 88 people in a movie theater.
127 more people come into the theater.
How many people are in the theater now? 215 people

4 There are 78 biscuits.
The baker bakes 159 more biscuits.
How many biscuits are there now? 237 biscuits

5 The library has 500 books.
248 books are checked out.
How many books does the library have now? 252 books

6 Mr. Miller's toy store has 102 stuffed animals.
He sells 76 of them.
How many stuffed animals are there now? 26 stuffed animals

See Additional Answers

ON YOUR OWN
Go to Workbook A:
Practice 2, pages 77–80

Student Book A p. 108

Best Practices You may want to teach this lesson as two mini-lessons: addition as joining sets and subtraction as taking away. Put a blank transparency over the exercises. Circle the addition problems in red and the subtraction problems in blue.

Let's Practice (page 108)

These exercises provide children with additional practice in applying the adding on and taking away strategies, at the same time using bar models to solve addition and subtraction word problems. Have children write out the relevant number sentences and work backward to check their answers.

Exercises **1**, **3**, and **4** check if children can apply the strategy of adding on sets, while Exercises **2**, **5**, and **6** check if children can apply the strategy of taking away sets. See Additional Answers, page T64.

Struggling Learners Some children who do not understand the vertical form may add basic facts incorrectly. Mastering facts takes practice. Until all facts are mastered, allow these children to rely on fact tables or sheets.

ON YOUR OWN

Children practice applying the adding-on and taking-away strategies using bar models in Practice 2, pages 77 to 80 of **Workbook 2A**. These pages (with the answers) are shown on page 108A.

Differentiation Options

Struggling: Reteach 2A, pp. 87–90
On Level: Extra Practice 2A, pp. 43–46

Practice and Apply
Workbook pages for Chapter 4, Lesson 2

Name: _____   Date: _____

Practice 2   Adding On and Taking Away Sets
Solve.
Use the bar models to help you.

1. Luke has 83 toy cars.
His brother gives him 52 more toy cars.
How many toy cars does he have altogether?

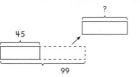

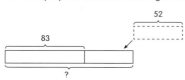

$83 + 52 =$ ____135____

He has ____135____ toy cars altogether.

2. Daniel has 228 craft sticks for his project.
He needs 350 more craft sticks.
How many craft sticks does he need for his project?

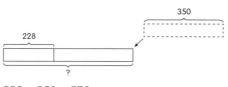

$228 + 350 = 578$

He needs ____578____ craft sticks for his project.

Lesson 2   Adding On and Taking Away Sets   **77**

Name: _____   Date: _____

Solve.
Use the bar models to help you.

5. Town Sports has 99 scooters.
The store sells some of them and has 45 scooters left.
How many scooters does Town Sports sell?

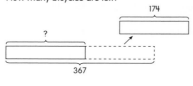

$99 - 45 =$ ____54____

Town Sports sold ____54____ scooters.

6. There were 367 bicycles at Ben's bicycle shop.
174 bicycles are rented.
How many bicycles are left?

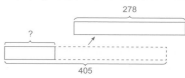

$367 - 174 = 193$

____193____ bicycles are left.

Lesson 2   Adding On and Taking Away Sets   **79**

Solve.
Draw bar models to help you.

3. The Bokil family drives 95 miles on the first day of their trip.
They drive another 105 miles on the next day.
How many miles do they drive in the two days?

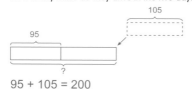

$95 + 105 = 200$

They drive ____200____ miles in the two days.

4. Kayla has 9 puzzles.
Her mother gives her 8 more puzzles.
Her uncle buys another 5 puzzles for her.
How many puzzles does Kayla have now?

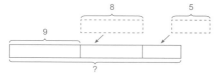

$9 + 8 + 5 = 17 + 5 = 22$

She has ____22____ puzzles now.

78   **Chapter 4**   *Using Bar Models: Addition and Subtraction*

Solve.
Draw bar models to help you.

7. Shawn has 405 stickers.
He gives 278 stickers away.
How many stickers does he have left?

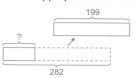

$405 - 278 = 127$

He has ____127____ stickers left.

8. There were 282 people in the park on Sunday afternoon.
In the evening, 199 people went home.
How many people were left in the park?

$282 - 199 = 83$

____83____ people were left in the park.

80   **Chapter 4**   *Using Bar Models: Addition and Subtraction*

LESSON 3 Comparing Two Sets

LESSON OBJECTIVES
• Model addition and subtraction as comparing sets.
• Apply the inverse operations of addition and subtraction.

TECHNOLOGY RESOURCES
• *Math in Focus* eBooks
• *Math in Focus* Teacher Resources CD
• *Math in Focus* Virtual Manipulatives

Vocabulary

compare

| DAY 1 | Student Book 2A, pp. 109–112 |

MATERIALS
• 1 set of Paper Strips (TRO7)
• scissors
• 1 index card
• 2 pieces of construction paper (optional)
• 1 set of counters (optional)

| DAY 2 | Student Book 2A, pp. 112–114
Workbook 2A, pp. 81–84 |

DIFFERENTIATION RESOURCES
• Reteach 2A, pp. 91–94
• Extra Practice 2A, pp. 47–48

5-minute Warm Up

• Randomly choose a number from 0 to 100 and the name of an item (for example, marbles).
• *Say:* I have *x* marbles.
• Ask a child to choose another number and say: I have *y* marbles.
• Ask another child: Who has more? Guide him or her to say: ___ has more marbles.
• Have a third child write the addition sentence for the model.
• Repeat with another group of three children – the first child gets to name the item. The children can take turns replying from where they are seated. You may wish to repeat the whole activity using *fewer* in place of *more*.

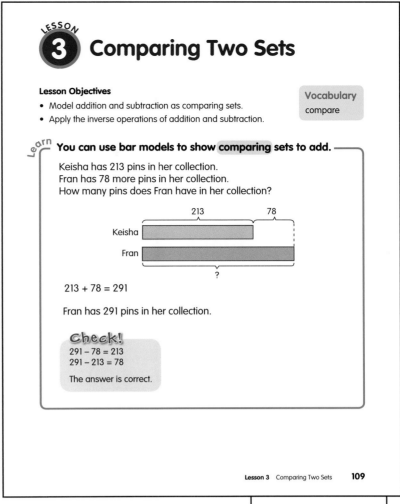

LESSON 3 Comparing Two Sets

Lesson Objectives
• Model addition and subtraction as comparing sets.
• Apply the inverse operations of addition and subtraction.

Vocabulary
compare

Learn **You can use bar models to show comparing sets to add.**

Keisha has 213 pins in her collection.
Fran has 78 more pins in her collection.
How many pins does Fran have in her collection?

213   78

Keisha

Fran

?

213 + 78 = 291

Fran has 291 pins in her collection.

Check!
291 − 78 = 213
291 − 213 = 78
The answer is correct.

Lesson 3 Comparing Two Sets   **109**

Student Book A p. 109

| DAY 1 | # Teach |

Learn

Use Bar Models to Show Comparing Sets to Add (page 109)

Bar models are used to illustrate comparing sets involving addition.

• Explain the story given in the problem.

• Represent the story with a model drawing and show how the information given in the story is related to the model. Use **Paper Strips** (TRO7) to help you, if necessary.

• Ask children to describe the difference between this model and the previous models in earlier lessons. (In this model, the bars are placed one on top of the other.)

• *Ask:* Who has more pins? (Fran) Point out to children that the longer bar is used to represent the set which has *more*.

• Guide children to write the addition sentence and to solve the problem. Then check the answer using subtraction.

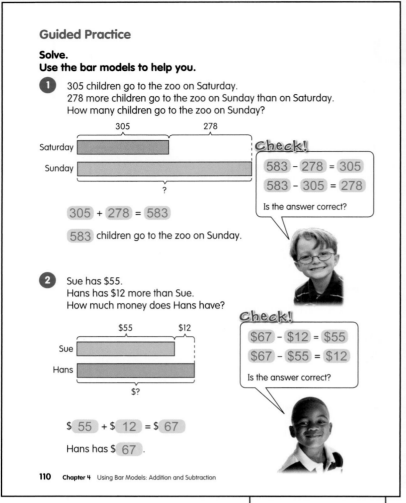

Guided Practice

Solve.
Use the bar models to help you.

1 305 children go to the zoo on Saturday.
278 more children go to the zoo on Sunday than on Saturday.
How many children go to the zoo on Sunday?

305   278

Saturday

Sunday

?

Check!

583 – 278 = 305

583 – 305 = 278

Is the answer correct?

305 + 278 = 583

583 children go to the zoo on Sunday.

2 Sue has $55.
Hans has $12 more than Sue.
How much money does Hans have?

$55 $12

Sue

Hans

$?

Check!

$67 – $12 = $55

$67 – $55 = $12

Is the answer correct?

$ 55 + $ 12 = $ 67

Hans has $ 67 .

110   Chapter 4   Using Bar Models: Addition and Subtraction

Student Book A p. 110

Differentiated Instruction

English Language Learners

Compare may be an unfamiliar word. Write *compare* on an index card. Form two groups of **counters** on the desk and place the word card between the two groups. Have children count each group of counters. Point to the card and say *compare*. Discuss the groups and say *compare* again to demonstrate the definition.

Check for Understanding
✓**Guided Practice** (page 110)

1 and **2** These exercises provide practice in comparing of sets involving addition. They also encourage children to write number sentences to solve the problems. Encourage children to read the problems aloud. Have them relate the information in the problems with the bar models first, then write and solve the addition sentences. Remind children to check each answer using subtraction.

Best Practices Cut out different lengths of paper strips from two different color pieces of construction paper. Use the longer strip of one color to represent the whole and the shorter strip of another color to represent the part. Compare the strips and decide which part is yet to be determined.

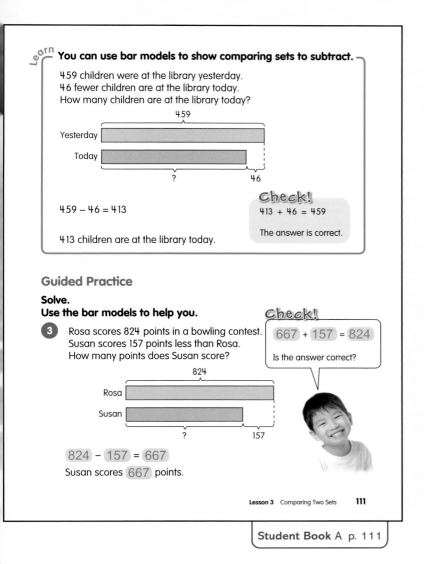

Learn You can use bar models to show comparing sets to subtract.

459 children were at the library yesterday.
46 fewer children are at the library today.
How many children are at the library today?

459 − 46 = 413

Check!
413 + 46 = 459
The answer is correct.

413 children are at the library today.

Guided Practice

Solve.
Use the bar models to help you.

3 Rosa scores 824 points in a bowling contest.
Susan scores 157 points less than Rosa.
How many points does Susan score?

Check!
667 + 157 = 824
Is the answer correct?

824 − 157 = 667
Susan scores 667 points.

4 In Store A, 300 video games are sold.
This is 126 more games sold than in Store B.
How many video games are sold in Store B?

Check!
174 + 126 = 300
Is your answer correct?

300 − 126 = 174

174 video games are sold in Store B.

Hands-On Activity

WORK IN PAIRS

Ask your friend to draw a bar model for the first problem.
You will then choose + or − and solve the problem.
Reverse your roles for the second problem.

1 95 cartons of milk are sold on Monday.
68 more cartons of milk are sold on Monday than on Tuesday.
How many cartons of milk are sold on Tuesday? subtract;
27 cartons

2 Ben can put 150 photos into a photo album.
He can put 28 fewer photos into a scrapbook.
How many photos can Ben put into the scrapbook? subtract;
122 photos

Use Bar Models to Show Comparing Sets to Subtract (page 111)

Bar models are used to illustrate the comparing of sets involving subtraction.

- Explain the story given in the problem.

- Represent the story with a model drawing and show how the information given in the story is related to the model. Use **Paper Strips** (TR07) to help you, if necessary.

- Point out to children that the word *fewer* is used instead of *more*.

- *Ask:* Which day has fewer children? (today) Point out to children that the shorter bar is used to represent the set that has *fewer*.

- Guide children to write the subtraction sentence and to solve the problem, then check the answer using addition.

✓Guided Practice (pages 111 and 112)

3 and **4** These exercises provide practice in comparing of sets involving subtraction. They also encourage children to write number sentences to solve the problems. Encourage children to read the problems aloud. Have them relate the information in the problems with the bar models first then write and solve the subtraction sentences. Remind children to check each answer using addition. In Exercise **4**, ensure that children understand that, because there are more games sold in Store A than in Store B, Store B has fewer games and the bar is shorter.

DAY 2 **Teach** See the Lesson Organizer on page 109 for Day 2 resources.

WORK IN PAIRS

Hands-On Activity:

Show Real-World Problems with Bar Models (page 112)

This activity reinforces the use of bar models to compare sets involving addition or subtraction. Have children work in pairs and take turns drawing the bar models and solving the problem. Emphasize the difference between the words *more* and *fewer*.

Guided Practice

Solve.
Choose + or − to solve the problems.
Draw bar models to help you.

5 Mika uses 56 beads to make a bracelet.
Emma uses 9 fewer beads than Mika.
How many beads does Emma use?
47 beads

6 There are 305 girls at the high school play.
There are 48 fewer boys than girls.
How many boys are at the play?
257 boys

7 A fruit seller has 140 strawberries.
He has 29 fewer pears than strawberries.
How many pears does he have?
111 pears

8 Pepe spends $78 on clothing.
He spends $49 less than John.
How much does John spend?
$127

9 Uncle Denzel and Uncle Mark work at a coffee shop.
Uncle Denzel works 210 hours.
Uncle Denzel works 34 fewer hours than Uncle Mark.
How many hours does Uncle Mark work?
244 hours

10 There are 78 chickens at a farm.
There are 39 more geese than chickens.
How many geese are there?
117 geese

See Additional Answers

Student Book A p. 113

Let's Practice

Solve.
Use bar models to help you.

1 The length of Pole A is 36 feet.
Pole B is 9 feet shorter than Pole A.
How long is Pole B? 27 feet

2 Lucy uses 64 inches of ribbon.
She uses 37 inches less than Wendy.
How many inches of ribbon does Wendy use? 101 inches

3 Carlos sells 478 tickets for the school fair.
Marissa sells 129 more tickets than Carlos.
How many tickets does Marissa sell? 607 tickets

4 A red box has 326 pencils.
The red box has 78 fewer pencils than the blue box.
How many pencils are in the blue box? 404 pencils

5 There are 586 red counters.
There are 137 fewer white counters than red counters.
How many white counters are there? 449 white counters

6 Julian drives 259 miles in one day.
He drives 109 more miles than Larry.
How many miles does Larry drive? 150 miles

See Additional Answers

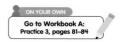

ON YOUR OWN
Go to Workbook A:
Practice 3, pages 81–84

Student Book A p. 114

✔ Guided Practice (page 113)

5 to **10** These exercises provide further practice in comparing sets involving addition or subtraction. Ask children to explain how they chose whether to add or subtract to solve each problem. Encourage children to draw bar models to represent each problem, and then write the addition or subtraction sentence to solve the problem. Remind children to check their answers with their partners by working backward. See Additional Answers, page T65.

Let's Practice (page 114)

Exercises **1** to **6** reinforce the skill of using bar models to solve comparison problems involving addition and subtraction. Have children work on problems individually and check their answers with their partners by working backward. See Additional Answers, page T65.

Common Error Some children may not understand what the problem is asking for. Write the problem on the board, and then read it aloud. Ask some children to circle the comparison terms *fewer* and *more*.

ON YOUR OWN

Children practice addition and subtraction with the comparing concept using bar models in Practice 3, pages 81 to 84 of **Workbook 2A**. These pages (with the answers) are shown on page 114A.

Differentiation Options

Struggling: Reteach 2A, pp. 91–94
On Level: Extra Practice 2A, pp. 47–48

Practice and Apply

Workbook pages for Chapter 4, Lesson 3

Name: _____ Date: _____

Practice 3 Comparing Two Sets

Solve.
Complete the bar models to help you.

1. 102 children at a swimming pool do not wear goggles.
23 more children wear goggles than those who do
not wear goggles.
How many children wear goggles?

without goggles ⟨102⟩ ⟨23⟩

with goggles

?

102 + 23 = 125

_____125_____ children wear goggles.

2. Alice made 166 ham sandwiches for a party.
She made 77 fewer cheese sandwiches than ham
sandwiches for the party.
How many cheese sandwiches did Alice make?

⟨166⟩

ham sandwiches

cheese sandwiches

? ⟨77⟩

166 − 77 = 89

Alice made _____89_____ cheese sandwiches.

Workbook A p. 81

Name: _____ Date: _____

Solve.
Complete the bar models to help you.

5. Mr. Diaz has 347 apple trees in his orchard.
He has 162 more apple trees than peach trees in his orchard.
How many peach trees does Mr. Diaz have in his orchard?

⟨347⟩

apple trees

peach trees

? ⟨162⟩

347 − 162 = 185

Mr. Diaz has _____185_____ peach trees in his orchard.

6. Shop A sells 97 television sets in December.
It sells 166 fewer television sets than Shop B in December.
How many television sets does Shop B sell in December?

⟨97⟩ ⟨166⟩

Shop A

Shop B

?

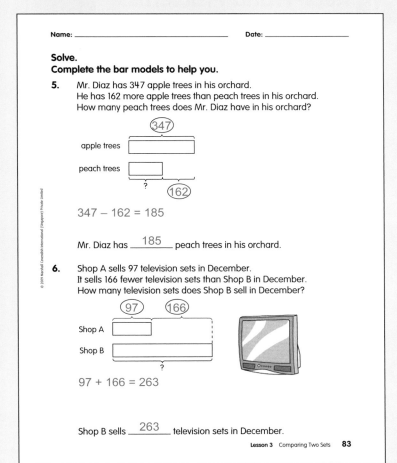

97 + 166 = 263

Shop B sells _____263_____ television sets in December.

Workbook A p. 83

Solve.
Draw bar models to help you.

3. Sam makes 123 party favors.
Lily makes 87 more party favors than Sam.
How many party favors does Lily make?

123   87

Sam

Lily

?

123 + 87 = 210

Lily makes _____210_____ party favors.

4. 952 children watch a funny movie.
265 fewer adults than children watch the funny movie.
How many adults watch the funny movie?

952

children

adults

?   265

952 − 265 = 687

_____687_____ adults watch the funny movie.

Workbook A p. 82

Solve.
Draw bar models to help you.

7. The school cook orders 219 hamburgers.
He orders 120 more hamburgers than hot dogs.
How many hot dogs does the school cook order?

219

hamburgers

hot dogs

?   120

219 − 120 = 99

The school cook orders _____99_____ hot dogs.

8. 234 flag twirlers march in the Fourth of July parade.
There are 159 fewer flag twirlers than band members at the parade.
How many band members are at the parade?

234   159

flag twirlers

band members

?

234 + 159 = 393

_____393_____ band members are at the parade.

Workbook A p. 84

LESSON 4 Real-World Problems: Two-Step Problems

LESSON OBJECTIVES

- Use bar models to solve two-step addition and subtraction problems.
- Apply the inverse operations of addition and subtraction.

TECHNOLOGY RESOURCES

- *Math in Focus* eBooks
- *Math in Focus* Teacher Resources CD
- *Math in Focus* Virtual Manipulatives

DAY 1   Student Book 2A, pp. 115–121
Workbook 2A, pp. 85–92

DIFFERENTIATION RESOURCES

- Reteach 2A, pp. 95–98
- Extra Practice 2A, pp. 49–52

5-minute Warm Up

Have children tell you three different 2-digit numbers. Add the two larger numbers. Then, subtract the smallest number from the value found earlier.

For example, if the numbers are 30, 94, and 58:
94 + 58 = 152
152 − 30 = 122

Repeat the exercise using different numbers.

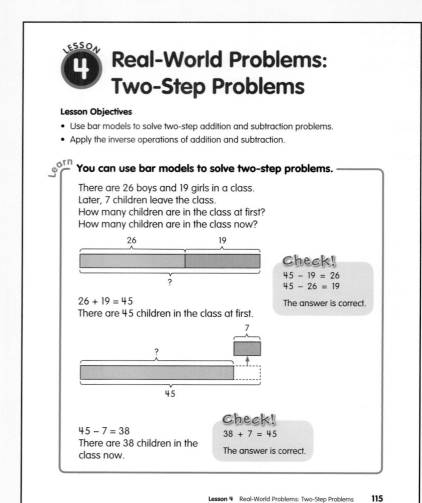

LESSON 4 Real-World Problems: Two-Step Problems

Lesson Objectives

- Use bar models to solve two-step addition and subtraction problems.
- Apply the inverse operations of addition and subtraction.

Learn   You can use bar models to solve two-step problems.

There are 26 boys and 19 girls in a class.
Later, 7 children leave the class.
How many children are in the class at first?
How many children are in the class now?

26 + 19 = 45
There are 45 children in the class at first.

Check!
45 − 19 = 26
45 − 26 = 19
The answer is correct.

45 − 7 = 38
There are 38 children in the class now.

Check!
38 + 7 = 45
The answer is correct.

Lesson 4   Real-World Problems: Two-Step Problems   **115**

Student Book A p. 115

DAY 1 # Teach

Learn

Use Bar Models to Solve Two-Step Problems
(page 115)

Bar models are used to illustrate the adding on, taking away, part-part-whole and comparison concepts related to computation in addition and subtraction.

- Read the story given in the problem.

- Read the first line again, and draw the bar model to illustrate the part-part-whole relationship described in that line.

- Have children provide the addition sentence that shows that relationship: 26 + 19 = 45.

- Point out that the total or whole, 45, is the answer to the first question in the problem.

- Read the second line and show the 'taking away' of 7 from the bar model by erasing and drawing it above the original position.

- Have children provide the subtraction sentence. Point out that this solution is the answer to the second question in the problem.

- Help children to check the answers by working backward.

Student Book A p. 116

Guided Practice

Solve.
Use the bar models to help you.

1. Mr. Castro drives 341 miles.
   Mrs. Castro drives 279 miles more than Mr. Castro.

   a How far does Mrs. Castro drive?

   b How far do Mr. and Mrs. Castro drive altogether?

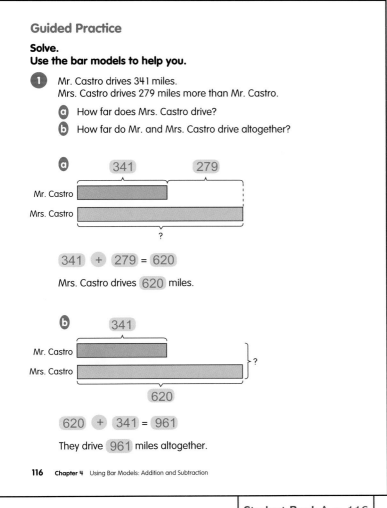

a

341 + 279 = 620

Mrs. Castro drives 620 miles.

b

620 + 341 = 961

They drive 961 miles altogether.

116   Chapter 4   Using Bar Models: Addition and Subtraction

Problem of the Lesson

Sally has 127 marbles. David gave Sally 219 marbles. Sally then gave away some of her marbles, leaving her with only 185 marbles. How many marbles did Sally give away?
Use bar models to help you solve this problem.

Solution:

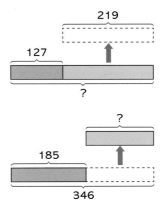

127 + 219 = 346
346 − 185 = 161

Answer: Sally gave away 161 marbles.

Check for Understanding
Guided Practice (pages 116 and 117)

1 and **2** These exercises guide children to use bar models to solve a two-step problem one step at a time. In later grades, children will need to figure out what the first step is, without being asked.

1 Lead children to compare the bars that represent the distances travelled by Mr. and Mrs. Castro, and add 341 and 279 to find the distance travelled by Mrs Castro.

Differentiated Instruction

English Language Learners

Have children work in pairs for the exercises on pages 119 and 120. Have one partner describe each step in the process as it is completed. The other partner follows along and checks the work. Switch roles and complete additional problems.

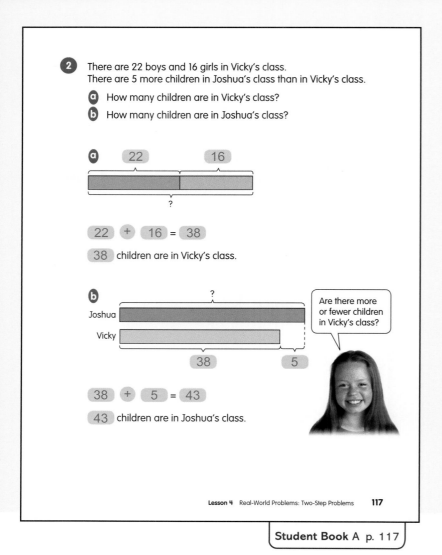

2 There are 22 boys and 16 girls in Vicky's class.
There are 5 more children in Joshua's class than in Vicky's class.

a How many children are in Vicky's class?

b How many children are in Joshua's class?

a   22   16

$22 + 16 = 38$

38 children are in Vicky's class.

b   ?

Joshua

Vicky

38   5

Are there more or fewer children in Vicky's class?

$38 + 5 = 43$

43 children are in Joshua's class.

Student Book A p. 117

3 Anya has 264 United States and Mexican stamps in all.
93 stamps are Mexican stamps.

a How many United States stamps does Anya have?

b How many more United States stamps than Mexican stamps does Anya have?

a   264

?   93

$264 - 93 = 171$

Anya has **171** United States stamps.

Do I add or subtract?

b   171

United States stamps

Mexican stamps

93   ?

$171 - 93 = 78$

Anya has **78** more United States stamps than Mexican stamps.

Student Book A p. 118

2 First, lead children to add two parts to form a whole. Then, lead children to compare two sets before adding to find the larger set.

Best Practices You may want to have children work in groups of four for this lesson. One child in the group draws the bar model. Another child solves the first step of the problem. The third child solves the second step of the problem. The fourth child uses the inverse operation to check the answer. Remind groups to reread the question and see if the answer makes sense.

✓ Guided Practice (pages 118 to 120)

3 This exercise provides practice for children to use bar models to solve a two-step problem, one step at a time.

- First, help children to see that they can apply the part-whole concept, and subtract one part (number of Mexican stamps) from the total to find the other part (number of United States stamps).

- Then, lead children to compare the two sets before subtracting again to find the difference between the sets (*how many more*).

4 Barry has 345 marbles.
He gives Andy 78 marbles.
Now, Barry has 183 blue marbles and some red marbles.
How many red marbles does Barry have now?

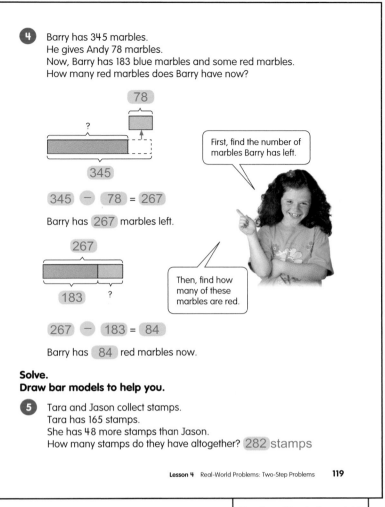

First, find the number of marbles Barry has left.

$345 - 78 = 267$

Barry has 267 marbles left.

Then, find how many of these marbles are red.

$267 - 183 = 84$

Barry has 84 red marbles now.

Solve.
Draw bar models to help you.

5 Tara and Jason collect stamps.
Tara has 165 stamps.
She has 48 more stamps than Jason.
How many stamps do they have altogether? 282 stamps

Student Book A p. 119

Solve.
Draw bar models to help you.

6 A tall bookcase has 56 math books and 78 reading books.
A short bookcase has 39 fewer books.
How many books are in the short bookcase? 95 books

READING AND WRITING MATH
Math Journal

Kelly	327	sells	stickers	Rashid
753	stamps	Sal	in all	how many
left	Kevin	468	buys	buttons

Use the words and numbers above to write:
1 two real-world addition problems.   Answers vary.
2 two real-world subtraction problems.

Let's Practice

Solve.
Draw bar models to help you.

1 The paper store receives 528 newspapers in a week.
Ms. Diaz delivers 274 newspapers to local homes.
Mr. Miguel sells all except 56 of the remaining papers.

  a How many newspapers are not delivered? 254 newspapers

  b How many of these does Mr. Miguel sell? 198 newspapers

Student Book A p. 120

---

4 This exercise provides practice for children to use bar models to solve a two-step problem, one step at a time.

• First, lead children to subtract one set from the whole.

• Then, help children to see the remaining set as the new whole, and subtract again to find the second part (number of red marbles), given one of the parts (number of blue marbles).

5 and **6** These exercises provide children with the opportunity to draw bar models on their own to solve two-step problems.

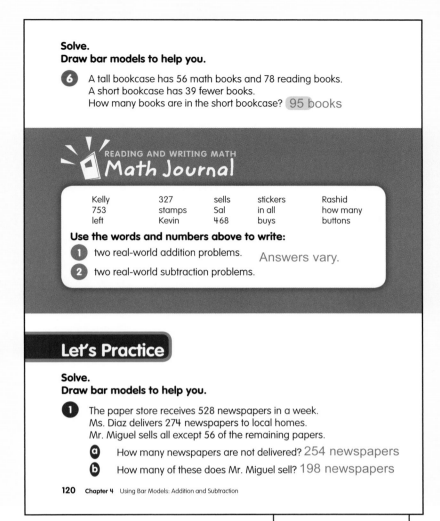

WORKING TOGETHER

READING AND WRITING MATH
Math Journal (page 120)

This section allows children to reflect on their understanding of using bar models to solve real-world problems.

• Children work in groups of three or four.

• Have them write two real-world addition and two real-world subtraction problems using the given words and numbers.

• Have children show the other groups their solutions using bar models.

Let's Practice (pages 120 and 121)

Exercises **1** to **5** reinforce the skills of using bar models, the adding-on and taking-away strategies, as well as part-whole and comparison concepts in solving two-step real-world problems. Exercises **1** and **3** involve subtraction in the two steps while Exercises **2** and **4** involve addition in the two steps.

Exercise **5** requires children to use the bar models to show that the solution can be obtained in two steps: first addition (275 + 82), and then subtraction of 148 from the answer in the first step. Encourage children to check their answers with their partners by working backward.

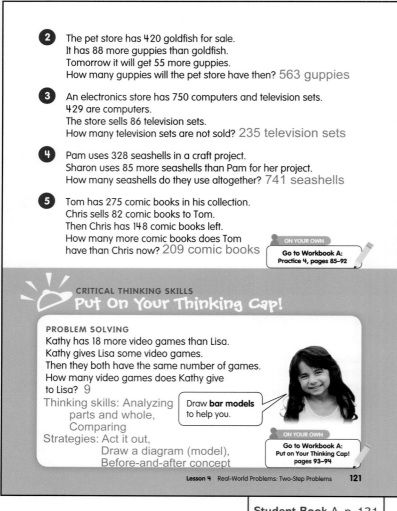

2 The pet store has 420 goldfish for sale.
It has 88 more guppies than goldfish.
Tomorrow it will get 55 more guppies.
How many guppies will the pet store have then? 563 guppies

3 An electronics store has 750 computers and television sets.
429 are computers.
The store sells 86 television sets.
How many television sets are not sold? 235 television sets

4 Pam uses 328 seashells in a craft project.
Sharon uses 85 more seashells than Pam for her project.
How many seashells do they use altogether? 741 seashells

5 Tom has 275 comic books in his collection.
Chris sells 82 comic books to Tom.
Then Chris has 148 comic books left.
How many more comic books does Tom have than Chris now? 209 comic books

ON YOUR OWN
Go to Workbook A:
Practice 4, pages 85–92

CRITICAL THINKING SKILLS
Put On Your Thinking Cap!

PROBLEM SOLVING
Kathy has 18 more video games than Lisa.
Kathy gives Lisa some video games.
Then they both have the same number of games.
How many video games does Kathy give to Lisa? 9

Thinking skills: Analyzing parts and whole, Comparing
Strategies: Act it out,
Draw a diagram (model),
Before-and-after concept

Draw **bar models** to help you.

ON YOUR OWN
Go to Workbook A:
Put on Your Thinking Cap!
pages 93–94

Lesson 4   Real-World Problems: Two-Step Problems   **121**

Student Book A p. 121

Common Error Some children may stop after solving the first step of the problem. After children have solved the problem, have them reread the question and see if the answer makes sense.

ON YOUR OWN

Children practice using bar models to solve two-step real-world problems in Practice 4, pages 85 to 90 of **Workbook 2A**. These pages (with the answers) are shown on pages 121A and 121B. The Math Journal on pages 91 and 92 of **Workbook 2A**, consolidates Lessons 1 to 4. These pages (with the answers) are shown on page 121B.

Differentiation Options

Struggling: Reteach 2A, pp. 95–98
On Level: Extra Practice 2A, pp. 49–52

CRITICAL THINKING AND PROBLEM SOLVING
Put on Your Thinking Cap! (page 121)

This problem solving exercise involves multi-step addition and subtraction using bar models and other concepts from this chapter. Children may work individually or in groups to answer the question and present the solution to the class. Remind children to check their answer by working backward.

Thinking Skills

• Analyzing parts and whole
• Comparing

Problem Solving Strategies

• Act it out
• Use a diagram/model
• Use before-and-after concept

ON YOUR OWN

Because all children should be challenged, have all children try the Problem Solving pages in **Workbook 2A**, pages 93 and 94. These pages (with the answers) are shown on page 121C.

Differentiation Options

On Level: Extra Practice 2A, pp. 53–54
Advanced: Enrichment 2A, pp. 31–37

Practice and Apply
Workbook pages for Chapter 4, Lesson 4

Name: _____ Date: _____

Practice 4   Real-World Problems: Two-Step Problems

Solve.
Complete the bar models to help you.

1. Mr. Kim has 78 boxes of apples and 130 boxes of oranges.
   He sells some boxes of oranges.
   Now he has 159 boxes of apples and oranges left.
   a. How many boxes of apples and oranges did Mr. Kim have
   at first?
   b. How many boxes of oranges did Mr. Kim sell?

   a.
   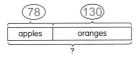

78	130
apples	oranges
   ?

   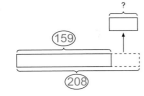

   78 + 130 = 208

   Mr. Kim had ___208___ boxes of apples and oranges at first.

   b.
   ?

   159
   208

   208 − 159 = 49

   Mr. Kim sold ___49___ boxes of oranges.

Workbook A p. 85

Name: _____ Date: _____

Solve.
Draw bar models to help you.

3. Kennedy Elementary School has 784 students.
   325 students are boys.
   a. How many girls are in the school?
   b. How many more girls than boys are in the school?

   325   ?
   boys [   ]
   784
   girls [   ]
   ?

   784 − 325 = 459

   a. ___459___ girls are in the school.

   459 − 325 = 134

   b. ___134___ more girls are in the school than boys.

Workbook A p. 87

Solve.
Complete the bar models to help you.

2. Sophie has 356 stamps in her collection.
   Rita has 192 stamps more than Sophie.
   a. How many stamps does Rita have?
   b. How many stamps do they have in all?

   356   192

   Sophie [   ]
   ?
   Rita [   ]
   ?

   356 + 192 = 548

   a. Rita has ___548___ stamps.

   356 + 548 = 904

   b. They have ___904___ stamps in all.

Workbook A p. 86

Solve.
Draw bar models to help you.

4. Club A has 235 male members, and 172 female members.
   45 new members join the club.
   a. How many members were in the club at first?
   b. How many members are in the club now?

   235 male members   172 female members
   [|]
   ?

   235 + 172 = 407

   a. ___407___ members were in the club at first.

   45
   new
   407 members   members
   [|]
   ?

   407 + 45 = 452

   b. ___452___ members are in the club now.

Workbook A p. 88

Page 89 (top left)

5. Kate's grandmother had $245.
She spends $78.
Then she gives $36 to Kate.
How much money does Kate's grandmother have now?

First, find how much she has left after spending $78.

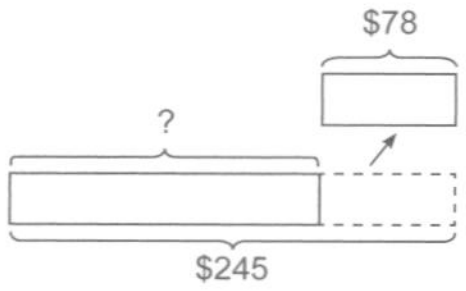

$245 – $78 = $167

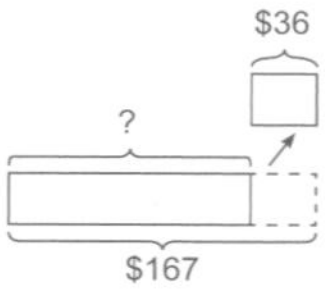

$167 – $36 = $131

She has ___$131___ now.

Workbook A p. 89

Page 91 (top right)

Math Journal

**Write an addition story or a subtraction story for each bar model.
Then solve.**

1.   36   16   ?

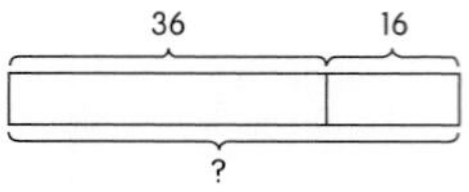

Answers vary.

_____
_____
_____
_____

2.   ?   44   63

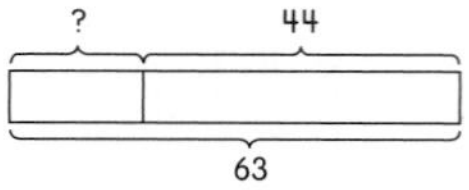

Answers vary.

_____
_____
_____
_____

Workbook A p. 91

Page 90 (bottom left)

**Solve.
Draw bar models to help you.**

6. There are 147 daisy plants and 32 tulip plants in Nursery X.
Nursery Y has 66 fewer daisy and tulip plants than Nursery X.
How many daisy and tulip plants are there in Nursery Y?

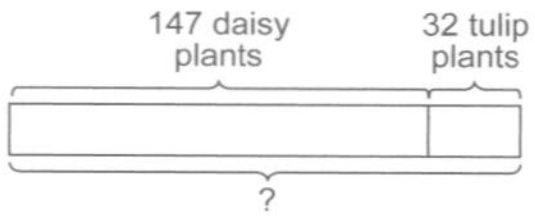

147 daisy plants   32 tulip plants   ?

147 + 32 = 179
There are 179 daisy and tulip plants in Nursery X.

179

Nursery X

Nursery Y

?   66

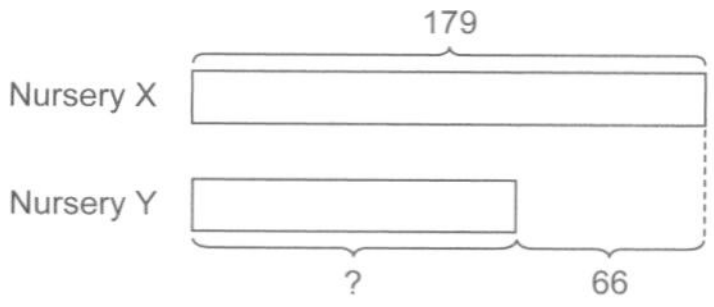

179 – 66 = 113

There are ___113___ daisy and tulip plants in Nursery Y.

Workbook A p. 90

Page 92 (bottom right)

**Write an addition story or a subtraction story for the bar model.
Then solve.**

3.   92

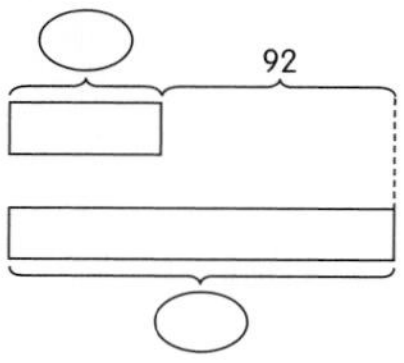

Answers vary.

_____
_____
_____
_____

Workbook A p. 92

Practice and Apply
Workbook pages for Put on Your Thinking Cap!

Name: _____   Date: _____

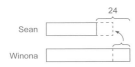

Put On Your Thinking Cap!

Problem Solving

Solve.

1. Sean has 24 fewer toys than Winona.
    After Winona gives some toys to Sean, both of them have
    the same number of toys.
    How many toys does Winona give Sean?

$12 + 12 = 24$

Thinking skills: Analyzing parts and whole,
                 Comparing
Strategies: Act it out, Before-and-after concept,
            Draw a diagram

Winona gives Sean ____12____ toys.

Chapter 4 Using Bar Models: Addition and Subtraction   **93**

Workbook A p. 93

---

2. Nadia has 20 more postcards than Pete.
    After Nadia gives Pete some postcards,
    Pete has 2 more postcards than Nadia.
    How many postcards does Nadia give to Pete?

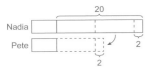

$20 - 2 = 18$
$9 + 9 = 18$
$9 + 2 = 11$

Thinking skills: Analyzing parts and wholes,
                 Comparing
Strategies: Act it out, Before-and-after concept,
            Draw a diagram

Nadia gives Pete ____11____ postcards.

94   **Chapter 4**   Using Bar Models: Addition and Subtraction

Workbook A p. 94

Notes

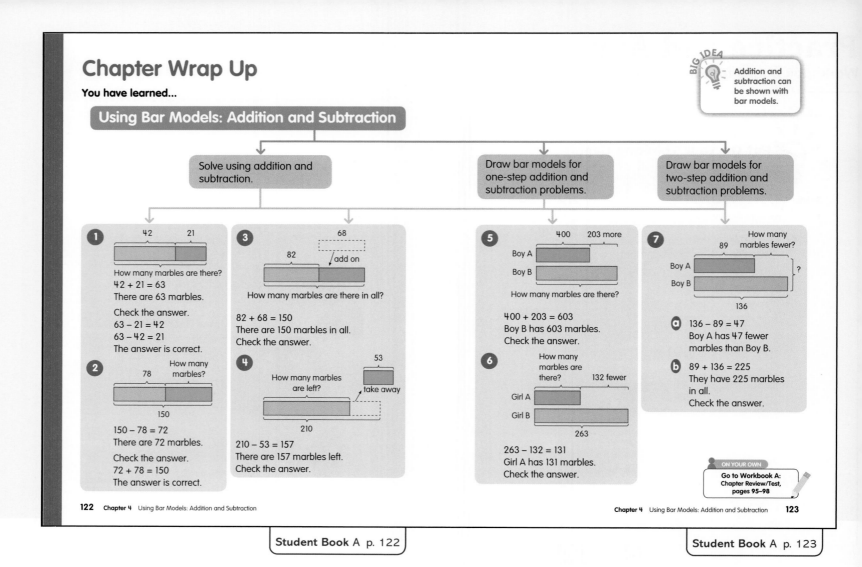

Chapter Wrap Up

You have learned...

Using Bar Models: Addition and Subtraction

> **BIG IDEA**
> Addition and subtraction can be shown with bar models.

Solve using addition and subtraction.

Draw bar models for one-step addition and subtraction problems.

Draw bar models for two-step addition and subtraction problems.

1 42 21
How many marbles are there?
42 + 21 = 63
There are 63 marbles.
Check the answer.
63 − 21 = 42
63 − 42 = 21
The answer is correct.

2 78 How many marbles?
150
150 − 78 = 72
There are 72 marbles.
Check the answer.
72 + 78 = 150
The answer is correct.

3 82 68 / add on
How many marbles are there in all?
82 + 68 = 150
There are 150 marbles in all.
Check the answer.

4 How many marbles are left? 53 / take away
210
210 − 53 = 157
There are 157 marbles left.
Check the answer.

5 400 203 more
Boy A
Boy B
How many marbles are there?
400 + 203 = 603
Boy B has 603 marbles.
Check the answer.

6 How many marbles are there? 132 fewer
Girl A
Girl B
263
263 − 132 = 131
Girl A has 131 marbles.
Check the answer.

7 89 How many marbles fewer?
Boy A
Boy B ?
136
a 136 − 89 = 47
Boy A has 47 fewer marbles than Boy B.
b 89 + 136 = 225
They have 225 marbles in all.
Check the answer.

> **ON YOUR OWN**
> Go to Workbook A:
> Chapter Review/Test,
> pages 95–98

Student Book A p. 122

Student Book A p. 123

Chapter Wrap Up (pages 122 and 123)

Use the examples on pages 122 and 123 to review using bar models to solve one-step and two-step addition and subtraction problems. Encourage children to use the chapter vocabulary:

- join
- take away
- set
- compare

> **ON YOUR OWN**
>
> Have children review the vocabulary, concepts, and skills from Chapter 4 with the Chapter Review/Test in **Workbook 2A**, pages 95 to 98. These pages (with the answers) are shown on page 123A.
>
> You may also wish to use the Cumulative Review for Chapters 1 to 4 from **Workbook 2A**, pages 99 to 106. These pages (with the answers) are shown on pages 123C and 123D.

Assessment

Use the Chapter 4 Test Prep on pages 19 to 24 of **Assessments 2** to assess how well children have learned the material of this chapter. This assessment is appropriate for reporting results to adults at home and administrators. This test is shown on page 123B.

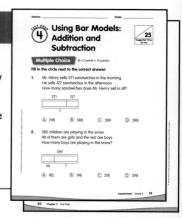

Assessments 2 pp. 19–24

Workbook pages for Chapter Review/Test

Workbook A p. 95

Name: _____   Date: _____

Chapter Review/Test
Vocabulary
Fill in the blanks.
Use the words in the box.

add	subtract	compare	sets

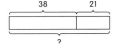

1. In this model, you __compare__ two __sets__ of data.

2. To find how many more apricots there are than peaches, you __subtract__.

3. To find the total number of apricots and peaches, you __add__.

Workbook A p. 95

Concepts and Skills

Fill in each ◯ with + or −.
Then fill in the blanks.

4.

   38 ⊕ 21 = __59__

5.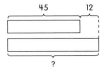

   50 ⊖ 38 = __12__

6.
   45 ⊕ 12 = __57__

7.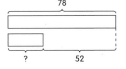

   78 ⊖ 52 = __26__

Workbook A p. 96

Name: _____   Date: _____

Problem Solving
Solve.
Draw bar models to help you.

8. A jewelry store has 198 rings and bracelets altogether.
   It has 89 bracelets.
   How many more rings than bracelets does the store have?

   $198 - 89 = 109$
   $109 - 89 = 20$

   The store has __20__ more rings than bracelets.

9. Andy reads 56 more pages of his book on Monday than on Tuesday.
   He reads 125 pages on Monday.
   How many pages in all does he read on Monday and Tuesday?

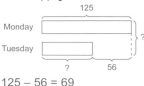

   $125 - 56 = 69$
   $125 + 69 = 194$

   He reads __194__ pages in all.

Workbook A p. 97

---

10. An office has 223 workers.
    132 of the workers are men.
    How many more men work in the office than women?

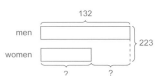

    $223 - 132 = 91$
    $132 - 91 = 41$

    __41__ more men work in the office than women.

11. A furniture shop has 581 tables and chairs in all.
    There are 125 tables.
    How many more chairs than tables are there in the shop?

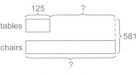

    $581 - 125 = 456$
    $456 - 125 = 331$

    There are __331__ more chairs than tables in the shop.

Workbook A p. 98

Assessments Book pages for Chapter 4 Test Prep

Answer key appears in Assessments Book.

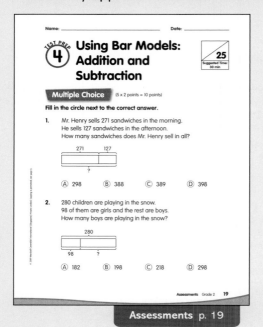

Name: _____ Date: _____

TEST PREP 4 Using Bar Models: Addition and Subtraction

Suggested Time: 30 min **25**

Multiple Choice (5 x 2 points = 10 points)

Fill in the circle next to the correct answer.

1. Mr. Henry sells 271 sandwiches in the morning.
He sells 127 sandwiches in the afternoon.
How many sandwiches does Mr. Henry sell in all?

271	127

?

(A) 298   (B) 388   (C) 389   (D) 398

2. 280 children are playing in the snow.
98 of them are girls and the rest are boys.
How many boys are playing in the snow?

280

98	?

(A) 182   (B) 198   (C) 218   (D) 298

Assessments   Grade 2   **19**

Assessments p. 19

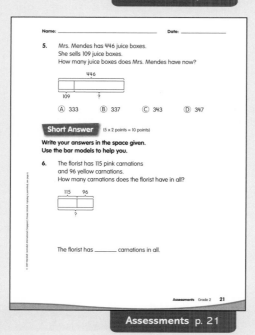

Name: _____ Date: _____

3. Sue has 274 baseball cards in her collection.
Her uncle gives her another 87 baseball cards.
How many baseball cards does Sue have now?

274	87

?

(A) 113   (B) 187   (C) 251   (D) 361

4. Meg has 272 stickers.
She gives some stickers to her friend.
Now she has 137 stickers left.
How many stickers did Meg give her friend?

272

?	137

(A) 135   (B) 145   (C) 145   (D) 409

20   Chapter 4   Test Prep

Assessments p. 20

Name: _____ Date: _____

5. Mrs. Mendes has 446 juice boxes.
She sells 109 juice boxes.
How many juice boxes does Mrs. Mendes have now?

446

109	?

(A) 333   (B) 337   (C) 343   (D) 347

Short Answer (5 x 2 points = 10 points)

Write your answers in the space given.
Use the bar models to help you.

6. The florist has 115 pink carnations
and 96 yellow carnations.
How many carnations does the florist have in all?

115	96

?

The florist has _____ carnations in all.

Assessments   Grade 2   **21**

Assessments p. 21

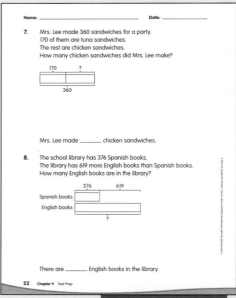

Name: _____ Date: _____

7. Mrs. Lee made 360 sandwiches for a party.
170 of them are tuna sandwiches.
The rest are chicken sandwiches.
How many chicken sandwiches did Mrs. Lee make?

170	?

360

Mrs. Lee made _____ chicken sandwiches.

8. The school library has 376 Spanish books.
The library has 619 more English books than Spanish books.
How many English books are in the library?

Spanish books | 376 | 619

English books

?

There are _____ English books in the library.

22   Chapter 4   Test Prep

Assessments p. 22

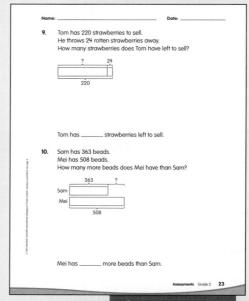

Name: _____ Date: _____

9. Tom has 220 strawberries to sell.
He throws 24 rotten strawberries away.
How many strawberries does Tom have left to sell?

?	24

220

Tom has _____ strawberries left to sell.

10. Sam has 363 beads.
Mei has 508 beads.
How many more beads does Mei have than Sam?

Sam | 363 | ? |

Mei

508

Mei has _____ more beads than Sam.

Assessments   Grade 2   **23**

Assessments p. 23

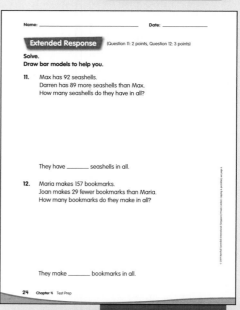

Name: _____ Date: _____

Extended Response (Question 11: 2 points, Question 12: 3 points)

Solve.
Draw bar models to help you.

11. Max has 92 seashells.
Darren has 89 more seashells than Max.
How many seashells do they have in all?

They have _____ seashells in all.

12. Maria makes 157 bookmarks.
Joan makes 29 fewer bookmarks than Maria.
How many bookmarks do they make in all?

They make _____ bookmarks in all.

24   Chapter 4   Test Prep

Assessments p. 24

Cumulative Review for Chapters 1 to 4

Cumulative Review
for Chapters 1 to 4

Name: _____ Date: _____

Cumulative Review
for Chapters 1 to 4

Concepts and Skills

Write in standard form.

1. Seven hundred sixteen __716__

2. Four hundred five __405__

Count on or count back.
Find the missing numbers.

3. 820, 810, 800, __790__, __780__, __770__

4. 600, 700, 800, __900__, __1,000__

5. 500, 400, 300, __200__, __100__, __0__

Find the missing numbers.

6. In 632, the digit __3__ is in the tens place.

7. In 591, the digit 5 is in the __hundreds__ place.

8. $743 = 700 + $ __40__ $+ 3$

9. 200 and 2 make __202__.

Write > or <.

10. 235 $<$ 325

11. 891 $>$ 889

Cumulative Review for Chapters 1 to 4 **99**

Workbook A p. 99

Name: _____ Date: _____

Add.

23.
```
  2 5 7
+   4 2
-------
  2 9 9
```

24.
```
  2 3 4
+ 7 1 3
-------
  9 4 7
```

25.
```
  7 0 8
+   3 6
-------
  7 4 4
```

26.
```
  2 5 6
+ 1 3 8
-------
  3 9 4
```

27.
```
  6 5 1
+ 2 8 6
-------
  9 3 7
```

28.
```
  6 5 7
+ 1 8 5
-------
  8 4 2
```

Subtract.

29.
```
  7 5 9
-   4 2
-------
  7 1 7
```

30.
```
  3 6 8
- 2 1 4
-------
  1 5 4
```

31.
```
  5 4 1
- 2 3 8
-------
  3 0 3
```

32.
```
  4 2 7
- 1 3 4
-------
  2 9 3
```

33.
```
  8 3 1
- 6 9 8
-------
  1 3 3
```

34.
```
  2 0 0
-   4 8
-------
  1 5 2
```

Subtract.
Check by adding.

35.
```
  5 1 0          385
- 3 8 5    +     125
-------
  1 2 5          510
```

36.
```
  4 0 8          219
- 2 1 9    +     189
-------
  1 8 9          408
```

Subtract.
Check by adding.

37. $400 - 57 = $ __343__

38. $500 - 493 = $ __7__

Cumulative Review for Chapters 1 to 4 **101**

Workbook A p. 101

Order the numbers from least to greatest.

12. 690   106   815   699

__106__, __690__, __699__, __815__

Find the missing numbers.

13.

873 883 [893] 903 913 [923] 933 943

Fill in the blanks.

14. 1 more than 638 is __639__.

15. 10 less than 286 is __276__.

16. 100 more than 899 is __999__.

17. __359__ is 1 less than 360.

18. __900__ is 10 more than 890.

19. __900__ is 100 less than 1,000.

Complete each pattern.

20. 240, 220, __200__, __180__, 160, __140__, __120__

21. 350, 390, 430, __470__, __510__, __550__, __590__

22. __654__, __554__, 454, 354, 254, __154__, __54__

100 Cumulative Review for Chapters 1 to 4

Workbook A p. 100

Find the missing numbers.

39.
```
  2 5 6
- [9] 4
-------
  1 6 2
```

40.
```
  [5] 0 8
+   3 9 9
---------
    9 0 7
```

Problem Solving
Solve.
Draw bar models to help you.
Check your answers.

41. Manuel drives 215 miles on Monday.
He drives 685 miles on Tuesday.
How many miles does he drive in all?

215 | 685
?

$215 + 685 = 900$

He drives __900__ miles in all.

42. Mrs. King has $200 in the bank.
She spends $45.
How much does she have left?

$200
$45 | ?

$\$200 - \$45 = \$155$

She has $__155__ left.

102 Cumulative Review for Chapters 1 to 4

Workbook A p. 102

Name: _____ Date: _____

Solve.
Draw bar models to help you.
Check your answers.

43. Jeremy has 430 black beads.
He has 50 more red beads than black beads.
How many red beads does he have?

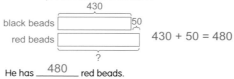

430 + 50 = 480

He has ___480___ red beads.

44. There are 356 sheep on a farm.
There are 100 fewer cows than sheep.
How many cows are there?

356 − 100 = 256

There are ___256___ cows.

45. Mike has 515 stickers in his album.
Shateel has 488 stickers in his.
Who has more stickers?
How many more stickers?

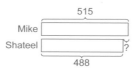

___Mike___ has more stickers.

___27___ more stickers.

515 − 488 = 27

Workbook A p. 103

Name: _____ Date: _____

Solve.
Draw bar models to help you.
Check your answers.

48. 339 passengers are on a train.
196 of them are children.
The others are adults.
How many adults are on the train?

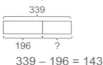

339 − 196 = 143

There are ___143___ adults on the train.

49. The Hat Store sold 265 caps last week.
It sold 97 fewer caps this week.
a. How many caps did the Hat Store sell this week?
b. How many caps did the Hat Store sell for the two weeks?

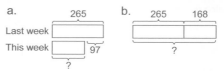

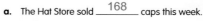

265 − 97 = 168   265 + 168 = 433

a. The Hat Store sold ___168___ caps this week.

b. The Hat Store sold ___433___ caps for the two weeks.

Workbook A p. 105

Solve.
Draw bar models to help you.
Check your answers.

46. Nick scores 715 points in a game.
He scores 100 fewer points than his sister.
How many points does his sister score?

715 + 100 = 815

His sister scores ___815___ points.

47. Beth reads for 60 minutes in the morning.
She reads for 42 minutes at night.
How many minutes does she read in all?

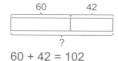

60 + 42 = 102

Beth reads for ___102___ minutes in all.

Workbook A p. 104

Solve.
Draw bar models to help you.
Check your answers.

50. The theater sold 343 tickets on Friday.
This is 192 fewer tickets than those sold on Saturday.
How many tickets were sold altogether?

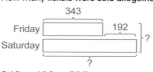

343 + 192 = 535
343 + 535 = 878

___878___ tickets were sold altogether.

51. 365 people watch a show on Monday.
78 more people watch the show on Tuesday.
105 more people watch the show on Tuesday than on Wednesday.
How many people watch the show on Wednesday?

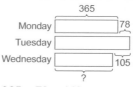

365 + 78 = 443
443 − 105 = 338

___338___ people watch the show on Wednesday.

Workbook A p. 106

Chapter Overview

Multiplication and Division

Math Background

Children learned basic multiplication and division concepts using manipulatives in Grade 1. Children have also been taught to relate and apply the concepts to real-world problems.

In this chapter, students move to the pictorial and symbolic phases through the emphasis on equal groups. Multiplication is used to find the number of items in a number of equal groups. Children are led to see that the computation can be done either by multiplying the number of items in each group by the number of groups, or by multiplying the number of groups by the number of items in each group. In both cases, the strategy of repeated addition, taught in Grade 1, is reviewed. For example, 3 groups of 5 can be written as 5 + 5 + 5.

Division is used in two ways. First, in sharing a number of items among a number of groups, divide to find the number of items in each group. Second, from a number of items that each group receives, to find the number of equal groups that can be formed. For the latter, the strategy of repeated subtraction is used to explicate the concept of division.

In repeated subtraction, a certain number (the number of items in each group) is subtracted from the total number of items repeatedly until zero value is obtained. The number of times the same number is subtracted gives the number of equal groups. For instance, if the total is 12 and each group gets 3 items, repeated subtraction is as follows: 12 − 3 − 3 − 3 − 3 = 0. Since there are 4 repeated subtractions, the number of equal groups is 4.

Cross-Curricular Connections

Reading/Language Arts Read aloud *The Doorbell Rang* by Pat Hutchins (HarperTrophy, © 1989) about a mother who makes a dozen cookies for Sam and Victoria to share. Each time the doorbell rings, they need to divide the cookies so everyone will have an equal amount.

Music Have children add numbers and a word to this simple song. Children can exchange songs with a partner and solve.

_____ _____ *in a set.*
Make _____ *equal groups.*
How many do you get?

For example:
16 cards in a set.
Make 2 equal groups.
How many do you get? (8)

Skills Trace

Grade 1	Relate repeated addition to the concept of multiplication. Relate sharing equally to the concept of division. (Chap. 18)
Grade 2	Understand the concept of multiplication as repeated addition and division as grouping or sharing. Use objects and picturees to show the concept of division as finding the number of equal groups. (Chap. 5)
Grade 3	Multiply and divide 2-digit and 3-digit numbers with and without regrouping. (Chaps. 6 to 9)

EVERY DAY COUNTS®
Calendar Math

The November activities provide...

Review of recognizing and extending a pattern

Preview of recognizing and extending a number pattern using rules (Chapter 1)

Practice of relating word problems to symbolic number sentences (Lesson 3 in this chapter)

Differentiation Resources

Differentiation for Special Populations

	English Language Learners	Struggling Reteach 2A	On Level Extra Practice 2A	Advanced Enrichment 2A
Lesson 1	p. 128	pp. 99–104	pp. 55–58	Enrichment pages can be used to challenge advanced children.
Lesson 2	p. 135	pp. 105–110	pp. 59–62	
Lesson 3	p. 143	pp. 111, 112	pp. 63–64	

Additional Support

For English Language Learners

Select activities that reinforce the chapter vocabulary and the connections among these words, such as having children

- add terms, definitions, and examples to the Word Wall
- create flash cards for terms and have children classify words as multiplication or division terms
- answer yes/no questions about terms, definitions, and examples
- discuss the Chapter Wrap Up, encouraging children to use the chapter vocabulary

For Struggling Learners

Select activities that go back to the appropriate stage of the Concrete-Pictorial-Abstract spectrum, such as having children

- act out finding products and quotients
- draw pictures to illustrate multiplication and division stories
- identify given oral number stories as multiplication or division stories
- create and solve new stories using those in the chapter as models

See also pages 128 and 135

If necessary, review

- Chapter 4 (Using Bar Models: Addition and Subtraction).

For Advanced Learners

See suggestions on pages 130–131 and 138–139.

Assessment and Remediation

Chapter 5 Assessment

Prior Knowledge		
	Resource	**Page numbers**
Quick Check	Student Book 2A	p. 126
Pre-Test	Assessments 2	pp. 25–26
Ongoing Diagnostic		
Guided Practice	Student Book 2A	pp. 128, 130, 135, 138, 142, 143, 144
Common Error	Teacher's Edition 2A	pp. 129, 140–141
Formal Evaluation		
Chapter Review/Test	Workbook 2A	pp. 121–126
Chapter 5 Test Prep	Assessments 2	pp. 27–31

Problems with these items...   Can be remediated with...

Remediation Options

Objective	Review/Test Items	Chapter Assessment Items	Reteach	Student Book
	Workbook 2A pp. 121-126	**Assessments 2 pp. 27–31**	**Reteach 2A**	**Student Book 2A**
Use chapter vocabulary correctly.	1	Not assessed	In context as needed	pp. 127, 134
Use equal groups and repeated addition to multiply.	2–4	1, 2, 7	pp. 99–104	Lesson 1
Make multiplication stories about pictures.	8–11		pp. 99–104	Lesson 1
Make multiplication sentences.	2–4	4, 7–9	pp. 99–104	Lesson 1
Divide to share equally.	12–13	3, 8, 9	pp. 105–110	Lesson 2
Divide by repeated subtraction of equal groups.	14–15		pp. 108–110	Lesson 2
Solve multiplication word problems.	17	6, 11	p. 111	Lesson 3
Solve division word problems.	16	5, 10, 12	p. 112	Lesson 3

Chapter Planning Guide

CHAPTER 5 Multiplication and Division

Lesson	Pacing	Instructional Objectives	Vocabulary
Chapter Opener pp. 124–126 Recall Prior Knowledge Quick Check	*1 day	💡**Big Idea** Multiplication and division use equal groups.	
Lesson 1, pp. 127–133 How to Multiply	2 days	• Use equal groups and repeated addition to multiply. • Make multiplication stories about pictures. • Make multiplication sentences.	• times • equal • group • multiply • repeated addition • multiplication sentence • multiplication story
Lesson 2, pp. 134–141 How to Divide	2 days	• Divide to share equally. • Divide by repeated subtraction of equal groups.	• share • divide • equal groups • division sentence • repeated subtraction
Lesson 3, pp. 142–147 Real-World Problems: Multiplication and Division	1 day	• Solve multiplication word problems. • Solve division word problems.	
Problem Solving, p. 147 ☀ Put on Your Thinking Cap!	$\frac{1}{2}$ day	**Thinking Skill** • Identifying patterns and relationships **Problem Solving Strategy** • Use a diagram/model	
Chapter Wrap Up p. 148	$\frac{1}{2}$ day	• Reinforce and consolidate chapter skills and concepts.	
Chapter Assessment	1 day		

*Assume that 1 day is a 45–55 minute period.

Resources	Materials	NCTM Focal Points	NCTM Process Standards
Student Book 2A, pp. 124–126 **Assessments 2,** pp. 25–26			
Student Book 2A, pp. 127–133 **Workbook 2A,** pp. 107–110 **Extra Practice 2A,** pp. 55–58 **Reteach 2A,** pp. 99–104	• 1 set of counters per group (optional) • 1 set of connecting cubes per group (optional)	***Number and Operations*** Develop initial understanding of multiplication as repeated addition.	Communication Problem Solving Reasoning/Proof Connections Representation
Student Book 2A, pp. 134–141 **Workbook 2A,** pp. 111–114 **Extra Practice 2A,** pp. 59–62 **Reteach 2A,** pp. 105–110	• 24 counters per group • 20 craft sticks per group • 20 index cards per group (optional)	***Number and Operations*** Apply relationships and properties of numbers.	Problem Solving Connections Representation
Student Book 2A, pp. 142–147 **Workbook 2A,** pp. 115–118 **Extra Practice 2A,** pp. 63–64 **Reteach 2A,** pp. 111–112	• 12 counters per group • index cards (optional)	***Number and Operations*** Develop initial understanding of multiplication as repeated addition. ***Number and Operations and Algebra*** Use procedures to solve problems.	Problem Solving Reasoning/Proof Representation
Student Book 2A, p. 147 **Workbook 2A,** pp. 119–120 **Extra Practice 2A,** pp. 65–66 **Enrichment 2A,** pp. 38–44		***Number and Operations and Algebra*** Use procedures to solve problems.	Problem Solving Reasoning/Proof
Student Book 2A, p. 148 **Workbook 2A,** pp. 121–126			
Assessments 2, pp. 27–31			

> **Technology Resources for easy classroom management**
> • *Math in Focus* eBooks
> • *Math in Focus* Teacher Resources CD
> • *Math in Focus* Virtual Manipulatives
> • Online Assessment Generator

Chapter Introduction

CHAPTER 5 Multiplication and Division

Chapter 5 Vocabulary

times	*see multiply*	Lesson 1
equal	having the same amount or number	Lesson 1
group	a set of things	Lesson 1
multiply	put all the equal groups together	Lesson 1
repeated addition	$3 + 3 + 3 + 3 = 12$ Groups of 3 are added 4 times. You can use repeated addition to find the number of things in all.	Lesson 1
multiplication sentence	a number sentence involving multiplication	Lesson 1
multiplication story	a number story involving multiplication	Lesson 1
share	put into groups	Lesson 2
divide	put into equal groups or share equally	Lesson 2
equal groups	groups or sets that have the same amount	Lesson 2
division sentence	a number sentence involving division	Lesson 2
repeated subtraction	$6 - 2 - 2 - 2 = 0$ Groups of 2 are subtracted 3 times. You can use repeated subtraction to find the number of groups.	Lesson 2

Student Book A p. 124

Big Idea (page 124)

Introducing the basics of multiplication and division is the main focus of this chapter.

- Children learn that multiplication and division involve the concept of equal groups.

- They learn to make multiplication and division stories and sentences about pictures.

- They learn to interpret real-world problems and use multiplication and division to solve them.

Chapter Opener (page 124)

The picture illustrates a boy planning lunch for 8 guests. He holds the recipe to make a salad that serves 4 people. This picture serves as a simple problem that prepares children for the basic multiplication and division concepts they will learn in this chapter.

- Show children the picture.

- Read the speech bubble as well as the salad recipe.

- *Ask:* How many guests is the boy having for lunch? (8) How many people does his salad recipe serve? (4)

- *Ask:* If he follows the amounts of ingredients given in the recipe, will the salad prepared be enough for 8 guests? (No)

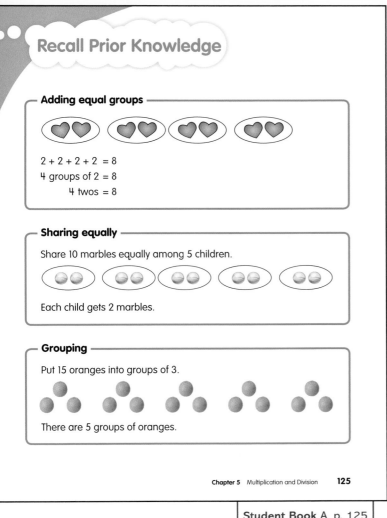

Adding equal groups

2 + 2 + 2 + 2 = 8
4 groups of 2 = 8
    4 twos = 8

Sharing equally

Share 10 marbles equally among 5 children.

Each child gets 2 marbles.

Grouping

Put 15 oranges into groups of 3.

There are 5 groups of oranges.

Chapter 5 *Multiplication and Division* **125**

Student Book A p. 125

• Using the grouping concept, lead children to see that the boy needs 2 times the amount of ingredients listed.

• Ask some children to say how many cups of each ingredient the boy will need to serve 8 guests. Lead them to the following answers:

6 cups + 6 cups = 12 cups of lettuce, 3 cups + 3 cups = 6 cups of carrots, 2 cups + 2 cups = 4 cups of tomatoes, 1 cup + 1 cup = 2 cups of sunflower seeds and 1 cup + 1 cup = 2 cups of salad dressing. This will lead into the repeated addition in Lesson 1.

Recall Prior Knowledge (page 125)

Adding Equal Groups

Children learned to add the same number in equal groups in Grade 1.

• Show children the picture and *ask:* How many groups of hearts are there? (4) How many hearts are in each group? (2)

• Guide children to see that 2 + 2 + 2 + 2 is the same as 4 twos, which is 8.

Sharing Equally

Children learned to divide items into equal groups in Grade 1.

• Show children the picture and *ask:* How many marbles are there in all? (10)

• *Ask:* How many children or groups of marbles are there? (5)

• *Ask:* How many marbles are in each group? (2)

• Have children read together: "Each child gets 2 marbles."

Grouping

Children learned to divide items into equal groups and find the number of groups in Grade 1.

• Show children the picture and *ask:* How many oranges are there in all? (15)

• *Ask:* How many oranges are in each group? (3)

• *Ask:* How many groups of oranges are there? (5)

• Have children read together: "There are 5 groups of oranges."

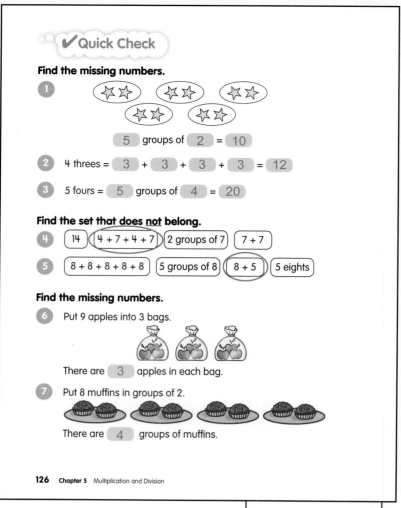

✔Quick Check

Find the missing numbers.

1.
   5 groups of 2 = 10

2. 4 threes = 3 + 3 + 3 + 3 = 12

3. 5 fours = 5 groups of 4 = 20

Find the set that does not belong.

4. | 14 | (4 + 7 + 4 + 7) | 2 groups of 7 | 7 + 7 |

5. | 8 + 8 + 8 + 8 + 8 | 5 groups of 8 | (8 + 5) | 5 eights |

Find the missing numbers.

6. Put 9 apples into 3 bags.

   There are 3 apples in each bag.

7. Put 8 muffins in groups of 2.

   There are 4 groups of muffins.

126 **Chapter 5** Multiplication and Division

Student Book A p. 126

✔Quick Check (page 126)

Use this section as a diagnostic tool to assess children's level of prerequisite knowledge before they progress to this chapter.

Exercises ❶ to ❸ assess children's understanding of repeated addition and equal groups.

Exercises ❹ and ❺ assess if children can express the concept of adding the same number repeatedly as an addition sentence as well as in words.

Exercise ❻ assesses sharing equally while Exercise ❼ assesses the concept of grouping.

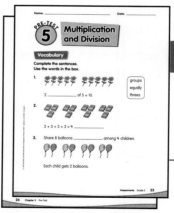

Assessments 2 pp. 25–26

Assessment

For additional assessment of children's prior knowledge and chapter readiness, use the Chapter 5 Pre-Test on pages 25 and 26 of **Assessments 2**.

LESSON 1 How to Multiply

LESSON OBJECTIVES
• Use equal groups and repeated addition to multiply.
• Make multiplication stories about pictures.
• Make multiplication sentences.

TECHNOLOGY RESOURCES
• *Math in Focus* eBooks
• *Math in Focus* Teacher Resources CD
• *Math in Focus* Virtual Manipulatives

Vocabulary

times	repeated addition
equal	multiplication sentence
group	multiplication story
multiply	

DAY 1 Student Book 2A, pp. 127–129
Workbook 2A, pp. 107–108

MATERIALS
• 1 set of counters per group (optional)
• 1 set of connecting cubes per group (optional)

DIFFERENTIATION RESOURCES
• Reteach 2A, pp. 99–102
• Extra Practice 2A, pp. 55–56

DAY 2 Student Book 2A, pp. 130–133
Workbook 2A, pp. 109–110

DIFFERENTIATION RESOURCES
• Reteach 2A, pp. 103–104
• Extra Practice 2A, pp. 57–58

5-minute Warm Up

• Have children work in groups of four or five.

• Ask each child to count the fingers on his or her hand. *Ask:* How many fingers do you have on two hands? (10) Point out that they each have 5 + 5 = 10 fingers.

• Then *ask:* How many fingers do you have in your group? Have them race to be the group that gives the answer first.

• Repeat the activity with number of other parts or items such as eyes, noses, or buttons.

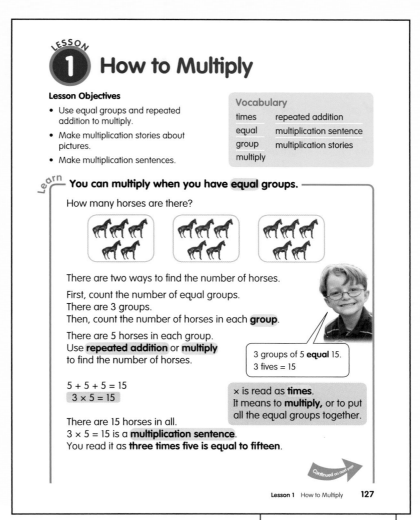

Student Book A p. 127

DAY 1 # Teach

Multiply Using Equal Groups (pages 127 and 128)

Children learn to multiply using repeated addition of equal groups.

• Explain the concept of multiplication as adding equal groups of items. Tell children that they can start by counting the number of groups. *Ask:* How many groups of horses are there? (3)

• *Ask:* How many horses are in each group? (5)

• Write the addition number sentence on the board.

• Help children recall that repeated addition is multiplication, and that 3 groups of 5 is the same as 3 times 5. Then write $3 \times 5 = 15$. *Say:* Three times five is equal to fifteen.

• Write 5×3 and ask: How much is five times three? (15)

• Point out that 5 + 5 + 5 can also be seen as 5 multiplied 3 times, that is, 5×3.

• Explain that it depends on whether you start counting the number of groups before multiplying (3×5), or if you start counting the number in each group before multiplying (5×3). In either case, the answer is 15.

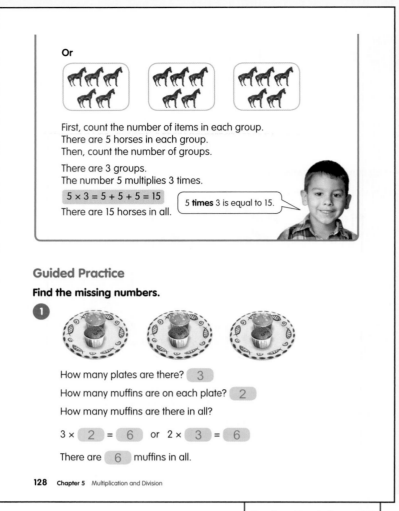

Or

First, count the number of items in each group.
There are 5 horses in each group.
Then, count the number of groups.

There are 3 groups.
The number 5 multiplies 3 times.

$5 \times 3 = 5 + 5 + 5 = 15$

There are 15 horses in all.

> 5 **times** 3 is equal to 15.

Guided Practice

Find the missing numbers.

1

How many plates are there? ⬚ 3

How many muffins are on each plate? ⬚ 2

How many muffins are there in all?

$3 \times$ ⬚ 2 $=$ ⬚ 6 or $2 \times$ ⬚ 3 $=$ ⬚ 6

There are ⬚ 6 muffins in all.

128 Chapter 5 Multiplication and Division

Student Book A p. 128

Problem of the Lesson

Write one or more multiplication sentences for each of the pictures below.

(a)

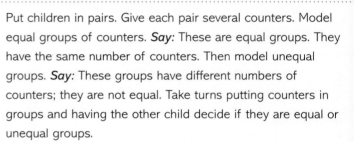

(b)

Solution:
(a) 2 groups of 6 = 12: 2 x 6 = 12 and 6 x 2 = 12
(b) 4 groups of 4 = 16: 4 x 4 = 16

Differentiated Instruction

English Language Learners

Put children in pairs. Give each pair several counters. Model equal groups of counters. *Say:* These are equal groups. They have the same number of counters. Then model unequal groups. *Say:* These groups have different numbers of counters; they are not equal. Take turns putting counters in groups and having the other child decide if they are equal or unequal groups.

Check for Understanding

✓**Guided Practice** (page 128)

1 This exercise checks that children have understood multiplication as a relationship between the number of things in a group and the number of equal groups.

For Struggling Learners Write the following sentences on separate strips of paper:

There are _____ groups of _____.

_____ groups of _____ = _____

_____ × _____ = _____

There are _____ groups in all.

Present different groups of objects. Model the use of this language with the groups of objects. Have children practice filling in the blanks to describe the different groups of objects.

Best Practices You may want to teach this lesson as three mini-lessons: creating equal groups, writing repeated addition sentences, and writing multiplication sentences. Use a three-column chart to record the relationship. In the first column show pictures of the equal groups, in the middle column show the repeated addition sentence, and in the third column record the multiplication sentence.

Let's Practice

Find the missing numbers.

1 How many chairs are there?

$4 + 4 = \boxed{8}$

$2 \times 4 = \boxed{8}$

2 How many crayons are there?

$7 + 7 = \boxed{14}$

$2 \times \boxed{7} = \boxed{14}$

3 How many beads are there?

$\boxed{10} + \boxed{10} + \boxed{10} + \boxed{10} + \boxed{10} = \boxed{50}$

$\boxed{5} \times \boxed{10} = \boxed{50}$

ON YOUR OWN
Go to Workbook A:
Practice 1, pages 107–108

Lesson 1 How to Multiply **129**

Student Book A p. 129

Let's Practice (page 129)

This practice reinforces the concept of multiplying as repeated addition in Exercises **1** to **3**.

Common Error Some children may miscount items in each group. On an overhead transparency, cross out each object as the children count.

ON YOUR OWN

Children practice the strategies used in multiplication in Practice 1, pages 107 and 108 of **Workbook 2A**. These pages (with the answers) are shown at the right.

Differentiation Options Depending on children's success with the Workbook pages, use these materials as needed.
Struggling: Reteach 2A, pp. 99–102
On Level: Extra Practice 2A, pp. 55–56

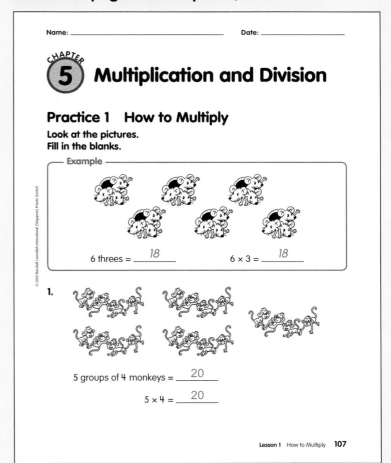

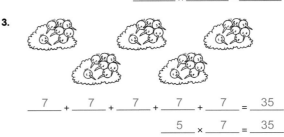

Name: _____ Date: _____

CHAPTER 5 Multiplication and Division

Practice 1 How to Multiply
Look at the pictures.
Fill in the blanks.

Example

6 threes = _18_   6 × 3 = _18_

1.

5 groups of 4 monkeys = _20_

5 × 4 = _20_

Lesson 1 How to Multiply **107**

Workbook A p. 107

Count and add the number of animals in each group.
Then multiply.

Example

$2 + 2 + 2 + 2 =$ _8_

$4 \times$ _2_ $=$ _8_

2.

_10_ + _10_ + _10_ + _10_ = _40_

_4_ × _10_ = _40_

3.

_7_ + _7_ + _7_ + _7_ + _7_ = _35_

_5_ × _7_ = _35_

108 Chapter 5 Multiplication and Division

Workbook A p. 108

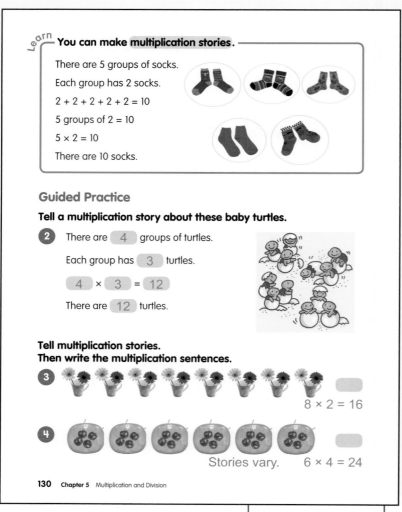

DAY 2 **Teach** See the Lesson Organizer on page 127 for Day 2 resources.

Learn

Make Multiplication Stories (page 130)

Children identify equal groups in pictures to make multiplication stories and write multiplication sentences.

- Help children recall the concept of multiplication as repeated addition of equal groups of items.

- Guide children in making a multiplication story from the pictures provided by:
  (1) Identifying the number of groups.
  (2) Identifying the number of socks in each group.

- Interpret the multiplication sentence $5 \times 2 = 10$ as: 5 groups of $2 = 10$.

✓ Guided Practice (page 130)

2 This exercise guides children to create multiplication stories from pictures. You may want to have children write their multiplication sentences on the board.

3 and **4** These exercises check if children can create multiplication stories and write multiplication sentences from the pictures.

ℚ Let's Explore!

Multiplication is Counting Equal Groups
(page 131)

This exploration checks children's understanding of using equal groups and repeated addition in multiplication. Highlight to children that the groups must be equal to write a multiplication sentence.

For Advanced Learners Have children work in groups and use **counters** or **connecting cubes** to explore redistributing the objects in equal groups.

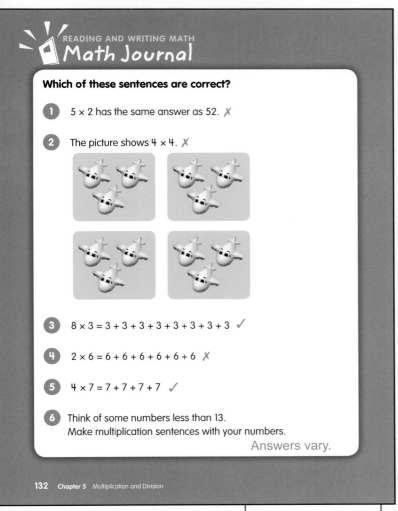

READING AND WRITING MATH

Math Journal (page 132)

This section allows children to reflect on their observations and understanding of the concepts of multiplication covered so far.

Ask children to explain why the statements in Exercises **1**, **2**, and **4** are incorrect. Take this opportunity to observe, diagnose, and correct possible misconceptions that children may have about multiplication.

Let's Practice (page 133)

This practice reinforces the concept of making multiplication stories and writing multiplication sentences to further enhance children's understanding of multiplication. Children may work in pairs to tell or write stories. They may also wish to illustrate their stories to share with other pairs.

ON YOUR OWN

Children practice the strategies used in multiplication in Practice 2, pages 109 and 110 of **Workbook 2A**. These pages (with the answers) are shown on page 133A.

Differentiation Options Depending on children's success with the Workbook pages, use these materials as needed.

Struggling: Reteach 2A, pp. 103–104

On Level: Extra Practice 2A, pp. 57–58

Practice and Apply
Workbook pages for Chapter 5, Lesson 1

Name: _____ Date: _____

Practice 2   How to Multiply

Look at the addition and multiplication sentences.
Fill in the blanks.

Example

8 + 8 = 16

2 × 8 = 16

Mary has ____2____ groups of books.

Each group has ____8____ books.

There are ____16____ books in all.

1.   5 + 5 + 5 = 15

3 × 5 = 15

Patrick has ____3____ groups of balloons.

Each group has ____5____ balloons.

There are ____15____ balloons in all.

Write the addition and multiplication sentences.
Fill in the blanks.

2.   3 + 3 + 3 = 9

3 × 3 = 9

Marcus has ____3____ groups of ties.

Each group has ____3____ ties.

There are ____9____ ties in all.

Fill in the blanks.

3.

How many bowls are there? ____2____

How many fish are in each bowl? ____6____

How many fish are there in all?

____2____ × ____6____ = ____12____

There are ____12____ fish in all.

Notes

LESSON 2 How to Divide

LESSON OBJECTIVES
- Divide to share equally.
- Divide by repeated subtraction of equal groups.

TECHNOLOGY RESOURCES
- *Math in Focus* eBooks
- *Math in Focus* Teacher Resources CD
- *Math in Focus* Virtual Manipulatives

Vocabulary

share	division sentence
divide	repeated subtraction
equal groups	

DAY 1	Student Book 2A, pp. 134–138	

MATERIALS
- 24 counters per group
- 20 craft sticks per group
- 20 index cards per group (optional)

DAY 2	Student Book 2A, pp. 139–141 Workbook 2A, pp. 111–114	

DIFFERENTIATION RESOURCES
- Reteach 2A, pp. 105–110
- Extra Practice 2A, pp. 59–62

5-minute Warm Up

Place children in groups of three or four. Provide each group with 12 **counters**. Introduce the method of grouping by separation. Have them separate the counters into groups of 2. Have children repeat the activity by grouping counters into groups of 3 and 4.

LESSON 2 How to Divide

Lesson Objectives
- Divide to share equally.
- Divide by repeated subtraction of equal groups.

Vocabulary
share   division sentences
divide   repeated subtraction
equal groups

Learn **You divide when you share equally.**

David has 6 apples.
He wants to **divide** the apples into 2 **equal groups**.
How many apples are there in each group?

$6 \div 2 = 3$ ÷ is read as **divided by**, and stands for **division**.

Read $6 \div 2 = 3$ as **six divided by two is equal to three**.
There are 3 apples in each group.

Now David wants to divide the 6 apples into 3 equal groups.
How many apples are there in each group?

$6 \div 3 = 2$ How do I read $6 \div 3 = 2$?

There are 2 apples in each group.

$6 \div 2 = 3$ and $6 \div 3 = 2$ are **division sentences**.

134   **Chapter 5** Multiplication and Division

Student Book A p. 134

DAY 1 Teach

Learn **Share Equally in Division** (page 134)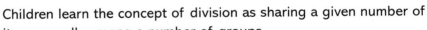

Children learn the concept of division as sharing a given number of items equally among a number of groups.

- Show children the picture and use **counters** or **craft sticks** to model how to divide the apples into 2 equal groups. One technique of dividing items into equal groups is to distribute the items one by one until all the items are distributed.

- Next, write the division sentence $6 \div 2 = 3$.

- ***Say:*** $6 \div 2 = 3$ means dividing 6 apples into 2 equal groups. Each group has 3 apples.

- Now ask a volunteer to divide the counters into 3 equal groups. ***Ask:*** How many apples are in each group? (2)

- Write the division sentence $6 \div 3 = 2$.

- ***Say:*** $6 \div 3 = 2$ means dividing 6 apples into 3 equal groups. Each group has 2 apples.

Guided Practice

Solve.

 Al takes 15 dog biscuits from a tin.
He gives an equal number of biscuits to each of his 3 dogs.
How many biscuits does each dog get?

15 ÷ 3 = 5

Each dog gets 5 biscuits.

 Then Al takes another 15 dog biscuits from the tin.
He gives an equal number of biscuits to each of his 5 puppies.
How many biscuits does each puppy get?

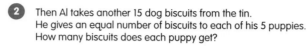

15 ÷ 5 = 3

Each puppy gets 3 biscuits.

Student Book A p. 135

Problem of the Lesson

Write as many division sentences as you can from the diagram below.

Solution:

24 = 1 group of 24 = 24 groups of 1
    24 ÷ 1 = 24; 24 ÷ 24 = 1

  = 2 groups of 12 = 12 groups of 2
    24 ÷ 2 = 12; 24 ÷ 12 = 2

  = 3 groups of 8 = 8 groups of 3
    24 ÷ 3 = 8; 24 ÷ 8 = 3

  = 4 groups of 6 = 6 groups of 4
    24 ÷ 4 = 6; 24 ÷ 6 = 4

For Struggling Learners It is often easier for children to learn a new concept when they can relate it to a concrete experience. Before assigning the exercises, divide the class into groups. Give each group a number of objects and ask them to share them equally among all group members. Visit each group and observe the methods children use.

Check for Understanding
✓**Guided Practice** (page 135)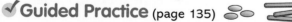

❶ and ❷ These exercises provide practice to check if children understand the concept of sharing equally in division. Encourage children to use **counters** or **craft sticks** to help them divide, if necessary.

❶ In this exercise, 15 biscuits are shown in 3 equal groups. Lead children to find the number of biscuits each dog gets by asking:

How many biscuits are to be given? (15)

How many dogs are there? (3)

How many biscuits will each dog get? (5)

❷ For this exercise, repeat the above but with 15 biscuits to be shared equally among 5 puppies.

Differentiated Instruction

English Language Learners

Demonstrate the words *share* and *divide*. Work in small groups. Give each group four illustrations of the same pizza or pie. Tell children to share by dividing the pie into two equal pieces. Now ask the group to divide the pie into four equal pieces. Continue with the remaining pictures, having groups divide the pie into three and six equal pieces.

Student Book A p. 136

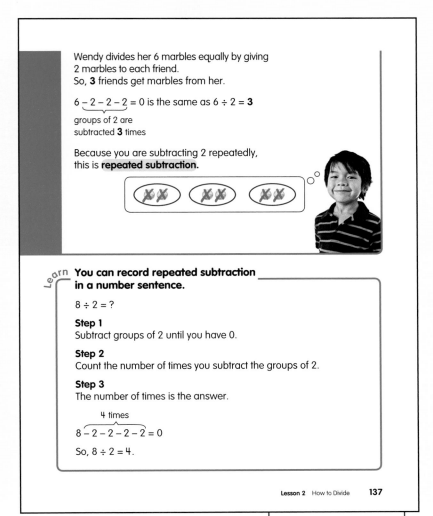

Student Book A p. 137

Divide by Using Repeated Subtraction of Equal Groups (pages 136 and 137)

Children learn division as repeated subtraction of equal groups.

- Use **counters** to model the given problem, with some children to help you. Explain that you are Wendy and the children are Wendy's friends.

- Have children read the problem. As you model the problem, *ask:* How many marbles does Wendy have? (6) How many marbles does Pete get? (2) After giving away 2 marbles, *ask:* How many marbles does Wendy have left? (4) Write $6 - 2 = 4$ on the board.

- Repeat this process until you have no more marbles.

- *Ask:* How many times did Wendy give away the marbles? (3) How many friends got 2 marbles each? (3) Recap by writing $6 - 2 - 2 - 2 = 0$.

- Explain that repeated subtraction is a way of putting the marbles into equal groups of 2, and that 3 groups are formed.

- Point out to children that $6 - 2 - 2 - 2 = 6 \div 2 = 3$.

Record Repeated Subtraction in a Number Sentence (page 137)

Children learn to record repeated subtraction of equal groups in a number sentence.

- Use **counters** to model the given problem, with some children to help you.

- Write $8 \div 2 = ?$ on the board and explain that you are going to use counters to model this.

- *Ask:* How many counters do I begin with? (8) How many counters do I give away to each child? (2)

- Give 2 counters to one child and write '$8 - 2$'. Then, as you give away 2 counters to each child, continue the number sentence with '$- 2$', until you have no more counters left.

- By that time, you will have $8 - 2 - 2 - 2 - 2 = 0$.

- Lead children to see that you subtract 2 four times.

- Explain to children that repeated subtraction is a way of sharing the counters in equal groups of 2, and that 4 groups are formed. Hence, lead children to see that $8 \div 2 = 4$.

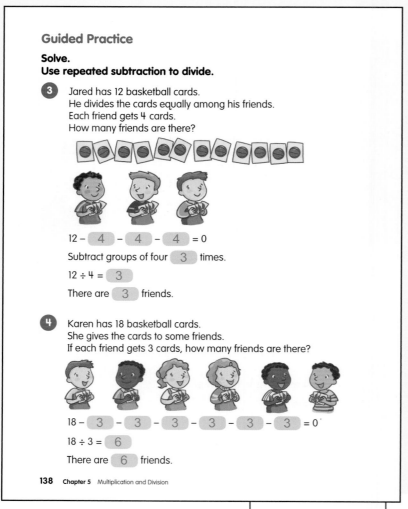

Guided Practice

Solve.
Use repeated subtraction to divide.

3 Jared has 12 basketball cards.
He divides the cards equally among his friends.
Each friend gets 4 cards.
How many friends are there?

12 – (4) – (4) – (4) = 0
Subtract groups of four (3) times.
12 ÷ 4 = (3)
There are (3) friends.

4 Karen has 18 basketball cards.
She gives the cards to some friends.
If each friend gets 3 cards, how many friends are there?

18 – (3) – (3) – (3) – (3) – (3) – (3) = 0
18 ÷ 3 = (6)
There are (6) friends.

Student Book A p. 138

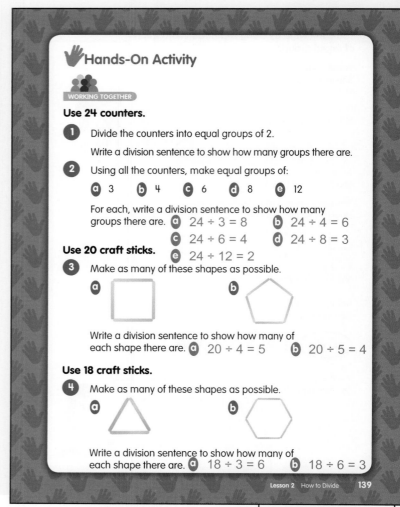

Hands-On Activity

WORKING TOGETHER

Use 24 counters.

1 Divide the counters into equal groups of 2.
Write a division sentence to show how many groups there are.

2 Using all the counters, make equal groups of:

ⓐ 3   **ⓑ** 4   **ⓒ** 6   **ⓓ** 8   **ⓔ** 12

For each, write a division sentence to show how many groups there are. **ⓐ** 24 ÷ 3 = 8   **ⓑ** 24 ÷ 4 = 6   **ⓒ** 24 ÷ 6 = 4   **ⓓ** 24 ÷ 8 = 3   **ⓔ** 24 ÷ 12 = 2

Use 20 craft sticks.

3 Make as many of these shapes as possible.

ⓐ    **ⓑ**

Write a division sentence to show how many of each shape there are. **ⓐ** 20 ÷ 4 = 5   **ⓑ** 20 ÷ 5 = 4

Use 18 craft sticks.

4 Make as many of these shapes as possible.

ⓐ   **ⓑ**

Write a division sentence to show how many of each shape there are. **ⓐ** 18 ÷ 3 = 6   **ⓑ** 18 ÷ 6 = 3

Student Book A p. 139

✓**Guided Practice** (page 138)

3 and **4** These exercises provide practice in division using repeated subtraction.

Best Practices For Exercises **3** and **4**, you may use **index cards** as concrete models. Have children physically divide the cards into equal groups. For example, in Exercise **3**, *say:* 4 children share the cards. Distribute the cards equally among 4 children. *Ask:* How many cards does each child get? Continue dividing cards by 2, 3, and 6 children.

For Advanced Learners If any child asks what happens if the number does not divide equally into the given number of groups, try this activity.

• Ask children to find the solution for Exercise **4**, beginning with 20 cards.

• Lead children to see that if the given number does not divide exactly, there will be a few remainder cards.

DAY 2 **Teach**

See the Lesson Organizer on page 134 for Day 2 resources.

WORKING TOGETHER

Hands-On Activity:
Make Equal Groups and Write the Division Sentences (page 139)

This activity allows children to explore the different ways in which a number may be divided into equal groups.

• Place children in groups of four to six. Distribute 24 **counters** and 20 **craft sticks** to each group.

• Exercises **1** and **2** ask children to explore the different ways of dividing 24 counters into equal groups. Lead children to see that 24 can be divided equally into groups of 2, 3, 4, 6, 8, or 12. Check that children can write the correct division sentence in each case.

• Exercises **3** and **4** guide children to see that 20 can be divided into equal groups of 4 or 5, while 18 can be divided into equal groups of 3 or 6. Check that children can write the correct division sentence in each case.

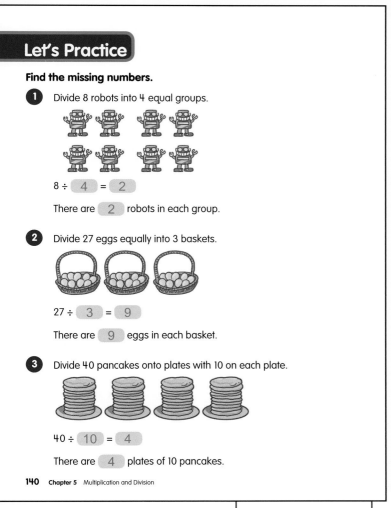

Let's Practice

Find the missing numbers.

1 Divide 8 robots into 4 equal groups.

$8 \div \boxed{4} = \boxed{2}$

There are $\boxed{2}$ robots in each group.

2 Divide 27 eggs equally into 3 baskets.

$27 \div \boxed{3} = \boxed{9}$

There are $\boxed{9}$ eggs in each basket.

3 Divide 40 pancakes onto plates with 10 on each plate.

$40 \div \boxed{10} = \boxed{4}$

There are $\boxed{4}$ plates of 10 pancakes.

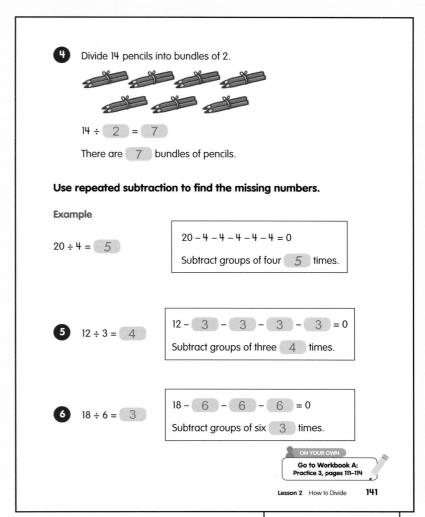

4 Divide 14 pencils into bundles of 2.

$14 \div \boxed{2} = \boxed{7}$

There are $\boxed{7}$ bundles of pencils.

Use repeated subtraction to find the missing numbers.

Example

$20 \div 4 = \boxed{5}$

| $20 - 4 - 4 - 4 - 4 - 4 = 0$ |
| Subtract groups of four $\boxed{5}$ times. |

5 $12 \div 3 = \boxed{4}$

| $12 - \boxed{3} - \boxed{3} - \boxed{3} - \boxed{3} = 0$ |
| Subtract groups of three $\boxed{4}$ times. |

6 $18 \div 6 = \boxed{3}$

| $18 - \boxed{6} - \boxed{6} - \boxed{6} = 0$ |
| Subtract groups of six $\boxed{3}$ times. |

ON YOUR OWN
Go to Workbook A:
Practice 3, pages 111–114

Let's Practice (pages 140 and 141)

This practice reinforces the strategies of division by grouping and repeated subtraction to further enhance children's understanding of division.

Exercises **1** to **4** check if children can divide by grouping. The pictures help them by showing the items in groups.

Exercises **5** and **6** guide children in division by repeated subtraction.

Common Error Some children may confuse objects and groups. Remind children to look at the illustration and read each problem carefully to determine what they are being asked to find.

ON YOUR OWN

Children practice grouping and repeated subtraction in division in Practice 3, pages 111 to 114 of **Workbook 2A**. These pages (with the answers) are shown on page 141A.

Differentiation Options Depending on children's success with the Workbook pages, use these materials as needed.
Struggling: Reteach 2A, pp. 105–110
On Level: Extra Practice 2A, pp. 59–62

Practice and Apply
Workbook pages for Chapter 5, Lesson 2

Name: _____ **Date:** _____

Practice 3   How to Divide
Find the number of items in each group.

Example

Divide 10 snails into 2 equal groups.

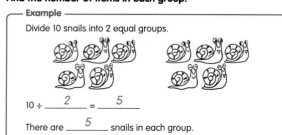

10 ÷ ___2___ = ___5___

There are ___5___ snails in each group.

1. Divide 15 books into 3 equal stacks.

15 ÷ ___3___ = ___5___

There are ___5___ books in each stack.

2. Divide 15 eggs equally into 5 nests.

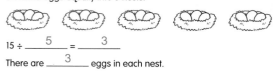

15 ÷ ___5___ = ___3___

There are ___3___ eggs in each nest.

Workbook A p. 111

Find the number of groups.
Fill in the blanks.

Example

Divide 15 pancakes so there are 3 pancakes in each group.

Subtract groups of 3 until there is nothing left.

15 – ___3___ – ___3___ – ___3___ – ___3___ – ___3___ = ___0___

How many times do you subtract groups of 3? ___5___

15 ÷ 3 = ___5___

There are ___5___ groups.

3. Divide 12 beads into groups of 4.

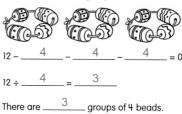

12 – ___4___ – ___4___ – ___4___ = 0

12 ÷ ___4___ = ___3___

There are ___3___ groups of 4 beads.

Workbook A p. 112

Name: _____ **Date:** _____

4. Divide 14 frozen yogurt cones into groups of 7.

14 – ___7___ – ___7___ = 0

14 ÷ ___7___ = ___2___

There are ___2___ groups of 7 frozen yogurt cones.

5. Put 20 oranges onto plates with 5 on each plate.

20 – ___5___ – ___5___ – ___5___ – ___5___ = 0

20 ÷ ___5___ = ___4___

There are ___4___ plates of 5 oranges.

Workbook A p. 113

Fill in the blanks.

6. Put 16 glasses onto trays with 4 on each tray.

16 – ___4___ – ___4___ – ___4___ – ___4___ = 0

16 ÷ ___4___ = ___4___

There are ___4___ trays of 4 glasses.

7. Put 8 cookies onto plates with 2 on each tray.

8 – ___2___ – ___2___ – ___2___ – ___2___ = 0

8 ÷ ___2___ = ___4___

There are ___4___ plates of 2 cookies.

Workbook A p. 114

LESSON 3 Real-World Problems: Multiplication and Division

LESSON OBJECTIVES
- Solve multiplication word problems.
- Solve division word problems.

TECHNOLOGY RESOURCES
- *Math in Focus* eBooks
- *Math in Focus* Teacher Resources CD
- *Math in Focus* Virtual Manipulatives

DAY 1	Student Book 2A, pp. 142–147
	Workbook 2A, pp. 115–118

MATERIALS
- 12 counters per group
- index cards (optional)

DIFFERENTIATION RESOURCES
- Reteach 2A, pp. 111–112
- Extra Practice 2A, pp. 63–64

 5-minute Warm Up

- Have children work in groups. Give each group 12 **counters**.

- Ask children to arrange the counters in 4 equal groups. Let the groups race to be the first to complete the division. Write the division sentence on the board: 12 ÷ 4 = 3.

- Have children write a multiplication sentence from the groups to relate the numbers. For example, 3 × 4 = 12.

- Repeat by asking children to arrange the counters in 2, 3, 6, and 12 equal groups.

 LESSON 3 Real-World Problems: Multiplication and Division

Lesson Objectives
- Solve multiplication word problems.
- Solve division word problems.

Learn Read, understand, and solve this word problem.

There are 3 children.
The teacher gives each child 6 seashells.
How many seashells does the teacher give out?

3 × 6 = 18
The teacher gives out 18 seashells.

Guided Practice

Solve.

1

Sandra has 2 pencil cases.
There are 4 erasers in each pencil case.
How many erasers does Sandra have?

2 × 4 = 8

Sandra has 8 erasers.

142 Chapter 5 Multiplication and Division

Student Book A p. 142

DAY 1 Teach

Learn

Read, Understand, and Solve Real-World Multiplication Problems (page 142)

Real-world problems are used to check children's ability to understand and apply the multiplication concepts learned in previous lessons.

- Have children identify the 3 children in the word problem as 3 groups and the 6 seashells as the number of items in each group. Lead children to the appropriate multiplication sentence: 3 × 6 = 18.

Best Practices You may wish to use real-world situations to teach these real-world problems. Use children and school supplies to model multiplication and division stories. Have volunteers write the corresponding number sentences on the board.

Check for Understanding
✓ **Guided Practice** (page 142)
1 This exercise provides practice in using multiplication to solve a real-world problem.

Read, understand, and solve this word problem.

Mrs. Carter has 14 markers.
She divides them equally among 7 children.
How many markers does each child get?

$14 \div 7 = 2$

Each child gets 2 marbles.

Guided Practice

Solve.

2

A clown has 18 balloons.
He gives an equal number to 9 children.
How many balloons does each child get?

$\boxed{18} \div \boxed{9} = \boxed{2}$

Each child gets $\boxed{2}$ balloons.

Student Book A p. 143

Problem of the Lesson

Sally has 18 stamps. Mandy has 6 stamps.

(a) How many times as many stamps does Sally have as Mandy?

(b) If Mandy shares her stamps equally with Bill, how many stamps will Bill get?

Solution:
(a) $18 \div 6 = 3$
(b) $6 \div 2 = 3$

Answer: (a) 3 times   (b) 3 stamps

Differentiated Instruction

English Language Learners

Children may need practice matching word problems and number sentences. Create several sets of word-problem cards. Use index cards. Write a word problem about equal groups on one card, draw a picture of it on another, and the related multiplication sentence on the third card. Read a word problem card aloud and ask children to find the matching picture and sentence. Continue until all problems have been matched.

Read, Understand, and Solve Real-World Division Problems (page 143)

Real-world problems are used to check children's ability to understand and apply the division concept of sharing in equal groups learned in previous lessons.

- Have children identify the 7 children in the word problem as 7 groups and the 14 markers as the total number of markers.

- Lead children to the appropriate division sentence: $14 \div 7 = 2$.

✓ Guided Practice (page 143)

2 This exercise provides practice in using division into equal groups to solve a real-world problem.

Learn Read, understand, and solve this word problem.

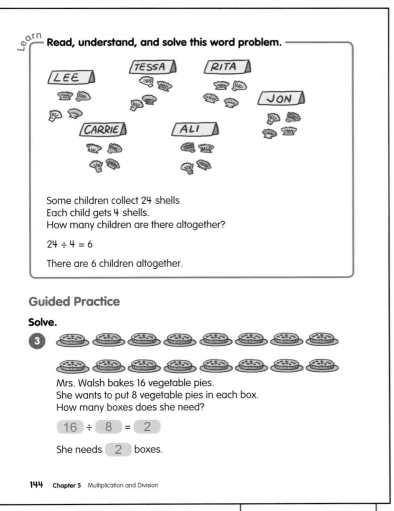

Some children collect 24 shells.
Each child gets 4 shells.
How many children are there altogether?

$24 \div 4 = 6$

There are 6 children altogether.

Guided Practice

Solve.

3

Mrs. Walsh bakes 16 vegetable pies.
She wants to put 8 vegetable pies in each box.
How many boxes does she need?

16 ÷ 8 = 2

She needs 2 boxes.

Student Book A p. 144

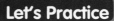

Let's Practice

Write a multiplication or division sentence for each problem. Then solve.

1 Juan has 3 jars.
He puts 6 almonds into each jar.
How many almonds does Juan have?

$3 \times 6 = 18$;
18 almonds

2 Mr. Wallace gives 7 books to each of his 2 sons. $7 \times 2 = 14$;
How many books does he give to his sons? 14 books

3 Melanie has 3 cups.
She puts 5 marbles in each cup.
How many marbles are in the cups?

$3 \times 5 = 15$;
15 marbles

Student Book A p. 145

Read, Understand, and Solve a Real-World Division Problem (page 144)

Real-world problems are used to check children's ability to understand and apply the concept of division as equal groups learned in previous lessons.

- Have children identify that the shells in the word problem are in groups of 4 and the 24 shells as the total number of shells.

- Lead children to the appropriate division sentence: 24 ÷ 4 = 6. Help children recall the strategy of repeated subtraction, if necessary.

✓ Guided Practice (page 144)

3 This exercise provides practice in using division as equal groups to solve a real-world problem.

Let's Practice (pages 145 and 146)

This practice reinforces choosing whether to use multiplication or division in solving real-world problems.

Exercises 1 to 3 require children to multiply.

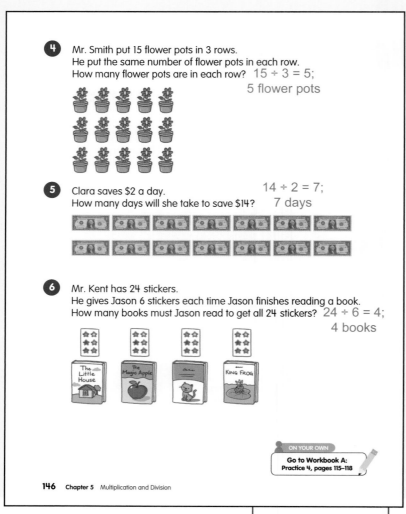

4 Mr. Smith put 15 flower pots in 3 rows.
He put the same number of flower pots in each row.
How many flower pots are in each row? $15 \div 3 = 5$;
5 flower pots

5 Clara saves $2 a day.
How many days will she take to save $14? $14 \div 2 = 7$;
7 days

6 Mr. Kent has 24 stickers.
He gives Jason 6 stickers each time Jason finishes reading a book.
How many books must Jason read to get all 24 stickers? $24 \div 6 = 4$;
4 books

ON YOUR OWN
Go to Workbook A:
Practice 4, pages 115–118

146 **Chapter 5** Multiplication and Division

Student Book A p. 146

Exercises **4** to **6** require children to divide.

Children write the multiplication or division sentence in each case before they solve the problem.

Common Error Some children may choose the wrong operation. Discuss words that help children determine whether to multiply or divide, such as *in all* and *each*. Remind children to reread the question and see if their answer makes sense.

ON YOUR OWN

Children practice using multiplication and division to solve real-world problems in Practice 4, pages 115 to 118 of **Workbook 2A**. These pages (with the answers) are shown at the right and on page 146A.

Differentiation Options Depending on children's success with the Workbook pages, use these materials as needed.
Struggling: Reteach 2A, pp. 111–112
On Level: Extra Practice 2A, pp. 63–64

Practice and Apply
Workbook pages for Chapter 5, Lesson 3

Name: _____ Date: _____

Practice 4 Real-World Problems: Multiplication and Division

Solve.

1. There are 2 plates.
Each plate has 5 strawberries.
How many strawberries are there?

   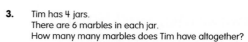

   $5 + 5 = \underline{10}$

   $2 \times 5 = \underline{10}$

   There are \underline{10} strawberries.

2. There are 6 bags.
Each bag has 3 pockets.
How many pockets are there?

   $\boxed{3} + \boxed{3} + \boxed{3} + \boxed{3} + \boxed{3} + \boxed{3} = \boxed{18}$

   $\boxed{6} \ \boxed{\times} \ \boxed{3} \ \boxed{=} \ \boxed{18}$

   There are \underline{18} pockets.

Lesson 3 Real-World Problems: Multiplication and Division **115**

Workbook A p. 115

3. Tim has 4 jars.
There are 6 marbles in each jar.
How many many marbles does Tim have altogether?

   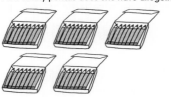

   $\boxed{4} \ \boxed{\times} \ \boxed{6} \ \boxed{=} \ \boxed{24}$

   Tim has \underline{24} marbles altogether.

4. Yanthi has 5 boxes.
There are 8 pencils in each box.
How many pencils does she have altogether?

   $\boxed{5} \ \boxed{\times} \ \boxed{8} \ \boxed{=} \ \boxed{40}$

   Yanthi has \underline{40} pencils altogether.

116 **Chapter 5** Multiplication and Division

Workbook A p. 116

Name: _____   **Date:** _____

5.

Aunt Emma has 3 nephews.
She buys 9 kites.
She gives each nephew an equal number of kites.
How many kites does each nephew get?

___9___ ÷ ___3___ = ___3___

Each nephew gets ___3___ kites.

6.

Mr. O'Brien catches 28 fish.
He puts 7 fish in each bucket.
How many buckets does he have?

___28___ – ___7___ – ___7___ – ___7___ – ___7___ = 0

___28___ ÷ ___7___ = ___4___

He has ___4___ buckets.

Workbook A p. 117

📖 **Math Journal**

Look at the picture.

Put 12 stars into equal groups in different ways.
What are the multiplication sentences and division sentences
that you can write?
Draw circles around the stars to help you.

☆ ☆ ☆ ☆ ☆ ☆ ☆ ☆ ☆ ☆ ☆ ☆

Answers vary.
Sample:

2 + 2 + 2 + 2 + 2 + 2 = 12	6 × 2 = 12
3 + 3 + 3 + 3 = 12	4 × 3 = 12
4 + 4 + 4 = 12	3 × 4 = 12
6 + 6 = 12	2 × 6 = 12
12 − 2 − 2 − 2 − 2 − 2 − 2 = 0	12 ÷ 2 = 6
12 − 3 − 3 − 3 − 3 = 0	12 ÷ 3 = 4
12 − 4 − 4 − 4 = 0	12 ÷ 4 = 3
12 − 6 − 6 = 0	12 ÷ 6 = 2

Workbook A p. 118

Notes

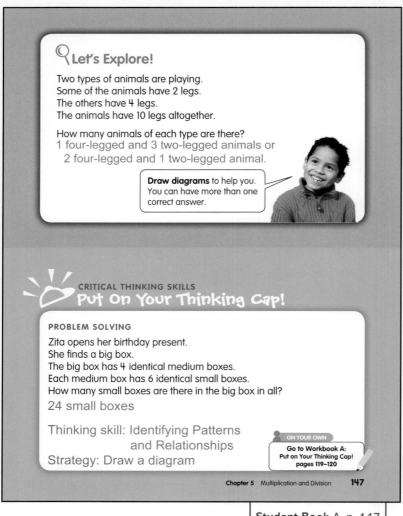

Let's Explore!

Two types of animals are playing.
Some of the animals have 2 legs.
The others have 4 legs.
The animals have 10 legs altogether.

How many animals of each type are there?
1 four-legged and 3 two-legged animals or
2 four-legged and 1 two-legged animal.

Draw diagrams to help you. You can have more than one correct answer.

CRITICAL THINKING SKILLS
Put on Your Thinking Cap!

PROBLEM SOLVING

Zita opens her birthday present.
She finds a big box.
The big box has 4 identical medium boxes.
Each medium box has 6 identical small boxes.
How many small boxes are there in the big box in all?

24 small boxes

Thinking skill: Identifying Patterns
                and Relationships
Strategy: Draw a diagram

ON YOUR OWN
Go to Workbook A:
Put on Your Thinking Cap!
pages 119–120

Chapter 5   Multiplication and Division   **147**

Student Book A p. 147

Let's Explore!
Draw Diagrams to Find Solutions to a Real-World Problem (page 147)

This activity allows children to explore combining the operations of addition and multiplication to solve the problem.

- Have children work in groups and suggest what the four-legged or two-legged animals might be.

- Encourage children to draw diagrams to help them solve the problem and think of all the possible answers for the problem.

CRITICAL THINKING AND PROBLEM SOLVING
Put on Your Thinking Cap! (page 147)

This problem solving exercise involves multiplication. Have children draw appropriate diagrams to solve the problem.

Thinking Skill

- Identifying patterns and relationships

Problem Solving Strategy

- Use a diagram/model

ON YOUR OWN

Because all children should be challenged, have all children try the Challenging Practice and Problem Solving pages in **Workbook 2A**, pages 119 and 120. These pages (with the answers) are shown on page 147A.

Differentiation Options Depending on children's success with the Workbook pages, use these materials as needed.
On Level: Extra Practice 2A, pp. 65–66
Advanced: Enrichment 2A, pp. 38–44

Practice and Apply
Workbook pages for Put on Your Thinking Cap!

Name: _____ Date: _____

Put On Your Thinking Cap!
Challenging Practice

Maya is making silly stuffed animals.
Study the number of eyes each stuffed animal has.
Find a pattern.
Then draw the eyes Maya will put on the last two stuffed animals.

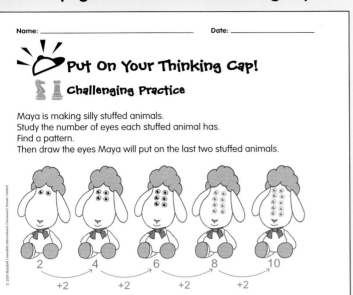

Thinking skills: Comparing, Deduction, Identifying
patterns and relationships, Sequencing
Strategies: Draw a diagram, Look for patterns

Chapter 5 Multiplication and Division **119**

Workbook A p. 119

Put On Your Thinking Cap!
Problem Solving

An open jar has 36 sugar cubes inside.
Mighty Ant takes 4 days to carry all the sugar cubes back to his nest.
He carries the same number of sugar cubes each day.
How many sugar cubes does he carry each day?

I can solve this problem by drawing a picture or by acting it out with cubes.

Mighty Ant carries 9 cubes
to his nest each day.

Thinking skill: Identifying patterns and relationships
Strategies: Act it out, Draw a diagram, Guess and
check

120 Chapter 5 Multiplication and Division

Workbook A p. 120

Notes

Chapter Wrap Up

Multiplication and division use equal groups.

You have learned...

to use repeated addition or multiply to find the total number of things in equal groups.

There are 3 groups.
There are 5 △ in each group.
$5 + 5 + 5 = 15$
$3 \times 5 = 15$

There are 5 △ in each group.
There are 3 groups.
$5 \times 3 = 5 + 5 + 5$
$= 15$

to divide a given number of objects equally to find:
- the number of things in each group.

Divide 12 things into 3 equal groups.
$12 \div 3 = 4$
There are 4 things in each group.

- the number of groups.

Divide 12 things so there are 4 things in each group.
$12 \div 4 = 3$
There are 3 groups.

$12 - 4 - 4 - 4 = 0$ is the same as $12 \div 4 = 3$
groups of four are subtracted **3** times

to solve real-world problems with multiplication and division.

ON YOUR OWN

Go to Workbook A:
Chapter Review/Test,
pages 121–126

148 Chapter 5 Multiplication and Division

Student Book A p. 148

Chapter Wrap Up (page 148)

Use the examples on page 148 to review multiplication and division using repeated addition and subtraction. Encourage children to use the chapter vocabulary:

- times
- equal
- group
- multiply
- repeated addition
- multiplication sentence

- share
- divide
- equal groups
- division sentence
- repeated subtraction
- multiplication story

ON YOUR OWN

Have children review the vocabulary, concepts, and skills from Chapter 5 with the Chapter Review/Test in **Workbook 2A**, pages 121 to 126. These pages (with the answers) are shown on pages 148A and 148B.

Assessment

Use the Chapter 5 Test Prep on pages 27 to 31 of **Assessments 2** to assess how well children have learned the material of this chapter. This assessment is appropriate for reporting results to adults at home and administrators. This test is shown on page 148C.

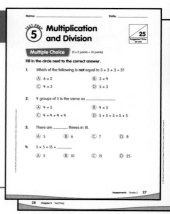

Assessments 2 pp. 27–31

Workbook pages for Chapter Review/Test

Name: _____ Date: _____

Chapter Review/Test
Vocabulary
Match.

1.

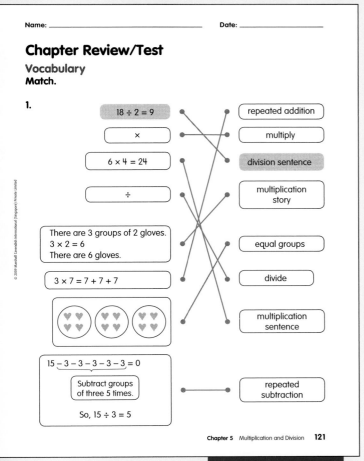

18 ÷ 2 = 9	repeated addition
×	multiply
6 × 4 = 24	division sentence
÷	multiplication story
There are 3 groups of 2 gloves. 3 × 2 = 6 There are 6 gloves.	equal groups
3 × 7 = 7 + 7 + 7	divide
♥♥♥ ♥♥♥ ♥♥♥	multiplication sentence
15 − 3 − 3 − 3 − 3 − 3 = 0 Subtract groups of three 5 times. So, 15 ÷ 3 = 5	repeated subtraction

Workbook A p. 121

Concepts and Skills

Fill in the ◯ with +, −, ×, or ÷.

2. 6 groups of 2 = 6 $\times$ 2

3. 8 $\times$ 4 = 32

4. 3 × 5 = 5 $+$ 5 $+$ 5

5. 20 $-$ 4 $-$ 4 $-$ 4 $-$ 4 $-$ 4 = 0

6. 20 $\div$ 5 = 4

7. 15 $\div$ 3 = 5

Find the missing numbers.

8.

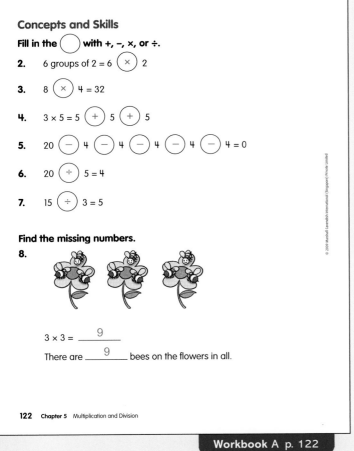

3 × 3 = ___9___

There are ___9___ bees on the flowers in all.

Workbook A p. 122

Name: _____ Date: _____

9.

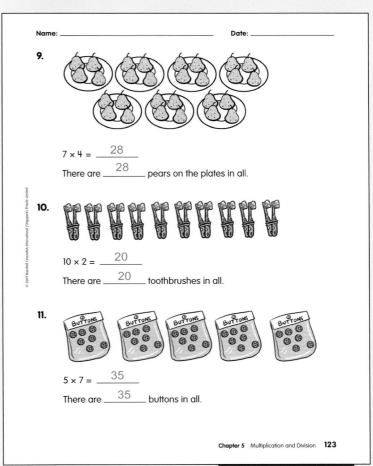

7 × 4 = ___28___

There are ___28___ pears on the plates in all.

10.

10 × 2 = ___20___

There are ___20___ toothbrushes in all.

11.

5 × 7 = ___35___

There are ___35___ buttons in all.

Workbook A p. 123

Find the missing numbers.

12. Divide 8 bananas onto 4 plates equally.

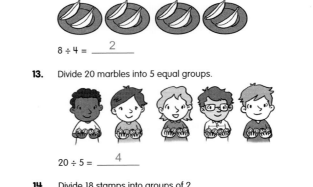

8 ÷ 4 = ___2___

13. Divide 20 marbles into 5 equal groups.

20 ÷ 5 = ___4___

14. Divide 18 stamps into groups of 2.

18 ÷ 2 = ___9___

15. Divide 24 almonds into groups of 3.

24 ÷ 3 = ___8___

Workbook A p. 124

Name: _____ **Date:** _____

Problem Solving
Solve.

16. Every day, Mr. Smith collects 3 eggs from his chickens.
How many eggs does he collect in a week?

There are 7 days in a week.
$3 \times 7 = 21$

Mr. Smith collects ____21____ eggs in a week.

17. There are 3 baskets.
Each basket contains 4 loaves of bread.
How many loaves of bread are there in all?

There are ____12____ loaves of bread in all.

Chapter 5 Multiplication and Division **125**

Workbook A p. 125

---

18. Meg has 35 stickers.
She has an album with 5 pages.
She puts an equal number of stickers on each page.
How many stickers are on each page?

$35 \div 5 = 7$

There are ____7____ stickers on each page.

19. Mrs. Barker has 30 star stickers.
She gives each student 5 star stickers.
How many students are there?

$30 \div 5 = 6$

There are ____6____ students.

126 Chapter 5 Multiplication and Division

Workbook A p. 126

Notes

Assessments Book pages for Chapter 5 Test Prep

Answer key appears in Assessments Book.

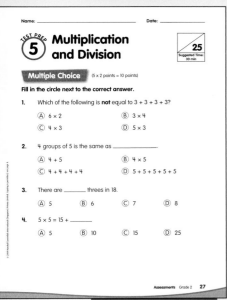

Name: _____ **Date:** _____

TEST PREP 5 — Multiplication and Division

/25

Suggested Time: 30 min

Multiple Choice (5 x 2 points = 10 points)

Fill in the circle next to the correct answer.

1. Which of the following is **not** equal to 3 + 3 + 3 + 3?

   Ⓐ 6 × 2   Ⓑ 3 × 4

   Ⓒ 4 × 3   Ⓓ 5 × 3

2. 4 groups of 5 is the same as _____

   Ⓐ 4 + 5   Ⓑ 4 × 5

   Ⓒ 4 + 4 + 4 + 4   Ⓓ 5 + 5 + 5 + 5 + 5

3. There are _____ threes in 18.

   Ⓐ 5   Ⓑ 6   Ⓒ 7   Ⓓ 8

4. 5 × 5 = 15 + _____

   Ⓐ 5   Ⓑ 10   Ⓒ 15   Ⓓ 25

Assessments Grade 2   **27**

Assessments p. 27

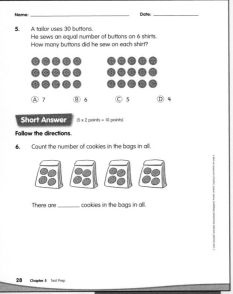

Name: _____ **Date:** _____

5. A tailor uses 30 buttons.
   He sews an equal number of buttons on 6 shirts.
   How many buttons did he sew on each shirt?

   Ⓐ 7   Ⓑ 6   Ⓒ 5   Ⓓ 4

Short Answer (5 x 2 points = 10 points)

Follow the directions.

6. Count the number of cookies in the bags in all.

   There are _____ cookies in the bags in all.

28 Chapter 5 Test Prep

Assessments p. 28

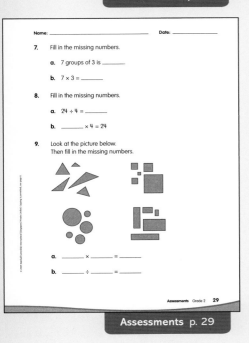

Name: _____ **Date:** _____

7. Fill in the missing numbers.

   a. 7 groups of 3 is _____

   b. 7 × 3 = _____

8. Fill in the missing numbers.

   a. 24 ÷ 4 = _____

   b. _____ × 4 = 24

9. Look at the picture below.
   Then fill in the missing numbers.

   a. _____ × _____ = _____

   b. _____ ÷ _____ = _____

Assessments Grade 2   **29**

Assessments p. 29

Name: _____ **Date:** _____

10. Jeron has 15 tubes of paint.
    He has 3 tubes of each color.
    How many different colors of paint does Jeron have?

    Jeron has _____ different colors of paint.

Extended Response (Question 11: 2 points, Question 12: 3 points)

Solve.
Show your work.

11. Each jar has 8 dog treats in it.
    There are 4 jars.
    How many dog treats are there in all?

    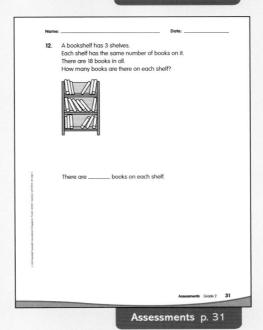

    There are _____ dog treats in all.

30 Chapter 5 Test Prep

Assessments p. 30

Name: _____ **Date:** _____

12. A bookshelf has 3 shelves.
    Each shelf has the same number of books on it.
    There are 18 books in all.
    How many books are there on each shelf?

    There are _____ books on each shelf.

Assessments Grade 2   **31**

Assessments p. 31

Notes

Chapter Overview

Multiplication Tables of 2, 5, and 10

Math Background

Children learned multiplication and division in Chapter 5, Grade 2, where they were taught basic properties of multiplication and division. Children were taught to multiply and divide using the concept of equal groups and relate it to the appropriate multiplication and division sentences. In addition, children were taught to identify number patterns in Chapter 1 which can be applied to multiplication and division.

In this chapter, children are taught multiplication tables of 2, 5, and 10 using the skip-counting and dot-paper strategies. Pictures and fingers illustrate the skip-counting strategy related to computation in multiplication. Using the skip-counting strategy, each finger is used to represent a specific value. For example, in the multiplication tables of 2, each finger represents 2 items. Dot paper can also be used to represent the group and item concept related to computation in multiplication. Using the dot paper, each column represents the number of groups while each row represents the number of items in each group.

Children also learn to use related multiplication facts to divide. Division here is conceptualized as the inverse of multiplication and as the equal sharing of items. A distinction is made between sharing a number of items into a given number of groups (for example, divide 20 marbles among 4 children) and putting an equal number of items into groups (for example, divide 20 marbles among some children such that each child has 4 marbles). Children learn to apply the Commutative Property of Multiplication as well as the inverse relationship of multiplication and division to form related multiplication facts. From there, they write multiplication and division sentences to solve real-world problems.

Cross-Curricular Connections

Reading/Language Arts Read aloud **Anno's Mysterious Multiplying Jar** by Mitsumasa Anno (Philomel, © 1983) about a jar that contains one island that has two countries, each of which has three mountains. This story teaches counting as well as factors.

Science Discuss and list the five senses. Ask a child to name the body part that helps you see. Line up the class and skip-count by 2s the number of eyes in the class. Now ask a child to name the body part that helps you touch and feel. Skip-count by 5s the number of fingers in the class.

Skills Trace

Grade 1	Relate repeated addition to the concept of multiplication. Relate sharing equally to the concept of division. (Chap. 18)
Grade 2	Multiply and divide with tables of 2, 3, 4, 5 and 10 using models and known multiplication facts. (Chaps. 6 and 15)
Grade 3	Multiply and divide with tables 6, 7, 8, and 9 using models and known multiplication facts. (Chap. 6)

EVERY DAY COUNTS®
Calendar Math

The November activities provide...

Review of recognizing, describing, and extending patterns (Chapter 1)
Preview of mental math strategies (Chapter 10)
Practice of skip-counting by 2, 5, and 10 (Lessons 1, 2, 3, 4, and 5 in this chapter)

Differentiation Resources

Differentiation for Special Populations

	English Language Learners	Struggling Reteach 2A	On Level Extra Practice 2A	Advanced Enrichment 2A
Lesson 1	p. 154	pp. 113–116	pp. 67–68	
Lesson 2	p. 157	pp. 117–124	pp. 69–72	
Lesson 3	p. 163	pp. 125–126	pp. 73–74	Enrichment pages can be used to challenge advanced children.
Lesson 4	p. 169	pp. 127–130	pp. 75–78	
Lesson 5	p. 174	pp. 131–134	pp. 79–82	
Lesson 6	p. 180	pp. 135–138	pp. 83–86	

Additional Support

For English Language Learners

Select activities that reinforce the chapter vocabulary and the connections among these words, such as having children

- add terms, definitions, and examples to the Word Wall
- create and practice with flash cards that have terms on one side and examples on the other
- draw pictures to illustrate each term
- discuss the Chapter Wrap Up, encouraging children to use the chapter vocabulary

For Struggling Learners

Select activities that go back to the appropriate stage of the Concrete-Pictorial-Abstract spectrum, such as having children

- use models to show related facts
- draw pictures to illustrate related facts
- have partners take turns acting out and identifying how to multiply using skip-counting and dot paper
- create and solve new stories for pairs of related facts

See also pages 157 and 164–165

If necessary, review

- Chapter 5 (Multiplication and Division).

For Advanced Learners

See suggestions on pages 157 and 174.

Assessment and Remediation

Chapter 6 Assessment

Prior Knowledge		
	Resource	**Page numbers**
Quick Check	Student Book 2A	pp. 151–152
Pre-Test	Assessments 2	pp. 32–34

Ongoing Diagnostic		
Guided Practice	Student Book 2A	pp. 154, 157, 158, 159, 160, 163, 165, 168, 170, 171, 173, 175, 177, 179–180, 181, 182–183
Common Error	Teacher's Edition 2A	pp. 155, 160–161, 166–167, 172, 177–178, 184–185

Formal Evaluation		
Chapter Review/Test	Workbook 2A	pp. 153–156
Chapter 6 Test Prep	Assessments 2	pp. 35–37
Cumulative Review for Chapters 5 and 6	Workbook 2A	pp. 157–164
Test Prep for Chapters 1 to 6	Extra Practice 2A	pp. 89–98
Benchmark Assessment 1 for Chapters 1 to 6	Assessments 2	pp. 38–45

Problems with these items...   **Can be remediated with...**

Remediation Options

Objective	Review/Test Items Workbook 2A pp. 153–156	Chapter Assessment Items Assessments 2 pp. 35–37	Reteach Reteach 2A	Student Book Student Book 2A
Use chapter vocabulary correctly.	1–2	Not assessed	In context as needed	pp. 153, 156
Skip-count by 2s, 5s, and 10s.	9	3, 6, 7, 9	pp. 113–116, 125–126, 131–134	Lessons 1, 3, and 5
Solve multiplication word problems.	4, 15	11	pp. 113–119, 126–127, 132, 135–136,138	Lessons 1 to 5
Use known multiplication facts to find new multiplication facts.	3–5	1	pp. 120–122, 129–130, 133–134	Lessons 2, 4, and 5
Use dot paper to multiply by 2, 5, and 10.	3–8	11	pp. 117–124, 127–130, 133–134	Lessons 2, 4, and 5
Identify related multiplication facts.	6–8		pp. 123–124, 129–130, 133–134	Lessons 2, 4, and 5
Use related multiplication facts to find related division facts.	10–17	2, 4, 5, 8, 10, 11	pp. 137	Lesson 6
Solve division word problems.	16, 17	10	pp. 135–136, 138	Lesson 6

Chapter Planning Guide

6 Multiplication Tables of 2, 5, and 10

Lesson	Pacing	Instructional Objectives	Vocabulary
Chapter Opener pp. 149–152 Recall Prior Knowledge Quick Check	*1 day	**Big Idea** Known multiplication facts can be used to find other multiplication and division facts.	
Lesson 1, pp.153–155 Multiplying 2: Skip-counting	1 day	• Skip-count by 2s. • Solve multiplication word problems.	• skip-count
Lesson 2, pp. 156–161 Multiplying 2: Using Dot Paper	2 days	• Use dot paper to multiply by 2. • Use known multiplication facts to find new multiplication facts. • Identify related multiplication facts. • Solve multiplication word problems.	• dot paper • related multiplication facts
Lesson 3, pp. 162–167 Multiplying 5: Skip-counting	1 day	• Skip-count by 5s. • Solve multiplication word problems.	

*Assume that 1 day is a 45–55 minute period.

Resources	Materials	NCTM Focal Points	NCTM Process Standards
Student Book, pp. 149–152 **Assessments 2,** pp. 32–34			
Student Book 2A, pp. 153–155 **Workbook 2A,** pp. 127–128 **Extra Practice 2A,** pp. 67–68 **Reteach 2A,** pp. 113–116	• 1 egg carton or ice cube tray per group (optional) • 10 beans per group (optional)	***Number and Operations*** Develop initial understanding of multiplication as repeated addition. ***Algebra*** Use number patterns.	Problem Solving Representation
Student Book 2A, pp. 156–161 **Workbook 2A,** pp. 129–132 **Extra Practice 2A,** pp. 69–72 **Reteach 2A,** pp. 117–124	• 10 counters per group • Dot Paper of 2 (TR08) per child	***Number and Operations*** Develop initial understanding of multiplication as repeated addition. ***Number and Operations and Algebra*** Apply relationships and properties of numbers. ***Algebra*** Use number patterns.	Problem Solving Connections Representation
Student Book 2A, pp. 162–167 **Workbook 2A,** pp. 133–136 **Extra Practice 2A,** pp. 73–74 **Reteach 2A,** pp. 125–126	• 1 Hundreds Chart (TR09) per group • 10 counters of one color per child • 1 calculator (optional) • 1 number cube per group • 1 set of Number Cards from 1 to 10 (TR06) per group • 1 Worksheet (TR10) per child • 1 coin per group • 2 stickers per group	***Number and Operations*** Develop initial understanding of multiplication as repeated addition. ***Algebra*** Use number patterns.	Problem Solving Communication Representation

Chapter Planning Guide

Lesson	Pacing	Instructional Objectives	Vocabulary
Lesson 4, pp. 168–172 Multiplying 5: Using Dot Paper	2 days	• Use dot paper to multiply by 5. • Use known multiplication facts to find new multiplication facts. • Identify related multiplication facts. • Solve multiplication word problems.	
Lesson 5, pp. 173–178 Multiplying 10: Skip-counting and Using Dot Paper	2 days	• Skip-count and use dot paper to multiply by 10. • Use known multiplication facts to find new multiplication facts. • Identify related multiplication facts. • Solve multiplication word problems.	
Lesson 6, pp. 179–185 Divide Using Related Multiplication Facts	1 day	• Use related multiplication facts to find related division facts. • Write a multiplication sentence and a related division sentence. • Solve division word problems.	
Problem Solving, p. 186 Put on Your Thinking Cap!	$\frac{1}{2}$ day	**Thinking Skills** • Deduction • Identifying patterns and relationships **Problem Solving Strategy** • Look for pattern(s)	
Chapter Wrap Up pp. 187–188	$\frac{1}{2}$ day	• Reinforce and consolidate chapter skills and concepts.	
Chapter Assessment	1 day		
Review Cumulative Review for Chapters. 5 and 6 Test Prep for Chapters. 1 to 6 Benchmark Assessment 1 for Chapters. 1 to 6			

*Assume that 1 day is a 45–55 minute period.

Resources	Materials	NCTM Focal Points	NCTM Process Standards
Student Book 2A, pp. 168–172 **Workbook 2A,** pp. 137–140 **Extra Practice 2A,** pp. 75–78 **Reteach 2A,** pp. 127–130	• Dot Paper of 5 (TR11) per child • 1 Spinner Card (TR12) per group • 1 transparent spinner • 1 paper clip per group • 1 pencil per group • index cards (optional)	***Number and Operations and Algebra*** Apply relationships and properties of numbers. Use procedures to solve problems.	Problem Solving Communication Connections Representation
Student Book 2A, pp. 173–178 **Workbook 2A,** pp. 141–144 **Extra Practice 2A,** pp. 79–82 **Reteach 2A,** pp. 131–134	• 1 Hundreds Chart (TR09) • Dot Paper of 10 (TR13) per child	***Number and Operations and Algebra*** Apply relationships and properties of numbers. Use procedures to solve problems. ***Algebra*** Use number patterns.	Problem Solving Connections Representation
Student Book 2A, pp. 179–185 **Workbook 2A,** pp. 145–150 **Extra Practice 2A,** pp. 83–86 **Reteach 2A,** pp. 135–138	• 35 counters • 12 craft sticks per group	***Number and Operations and Algebra*** Apply relationships and properties of numbers. Use procedures to solve problems.	Problem Solving Reasoning/Proof Connections Representation
Student Book 2A, p. 186 **Workbook 2A,** pp. 151–152 **Extra Practice 2A,** pp. 87–88 **Enrichment 2A,** pp. 45–56		***Number and Operations and Algebra*** Apply relationships and properties of numbers. Use number patterns.	Problem Solving Reasoning/Proof Connections Representation
Student Book 2A, pp. 187–188 **Workbook 2A,** pp. 153–156			
Assessments 2, pp. 35–37			
Workbook 2A, pp. 157–164 **Extra Practice 2A,** pp. 89–98 **Assessments 2,** pp. 38–45			

Technology Resources for easy classroom management
• *Math in Focus* eBooks
• *Math in Focus* Teacher Resources CD
• *Math in Focus* Virtual Manipulatives
• Online Assessment Generator

Multiplication Tables of 2, 5, and 10

Chapter 6
Vocabulary

	skip-counting by 2s:	
skip-count	0 2 4 6 8 10 Start	Lesson 1
dot paper	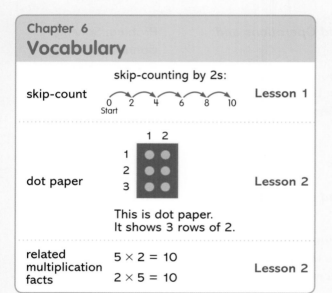 1 2 1 2 3 This is dot paper. It shows 3 rows of 2.	Lesson 2
related multiplication facts	$5 \times 2 = 10$ $2 \times 5 = 10$	Lesson 2

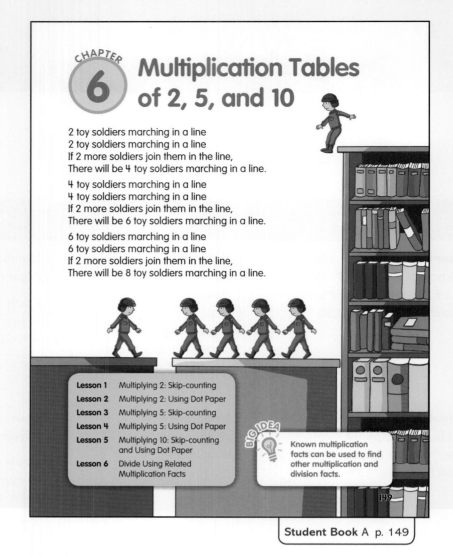

CHAPTER
6
Multiplication Tables of 2, 5, and 10

2 toy soldiers marching in a line
2 toy soldiers marching in a line
If 2 more soldiers join them in the line,
There will be 4 toy soldiers marching in a line.

4 toy soldiers marching in a line
4 toy soldiers marching in a line
If 2 more soldiers join them in the line,
There will be 6 toy soldiers marching in a line.

6 toy soldiers marching in a line
6 toy soldiers marching in a line
If 2 more soldiers join them in the line,
There will be 8 toy soldiers marching in a line.

Lesson 1 Multiplying 2: Skip-counting
Lesson 2 Multiplying 2: Using Dot Paper
Lesson 3 Multiplying 5: Skip-counting
Lesson 4 Multiplying 5: Using Dot Paper
Lesson 5 Multiplying 10: Skip-counting and Using Dot Paper
Lesson 6 Divide Using Related Multiplication Facts

BIG IDEA
Known multiplication facts can be used to find other multiplication and division facts.

149

Student Book A p. 149

💡 Big Idea (page 149)

Counting and comparing numbers to 10 are the main foci of this chapter.

* Children use the strategies of skip-counting and use dot paper as concrete representation to learn multiplication of 2, 5, and 10.

* Children learn to apply the inverse relationship of multiplication and division to write division sentences from related multiplication sentences.

Chapter Opener (page 149)

The picture illustrates several toy soldiers marching along the top of a bookshelf. Used together with the poem, it models skip-counting by 2.

* Show children the picture and the poem.

* Read the poem aloud and have children read each sentence after you.

* Write 2, 4, 6 on the board, and relate each stanza to each number.

* *Ask:* How many toy soldiers are there at first? (2)

* Invite volunteers to add stanzas to the poem until they reach 20.

Recall Prior Knowledge

Number patterns

① 2, 4, 6, 8, 10, 12, 14, 16, 18, 20

② 5, 10, 15, 20, 25, 30, 35, 40, 45, 50

③ 10, 20, 30, 40, 50, 60, 70, 80, 90, 100

Using equal groups to multiply

 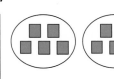

5 groups of 2 = 10
2 + 2 + 2 + 2 + 2 = 10
5 twos = 10
5 × 2 = 10

2 groups of 5 = 10
5 + 5 = 10
2 fives = 10
2 × 5 = 10

150   **Chapter 6**   Multiplication Tables of 2, 5, and 10

Student Book A p. 150

Recall Prior Knowledge (page 150)

Number Patterns

Children learned to identify number patterns in Chapter 1.

- Have children find the difference between consecutive numbers in each set of number patterns ① to ③.

Using Equal Groups to Multiply

Children learned to multiply the number of items in equal groups in Chapter 5.

- Show children the picture and *ask:* How many hearts are in each group? (2) *Ask:* How many groups are there? (5) *Ask:* How many hearts are there in all? (10)

- Help children recall that they can find the answer by repeated addition:

  2 + 2 + 2 + 2 + 2 = 10, or by multiplying: 5 × 2 = 10.

- Help children to see that if the same number of items were grouped as 2 equal groups of 5 squares, the number sentence would be 2 × 5 = 10.

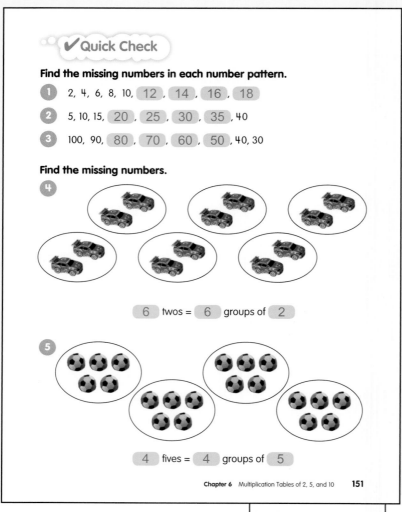

✔ Quick Check

Find the missing numbers in each number pattern.

1. 2, 4, 6, 8, 10, 12, 14, 16, 18

2. 5, 10, 15, 20, 25, 30, 35, 40

3. 100, 90, 80, 70, 60, 50, 40, 30

Find the missing numbers.

4.

6 twos = 6 groups of 2

5.

4 fives = 4 groups of 5

Student Book A p. 151

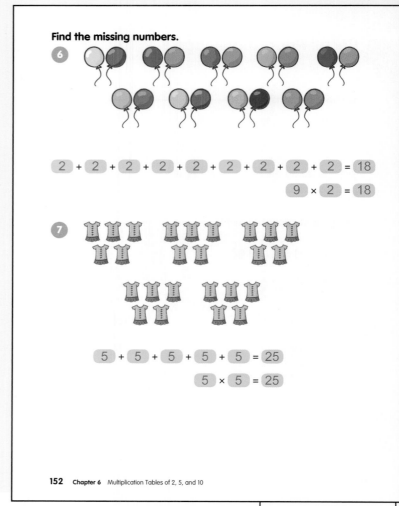

Find the missing numbers.

6.

2 + 2 + 2 + 2 + 2 + 2 + 2 + 2 + 2 = 18

9 × 2 = 18

7.

5 + 5 + 5 + 5 + 5 = 25

5 × 5 = 25

Student Book A p. 152

✔ Quick Check (pages 151 and 152)

Use this section as a diagnostic tool to assess children's level of prerequisite knowledge before they progress to this chapter.

Exercises 1 to 3 assess the children's ability in completing number patterns.

Exercises 4 to 7 assess the concept of using equal groups to multiply.

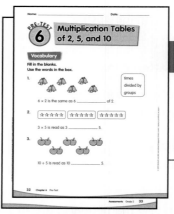

Assessments 2 pp. 32–34

Assessment

For additional assessment of children's prior knowledge and chapter readiness, use the Chapter 6 Pre-Test on pages 32 to 34 of **Assessments 2**.

Multiplying 2: Skip-counting

LESSON 1

LESSON OBJECTIVES
- Skip-count by 2s.
- Solve multiplication word problems.

TECHNOLOGY RESOURCES
- *Math in Focus* eBooks
- *Math in Focus* Teacher Resources CD
- *Math in Focus* Virtual Manipulatives

Vocabulary
skip-count

| DAY 1 | Student Book 2A, pp. 153–155
Workbook 2A, pp. 127–128 |

MATERIALS
- 1 egg carton or ice cube tray per group (optional)
- 10 beans per group (optional)

DIFFERENTIATION RESOURCES
- Reteach 2A, pp. 113–116
- Extra Practice 2A, pp. 67–68

5-minute Warm Up

Have children work in pairs. One child in each group holds up *n* fingers to show a number from 1 to 10. The other child holds up the same number of fingers and says what $2 \times n$ is. Children check the answer by counting the total number of fingers.

Student Book A p. 153

| DAY 1 | **Teach** |

Skip-count by 2s (pages 153 and 154)

Children learn to multiply 2 by skip-counting by 2s.

- Count the number of groups of scooters aloud, while children count with you.

- Model skip-counting by 2s by counting aloud the groups of scooters in the picture as 2, 4, 6, 8, …, 20. Have children count with you. Write $10 \times 2 = 20$ on the board.

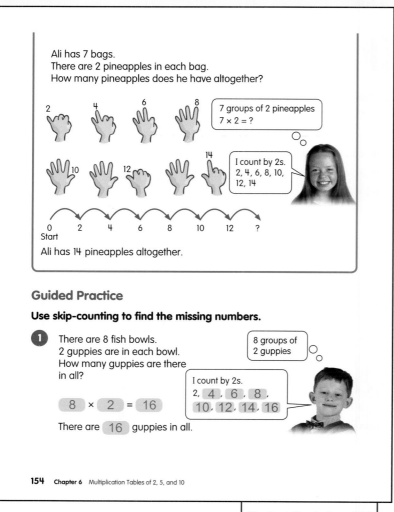

Ali has 7 bags.
There are 2 pineapples in each bag.
How many pineapples does he have altogether?

7 groups of 2 pineapples
7 × 2 = ?

I count by 2s.
2, 4, 6, 8, 10, 12, 14

0   2   4   6   8   10   12   ?
Start

Ali has 14 pineapples altogether.

Guided Practice

Use skip-counting to find the missing numbers.

1. There are 8 fish bowls.
2 guppies are in each bowl.
How many guppies are there in all?

8 groups of 2 guppies

I count by 2s.
2, 4, 6, 8, 10, 12, 14, 16

8 × 2 = 16

There are 16 guppies in all.

154 **Chapter 6** Multiplication Tables of 2, 5, and 10

Student Book A p. 154

Problem of the Lesson

(a) How many legs do 9 birds have in all?
(b) How many wheels do 8 bicycles have in all?

Solution:
(a) 9 × 2 = 18
(b) 8 × 2 = 16

Answer: (a) 18 legs   (b) 16 wheels

Differentiated Instruction

English Language Learners

Work in small groups. To explain skip-counting, give each group an egg carton or ice cube tray and several beans. Have children put 2 beans in each hole. *Say:* We are skipping counting every single bean; we are only counting the groups of beans. This is skip-counting.

- Read the second question and ask children to use their fingers to skip-count.

- Explain to children that they will use one finger to represent 2 pineapples.

- Model skip-counting using your fingers as shown in the Student Book, and have children do the same. Write 7 × 2 = 14 on the board.

- Lead children to recognize the following one-to-one correspondence in counting the number of groups and the number of items:

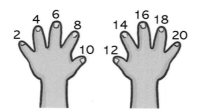

- Lead children to see 7 × 2 = ? as 7 fingers raised and each finger represents 2. So the 7 fingers represent 14.

- Have children recite the sequence of numbers while raising the corresponding fingers: 2, 4, 6, 8, 10, 12, 14, 16, 18, 20.

Best Practices You may want to teach this lesson as three mini-lessons: skip-counting by 2s, writing/drawing groups of 2, and writing the multiplication number sentence. Children can stand in a circle and count their feet to skip-count by 2s. *Ask:* How many feet do (number in class) children have?

Check for Understanding
✔ **Guided Practice** (page 154)

1 This exercise provides additional practice with skip-counting by 2s. Guide children to fill in the number of bowls (8) and the number of guppies in each bowl (2) in the multiplication sentence first before skip-counting to find the answer.

Let's Practice

Find the missing numbers.

1 2 groups of 2 = 2 × 2

2 6 groups of 2 = 6 × 2

3 1 group of 2 = 1 × 2

4 9 groups of 2 = 9 × 2

Use skip-counting to find the missing numbers.

Example

4 × 2 = ?

0 2 4 6 8
Start

4 × 2 = 8

5 3 × 2 = 6 **6** 10 × 2 = 20

Multiply by 2 to find the missing numbers.

7 7 × 2 = 14 **8** 5 × 2 = 10

9 6 × 2 = 12 **10** 8 × 2 = 16

Solve.

11 There are 9 girls.
Each girl wears 2 hairclips in her hair.
How many hairclips are there in all? 18 hairclips

12 Karan and Jose eat 2 tacos each for lunch.
How many tacos do they eat in all?
4 tacos

ON YOUR OWN
Go to Workbook A:
Practice 1, pages 127–128

Lesson 1 Multiplying 2: Skip-counting **155**

Student Book A p. 155

Let's Practice (page 155)

This provides children with more practice in multiplying 2 using the skip-counting strategy. Exercises **1** to **4** require children to form the correct number sentence given the number of groups of two. Exercises **5** to **10** provide practice in skip-counting. Exercises **11** and **12** require children to apply the skip-counting strategy when solving real-world problems.

Common Error Some children may add instead of multiply. Remind children to look at the operation symbol carefully. Display a list of math symbols and what they mean for children to refer to.

ON YOUR OWN

Children practice multiplying by 2 using the skip-counting strategy in Practice 1, pages 127 and 128 of **Workbook 2A**. These pages (with the answers) are shown at the right.

Differentiation Options Depending on children's success with the Workbook pages, use these materials as needed.
Struggling: Reteach 2A, pp. 113–116
On Level: Extra Practice 2A, pp. 67–68

Practice and Apply
Workbook pages for Chapter 6, Lesson 1

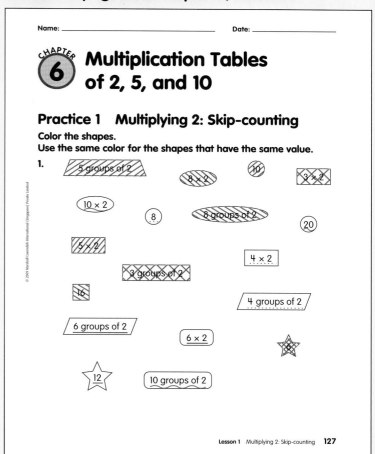

Name: _____ Date: _____

CHAPTER 6 Multiplication Tables of 2, 5, and 10

Practice 1 Multiplying 2: Skip-counting
Color the shapes.
Use the same color for the shapes that have the same value.

1.

5 groups of 2 · 8 × 2 · 10 · 3 × 2 · 10 × 2 · 8 · 8 groups of 2 · 20 · 5 × 2 · 4 × 2 · 3 groups of 2 · 16 · 4 groups of 2 · 6 groups of 2 · 6 × 2 · 12 · 10 groups of 2

Lesson 1 Multiplying 2: Skip-counting **127**

Workbook A p. 127

Count by 2s.
Then fill in the blanks.

Example

2, 4, 6 , 8 , 10   2 · 4 · 6 8 10

2. 6, 8, 10, 12 , 14 , 16 , 18

3. 8, 10 , 12, 14, 16 , 18 , 20

4. 6 , 8 , 10, 12, 14, 16 , 18

Fill in the blanks.

5. 6 × 2 = 12   6. 3 × 2 = 6

7. 7 × 2 = 14   8. 4 × 2 = 8

9. 9 × 2 = 18   10. 5 × 2 = 10

11. 8 × 2 = 16   12. 1 × 2 = 2

13. 10 × 2 = 20   14. 2 × 2 = 4

128 Chapter 6 Multiplication Tables of 2, 5, and 10

Workbook A p. 128

LESSON 2 Multiplying 2: Using Dot Paper

LESSON OBJECTIVES
• Use dot paper to multiply by 2.
• Use known multiplication facts to find new multiplication facts.
• Identify related multiplication facts.
• Solve multiplication word problems.

TECHNOLOGY RESOURCES
• *Math in Focus* eBooks
• *Math in Focus* Teacher Resources CD

Vocabulary

dot paper
related multiplication facts

DAY 1 Student Book 2A, pp. 156–158

MATERIALS
• 10 counters per group
• Dot Paper of 2 (TRO8) per child

DAY 2 Student Book 2A, pp. 159–161
Workbook 2A, pp. 129–132

DIFFERENTIATION RESOURCES
• Reteach 2A, pp. 117–124
• Extra Practice 2A, pp. 69–72

5-minute Warm Up

• Children work in pairs. Have one child say a single-digit number *n*. The partner says *n* groups of 2 = ___.

• For example, Child A says 5.
  Child B says: 5 groups of 2 = 10.
  Encourage children to use skip-counting with fingers to find the answer.

• Repeat the exercise using different numbers.

LESSON 2 Multiplying 2: Using Dot Paper

Lesson Objectives
• Use dot paper to multiply by 2.
• Use known multiplication facts to find new multiplication facts.
• Identify related multiplication facts.
• Solve multiplication word problems.

Vocabulary
dot paper
related multiplication facts

Learn **You can use dot paper to multiply by 2.**

lambs

Each sheep has 2 lambs.

How many lambs do the 3 sheep have in all?

This is **dot paper**. It shows 3 rows of 2.

$3 \times 2 = 6$

3 sheep have 6 lambs in all.

156 Chapter 6 Multiplication Tables of 2, 5, and 10

Student Book A p. 156

DAY 1 # Teach

Learn

Use Dot Paper to Multiply by 2 (page 156)

Children learn to relate the multiples of 2 with dot paper that has two dots on each row.

• Explain and apply the 'group and item' concept to lead children to recall multiplication facts.

• Explain that there are 3 groups (sheep) and 2 items (lambs) for each group. The number 2 is repeatedly added to get 6.

• You may use the 'multiplying' concept to explain the solution. Make a copy of the **Dot Paper of 2 (TRO8)** for each child. Use the dot paper to help children conceptualize the idea.

• *Say*: There are 3 groups and each group has 2 items. So, $3 \times 2 = 6$.

• Explain the 'multiplying' concept as follows: A fixed number, two, (2 dots) and it is being multiplied by 3.

Guided Practice

Use dot paper to find the missing numbers.

1 Sam has 4 bundles of pencils.
Each bundle has 2 pencils.
How many pencils does he have in all?

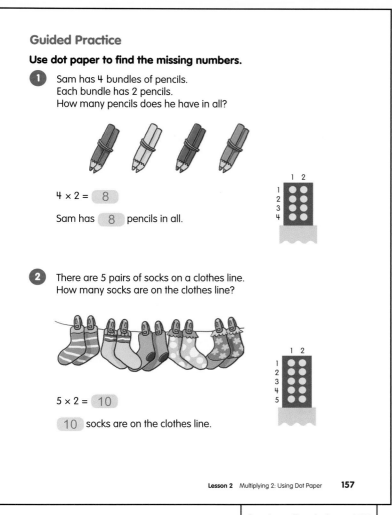

$4 \times 2 = \boxed{8}$

Sam has $\boxed{8}$ pencils in all.

2 There are 5 pairs of socks on a clothes line.
How many socks are on the clothes line?

$5 \times 2 = \boxed{10}$

$\boxed{10}$ socks are on the clothes line.

Lesson 2 Multiplying 2: Using Dot Paper   **157**

Student Book A p. 157

Each bicycle has 2 wheels. Using dot paper, find
the number of wheels on 6 bicycles.

Solution:

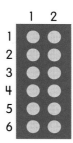

$6 \times 2 = 12$
Answer: 12 wheels

Differentiated Instruction

English Language Learners

On page 160, the term *related* may be unfamiliar vocabulary.
Draw a house with a door and two large windows. Explain
that people that are related often live in the same house. In
this house, children are going to identify related multiplication
facts, or facts that can be turned around. In one window,
write 2×6 and in the other window write 6×2. Say *related*
and have children repeat the word.

Check for Understanding
Guided Practice (page 157)

1 and **2** These exercises provide practice in using dot paper
for multiplying by 2 to solve real-world problems. Provide the
concrete objects and dot paper if necessary.

For Struggling Learners Have children work in pairs. The first
child comes up with a 2s fact, for example, $8 \times 2 =$ _____. The
partner then uses dot paper to show 8 groups of 2, and then
uses any method to find the answer (repeated addition,
skip-counting, etc.).

For Advanced Learners Have children work in pairs. One
child says, for example, "7×2". The partner has to say: "7×2
is 7 groups of 2. It is 5 groups of 2 plus 2 more groups of 2
$= 10 + 4 = 14$."
Ask children to switch roles. The objective of this activity is to
train children to verbalize and remember the strategy.

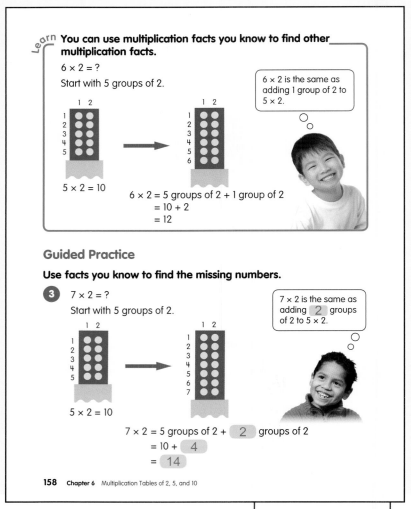

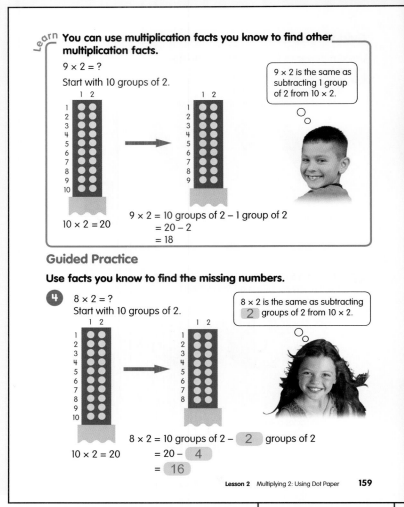

Learn

Use Known Multiplication Facts to Find Other Multiplication Facts (page 158)

Children use the 'connecting easier facts' strategy, starting from 5×2, to find a more difficult fact. (Note: In later grades, children will learn this strategy as the Distributive Property of Multiplication: $(5 + 1) \times 2 = (5 \times 2) + (1 \times 2)$.)

- Model the strategy using **counters** to build an array of 5×2. Explain that $5 \times 2 = 10$ is an easier fact.

- Point out to children that to find 6×2, you have to add one more group of 2, and model this by adding a row to the array.

- Lead children to see that
  $6 \times 2 = (5 \text{ groups of } 2) + (1 \text{ more group of } 2)$
  $= 10 + 2 = 12$

- Repeat the explanation using dot paper to reinforce the concept.

✓ Guided Practice (page 158)

3 This exercise provides practice with using known multiplication facts to find new facts. Have children work individually to solve the problem. Provide dot paper if necessary.

Learn

Use Known Multiplication Facts to Find Other Multiplication Facts (page 159)

Children use the 'connecting easier facts' strategy starting from 10×2 to find a more difficult fact.

- Show children how the strategy can be extended to first finding the groups of 2, and then subtracting.

- Model the strategy using dot paper:

  Start with 10 groups of 2. Then subtract 1 group of 2.

  $9 \times 2 = (10 \text{ groups of } 2) - (1 \text{ group of } 2)$
  $ = 20 - 2 = 18$

✓ Guided Practice (page 159)

4 This exercise provides practice with using known facts to find new facts. Have children work individually to solve the problem. Provide dot paper if necessary.

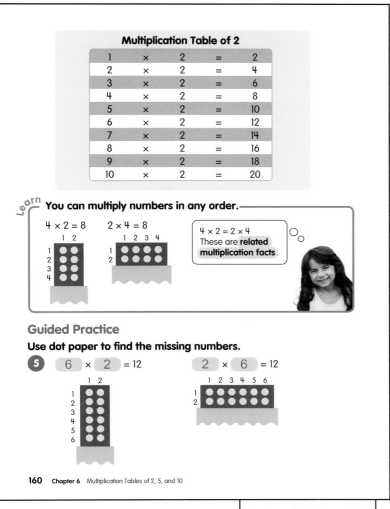

Multiplication Table of 2

1	×	2	=	2
2	×	2	=	4
3	×	2	=	6
4	×	2	=	8
5	×	2	=	10
6	×	2	=	12
7	×	2	=	14
8	×	2	=	16
9	×	2	=	18
10	×	2	=	20

Learn **You can multiply numbers in any order.**

4 × 2 = 8   2 × 4 = 8

4 × 2 = 2 × 4
These are **related multiplication facts**.

Guided Practice

Use dot paper to find the missing numbers.

5   6 × 2 = 12   2 × 6 = 12

160   Chapter 6   Multiplication Tables of 2, 5, and 10

Let's Practice

Find the missing numbers.

1   5 × 2 = 10   6 × 2 = 10 + 2 = 12

7 × 2 = 10 + 4 = 14

2   10 × 2 = 20   9 × 2 = 20 − 2 = 18

8 × 2 = 20 − 4 = 16

Use dot paper to find the missing numbers.

3   3 × 2 = 6   4   7 × 2 = 14

2 × 3 = 6   2 × 7 = 14

5   8 × 2 = 16   6   9 × 2 = 18

2 × 8 = 16   2 × 9 = 18

7   Andre, Brad, Cedric and Deon have 2 baseball caps each.
How many baseball caps do they have in all?
8 baseball caps

8   There are 6 pairs of shoes on a shelf.
How many shoes are there in all?
12 shoes

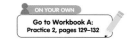

ON YOUR OWN
Go to Workbook A:
Practice 2, pages 129–132

Lesson 2   Multiplying 2: Using Dot Paper   **161**

Multiply Numbers in Any Order (page 160)

Children use the Commutative Property of Multiplication with dot paper to find two related facts.

- Help children understand that the Commutative Property of Multiplication means that they can multiply two numbers in any order and get the same answer.

- Using dot paper, show that 2 × 4 = 4 × 2.
  Say: 2 × 4 means 2 groups of 4.
  4 × 2 means 4 groups of 2.

- The two pieces of dot paper show the same number of dots.
  Say: 2 × 4 = 8 and 4 × 2 = 8 are related multiplication facts.

Guided Practice (page 160)

5 This exercise reinforces the concept of the Commutative Property of Multiplication. Provide dot paper if necessary.

Common Error Some children may have difficulty using dot paper. Display a multiplication table or give children individual multiplication tables for reference until facts are mastered.

Let's Practice (page 161)

This provides children with more practice in multiplying 2 using dot paper. Exercises 1 and 2 reinforce the strategy of using known multiplication facts of 2 to find unknown facts. Exercises 3 to 6 help reinforce the Commutative Property of Multiplication. Exercise 7 provides practice in applying multiplication strategies to solve real-world problems.

Best Practices You may want to have children work with a partner. Allow partners to use dot paper, a 2s multiplication table, or skip-counting. Have partners share how they solved each problem.

ON YOUR OWN

Children practice multiplying by 2 using dot paper in Practice 2, pages 129 to 132 of **Workbook 2A**. These pages (with the answers) are shown on page 161A.

Differentiation Options Depending on children's success with the Workbook pages, use these materials as needed.
Struggling: Reteach 2A, pp. 117–124
On Level: Extra Practice 2A, pp. 69–72

Practice and Apply
Workbook pages for Chapter 6, Lesson 2

Name: _____ Date: _____

Practice 2 Multiplying 2: Using Dot Paper

Use dot paper to solve.

1. There are 4 bags.
   2 rolls are in each bag.
   How many rolls are there in all?

$4 \times 2 = $ __8__

There are __8__ rolls in all.

2. 6 bicycles are in the shop.
   Each bicycle has 2 wheels.
   How many wheels are there in all?

__6__ $\times 2 = $ __12__

There are __12__ wheels in all.

Workbook A p. 129

Name: _____ Date: _____

Use dot paper to fill in the blanks.

┌─ Example ─────────────────────────────┐

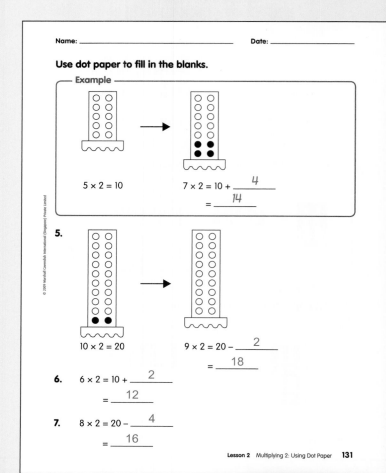

$5 \times 2 = 10$ $7 \times 2 = 10 + $ __4__

                           $= $ __14__
└───────────────────────────────────────┘

5.

$10 \times 2 = 20$ $9 \times 2 = 20 - $ __2__

                           $= $ __18__

6. $6 \times 2 = 10 + $ __2__

   $= $ __12__

7. $8 \times 2 = 20 - $ __4__

   $= $ __16__

Workbook A p. 131

Use dot paper to solve.

3. Mrs. Smith buys 5 burgers for her children.
   Each burger costs $2.
   How much do the 5 burgers cost in all?

__5__ $\times \$2 = \$ $ __10__

The 5 burgers cost $ __10__ in all.

4. Ed buys 9 pairs of socks.
   Each pair of socks costs $2.
   How much do the socks cost in all?

  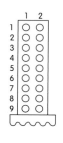

__9__ $\times \$ $ __2__ $= \$ $ __18__

The socks cost $ __18__ in all.

Workbook A p. 130

Use dot paper to find the missing numbers.

┌─ Example ─────────────────────────────┐

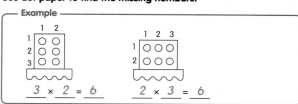

__3__ $\times$ __2__ $= $ __6__   __2__ $\times$ __3__ $= $ __6__
└───────────────────────────────────────┘

8.

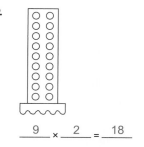

__5__ $\times$ __2__ $= $ __10__ $2 \times$ __5__ $= $ __10__

9.

__9__ $\times$ __2__ $= $ __18__   __2__ $\times$ __9__ $= $ __18__

Workbook A p. 132

Multiplying 5: Skip-counting

LESSON OBJECTIVES
• Skip-count by 5s.
• Solve multiplication word problems.

TECHNOLOGY RESOURCES
• *Math in Focus* eBooks
• *Math in Focus* Teacher Resources CD

 DAY 1 Student Book 2A, pp. 162–167
Workbook 2A, pp. 133–136

MATERIALS
• 1 Hundreds Chart (TR09) per group
• 10 counters of one color per child
• 1 calculator (optional)
• 1 number cube per group
• 1 set of Number Cards from 1 to 10 (TR06) per group
• 1 Worksheet (TR10) per child
• 1 coin per group
• 2 stickers per group

DIFFERENTIATION RESOURCES
• Reteach 2A, pp. 125–126
• Extra Practice 2A, pp. 73–74

 5-minute Warm Up

Hold up a certain number of fingers to represent a number from 1 to 10, for example, 4.

To find 5 × 4, have children count in 5s while raising each finger:

1,	2,	3,	4,	5
6,	7,	8,	9,	10
11,	12,	13,	14,	15
16,	17,	18,	19,	20

Therefore, 5 × 4 = 20. Repeat the exercise with another number. This simple activity prepares children for the skip-counting strategy used when multiplying by 5.

LESSON 3 **Multiplying 5: Skip-counting**

Lesson Objectives
• Skip-count by 5s.
• Solve multiplication word problems.

Student Book A p. 162

DAY 1 # Teach

 **Game:**
Skip Fives! (pages 162 and 163)

This game identifies the patterns of multiplication facts of 5.

• Place children in groups of four to six and give each child 10 **counters** of a specific color.

• Read and explain the instructions for the game.

• At the end of the game, ask children to identify the pattern on the **Hundreds Chart** (TR09). Help them to see that the multiples of 5 all end with a '5' or '0'.

Best Practices You may want to use a **Hundreds Chart** (TR09) to teach this lesson. Skip-count the 5s. Ask a child to mark every 5 with a colored marker. Children can mark individual hundreds charts with the same colored crayon. These charts can be used in the lesson if needed. You may also want to mark 2s and 10s in a different color.

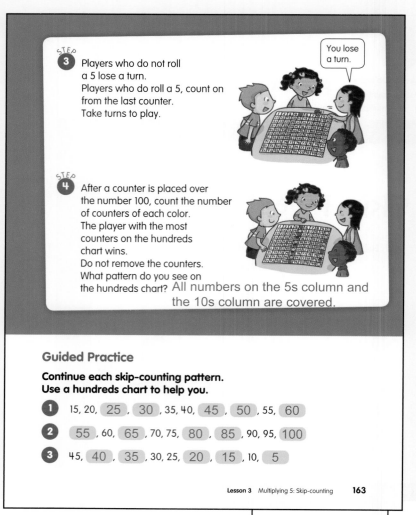

Guided Practice

Continue each skip-counting pattern.
Use a hundreds chart to help you.

1 15, 20, **25** , **30** , 35, 40, **45** , **50** , 55, **60**

2 **55** , 60, **65** , 70, 75, **80** , **85** , 90, 95, **100**

3 45, **40** , **35** , 30, 25, **20** , **15** , 10, **5**

Lesson 3   Multiplying 5: Skip-counting   **163**

Problem of the Lesson

Find the missing numbers in these multiplication sentences.
(a) $5 \times$ ___ $= 35$
(b) $9 \times 5 =$ ___
(c) ___ $\times$ ___ $= 25$ (missing numbers in the blanks are identical)

Answers:
(a) 7   (b) 45   (c) 5, 5

Differentiated Instruction

English Language Learners

Show children how to skip-count 5s using a calculator. Have a child press 5, then +, then 5 again. *Say:* 2 groups of 5 make 10. Continue with + 5. *Say:* 3 groups of 5 make 15. Continue this procedure, asking children to repeat after you.

Check for Understanding
✓ **Guided Practice** (page 163)

1 to **3** These exercises reinforce the number pattern children noticed in the previous game. Encourage children to use the hundreds chart from the game to complete these exercises.

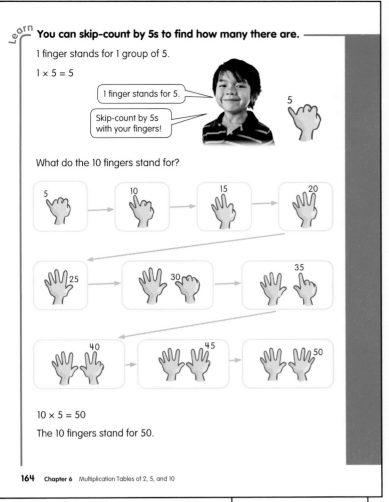

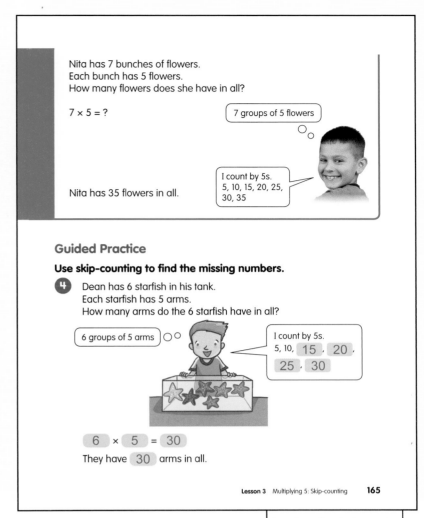

Skip-count by 5s (pages 164 and 165)

Children learn to multiply 5 by skip-counting by 5s.

- Help children recall the concept of multiplication as the number of groups multiplied by the number of items in each group.

- Model this concept using your fingers. Show children that 1 finger can represent one group of 5. Write $1 \times 5 = 5$ on the board.

- Show that 2 fingers represent 2 groups of 5. Write $2 \times 5 = 10$.

- Explain and show children the skip-counting strategy, using all 10 fingers to find the facts of 5 up to 50.

- Have children practice this skip-counting method with their friends. Encourage children to check one another's answers.

- Read and explain the problem on page 165.

- Help children identify the groups and number of items in each group from the question.

- *Say:* 7 groups of 5 flowers is 7×5.

- Have children use their fingers to skip-count by 5s to find the answer.

✓ Guided Practice (page 165)

4 This exercise provides practice in skip-counting by 5s to solve a real-world problem.

For Struggling Learners Have children work in pairs. Review the 'using fingers' strategy: 1 finger represents 5, 2 fingers represent 10, etc.
One child calls out a 5s fact and the partner finds the answer using the strategy.
Ask children to switch roles.

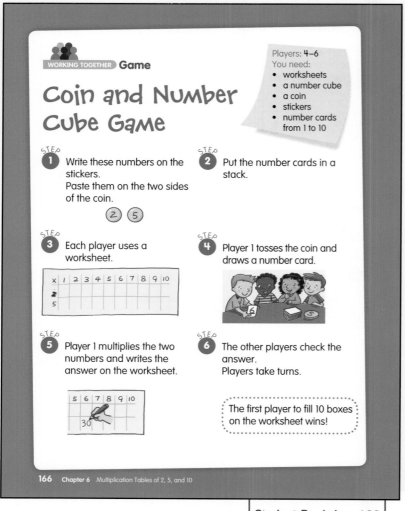

Student Book A p. 166

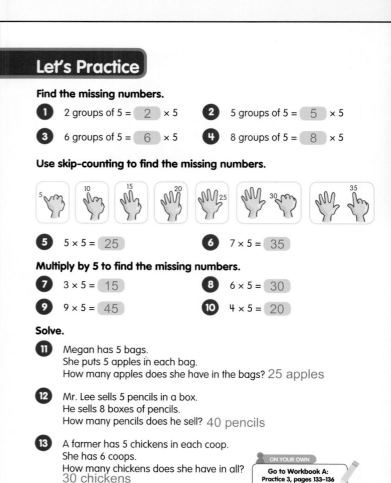

Student Book A p. 167

 **WORKING TOGETHER** **Game:**

Coin and Number Cube Game (page 166)

This game reinforces children's recall of multiplication facts for 2 and 5.

- Explain the steps in the Student Book and distribute the **Worksheets** (TR10).

- Encourage children to check one another's answers.

Let's Practice (page 167)

This provides children with more practice in multiplying 5 by using the skip-counting strategy. Exercises ❶ to ❹ require children to relate multiplication to the concept of equal groups. Exercises ❺ to ❿ provide practice in skip-counting by 5s. Exercises ⓫ to ⓭ provide practice in applying skip-counting by 5s to solve real-world problems.

Common Error Some children may skip-count incorrectly. Encourage children to use the finger chart on the page, their own fingers, or their hundreds chart if they need help with the 5s facts.

ON YOUR OWN

Children practice multiplying by 5 using the skip-counting strategy in Practice 3, pages 133 to 136 of **Workbook 2A**. These pages (with the answers) are shown on page 167A.

Differentiation Options Depending on children's success with the Workbook pages, use these materials as needed.

Struggling: Reteach 2A, pp. 125–126

On Level: Extra Practice 2A, pp. 73–74

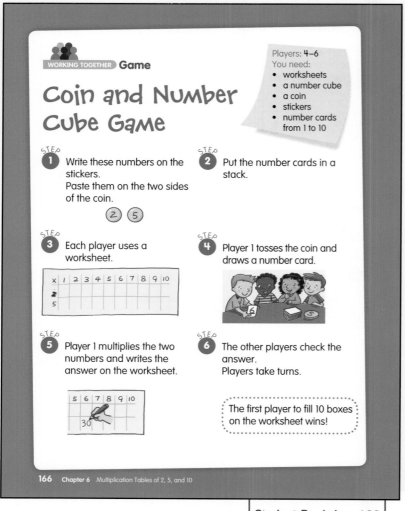

Student Book A p. 166

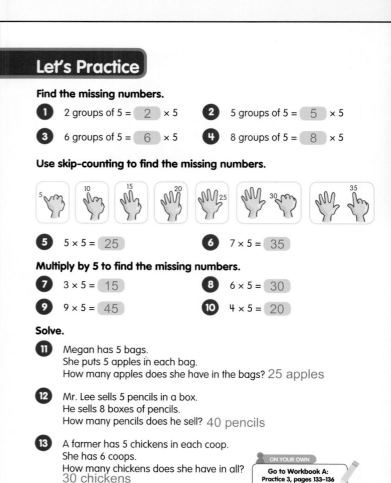

Student Book A p. 167

 **WORKING TOGETHER** **Game:**

Coin and Number Cube Game (page 166)

This game reinforces children's recall of multiplication facts for 2 and 5.

- Explain the steps in the Student Book and distribute the **Worksheets** (TR10).

- Encourage children to check one another's answers.

Let's Practice (page 167)

This provides children with more practice in multiplying 5 by using the skip-counting strategy. Exercises ❶ to ❹ require children to relate multiplication to the concept of equal groups. Exercises ❺ to ❿ provide practice in skip-counting by 5s. Exercises ⓫ to ⓭ provide practice in applying skip-counting by 5s to solve real-world problems.

Common Error Some children may skip-count incorrectly. Encourage children to use the finger chart on the page, their own fingers, or their hundreds chart if they need help with the 5s facts.

ON YOUR OWN

Children practice multiplying by 5 using the skip-counting strategy in Practice 3, pages 133 to 136 of **Workbook 2A**. These pages (with the answers) are shown on page 167A.

Differentiation Options Depending on children's success with the Workbook pages, use these materials as needed.

Struggling: Reteach 2A, pp. 125–126

On Level: Extra Practice 2A, pp. 73–74

Practice and Apply
Workbook pages for Chapter 6, Lesson 3

Name: ____________________ Date: ____________

Practice 3 Multiplying 5: Skip-counting

Jon is skip-counting by 5s.
He shades each number he counts on a hundreds chart.
He misses some numbers.
Circle the numbers he misses.

1.

1	2	3	4	⑤	6	7	8	9	⑩
11	12	13	14	15	16	17	18	19	20
21	22	23	24	25	26	27	28	29	㉚
31	32	33	34	㉟	36	37	38	39	40
41	42	43	44	㊺	46	47	48	49	50
51	52	53	54	55	56	57	58	59	(60)
61	62	63	64	(65)	66	67	68	69	70
71	72	73	74	75	76	77	78	79	80
81	82	83	84	(85)	86	87	88	89	(90)
91	92	93	94	95	96	97	98	99	(100)

Find the missing numbers.

Example

3 groups of 5 = __3__ × 5
= __15__

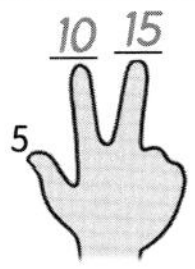

2. 4 groups of 5 = __4__ × 5
= __20__

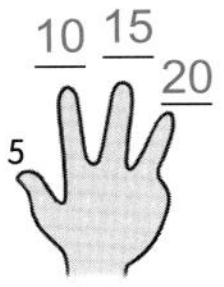

Workbook A p. 133

3. 5 groups of 5 = __5__ × __5__
= __25__

4. 7 groups of 5 = __7__ × __5__
= __35__

5. 8 groups of 5 = __8__ × __5__
= __40__

6. 9 groups of 5 = __9__ × __5__
= __45__

Count by 5s.
Then fill in the blanks.

7. 5, 10, 15, 20, 25, __30__

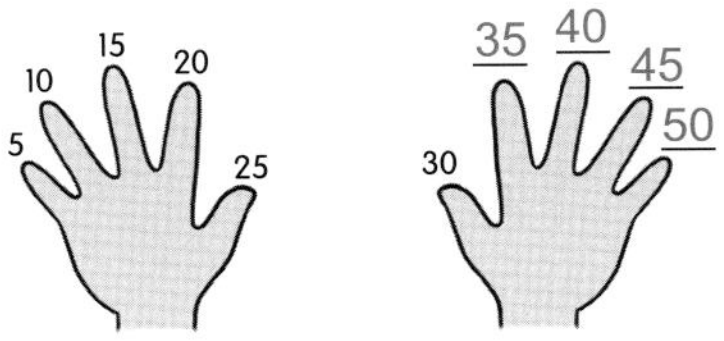

8. 20, 25, __30__, __35__, __40__, __45__, __50__

Workbook A p. 134

Name: ____________________ Date: ____________

Count by 5s.
Then fill in the blanks.

9. 20, __25__, 30, __35__, 40, 45

10. __15__, __20__, 25, 30, 35, __40__, __45__, __50__

Fill in the blanks.

11. 3 × 5 = __15__ **12.** 2 × 5 = __10__

13. 6 × 5 = __30__ **14.** 8 × 5 = __40__

15. 9 × 5 = __45__ **16.** 7 × 5 = __35__

17. 5 × 5 = __25__ **18.** 10 × 5 = __50__

Solve.

19. Three children raise both hands.
There are 5 fingers on each hand.
How many fingers do they raise in all?

6 × 5 = __30__

They raise __30__ fingers in all.

Workbook A p. 135

20. Jeff buys 7 books at the bookstore.
Each book costs $5.
How much does Jeff pay for the 7 books?

__7__ × $ __5__ = $ __35__

He pays $ __35__ for the 7 books.

21. There are 9 trays on the counter.
There are 5 plates on each tray.
How many plates are there in all?

__9__ × __5__ = __45__

There are __45__ plates in all.

Workbook A p. 136

LESSON 4 Multiplying 5: Using Dot Paper

LESSON OBJECTIVES

- Use dot paper to multiply by 5.
- Use known multiplication facts to find new multiplication facts.
- Identify related multiplication facts.
- Solve multiplication word problems.

TECHNOLOGY RESOURCES

- *Math in Focus* eBooks
- *Math in Focus* Teacher Resources CD

DAY 1 Student Book 2A, pp. 168–170

MATERIALS

- Dot Paper of 5 (TR11) per child
- 1 Spinner Card (TR12) per group
- 1 transparent spinner
- 1 paper clip per group
- 1 pencil per group
- index cards (optional)

DAY 2 Student Book 2A, pp. 171–172
Workbook 2A, pp. 137–140

DIFFERENTIATION RESOURCES

- Reteach 2A, pp. 127–130
- Extra Practice 2A, pp. 75–78

 5-minute Warm Up

Children work in pairs. One child calls out a single-digit number. His or her partner will use the fact recall or the skip-counting strategy to find that particular multiple of 5. Children switch roles and repeat.

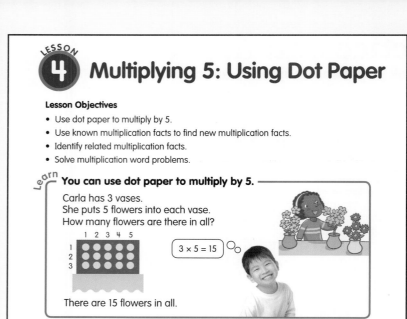

LESSON 4 Multiplying 5: Using Dot Paper

Lesson Objectives

- Use dot paper to multiply by 5.
- Use known multiplication facts to find new multiplication facts.
- Identify related multiplication facts.
- Solve multiplication word problems.

Learn **You can use dot paper to multiply by 5.**

Carla has 3 vases.
She puts 5 flowers into each vase.
How many flowers are there in all?

$3 \times 5 = 15$

There are 15 flowers in all.

Guided Practice

Use dot paper to find the missing numbers.

1 Tim has 2 fish tanks.
Each tank has 5 goldfish.
How many goldfish are there in all?

$2 \times 5 = 10$

There are 10 goldfish in all.

168   Chapter 6 Multiplication Tables of 2, 5, and 10

Student Book A p. 168

DAY 1 # Teach

Learn

Use Dot Paper to Multiply by 5 (page 168)

Children learn to relate the multiples of 5 with dot paper that have five dots on each row.

- Explain and apply the 'group and item' concept to help children recall multiplication facts.

- Explain that there are 3 groups (vases) and 5 items (flowers) in each group. The number 5 is repeatedly added to get 15: $5 + 5 + 5 = 15$. *Say:* There are 3 groups and each group has 5 items. So, $3 \times 5 = 15$.

- Copy and distribute the **Dot Paper of 5** (TR11). With the dot paper, show a fixed number of 5 dots in each row, and explain that 3 groups of 5 is the same as 3 rows of 5 dots.

Write on the board:
$$5 + 5 + 5 = 3 \text{ fives}$$
$$= 3 \times 5$$
$$= 15$$

Check for Understanding

✓ **Guided Practice** (page 168)

1 This exercise provides practice in using dot paper to multiply by 5 to solve a real-world problem.

Student Book A p. 169

In the list of numbers below, all the numbers are obtained by multiplying by 5, except two numbers. Cross out the two numbers that do not belong.

10 , 23 , 30 , 45 , 52 , 55 , 60.

Solution:
Numbers obtained by multiplying by 5 end with 5 or 0. Therefore, the numbers that do not belong are 23 and 52.

Answer: 23 and 52.

Differentiated Instruction

English Language Learners

Practice matching word problems and number sentences. Use three index cards. Write a multiplication word problem on one card, draw a dot paper of it on another, and the related multiplication sentence on the third card. Create several sets with different word problems. Read a word problem card to a child and ask him/her to find the matching dot paper and sentence. Continue with other word problems.

READING AND WRITING MATH
Math Journal (page 169)

This section allows children to reflect on and apply their understanding of multiplication by writing multiplication stories.

- In Exercise ❶, children are expected to write a multiplication sentence containing × 5 as there are 5 birds in each nest.

- For Exercise ❷, encourage children to use other numbers to make up a multiplication story for multiples of 2 and 5. Ask volunteers to write the corresponding multiplication sentence and solve it.

Use Short Cuts to Find Multiplication Facts
(page 169)

Children learn to multiply faster by skip-counting by 10s and 5s, using 2 fingers to represent 10.

- Demonstrate the new strategy for finding facts for 5. Explain the representation of fingers: 1 finger represents 5 and 2 fingers represent 10. The strategy is to count by 10s and 5s.

- To compute 3 × 5, we show 3 fingers: Two fingers is 10 and 3 fingers is 10 + 5 = 15.

$$3 × 5 = 10 + 5 = 15$$

- After your demonstration and explanation, have children explain the method in their own words.

- Have children solve 7 × 5 using finger computation.

  Ask children to raise 7 fingers.

  2 fingers make 10.

  4 fingers make 20.

  6 fingers make 30.

  7 fingers make 35.

  $$7 × 5 = 10 + 10 + 10 + 5$$
  $$= 35$$

Best Practices Use a three-column chart to teach this lesson. Use the first column to show a 5s fact on dot paper, the next column to show the corresponding multiplication fact, and the third column to show a related multiplication fact.

Guided Practice

Use a short cut to find the missing numbers.

2 $4 \times 5 = ?$ $4 \times 5 = 20$

WORKING TOGETHER Game

Spin and Multiply

Players: 4–6
You need:
• cards
• a paper clip
• a pencil

STEP 1 Each player has a card.

STEP 2 Place a pencil and a paper clip at the center of the card. Player 1 spins the paper clip.

STEP 3 The paper clip points towards a number. Player 1 multiplies the number by 5 and writes the answer on the card.

STEP 4 The other players check the answer.

STEP 5 Players take turns.

The first player to complete the card wins!

170   Chapter 6   Multiplication Tables of 2, 5, and 10

Student Book A p. 170

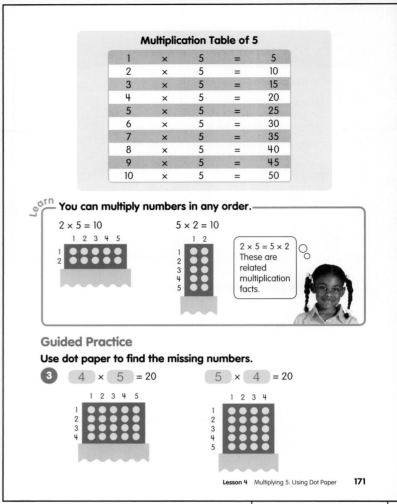

Multiplication Table of 5

1	×	5	=	5
2	×	5	=	10
3	×	5	=	15
4	×	5	=	20
5	×	5	=	25
6	×	5	=	30
7	×	5	=	35
8	×	5	=	40
9	×	5	=	45
10	×	5	=	50

Learn You can multiply numbers in any order.

$2 \times 5 = 10$ $5 \times 2 = 10$

$2 \times 5 = 5 \times 2$
These are related multiplication facts.

Guided Practice

Use dot paper to find the missing numbers.

3 $4 \times 5 = 20$ $5 \times 4 = 20$

Lesson 4   Multiplying 5: Using Dot Paper   **171**

Student Book A p. 171

✓ Guided Practice (page 170)

2 This exercise provides practice in using the finger computation strategy to find 4×5.

WORKING TOGETHER Game:

Spin and Multiply (page 170)

This game reinforces the short cut method using the finger computation strategy to find the 5s facts.

• Distribute the **Spinner Card** (TR12) and paper clips to each group. Have children follow the steps in the Student Book.

• Encourage children to use the finger computation strategy to find the answers.

For Advanced Learners You may want to use counters to review odd and even numbers. If the counters can be grouped in 2s they are even numbers. Even numbers have a 0, 2, 4, 6, or 8 in the ones place. If the counters cannot be grouped in 2s, they are odd numbers. Odd numbers have a 1, 3, 5, 7, or 9 in the ones place.

DAY 2 **Teach**   See the Lesson Organizer on page 168 for Day 2 resources.

At the start of the day, have children recite and remember the multiplication table of 5 on page 171. Help children recall the number pattern in the table, where the answer ends with either a '5' or '0'. Challenge children to commit the multiplication table of 5 to memory.

Learn

Multiply Numbers in Any Order (page 171)

Children use the Commutative Property of Multiplication with dot paper as a strategy to find the 5s facts.

• Help children recall that the Commutative Property of Multiplication means that they can multiply two numbers in any order to get the same answer.

• Demonstrate with the help of dot paper:

Show 2 rows of 5 $2 \times 5 = 10$.
Show 5 rows of 2 $5 \times 2 = 10$.

• Lead children to recognize that 5×2 is the same as 2×5. *Say:* $5 \times 2 = 10$ and $2 \times 5 = 10$ are related multiplication facts.

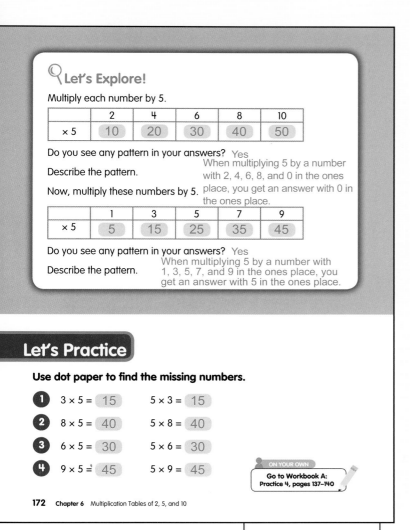

Let's Explore!

Multiply each number by 5.

	2	4	6	8	10
× 5	10	20	30	40	50

Do you see any pattern in your answers? Yes

Describe the pattern. When multiplying 5 by a number with 2, 4, 6, 8, and 0 in the ones place, you get an answer with 0 in the ones place.

Now, multiply these numbers by 5.

	1	3	5	7	9
× 5	5	15	25	35	45

Do you see any pattern in your answers? Yes

Describe the pattern. When multiplying 5 by a number with 1, 3, 5, 7, and 9 in the ones place, you get an answer with 5 in the ones place.

Let's Practice

Use dot paper to find the missing numbers.

1. 3 × 5 = 15   5 × 3 = 15
2. 8 × 5 = 40   5 × 8 = 40
3. 6 × 5 = 30   5 × 6 = 30
4. 9 × 5 = 45   5 × 9 = 45

ON YOUR OWN
Go to Workbook A:
Practice 4, pages 137–140

172   Chapter 6   Multiplication Tables of 2, 5, and 10

Student Book A p. 172

Guided Practice (page 171)

3 This exercise reinforces the concept of the Commutative Property of Multiplication. Provide dot paper if necessary.

Let's Explore!

Number Patterns in Multiplication Table of 5
(page 172)

• Have children work in groups of three or four.

• Have each group copy the table onto a piece of paper, complete the table, and then identify the number patterns.

• Lead children to deduce that when multiplying 5:
With an even number in the ones place, they will get an answer with 0 in the ones place.
With an odd number in the ones place, they will get an answer with 5 in the ones place.

Let's Practice (page 172)

Exercises **1** to **4** provide more practice multiplying 5 using dot paper. They also reinforce the Commutative Property of Multiplication.

Common Error Some children may misuse the dot paper. Tell children to count carefully and after circling the dots, recount their rows and columns.

ON YOUR OWN

Children practice multiplying by 5 using dot paper in Practice 4, pages 137 to 140 of **Workbook 2A**. These pages (with the answers) are shown on page 172A.

Differentiation Options Depending on children's success with the Workbook pages, use these materials as needed.
Struggling: Reteach 2A, pp. 127–130
On Level: Extra Practice 2A, pp. 75–78

Practice and Apply
Workbook pages for Chapter 6, Lesson 4

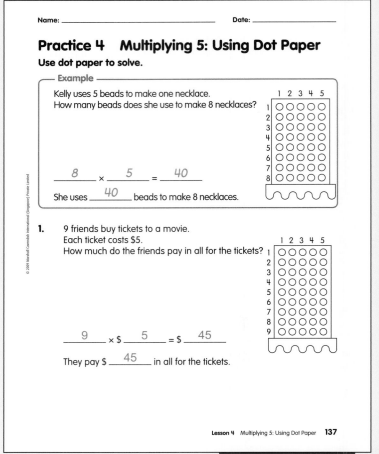

Name: _____ **Date:** _____

Practice 4 Multiplying 5: Using Dot Paper
Use dot paper to solve.

Example

Kelly uses 5 beads to make one necklace.
How many beads does she use to make 8 necklaces?

$\underline{\quad 8 \quad} \times \underline{\quad 5 \quad} = \underline{\quad 40 \quad}$

She uses __40__ beads to make 8 necklaces.

1. 9 friends buy tickets to a movie.
Each ticket costs $5.
How much do the friends pay in all for the tickets?

$\underline{\quad 9 \quad} \times \$ \underline{\quad 5 \quad} = \$ \underline{\quad 45 \quad}$

They pay $ __45__ in all for the tickets.

Lesson 4 Multiplying 5: Using Dot Paper **137**

Workbook A p. 137

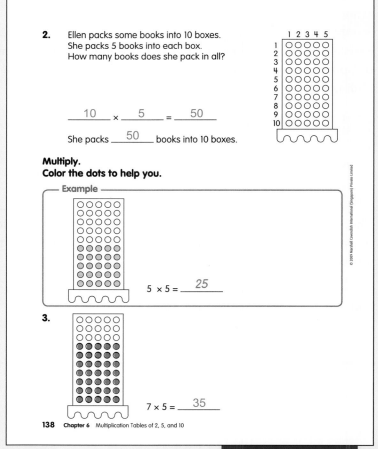

2. Ellen packs some books into 10 boxes.
She packs 5 books into each box.
How many books does she pack in all?

$\underline{\quad 10 \quad} \times \underline{\quad 5 \quad} = \underline{\quad 50 \quad}$

She packs __50__ books into 10 boxes.

Multiply.
Color the dots to help you.

Example

$5 \times 5 = \underline{\quad 25 \quad}$

3.

$7 \times 5 = \underline{\quad 35 \quad}$

138 Chapter 6 Multiplication Tables of 2, 5, and 10

Workbook A p. 138

Name: _____ **Date:** _____

Multiply.
Color the dots to help you.

4.

$3 \times 5 = \underline{\quad 15 \quad}$

Use dot paper to fill in the blanks.

5.

$\underline{\quad 4 \quad} \times \underline{\quad 5 \quad} = \underline{\quad 20 \quad}$

$\underline{\quad 5 \quad} \times \underline{\quad 4 \quad} = \underline{\quad 20 \quad}$

Lesson 4 Multiplying 5: Using Dot Paper **139**

Workbook A p. 139

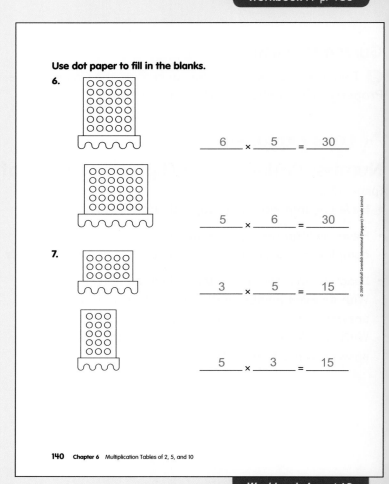

Use dot paper to fill in the blanks.

6.

$\underline{\quad 6 \quad} \times \underline{\quad 5 \quad} = \underline{\quad 30 \quad}$

$\underline{\quad 5 \quad} \times \underline{\quad 6 \quad} = \underline{\quad 30 \quad}$

7.

$\underline{\quad 3 \quad} \times \underline{\quad 5 \quad} = \underline{\quad 15 \quad}$

$\underline{\quad 5 \quad} \times \underline{\quad 3 \quad} = \underline{\quad 15 \quad}$

140 Chapter 6 Multiplication Tables of 2, 5, and 10

Workbook A p. 140

LESSON 5 Multiplying 10: Skip-counting and Using Dot Paper

LESSON OBJECTIVES
- Skip-count and use dot paper to multiply by 10.
- Use known multiplication facts to find new multiplication facts.
- Identify related multiplication facts.
- Solve multiplication word problems.

TECHNOLOGY RESOURCES
- *Math in Focus* eBooks
- *Math in Focus* Teacher Resources CD
- *Math in Focus* Virtual Manipulatives

DAY 1 Student Book 2A, pp. 173–175

MATERIALS
- 1 Hundreds Chart (TR09)
- Dot Paper of 10 (TR13) per child

DAY 2 Student Book 2A, pp. 176–178
Workbook 2A, pp. 141–144

DIFFERENTIATION RESOURCES
- Reteach 2A, pp. 131–134
- Extra Practice 2A, pp. 79–82

 5-minute Warm Up

Children work in pairs. One child says a single-digit number, for example, 4, and writes it on a piece of paper. His or her partner appends a zero behind the number then says the new number: Forty. Children switch roles and repeat with different numbers. This prepares children for skip-counting by 10s.

LESSON 5 Multiplying 10: Skip-counting and Using Dot Paper

Lesson Objectives
- Skip-count and use dot paper to multiply by 10.
- Use known multiplication facts to find new multiplication facts.
- Identify related multiplication facts.
- Solve multiplication word problems.

Learn You can use a hundreds chart to count by 10.

Carrie counts the animals at the zoo ten at a time. Then she colors the number on the hundreds chart. This is what her chart looks like.

1	2	3	4	5	6	7	8	9	10
11	12	13	14	15	16	17	18	19	20
21	22	23	24	25	26	27	28	29	30
31	32	33	34	35	36	37	38	39	40
41	42	43	44	45	46	47	48	49	50
51	52	53	54	55	56	57	58	59	60
61	62	63	64	65	66	67	68	69	70
71	72	73	74	75	76	77	78	79	80
81	82	83	84	85	86	87	88	89	90
91	92	93	94	95	96	97	98	99	100

What pattern do you see in the colored numbers on the chart?

Guided Practice

Continue each skip-counting pattern.
Use a hundreds chart to help you.

1 100, 90, 80, 70, 60, 50, 40, 30, 20, 10

Student Book A p. 173

DAY 1 Teach

Learn

Use a Hundreds Chart to Count by 10 (page 173)

A **Hundreds Chart** (TR09) is used to show the number pattern related to counting in 10s.

- Show children the Hundreds Chart and have them identify the multiplication facts of 10.

- Highlight the multiplication facts identified by children and prompt them to identify the number pattern formed.

- Children should deduce that all multiplication facts of 10 have the digit 0 in the ones place.

- Have children read the highlighted numbers aloud to prepare them for skip-counting by 10s.

Check for Understanding
✓ **Guided Practice** (page 173)

1 This practice reinforces the number pattern involving the multiplication facts of 10. Have children refer to the **Hundreds Chart** (TR09), if necessary.

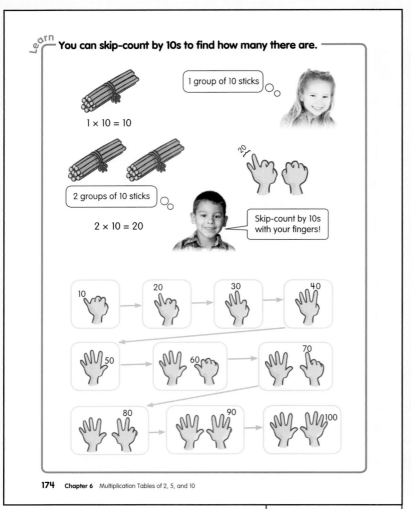

Student Book A p. 174

Problem of the Lesson

Solve the following multiplication sentences.

(a) _____ × 10 = 60

(b) 2 × 5 × 10 = _____

Answer:

(a) 6

(b) 100

Differentiated Instruction

English Language Learners

Have a native English-speaking child read aloud the word problems to the English Language learner. Have the two children work together to write the multiplication number sentence. Children solve the problem independently.

For Advanced Learners Have children work in groups. Each group comes up with some 10s facts. Children discuss if these facts form any pattern. If they find that there is a pattern, have them check if other 10s facts form the same pattern.

Skip-count by 10s (page 174)

Children use the skip-counting by 10s strategy to find the 10s facts.

- Help children recall the group and item concept in multiplication, using the example of sticks in the Student Book.

- Explain that 1 bundle (group) has 10 sticks: 1 × 10 = 10.

- Explain that 2 bundles have 20 sticks: 2 × 10 = 20.

- Model the skip-counting by 10s strategy using fingers:
  1 finger represents 1 group of 10 items (1 × 10 = 10).
  2 fingers represent 2 groups of 10 items (2 × 10 = 20),
  and so on.

- Have children recite the sequence of numbers while raising the corresponding number of fingers:
  10, 20, 30, 40, 50, 60, 70, 80, 90, 100.

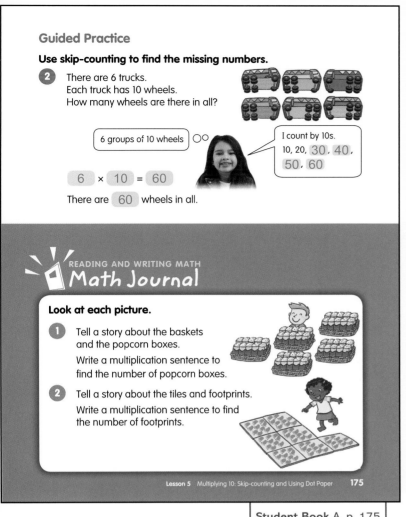

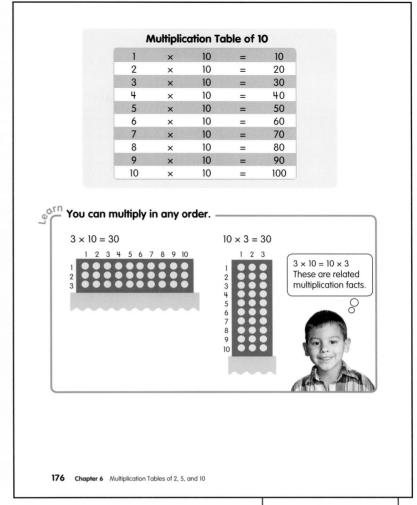

Guided Practice (page 175)

② This exercise provides practice in skip-counting by 10s to solve a real-world problem.

READING AND WRITING MATH

Math Journal (page 175)

This section allows children to reflect on and apply their understanding of multiplication by writing multiplication stories and sentences.

- Have children study the pictures.

- Highlight to children the group and item concept used, and lead children to identify the groups and the items in each picture.

- Encourage children to tell a multiplication story about each picture.

- Pair children up and ask them to take turns writing and solving multiplication stories based on the pictures.

Teach

See the Lesson Organizer on page 173 for Day 2 resources.

At the start of the lesson, have children recite and remember the multiplication table of 10 on page 176. Help children recall the number pattern in the table, where the answer always ends with 0. Challenge children to commit the multiplication table of 10 to memory.

Multiply Numbers in Any Order (page 176)

Children use the Commutative Property of Multiplication with **Dot Paper of 10 (TR13)** as a strategy to find the 10s facts.

- Help children recall that the Commutative Property of Multiplication means that they can multiply two numbers in any order to get the same answer.

- Demonstrate with the help of dot paper:

  Show 3 rows of 10 $3 \times 10 = 30$.
  Show 10 rows of 3 $10 \times 3 = 30$.

- Lead children to recognize that 10×3 is the same as 3×10. *Say:* $10 \times 3 = 30$ and $3 \times 10 = 30$ are related multiplication facts.

Guided Practice

Use dot paper to find the missing numbers.

3 8 × 10 = 80 10 × 8 = 80

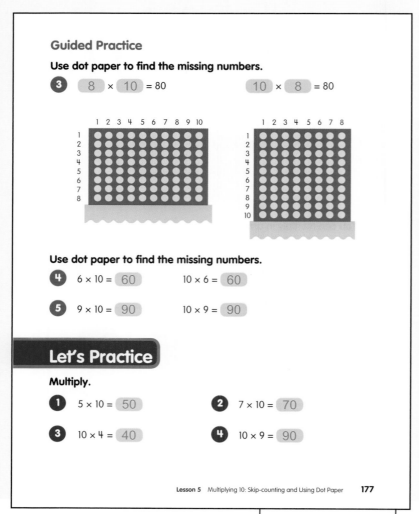

Use dot paper to find the missing numbers.

4 $6 \times 10 =$ 60 $10 \times 6 =$ 60

5 $9 \times 10 =$ 90 $10 \times 9 =$ 90

Let's Practice

Multiply.

1 $5 \times 10 =$ 50   **2** $7 \times 10 =$ 70

3 $10 \times 4 =$ 40   **4** $10 \times 9 =$ 90

Student Book A p. 177

Write multiplication sentences to find the number of dots.

5

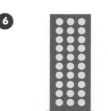

3 × 10 = 30

6

10 × 3 = 30

Solve.

7 4 groups of children visit a museum.
There are 10 children in each group.
How many children are there altogether? 40 children

8 Marlee and her 7 friends each have 10 tokens for a funfair.
How many tokens do they have altogether? 80 tokens

ON YOUR OWN
Go to Workbook A:
Practice 5, pages 141–144

Student Book A p. 178

✓ Guided Practice (page 177)

3 to **5** There exercises reinforce the concept of the Commutative Property of Multiplication. Provide dot paper if necessary.

Best Practices Use the **Dot Paper of 10** (TR13) to illustrate the Commutative Property of Multiplication. Have children cut out dot paper to show 4 × 10. Have children hold it both vertically and horizontally. Write on the board 4 × 10 = 10 × 4.

Let's Practice (pages 177 and 178)

This provides children with more practice in multiplying 10, using the various multiplication strategies. Exercises **1** to **4** check that children can recall the multiplication facts of 10. Exercises **5** and **6** check that children can use dot paper to multiply 10, and Exercises **7** and **8** check that children can solve real-world problems using the multiplication strategies learned.

Common Error Some children may still try to count dots or skip-count. Remind children that when multiplying by 10, they can simply tack a zero to the end of the number being multiplied by ten.

ON YOUR OWN

Children practice multiplying by 10, using the various strategies in Practice 5, pages 141 to 144 of **Workbook 2A**. These pages (with the answers) are shown on page 178A.

Differentiation Options Depending on children's success with the Workbook pages, use these materials as needed.
Struggling: Reteach 2A, pp. 131–134
On Level: Extra Practice 2A, pp. 79–82

Practice and Apply
Workbook pages for Chapter 6, Lesson 5

Practice 5   Multiplying 10: Skip-counting and Using Dot Paper

The numbers below the chart follow a pattern.
Use the hundreds chart to find the missing numbers.

1.

1	2	3	4	5	6	7	8	9	⑩
11	12	13	14	15	16	17	18	19	㉒
21	22	23	24	25	26	27	28	29	㉚
31	32	33	34	35	36	37	38	39	㊵
41	42	43	44	45	46	47	48	49	㊿
51	52	53	54	55	56	57	58	59	60
61	62	63	64	65	66	67	68	69	70
71	72	73	74	75	76	77	78	79	80
81	82	83	84	85	86	87	88	89	90
91	92	93	94	95	96	97	98	99	⑩⓪

10, __20__, __30__, 40, 50, __60__,

70, __80__, 90, __100__

Use patterns to fill in the blanks.

Example

$1 \times 1 =$ __1__

$1 \times 10 =$ __10__

2. $2 \times 1 =$ __2__

$2 \times 10 =$ __20__

3. $3 \times 1 =$ __3__

$3 \times 10 =$ __30__

Workbook A p. 141

Use patterns to fill in the blanks.

4. $4 \times 1 =$ __4__

$4 \times 10 =$ __40__

5. $5 \times 1 =$ __5__

$5 \times 10 =$ __50__

6. $6 \times 10 =$ __60__

7. $7 \times 10 =$ __70__

Solve.

8. There are 4 bundles of sticks.
Each bundle has 10 sticks.
How many sticks are there in all?

$4 \times 10 =$ __40__

There are __40__ sticks in all.

9. Megan makes 6 bracelets.
She needs 10 beads to make one bracelet.
How many beads are needed to make the 6 bracelets?

__6__ $\times 10 =$ __60__

__60__ beads are needed to make the 6 bracelets.

Workbook A p. 142

Solve.

10. During sports day, 10 children form a group for a relay race.
How many children are there in 8 groups?

__8__ $\times 10 =$ __80__

There are __80__ children in 8 groups.

11. The school band has 10 violins.
Each violin has 4 strings on it.
How many strings are on the 10 violins?

__4__ $\times$ __10__ $=$ __40__

There are __40__ strings on the 10 violins.

Workbook A p. 143

Use dot paper to multiply.

12.

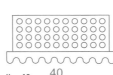

$4 \times 10 =$ __40__

$10 \times 4 =$ __40__

13.

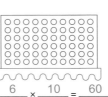

__6__ $\times$ __10__ $=$ __60__

__10__ $\times$ __6__ $=$ __60__

14.

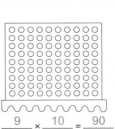

__9__ $\times$ __10__ $=$ __90__

__10__ $\times$ __9__ $=$ __90__

Workbook A p. 144

LESSON 6 Divide Using Related Multiplication Facts

LESSON OBJECTIVES
- Use related multiplication facts to find related division facts.
- Write a multiplication sentence and a related division sentence.
- Solve division word problems.

TECHNOLOGY RESOURCES
- *Math in Focus* eBooks
- *Math in Focus* Teacher Resources CD
- *Math in Focus* Virtual Manipulatives

DAY 1 Student Book 2A, pp. 179–185
Workbook 2A, pp. 145–150

MATERIALS
- 35 counters
- 12 craft sticks per group

DIFFERENTIATION RESOURCES
- Reteach 2A, pp. 135–138
- Extra Practice 2A, pp. 83–86

5-minute Warm Up

Children work in pairs to review multiplication tables of 2, 5, and 10. One child asks a multiplication question, for example, "What is 6 × 5?". His or her partner gives the answer. If the answer is correct, they switch roles. If the answer is incorrect, the child gets to ask another question.

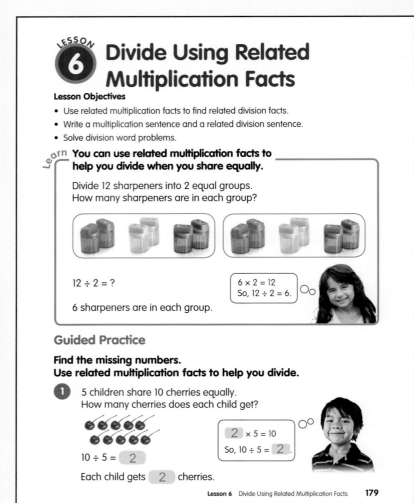

LESSON 6 Divide Using Related Multiplication Facts

Lesson Objectives
- Use related multiplication facts to find related division facts.
- Write a multiplication sentence and a related division sentence.
- Solve division word problems.

Learn **You can use related multiplication facts to help you divide when you share equally.**

Divide 12 sharpeners into 2 equal groups. How many sharpeners are in each group?

12 ÷ 2 = ?

6 × 2 = 12
So, 12 ÷ 2 = 6.

6 sharpeners are in each group.

Guided Practice

Find the missing numbers.
Use related multiplication facts to help you divide.

1. 5 children share 10 cherries equally. How many cherries does each child get?

10 ÷ 5 = 2

2 × 5 = 10
So, 10 ÷ 5 = 2.

Each child gets 2 cherries.

Lesson 6 Divide Using Related Multiplication Facts **179**

Student Book A p. 179

DAY 1 **Teach**

Learn

Use Related Multiplication Facts to Divide When Sharing Equally (page 179)

Children conceptualize division as the inverse of multiplication and as the equal sharing of items. Children learn to divide using related multiplication facts.

- Read the problem in the Student Book. Explain that it is a division problem that involves sharing. Help children see that there are 12 items to be divided into 2 equal groups.

- Write the division sentence 12 ÷ 2 = ___ on the board.

- Explain that one way to divide is to use related multiplication facts.

- Ask children to recall a related multiplication fact for 2 using the skip-counting strategy: 2, 4, 6, 8, 10, 12… to find the answer to 2 × ___ = 12.

- Children should give the answer 2 × **6** = 12, and deduce that 12 ÷ 2 = **6**.

2 Kelly puts 40 eggs equally on 10 trays.
How many eggs are on each tray?

$40 \div 10 = \boxed{4}$

$\boxed{4} \times 10 = 40$
So, $40 \div 10 = \boxed{4}$.

$\boxed{4}$ eggs are on each tray.

Learn You can use related multiplication facts to help you divide when you put things in equal groups.

Divide 35 cubes into equal groups.
There are 5 cubes in each group.
How many groups are there?

$7 \times 5 = 35$
So, $35 \div 5 = 7$.

$35 \div 5 = ?$

There are 7 groups.

180 Chapter 6 Multiplication Tables of 2, 5, and 10

Student Book A p. 180

Check for Understanding

Guided Practice (pages 179 and 180)

1 and **2** These exercises reinforce the concept of the inverse relationship between division and multiplication.

- Using a blank transparency or by drawing on the board, help the children group the cherries (or eggs) into 5 (or 10) equal groups by circling each group of 2 cherries (or 4 eggs).

- Point out that children can check their answers using multiplication.

n

Use Related Multiplication Facts to Divide When Putting Things in Equal Groups

(page 180)

Children conceptualize division as the inverse of multiplication and as the equal sharing of items. Children learn to divide using related multiplication facts.

- Read the problem in the Student Book. Explain that it is a division problem that involves putting a number of items into equal groups.

Sandy has 25 balloons. Derrick has 5 balloons.
(a) How many times as many balloons as Derrick does Sandy have?
(b) Sandy and Derrick combine all their balloons to be shared equally among 10 children. How many balloons will each child get?

Solution:
(a) The problem can be restated as: $5 \times \_\_ = 25$. The answer is 5.
(b) First, find the number of balloons they have in all:
$25 + 5 = 30$
They have 30 balloons in all.
Next, share or divide 30 equally by 10 children:
$30 \div 10 = 3$

Answer:
(a) Sandy has 5 times as many balloons as Derrick.
(b) Each child will get 3 balloons.

Differentiated Instruction

English Language Learners

Have children practice saying *multiplication* and *division*. Guide children to point to the multiplication symbol when they say *multiplication*. Repeat this procedure for the division symbol.

- Point out that this problem requires children to find the number of equal groups, while the problem in the previous Learn section required them to find the number of items in each equal group. Model the problems using **counters**, if necessary. Explain that division is used to solve both types of problem.

- Show children the groups and items that are shared.

35 cubes represent the total number of items

5 is the number of cubes in each group

- Write the sentence $35 \div 5 = _____$.

- Explain the strategy to find the related multiplication fact by recalling the multiplication facts of 5: 5, 10, 15, 20, 25, 30, 35, 40, 45, 50.

$7 \times 5 = 35$

So, $35 \div 5 = 7$

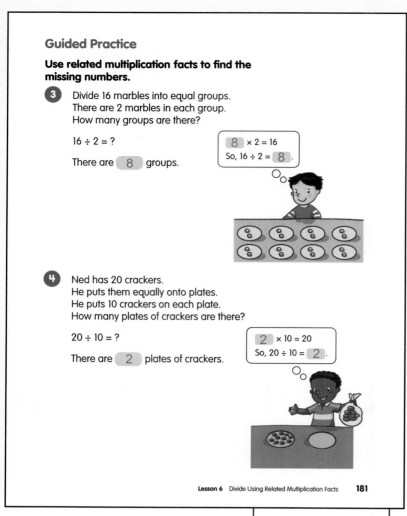

Guided Practice

Use related multiplication facts to find the missing numbers.

3 Divide 16 marbles into equal groups.
   There are 2 marbles in each group.
   How many groups are there?

   $16 \div 2 = ?$

   There are [8] groups.

   [8] $\times 2 = 16$
   So, $16 \div 2 =$ [8].

4 Ned has 20 crackers.
   He puts them equally onto plates.
   He puts 10 crackers on each plate.
   How many plates of crackers are there?

   $20 \div 10 = ?$

   There are [2] plates of crackers.

   [2] $\times 10 = 20$
   So, $20 \div 10 =$ [2].

Lesson 6 Divide Using Related Multiplication Facts **181**

Student Book A p. 181

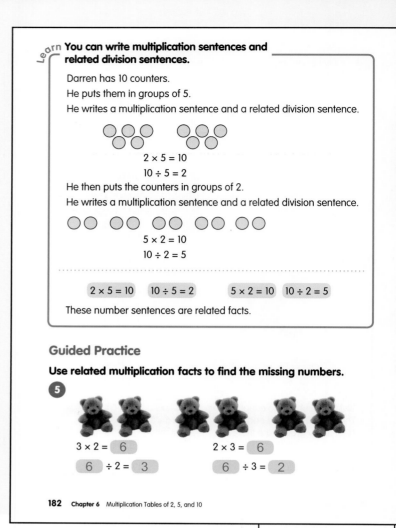

Learn You can write multiplication sentences and related division sentences.

Darren has 10 counters.
He puts them in groups of 5.
He writes a multiplication sentence and a related division sentence.

$2 \times 5 = 10$
$10 \div 5 = 2$

He then puts the counters in groups of 2.
He writes a multiplication sentence and a related division sentence.

$5 \times 2 = 10$
$10 \div 2 = 5$

$2 \times 5 = 10$ $10 \div 5 = 2$ $5 \times 2 = 10$ $10 \div 2 = 5$

These number sentences are related facts.

Guided Practice

Use related multiplication facts to find the missing numbers.

5

$3 \times 2 =$ [6] $2 \times 3 =$ [6]
[6] $\div 2 = 3$ [6] $\div 3 = 2$

182 Chapter 6 Multiplication Tables of 2, 5, and 10

Student Book A p. 182

✔ Guided Practice (page 181)

3 and 4 These exercises reinforce the concept of the inverse relationship between division and multiplication. Guide children to see how the items are grouped in the pictures in the Student Book. Remind children to use related multiplication facts to check their answers.

Best Practices Have children work in groups of four. Give each group several **counters**. Have one child use the counters to make two to five equal groups. Have the next child write the multiplication sentence that represents the groups of counters. Have the third child write the other multiplication sentence. Have the fourth child write both related division sentences.

Learn
Write Multiplication Sentences and Related Division Sentences (page 182)

Children conceptualize division as the inverse of multiplication and as the equal sharing of items. Children learn to write multiplication sentences and related division sentences.

- Help children relate the group and item concept in division to the context of the problem.

- Write the multiplication sentence $2 \times 5 = 10$, and lead children to see how the related division sentence $10 \div 5 = 2$ can be formulated from the same context.

- Do the same for the other multiplication sentence.

- Emphasize that all these sentences are called related facts.

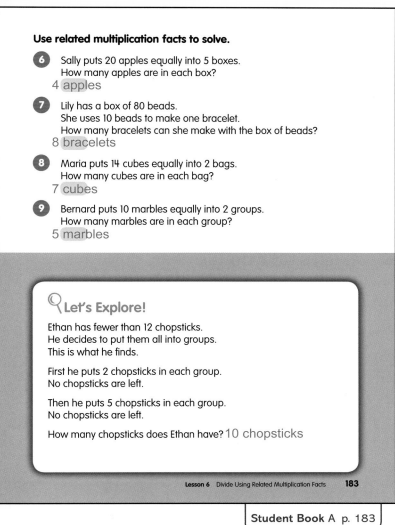

Use related multiplication facts to solve.

6 Sally puts 20 apples equally into 5 boxes.
How many apples are in each box?
4 apples

7 Lily has a box of 80 beads.
She uses 10 beads to make one bracelet.
How many bracelets can she make with the box of beads?
8 bracelets

8 Maria puts 14 cubes equally into 2 bags.
How many cubes are in each bag?
7 cubes

9 Bernard puts 10 marbles equally into 2 groups.
How many marbles are in each group?
5 marbles

Let's Explore!

Ethan has fewer than 12 chopsticks.
He decides to put them all into groups.
This is what he finds.

First he puts 2 chopsticks in each group.
No chopsticks are left.

Then he puts 5 chopsticks in each group.
No chopsticks are left.

How many chopsticks does Ethan have? 10 chopsticks

Lesson 6   Divide Using Related Multiplication Facts   **183**

Student Book A p. 183

Guided Practice (pages 182 and 183)

5 This exercise reinforces the concept of the inverse relationship between division and multiplication, and provides practice in writing related multiplication and division sentences.

6 to **9** These exercises require children to apply the strategy of using related multiplication and division sentences to solve real-world problems.

Let's Explore!

Find the Number of Items Given Different Ways of Grouping Them (page 183)

- Have children work in groups of three or four. Explain the question and give each group 12 **craft sticks**.

- Encourage children to model what Ethan did and explore with a different number of sticks to get the answer.

- After most groups have worked out the answer, discuss the activity. Lead children to deduce that the total number of chopsticks (fewer than 12) can be grouped into both 2s and 5s.

- Ask children to recite the multiplication facts of 2 and 5, and write:
  2: 2, 4, 6, 8, 10, 12
  5: 5, 10, 15

- Circle the common numbers in each row, and lead children to see that the number of chopsticks is 10.

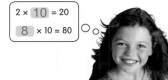

Let's Practice

Use related multiplication facts to find the missing numbers.

1 20 ÷ 2 = 10

2 80 ÷ 10 = 8

2 × 10 = 20
8 × 10 = 80

Divide.

3 45 ÷ 5 = 9

4 50 ÷ 10 = 5

Use related multiplication facts to find the missing numbers.

5 4 × 2 = 8   2 × 4 = 8   8 ÷ 2 = 4   8 ÷ 4 = 2

6 7 × 5 = 35   5 × 7 = 35   35 ÷ 5 = 7   35 ÷ 7 = 5

7 9 × 10 = 90   10 × 9 = 90   90 ÷ 10 = 9   90 ÷ 9 = 10

Find the missing number.
Then, write a related multiplication sentence and two related division sentences for the multiplication sentences.

8   4 × 5 = 20   5 × 4 = 20
       20 ÷ 5 = 4   20 ÷ 4 = 5

9   6 × 10 = 60   10 × 6 = 60
       60 ÷ 10 = 6   60 ÷ 10 = 6

Student Book A p. 184

Use related multiplication facts to solve.

10 Grandma shares 12 apples equally among her grandchildren.
Each grandchild gets 2 apples.
How many grandchildren are there? 6 grandchildren

11 Shara has 18 meatballs.
She puts an equal number of meatballs on 2 plates.
How many meatballs are on each plate? 9 meatballs

12 Raja divides 25 chairs equally among 5 tables.
How many chairs are at each table? 5 chairs

13 Mom makes 50 granola bars.
She packs them into bags of 5.
How many bags of granola bars are there? 10 bags

14 The second grade class goes on a bus trip.
There are 40 children in the class.
Each bus can seat 10 children.
How many buses do they need in all? 4 buses

15 Sharon picks 90 apples from 10 trees.
She picks the same number of apples from each tree.
How many apples does Sharon pick from each tree? 9 apples

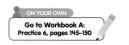

ON YOUR OWN
Go to Workbook A:
Practice 6, pages 145–150

Student Book A p. 185

Let's Practice (pages 184 and 185)

This provides more practice in using the inverse relationship of multiplication and division to deduce one from the other.

Exercises **1** and **2** prompt children to use a related multiplication fact.

Exercises **3** and **4** require children to think of the related multiplication fact on their own.

Exercises **5** to **9** allow children to complete sentences that involve related multiplication and division facts. You may want to encourage children to draw diagrams and circles to represent the items in groups to show division.

Exercises **10** to **15** provide additional practice in using related multiplication facts to solve real-world division problems.

Common Error Some children may choose incorrect related multiplication facts. Direct children who still have difficulty remembering basic facts to practice daily.

ON YOUR OWN

Children practice division using the related multiplication facts and sentences in Practice 6, pages 145 to 148. These pages (with the answers) are shown on page 185A. The Math Journal on pages 149 and 150 of **Workbook 2A** consolidates Lessons 1 to 6. These pages (with the answers) are shown on page 185B.

Differentiation Options Depending on children's success with the Workbook pages, use these materials as needed.
Struggling: Reteach 2A, pp. 135–138
On Level: Extra Practice 2A, pp. 83–86

Practice and Apply
Workbook pages for Chapter 6, Lesson 6

Name: _____ **Date:** _____

Practice 6 Divide Using Related Multiplication Facts

Complete the multiplication sentences.
Then complete the division sentences.

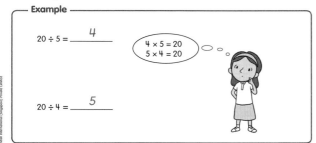

Example

$20 \div 5 = \underline{4}$

$4 \times 5 = 20$
$5 \times 4 = 20$

$20 \div 4 = \underline{5}$

1. $4 \times \underline{2} = 8$

$\underline{2} \times 4 = 8$

$8 \div 2 = \underline{4}$

$8 \div 4 = \underline{2}$

2. $5 \times \underline{5} = 25$

$\underline{5} \times 5 = 25$

$25 \div 5 = \underline{5}$

Workbook A p. 145

Name: _____ **Date:** _____

Use related multiplication facts to solve.

9. The art teacher divides 30 beads equally among 5 children.
How many beads does each child get?

$\underline{30} \div \underline{5} = \underline{6}$

Each child gets __6__ beads.

10. Jeff uses 40 craft sticks to make squares of the same size.
He makes 10 squares like the one shown.
How many craft sticks does he use to make 1 square?

$\underline{40} \div \underline{10} = \underline{4}$

He uses __4__ craft sticks to make 1 square.

11. Mr. Lee has 16 notebooks.
He gives each student 2 notebooks.
How many students does Mr. Lee have?

$\underline{16} \div \underline{2} = \underline{8}$

Mr. Lee has __8__ students.

Workbook A p. 147

---

3. $\underline{6} \times 2 = 12$

$2 \times \underline{6} = 12$

$12 \div 2 = \underline{6}$

$12 \div 6 = \underline{2}$

4. $\underline{3} \times 5 = 15$

$5 \times \underline{3} = 15$

$15 \div 5 = \underline{3}$

$15 \div 3 = \underline{5}$

5. $\underline{7} \times 10 = 70$

$10 \times \underline{7} = 70$

$70 \div 10 = \underline{7}$

$70 \div 7 = \underline{10}$

6. $\underline{7} \times 2 = 14$

$2 \times \underline{7} = 14$

$14 \div 2 = \underline{7}$

$14 \div 7 = \underline{2}$

7. $\underline{6} \times 10 = 60$

$10 \times \underline{6} = 60$

$60 \div 10 = \underline{6}$

$60 \div 6 = \underline{10}$

8. $\underline{7} \times 5 = 35$

$5 \times \underline{7} = 35$

$35 \div 5 = \underline{7}$

$35 \div 7 = \underline{5}$

Workbook A p. 146

Find the missing number.
Then, write one related multiplication sentence.
Write two related division sentences.

Example

$\underline{3} \times 2 = 6$ $2 \times \underline{3} = 6$

$6 \div \underline{2} = \underline{3}$ $6 \div \underline{3} = \underline{2}$

12. $\underline{6} \times 5 = 30$ $5 \times \underline{6} = 30$

$30 \div \underline{5} = \underline{6}$ $30 \div \underline{6} = \underline{5}$

13. $\underline{3} \times 5 = 15$ $5 \times \underline{3} = 15$

$15 \div \underline{5} = \underline{3}$ $15 \div \underline{3} = \underline{5}$

14. $\underline{7} \times 10 = 70$ $\underline{10} \times 7 = 70$

$70 \div \underline{10} = \underline{7}$ $70 \div \underline{7} = \underline{10}$

15. $\underline{10} \times 5 = 50$ $5 \times \underline{10} = 50$

$50 \div \underline{5} = \underline{10}$ $50 \div \underline{10} = \underline{5}$

16. $\underline{8} \times 2 = 16$ $2 \times \underline{8} = 16$

$16 \div \underline{2} = \underline{8}$ $16 \div \underline{8} = \underline{2}$

Workbook A p. 148

Notes

Name: _____ Date: _____

📖 Math Journal

$5
diary

$2
pen

$10
dictionary

Look at the pictures.
Write multiplication stories.
Use multiplication tables of 5 and 10.

— Example —

Mandy bought 10 pens.

She paid $2 for each pen.

How much did she pay altogether?

_____

— Story A —

Answers vary.

Workbook A p. 149

Look at the pictures on page 149.
Write multiplication stories.
Use multiplication tables of 5 and 10.

— Story B —

Answers vary.

— Story C —

Answers vary.

Workbook A p. 150

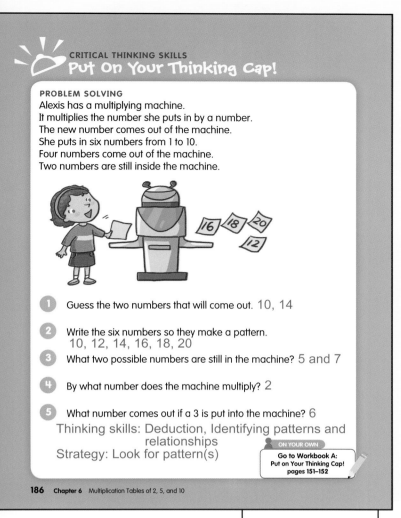

CRITICAL THINKING SKILLS
Put On Your Thinking Cap!

PROBLEM SOLVING

Alexis has a multiplying machine.
It multiplies the number she puts in by a number.
The new number comes out of the machine.
She puts in six numbers from 1 to 10.
Four numbers come out of the machine.
Two numbers are still inside the machine.

1. Guess the two numbers that will come out. 10, 14

2. Write the six numbers so they make a pattern.
   10, 12, 14, 16, 18, 20

3. What two possible numbers are still in the machine? 5 and 7

4. By what number does the machine multiply? 2

5. What number comes out if a 3 is put into the machine? 6

Thinking skills: Deduction, Identifying patterns and relationships
Strategy: Look for pattern(s)

ON YOUR OWN
Go to Workbook A:
Put on Your Thinking Cap!
pages 151–152

Student Book A p. 186

 CRITICAL THINKING AND PROBLEM SOLVING

Put on Your Thinking Cap! (page 186)

This problem solving exercise involves a multiplying machine with a rule of "multiply by 2." Children work individually or in groups to answer the questions and to present the solutions to the class.

- Pose the problems to children. Allow children to work on the solutions in their groups.

- If necessary, help children by writing the numbers 16, 18, 20, and 12 (from the picture in the Student Book) on the board. Have them arrange the numbers in ascending order and guide them to see the number pattern.

- Discuss the answers to the exercises with the class.

Thinking Skills

- Deduction
- Identifying patterns and relationships

Problem Solving Strategy

- Look for pattern(s)

ON YOUR OWN

Because all children should be challenged, have all children try the Challenging Practice and Problem Solving pages in **Workbook 2A,** pages 151 and 152. These pages (with the answers) are shown on page 186A.

Differentiation Options

On Level: Extra Practice 2A, pp. 87–88
Advanced: Enrichment 2A, pp. 45–56

Practice and Apply

Workbook pages for Put on Your Thinking Cap!

Name: _____ Date: _____

Put On Your Thinking Cap!

Challenging Practice

Fill in the blanks with the correct numbers.

Thinking skill: Identifying patterns and relationships
Strategy: Solve part of the problem

Chapter 6   Multiplication Tables of 2, 5, and 10   **151**

Workbook A p. 151

Put On Your Thinking Cap!

Problem Solving

Solve.

A shop sells oranges and apples packed as shown.

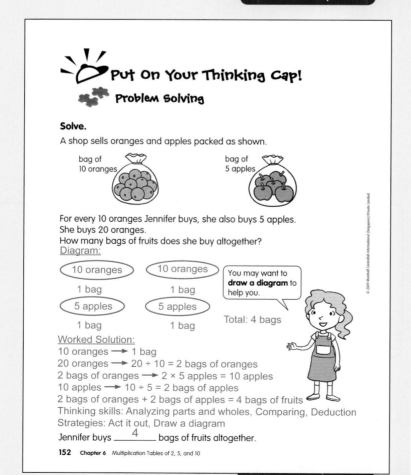

bag of
10 oranges

bag of
5 apples

For every 10 oranges Jennifer buys, she also buys 5 apples.
She buys 20 oranges.
How many bags of fruits does she buy altogether?

Diagram:

10 oranges	10 oranges
1 bag	1 bag
5 apples	5 apples
1 bag	1 bag

You may want to **draw a diagram** to help you.

Total: 4 bags

Worked Solution:
10 oranges ➝ 1 bag
20 oranges ➝ 20 ÷ 10 = 2 bags of oranges
2 bags of oranges ➝ 2 × 5 apples = 10 apples
10 apples ➝ 10 ÷ 5 = 2 bags of apples
2 bags of oranges + 2 bags of apples = 4 bags of fruits
Thinking skills: Analyzing parts and wholes, Comparing, Deduction
Strategies: Act it out, Draw a diagram

Jennifer buys ___4___ bags of fruits altogether.

152   Chapter 6   Multiplication Tables of 2, 5, and 10

Workbook A p. 152

Notes

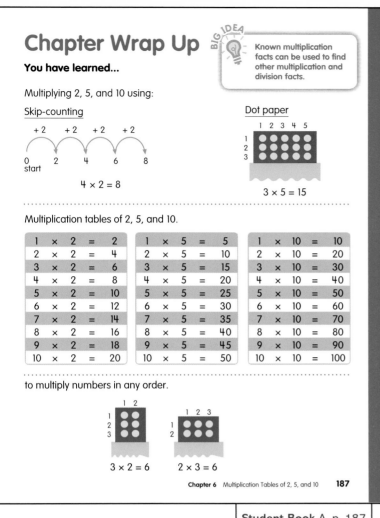

Chapter Wrap Up

You have learned...

BIG IDEA
Known multiplication facts can be used to find other multiplication and division facts.

Multiplying 2, 5, and 10 using:

Skip-counting

+ 2   + 2   + 2   + 2

0   2   4   6   8
start

$4 \times 2 = 8$

Dot paper

1 2 3 4 5

$3 \times 5 = 15$

Multiplication tables of 2, 5, and 10.

1	×	2	=	2		1	×	5	=	5		1	×	10	=	10
2	×	2	=	4		2	×	5	=	10		2	×	10	=	20
3	×	2	=	6		3	×	5	=	15		3	×	10	=	30
4	×	2	=	8		4	×	5	=	20		4	×	10	=	40
5	×	2	=	10		5	×	5	=	25		5	×	10	=	50
6	×	2	=	12		6	×	5	=	30		6	×	10	=	60
7	×	2	=	14		7	×	5	=	35		7	×	10	=	70
8	×	2	=	16		8	×	5	=	40		8	×	10	=	80
9	×	2	=	18		9	×	5	=	45		9	×	10	=	90
10	×	2	=	20		10	×	5	=	50		10	×	10	=	100

to multiply numbers in any order.

$3 \times 2 = 6$ $2 \times 3 = 6$

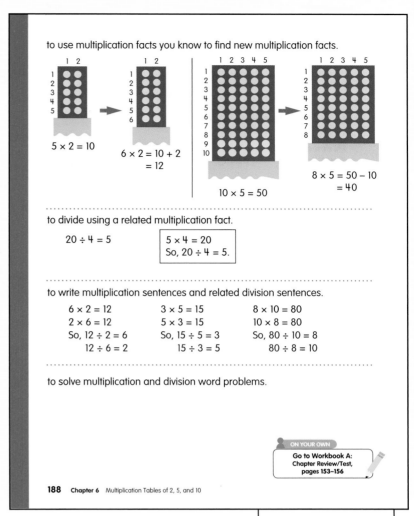

to use multiplication facts you know to find new multiplication facts.

$5 \times 2 = 10$

$6 \times 2 = 10 + 2$
$\qquad = 12$

$10 \times 5 = 50$

$8 \times 5 = 50 - 10$
$\qquad = 40$

to divide using a related multiplication fact.

$20 \div 4 = 5$

$5 \times 4 = 20$
So, $20 \div 4 = 5$.

to write multiplication sentences and related division sentences.

$6 \times 2 = 12$ $3 \times 5 = 15$ $8 \times 10 = 80$
$2 \times 6 = 12$ $5 \times 3 = 15$ $10 \times 8 = 80$
So, $12 \div 2 = 6$ So, $15 \div 5 = 3$ So, $80 \div 10 = 8$
$12 \div 6 = 2$ $15 \div 3 = 5$ $80 \div 8 = 10$

to solve multiplication and division word problems.

ON YOUR OWN
Go to Workbook A:
Chapter Review/Test,
pages 153–156

Chapter Wrap Up (pages 187 and 188)

Use the examples on pages 187 and 188 to review multiplication by 2, 5, and 10. As you work through the examples, encourage children to use the chapter vocabulary:

- skip-count
- dot paper
- related multiplication facts

ON YOUR OWN

Have children review the vocabulary, concepts, and skills from Chapter 6 with the Chapter Review/Test in **Workbook 2A**, pages 153 to 156. These pages (with the answers) are shown on page 188A.

You may also want to use the Cumulative Review for Chapters 5 and 6 from **Workbook 2A**, pages 157 to 164. These pages (with the answers) are shown on pages 188C and 188D.

Assessment

Use the Chapter 6 Test Prep on pages 35 to 37 of **Assessments 2** to assess how well children have learned the material of this chapter.

This assessment is appropriate for reporting results to adults at home and administrators.

This test is shown on page 188B.

You may also wish to use Benchmark Assessment 1 for Chapters 1 to 6 on pages 38 to 45 of **Assessments 2**.

This test is shown on page 188E

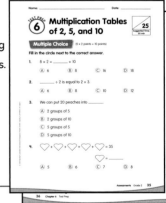

Assessments 2 pp. 35–37

Workbook pages for Chapter Review/Test

Name: _____ **Date:** _____

Chapter Review/Test

Vocabulary
Fill in the blanks.
Circle the words that belong.

1. 15, __20__, 25, 30, __35__, 40

   To find the answer, (multiply / skip-count) by fives.

2. | 5 × 2 = 10 | | 2 × 5 = 10 |

   These are (addition facts / related multiplication facts).

Concepts and Skills
Use dot paper to find the missing numbers.

3.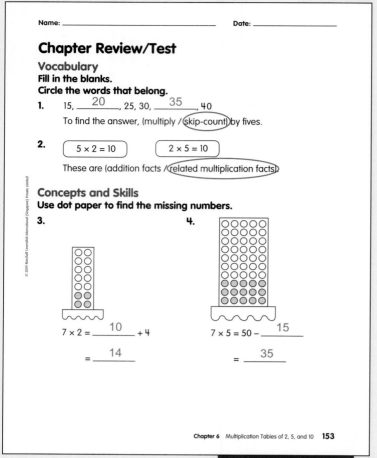

   7 × 2 = __10__ + 4

   = __14__

4.

   7 × 5 = 50 – __15__

   = __35__

Chapter 6 Multiplication Tables of 2, 5, and 10 **153**

Name: _____ **Date:** _____

Use dot paper to find the missing numbers.

8. 7 × 10 = __70__   10 × 7 = __70__

Find the missing numbers.
Then match the numbers to the letters to answer the riddle.

9. | 6 × 2 = 12 **A** | 5 × 3 = 15 **E** | 7 × 2 = 14 **I** |
   | 8 × 5 = 40 **L** | 10 × 9 = 90 **N** | 10 × 5 = 50 **P** |
   | 9 × 2 = 18 **S** | 8 × 10 = 80 **V** | 3 × 10 = 30 **Y** |

   I am named after Admiral Penn.
   What state am I?

   $\underset{50}{P}\ \underset{15}{E}\ \underset{90}{N}\ \underset{90}{N}\ \underset{18}{S}\ \underset{30}{Y}\ \underset{40}{L}\ \underset{80}{V}\ \underset{12}{A}\ \underset{90}{N}\ \underset{14}{I}\ \underset{12}{A}$!

Use related multiplication facts to find the missing numbers.

10. 4 × 2 = 8
    So, 8 ÷ 2 = __4__.

11. 3 × 5 = 15
    So, 15 ÷ 3 = __5__.

12. 9 × 10 = 90
    So, 90 ÷ 10 = __9__.

13. 5 × 10 = 50
    So, 50 ÷ 5 = __10__.

Chapter 6 Multiplication Tables of 2, 5, and 10 **155**

Use dot paper to find the missing numbers.

5.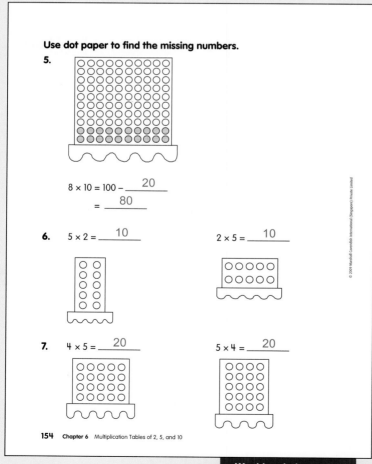

   8 × 10 = 100 – __20__

   = __80__

6. 5 × 2 = __10__   2 × 5 = __10__

7. 4 × 5 = __20__   5 × 4 = __20__

154 Chapter 6 Multiplication Tables of 2, 5, and 10

Problem Solving
Use skip-counting or dot paper to solve.

14. Teddy grills 8 skewers of chicken.
    Each skewer has 2 pieces of chicken.
    How many pieces of chicken does he grill?

    8 × 2 = 16

    He grills __16__ pieces of chicken.

15. Naomi pastes 9 star stickers on each piece of paper.
    There are 5 pieces of paper.
    How many star stickers are on the pieces of paper?

    9 × 5 = 45

    There are __45__ star stickers on the pieces of paper.

Use related multiplication facts to solve.

16. Mr. Wilson picks 60 strawberries.
    He gives an equal number of strawberries to 10 children.
    How many strawberries does each child get?

    60 ÷ 10 = 6

    Each child gets __6__ strawberries.

17. Jess gives away 20 pennies.
    She gives each friend 5 pennies.
    How many friends are there?

    20 ÷ 5 = 4

    There are __4__ friends.

156 Chapter 6 Multiplication Tables of 2, 5, and 10

Assessments Book pages for Chapter 6 Test Prep
Answer key appears in Assessments Book.

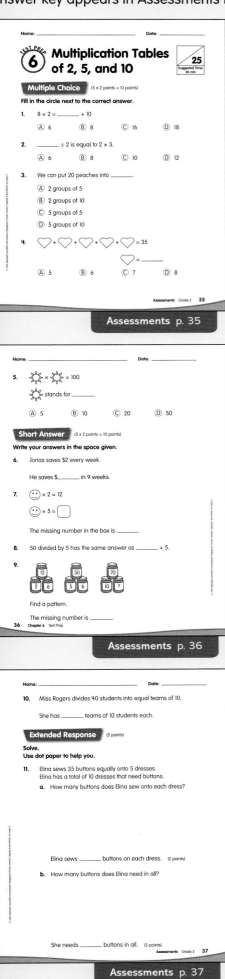

Name: _____ Date: _____

TEST PREP 6 Multiplication Tables of 2, 5, and 10

25 Suggested Time: 30 min

Multiple Choice (5 × 2 points = 10 points)

Fill in the circle next to the correct answer.

1. $8 \times 2 = $ _____ $+ 10$

   Ⓐ 6   Ⓑ 8   Ⓒ 16   Ⓓ 18

2. _____ ÷ 2 is equal to 2 × 3.

   Ⓐ 6   Ⓑ 8   Ⓒ 10   Ⓓ 12

3. We can put 20 peaches into _____

   Ⓐ 2 groups of 5
   Ⓑ 2 groups of 10
   Ⓒ 5 groups of 5
   Ⓓ 5 groups of 10

4. ♡ + ♡ + ♡ + ♡ + ♡ = 35

   ♡ = _____

   Ⓐ 5   Ⓑ 6   Ⓒ 7   Ⓓ 8

Assessments Grade 2 **35**

Assessments p. 35

Name: _____ Date: _____

5. ✳ × ✳ = 100

   ✳ stands for _____

   Ⓐ 5   Ⓑ 10   Ⓒ 20   Ⓓ 50

Short Answer (5 × 2 points = 10 points)

Write your answers in the space given.

6. Jonas saves $2 every week.

   He saves $_____ in 9 weeks.

7. ☺ × 2 = 12

   ☺ × 5 = ☐

   The missing number in the box is _____

8. 50 divided by 5 has the same answer as _____ + 5.

9. [12 | 2 6] [30 | 5 6] [70 | 10 ?]

   Find a pattern.

   The missing number is _____

36 Chapter 6 Test Prep

Assessments p. 36

Name: _____ Date: _____

10. Miss Rogers divides 40 students into equal teams of 10.

    She has _____ teams of 10 students each.

Extended Response (5 points)

Solve.
Use dot paper to help you.

11. Elina sews 35 buttons equally onto 5 dresses.
    Elina has a total of 10 dresses that need buttons.

    a. How many buttons does Elina sew onto each dress?

    Elina sews _____ buttons on each dress. (2 points)

    b. How many buttons does Elina need in all?

    She needs _____ buttons in all. (3 points)

Assessments Grade 2 **37**

Assessments p. 37

Cumulative Review for Chapters 5 and 6

Name: _____ Date: _____

Cumulative Review
for Chapters 5 and 6

Concepts and Skills

Draw ☺.

1. Draw 4 groups of 3 ☺.

☺ ☺   ☺ ☺   ☺ ☺   ☺ ☺
☺   ☺   ☺   ☺

2. Draw 3 groups of 4 ☺.

☺ ☺   ☺ ☺   ☺ ☺
☺ ☺   ☺ ☺   ☺ ☺

Find the missing numbers.

3. 2 + 2 + 2 + 2 + 2 + 2 = __6__ × 2

4. 3 + 3 + 3 + 3 + 3 is __5__ groups of __3__.

5.    3 × 4 = __12__

12 ÷ __4__ = 3

6. ♥ ♥ ♥ ♥   ♥ ♥ ♥ ♥   ♥ ♥ ♥ ♥   24 ÷ 3 = __8__
♥ ♥ ♥ ♥   ♥ ♥ ♥ ♥   ♥ ♥ ♥ ♥   24 ÷ 8 = __3__

Workbook A p. 157

Find the missing numbers.

7. Divide 20 socks so there are 5 socks in each group.

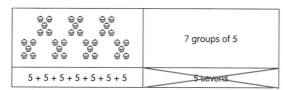

Subtract groups of 5 until there is nothing left.

20 − __5__ − __5__ − __5__ − __5__ = __0__

Groups of five are subtracted __4__ times.

20 ÷ 5 = __4__

Cross out what does not belong.

8.

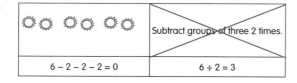

| | 7 groups of 5 |
| 5 + 5 + 5 + 5 + 5 + 5 + 5 | ~~5 sevens~~ |

9.

| ✺✺ ✺✺ ✺✺ | ~~Subtract groups of three 2 times.~~ |
| 6 − 2 − 2 − 2 = 0 | ~~6 ÷ 2 = 3~~ |

Workbook A p. 158

Name: _____ Date: _____

Fill in the blanks.

10. Divide 16 fruit bars equally on 4 trays.

16 ÷ __4__ = __4__

There are __4__ fruit bars on each tray.

11. 6 bugs are on each of the 3 branches.

6 × __3__ = __18__

There are __18__ bugs altogether.

12. Divide 20 crayons equally among 5 children.

20 ÷ __5__ = __4__

Each child gets __4__ crayons.

Workbook A p. 159

Skip-count.

13. 2, 4, 6, __8__, __10__, __12__, __14__, __16__, __18__, __20__

14. 5, 10, 15, __20__, __25__, __30__, __35__, __40__, __45__, __50__

15. 10, 20, 30, __40__, __50__, __60__, __70__, __80__, __90__, __100__

Fill in the blanks.

16. 2 groups of 2 = __2__ × __2__ = __4__

17. 5 groups of 2 = __5__ × __2__ = __10__

18. 6 groups of 5 = __6__ × __5__ = __30__

19. 7 groups of 5 = __7__ × __5__ = __35__

Use the dot paper to find the missing numbers.

20.

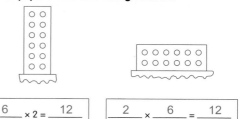

| __6__ × 2 = __12__ |

| __2__ × __6__ = __12__ |

Workbook A p. 160

Name: _____ **Date:** _____

21.

$\underline{4} \times \underline{5} = \underline{20}$ $\underline{5} \times \underline{4} = \underline{20}$

Complete the multiplication sentences.

22. $4 \times 2 = \underline{8}$ **23.** $7 \times 2 = \underline{14}$

$2 \times 4 = \underline{8}$ $2 \times 7 = \underline{14}$

24. $3 \times 5 = \underline{15}$ **25.** $9 \times 5 = \underline{45}$

$5 \times 3 = \underline{15}$ $5 \times 9 = \underline{45}$

26. $4 \times 10 = \underline{40}$ **27.** $6 \times 10 = \underline{60}$

$10 \times 4 = \underline{40}$ $10 \times 6 = \underline{60}$

Fill in the blanks.

28. $\underline{8} \times 2 = 16$ **29.** $\underline{9} \times 2 = 18$

30. $\underline{8} \times 5 = 40$ **31.** $\underline{5} \times 5 = 25$

32. $\underline{7} \times 10 = 70$ **33.** $\underline{5} \times 10 = 50$

Complete the multiplication and division sentences.

34. $\underline{5} \times 2 = 10$ $10 \div 2 = \underline{5}$

35. $\underline{6} \times 5 = 30$ $30 \div 5 = \underline{6}$

36. $\underline{2} \times 10 = 20$ $20 \div 10 = \underline{2}$

Workbook A p. 161

Problem Solving

Solve.

37. A grocer sells 5 oranges in a bag.
Mr. Diaz buys 6 bags of oranges.
How many oranges does he buy in all?

$6 \times 5 = 30$

He buys $\underline{30}$ oranges in all.

38. Shauna puts some chairs in rows of 9.
There are 2 rows of chairs.
How many chairs are there?

$9 \times 2 = 18$

There are $\underline{18}$ chairs.

Workbook A p. 162

Name: _____ **Date:** _____

39. Ling's Travel has 10 new alarm clocks.
Each clock needs 4 batteries.
How many batteries are needed in all?

$10 \times 4 = 40$

$\underline{40}$ batteries are needed in all.

40. There are 18 seashells.
They are divided into 2 equal groups.
How many seashells are in each group?

$18 \div 2 = 9$

$\underline{9}$ seashells are in each group.

Workbook A p. 163

---

41. Mr. Jenkins spends $30 on books.
Each book costs $10.
How many books does Mr. Jenkins buy?

$30 \div 10 = 3$

Mr. Jenkins buys $\underline{3}$ books.

42. The school chef has 30 mini pizzas.
She divides them equally among a few children.
  a. If each child gets 5 mini pizzas, how many children are there?
  b. If there are 10 children, how many mini pizzas will each
     child get?

$30 \div 5 = 6$

  a. There are $\underline{6}$ children.

$30 \div 10 = 3$

  b. Each child will get $\underline{3}$ mini pizzas.

Workbook A p. 164

Assessments Book pages for Benchmark Assessment 1 for Chapters 1 to 6

Answer key appears in Assessments Book.

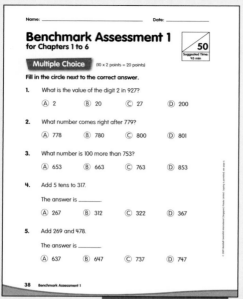

Assessments p. 38

Name: _____ Date: _____

Benchmark Assessment 1
for Chapters 1 to 6

50
Suggested Time: 45 min

Multiple Choice (10 × 2 points = 20 points)

Fill in the circle next to the correct answer.

1. What is the value of the digit 2 in 927?
   (A) 2 (B) 20 (C) 27 (D) 200

2. What number comes right after 779?
   (A) 778 (B) 780 (C) 800 (D) 801

3. What number is 100 more than 753?
   (A) 653 (B) 663 (C) 763 (D) 853

4. Add 5 tens to 317.
   The answer is _____
   (A) 267 (B) 312 (C) 322 (D) 367

5. Add 269 and 478.
   The answer is _____
   (A) 637 (B) 647 (C) 737 (D) 747

38 Benchmark Assessment 1

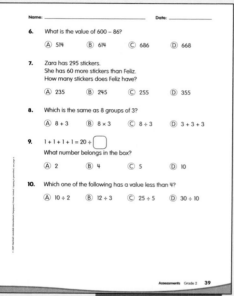

Assessments p. 39

Name: _____ Date: _____

6. What is the value of 600 − 86?
   (A) 514 (B) 614 (C) 686 (D) 668

7. Zara has 295 stickers.
   She has 60 more stickers than Feliz.
   How many stickers does Feliz have?
   (A) 235 (B) 245 (C) 255 (D) 355

8. Which is the same as 8 groups of 3?
   (A) 8 + 3 (B) 8 × 3 (C) 8 ÷ 3 (D) 3 + 3 + 3

9. 1 + 1 + 1 + 1 = 20 ÷ ☐
   What number belongs in the box?
   (A) 2 (B) 4 (C) 5 (D) 10

10. Which one of the following has a value less than 4?
    (A) 10 ÷ 2 (B) 12 ÷ 3 (C) 25 ÷ 5 (D) 30 ÷ 10

Assessments Grade 2 39

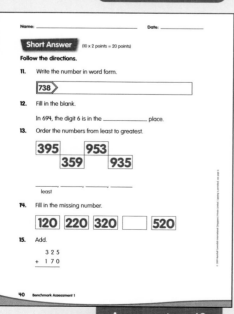

Assessments p. 40

Name: _____ Date: _____

Short Answer (10 × 2 points = 20 points)

Follow the directions.

11. Write the number in word form.
    738 ▷ _____

12. Fill in the blank.
    In 694, the digit 6 is in the _____ place.

13. Order the numbers from least to greatest.
    395 **953**
    359 **935**
    _____ _____ _____ _____
    least

14. Fill in the missing number.
    120 **220** **320** **☐** **520**

15. Add.
    ```
      3 2 5
    + 1 7 0
    ```

40 Benchmark Assessment 1

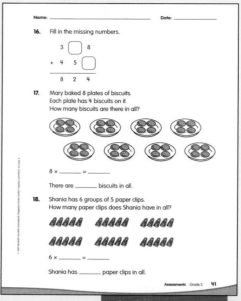

Assessments p. 41

Name: _____ Date: _____

16. Fill in the missing numbers.
    ```
       3 ☐ 8
    +  4 5 ☐
    ───────
       8 2 4
    ```

17. Mary baked 8 plates of biscuits.
    Each plate has 4 biscuits on it.
    How many biscuits are there in all?

    8 × _____ = _____
    There are _____ biscuits in all.

18. Shania has 6 groups of 5 paper clips.
    How many paper clips does Shania have in all?

    6 × _____ = _____
    Shania has _____ paper clips in all.

Assessments Grade 2 41

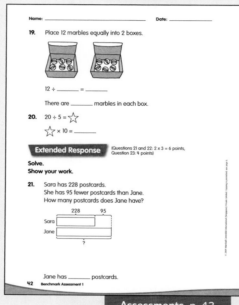

Assessments p. 42

Name: _____ Date: _____

19. Place 12 marbles equally into 2 boxes.

    12 ÷ _____ = _____
    There are _____ marbles in each box.

20. 20 ÷ 5 = ☆
    ☆ × 10 = _____

Extended Response (Questions 21 and 22: 2 × 3 = 6 points, Question 23: 4 points)

Solve.
Show your work.

21. Sara has 228 postcards.
    She has 95 fewer postcards than Jane.
    How many postcards does Jane have?

    Sara | 228 | 95 |
    Jane | |
           ?

    Jane has _____ postcards.

42 Benchmark Assessment 1

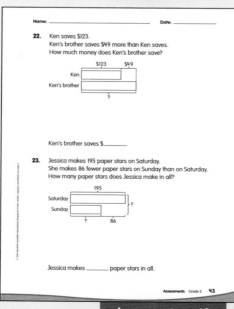

Assessments p. 43

Name: _____ Date: _____

22. Ken saves $123.
    Ken's brother saves $49 more than Ken saves.
    How much money does Ken's brother save?

    Ken | $123 | $49 |
    Ken's brother | |
                    ?

    Ken's brother saves $_____.

23. Jessica makes 195 paper stars on Saturday.
    She makes 86 fewer paper stars on Sunday than on Saturday.
    How many paper stars does Jessica make in all?

    Saturday | 195 |
    Sunday | | ?
           ?   86

    Jessica makes _____ paper stars in all.

Assessments Grade 2 43

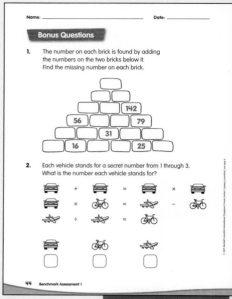

Assessments p. 44

Name: _____ Date: _____

Bonus Questions

1. The number on each brick is found by adding
   the numbers on the two bricks below it.
   Find the missing number on each brick.

   ☐
   ☐ 142
   56 ☐ 79
   ☐ 31 ☐
   16 ☐ 25

2. Each vehicle stands for a secret number from 1 through 3.
   What is the number each vehicle stands for?

   🚗 + 🚗 = 🚗 × 🚗
   🚗 × 🚲 = ✈ − 🚲
   ✈ ÷ ✈ = 🚲

   🚗 🚲 ✈
   ☐   ☐   ☐

44 Benchmark Assessment 1

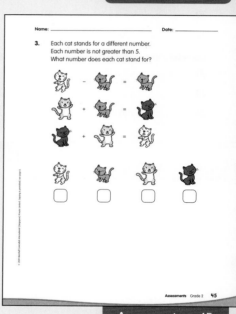

Assessments p. 45

Name: _____ Date: _____

3. Each cat stands for a different number.
   Each number is not greater than 5.
   What number does each cat stand for?

   ☐ ☐ ☐ ☐

Assessments Grade 2 45

188E CHAPTERS 1 TO 6: ASSESSMENT ANCILLARY

Chapter Overview

Metric Measurement of Length

Math Background

Children learned how to find and compare lengths in Grade 1 using non-standard units of measure. For example, they learned to estimate and compare length with reference to a non-standard unit such as a paper clip. In Grade 2, children also learned addition and subtraction up to 1,000 with and without regrouping in Chapters 2 and 3, as well as using bar models in Chapter 4 to solve real-world problems.

In this chapter, children learn to estimate and measure medium and short lengths using the standard metric units of meters (m) and centimeters (cm). The meterstick and centimeter ruler are used to illustrate length as a concept of measure to determine how long or short an object is. The length of curved lines can be measured with the help of a piece of string which is placed along the curved line and then measured with a ruler. Children are also led to see that the standard units of measure provide a basis for the comparison of lengths. To further reinforce children's understanding of length, children are taught to draw lines of specific lengths.

Also, children learn to apply addition and subtraction concepts taught in earlier chapters to real-world problems involving metric length. Children use bar models to represent the part-whole concept to help them solve real-world problems involving length and short distances.

Cross-Curricular Connections

Reading/Language Arts Read aloud **Measuring Penny** by Loreen Leedy (Henry Holt, © 2000) about Lisa and her Boston terrier dog, Penny. Lisa's teacher gave her an assignment to measure something in as many ways as possible. Lisa decides to measure Penny many different ways.

Social Studies Display a map of your school, neighborhood, or city. Look at the map scale. Duplicate this scale on the edge of a sheet of paper and have children practice measuring the distances between places, streets, and so on.

Skills Trace

Grade 1	Compare the height and length of more than two things. Measure and compare using non-standard units. (Chap. 9)
Grade 2	Measure and compare length in meters and centimeters. Add and subtract length with the help of bar models. (Chap. 7)
Grade 3	Measure length, mass, and volume using metric units of measurement. Then, solve one- and two-step problems on measurements using bar models. (Chaps. 11 and 12) Measure length, weight and capacity in customary units and solve real-world problems. (Chap. 15)

EVERY DAY COUNTS®
Calendar Math

The December activities provide...

Review of the relationship between addition and subtraction (Chapter 4)

Preview of organizing and analyzing data (Chapter 17)

Practice of relating word problems to symbolic number sentences (Lesson 5 in this chapter)

Differentiation Resources

Differentiation for Special Populations

	English Language Learners	Struggling Reteach 2A	On Level Extra Practice 2A	Advanced Enrichment 2A
Lesson 1	p. 193	pp. 139–142	pp. 99–102	Enrichment pages can be used to challenge advanced children.
Lesson 2	p. 197	pp. 143–144	pp. 103–104	
Lesson 3	p. 202	pp. 145–150	pp. 105–106	
Lesson 4	p. 212	pp. 151–152	pp. 107–108	
Lesson 5	p. 217	pp. 153–156	pp. 109–114	

Additional Support

For English Language Learners

Select activities that reinforce the chapter vocabulary and the connections among these words, such as having children

- add terms, definitions, and examples to the Word Wall

- act out measuring length and height and use vocabulary terms to describe actions

- draw and label pictures to illustrate each term

- discuss the Chapter Wrap Up, encouraging children to use the chapter vocabulary

For Struggling Learners

Select activities that go back to the appropriate stage of the Concrete-Pictorial-Abstract spectrum, such as having children

- identify classroom objects to represent different measures of length

- draw pictures to illustrate comparisons of different measures of length

- order classroom objects from least to greatest length and/or heights

- create and solve new stories for given measures

See also pages 197 and 203–204

If necessary, review

- Chapter 1 (Addition to 1,000).

For Advanced Learners

See suggestions on pages 209–210 and 221.

Practice and Apply
Workbook pages for Chapter 7, Lesson 1

Name: _____ Date: _____

Metric Measurement of Length

Practice 1   Measuring in Meters

Look at the pictures.
Fill in the blanks with *more* or *less*.

1.

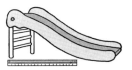

The length of the rope is ___less___ than 1 meter.

2.

The length of the slide is ___more___ than 1 meter.

3.

The height of the bookcase is ___more___ than 1 meter.

Workbook A p. 165

Name: _____ Date: _____

Look at the list below.
Check (✔) the columns that are true.
You will need a meterstick or a 1-meter string to measure some items.

Answers vary.

6.

Object	Less than 1 meter	More than 1 meter	More than 1 meter but less than 2 meters	More than 2 meters
Door				
Desk				
Bed				
Computer monitor				
Trash can				

Workbook A p. 167

Fill in the blanks.

4. Metersticks are placed against two boxes.

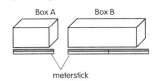

Box A   Box B

meterstick

a. Which box is about 1 meter long? Box ___A___

Fill in the blanks with *more* or *less*.

b. Box A is ___less___ than 1 meter long.

c. Box B is ___more___ than 1 meter long.

5. Metersticks are placed against a board.

Side A
Side B
meterstick

a. Which side of the board is about 3 meters long?

Side ___B___

b. Side A is shorter than ___1___ meter.

c. Side B is shorter than ___3___ meters.

Workbook A p. 166

Name three things that match each length.
Answers vary.

7.

Length	Things
Less than 1 meter long	
About 1 meter long	
More than 1 meter long	

Fill in the blanks.
Use string and a meterstick.   Answers vary.

8. Mark on the string with a pencil how long you think 1 meter is.
Then use a meterstick to measure this length.
Did you mark more or less than 1 meter on your string?

_____

9. Next, mark on the string how long you think 2 meters are.
Then use a meterstick to measure this length.
Did you mark more or less than 2 meters on your string?

_____

Workbook A p. 168

LESSON 2 Comparing Lengths in Meters

LESSON OBJECTIVES
- Compare lengths.
- Find the difference in lengths of objects.

TECHNOLOGY RESOURCES
- *Math in Focus* eBooks
- *Math in Focus* Teacher Resources CD

Vocabulary

taller	tallest
shorter	shortest
longer	longest

DAY 1 Student Book 2A, pp. 196–200
Workbook 2A, pp. 169–170

MATERIALS
- 1 meterstick or measuring tape per group
- 6 index cards per pair (optional)

DIFFERENTIATION RESOURCES
- Reteach 2A, pp. 143–144
- Extra Practice 2A, pp. 103–104

5-minute Warm Up

Use this activity to help children revise the terms *longer*, *shorter*, and *taller*.

- Ask children to identify which is longer, the board or the table. After they have answered, *say:* The board is *longer* than the table. The table is *shorter* than the board.

- Write *longer* and *shorter* on the board.

- Ask children to tell you who is taller, you or (name of a child). *Say:* I am taller than _____.

- Ask children to say that in another way, using *shorter than*.

- Ask children to make similar sentences using *longer*, *shorter*, or *taller* with the objects and people in the classroom.

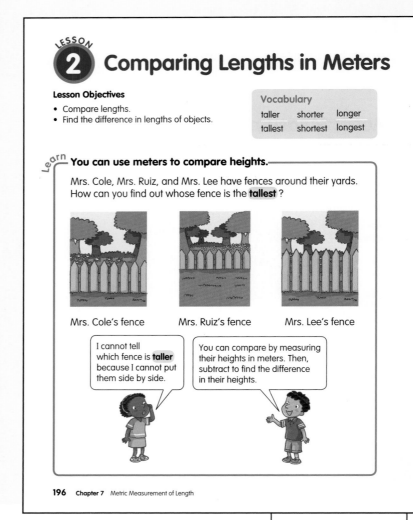

Student Book A p. 196

DAY 1 # Teach

Use Meters to Compare Heights (page 196)

Children learn to compare heights of objects using meters.

- Explain to children that the heights and lengths of many things can be compared by putting them side by side. However, if things cannot be put side by side, they will need a medium for measuring and comparing.

- Illustrate this concept with the examples in the Student Book.

- Point out that when you know the individual heights in meters, you can subtract the heights to find how much taller or shorter one object is compared to another.

Learn You can use meters to compare lengths.

This fence is 2 meters tall.

This fence is 1 meter tall.
2 − 1 = 1
So, Mrs. Cole's fence is 1 meter taller than Mrs. Ruiz's fence.

This fence is more than 2 meters tall. Mrs. Lee's fence is the tallest and Mrs. Ruiz's fence is the **shortest**.

This car is about 3 meters long.

This van is about 5 meters long.
5 − 3 = 2
The car is 2 meters **shorter** than the van.
The van is 2 meters **longer** than the car.

This truck is the **longest**. It is about 11 meters long!

1 m

Lesson 2 Comparing Lengths in Meters **197**

Student Book A p. 197

Use Meters to Compare Lengths (page 197)

Children learn to compare lengths and heights of objects using meters. They learn to find the difference in the lengths of objects by subtracting.

- Have children compare the heights of the fences and subtract to find the difference in terms of meters.
- Have children identify the tallest and shortest fences.
- Have children compare the lengths of the vehicles and subtract to find the difference in terms of meters.
- Have children identify the longest and shortest vehicles.

For Struggling Learners Paste a strip of adhesive tape 1 meter off the floor. Have children stand by the mark. Ask children if they are 1 meter tall. Have them say, "I am more than 1 meter tall," or, "I am less than 1 meter tall".

Problem of the Lesson

Sarah has a 7-meter long string. She cuts out part of the string to form a square. Each side of the square is 1 meter. Find the remaining length of the string.

Solution:
Length of 4 sides of the square
= 1 m + 1 m + 1 m + 1 m = 4 meters

Length of remaining string = 7 m − 4 m
= 3 meters

Answer:
The remaining length of the string is 3 meters.

Differentiated Instruction

English Language Learners

On pages 196 and 197, *shorter*, *taller*, *longer*, *shortest*, *tallest*, and *longest* may be unfamiliar vocabulary. Write these terms on index cards. Have children work in pairs and give each pair several objects and six index cards. Have children compare and discuss the objects using the new vocabulary and then label the objects with the cards.

Best Practices You may want to have children work with a partner. Have partners find and compare the length of items around the room or school. Encourage them to use the vocabulary words in their discussion.

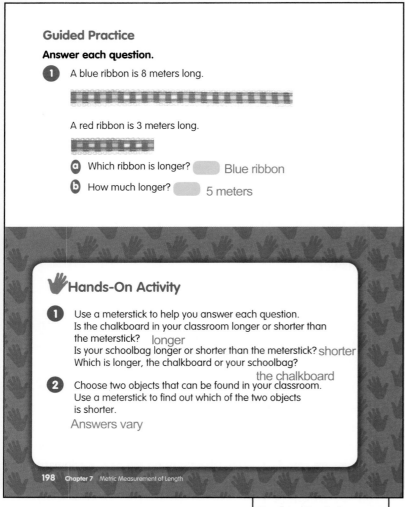

Guided Practice

Answer each question.

1 A blue ribbon is 8 meters long.

A red ribbon is 3 meters long.

a Which ribbon is longer? Blue ribbon

b How much longer? 5 meters

🖐 Hands-On Activity

1 Use a meterstick to help you answer each question.
Is the chalkboard in your classroom longer or shorter than the meterstick? longer
Is your schoolbag longer or shorter than the meterstick? shorter
Which is longer, the chalkboard or your schoolbag?
the chalkboard

2 Choose two objects that can be found in your classroom.
Use a meterstick to find out which of the two objects is shorter.
Answers vary

198 **Chapter 7** Metric Measurement of Length

Student Book A p. 198

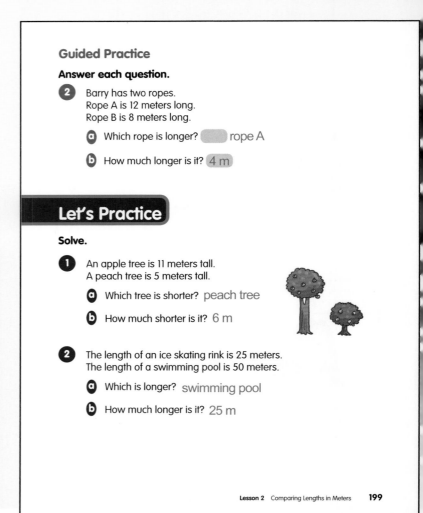

Guided Practice

Answer each question.

2 Barry has two ropes.
Rope A is 12 meters long.
Rope B is 8 meters long.

a Which rope is longer? rope A

b How much longer is it? 4 m

Let's Practice

Solve.

1 An apple tree is 11 meters tall.
A peach tree is 5 meters tall.

a Which tree is shorter? peach tree

b How much shorter is it? 6 m

2 The length of an ice skating rink is 25 meters.
The length of a swimming pool is 50 meters.

a Which is longer? swimming pool

b How much longer is it? 25 m

Lesson 2 Comparing Lengths in Meters **199**

Student Book A p. 199

Check for Understanding

✓Guided Practice (page 198)

1 This exercise reinforces the concept of length measurement in meters and provides practice in comparing lengths. Help children to see that they should subtract to find the exact difference in the lengths of the ribbons.

🖐Hands-On Activity:

Compare Lengths of Objects in the Classroom with a Meterstick (page 198)

This activity provides children with additional practice in comparing lengths in meters using the **meterstick** (or **measuring tape**).

- Children work in groups of four.

- Encourage children to observe and guess the answers to the questions before using the meterstick or measuring tape to check their guesses.

✓Guided Practice (page 199)

2 This exercise reinforces the concept of length measurement in meters and provides practice in comparing lengths. Guide children to compare the numbers to determine which rope is longer, and to see that they should subtract to find the difference in the lengths of the ropes.

Let's Practice (pages 199 and 200)

These exercises reinforce the concept of length measurement in meters and provide practice in comparing lengths.

Exercises **1** and **2** compare two lengths.

Solve.

3

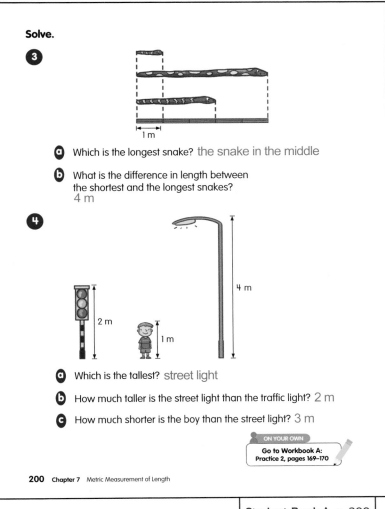

    a Which is the longest snake? the snake in the middle

    b What is the difference in length between the shortest and the longest snakes?
      4 m

4

    a Which is the tallest? street light

    b How much taller is the street light than the traffic light? 2 m

    c How much shorter is the boy than the street light? 3 m

> ON YOUR OWN
> **Go to Workbook A:**
> **Practice 2, pages 169–170**

200   Chapter 7   Metric Measurement of Length

Student Book A p. 200

Exercises **3** and **4** compare three lengths. Children also practice using subtraction to find the difference in lengths of various objects.

Common Error Some children may have difficulty understanding what is being asked. Help children look for key words such as *longer than* and *shorter than* as well as the objects so children know what is being compared.

ON YOUR OWN

Children practice comparing length in meters in Practice 2, pages 169 and 170 of **Workbook 2A**. These pages (with the answers) are shown at the right.

Differentiation Options Depending on children's success with the Workbook pages, use these materials as needed.
Struggling: Reteach 2A, pp. 143–144
On Level: Extra Practice 2A, pp. 103–104

Practice and Apply
Workbook pages for Chapter 7, Lesson 2

Name: _____   Date: _____

Practice 2   Comparing Lengths in Meters
Fill in the blanks.

1. Look at the two ropes.

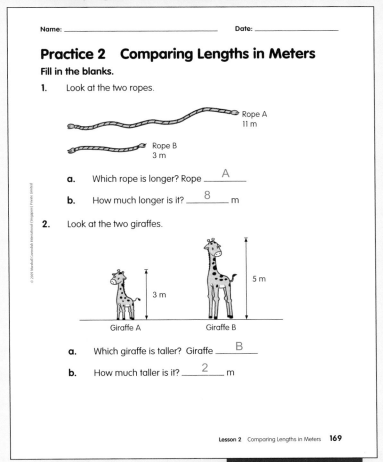

    a. Which rope is longer? Rope ___A___

    b. How much longer is it? ___8___ m

2. Look at the two giraffes.

    a. Which giraffe is taller? Giraffe ___B___

    b. How much taller is it? ___2___ m

Lesson 2   Comparing Lengths in Meters   **169**

Workbook A p. 169

---

3. Look at the sides of the rectangle.

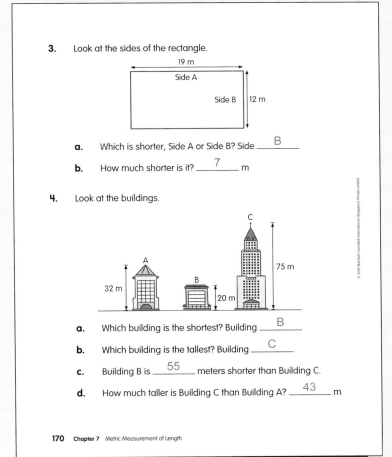

    a. Which is shorter, Side A or Side B? Side ___B___

    b. How much shorter is it? ___7___ m

4. Look at the buildings.

    a. Which building is the shortest? Building ___B___

    b. Which building is the tallest? Building ___C___

    c. Building B is ___55___ meters shorter than Building C.

    d. How much taller is Building C than Building A? ___43___ m

170   Chapter 7   Metric Measurement of Length

Workbook A p. 170

3 Measuring in Centimeters

LESSON OBJECTIVES
• Use a centimeter ruler to measure length.
• Draw a line of given length.

TECHNOLOGY RESOURCES
• *Math in Focus* eBooks
• *Math in Focus* Teacher Resources CD

Vocabulary

centimeter (cm)

DAY 1 Student Book 2A, pp. 201–206

MATERIALS
• 1 meterstick or measuring tape
• 1 centimeter ruler per child
• 2 Paper Strips of Varying Lengths (TR15) per child
• 1 roll of string

DAY 2 Student Book 2A, pp. 207–210
Workbook 2A, pp. 171–174

DIFFERENTIATION RESOURCES
• Reteach 2A, pp. 145–150
• Extra Practice 2A, pp. 105–106

 5-minute Warm Up

• Show children 5 pieces of string or rope of different lengths, all shorter than a meter.

• Ask whether the length of each piece is less than 1 m, between 1 m and 2 m, or more than 2 m. (all less than 1 m)

• *Say:* They are all shorter than 1 m. Are they the same length? (no)

• Ask a volunteer to arrange them in order of length from the shortest to the longest.

• *Ask:* Can you find the difference in lengths using a meterstick? (no)

• Explain that you need to use a unit smaller than a meter to measure shorter lengths. Use this to introduce the lesson.

---

3 Measuring in Centimeters

Lesson Objectives
• Use a centimeter ruler to measure length.
• Draw a line of given length.

Vocabulary
centimeter (cm)

Learn **You can use centimeters to measure lengths of shorter objects.**
This is a centimeter ruler.

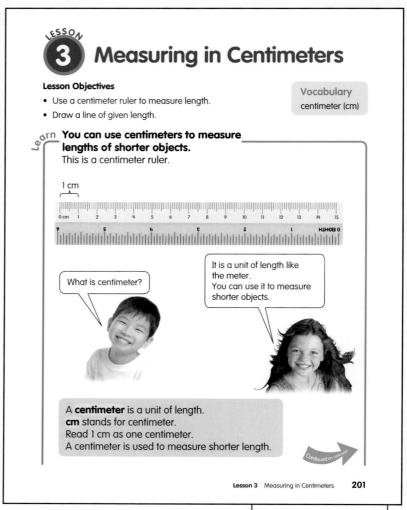

What is centimeter?

It is a unit of length like the meter.
You can use it to measure shorter objects.

A **centimeter** is a unit of length.
cm stands for centimeter.
Read 1 cm as one centimeter.
A centimeter is used to measure shorter length.

Continued on next page

Lesson 3 Measuring in Centimeters **201**

Student Book A p. 201

DAY 1 **Teach**

Learn
Use Centimeters to Measure Lengths of Shorter Objects (pages 201 and 202)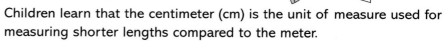

Children learn that the centimeter (cm) is the unit of measure used for measuring shorter lengths compared to the meter.

• Show children a **meterstick**. Explain that a smaller unit of measure is needed for measuring lengths shorter than a meter.

• Show children a **centimeter ruler**, and with the help of the overhead projector, show children the length of 1cm on a centimeter ruler.

• Say and write the word *centimeter* on the board and point out that *cm* stands for centimeter.

• Emphasize that the scale on the ruler is divided equally into centimeter units.

• Model how to measure the length of a pencil or crayon using the centimeter ruler. Demonstrate the correct technique for reading length on a centimeter ruler. Point out the 'O' mark. Children should be told to start from the 'O' mark and not from the edge of the ruler, as most rulers have a space before the 'O' mark.

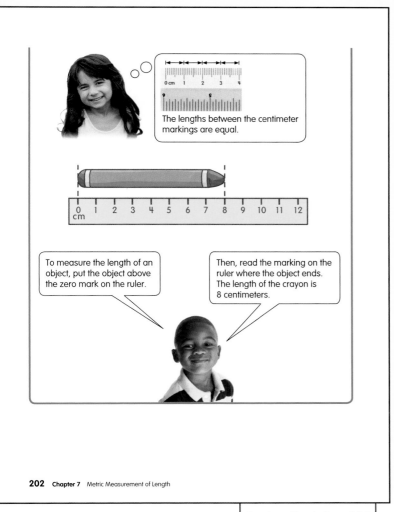

The lengths between the centimeter markings are equal.

To measure the length of an object, put the object above the zero mark on the ruler.

Then, read the marking on the ruler where the object ends. The length of the crayon is 8 centimeters.

Student Book A p. 202

Use a centimeter ruler to find the length of the path below.

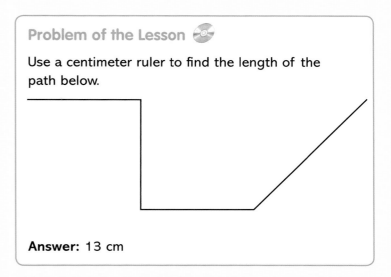

Answer: 13 cm

Differentiated Instruction

English Language Learners

Centimeter may be unfamiliar vocabulary. Display a centimeter ruler. Point to each mark on the ruler and *say:* one centimeter, two centimeters, etc. Encourage children to count increments with you as you continue. Measure the length of several small items and ask children to repeat the measurement.

Best Practices You may want to have children work in pairs. Give each pair a centimeter ruler and a list of common items on their desk to measure. Partners can verify that they are lining up the object with the '0' on their ruler. Invite children to share their findings with the class.

Guided Practice

Look at the pictures.

1. Which shows the correct way of measuring objects?
A, B, or C? C

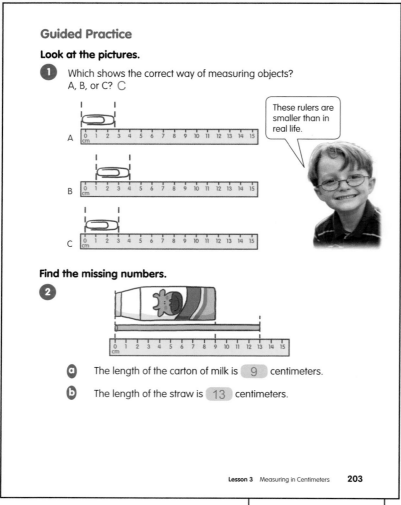

These rulers are smaller than in real life.

Find the missing numbers.

2.

a. The length of the carton of milk is 9 centimeters.

b. The length of the straw is 13 centimeters.

Guess the lengths of the objects in centimeters.
Then measure the objects.
Write your answers in a chart. Answers vary

3.

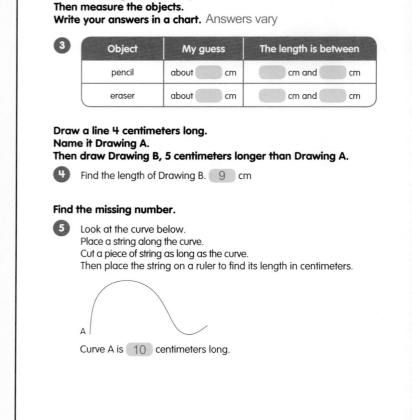

Object	My guess	The length is between
pencil	about ___ cm	___ cm and ___ cm
eraser	about ___ cm	___ cm and ___ cm

Draw a line 4 centimeters long.
Name it Drawing A.
Then draw Drawing B, 5 centimeters longer than Drawing A.

4. Find the length of Drawing B. 9 cm

Find the missing number.

5. Look at the curve below.
Place a string along the curve.
Cut a piece of string as long as the curve.
Then place the string on a ruler to find its length in centimeters.

A

Curve A is 10 centimeters long.

Check for Understanding
✓ **Guided Practice** (pages 203 and 204)

1 and **2** These exercises provide children with practice in measuring the exact lengths of objects using a centimeter ruler, and reinforce the proper technique for measuring.

For Struggling Learners Tell children that the 'O' mark is the starting point. Draw a line 1 cm long. Tell children that it is 1 cm long and place the ruler below it to show this. The line ends at the '1' mark. Have children say, "The line is 1 centimeter long".

3 This exercise gives children hands-on practice in measuring the length of objects and recording each length in centimeters.

4 Guide children to draw Drawing A using a centimeter ruler. Show children how they can count on 5 centimeter units to draw Drawing B. Then have them check their answer by adding: 4 cm + 5 cm = 9 cm.

5 Explain that you can use a piece of string to measure the length of a curve, as shown in this exercise. Compare the answers from different children and check that they have used the correct technique.

Hands-On Activity

STEP 1 Use two strips of paper of different lengths.

STEP 2 Measure the length of each strip with a ruler. Write the length of each strip on the strip.

STEP 3 Find out who else in the class has strips that are the same length as yours.

Answers vary.

Student Book A p. 205

READING AND WRITING MATH
Math Journal

Jerome and Tracie are measuring the lengths of their books.

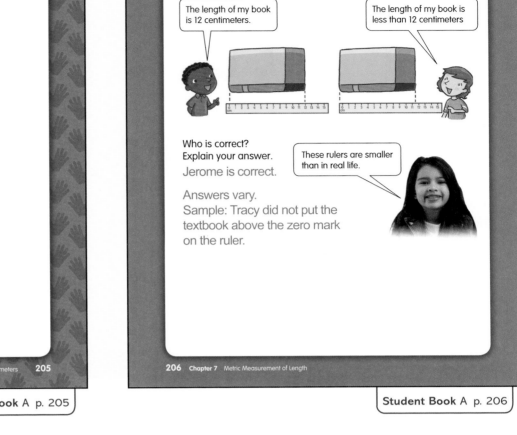

The length of my book is 12 centimeters.

The length of my book is less than 12 centimeters

Who is correct?
Explain your answer.
Jerome is correct.

These rulers are smaller than in real life.

Answers vary.
Sample: Tracy did not put the textbook above the zero mark on the ruler.

Student Book A p. 206

Hands-On Activity:
Measure Lengths of Strips of Paper (page 205)

This activity provides children with additional hands-on practice in measuring length using the centimeter ruler.

- Have children work in groups of six.

- Provide each child with two **Paper Strips of Varying Lengths** (TR15).

- Have children measure and record the length of each strip using their **centimeter ruler**.

- Have children find out who else in their group has strips that are the same length. Encourage children to compare the length of both strips as well as what they have written to check that they match.

READING AND WRITING MATH
Math Journal (page 206)

This section allows children to reflect on their observations and understanding of the measurements of lengths in centimeters, specifically the proper technique for measuring with a centimeter ruler.

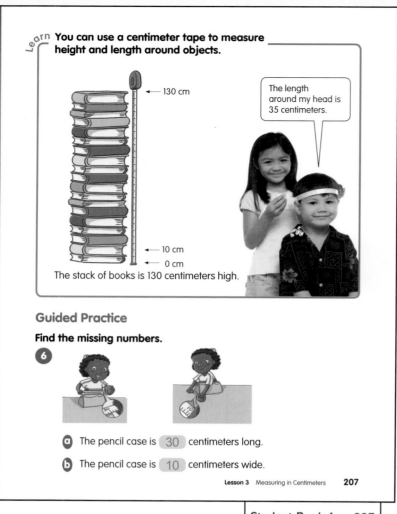

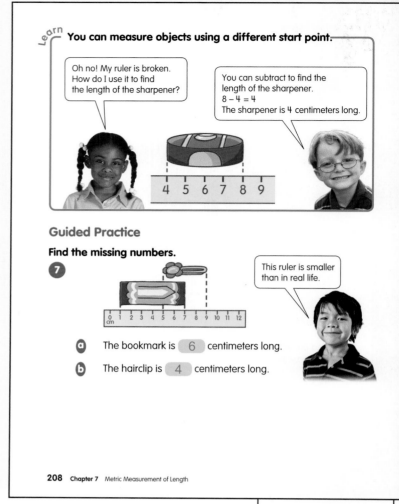

See the Lesson Organizer on page 201 for Day 2 resources.

Use a Centimeter Tape to Measure Height and Length Around Objects (page 207)

Children learn that a centimeter tape can be used to measure height and length around objects.

- Explain to children that a **measuring tape** with cm and m markings can be used to measure round things such as a ball or the head of a person. Alternatively, a string can be used, and a ruler or measuring tape can then be used to measure the length of the string.

- *Ask:* Whose head do you think is bigger than that of the boy on the page? *Say:* Let's use the centimeter tape to find out. Invite a volunteer to the front of the class. Measure the circumference of the child's head and record it on the board to check if the children guessed correctly.

✓ Guided Practice (page 207)

6 This exercise checks children's ability to read a scale to find the length and width of the pencil case in centimeters.

207–208 CHAPTER 7: LESSON 3

Measure Objects Using a Different Start Point (page 208)

Children learn to find the length of an object using a centimeter ruler when the object is not placed at the '0' mark.

- Explain to children the object to be measured does not always have to be placed at the '0' mark as the start point.

- Model on the overhead projector how children can use either the 'count on' strategy from the start point to the end or use the 'subtraction' strategy by subtracting the beginning mark from the end mark. For example, the sharpener is (8 − 4) cm = 4 cm long.

✓ Guided Practice (page 208)

7 This exercise provides children with practice in measuring objects using a different start point. Remind children of the possible strategies that may be used.

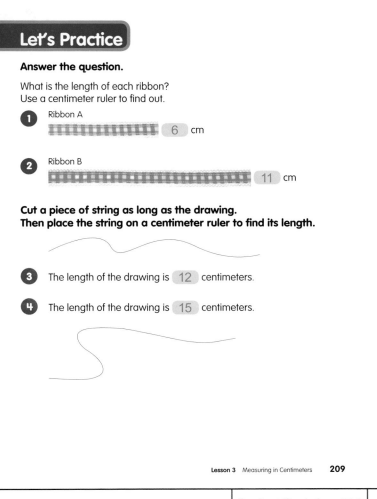

Let's Practice

Answer the question.

What is the length of each ribbon?
Use a centimeter ruler to find out.

1. Ribbon A

   [6] cm

2. Ribbon B

   [11] cm

Cut a piece of string as long as the drawing.
Then place the string on a centimeter ruler to find its length.

3. The length of the drawing is [12] centimeters.

4. The length of the drawing is [15] centimeters.

Student Book A p. 209

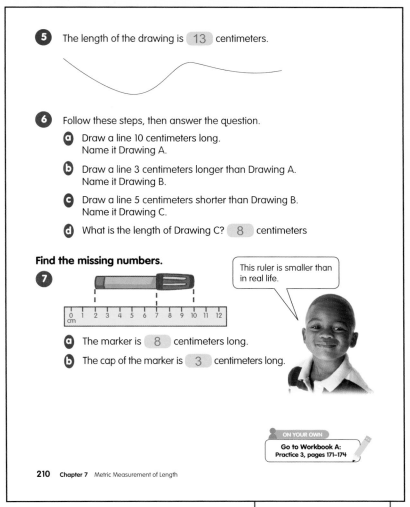

5. The length of the drawing is [13] centimeters.

6. Follow these steps, then answer the question.

   a. Draw a line 10 centimeters long.
      Name it Drawing A.

   b. Draw a line 3 centimeters longer than Drawing A.
      Name it Drawing B.

   c. Draw a line 5 centimeters shorter than Drawing B.
      Name it Drawing C.

   d. What is the length of Drawing C? [8] centimeters

Find the missing numbers.

7.

   > This ruler is smaller than in real life.

   a. The marker is [8] centimeters long.

   b. The cap of the marker is [3] centimeters long.

   ON YOUR OWN
   Go to Workbook A:
   Practice 3, pages 171–174

Student Book A p. 210

Let's Practice (pages 209 and 210)

These exercises provide more practice with measurements in centimeters.

Exercises **1** and **2** check children's ability to read the length of an object shown by a centimeter ruler.

Exercises **3** to **5** require an additional step where children use string to measure the length of curves.

Exercise **6** also requires children to count on and count back while drawing longer and shorter lines.

Exercise **7** checks children's ability to measure objects using different starting points.

For Advanced Learners Have children work in groups. Show them an 8 cm long piece of string. Ask children to estimate the length of the string. Then ask them to cut a strip of paper with the same length as the string. (They should use rulers to measure the lengths of the strips of paper.) The child whose strip of paper is closest in length to the string wins.

Common Error Some children will still have trouble aligning the ruler. Demonstrate how to align the left end of the ruler with the left end of the object being measured. Have children practice alignment.

ON YOUR OWN

Children practice measuring in centimeters in Practice 3, pages 171 to 174 of **Workbook 2A**. These pages (with the answers) are shown on page 210A.

Differentiation Options Depending on children's success with the Workbook pages, use these materials as needed.
Struggling: Reteach 2A, pp. 145–150
On Level: Extra Practice 2A, pp. 105–106

Practice and Apply

Workbook pages for Chapter 7, Lesson 3

Name: _____   Date: _____

Practice 3   Measuring in Centimeters

Check (✔) the correct way to measure
the length of the pencil.

1.

☐

✔

Use your centimeter ruler to draw.

2.   A line that is 5 centimeters long

3.   A line that is 12 centimeters long

4.   A line that is 9 centimeters long

Workbook A p. 171

Name: _____   Date: _____

Cut a piece of string as long as the drawing below.
Then place the string on a centimeter ruler to find its length.

11.   **a.** How long is the string? _____9_____ cm

string

b. This string is used to form the following shapes.
Use a string and a centimeter ruler to measure each of them.

A   B   C

___9___ cm   ___9___ cm   ___9___ cm

Do they all have the same length? ___yes___

Explain your answer.

The length of the string does not change even

when the shape is changed.

Workbook A p. 173

Use your centimeter ruler to draw.

5.   A line that is 6 centimeters long

6.   A line that is 2 centimeters shorter than the line in Exercise 4.

7.   A line that is 2 centimeters longer than the line in Exercise 5.

Use a piece of string to find the length.

8.

___7___ cm

9.

___8___ cm

10.

___4___ cm

Workbook A p. 172

Find the missing numbers.

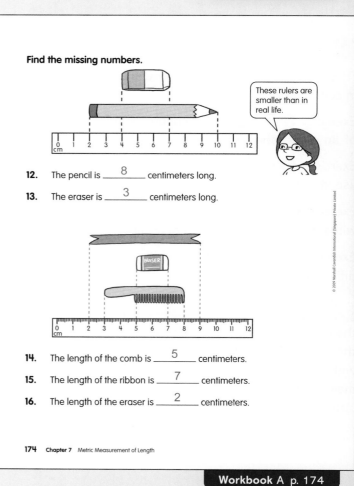

These rulers are smaller than in real life.

12.   The pencil is ___8___ centimeters long.

13.   The eraser is ___3___ centimeters long.

14.   The length of the comb is ___5___ centimeters.

15.   The length of the ribbon is ___7___ centimeters.

16.   The length of the eraser is ___2___ centimeters.

Workbook A p. 174

Comparing Lengths in Centimeters

LESSON OBJECTIVES

- Use a centimeter ruler to measure and compare lengths of objects.
- Find the difference in centimeters in lengths of objects.

TECHNOLOGY RESOURCES

- *Math in Focus* eBooks
- *Math in Focus* Teacher Resources CD

DAY 1 Student Book 2A, pp. 211–215
Workbook 2A, pp. 175–178

MATERIALS

- 1 centimeter ruler per child
- 1 meterstick

DIFFERENTIATION RESOURCES

- Reteach 2A, pp. 151–152
- Extra Practice 2A, pp. 107–108

 5-minute Warm Up

Show children five pieces of string of different lengths, all shorter than 15 cm. Ask 5 volunteers to each measure the length of their strings using centimeter rulers and write the lengths on the board. Then as a class, arrange the strings in order of length. Also arrange the numbers on the board in order from least to greatest. Show that the order in each case is the same.

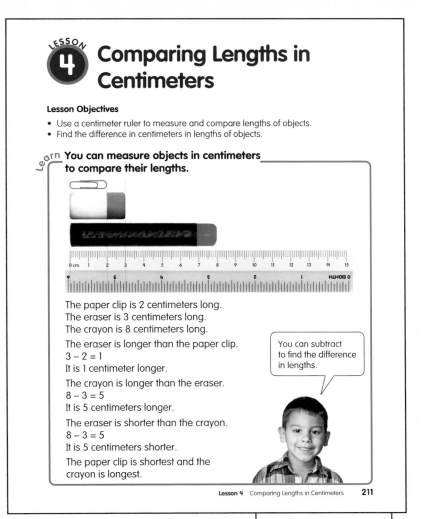

 Comparing Lengths in Centimeters

Lesson Objectives

- Use a centimeter ruler to measure and compare lengths of objects.
- Find the difference in centimeters in lengths of objects.

Learn You can measure objects in centimeters to compare their lengths.

The paper clip is 2 centimeters long.
The eraser is 3 centimeters long.
The crayon is 8 centimeters long.
The eraser is longer than the paper clip.
$3 - 2 = 1$
It is 1 centimeter longer.
The crayon is longer than the eraser.
$8 - 3 = 5$
It is 5 centimeters longer.
The eraser is shorter than the crayon.
$8 - 3 = 5$
It is 5 centimeters shorter.
The paper clip is shortest and the crayon is longest.

You can subtract to find the difference in lengths.

Lesson 4 Comparing Lengths in Centimeters **211**

Student Book A p. 211

DAY 1 **Teach**

Learn

Measure Objects in Centimeters to Compare Their Lengths (page 211)

Children learn to compare the lengths of objects in centimeters and find the difference in lengths of objects.

- Explain that a ruler can be used to help compare the lengths of the eraser, paper clip, and crayon.

- With the help of an overhead projector and **centimeter ruler**, have children measure and record the length of each item. Then ask children to compare the lengths. *Ask:* Which is longer, the crayon or the eraser? How much longer? Which is shorter, the paper clip or the eraser? How much shorter?

- Have children identify the longest and shortest object.

Guided Practice

Find the missing numbers.

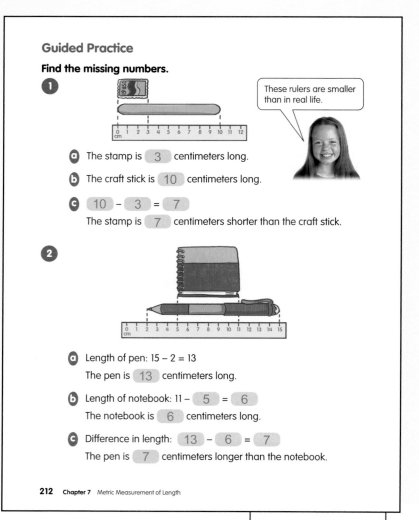

1

> These rulers are smaller than in real life.

ⓐ The stamp is `3` centimeters long.

ⓑ The craft stick is `10` centimeters long.

ⓒ `10` – `3` = `7`
The stamp is `7` centimeters shorter than the craft stick.

2

ⓐ Length of pen: 15 – 2 = 13
The pen is `13` centimeters long.

ⓑ Length of notebook: 11 – `5` = `6`
The notebook is `6` centimeters long.

ⓒ Difference in length: `13` – `6` = `7`
The pen is `7` centimeters longer than the notebook.

212   **Chapter 7** *Metric Measurement of Length*

Student Book A p. 212

Problem of the Lesson

Jenna's eraser is 6 centimeters long. Charlie's pen is 8 centimeters long.
(a) Which object is longer? How much longer?
(b) What is the total length of the two objects?

Solution:
(a) 8 – 6 = 2
(b) 6 + 8 = 14

Answer:
(a) Charlie's pen is longer by 2 centimeters.
(b) The total length is 14 centimeters.

Differentiated Instruction

English Language Learners

Children may require help understanding part c of each problem on page 212 (finding how much shorter or longer). Explain what is being asked. Read aloud the sentence without using the numbers. Ask children to work with a partner to solve the problem.

Check for Understanding

✓**Guided Practice** (pages 212 and 213)

1 to **3** These exercises provide practice with measurement and comparison of length in centimeters. Children should identify subtraction as the method used to find the exact difference between the lengths of the various objects.

Children also practice comparing lengths of objects using appropriate terms such as *longer* and *shorter*. Emphasize that different starting points are used when measuring objects in Exercise **2**.

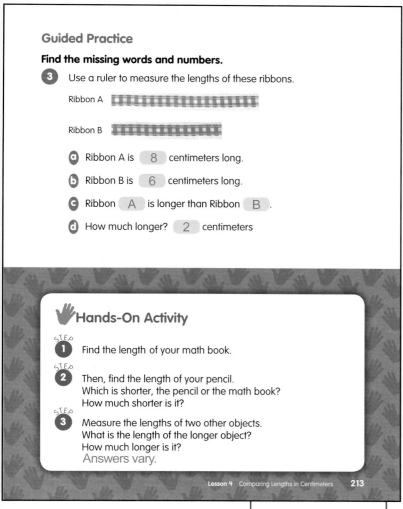

Guided Practice

Find the missing words and numbers.

3 Use a ruler to measure the lengths of these ribbons.

Ribbon A

Ribbon B

ⓐ Ribbon A is ⟨ 8 ⟩ centimeters long.

ⓑ Ribbon B is ⟨ 6 ⟩ centimeters long.

ⓒ Ribbon ⟨ A ⟩ is longer than Ribbon ⟨ B ⟩.

ⓓ How much longer? ⟨ 2 ⟩ centimeters

✋Hands-On Activity

STEP 1 Find the length of your math book.

STEP 2 Then, find the length of your pencil.
Which is shorter, the pencil or the math book?
How much shorter is it?

STEP 3 Measure the lengths of two other objects.
What is the length of the longer object?
How much longer is it?
Answers vary.

Lesson 4 Comparing Lengths in Centimeters **213**

Student Book A p. 213

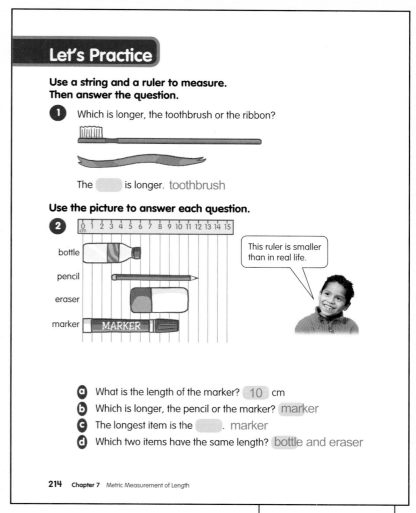

Let's Practice

Use a string and a ruler to measure.
Then answer the question.

1 Which is longer, the toothbrush or the ribbon?

The ⟨ ⟩ is longer. toothbrush

Use the picture to answer each question.

2

bottle

pencil

eraser

marker MARKER

This ruler is smaller than in real life.

ⓐ What is the length of the marker? ⟨ 10 ⟩ cm
ⓑ Which is longer, the pencil or the marker? marker
ⓒ The longest item is the ⟨ ⟩. marker
ⓓ Which two items have the same length? bottle and eraser

214 Chapter 7 Metric Measurement of Length

Student Book A p. 214

✋Hands-On Activity:
Compare Lengths of Objects in Centimeters (page 213)

This activity provides children with additional hands-on practice measuring and comparing lengths using the **centimeter ruler.**

- Guide children to follow the steps to measure and compare the lengths of objects.

Best Practices You may want to teach this lesson as three mini-lessons: measuring lengths of objects in centimeters, comparing the lengths of the objects, and finding the difference in centimeters between the lengths of the objects.

Let's Practice (pages 214 and 215)

These exercises provide practice in comparing lengths of objects in centimeters.

Exercises **1** and **2** provide practice for children to measure and compare the lengths of objects using the centimeter scale.

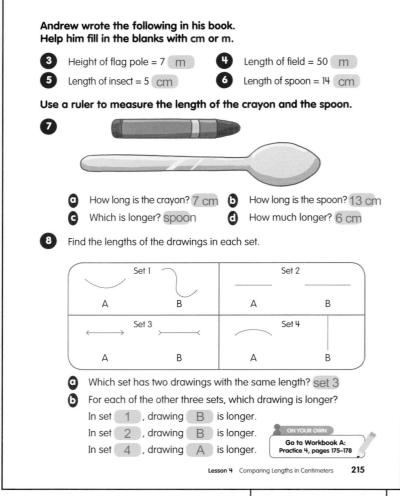

Andrew wrote the following in his book.
Help him fill in the blanks with cm or m.

3 Height of flag pole = 7 **m**   **4** Length of field = 50 **m**

5 Length of insect = 5 **cm**   **6** Length of spoon = 14 **cm**

Use a ruler to measure the length of the crayon and the spoon.

7

a How long is the crayon? **7 cm**   **b** How long is the spoon? **13 cm**

c Which is longer? **spoon**   **d** How much longer? **6 cm**

8 Find the lengths of the drawings in each set.

Set 1	Set 2
A B	A B
Set 3	Set 4
A B	A B

a Which set has two drawings with the same length? **set 3**

b For each of the other three sets, which drawing is longer?

In set **1**, drawing **B** is longer.

In set **2**, drawing **B** is longer.   **ON YOUR OWN**
Go to Workbook A:
Practice 4, pages 175–178

In set **4**, drawing **A** is longer.

Lesson 4   Comparing Lengths in Centimeters   **215**

Student Book A p. 215

Exercises **3** to **6** require children to identify the lengths of various objects using the correct units. Exercises **7** and **8** reinforce the technique of measuring using a centimeter ruler.

Common Error Some children may confuse meters and centimeters. Display and label a centimeter ruler and a meterstick for children to observe.

ON YOUR OWN

Children practice comparing lengths in centimeters in Practice 4, pages 175 to 178 of **Workbook 2A**. These pages (with the answers) are shown at the right and on page 215A.

Differentiation Options Depending on children's success with the Workbook pages, use these materials as needed.

Struggling: Reteach 2A, pp. 151–152
On Level: Extra Practice 2A, pp. 107–108

Practice and Apply
Workbook pages for Chapter 7, Lesson 4

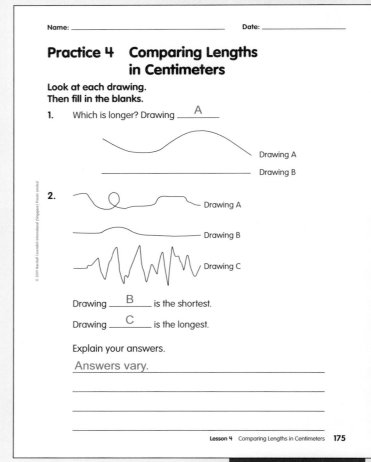

Name: _____   Date: _____

Practice 4 Comparing Lengths in Centimeters

Look at each drawing.
Then fill in the blanks.

1. Which is longer? Drawing ___**A**___

Drawing A
Drawing B

2.

Drawing A
Drawing B
Drawing C

Drawing ___**B**___ is the shortest.

Drawing ___**C**___ is the longest.

Explain your answers.

Answers vary. _____

Lesson 4   Comparing Lengths in Centimeters   **175**

Workbook A p. 175

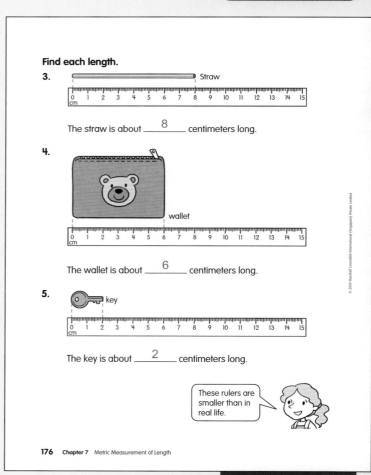

Find each length.

3.   Straw

The straw is about ___**8**___ centimeters long.

4.   wallet

The wallet is about ___**6**___ centimeters long.

5.   key

The key is about ___**2**___ centimeters long.

These rulers are smaller than in real life.

176   Chapter 7   Metric Measurement of Length

Workbook A p. 176

Name: _____ **Date:** _____

Find each length.

6.

The pen is about ___12___ centimeters long.

7.

bracelet

These rulers are smaller than in real life.

The bracelet is about ___5___ centimeters wide.

Use your answers for Exercises 3 to 6.
Fill in the blanks with *longer* or *shorter*.

8. The pen is __longer__ than the straw.

9. The key is __shorter__ than the pen.

10. The wallet is __shorter__ than the straw.

Workbook A p. 177

Use your answers for Exercises 3 to 7.
Fill in the blanks.

11. The straw is ___6___ centimeters longer than the key.

12. The straw is ___4___ centimeters shorter than the pen.

13. The pen is ___10___ centimeters longer than the key.

14. The bracelet is ___1___ centimeter shorter than the wallet.

15. The longest object is the ___pen___.

16. The shortest object is the ___key___.

Workbook A p. 178

LESSON 5 Real-World Problems: Metric Length

LESSON OBJECTIVES

- Solve one-step and two-step problems involving length.
- Draw models to solve real-world problems.

TECHNOLOGY RESOURCES

- *Math in Focus* eBooks
- *Math in Focus* Teacher Resources CD

DAY 1 Student Book 2A, pp. 216–220
Workbook 2A, pp. 179–182

MATERIALS

- 3 paper or magnetic strips for the teacher

DIFFERENTIATION RESOURCES

- Reteach 2A, pp. 153–156
- Extra Practice 2A, pp. 109–114

5-minute Warm Up

Have children work in pairs. Each child writes a two-digit number on a piece of paper. One child adds the two numbers, and the partner subtracts one of the numbers from the total to check the answer. Reverse roles and repeat.

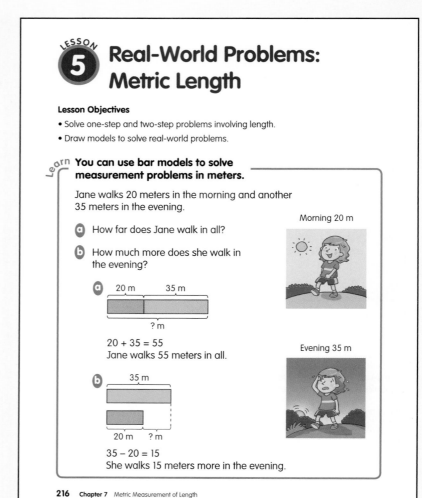

Student Book A p. 216

DAY 1 # Teach

Learn Use Bar Models to Solve Measurement Problems in Meters (page 216)

Children learned to use bar models to solve real-world problems involving addition and subtraction in Chapter 4. In this lesson, children will use bar models to solve problems involving length in meters.

- Write an addition sentence and subtraction sentence involving 2-digit numbers on the board. Explain that the addition and subtraction of lengths follow the same procedure, but you show the unit of measurement, which in this case is either *cm* or *m*.

- Have children recall the 'part-whole' and 'comparing' concepts and models.

- Place two paper strips on the overhead projector or magnetic strips on the board. Ask some children to measure the length of each strip in centimeters.

- *Say:* Let's find the total length of the two strips. Draw the corresponding bar model, and add.

- Then, place the strips end to end, and ask a child to measure the total length to check the answer.

Guided Practice

Solve.

1

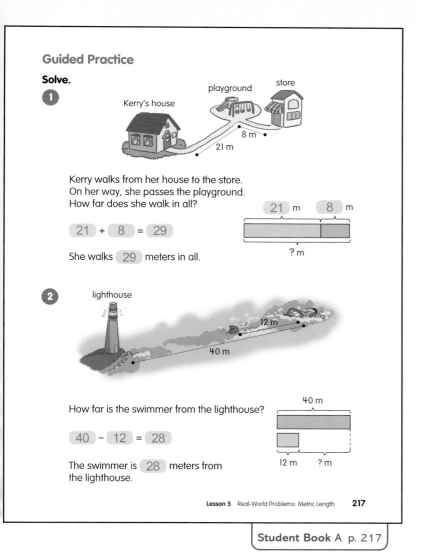

Kerry walks from her house to the store. On her way, she passes the playground. How far does she walk in all?

$21 + 8 = 29$

She walks 29 meters in all.

2

How far is the swimmer from the lighthouse?

$40 - 12 = 28$

The swimmer is 28 meters from the lighthouse.

Student Book A p. 217

- Now place one strip above the other to compare the lengths. Ask a child to find the difference. Draw a corresponding bar model to illustrate this.

- Direct children to the problem in the Student Book, and apply the above concepts to the word problem there.

Check for Understanding

Guided Practice (page 217)

1 and **2** These exercises provide practice in using addition and subtraction to solve real-world problems involving length and distance. They also reinforce the part-whole concept related to addition and the comparing concept related to subtraction, both illustrated with bar models.

Problem of the Lesson

Elaine has a piece of yarn. She wants to outline a triangle that has equal sides of 5 centimeters, and a square with sides of 9 centimeters. She needs 13 centimeters more yarn to outline the shapes. Find the length of the piece of yarn that Elaine has.

Solution:

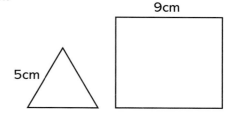

Length of yarn (in cm) needed to make triangle $= 5 + 5 + 5 = 15$.

Length of yarn (in cm) needed to make square $= 9 + 9 + 9 + 9 = 36$

Total length of yarn required = 15 cm + 36 cm = 51 cm
Length of yarn that Elaine has = 51 cm − 13 cm = 38 cm

Answer: The length of the yarn Elaine has is 38 centimeters.

Differentiated Instruction

English Language Learners

Some children will have difficulty understanding word problems. Pair each child with a native English speaker who reads aloud each word problem. Have each pair discuss how to solve each problem and work together to find the solution.

Best Practices You may want to have children work in groups of two or three. Give each group paper strips (or strips of construction paper) in two different colors to use as bar models. Have one partner duplicate the problem on paper strips and ask the others in the group to solve the problem.

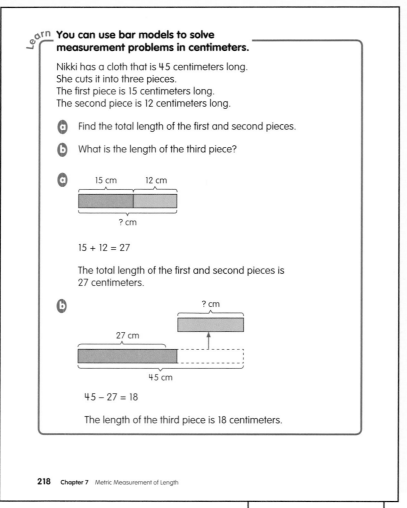

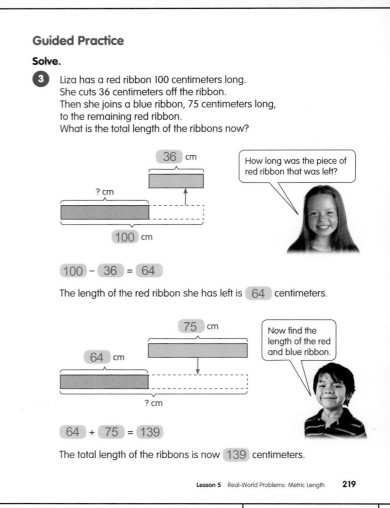

 Learn

Use Bar Models to Solve Measurement Problems in Centimeters (page 218)

Children use bar models to solve problems involving lengths in centimeters.

- Model the problem in the Student Book using three paper or magnetic strips of proportionate length matching those in the problem.

- With the help of the strips, show children how to apply the 'part-whole' concept in addition and subtraction to solve the problem.

✓ Guided Practice (page 219)

❸ This exercise provides practice in using addition and subtraction to solve real-world problems involving length. It also reinforces the 'taking away' and 'adding on' strategies illustrated by bar models.

Let's Practice

Solve.

1 Tony jogs two times around a 400-meter track.
How far does he jog in meters? 800 m

2 The length of Adam's notebook is 21 centimeters.
Hector's notebook is 5 centimeters longer.
How long is Hector's notebook? 26 cm

3 A string that is 20 centimeters long is cut into two pieces.
One piece is 8 centimeters long.
How long is the other piece? 12 cm

4 Harry's string is 25 centimeters long.
Keisha's string is 12 centimeters longer.
How long is Keisha's string? 37 cm

5 A tall room has two windows, one above the other.
The bottom window is 162 centimeters tall.
The top window is 47 centimeters shorter.

   a How tall is the top window? 115 cm

   b What is the height of both windows? 277 cm

6 A rope 42 meters long is cut into two pieces.
The first piece is 14 meters.

   a How long is the second piece? 28 m

   b What is the difference in length
between the two pieces? 14 m

ON YOUR OWN

Go to Workbook A:
Practice 5, pages 179–182

220 Chapter 7 Metric Measurement of Length

Student Book A p. 220

Let's Practice (page 220)

These exercises provide practice in solving real-world measurement problems using the relevant addition and subtraction concepts.

Exercises **1** to **4** check that children can solve one-step addition and subtraction word problems. Exercises **5** and **6** require children to solve the problems in two steps. Encourage children to draw bar models to help them solve the problems.

Common Error Some children may choose the wrong operation. Remind children to read each word problem carefully and understand what is being asked before they begin trying to solve the problem.

ON YOUR OWN

Children practice solving real-world metric problems in Practice 5, pages 179 to 182 of **Workbook 2A**. These pages (with the answers) are shown on page 220A.

Differentiation Options Depending on children's success with the Workbook pages, use these materials as needed.
Struggling: Reteach 2A, pp. 153–156
On Level: Extra Practice 2A, pp. 109–114

Practice and Apply
Workbook pages for Chapter 7, Lesson 5

Name: _____ Date: _____

Practice 5 Real-World Problems: Metric Length

Solve.

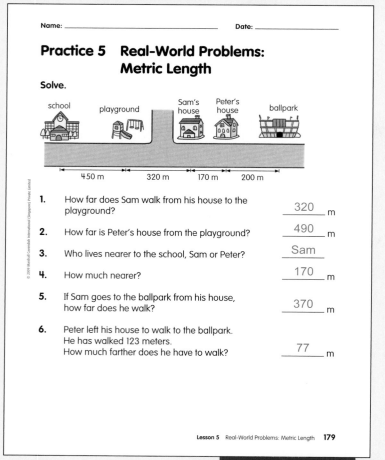

school   playground   Sam's house   Peter's house   ballpark

|← 450 m →|← 320 m →|← 170 m →|← 200 m →|

1. How far does Sam walk from his house to the playground?

____320____ m

2. How far is Peter's house from the playground?

____490____ m

3. Who lives nearer to the school, Sam or Peter?

____Sam____

4. How much nearer?

____170____ m

5. If Sam goes to the ballpark from his house, how far does he walk?

____370____ m

6. Peter left his house to walk to the ballpark.
He has walked 123 meters.
How much farther does he have to walk?

____77____ m

Lesson 5 Real-World Problems: Metric Length **179**

Workbook A p. 179

Name: _____ Date: _____

Solve.

10. A flag pole is 450 centimeters tall.
The top of the flag is 345 centimeters from the ground.
How much farther must it be raised to reach the top?

450 − 345 = 105

The flag must be raised ____105____
centimeters farther to reach the top.

? cm
450 cm
345 cm

11. The total length of two pieces of wood is 215 centimeters.
The first piece is 135 centimeters long.

a. What is the length of the second piece?

The length of the second piece is ____80____ centimeters.

b. How much shorter is the second piece than the first piece?

The second piece is ____55____ centimeters shorter than the first piece.

12. Max is 135 centimeters tall.
He is 18 centimeters taller than Rita.
Rita is 30 centimeters shorter than Jan.
How tall is Jan?

135 − 18 = 117

117 + 30 = 147

Jan is ____147____ centimeters tall.

Lesson 5 Real-World Problems: Metric Length **181**

Workbook A p. 181

Solve.

7. There are two pictures.
One of them is 35 centimeters long.
The other is 86 centimeters long.
They are placed side by side.
What is the length of the two pictures?

35 + 86 = 121

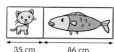

35 cm   86 cm

The length is ____121____ centimeters.

8. A ribbon is cut into three pieces.
They are 4 meters, 6 meters, and 2 meters long.
How long was the ribbon before it was cut?

4 + 6 + 2 = 12

The ribbon was ____12____ meters long.

9. Mrs. Chu has 2 pairs of chopsticks.
Each red chopstick is 19 centimeters long.
Each yellow chopstick is 22 centimeters long.

a. Which pair of chopsticks is longer?
The ____yellow____ chopsticks

b. How much longer? ____3____ cm

180 Chapter 7 Metric Measurement of Length

Workbook A p. 180

---

13. Cody has a strip of paper 10 centimeters long.
He cuts it into three pieces.
One piece is 4 centimeters long.
The second piece is 3 centimeters long.
How long is the third piece of paper?

10 − 4 − 3 = 3

The third piece of paper is ____3____ centimeters long.

14. A string is 200 centimeters long.
Kaly uses 63 centimeters of it to tie a box.
She gives 48 centimeters of it to Susan.
How long is the string that Kaly has left?

200 − 63 − 48 = 89

The length of the string that Kaly has left is ____89____ centimeters.

182 Chapter 7 Metric Measurement of Length

Workbook A p. 182

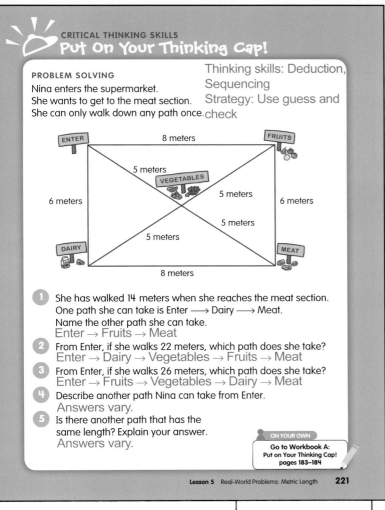

CRITICAL THINKING AND PROBLEM SOLVING

Put on Your Thinking Cap! (page 221)

This problem solving exercise requires children to deduce and sequence the correct paths taken by Nina using the 'guess and check' strategy. Children work individually or in groups to answer the questions and present the solutions to the class.

Thinking Skills

- Deduction
- Sequencing

Problem Solving Strategy

- Use guess and check

For Advanced Learners Have children find all the possible paths that Nina can take to visit every section in the supermarket once. Then, ask children which of these is the shortest path, and how long it is. (Enter → Dairy → Vegetables → Fruits → Meat: 22 meters)

ON YOUR OWN

Because all children should be challenged, have all children try the Challenging Practice and Problem Solving pages in **Workbook 2A**, pages 183 and 184. These pages (with the answers) are shown on page 221A.

Differentiation Options Depending on children's success with the Workbook pages, use these materials as needed.

On Level: Extra Practice 2A, pp. 115–116
Advanced: Enrichment 2A, pp. 57–65

Practice and Apply
Workbook pages for Put on Your Thinking Cap!

Name: _____   Date: _____

Put On Your Thinking Cap!
Challenging Practice

Solve.

1. There are three drawings—A, B, and C.
   Drawing A is shown below.

   _____ Drawing A

   Drawing B is 2 centimeters longer than Drawing A.
   Drawing C is 3 centimeters shorter than Drawing B.
   How long is Drawing C?

   8 + 2 = 10
   10 − 3 = 7
   Drawing C is 7 centimeters long.

2. Sara bought three pieces of ribbon.
   She bought 90 centimeters of ribbon in all.
   Check (✔) to show which three pieces of ribbon she bought.

Ribbon	Length of Ribbon	Check
A	25 cm	
B	42 cm	✔
C	38 cm	✔
D	15 cm	
E	10 cm	✔
F	20 cm	

   Thinking skills: Comparing, Deduction
   Strategy: Act it out

   Chapter 7 Metric Measurement of Length   **183**

Workbook A p. 183

Put On Your Thinking Cap!
Problem Solving

The picture shows the shadows of two trees.

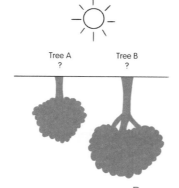

Tree A   Tree B
  ?   ?

Look at the shadows. Which tree is taller? Tree ____B____

Explain your answer.

Answers vary.

Thinking skills: Comparing, Deduction

Strategy: Make suppositions.

184   Chapter 7 Metric Measurement of Length

Workbook A p. 184

Notes

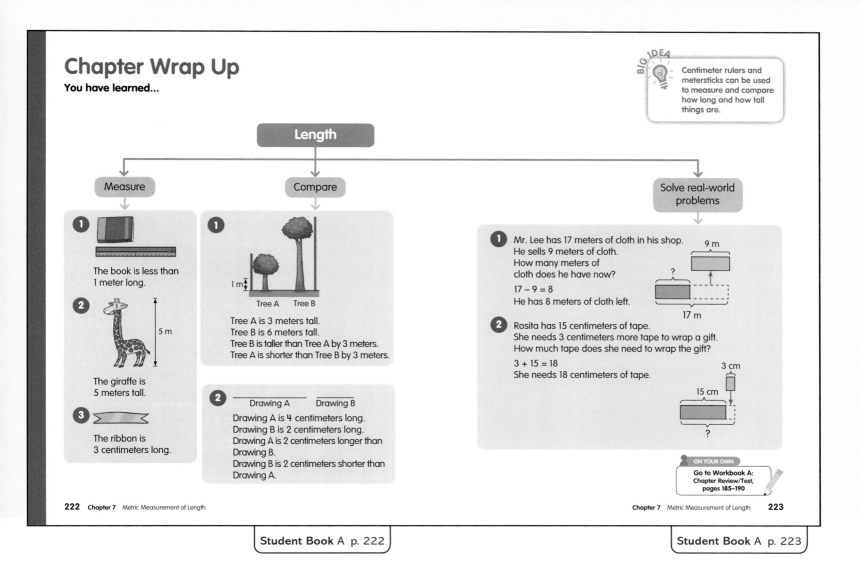

Chapter Wrap Up

You have learned...

BIG IDEA — Centimeter rulers and metersticks can be used to measure and compare how long and how tall things are.

Length

Measure

1. The book is less than 1 meter long.

2. The giraffe is 5 meters tall. (5 m)

3. The ribbon is 3 centimeters long.

Compare

1. Tree A — Tree B (1 m)
Tree A is 3 meters tall.
Tree B is 6 meters tall.
Tree B is taller than Tree A by 3 meters.
Tree A is shorter than Tree B by 3 meters.

2. Drawing A — Drawing B
Drawing A is 4 centimeters long.
Drawing B is 2 centimeters long.
Drawing A is 2 centimeters longer than Drawing B.
Drawing B is 2 centimeters shorter than Drawing A.

Solve real-world problems

1. Mr. Lee has 17 meters of cloth in his shop.
He sells 9 meters of cloth.
How many meters of cloth does he have now?
$17 - 9 = 8$
He has 8 meters of cloth left.
(9 m, ?, 17 m)

2. Rosita has 15 centimeters of tape.
She needs 3 centimeters more tape to wrap a gift.
How much tape does she need to wrap the gift?
$3 + 15 = 18$
She needs 18 centimeters of tape.
(3 cm, 15 cm, ?)

ON YOUR OWN
Go to Workbook A:
Chapter Review/Test,
pages 185–190

Student Book A p. 222

Student Book A p. 223

Chapter Wrap Up (pages 222 and 223)

Use the examples on pages 222 and 223 to review metric measurement of length. As you work through the examples, encourage children to use the chapter vocabulary.

- meterstick
- meter (m)
- width
- taller
- shorter
- longer
- centimeter (cm)
- length
- unit
- height
- tallest
- shortest
- longest

ON YOUR OWN

Have children review the vocabulary, concepts, and skills from Chapter 7 with the Chapter Review/Test on Workbook pages 185 to 190. These pages (with the answers) are shown on pages 223A and 223B.

Assessment

Use the Chapter 7 Test Prep on pages 48 to 53 of **Assessments 2** to assess how well children have learned the material of this chapter. This assessment is appropriate for reporting results to adults at home and administrators. This test is shown on page 223C.

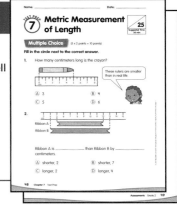

Assessments 2 pp. 48–53

Workbook pages for Chapter Review/Test

Name: _____ Date: _____

Chapter Review/Test
Vocabulary
Fill in the blanks with the words in the box.

| meters | meterstick | height | centimeters | width | length |

1.

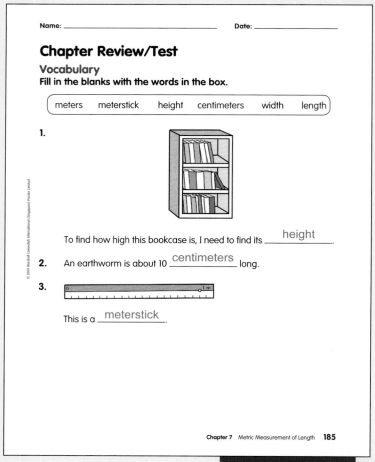

To find how high this bookcase is, I need to find its ___height___

2. An earthworm is about 10 ___centimeters___ long.

3.

This is a ___meterstick___

Workbook A p. 185

Name: _____ Date: _____

Concepts and Skills
Check (✔) the correct answers.

7. What is the length of your math textbook?

Length	Check
About 1 meter	
Less than 1 meter	✔
More than 1 meter	

8. What is the height of your desk?

Height	Check
About 1 meter	
Less than 1 meter	✔
More than 8 meters	
Less than 3 meters	

9. What is the height of your classroom?

Height	Check
About 1 meter	
Less than 1 meter	
More than 8 meters	
Less than 8 meters	✔

Workbook A p. 187

Fill in the blanks with the words in the box.

| meters | meterstick | height | centimeters | width | length |

4.

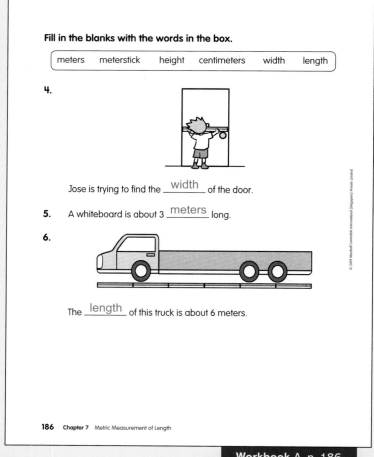

Jose is trying to find the ___width___ of the door.

5. A whiteboard is about 3 ___meters___ long.

6.

The ___length___ of this truck is about 6 meters.

Workbook A p. 186

Look at the objects measured.
Then fill in the blanks.

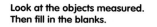

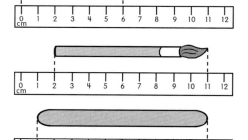

What are the lengths of the

10. spoon: ___6___ cm

11. brush: ___9___ cm

12. craftstick: ___10___ cm

13. The craftstick is ___4___ centimeters longer than the spoon.

14. The ___spoon___ is the shortest.

Workbook A p. 188

Name: _____   Date: _____

Solve.

15. Shane has 5 meters of cloth.
He needs 16 meters more cloth to make some curtains.
How many meters of cloth are needed to make the curtains?

5 + 16 = 21

_____21_____ meters of cloth are needed to make the curtains.

16. Two boards are 26 meters long altogether.
One board is 8 meters long.
How long is the other board?

26 − 8 = 18

The other board is ____18____ meters long.

Chapter 7   Metric Measurement of Length   **189**

Workbook A p. 189

17. Bella is 161 centimeters tall.
She is 12 centimeters taller than Joshua.
How tall is Joshua?

161 − 12 = 149

Joshua is ____149____ centimeters tall.

18. Raul has a box that is 9 centimeters wide.
Ling's box is 3 centimeters wider than Raul's box.
Will both their boxes fit on a shelf that is 30 centimeters wide?
Explain why.

9 + 3 = 12

Ling's box is 12 centimeters wide.

12 + 9 = 21

Yes, both their boxes will fit on a shelf that is

30 centimeters wide because the total width of the

boxes (21 cm) is shorter than the width of the shelf

(30 cm).

_____

_____

190   Chapter 7   Metric Measurement of Length

Workbook A p. 190

Notes

Assessments Book pages for Chapter 7 Test Prep

Answer key appears in Assessments Book.

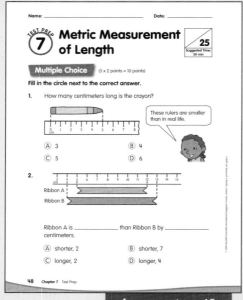

Assessments p. 48

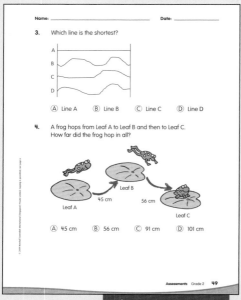

Assessments p. 49

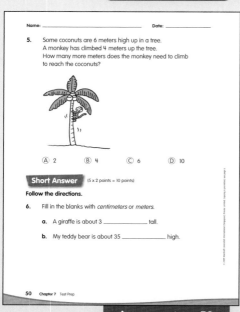

Assessments p. 50

Assessments p. 51

Assessments p. 52

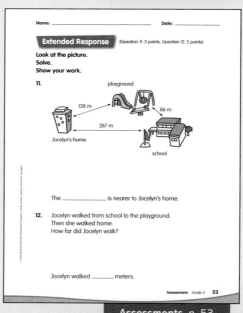

Assessments p. 53

Chapter Overview

Mass

Math Background

Children learned how to find and compare mass in Grade 1. They learned to estimate and compare mass using a non-standard unit, such as a marble or a nickel. Children also learned addition and subtraction to 1,000 with and without regrouping in Chapters 2 and 3 of Grade 2, as well as using bar models in Chapter 4.

In this chapter, children learn to estimate and measure the mass of objects using the standard metric units of kilograms (kg) and grams (g). Children read the masses of objects from measuring scales in these units. Another way of finding the mass of objects involves using a balance with 1-kilogram and 1-gram masses. Children conduct experiments using the measuring scale to compare the masses of two objects, as well as to determine the masses of objects using addition and subtraction of masses.

Cross-Curricular Connections

Reading/Language Arts Read aloud **Weight** by Henry Pluckrose (Children's Press, © 1995). This book discusses how objects are weighed, compares the weight of familiar objects, and teaches the units in which we weigh objects.

Art Create a kilogram collage. Use a large piece of butcher paper. At the top of the left side of the paper write *More Than 1 Kilogram*; at the top of the right side write *Less Than 1 Kilogram*. Invite children to cut out pictures of objects from magazines, estimate the mass of the objects, and glue them on the correct side of the collage.

Skills Trace

Grade 1	Measure and compare masses in non-standard units. (Chap. 10)
Grade 2	Measure and compare masses in kilograms and grams. Add and subtract masses with the help of bar models. (Chap. 8)
Grade 3	Measure and convert length, mass and volume in metric units. (Chap. 11) Solve real-world problems involving metric units of measurements. (Chap. 12) Measure length, weight and capacity in customary units and solve real-world problems. (Chap. 15)

EVERY DAY COUNTS®
Calendar Math
The December activities provide...

Review of comparing and ordering quantities (Chapter 1)

Preview of reading a clock (Chapter 14)

Practice of relating word problems to symbolic number sentences (Lesson 5 in this chapter)

Differentiation Resources

Differentiation for Special Populations

	English Language Learners	Struggling Reteach 2A	On Level Extra Practice 2A	Advanced Enrichment 2A
Lesson 1	p. 229	pp. 157–162	pp. 117–118	Enrichment pages can be used to challenge advanced children.
Lesson 2	p. 238	pp. 163–164	pp. 119–120	
Lesson 3	p. 241	pp. 165–168	pp. 121–122	
Lesson 4	p. 246	pp. 169–170	pp. 123–124	
Lesson 5	p. 254	pp. 171–174	pp. 125–127	

Additional Support

For English Language Learners

Select activities that reinforce the chapter vocabulary and the connections among these words, such as having children

- add terms, definitions, and examples to the Word Wall

- act out measuring mass and use vocabulary terms to describe actions

- draw and label pictures to illustrate each term

- discuss the Chapter Wrap Up, encouraging children to use the chapter vocabulary

For Struggling Learners

Select activities that go back to the appropriate stage of the Concrete-Pictorial-Abstract spectrum, such as having children

- identify classroom objects to represent different measures of mass

- draw pictures to illustrate comparisons of different measures of mass

- order classroom objects from least to greatest mass

- create and solve new stories for given measures of mass

If necessary, review

- Chapter 2 (Addition up to 1,000)

- Chapter 3 (Subtraction up to 1,000)

For Advanced Learners

See page 254 for suggestions.

Assessment and Remediation

Chapter 8 Assessment

Prior Knowledge		
	Resource	**Page numbers**
Quick Check	Student Book 2A	pp. 226–227
Pre-Test	Assessments 2	pp. 54–55
Ongoing Diagnostic		
Guided Practice	Student Book 2A	pp. 231–232, 233, 236–237, 241, 242, 246, 248, 254, 257
Common Error	Teacher's Edition 2A	pp. 238, 244, 249–250, 257–258
Formal Evaluation		
Chapter Review/Test	Workbook 2A	pp. 211–216
Chapter 8 Test Prep	Assessments 2	pp. 56–60

Remediation Options

Problems with these items...   Can be remediated with...

	Review/Test Items	Chapter Assessment Items	Reteach	Student Book
Objective	**Workbook 2A pp. 211–216**	**Assessments 2 pp. 56–60**	**Reteach 2A**	**Student Book 2A**
Use chapter vocabulary correctly.	1–5	Not assessed	In context as needed	pp. 228, 235, 240
Use a measuring scale to measure mass in kilograms.	6–8	1	pp. 157–162	Lesson 1
Compare and order masses.	6–8	6	pp. 163–164	Lesson 2
Use a measuring scale to measure mass in grams.	9–12	2, 7, 8, 11, 12	pp. 165–168	Lesson 3
Compare and order masses in grams.	9–12	3, 4, 9	pp. 169–170	Lesson 4
Use bar models to solve problems about mass.	13–18	3, 4, 5, 10, 13	pp. 171–174	Lesson 5

Chapter Planning Guide

CHAPTER 8 Mass

Lesson	Pacing	Instructional Objectives	Vocabulary
Chapter Opener pp. 224–227 Recall Prior Knowledge Quick Check	*1 day	💡**Big Idea** A scale can be used to measure and compare masses in kilograms and grams.	
Lesson 1, pp. 228–234 Measuring in Kilograms	1 day	• Use a measuring scale to measure mass in kilograms.	• kilogram (kg) • mass • measuring scale • as heavy as • less than • more than
Lesson 2, pp. 235–239 Comparing Masses in Kilograms	1 day	• Compare and order masses.	• heavier than • lighter than • heaviest • lightest
Lesson 3, pp. 240–244 Measuring in Grams	1 day	• Use a measuring scale to measure mass in grams.	• gram (g)
Lesson 4, pp. 245–252 Comparing Masses in Grams	1 day	• Compare and order masses in grams.	

*Assume that 1 day is a 45–55 minute period.

Resources	Materials	NCTM Focal Points	NCTM Process Standards
Student Book 2A, pp. 224–227 **Assessments 2,** pp. 54–55			
Student Book 2A, pp. 228–234 **Workbook 2A,** pp. 191–192 **Extra Practice 2A,** pp. 117–118 **Reteach 2A,** pp. 157–162	• 1-kg mass • 1 measuring scale • 1 balance scale • 1 Mass of Objects Chart (TR16) per group • 1 copy of Kilogram Scales (TR17) per child (optional)	*Measurement* Develop an understanding of the meaning and processes of measurement. Understand partitioning and transitivity. Use rulers and other measurement tools.	Problem Solving Reasoning/Proof Connections
Student Book 2A, pp. 235–239 **Workbook 2A,** pp. 193–196 **Extra Practice 2A,** pp. 119–120 **Reteach 2A,** pp. 163–164	• 1 measuring scale • 1 balance scale • 1 copy of Kilogram Scales (TR17) per child (optional) • index cards (optional)	*Measurement* Develop an understanding of the meaning and processes of measurement. Use rulers and other measurement tools.	Problem Solving Connections
Student Book 2A, pp. 240–244 **Workbook 2A,** pp. 197–202 **Extra Practice 2A,** pp. 121–122 **Reteach 2A,** pp. 165–168	• 1-gram mass • 1 measuring scale • 1-kg bag of beans • 1 copy of Kilogram Scales (TR17) • 1 copy of Gram Scale (TR18)	*Measurement* Use rulers and other measurement tools.	Problem Solving Connections
Student Book 2A, pp. 245–252 **Workbook 2A,** pp. 203–204 **Extra Practice 2A,** pp. 123–124 **Reteach 2A,** pp. 169–170	• 3 bags of marbles per group • 1 measuring scale • 3 index cards • 3 fruits per group • 1 Chart for Recording Mass (TR19) per group	*Number and Operations* Add and subtract to solve a variety of problems. *Measurement* Use rulers and other measurement tools.	Problem Solving Reasoning/Proof Connections

Chapter Planning Guide

Lesson	Pacing	Instructional Objectives	Vocabulary
Lesson 5, pp. 253–258 Real-World Problems: Mass	1 day	• Use bar models to solve problems about mass.	
Problem Solving p. 259 Put on Your Thinking Cap!	$\frac{1}{2}$ day	**Thinking Skills** • Analyzing parts and whole • Induction **Problem Solving Strategy** • Use a diagram/model	
Chapter Wrap Up pp. 260–261	$\frac{1}{2}$ day	• Reinforce and consolidate chapter skills and concepts	
Chapter Assessment	1 day		

*Assume that 1 day is a 45–55 minute period.

Resources	Materials	NCTM Focal Points	NCTM Process Standards
Student Book 2A, pp. 253–258 **Workbook 2A,** pp. 205–208 **Extra Practice 2A,** pp. 125–127 **Reteach 2A,** pp. 171–174	• 1 measuring scale per group • Paper Strips (TR07) (optional)	***Number and Operations*** Add and subtract to solve a variety of problems. ***Measurement*** Develop an understanding of the meaning and processes of measurement.	Problem Solving Reasoning/Proof Connections Representation
Student Book 2A, p. 259 **Workbook 2A,** pp. 209–210 **Extra Practice 2A,** p. 128 **Enrichment 2A,** pp. 66–75		***Number and Operations*** Add and subtract to solve a variety of problems. ***Measurement*** Develop an understanding of the meaning and processes of measurement.	Problem Solving Reasoning/Proof Connections Representation
Student Book 2A, pp. 260–261 **Workbook 2A,** pp. 211–216			
Assessments 2, pp. 56–60			

Technology Resources for easy classroom management
- *Math in Focus* eBooks
- *Math in Focus* Teacher Resources CD
- Online Assessment Generator

CHAPTER 8: PLANNING GUIDE **224G**

Chapter Introduction

8 Mass

Chapter 8 Vocabulary

kilogram (kg)	a metric unit of mass	Lesson 1
mass	how heavy an object or a set of objects is	Lesson 1
measuring scale	a tool for measuring the mass of an object	Lesson 1
as heavy as	having the same mass as	Lesson 1
less than	of a smaller value than	Lesson 1
more than	of a greater value than	Lesson 1
heavier than	having a greater mass than	Lesson 2
lighter than	having a lesser mass than	Lesson 2
heaviest	having the greatest mass	Lesson 2
lightest	having the lowest mass	Lesson 2
gram (g)	a metric unit of mass	Lesson 3

Student Book A p. 224

Big Idea (page 224)

Measuring and comparing mass accurately in kilograms and grams using a measuring scale is the main focus of this chapter.

- Children learn that mass is a concept of measure to describe how heavy an object is.

- They learn that kilogram (kg) and gram (g) are units of measure for mass in the metric system.

Chapter Opener (page 224)

The pictures illustrate a story of a mother and two children measuring ingredients for a muffin recipe. Use the story to help introduce the concept of measurement of mass using a measuring scale.

- Have children read the text in the speech bubbles on their own.

- Ask some children to read the text aloud, taking different roles.

- Using a **measuring scale** and a 1-kg mass, demonstrate how the scale records the mass of a kilogram.

- Point out that there are scales that measure weight in pounds and ounces, which are customary units of measure to describe how heavy an object is.

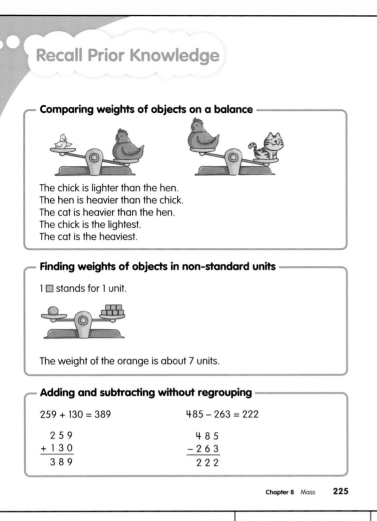

Recall Prior Knowledge (pages 225 and 226)

Comparing Weights of Objects on a Balance

Children learned to estimate and compare weight with reference to a weighing balance in Grade 1.

- Direct children's attention to one scale at a time, and have them tell you which is heavier and lighter in each case.

- Then compare the masses of all three animals and *ask:* Which is the heaviest? Which is the lightest?

Finding Weights of Objects in Non-Standard Units

Children learned to estimate weights with reference to non-standard units in Grade 1.

- Have children count the number of pink unit cubes to find the weight of the orange.

Adding and Subtracting Without Regrouping

Children learned addition and subtraction up to 1,000 without regrouping in Chapters 2 and 3 of Grade 2.

- Show children the number sentences without the answers.

- Have children solve and complete the number sentences in horizontal and vertical forms.

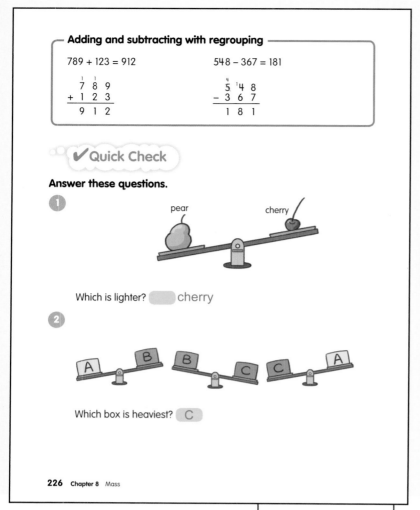

Adding and subtracting with regrouping

$789 + 123 = 912$

$$\begin{array}{r} \overset{1}{7}\overset{1}{8}9 \\ +\ 1\ 2\ 3 \\ \hline 9\ 1\ 2 \end{array}$$

$548 - 367 = 181$

$$\begin{array}{r} \overset{4}{5}\overset{1}{4}8 \\ -\ 3\ 6\ 7 \\ \hline 1\ 8\ 1 \end{array}$$

✔Quick Check

Answer these questions.

1

pear   cherry

Which is lighter? cherry

2

A   B   B   C   C   A

Which box is heaviest? C

Student Book A p. 226

Find the weight of each object.
1 ● represents 1 unit.

3

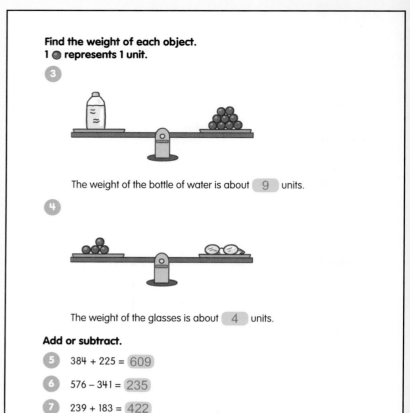

The weight of the bottle of water is about 9 units.

4

The weight of the glasses is about 4 units.

Add or subtract.

5 $384 + 225 = $ 609

6 $576 - 341 = $ 235

7 $239 + 183 = $ 422

8 $617 - 424 = $ 193

Student Book A p. 227

Adding and Subtracting with Regrouping

Children learned addition and subtraction up to 1,000 with regrouping in Chapters 2 and 3 of Grade 2.

- Show children the number sentences without the answers.

- Have children solve and complete the number sentences in horizontal and vertical form.

✔Quick Check (pages 226 and 227)

Use this section as a diagnostic tool to assess children's level of prerequisite knowledge before they progress to this chapter.

Exercises **1** and **2** assess children's ability to compare weights of objects on a balance.

Exercises **3** and **4** assess children's ability to measure weight in non-standard units.

Exercises **5** and **6** assess children's ability to add and subtract without regrouping.

Exercises **7** and **8** assess children's ability to add and subtract with regrouping.

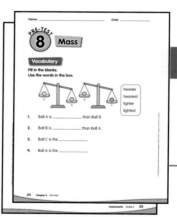

Assessments 2 pp. 54–55

Assessment

For additional assessment of children's prior knowledge and chapter readiness, use the Chapter 8 Pre-Test on pages 54 and 55 of **Assessments 2**.

Chapter 8

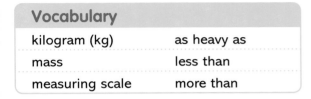
1 Measuring in Kilograms

LESSON OBJECTIVE
• Use a measuring scale to measure mass in kilograms.

TECHNOLOGY RESOURCES
• *Math in Focus* eBooks
• *Math in Focus* Teacher Resources CD
• *Math in Focus* Virtual Manipulatives

Vocabulary	
kilogram (kg)	as heavy as
mass	less than
measuring scale	more than

DAY 1 | Student Book 2A, pp. 228–234
Workbook 2A, pp. 191–192

MATERIALS
• 1-kg mass
• 1 measuring scale
• 1 balance scale
• 1 Mass of Objects Chart (TR16) per group
• 1 copy of Kilogram Scales (TR17) per child (optional)

DIFFERENTIATION RESOURCES
• Reteach 2A, pp. 157–162
• Extra Practice 2A, pp. 117–118

5-minute Warm Up

Try this activity to check that children understand the concept of comparing weights.

• Draw a balance in the middle of the board. Ask children to stand and hold their arms out on both sides to act as a balance.

• Draw or write the names of objects one at a time on each of the pans, and ask children to tip left or right depending on the objects you add to each side. For example, when you first add anything to the right pan, children should dip the right arm down and raise the left arm. Add distinctly heavier or lighter objects such as a bowling ball or feathers.

---

1 Measuring in Kilograms

Lesson Objective
• Use a measuring scale to measure mass in kilograms.

Vocabulary		
kilogram (kg)	measuring scale	less than
mass	as heavy as	more than

Learn **You can use a kilogram as a unit of measurement to compare the mass of different objects.**

Use a 1-kilogram mass.

Step 1
Hold the 1-kilogram mass in your hand.

Step 2
Next, hold a notebook in your other hand. Which is heavier, the 1-kilogram mass or the notebook?

Step 3
Put the notebook down. Carry your school bag. Which is heavier, the 1-kilogram mass or the school bag?

> The kilogram is a unit of mass.
> **kg** stands for kilogram.
> Read 1 kg as one kilogram.
> A kilogram is used to measure the mass of heavier objects.

228 Chapter 8 Mass

Student Book A p. 228

DAY 1 # Teach

Learn
Compare Mass Using Kilograms (page 228)

Children develop a sense of how heavy 1 kilogram is using a 1-kilogram mass.

• Show children an object that has a mass of about 1 kilogram such as a 1-liter bottle of soda. Pass it around the class for children to hold and feel how heavy 1 kilogram is.

• Have children compare the 1-kilogram mass with a notebook and a bag. This helps them tell how heavy 1 kilogram is.

• Explain that a unit of measure for mass is 1 kilogram (kg). It is used in most countries around the world and by scientists in the U.S. Ask in what units their weights are measured. (pounds) Tell them that the kilogram is a unit to measure the mass of heavy things in the metric system.

• Point out that although they write 'kg', they read it in full as 'kilogram'.

• Explain that they will learn about measuring weight in pounds in Grade 3 after they learn about fractions.

The bag of flour is **as heavy as** a mass of 1 kilogram.

The mass of the box of tissues is **less than** 1 kilogram.

Student Book A p. 229

Problem of the Lesson

Without using a measuring scale, sort these items by their mass: notebook, pen, math textbook, stapler, watermelon, marker.

Complete the table below.

Masses less than 1 kg	Masses more than 1 kg

Answer:

Masses less than 1 kg	Masses more than 1 kg
notebook, pen, stapler, marker	math textbook, watermelon

The Mass of an Object Can Be Equal to 1 Kilogram (page 229)

Children read a measuring scale that shows '1 kg'.

- Have children look at the picture of the measuring scale with a bag of flour in the Student Book and direct children's attention to the reading on the scale: 1 kg.

- Explain that a scale usually has small markings on it that represent the units of measure. Help them recall that the meterstick and centimeter rulers in Chapter 7 also make use of scales for measurement.

- Explain that the measuring scale measures the mass of the bag of flour, which is 1 kg. Have children say after you: *The bag of flour is as heavy as the mass of 1 kg.*

- You may want to bring a 2-pound bag of sugar to class and have children note that its mass is almost 1 kilogram.

Differentiated Instruction

English Language Learners

Use a kilogram measuring scale and various objects to discuss the terms *measuring scale, mass, kilogram, more than, less than,* and *as heavy as.* For example, show two objects and say, "This (object) has a mass that is less than this (object)". Ask children to repeat the phrase *less than.* Repeat with other objects and terms.

The Mass of an Object Can Be Less Than 1 Kilogram (page 229)

- Have children look at the picture of the measuring scale with the box of tissues in the Student Book and direct children's attention to the reading on the scale: less than 1 kg.

- Explain that the measuring scale measures the mass of the box of tissues, which is less than 1 kg. Have children say after you: *The mass of the box of tissues is less than 1 kg.*

- You could bring a 1-pound package of butter to class to have children feel that its mass is less than 1 kilogram.

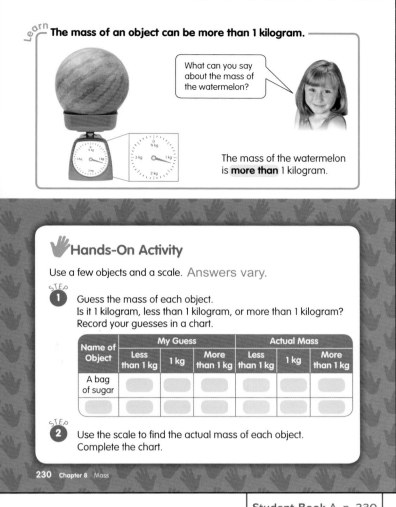

The mass of an object can be more than 1 kilogram.

What can you say about the mass of the watermelon?

The mass of the watermelon is **more than** 1 kilogram.

Hands-On Activity

Use a few objects and a scale. Answers vary.

STEP 1 Guess the mass of each object.
Is it 1 kilogram, less than 1 kilogram, or more than 1 kilogram?
Record your guesses in a chart.

Name of Object	My Guess			Actual Mass		
	Less than 1 kg	1 kg	More than 1 kg	Less than 1 kg	1 kg	More than 1 kg
A bag of sugar						

STEP 2 Use the scale to find the actual mass of each object.
Complete the chart.

Student Book A p. 230

The Mass of an Object Can Be More Than 1 Kilogram (page 230)

- Have children look at the picture of the kitchen scale with a watermelon and direct children's attention to the scale reading: more than 1 kg.

- Explain that the measuring scale measures the mass of the watermelon, which is more than 1 kilogram. Have children say after you: *The mass of the watermelon is more than 1 kilogram.*

Hands-On Activity:

WORKING TOGETHER

Guess and Measure the Mass of Objects
(page 230)

This activity provides additional practice in estimating mass using a **measuring scale**.

- Have children complete the activity using the steps in the Student Book, and record the masses using a copy of the **Mass of Objects Chart** (TR16).

- Children should use various objects given to them such as bags of sugar, red beans, green beans, canned food, empty cans, and so on.

Best Practices You may want to have children work in small groups and send them to the Math Center one group at a time. After all the groups have completed the activity, create a three-column chart on chart paper with the headings *Equal To 1 Kilogram*, *More Than 1 Kilogram*, and *Less Than 1 Kilogram*. Discuss items from each group's chart and compile a large three-column class chart.

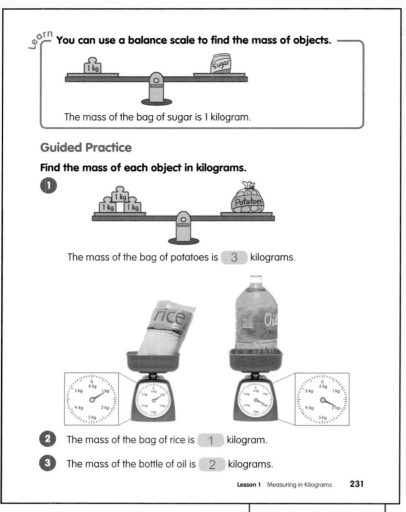

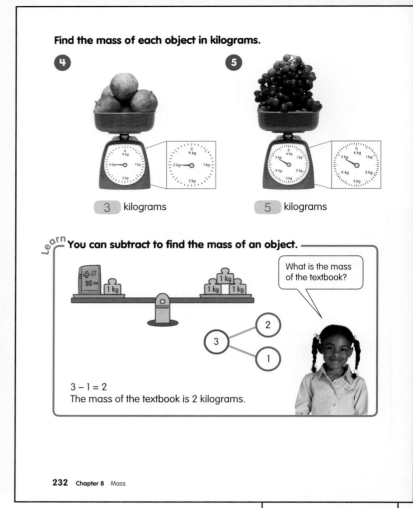

The content shown on Student Book pages:

Student Book A p. 231

Learn **You can use a balance scale to find the mass of objects.**

The mass of the bag of sugar is 1 kilogram.

Guided Practice

Find the mass of each object in kilograms.

❶

The mass of the bag of potatoes is [3] kilograms.

❷ The mass of the bag of rice is [1] kilogram.

❸ The mass of the bottle of oil is [2] kilograms.

Lesson 1 Measuring in Kilograms **231**

Student Book A p. 232

Find the mass of each object in kilograms.

❹ [3] kilograms

❺ [5] kilograms

Learn **You can subtract to find the mass of an object.**

What is the mass of the textbook?

3 — 2 — 1

$3 - 1 = 2$
The mass of the textbook is 2 kilograms.

232 Chapter 8 Mass

Learn

Use a Balance Scale to Find the Mass of Objects (page 231)

Children learn to find the mass of an object in kilograms using the balance with 1-kilogram masses.

- Point out that the **balance scale** is another weighing scale, which is different from the measuring scale.

- You may want to display a balance scale and use it to show the equality and inequality of some masses.

- Explain that in this picture, the 1-kilogram mass balances the bag of sugar. Hence the mass of the sugar is 1 kilogram.

- Explain to children that if the mass does not balance the bag of sugar, then the mass of the sugar is not 1 kilogram.

Check for Understanding

✓ **Guided Practice** (pages 231 and 232)

❶ This exercise provides practice in measuring the mass of an object using a balance scale with 1-kilogram masses.

❷ to ❺ These exercises provide practice in reading the measuring scale to find the mass of objects placed on the scale.

Learn

Subtract to Find the Mass of an Object
(page 232)

Children learn to find the mass of an object in kilograms using the balance with 1-kg masses.

- Direct children's attention to the example in the Student Book.

- Point out that the textbook and the 1-kilogram mass balance the three 1-kilogram masses.

- Explain that since there are 1-kg masses on both sides, the extra 1-kilogram mass must be subtracted from both sides to find the actual mass of the textbook.

You may use the number bond 3–2–1 to help children see how the three 1-kilogram masses can be broken into 2 parts:
2 kilograms and 1 kilogram.

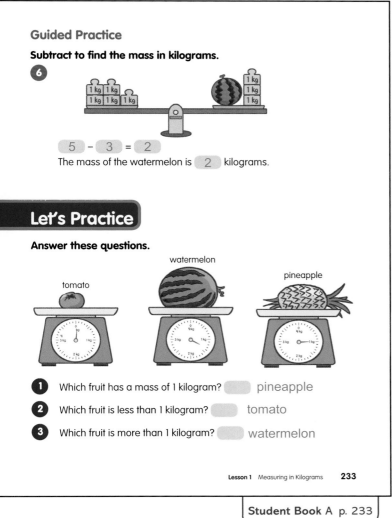

Guided Practice

Subtract to find the mass in kilograms.

6

$5 - 3 = 2$

The mass of the watermelon is 2 kilograms.

Let's Practice

Answer these questions.

tomato

watermelon

pineapple

1 Which fruit has a mass of 1 kilogram? pineapple

2 Which fruit is less than 1 kilogram? tomato

3 Which fruit is more than 1 kilogram? watermelon

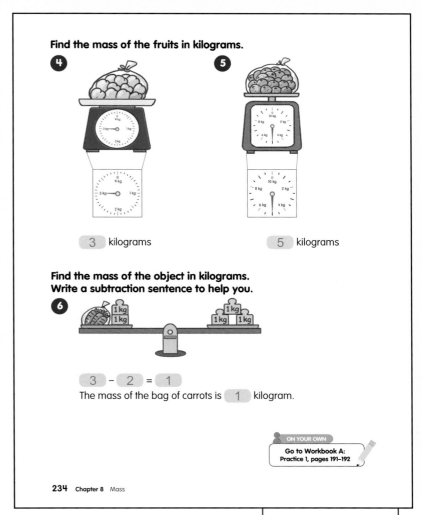

Find the mass of the fruits in kilograms.

4

5

3 kilograms

5 kilograms

Find the mass of the object in kilograms. Write a subtraction sentence to help you.

6

$3 - 2 = 1$

The mass of the bag of carrots is 1 kilogram.

ON YOUR OWN

Go to Workbook A:
Practice 1, pages 191–192

Guided Practice (page 233)

6 This exercise provides practice in subtracting to find the mass of an object using a balance scale with 1-kilogram masses on both sides.

Let's Practice (pages 233 and 234)

These exercises provide more practice in measuring mass in kilograms.

Exercises **1** to **3** check that children understand that the mass of objects can be expressed as 1 kilogram, more than 1 kilogram, or less than 1 kilogram.

Exercises **4** and **5** check that children can read the measuring scale to find the mass of objects placed on it.

Exercise **6** checks that children can subtract to find the mass of an object using a balance scale with 1-kilogram masses on both sides.

Best Practices Some children may have difficulty in reading the scales. You may want to have these children work in small groups. You can use copies of the **Kilogram Scales** (TR17) to demonstrate how to read the measuring scales in Exercises **1** to **5**.

ON YOUR OWN

Children practice measuring in kilograms in Practice 1, pages 191 and 192 of **Workbook 2A**. These pages (with the answers) are shown on page 234A.

Differentiation Options Depending on children's success with the Workbook pages, use these materials as needed.
Struggling: Reteach 2A, pp. 157–162
On Level: Extra Practice 2A, pp. 117–118

Practice and Apply

Workbook pages for Chapter 8, Lesson 1

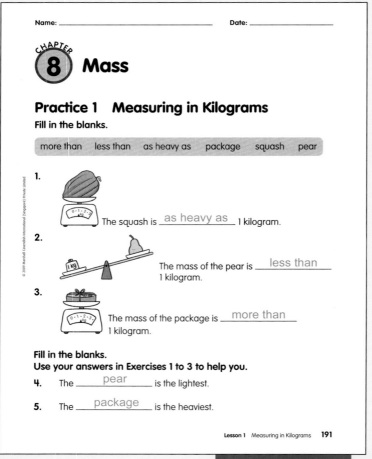

Name: _____ Date: _____

CHAPTER 8 Mass

Practice 1   Measuring in Kilograms

Fill in the blanks.

| more than | less than | as heavy as | package | squash | pear |

1. The squash is _as heavy as_ 1 kilogram.

2. The mass of the pear is _less than_ 1 kilogram.

3. The mass of the package is _more than_ 1 kilogram.

Fill in the blanks.
Use your answers in Exercises 1 to 3 to help you.

4. The ___pear___ is the lightest.

5. The ___package___ is the heaviest.

Lesson 1   Measuring in Kilograms   **191**

Workbook A p. 191

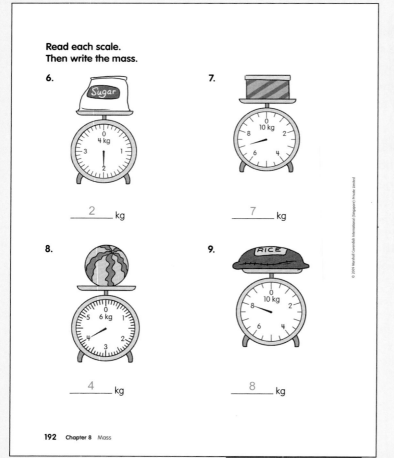

Read each scale.
Then write the mass.

6. ___2___ kg

7. ___7___ kg

8. ___4___ kg

9. ___8___ kg

192   Chapter 8   Mass

Workbook A p. 192

Notes

LESSON 2 Comparing Masses in Kilograms

LESSON OBJECTIVE
• Compare and order masses.

TECHNOLOGY RESOURCES
• *Math in Focus* eBooks
• *Math in Focus* Teacher Resources CD

Vocabulary

heavier than	heaviest
lighter than	lightest

DAY 1 Student Book 2A, pp. 235–239
Workbook 2A, pp. 193–196

MATERIALS
• 1 measuring scale
• 1 balance scale
• 1 copy of Kilogram Scales (TR17) per child (optional)
• index cards (optional)

DIFFERENTIATION RESOURCES
• Reteach 2A, pp. 163–164
• Extra Practice 2A, pp. 119–120

 5-minute Warm Up

Have children work in pairs. Ask each child to choose a number from 20 to 40.

Tell the children to pretend that the number they chose is their mass in kilograms. Have them write their 'mass' on an index card or small piece of paper they can hold up to show the others.

Write *heavier than* and *lighter than* on the board. Ask each pair of children to say a sentence using the phrases *heavier than* or *lighter than*. For example, "I am heavier/lighter than (name)." The other children can check if the pair is correct by looking at the cards held up by the pair.

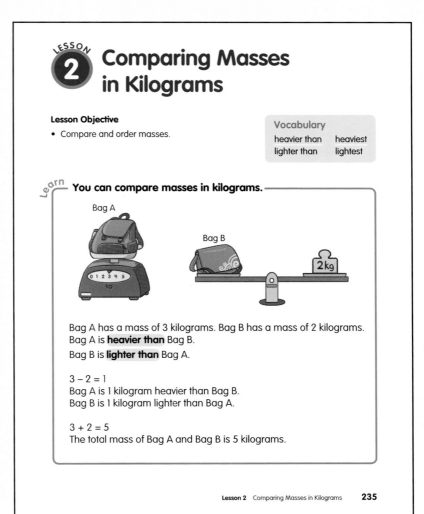

LESSON 2 Comparing Masses in Kilograms

Lesson Objective
• Compare and order masses.

Vocabulary
heavier than   heaviest
lighter than   lightest

Learn **You can compare masses in kilograms.**

Bag A

Bag B

2 kg

Bag A has a mass of 3 kilograms. Bag B has a mass of 2 kilograms.
Bag A is **heavier than** Bag B.
Bag B is **lighter than** Bag A.

3 – 2 = 1
Bag A is 1 kilogram heavier than Bag B.
Bag B is 1 kilogram lighter than Bag A.

3 + 2 = 5
The total mass of Bag A and Bag B is 5 kilograms.

Lesson 2   Comparing Masses in Kilograms   **235**

Student Book A p. 235

DAY 1 **Teach**

Learn **Compare Masses in Kilograms** (page 235)

Children learn to compare the masses of objects and tell which is heavier or lighter.

• Explain and show children how to read the scales and balance to find the masses of Bags A and B in kilograms.

• Lead children to realize that masses of objects are compared using the numerical values of the masses.

• Ask children which bag is heavier and by how much. (Answer: Bag A, by 1 kilogram.)

Best Practices You may want to have children work in small groups at the Math Center during the day. Have groups find and compare the masses of items around the room or school. Invite them to order three of the objects from lightest to heaviest. Remind them to use the vocabulary words in their discussion.

Guided Practice

**Read the measuring scale to find the mass of each object.
Then answer the questions.**

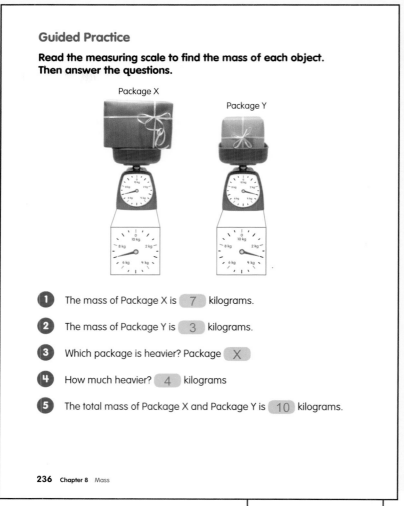

Package X

Package Y

1. The mass of Package X is **7** kilograms.

2. The mass of Package Y is **3** kilograms.

3. Which package is heavier? Package **X**

4. How much heavier? **4** kilograms

5. The total mass of Package X and Package Y is **10** kilograms.

Student Book A p. 236

**Look at the pictures.
Then answer the questions.**

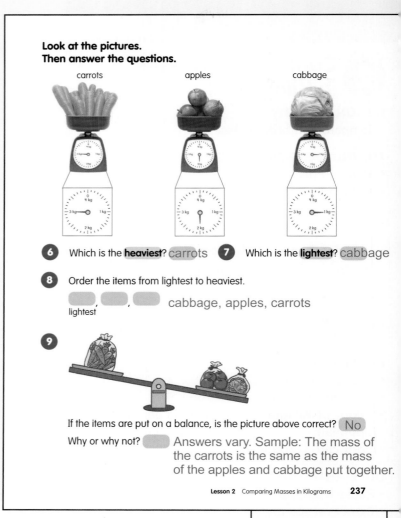

carrots   apples   cabbage

6. Which is the **heaviest**? carrots   7. Which is the **lightest**? cabbage

8. Order the items from lightest to heaviest.

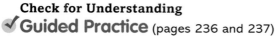 cabbage, apples, carrots

lightest

9.

If the items are put on a balance, is the picture above correct? No

Why or why not?   Answers vary. Sample: The mass of the carrots is the same as the mass of the apples and cabbage put together.

Student Book A p. 237

Check for Understanding

✓ Guided Practice (pages 236 and 237)

1 to **3** These exercises provide practice in reading a measuring scale to find and compare the masses of objects.

4 Children should identify subtraction as the method used to find the difference in mass.

5 Children should identify addition as the method used to find the total mass.

6 to **9** These exercises provide practice in comparing and ordering the masses of three objects using measuring scales.

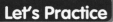

Let's Practice

**Read the measuring scale to find the mass of each object.
Then answer the questions.**

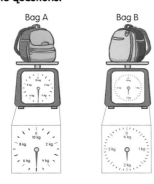

Bag A   Bag B

1 The mass of Bag A is (5) kilograms.

2 The mass of Bag B is (2) kilograms.

3 Which bag is heavier? Bag (A)

4 How much heavier? (3) kilograms heavier

238   Chapter 8   Mass

Student Book A p. 238

Problem of the Lesson

The total mass of a watermelon and a pumpkin is 7 kilograms. The mass of the watermelon is 1 kilogram more than the mass of the pumpkin.

Find the mass of each fruit. Use the bar models to help you solve the problem.

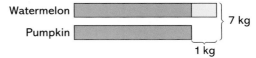

Watermelon

Pumpkin

7 kg

1 kg

Solution:

$7 - 1 = 6$

$6 \div 2 = 3$

$3 + 1 = 4$

Answers:

Mass of watermelon: 4 kg

Mass of pumpkin: 3 kg

Let's Practice (pages 238 and 239)

Exercises ❶ to ⓫ reinforce children's ability to read a measuring scale to find, compare, and order masses of objects.

Exercises ❹ and ❽ to ❿ require children to also use subtraction and addition to find differences in mass and total mass.

Common Error Some children will not understand that the two scales on page 238 are different. They may see both arrows pointing down and think the bags have the same mass. Remind children to read the numbers on the scales. You may wish to have copies of the **Kilogram Scales** (TR17) available to help children notice the difference.

Differentiated Instruction

English Language Learners

Heaviest, lightest, heavier than, and *lighter than* may be unfamiliar terms. Give groups of children several objects of varying mass. Have children compare and talk about the objects using the new vocabulary.

Look at the pictures.
Then answer the questions.

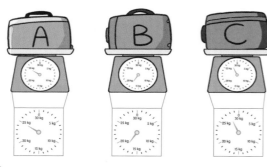

5. The mass of Bag A is 25 kilograms.

6. The mass of Bag B is 18 kilograms.

7. The mass of Bag C is 28 kilograms.

8. Bag A is 7 kilograms heavier than Bag B.

9. Bag B is 10 kilograms lighter than Bag C.

10. The total mass of Bag A and Bag C is 53 kilograms.

11. Order the bags from heaviest to lightest.

C , A , B
heaviest

ON YOUR OWN
Go to Workbook A:
Practice 2, pages 193–196

Lesson 2 Comparing Masses in Kilograms **239**

Student Book A p. 239

ON YOUR OWN

Children practice reading measuring scales and comparing
mass in kilograms in Practice 2, pages 193 to 196 of
Workbook 2A. These pages (with the answers) are shown at
the right and on page 239A.

Differentiation Options Depending on children's success
with the Workbook pages, use these materials as needed.
Struggling: Reteach 2A, pp. 163–164
On Level: Extra Practice 2A, pp. 119–120

Practice and Apply
Workbook pages for Chapter 8, Lesson 2

Name: _____ Date: _____

Practice 2 Comparing Masses in Kilograms
Look at the pictures.
Then fill in the blanks.

bag of oranges bag of potatoes

1. The mass of the bag of oranges is _____ 2 _____ kilograms.

2. The mass of the bag of potatoes is _____ 3 _____ kilograms.

3. Which bag is heavier? The bag of ___ potatoes ___

4. How much heavier? _____ 1 _____ kg

5. The total mass of the bag of oranges and the bag of
   potatoes is _____ 5 _____ kilograms.

Lesson 2 Comparing Masses in Kilograms **193**

Workbook A p. 193

Look at the pictures.
Then answer the questions.

chicken fish vegetables

6. Which is the heaviest? The ___ chicken ___

7. Which is the lightest? The ___ vegetables ___

8. Order the items from lightest to heaviest.

   ___ vegetables ___ , ___ fish ___ , ___ chicken ___
   lightest

9.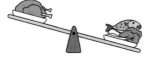

   If the items are put on a balance scale, do you think the picture
   above is correct? ___ No ___

   Why or why not? Answers vary.
   Sample: The weight of the chicken equals the
   combined weights of the fish and the vegetables.

194 Chapter 8 Mass

Workbook A p. 194

Notes

Name: _____ **Date:** _____

Fill in the blanks.
The pictures show Ally's and Roger's mass.

Ally   Roger

10. Ally has a mass of _____54_____ kilograms.

11. Roger has a mass of _____74_____ kilograms.

12. Who is heavier, Roger or Ally? _____Roger_____

13. How much heavier? _____20_____ kg

14. What is the total mass of Roger and Ally?

_____128_____ kg

Workbook A p. 195

Read each sentence.
Write *True* or *False*.

Bag A

Bag B   Bag A and Bag C

15. The mass of Bag A is 2 kilograms. _____True_____

16. Bag B has the same mass as the total mass of both
Bag A and Bag C. _____True_____

17. The mass of Bag A is different from the mass of Bag B.
_____True_____

18. Bag B is heavier than Bag C. _____True_____

Workbook A p. 196

Chapter 8

LESSON 3 Measuring in Grams

LESSON OBJECTIVE
• Use a measuring scale to measure mass in grams.

TECHNOLOGY RESOURCES
• *Math in Focus* eBooks
• *Math in Focus* Teacher Resources CD

Vocabulary
gram (g)

DAY 1 Student Book 2A, pp. 240–244
Workbook 2A, pp. 197–202

MATERIALS
• 1-gram mass
• 1 measuring scale
• 1-kg bag of beans
• 1 copy of Kilogram Scales (TR17)
• 1 copy of Gram Scale (TR18)

DIFFERENTIATION RESOURCES
• Reteach 2A, pp. 165–168
• Extra Practice 2A, pp. 121–122

 5-minute Warm Up

To familiarize children with reading the measuring scale in kilograms, use large cut-outs of the **Kilogram Scales** (TR17) and a pointer to point out different readings.

Ask children to read the mass. (You may also use an overhead projector and a pointer to point at the different markings.)

This helps to prepare them for reading the gram scale in this chapter.

LESSON 3 Measuring in Grams

Lesson Objective
• Use a measuring scale to measure mass in grams.

Vocabulary
gram (g)

Learn You can use smaller units to measure the mass of lighter objects.

These are some objects that are lighter than 1 kilogram.

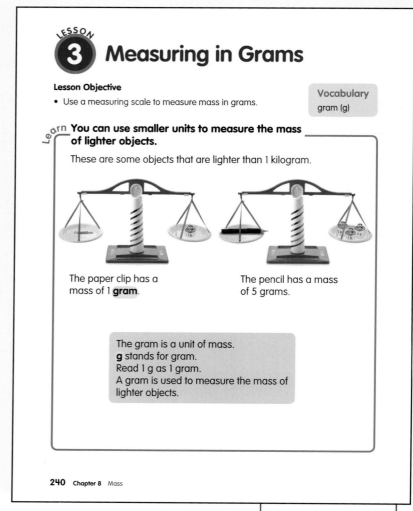

The paper clip has a mass of 1 **gram**.

The pencil has a mass of 5 grams.

> The gram is a unit of mass.
> **g** stands for gram.
> Read 1 g as 1 gram.
> A gram is used to measure the mass of lighter objects.

240 Chapter 8 Mass

Student Book A p. 240

DAY 1 Teach

Learn

Use Smaller Units to Measure the Mass of Lighter Objects (page 240)

Children develop a sense of how heavy 1 gram is and find the mass of an object in grams using the balance with 1-gram masses.

• Show children objects that are lighter than 1 kilogram. Explain to children that these objects are lighter than 1 kilogram and their masses are measured in grams (g).

• Show children a nickel coin. Pass it around the class for children to hold and feel how heavy a 5-gram mass is.

• Ask children to refer to the pictures in the Student Book and point out that the mass of the paper clip is 1 gram. Have children count the masses on the other balance to find the mass of the pencil.

• Inform children that 'gram' is the unit of measure for mass of objects that are less than 1 kilogram.

• Highlight to children that '1 g' is read in full as '1 gram'.

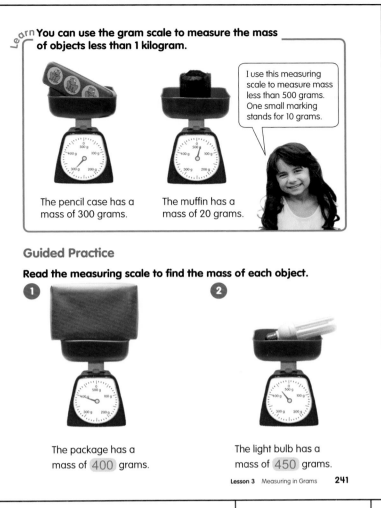

Learn You can use the gram scale to measure the mass of objects less than 1 kilogram.

I use this measuring scale to measure mass less than 500 grams. One small marking stands for 10 grams.

The pencil case has a mass of 300 grams.

The muffin has a mass of 20 grams.

Guided Practice

Read the measuring scale to find the mass of each object.

1

The package has a mass of 400 grams.

2

The light bulb has a mass of 450 grams.

Lesson 3   Measuring in Grams   **241**

Student Book A p. 241

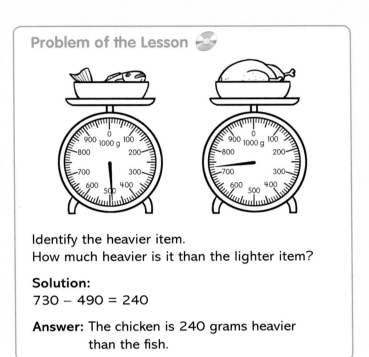

Problem of the Lesson

Identify the heavier item.
How much heavier is it than the lighter item?

Solution:
730 − 490 = 240

Answer: The chicken is 240 grams heavier than the fish.

Best Practices   You may want to have children work in small groups at the Math Center. Give each group a list of common items in their desk to measure. Groups can add gram weights or nickels as needed to determine the mass of objects. Have children discuss results with other groups.

Learn

Use the Measuring Scale to Measure the Mass of Objects Less Than 1 Kilogram

(page 241)

Children learn to read the measuring scale to find the mass of an object less than 500 g.

• Explain and show how to read the scales to find the masses of the objects in grams.

• Emphasize that one small marking on the scale stands for 10 grams.

• You can use cut-outs of a measuring scale or an overhead projector to let children practice reading a measuring scale. (See **Gram Scale** (TR18) for a copy of the 500-gram scale.)

Differentiated Instruction

English Language Learners

To help children understand and learn the word *gram*, use a balance scale. Have children place a light object on one side and add 1-g masses one at a time on the other side until the scale is close to being balanced. Have children say the phrases one *gram*, two *grams*... as they add 1-g masses. If you are using nickel coins as weights, have them count by 5s: 5 grams, 10 grams, ... as they add nickels.

Check for Understanding
✓**Guided Practice** (page 241)

1 and **2** These exercises provide practice in measuring the mass of objects using a gram scale and reinforce the proper technique used in such measurements.

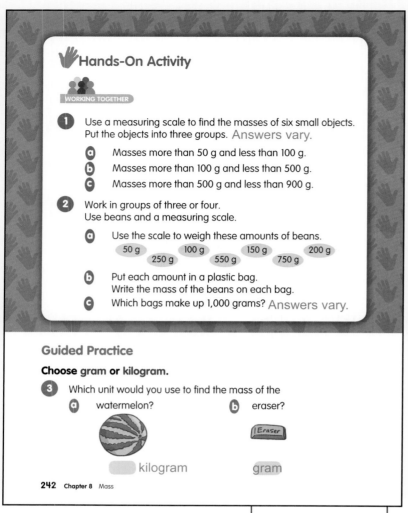

Student Book A p. 242

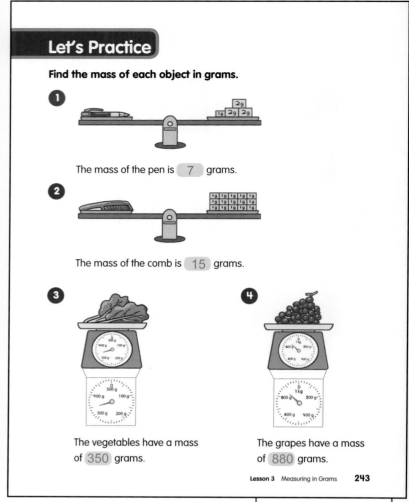

Student Book A p. 243

Hands-On Activity:

![WORKING TOGETHER]

Use a Measuring Scale to Find Mass
(page 242)

This activity provides practice in using a scale to measure mass.

- Place children in groups of four.

- Children find the masses of various items, for example, a stapler, and classify these items according to mass.

- Children measure out the required amounts of beans using the **measuring scale** and put them in different plastic bags.

✓ Guided Practice (page 242)

3 This exercise checks that children can choose the appropriate units to find the mass of different objects.

Let's Practice (pages 243 and 244)

These exercises provide more practice in measurement using grams.

Exercises 1 and 2 check children's ability to find mass using a balance and 1-gram masses.

Exercises 3 and 4 check children's ability to read a measuring scale.

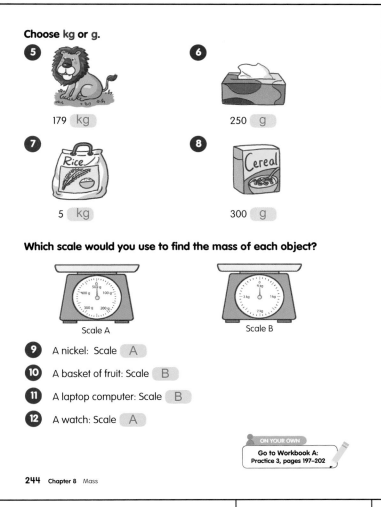

Choose kg or g.

5 179 kg

6 250 g

7 5 kg

8 300 g

Which scale would you use to find the mass of each object?

Scale A

Scale B

9 A nickel: Scale A

10 A basket of fruit: Scale B

11 A laptop computer: Scale B

12 A watch: Scale A

ON YOUR OWN
Go to Workbook A:
Practice 3, pages 197–202

244 Chapter 8 Mass

Student Book A p. 244

Practice and Apply
Workbook pages for Chapter 8, Lesson 3

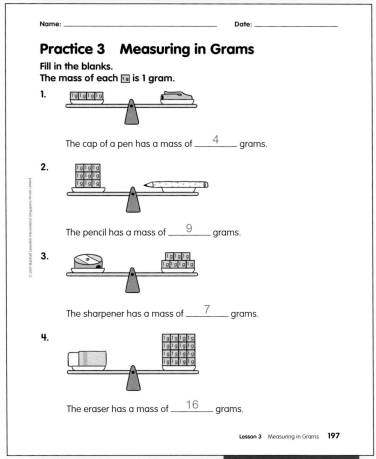

Name: _____ Date: _____

Practice 3   Measuring in Grams

Fill in the blanks.
The mass of each ⊡ is 1 gram.

1. The cap of a pen has a mass of _____4_____ grams.

2. The pencil has a mass of _____9_____ grams.

3. The sharpener has a mass of _____7_____ grams.

4. The eraser has a mass of _____16_____ grams.

Lesson 3 Measuring in Grams **197**

Workbook A p. 197

Exercises **5** to **12** check children's ability to choose the appropriate units (g) or (kg) when measuring the mass of various items.

Common Error Some children may confuse kilograms and grams. Tell children that kilogram (kg) is a bigger word than gram (g) to help them remember that kilogram is used to measure heavier objects.

ON YOUR OWN

Children practice measuring in grams in Practice 3, pages 197 to 202 of **Workbook 2A**. These pages (with the answers) are shown at the right and on page 244A.

Differentiation Options Depending on children's success with the Workbook pages, use these materials as needed.
Struggling: Reteach 2A, pp. 165–168
On Level: Extra Practice 2A, pp. 121–122

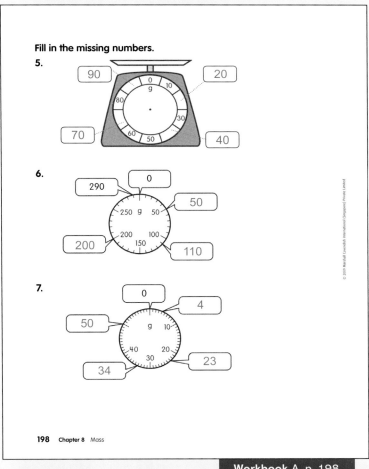

Fill in the missing numbers.

5. 90   20   70   40

6. 290   0   50   200   110

7. 0   4   50   34   23

198 Chapter 8 Mass

Workbook A p. 198

Workbook A p. 199

Name: _____ Date: _____

Fill in the missing numbers.

8.

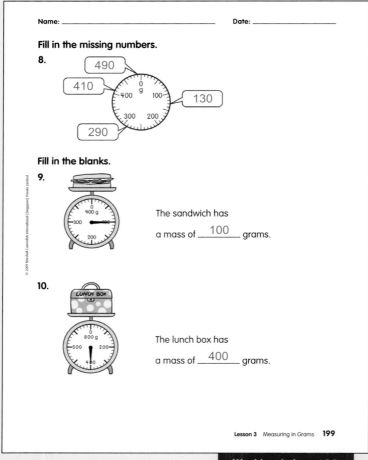

490
410
130
290

Fill in the blanks.

9. The sandwich has a mass of __100__ grams.

10. The lunch box has a mass of __400__ grams.

Workbook A p. 199

Workbook A p. 201

Name: _____ Date: _____

Fill in the blanks.

13.

The bag of peanuts has a mass of __170__ grams.

14.

The box of crackers has a mass of __370__ grams.

Workbook A p. 201

Workbook A p. 200

Fill in the blanks.

11.

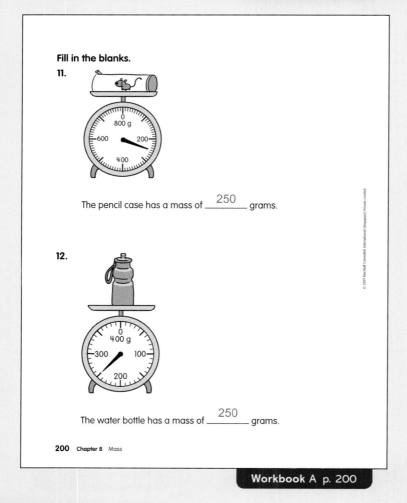

The pencil case has a mass of __250__ grams.

12.

The water bottle has a mass of __250__ grams.

Workbook A p. 200

Workbook A p. 202

Fill in the blanks.

15. The empty bowl has a mass of __300__ grams.

16. Some marbles are put into the bowl.

The bowl and the marbles have a mass of __480__ grams

17. What is the mass of the marbles? __180__ grams

Workbook A p. 202

Comparing Masses in Grams

LESSON OBJECTIVE
• Compare and order masses in grams.

TECHNOLOGY RESOURCES
• *Math in Focus* eBooks
• *Math in Focus* Teacher Resources CD

DAY 1
Student Book 2A, pp. 245–252
Workbook 2A, pp. 203–204

MATERIALS
• 3 bags of marbles per group
• 1 measuring scale
• 3 index cards
• 3 fruits per group
• 1 Chart for Recording Mass (TR19) per group

DIFFERENTIATION RESOURCES
• Reteach 2A, pp. 169–170
• Extra Practice 2A, pp. 123–124

 5-minute Warm Up

• This activity gives children a chance to estimate mass. Show the class any three objects in the classroom that you have weighed beforehand. Choose objects that have a mass of less than 1 kilogram, and write their mass on an index card.

• For each object, have five children take turns holding the object and estimating its mass in grams. Children then write their estimates on the board.

• Show the actual mass on the index card to see who has made the best guess.

 Comparing Masses in Grams

Lesson Objective
• Compare and order masses in grams.

Learn **You can compare masses in grams.**

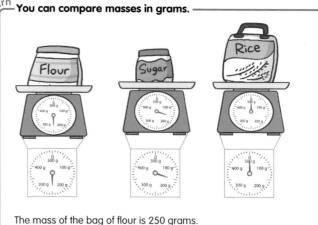

The mass of the bag of flour is 250 grams.
The mass of the bag of sugar is 150 grams.
The mass of the bag of rice is 500 grams.

The bag of sugar is the lightest object.
The bag of rice is the heaviest object.
From lightest to heaviest, the objects are: sugar, flour, rice.

You can find the total mass of the bag of flour and the bag of sugar.
250 + 150 = 400
The total mass of the bag of flour and the bag of sugar is 400 grams.

Lesson 4 Comparing Masses in Grams **245**

Student Book A p. 245

 **Teach**

Learn

Compare Masses in Grams (page 245)

Children learn to compare masses and order them. Children also learn to find the total mass of two objects by adding in grams.

• Have children read the measuring scale to find the mass of each item in the Student Book. Then ask children to compare and order the masses.

• Help children recall that they can add any two masses to find the total mass of two items. Use examples from the Learn section to model the addition.

Best Practices You may want to teach this lesson as four mini-lessons: comparing mass, ordering objects by mass, finding the total mass of several objects, and finding the difference in mass of two objects.

Guided Practice

Ben is finding the masses of his tape dispenser, stapler, and notebook using a measuring scale.

This is what Ben writes on a piece of paper.

> The mass of my tape dispenser is 320 grams.
> The mass of my stapler is 100 grams.
> The mass of my notebook is 250 grams.
> The lightest object is my stapler.
> The heaviest object is my tape dispenser.

Help Ben complete each sentence.
Use lighter or heavier.

1. The notebook is __heavier__ than the stapler.

2. The stapler is __lighter__ than the tape dispenser.

3. Order the stapler, tape dispenser, and notebook from heaviest to lightest.
   __tape dispenser__, __notebook__, __stapler__
   heaviest   lighter

   > 100 + 250 = 350
   > The total mass of the stapler and notebook is 350 grams.

4. The tape dispenser is __lighter__ than the total mass of the stapler and the notebook.

246 Chapter 8 Mass

Student Book A p. 246

Box A is heavier than Box B.
Box C is lighter than Box D.
Boxes C and D have a total mass equal to that of Box B.
Arrange the boxes in order of their masses from the lightest to heaviest.

Solution:
Boxes C and D are lighter than Box B because their total mass is that of B. Combining this with the first and third sentences in the problem, the order is: Box C, Box D, Box B, Box A.

Answer: Box C, Box D, Box B, Box A (lightest to heaviest)

Differentiated Instruction

English Language Learners

Some children may have difficulty reading page 246. Label the objects with a name and arrow on a sheet of paper or label real physical objects that can be displayed on the child's desk. Have children order the real objects from heaviest to lightest on their desk.

Check for Understanding
✓ Guided Practice (page 246)

1 to **3** These exercises provide practice in the comparison of mass using the appropriate terms such as 'heavier', 'heaviest', 'lighter', and 'lightest'.

4 This is a problem that requires a two-step solution. Guide children to find the total mass of the stapler and notebook by adding the two individual masses before finding the answer to the second step.

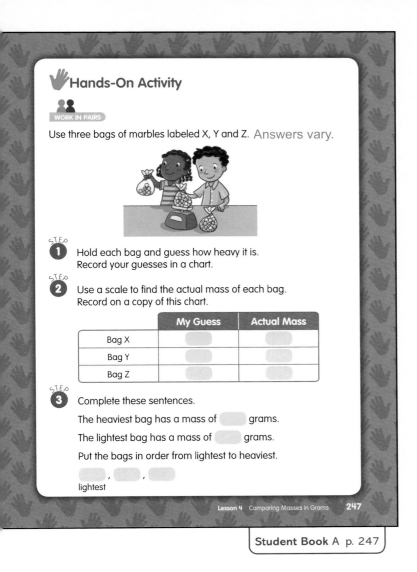

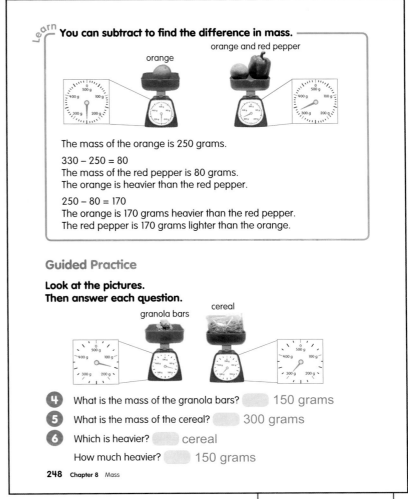

Student Book A p. 247

Student Book A p. 248

 Hands-On Activity:

WORKING TOGETHER

Guess, Measure, and Compare Masses of Objects (page 247)

This activity provides children with practice in estimating and measuring masses using the measuring scale.

- Prepare bags of marbles (of different masses, not exceeding 1 kilogram). Label them Bags X, Y, and Z. You may replace the marbles with other objects such as beans if necessary.

- Children work in groups of four at the Math Center. Give each group a copy of the **Chart for Recording Mass** (TR19).

- Have children follow the steps in the activity.

- Ask children to estimate the mass of each bag of marbles. Then have children use the **measuring scale** to confirm their estimates.

- Ask children to find out which are the heaviest and lightest bags, and then to arrange them in order of their masses.

Subtract to Find the Difference in Mass
(page 248)

Children find the difference in masses of two objects by subtracting.

- Explain the example in the Student Book. Point out that the orange is common to both cases.

- Have children read the mass of the orange, and that of the orange and red pepper together.

- Explain that the heavier mass contains the masses of both objects. Lead children to find the mass of the red pepper, which is the object not common to both measurements.

- Ask children to compare the masses of the orange and the red pepper.

✓ Guided Practice (page 248)

④ to ⑥ These exercises provide practice in comparing masses and subtracting to find the difference in masses.

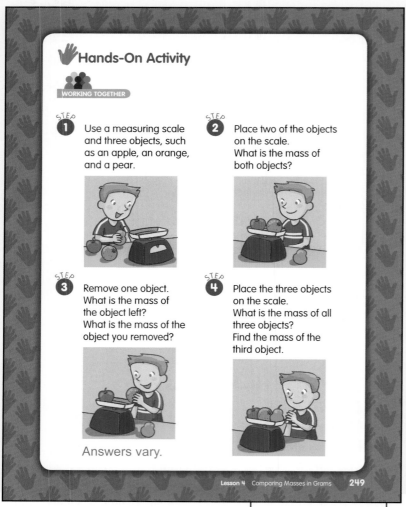

Hands-On Activity:

WORKING TOGETHER

Subtract to Find the Difference in Mass

(page 249)

This activity provides further practice in measuring masses using the **measuring scale**.

- Children work in groups of four at the Math Center. Give each group 3 fruits, such as an apple, orange, and pear.

- Have children follow the steps to find the mass of the fruits.

- Have children record the masses at each step, for example:

Mass of apple and orange is _____.

Mass of apple only is _____.

Mass of 3 fruits (apple, orange, and pear) is _____.

Mass of the pear is _____.

Let's Practice (pages 250 to 252)

Exercises ❶ to ⓰ provide more practice in measuring and comparing masses of objects in grams. Then check that children can use addition and subtraction appropriately to find the mass of different objects.

Common Error Some children may not be able to identify and name the various fruits. Discuss and write the names of the fruits on the board as they appear from left to right.

Look at the pictures.
Then answer the questions.

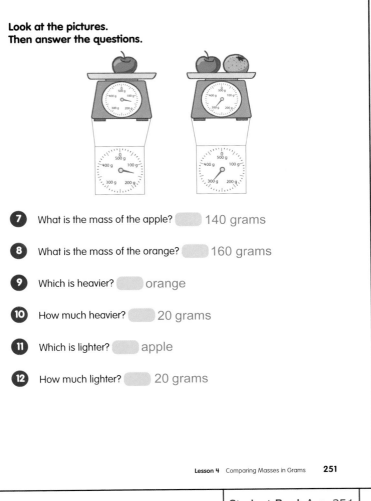

7 What is the mass of the apple? 140 grams

8 What is the mass of the orange? 160 grams

9 Which is heavier? orange

10 How much heavier? 20 grams

11 Which is lighter? apple

12 How much lighter? 20 grams

Look at the pictures.
Then answer the questions.

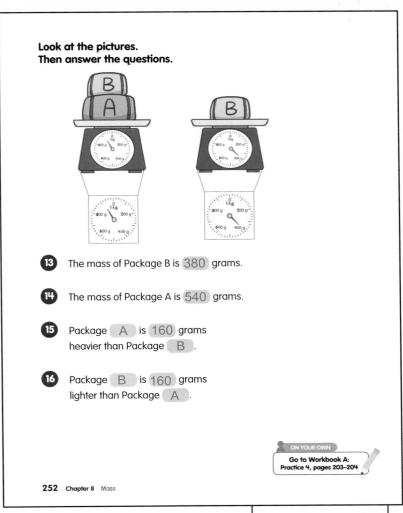

13 The mass of Package B is 380 grams.

14 The mass of Package A is 540 grams.

15 Package A is 160 grams
heavier than Package B.

16 Package B is 160 grams
lighter than Package A.

ON YOUR OWN
Go to Workbook A:
Practice 4, pages 203–204

ON YOUR OWN

Children practice comparing masses in grams in Practice 4, pages 203 and 204 of **Workbook 2A**. These pages (with the answers) are shown on page 252A.

Differentiation Options Depending on children's success with the Workbook pages, use these materials as needed.
Struggling: Reteach 2A, pp. 169–170
On Level: Extra Practice 2A, pp. 123–124

Practice and Apply
Workbook pages for Chapter 8, Lesson 4

Name: _____ Date: _____

Practice 4 Comparing Masses in Grams

Find the mass of each vegetable.
Then fill in the blanks.

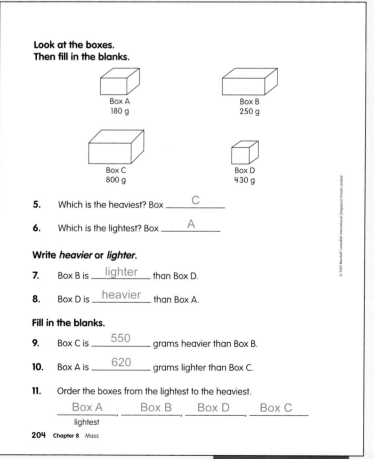

celery

[200] g

pumpkin

[750] g

carrots

[250] g

peppers

[100] g

1. The ___pumpkin___ is the heaviest.

2. The ___peppers___ are the lightest.

3. The pumpkin is ___550___ grams heavier than the celery.

4. The ___celery___ is heavier than the bag of peppers but lighter than the bag of carrots.

Workbook A p. 203

Look at the boxes.
Then fill in the blanks.

Box A
180 g

Box B
250 g

Box C
800 g

Box D
430 g

5. Which is the heaviest? Box ___C___

6. Which is the lightest? Box ___A___

Write *heavier* or *lighter*.

7. Box B is ___lighter___ than Box D.

8. Box D is ___heavier___ than Box A.

Fill in the blanks.

9. Box C is ___550___ grams heavier than Box B.

10. Box A is ___620___ grams lighter than Box C.

11. Order the boxes from the lightest to the heaviest.

___Box A___ ___Box B___ ___Box D___ ___Box C___
lightest

Workbook A p. 204

Notes

Chapter 8

LESSON 5 Real-World Problems: Mass

LESSON OBJECTIVE
• Use bar models to solve problems about mass.

TECHNOLOGY RESOURCES
• *Math in Focus* eBooks
• *Math in Focus* Teacher Resources CD

DAY 1 Student Book 2A, pp. 253–258
Workbook 2A, pp. 205–208

MATERIALS
• 1 measuring scale per group
• Paper Strips (TR07) (optional)

DIFFERENTIATION RESOURCES
• Reteach 2A, pp. 171–174
• Extra Practice 2A, pp. 125–127

5-minute Warm Up

• Review using bar models to solve real-world addition and subtraction problems. Draw a bar model similar to those in this lesson, with the numbers but without the units of measure.

• Children work in pairs. Have each pair write an addition or subtraction story based on the model.

• The stories do not need to be on measurement, since this activity is meant to prepare children for addition and subtraction of mass using bar models in this lesson.

• Invite pairs to share their stories.

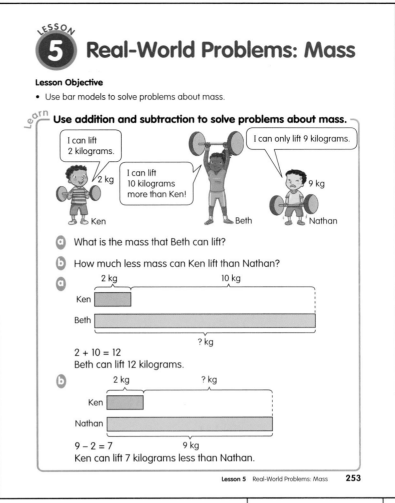

Student Book A p. 253

DAY 1 # Teach

Use Addition and Subtraction to Solve Problems About Mass (page 253)

Children solve problems and determine the operations used based on the addition and subtraction concepts.

• Write a few addition and subtraction sums on the board and have children solve them.

• Tell children that adding and subtracting mass follows the same procedure. Then remind them that they have to include the unit, which is either kilograms or grams, in their answers.

• Explain the examples in the Student Book, pointing out why addition or subtraction is used to solve each comparison problem.

Best Practices Have children work in pairs. Give children **Paper Strips** (TR07) to use as bar models. Have children use the strips to model the problem.

Guided Practice

Solve.
Use the bar models to help you.

1 A grocer has 78 kilograms of potatoes.
He sells 12 kilograms of potatoes.
How many kilograms of potatoes does he have left?

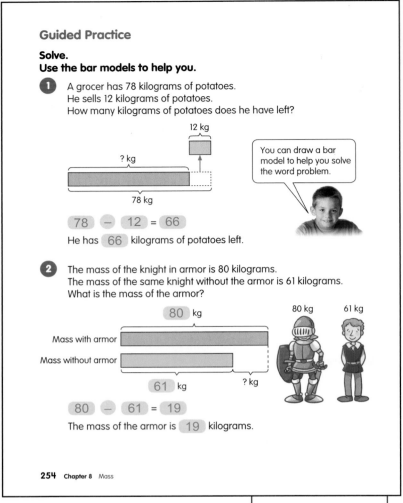

You can draw a bar model to help you solve the word problem.

78 − 12 = 66

He has 66 kilograms of potatoes left.

2 The mass of the knight in armor is 80 kilograms.
The mass of the same knight without the armor is 61 kilograms.
What is the mass of the armor?

80 − 61 = 19

The mass of the armor is 19 kilograms.

254 Chapter 8 Mass

Student Book A p. 254

Student Book A p. 254

Problem of the Lesson

Albert is 15 kilograms lighter than Benny.
Charlie is 31 kilograms heavier than Benny.
If their total mass is 148 kilograms, find their individual masses.

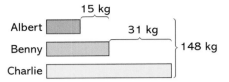

Solution:
148 − 31 − 15 − 15 = 87
87 ÷ 3 = 29
29 + 15 = 44
44 + 31 = 75

Answer: Albert: 29 kg; Benny: 44 kg;
Charlie: 75 kg

Differentiated Instruction

English Language Learners

Pair each child with a native English speaker. Have the English language learner read aloud each word problem. Pairs can discuss the numbers and operations that are needed to solve each problem. Have children work together to find a solution.

Check for Understanding
✓ **Guided Practice** (page 254)

1 and **2** These exercises provide practice in relating real-world measurement problems to addition and subtraction These exercises also reinforce the 'part-whole', 'comparing', and 'taking away' concepts and strategies related to addition and subtraction acquired by children in Grades 1 and 2.

For Advanced Learners Challenge children to find the mass of just the sugar in a container. Tell them they can use the measuring scale and another container (large enough to hold the sugar) to figure this out. They will need to subtract the mass of the container from the total mass.

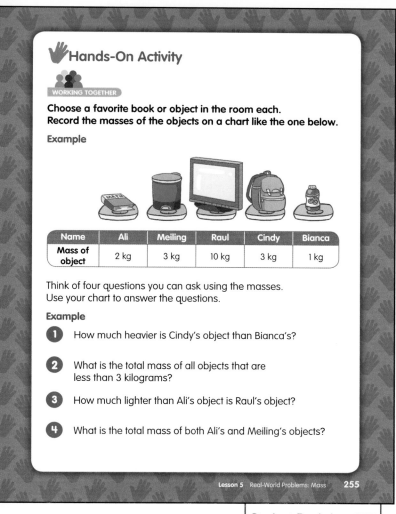

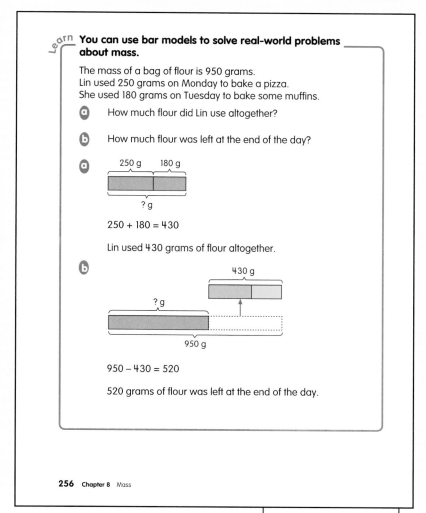

Student Book A p. 255

Student Book A p. 256

**Hands-On Activity:**

Write and Solve Real-World Problems about Mass (page 255)

This activity provides further practice in measuring mass in kilograms, using a **measuring scale**.

• Children work in groups of four at the Math Center.

• Children find the masses of the objects using a measuring scale, and formulate problems as shown in the Student Book.

• Guide children to formulate problems that require addition and subtraction involving 'part-whole', 'adding on', 'taking away', and 'comparing' to solve.

Use Bar Models to Solve Real-World Problems About Mass (page 256)

Children use bar models to help them solve addition and subtraction problems involving mass in grams.

• Explain the concepts involved in solving the two-step problem in the Student Book: 'part-whole' in addition and 'taking away' in subtraction.

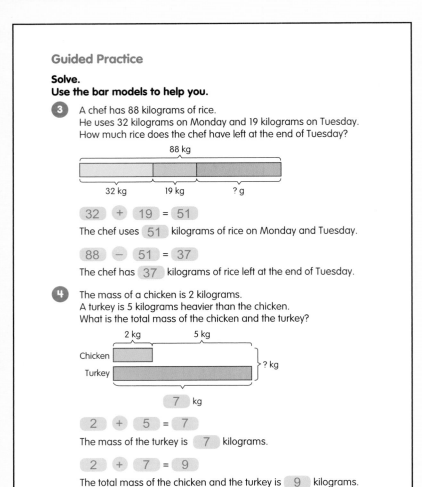

Guided Practice

Solve.
Use the bar models to help you.

3 A chef has 88 kilograms of rice.
He uses 32 kilograms on Monday and 19 kilograms on Tuesday.
How much rice does the chef have left at the end of Tuesday?

88 kg

32 kg   19 kg   ? g

32 + 19 = 51

The chef uses 51 kilograms of rice on Monday and Tuesday.

88 − 51 = 37

The chef has 37 kilograms of rice left at the end of Tuesday.

4 The mass of a chicken is 2 kilograms.
A turkey is 5 kilograms heavier than the chicken.
What is the total mass of the chicken and the turkey?

2 kg   5 kg

Chicken

Turkey   ? kg

7 kg

2 + 5 = 7

The mass of the turkey is 7 kilograms.

2 + 7 = 9

The total mass of the chicken and the turkey is 9 kilograms.

Lesson 5 Real-World Problems: Mass   **257**

Student Book A p. 257

Let's Practice

Solve.
Use bar models to help you.

1 A box of cereal has a mass of 850 grams.
The mass of the cereal is 670 grams.
What is the mass of the empty box?   180 grams

2 A bag of onions has a mass of 240 grams.
A bag of carrots has a mass of 470 grams.
How much lighter is the bag of onions than the bag of carrots?
230 grams

3 A bag of peaches has a mass of 540 grams.
A bag of tomatoes has a mass of 150 grams.
How much heavier is the bag of peaches than
the bag of tomatoes? 390 grams

4 The mass of a chair is 10 kilograms.
A table is 22 kilograms heavier than the chair.
What is the total mass of the table and the chair? 42 kilograms

5 Sara has 630 grams of strawberries.
She eats 120 grams of strawberries.
She gives 350 grams of strawberries to Jose.
What is the mass of the strawberries left? 160 grams

See Additional Answers

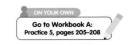

ON YOUR OWN
Go to Workbook A:
Practice 5, pages 205–208

258   Chapter 8   Mass

Student Book A p. 258

✓**Guided Practice** (page 257)

3 and **4** These exercises provide practice in relating
real-world problems about mass to bar models and addition
and subtraction concepts.

Let's Practice (page 258)

Exercises **1** to **5** provide more practice in solving real-world
problems about mass. Encourage children to use bar models to
help them. See Additional Answers, pages T66.

Common Error Some children may choose the wrong
numbers to solve the word problems. Tell children to read each
word problem carefully and choose the correct numbers to add
or subtract.

ON YOUR OWN

Children practice solving real-world mass problems in Practice
5, pages 205 and 206 of **Workbook 2A**. These pages (with
the answers) are shown on page 258A. The Math Journal on
Workbook 2A, pages 207 and 208, consolidate Lessons 1 to 5.
These pages (with the answers) are shown on page 258A.

Differentiation Options Depending on children's success
with the Workbook pages, use these materials as needed.
Struggling: Reteach 2A, pp. 171–174
On Level: Extra Practice 2A, pp. 125–127

Practice and Apply
Workbook pages for Chapter 8, Lesson 5

Name: _____ Date: _____

Practice 5 Real-World Problems: Mass

Solve.
Use bar models to help you.

1. Angelina has two dogs.
The masses of the two dogs are 35 kilograms
and 67 kilograms.
What is the total mass of the two dogs?

$35 + 67 = 102$

35 kg   67 kg

?

The total mass of the two dogs is __102__ kilograms.

2. Miguel has a mass of 32 kilograms.
He is 5 kilograms lighter than Sal.
What is Sal's mass?

$32 + 5 = 37$

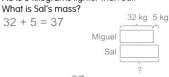

32 kg   5 kg

Miguel

Sal

?

Sal's mass is __37__ kilograms.

3. Mr. Souza needs 400 grams of clay to make a small statue.
He has only 143 grams of clay.
How much more clay does he need?

$400 - 143 = 257$

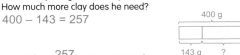

400 g

143 g   ?

He needs __257__ grams more clay.

Solve.

4. Ali has a mass of 25 kilograms.
Tyrone is 6 kilograms heavier than Ali.
What is their total mass?

$25 + 6 = 31$
$31 + 25 = 56$

25 kg   6 kg

Ali

Tyrone

?

?

Their total mass is __56__ kilograms.

5. Twyla buys a bag of onions with a mass of 750 grams.
She uses 100 grams of the onions for lunch.
She uses 480 grams of the onions for dinner.
What is the mass of the onions that are left?

$750 - 100 - 480 = 170$

750 g

100 g   480 g   ?

The mass of onions left is __170__ grams.

6. Tim sells 45 kilograms of rice on Monday.
He sells 18 kilograms less rice on Tuesday than on Monday.
How much rice does he sell in all on the two days?

$45 - 18 = 27$
$45 + 27 = 72$

45 kg

Monday

Tuesday   18 kg

?

?

He sells __72__ kilograms of rice in all on the two days.

Name: _____ Date: _____

Math Journal

Look at the pictures.

1. Write sentences to compare the mass of the boxes.
Use the words *lighter*, *heavier*, *lightest* and *heaviest*.

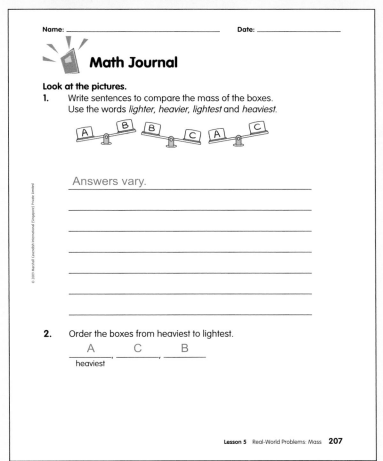

Answers vary.

_____

_____

_____

_____

_____

_____

2. Order the boxes from heaviest to lightest.

__A__   __C__ , __B__
heaviest

Write *True* or *False*.

─ **Example** ─────────────
The stapler is as heavy as the pen.

False
────────────────────────

3. The pen has a mass of 60 grams.
True

4. The stapler is 70 grams lighter than the pen.
False

5. The book is the heaviest.
True

6. The total mass of the stapler and the pen is 190 grams.
True

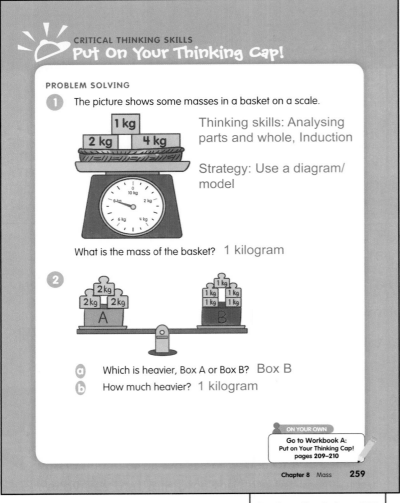

CRITICAL THINKING SKILLS
Put On Your Thinking Cap!

PROBLEM SOLVING

1. The picture shows some masses in a basket on a scale.

Thinking skills: Analysing parts and whole, Induction

Strategy: Use a diagram/model

What is the mass of the basket? 1 kilogram

2.

a. Which is heavier, Box A or Box B? Box B
b. How much heavier? 1 kilogram

ON YOUR OWN
Go to Workbook A: Put on Your Thinking Cap! pages 209–210

Chapter 8 Mass **259**

Student Book A p. 259

CRITICAL THINKING SKILLS
Put on Your Thinking Cap! (page 259)

This problem solving exercise requires children to infer and deduce the mass of the basket and boxes. Children work individually or in groups to answer the questions and present their solutions to the class.

Thinking Skills

• Analyzing parts and whole
• Induction

Problem Solving Strategy

• Use a diagram/model

ON YOUR OWN

Because all children should be challenged, have all children try the Challenging Practice and Problem Solving pages in **Workbook 2A**, pages 209 and 210. These pages (with the answers) are shown at the right.

Differentiation Options Depending on children's success with the Workbook pages, use these materials as needed.
On Level: Extra Practice 2A, p. 128
Advanced: Enrichment 2A, pp. 66–75

Practice and Apply
Workbook pages for Put on Your Thinking Cap!

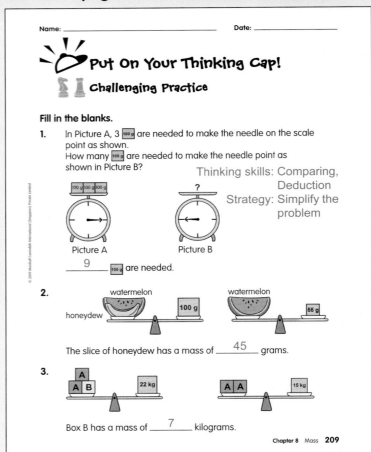

Name: _____   Date: _____

Put On Your Thinking Cap!
Challenging Practice

Fill in the blanks.

1. In Picture A, 3 [100 g] are needed to make the needle on the scale point as shown.
How many [100 g] are needed to make the needle point as shown in Picture B?

Thinking skills: Comparing, Deduction
Strategy: Simplify the problem

Picture A   Picture B

____9____ [100 g] are needed.

2.   watermelon   watermelon
honeydew   100 g   55 g

The slice of honeydew has a mass of ____45____ grams.

3.

Box B has a mass of ____7____ kilograms.

Chapter 8 Mass **209**

Workbook A p. 209

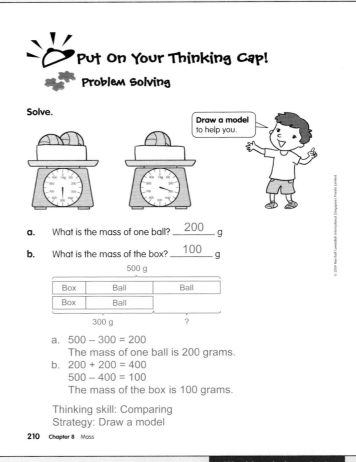

Put On Your Thinking Cap!
Problem Solving

Solve.

Draw a model to help you.

a. What is the mass of one ball? ____200____ g
b. What is the mass of the box? ____100____ g

	500 g	
Box	Ball	Ball
Box	Ball	
	300 g	?

a. 500 − 300 = 200
   The mass of one ball is 200 grams.
b. 200 + 200 = 400
   500 − 400 = 100
   The mass of the box is 100 grams.

Thinking skill: Comparing
Strategy: Draw a model

210 Chapter 8 Mass

Workbook A p. 210

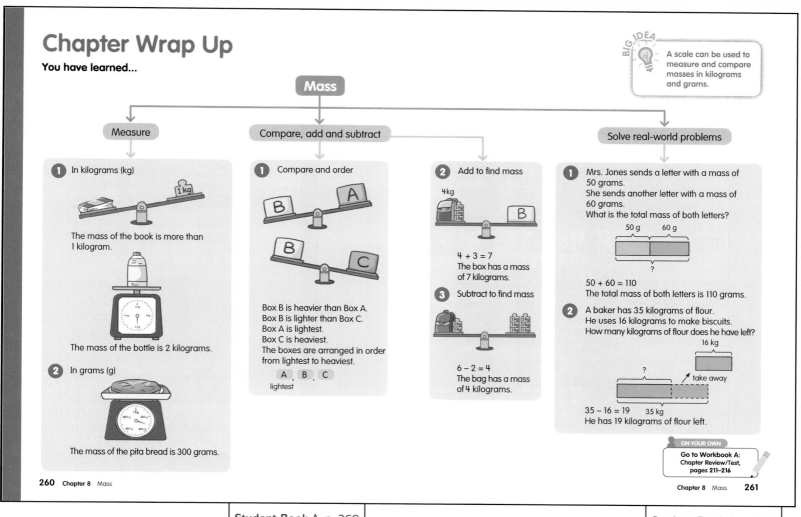

Chapter Wrap Up

You have learned...

Mass

Measure

1 In kilograms (kg)

The mass of the book is more than 1 kilogram.

The mass of the bottle is 2 kilograms.

2 In grams (g)

The mass of the pita bread is 300 grams.

Compare, add and subtract

1 Compare and order

Box B is heavier than Box A.
Box B is lighter than Box C.
Box A is lightest.
Box C is heaviest.
The boxes are arranged in order from lightest to heaviest.

A , B , C
lightest

2 Add to find mass

4 kg

$4 + 3 = 7$
The box has a mass of 7 kilograms.

3 Subtract to find mass

$6 - 2 = 4$
The bag has a mass of 4 kilograms.

Solve real-world problems

1 Mrs. Jones sends a letter with a mass of 50 grams.
She sends another letter with a mass of 60 grams.
What is the total mass of both letters?

50 g   60 g
?

$50 + 60 = 110$
The total mass of both letters is 110 grams.

2 A baker has 35 kilograms of flour.
He uses 16 kilograms to make biscuits.
How many kilograms of flour does he have left?

16 kg
?   take away
35 kg

$35 - 16 = 19$
He has 19 kilograms of flour left.

ON YOUR OWN
Go to Workbook A:
Chapter Review/Test,
pages 211–216

260   Chapter 8   Mass

Chapter 8   Mass   **261**

Student Book A p. 260

Student Book A p. 261

Chapter Wrap Up (pages 260 and 261)

Use the examples on pages 260 and 261 to review metric measurement of mass. Encourage children to use the chapter vocabulary:

- kilogram
- mass
- measuring scale
- as heavy as
- less than
- more than
- heavier than
- lighter than
- heaviest
- lightest
- gram (g)

ON YOUR OWN

Have children review the vocabulary, concepts, and skills from Chapter 8 with the Chapter Review/Test in **Workbook 2A**, pages 211 to 216. These pages (with the answers) are shown on pages 261A and 261B.

Assessment

Use the Chapter 8 Test Prep on pages 56 to 60 of **Assessments 2** to assess how well children have learned the material of this chapter. This assessment is appropriate for reporting results to adults at home and administrators. This test is shown on page 261C.

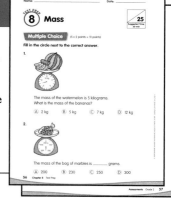

Assessments 2 pp. 56–60

Workbook pages for Chapter Review/Test

Name: _____   Date: _____

Chapter Review/Test
Vocabulary
Fill in the blanks with the words below.

kilogram	heavier than	mass
lightest	gram	measuring scale

1. A table is _____heavier than_____ a watch.

2. A _____kilogram_____ is a bigger unit of mass and a
    _____gram_____ is a smaller unit of mass.

3. To measure how heavy an object is, you find its _____mass_____.

4. You use a _____measuring scale_____ to measure the mass of an object.

5.
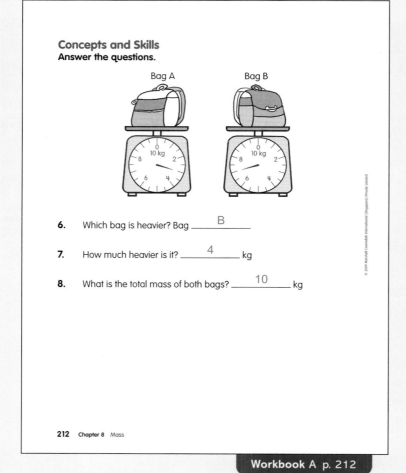

The spoon is the _____lightest_____.

Workbook A p. 211

Name: _____   Date: _____

9. Which bottle is the lightest? Bottle _____C_____

10. What is the difference in mass between the heaviest
    and lightest bottle? _____790_____ g

11. What is the total mass of Bottle A and Bottle C? _____470_____ g

12. Order the bottles from lightest to heaviest.
    Bottle C, _Bottle A_, _Bottle B_
    lightest

Workbook A p. 213

Concepts and Skills
Answer the questions.

Bag A   Bag B

6. Which bag is heavier? Bag _____B_____

7. How much heavier is it? _____4_____ kg

8. What is the total mass of both bags? _____10_____ kg

Workbook A p. 212

Problem Solving
Solve.
Use bar models to help you.

13. Mr. Shepherd has 5 kilograms of rice.
    He buys another 8 kilograms of rice.
    How many kilograms of rice does he have?

    $5 + 8 = 13$

    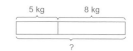

    Mr. Shepherd has _____13_____ kilograms of rice.

14. Claudia has two boxes.
    The mass of Box A is 980 grams.
    The mass of Box B is 750 grams.
    What is the difference in masses between the two boxes?

    $980 - 750 = 230$

    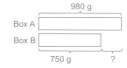

    The difference in masses between the two boxes is
    _____230_____ grams.

Workbook A p. 214

---

15. Casey has 500 grams of carrots.
He buys another 400 grams of carrots.
He uses 725 grams of carrots for a recipe.
How many grams of carrots does he have left?

$$500 + 400 = 900$$
$$900 - 725 = 175$$

500 g   400 g

725 g   ?

Casey has ____175____ grams of carrots left.

16. Lily's dog weighs 27 kilograms.
Her dog is 2 kilograms heavier than Ben's dog.
Joe's dog is 5 kilograms heavier than Ben's dog.
What is the mass of Joe's dog?

$$27 - 2 = 25$$
$$25 + 5 = 30$$

27 kg
Lily's dog
Ben's dog   2 kg
?

?   5 kg
Ben's dog
Joe's dog
?

The mass of Joe's dog is ____30____ kilograms.

Chapter 8 Mass **215**

Workbook A p. 215

17. A chef buys 45 kilograms of chicken.
He uses 7 kilograms of chicken on Tuesday.
He buys another 5 kilograms of chicken on Wednesday.
How many kilograms of chicken does he have left?

$$45 - 7 = 38$$
$$38 + 5 = 43$$

45 kg

?   7 kg

?   5 kg

?

He has ____43____ kilograms of chicken left.

18. The mass of Nadia's pencil case is 87 grams.
The mass of Pete's pencil case is 12 grams more than
the mass of Nadia's pencil case.
The mass of Felix's pencil case is 10 grams less than
the mass of Pete's pencil case.
Find the mass of Felix's pencil case.

$$87 + 12 = 99$$
$$99 - 10 = 89$$

87 g   12 g
Pete
?

Felix   10 g
?

The mass of Felix's pencil case is ____89____ grams.

Workbook A p. 216

Notes

Assessments Book pages for Chapter 8 Test Prep

Answer key appears in Assessments Book.

Assessments p. 56

Name: _____ Date: _____

TEST PREP 8 Mass

25
Suggested Time: 30 min

Multiple Choice (5 x 2 points = 10 points)

Fill in the circle next to the correct answer.

1.

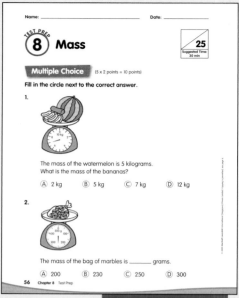

The mass of the watermelon is 5 kilograms.
What is the mass of the bananas?

Ⓐ 2 kg   Ⓑ 5 kg   Ⓒ 7 kg   Ⓓ 12 kg

2.

The mass of the bag of marbles is _____ grams.

Ⓐ 200   Ⓑ 230   Ⓒ 250   Ⓓ 300

56   Chapter 8   Test Prep

Assessments p. 57

Name: _____ Date: _____

3. How much heavier is the can of tuna than the bagel?

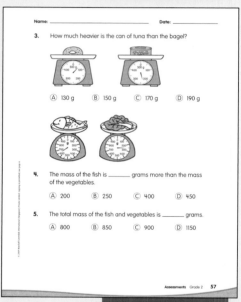

Ⓐ 130 g   Ⓑ 150 g   Ⓒ 170 g   Ⓓ 190 g

4. The mass of the fish is _____ grams more than the mass of the vegetables.

Ⓐ 200   Ⓑ 250   Ⓒ 400   Ⓓ 450

5. The total mass of the fish and vegetables is _____ grams.

Ⓐ 800   Ⓑ 850   Ⓒ 900   Ⓓ 1150

Assessments   Grade 2   57

Assessments p. 58

Name: _____ Date: _____

Short Answer (5 x 2 points = 10 points)

Follow the directions.

6. Fill in the blanks with *more* or *less*.

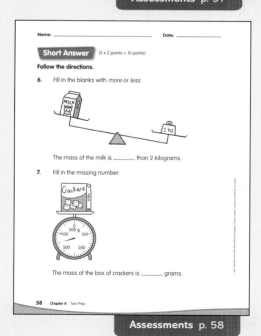

The mass of the milk is _____ than 2 kilograms.

7. Fill in the missing number.

The mass of the box of crackers is _____ grams.

58   Chapter 8   Test Prep

Assessments p. 59

Name: _____ Date: _____

Look at the pictures.
Then fill in the blanks.

8. Box A has a mass of _____ grams.

9. Box _____ is the lightest.

10. Box B is _____ grams lighter than Box C.

Assessments   Grade 2   59

Assessments p. 60

Name: _____ Date: _____

Extended Response (Question 11: 1 point, Questions 12 and 13: 2 x 2 = 4 points)

Look at the pictures.
Then fill in the blanks.

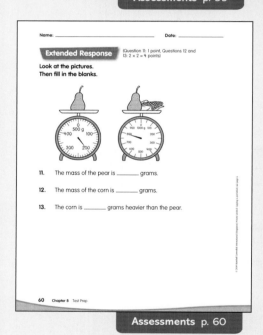

11. The mass of the pear is _____ grams.

12. The mass of the corn is _____ grams.

13. The corn is _____ grams heavier than the pear.

60   Chapter 8   Test Prep

Chapter Overview

Volume

Math Background

Children learned to measure and compare length and mass respectively in standard units in Grade 2, Chapters 7 and 8. Children learned that the standard units of length are meters and centimeters, and those of mass are kilograms and grams. In addition, children also learned addition and subtraction up to 1,000 with and without regrouping in Grade 2, Chapters 2 and 3, as well as using bar models to solve real-world problems in Chapter 4.

Getting to know volume, its units and properties is the main focus of this chapter. In Singapore Math, there is a distinction made between capacity of a container (amount of space in a container) and volume of liquid (amount of liquid in a container). This distinction is not made in this chapter because the emphasis here is on the amount or volume of liquids, and not containers. Children learn that the liter (L) is the unit of measure that provides a basis for the comparison of volume. The volume of liquid in a container can be measured by using one or more measuring cups. The liquid can be poured into the measuring cup(s) to determine its volume, regardless of the capacity of the original container. The volume of liquid in different containers can be compared by comparing the number of these measuring cups needed to contain all the liquid. Children learn through various hands-on activities to illustrate the concept that the volume of a liquid remains unchanged (or is conserved) when poured into different containers.

In addition, children also learn to apply the concepts of addition and subtraction to one- and two-step real-world problems involving volume. Children are taught to draw appropriate bar models to aid them in solving these problems.

Cross-Curricular Connections

Reading/Language Arts Read aloud *Millions to Measure* by David Schwartz (Harper Collins, © 2003) about Marvelosissimo the Mathematical Magician. He teaches four children the history of measurement and explains both standard and metric measurement systems.

Music Produce a musical scale. Gather eight similar-sized drinking glasses and arrange them in a row. Pour just a bit of water into the second glass from the left. Now pour water into each of the other glasses, with each glass having slightly more water than the previous one. Strike each glass with a spoon, starting with the empty glass. Add or take away water as needed to get the tones in order.

Skills Trace

Grade 1	
Grade 2	Measure and compare volume in liters using identical containers as well as measuring cups. Add and subtract volume with the help of bar models. (Chap. 9)
Grade 3	Measure and convert length, mass and volume in metric units. (Chap. 11) Solve real-world problems involving metric units of measurements. (Chap. 12)

EVERY DAY COUNTS®
Calendar Math

The January activities provide...

Review of using greater than and less than symbols to compare quantities (Chapter 1)

Preview of mental math addition strategies (Chapter 10)

Practice of relating word problems to symbolic number sentences (Lesson 3 in this chapter)

Differentiation Resources

Differentiation for Special Populations

	English Language Learners	Struggling Reteach 2A	On Level Extra Practice 2A	Advanced Enrichment 2A
Lesson 1	p. 267	pp. 175–178	pp. 129–132	Enrichment pages can be used to challenge advanced children.
Lesson 2	p. 274	pp. 179–182	pp. 133–136	
Lesson 3	p. 279	pp. 183–186	pp. 137–138	

Additional Support

For English Language Learners

Select activities that reinforce the chapter vocabulary and the connections among these words, such as having children

- add terms, definitions, and examples to the Word Wall

- act out measuring and comparing volume and use vocabulary terms to describe actions

- draw and label pictures to illustrate each term

- discuss the Chapter Wrap Up, encouraging children to use the chapter vocabulary

For Struggling Learners

Select activities that go back to the appropriate stage of the Concrete-Pictorial-Abstract spectrum, such as having children

- identify classroom objects to represent and compare different measures of volume

- draw pictures to compare and order volumes of different containers

- guess and check predictions of how volumes of various containers compare

- create and share stories about finding volume in real-life situations

See also pages 268–269 and 274

If necessary, review

- Chapter 7 (Metric Measurement of Length)

- Chapter 8 (Mass)

For Advanced Learners

See suggestions on pages 267 and 270–271.

Assessment and Remediation

Chapter 9 Assessment

Prior Knowledge

	Resource	Page numbers
Quick Check	Student Book 2A	p. 265
Pre-Test	Assessments 2	pp. 61–62

Ongoing Diagnostic

	Resource	Page numbers
Guided Practice	Student Book 2A	pp. 269, 271, 274, 275, 279–280
Common Error	Teacher's Edition 2A	pp. 272, 277, 280–281

Formal Evaluation

	Resource	Page numbers
Chapter Review/Test	Workbook 2A	pp. 233–236
Chapter 9 Test Prep	Assessments 2	pp. 63–67
Cumulative Review for Chapters 7 to 9	Workbook 2A	pp. 237–244
Mid-Year Review	Workbook 2A	pp. 245–256
Mid-Year Test Prep	Extra Practice 2A	pp. 141–156
Mid-Year Test	Assessments 2	pp. 68–82

Problems with these items...   Can be remediated with...

Remediation Options

Objective	Review/Test Items Workbook 2A pp. 233–236	Chapter Assessment Items Assessments 2 pp. 63–67	Reteach Reteach 2A	Student Book Student Book 2A
Use chapter vocabulary correctly.	1, 2, 3	Not assessed	In context as needed	pp. 266, 273
Explore and compare volume.	4, 5	1, 2, 5, 6, 7	pp. 175–178	Lesson 1
Use liters to estimate, measure, and compare volume.	6, 7, 8, 9	3, 4, 8, 9, 10	pp. 179–182	Lesson 2
Use bar models, addition, and subtraction to solve real-world problems about volume.	10, 11, 12, 13	11, 12	pp. 183–186	Lesson 3

Chapter Planning Guide

CHAPTER 9 Volume

Lesson	Pacing	Instructional Objectives	Vocabulary
Chapter Opener pp. 262–265 Recall Prior Knowledge Quick Check	*1 day	💡**Big Idea** Volume is the amount of liquid in a container. Liters can be used to measure volume.	
Lesson 1, pp. 266–272 Getting to Know Volume	2 days	• Explore and compare volume.	• volume • less than • most • more than • as much as • least
Lesson 2, pp. 273–277 Measuring in Liters	2 days	• Use liters to estimate, measure, and compare volume.	• liter (L) • measuring cup
Lesson 3, pp. 278–281 Real-World Problems: Volume	1 day	• Use bar models, addition, and subtraction to solve real-world problems about volume.	
Problem Solving, p. 281 🖐 Put on Your Thinking Cap!	$\frac{1}{2}$ day	**Thinking Skills** • Comparing • Deduction **Problem Solving Strategy** • Use a diagram/model	

*Assume that 1 day is a 45–55 minute period.

Resources	Materials	NCTM Focal Points	NCTM Process Standards
Student Book 2A, pp. 262–265 **Assessments 2,** pp. 61–62			
Student Book 2A, pp. 266–272 **Workbook 2A,** pp. 217–222 **Extra Practice 2A,** pp. 129–132 **Reteach 2A,** pp. 175–178	• empty containers of various shapes and sizes • 5 identical glasses per group • 1 large pitcher of water (optional)	**Measurement** Develop an understanding of the meaning and processes of measurement.	Connections Representation
Student Book 2A, pp. 273–277 **Workbook 2A,** pp. 223–226 **Extra Practice 2A,** pp. 133–136 **Reteach 2A,** pp. 179–182	• a 1-liter milk carton • empty containers of various shapes and sizes • 1 measuring cylinder • 1 measuring cup per pair (optional) • 1 small pitcher of water per pair (optional) • 1 ladle per pair (optional)	**Measurement** Use rulers and other measurement tools. Use standard units of measure.	Problem Solving Connections Representation
Student Book 2A, pp. 278–281 **Workbook 2A,** pp. 227–230 **Extra Practice 2A,** pp. 137–138 **Reteach 2A,** pp. 183–186	• Strips of construction paper in two different colors per pair	**Number and Operations** Add and subtract to solve a variety of problems. **Measurement** Develop an understanding of the meaning and processes of measurement.	Problem Solving Reasoning/Proof Representation
Student Book 2A, p. 281 **Workbook 2A,** pp. 231–232 **Extra Practice 2A,** pp. 139–140 **Enrichment 2A,** pp. 76–81		**Number and Operations** Add and subtract to solve a variety of problems. **Measurement** Develop an understanding of the meaning and processes of measurement.	Problem Solving Reasoning/Proof

Chapter Planning Guide

Lesson	Pacing	Instructional Objectives	Vocabulary
Chapter Wrap Up pp. 282–283	$\frac{1}{2}$ day	• Reinforce and consolidate chapter skills and concepts.	
Chapter Assessment	1 day		
Review Cumulative Review for Chapters. 7 to 9 Mid-Year Review Mid-Year Test Prep Mid-Year Test			

*Assume that 1 day is a 45–55 minute period.

Resources	Materials	NCTM Focal Points	NCTM Process Standards
Student Book 2A, pp. 282–283 **Workbook 2A,** pp. 233–236			
Assessments 2, pp. 63–67			
Workbook 2A, pp. 237–244 **Workbook 2A,** pp. 245–256 **Extra Practice 2A,** pp. 141–156 **Assessments 2,** pp. 68–82			

Technology Resources for easy classroom management
- *Math in Focus* eBooks
- *Math in Focus* Teacher Resources CD
- Online Assessment Generator

Chapter Introduction

Chapter 9
Vocabulary

volume	the amount of liquid a container has	Lesson 1
more than	having a greater amount than, e.g. 7 liters is more than 2 liters	Lesson 1
less than	having a smaller amount than, e.g. 2 liters is less than 5 liters	Lesson 1
as much as	having the same amount as	Lesson 1
most	having the greatest amount	Lesson 1
least	having the smallest amount	Lesson 1
liter (L)	a metric unit of volume	Lesson 2
measuring cup	a container for measuring a fixed amount of liquid	Lesson 2

Student Book A p. 262

Big Idea (page 262)

Getting to know volume and its metric unit of measure is the main focus of the chapter.

- Children learn that volume is the amount of liquid in a container.

- Children compare volumes of liquids in identical and non-identical containers.

- Children learn that the metric unit of measure for volume is liters.

- Children apply the concepts of addition and subtraction to solve problems involving volume.

Chapter Opener (page 262)

The picture illustrates two children tapping glass containers filled with varying volumes of water to create different sounds. It models comparing volumes of liquids.

- Show children the picture. Read and explain the text in the speech bubbles.

- Point out the different volumes of liquids in the containers.

- *Ask:* Which container has the smallest amount of liquid?

- *Ask:* Which container has the largest amount of liquid?

- You may try this activity in the classroom using glasses filled with different amounts of water.

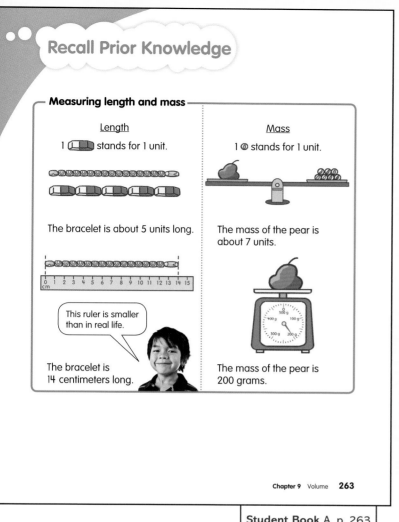

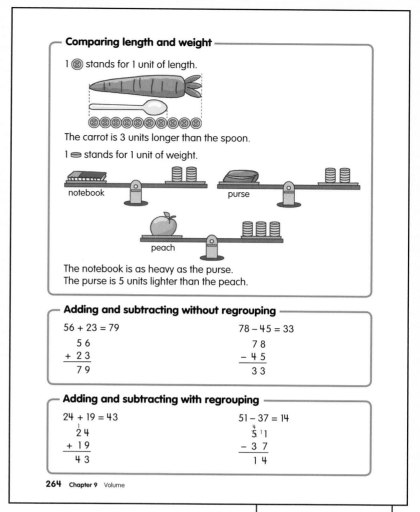

Recall Prior Knowledge (pages 263 and 264)

Measuring Length and Mass
Children learned to measure length and mass using metric units in Chapters 7 and 8.

- Show children the measurements of the length of the bracelet and mass of the pear.
- Have children identify the units for length and mass.

Comparing Length and Weight
Children learned to compare length and mass using non-standard units in Grade 1.

- Have children identify the length and mass of the items shown.
- Help children recall how to compare the lengths of the two objects.
- Help children recall how to compare weight using a balance with unit weights.

Adding and Subtracting Without Regrouping
Children learned addition and subtraction up to 100 without regrouping in Grade 1.

- Show children the number sentences without the answers.
- Help children recall the strategy for adding and subtracting numbers in vertical form: Add/Subtract from right to left (first add/subtract ones, and then the tens).
- Have children complete the number sentences.

Adding and Subtracting with Regrouping
Children learned addition and subtraction up to 100 with regrouping in Grade 1.

- Show children the number sentences without the answers.
- Help children recall the regrouping strategy: 10 ones = 1 ten and 1 ten = 10 ones.
- Have children complete the number sentences.

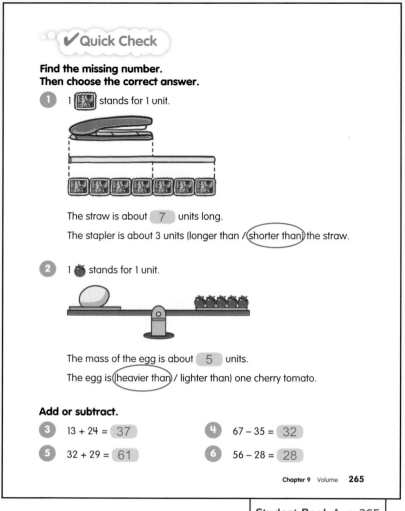

✔ Quick Check

**Find the missing number.
Then choose the correct answer.**

1. 1 🖼 stands for 1 unit.

The straw is about ⬚7⬚ units long.

The stapler is about 3 units (longer than / (shorter than)) the straw.

2. 1 🍅 stands for 1 unit.

The mass of the egg is about ⬚5⬚ units.

The egg is ((heavier than) / lighter than) one cherry tomato.

Add or subtract.

3. 13 + 24 = ⬚37⬚

4. 67 − 35 = ⬚32⬚

5. 32 + 29 = ⬚61⬚

6. 56 − 28 = ⬚28⬚

Chapter 9 Volume **265**

Student Book A p. 265

✔ Quick Check (page 265)

Use this section as a diagnostic tool to assess children's level of prerequisite knowledge before they progress to this chapter.

Exercises 1 and 2 assess measuring and comparing length and mass in non-standard units.

Exercises 3 to 6 assess children's ability to add and subtract with and without grouping.

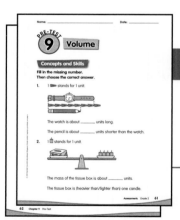

Assessments 2 pp. 61–62

Assessment

For additional assessment of children's prior knowledge and chapter readiness, use the Chapter 9 Pre-Test on pages 61 and 62 of **Assessments 2**.

Chapter 9

LESSON 1 Getting to Know Volume

LESSON OBJECTIVE
- Explore and compare volume.

TECHNOLOGY RESOURCE
- *Math in Focus* eBooks
- *Math in Focus* Teacher Resources CD
- *Math in Focus* Virtual Manipulatives

Vocabulary

volume	more than
less than	as much as
most	least

DAY 1 Student Book 2A, pp. 266–269

MATERIALS
- empty containers of various shapes and sizes
- 5 identical glasses per group
- 1 large pitcher of water (optional)

DAY 2 Student Book 2A, pp. 270–272
Workbook 2A, pp. 217–222

DIFFERENTIATION RESOURCES
- Reteach 2A, pp. 175–178
- Extra Practice 2A, pp. 129–132

5-minute Warm Up

- Have children fill two identical containers with different amounts of water.

- Ask them to discuss methods to find out whether the containers have the same or different amounts of water.

- Encourage children to offer as many suggestions as possible.

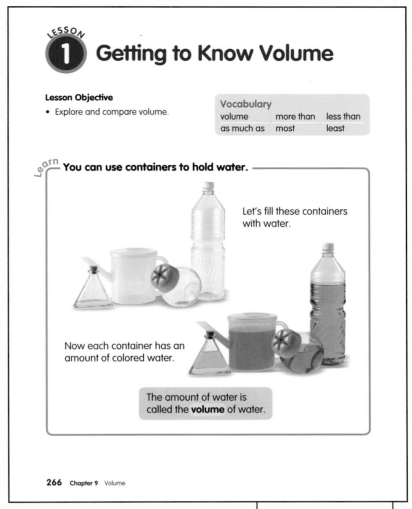

Student Book A p. 266

DAY 1 Teach

Volume is the Amount of Water in a Container
(page 266)

Children learn that the volume of water is the amount of water in a container, and that the volume is conserved no matter which container is used.

- Point out to children that the different containers hold different amounts of water.

- *Say:* The amount of water in a container is called the volume of water. Have children repeat this statement.

Best Practices Have children work in small groups. Give each group several different-sized containers and a large pitcher of water. Have groups explore volume by noting that liquids have volumes and the amount of liquid in a container is its volume.

Student Book A p. 267

Which container has more water?
How many glasses of water must be poured from Container A to Container B so that they both contain the same amount of water?

Solution:
Container A holds 9 glasses of water; Container B holds 5 glasses of water.

Container A: 9 − 2 = 7; Container B: 5 + 2 = 7

Answer: Container A; 2 glasses

Differentiated Instruction

English Language Learners

Use water and five identical glasses to discuss the terms *more than, less than, as much as, most,* and *least*. For example, fill one glass with more water than another glass, point to the glass with more water and **say:** This glass has *more than* this glass. Ask children to repeat the phrase *more than*. Repeat for other terms.

Hands-On Activity:

Conservation of Volume (page 267)

This activity shows that the volume of a liquid remains unchanged when poured into different containers.

• Children work in groups of three or four.

• Prepare water and three containers of different sizes for each group. (You may wish to ask children to bring these containers from home.)

• Use this activity to highlight to children the conservation of volume.

For Advanced Learners Have children fill two similar containers with different amounts of water. Ask them to discuss methods to find out if the containers have the same or different amounts of water.

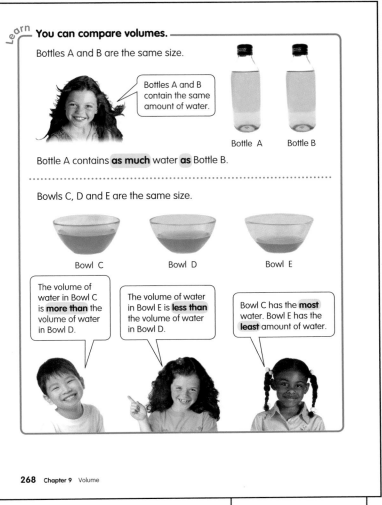

You can compare volumes.

Bottles A and B are the same size.

Bottles A and B contain the same amount of water.

Bottle A   Bottle B

Bottle A contains **as much** water **as** Bottle B.

Bowls C, D and E are the same size.

Bowl C   Bowl D   Bowl E

The volume of water in Bowl C is **more than** the volume of water in Bowl D.

The volume of water in Bowl E is **less than** the volume of water in Bowl D.

Bowl C has the **most** water. Bowl E has the **least** amount of water.

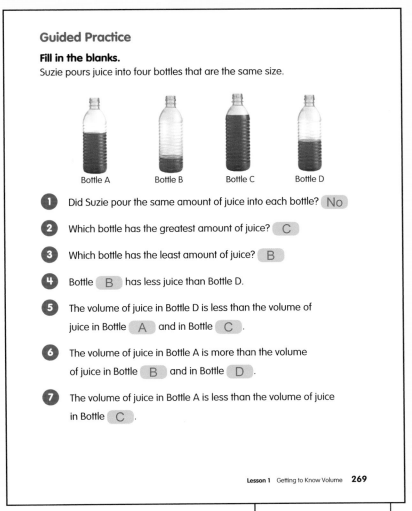

Guided Practice

Fill in the blanks.
Suzie pours juice into four bottles that are the same size.

Bottle A   Bottle B   Bottle C   Bottle D

1 Did Suzie pour the same amount of juice into each bottle? No

2 Which bottle has the greatest amount of juice? C

3 Which bottle has the least amount of juice? B

4 Bottle B has less juice than Bottle D.

5 The volume of juice in Bottle D is less than the volume of juice in Bottle A and in Bottle C .

6 The volume of juice in Bottle A is more than the volume of juice in Bottle B and in Bottle D .

7 The volume of juice in Bottle A is less than the volume of juice in Bottle C .

Compare Volumes (page 268)

Children learn to compare the volumes of water in identical containers by comparing the levels of water in the containers.

- Fill two identical bottles with the same amount of water.

- *Ask:* Do the bottles contain the same amount of water? How can you tell?

- Help children see that the levels of water are the same.

- Emphasize that they can only make this conclusion because the containers have the same shape and size.

- *Say:* Bottle A has as much water as Bottle B. Have children repeat after you.

- *Ask:* Are Bowls C, D, and E the same size? (Yes)

- Explain and show children that Bowl C has more water than Bowl D, which has more water than Bowl E.

- Help children understand the terms *more than*, *less than*, *most,* and *least* in this example.

Check for Understanding
✓ **Guided Practice** (page 269)

1 to **7** Emphasize that the bottles in these exercises have the same shape and size. These exercises provide additional practice in comparing volumes in more than two identical containers.

For Struggling Learners Fill several containers of different shapes with water. Ask children if they can tell which container has the most amount of water. Have them suggest how they can compare:

(a) by pouring all the water from each container into one common container in turn and marking the level for each for comparision

(b) by pouring all the water into smaller similar glasses and filling them to the brim and counting the number of glasses to compare

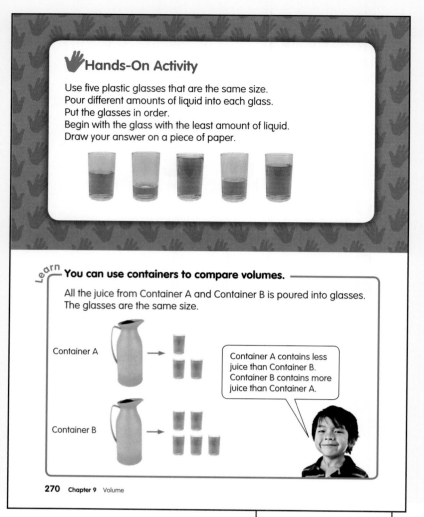

Student Book A p. 270

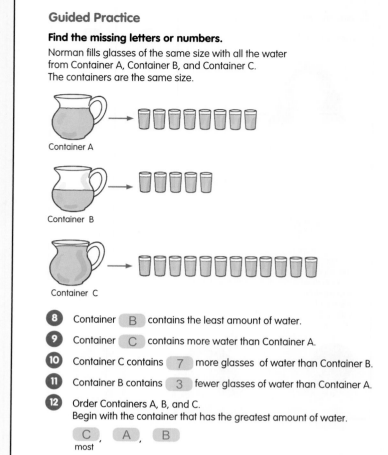

Student Book A p. 271

Teach

See the Lesson Organizer on page 266 for Day 2 resources.

Hands-On Activity:

Order Different Amounts of Water From Least to Greatest (page 270)

This activity provides children with additional practice in comparing volumes of liquids using identical containers. Children are also expected to arrange the glasses in order of the amounts of liquids they contain.

- Children work in groups of three or four.

- Pour different amounts of water into five identical glasses.

- Have children arrange the glasses in ascending order of volume of liquid.

For Advanced Learners Have children work in groups of five. Each child is given a similar container and asked to fill it with some water. Ask the children in each group to arrange their containers in increasing or decreasing order according to the volumes of water in their containers.

Use Containers to Compare Volumes
(page 270)

Children learn to compare the amounts of water in identical containers by counting the number of non-standard units (glasses) that fill each container.

- Explain that this activity provides another method of determining which container has more or less water.

- Explain that each glass full of water is a non-standard unit of measurement.

✓ Guided Practice (page 271)

8 to **12** These exercises provide additional practice in comparing volumes in identical containers, using non-standard units of measure.

Let's Practice

Use the picture to answer each question.

The picture shows four glasses, A, B, C, and D.
The glasses are the same size.

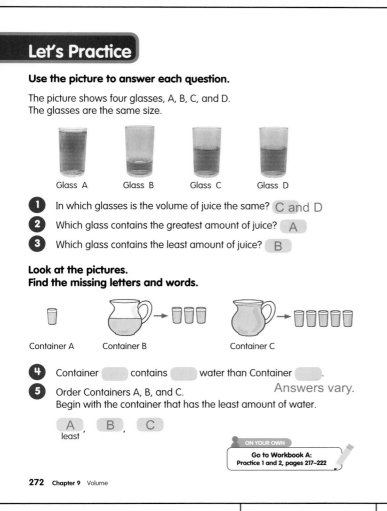

Glass A   Glass B   Glass C   Glass D

1 In which glasses is the volume of juice the same? C and D

2 Which glass contains the greatest amount of juice? A

3 Which glass contains the least amount of juice? B

Look at the pictures.
Find the missing letters and words.

Container A   Container B   Container C

4 Container ____ contains ____ water than Container ____.

5 Order Containers A, B, and C.
Begin with the container that has the least amount of water.

Answers vary.

A , B , C
least

ON YOUR OWN
Go to Workbook A:
Practice 1 and 2, pages 217–222

272 Chapter 9 Volume

Student Book A p. 272

Let's Practice (page 272)

This provides more practice in comparing volumes using the appropriate terms and units. Exercises **1** to **3** check that children can compare the volumes of water in identical containers by comparing the levels of water in the containers. Exercises **4** and **5** check that children can compare volumes in identical containers using non-standard units of measurement.

Common Error Some children may have trouble understanding that in Exercise **4** they can choose any container to write in the first space. What they write in the rest of the sentence depends on the container they choose. For children who need help choosing a container, suggest they choose Container A.

ON YOUR OWN

Children practice comparing volume in Practice 1 and 2, pages 217 to 222 of **Workbook 2A**. These pages (with the answers) are shown at the right and on page 272A.

Differentiation Options Depending on children's success with the Workbook pages, use these materials as needed.
Struggling: Reteach 2A, pp. 175–178
On Level: Extra Practice 2A, pp. 129–132

Practice and Apply
Workbook pages for Chapter 9, Lesson 1

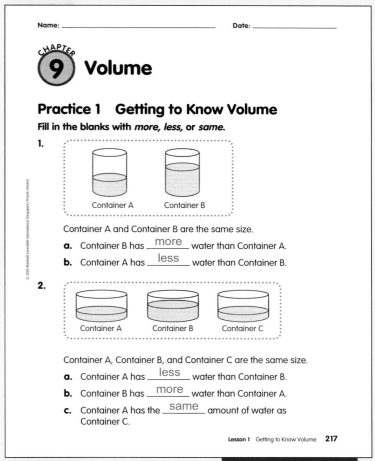

Name: _____   Date: _____

CHAPTER 9 Volume

Practice 1 Getting to Know Volume
Fill in the blanks with more, less, or same.

1.

Container A   Container B

Container A and Container B are the same size.

a. Container B has ___more___ water than Container A.

b. Container A has ___less___ water than Container B.

2.

Container A   Container B   Container C

Container A, Container B, and Container C are the same size.

a. Container A has ___less___ water than Container B.

b. Container B has ___more___ water than Container A.

c. Container A has the ___same___ amount of water as Container C.

Lesson 1 Getting to Know Volume **217**

Workbook A p. 217

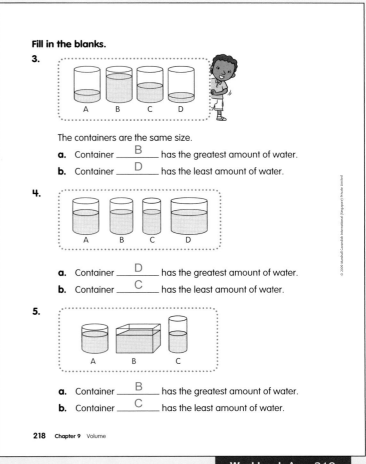

Fill in the blanks.

3.

A   B   C   D

The containers are the same size.

a. Container ___B___ has the greatest amount of water.

b. Container ___D___ has the least amount of water.

4.

A   B   C   D

a. Container ___D___ has the greatest amount of water.

b. Container ___C___ has the least amount of water.

5.

A   B   C

a. Container ___B___ has the greatest amount of water.

b. Container ___C___ has the least amount of water.

218 Chapter 9 Volume

Workbook A p. 218

Practice 2   Getting to Know Volume

Fill in the blanks.

Water is scooped out of a pail and poured into these containers.
Each ⌐ is one scoop.

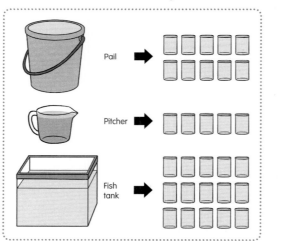

1. Container __S__ has the greatest amount of water.
2. Container __T__ has the least amount of water.
3. Containers __U__ and __V__ have the same amount of water.
4. Container __S__ has more water than Container U.
5. Container V has more water than Container __T__.

Fill in the blanks.

All the water in each container is used to fill the glasses.

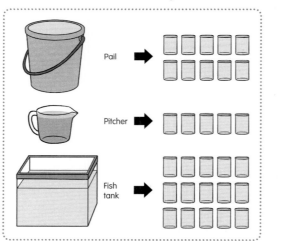

6. Which container has the most water? The __fish tank__
7. Which container has the least water? The __pitcher__
8. Which container has a lesser volume of water,
   the pail or the pitcher? The __pitcher__

Fill in the blanks.

Luisa fills glasses of the same size with all the water
from the pitcher, flask, and mug.

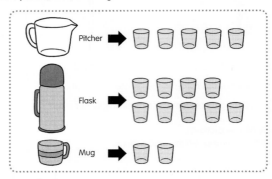

9. The __flask__ has the most water.
10. The __mug__ has the least water.
11. There are __4__ more glasses of water in the flask
    than in the pitcher.
12. There are __7__ fewer glasses of water in the mug than
    in the flask.
13. Order the pitcher, flask, and mug.
    Begin with the container that has the most water.
    __flask__, __pitcher__, __mug__
    most

Fill in the blanks.

Brad fills glasses of the same size with all the water from
Kettle A, Kettle B, Kettle C, and Kettle D.

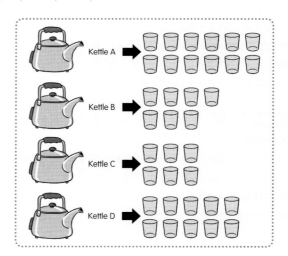

14. Kettle __A__ had the most water.
15. Kettle __C__ had the least water.
16. Kettle A had __5__ more glasses of water than Kettle B.
17. Kettle C had 4 fewer glasses of water than Kettle __D__.

LESSON 2 Measuring in Liters

LESSON OBJECTIVE
• Use liters to estimate, measure, and compare volume.

TECHNOLOGY RESOURCES
• *Math in Focus* eBooks
• *Math in Focus* Teacher Resources CD
• *Math in Focus* Virtual Manipulatives

Vocabulary

liter (L)	measuring cup

DAY 1 Student Book 2A, pp. 273–274

MATERIALS
• a 1-liter milk carton
• empty containers of various shapes and sizes
• 1 measuring cylinder
• 1 measuring cup per pair (optional)
• 1 small pitcher of water per pair (optional)
• 1 ladle per pair (optional)

DAY 2 Student Book 2A, pp. 275–277
Workbook 2A, pp. 223–226

DIFFERENTIATION RESOURCES
• Reteach 2A, pp. 179–182
• Extra Practice 2A, pp. 133–136

5-minute Warm Up

Show children a filled 1-liter bottle. Then show children different volumes of water in different containers, and have them guess whether the volumes are less than or more than the amount of water in the bottle. Pour the water from each of these containers into the 1-liter bottle to check their estimates. This activity prepares children for estimation of volumes.

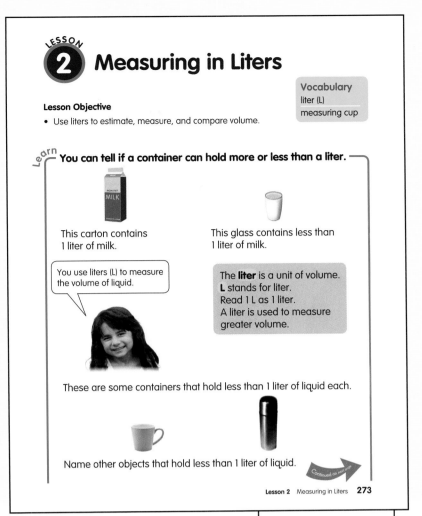

LESSON 2 Measuring in Liters

Vocabulary
liter (L)
measuring cup

Lesson Objective
• Use liters to estimate, measure, and compare volume.

Learn You can tell if a container can hold more or less than a liter.

This carton contains 1 liter of milk.

This glass contains less than 1 liter of milk.

You use liters (L) to measure the volume of liquid.

The **liter** is a unit of volume. **L** stands for liter. Read 1 L as 1 liter. A liter is used to measure greater volume.

These are some containers that hold less than 1 liter of liquid each.

Name other objects that hold less than 1 liter of liquid.

Continued on next page

Lesson 2 Measuring in Liters **273**

Student Book A p. 273

DAY 1 Teach

Learn

Compare the Amount of Liquid a Container Can Hold to a Liter (pages 273 and 274)

Children are given a sense of how much 1 liter of liquid is and given examples of containers that can hold 1 liter of liquid.

• Have children recall the metric units of measurement for length and mass (meter and centimeter, kilogram and gram).

• Inform children that the unit of measurement for volume is liter, and introduce the symbol L.

• Show children a 1-liter milk carton and pour its contents into a transparent container. Explain to children that the volume of milk is 1 liter or 1 L.

• Show children another smaller container with a lesser amount of milk, and point out that the volume of milk in the smaller container is less than 1 liter.

• Show some containers filled with less than 1 liter of liquid.

• Use any method to show that the volume of water is less than 1 liter; for example, pour it into a measuring cup.

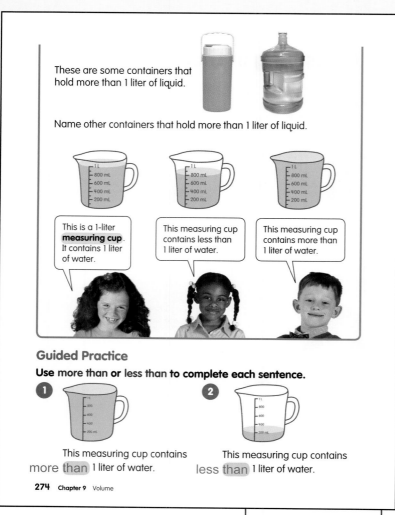

These are some containers that hold more than 1 liter of liquid.

Name other containers that hold more than 1 liter of liquid.

This is a 1-liter **measuring cup**. It contains 1 liter of water.

This measuring cup contains less than 1 liter of water.

This measuring cup contains more than 1 liter of water.

Guided Practice

Use more than or less than to complete each sentence.

1 This measuring cup contains more than 1 liter of water.

2 This measuring cup contains less than 1 liter of water.

274 Chapter 9 Volume

Student Book A p. 274

Student Book A p. 274

Problem of the Lesson

(a) Sammy has two water tanks filled with water. Tank A contains 12 liters. Tank B contains 19 liters more than Tank A. Find the volume of water in Tank B.

(b) Sammy pours half the amount of water in Tank A and all the water in Tank B into Tank C to fill it to the brim. Find the volume of water in Tank C.

Solutions:
(a) Tank B: 12 L + 19 L = 31 L
(b) Half of Tank A: 12 L ÷ 2 = 6 L
   Tank C = 6 L + 31L = 37 L

Answer: (a) 31 L
   (b) 37 L

Differentiated Instruction

English Language Learners

Liter may be an unfamiliar word. Display a 1-liter water bottle. Say the word *liter* and ask children to repeat the word. Stand a poster board behind the bottle, write the word *liter*, and draw a mark at the top of the bottle. Now empty the bottle. Fill familiar containers (e.g. a small milk carton, juice can, quart carton) with water and pour each into the bottle (emptying the container each time) to show how much of the bottle each container fills. Mark the bottle and label the amount for each container on the poster board.

- Show some containers filled with more than 1 liter of liquid.

- Use any method to show that the volume of water is more than 1 liter; for example, pour it into a measuring cup.

- Introduce a measuring cup that can measure more than 1 liter. Point out the marks on the cylinder. You can use empty 2- and 3-liter soft drink containers if you do not have access to a measuring cup.

- Fill two identical measuring cups, one with more than 1 liter of water and the other with less than 1 liter. Have children point out which has more and which has less.

- Have children handle 1-liter containers to help them get a sense of how much 1 liter is so that they can estimate volume of liquids.

- Direct children's attention to the mL markings on the side of the measuring cup and explain that those markings are used to measure volumes of less than 1 liter.

Best Practices You may want to have the class work in pairs for this activity. Give each pair a measuring cup, a small pitcher of water, and a ladle. One partner pours the water into the measuring cup while the other says whether the volume is more or less than 1 liter.

Check for Understanding
✓ Guided Practice (page 274)

1 and **2** These exercises check children's ability to use measuring cups to determine whether the volume of the water is more than or less than 1 liter.

For Struggling Learners You may wish to help children consolidate their understanding of the concepts of volume, estimation, and measuring using this activity.

- Mark the outside of a pail or a small wastebasket with A, B, and C labels. Show children empty 1-, 2-, and 3-liter soft drink containers.

- Have children use the containers as benchmarks to guess how many liters of water are needed to reach each marking. Write the guesses on the board.

- Use the containers to pour water into the pail up to the different markings. Children can count the liters as you pour.

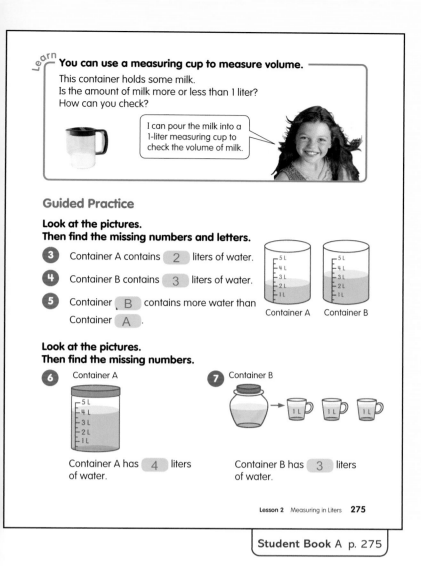

Learn **You can use a measuring cup to measure volume.**

This container holds some milk.
Is the amount of milk more or less than 1 liter?
How can you check?

I can pour the milk into a 1-liter measuring cup to check the volume of milk.

Guided Practice

Look at the pictures.
Then find the missing numbers and letters.

3 Container A contains `2` liters of water.

4 Container B contains `3` liters of water.

5 Container `B` contains more water than Container `A`.

Container A   Container B

Look at the pictures.
Then find the missing numbers.

6 Container A

Container A has `4` liters of water.

7 Container B

Container B has `3` liters of water.

Lesson 2 Measuring in Liters **275**

Student Book A p. 275

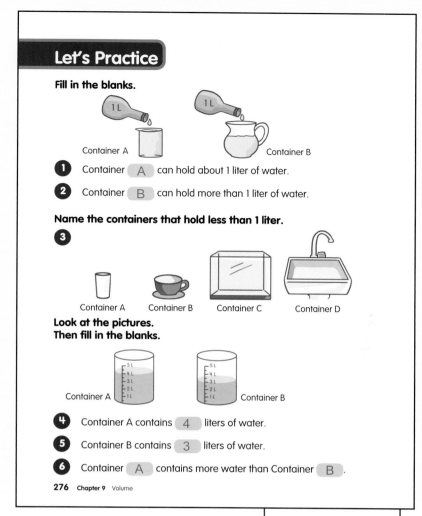

Let's Practice

Fill in the blanks.

Container A   Container B

1 Container `A` can hold about 1 liter of water.

2 Container `B` can hold more than 1 liter of water.

Name the containers that hold less than 1 liter.

3

Container A   Container B   Container C   Container D

Look at the pictures.
Then fill in the blanks.

Container A   Container B

4 Container A contains `4` liters of water.

5 Container B contains `3` liters of water.

6 Container `A` contains more water than Container `B`.

276 **Chapter 9** Volume

Student Book A p. 276

DAY 2 **Teach**   See the Lesson Organizer on page 273 for Day 2 resources.

n

Use a Measuring Cup to Measure Volume
(page 275)

Children learn to use a measuring cup to determine whether the volume of a liquid in a container is more than or less than 1 liter.

• Ask children to think of ways to check if the amount of milk is more than or less than 1 liter.

• Have children see that they can pour the milk into a 1-liter measuring cup to check.

• Another way to check is this: Mark the water level in a filled transparent 1-liter bottle, then pour out the water, and pour the milk into this bottle. Check to see whether the milk reaches the same level that was marked.

✓**Guided Practice** (page 275)

3, **4** and **6** These exercises check children's ability to read the volume of liquids from a measuring cup using the liter markings.

5 This exercise checks that children can compare the volumes of liquids in two containers.

7 This exercise checks that children are able to measure the volume of liquid in a container by pouring it out into measuring cups.

Let's Practice (page 276)

Exercises **1** to **6** provide additional practice in comparing volumes using the appropriate terms and units, as well as in reading the scales on containers to say the amounts of water in them in liters.

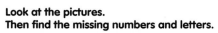

Look at the pictures.
Then find the missing numbers and letters.

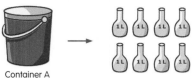

Container A

Container B

Container C

7 Container A has **8** liters of water.

8 Container **B** has the least amount of water.

9 Container B has **2** liters of water less than Container C.

10 Container A contains twice as much water as Container **C**.

11 Order the containers.
Begin with the container that has the greatest amount of water.

A , **C** , **B**
most

> **ON YOUR OWN**
> Go to Workbook A:
> Practice 3, pages 223–226

Lesson 2 Measuring in Liters **277**

Student Book A p. 277

Let's Practice (page 277)

Exercises **7** to **10** provide additional practice in measuring and comparing volumes using 1-liter containers. Exercise **11** requires children to arrange the containers in order of the amount of water each contains.

Common Error Some children may have difficulty grasping the idea of one liter. Display and label a 1-liter water bottle for reference.

ON YOUR OWN

Children practice measuring in liters in Practice 3, pages 223 to 226 of **Workbook 2A**. These pages (with the answers) are shown at the right and on page 277A.

Differentiation Options Depending on children's success with the Workbook pages, use these materials as needed.
Struggling: Reteach 2A, pp. 179–182
On Level: Extra Practice 2A, pp. 133–136

Practice and Apply
Workbook pages for Chapter 9, Lesson 2

Name: _____ Date: _____

Practice 3   Measuring in Liters
Find the volume of water in each container.

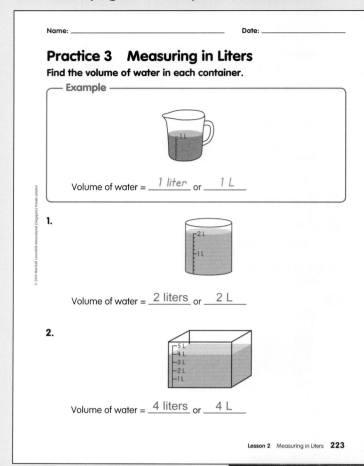

— Example —

Volume of water = _1 liter_ or _1 L_

1.

Volume of water = _2 liters_ or _2 L_

2.

Volume of water = _4 liters_ or _4 L_

Lesson 2 Measuring in Liters **223**

Workbook A p. 223

Find the volume of water in each container.

3.

Volume of water = _8 liters_ or _8 L_

4.

Volume of water = _3 liters_ or _3 L_

5.

Volume of water = _8 liters_ or _8 L_

6.

Volume of water = _18 liters_ or _18 L_

224 Chapter 9 Volume

Workbook A p. 224

Fill in the blanks.

7.

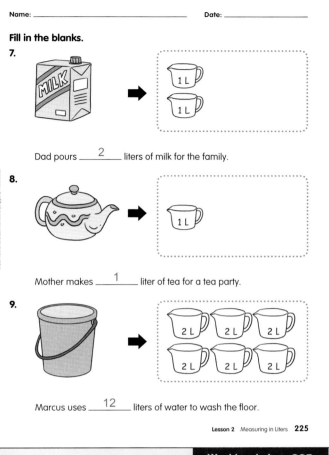

Dad pours ___2___ liters of milk for the family.

8.

Mother makes ___1___ liter of tea for a tea party.

9.

Marcus uses ___12___ liters of water to wash the floor.

Workbook A p. 225

Fill in the blanks.

10. Susan uses these volumes of juices to make fruit punch. Write the volume of each juice.

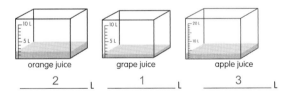

orange juice   grape juice   apple juice

___2___ L   ___1___ L   ___3___ L

11. The volume of ___apple___ juice is more than the volume of orange juice.

12. Susan used ___2___ liters more apple juice than grape juice.

13. Susan used ___1___ liter less orange juice than apple juice.

14. Order the volumes of the juices from least to greatest in liters.

___grape juice___ , ___orange juice___ , ___apple juice___
    least

Workbook A p. 226

Notes

3 Real-World Problems: Volume

LESSON OBJECTIVE

• Use bar models, addition, and subtraction to solve real-world problems about volume.

TECHNOLOGY RESOURCES

• *Math in Focus* eBooks
• *Math in Focus* Teacher Resources CD
• *Math in Focus* Virtual Manipulatives

DAY 1	Student Book 2A, pp. 278–281
	Workbook 2A, pp. 227–230

MATERIALS

• Strips of construction paper in two different colors per pair

DIFFERENTIATION RESOURCES

• Reteach 2A, pp. 183–186
• Extra Practice 2A, pp. 137–138

5-minute Warm Up

• Have small groups of children write one-step word problems involving addition or subtraction. Groups exchange and solve one another's problems.

• Repeat for two-step word problems.

• Remind children to draw bar models to help them solve the problems.

• This activity prepares children for the addition and subtraction that they will encounter in this lesson.

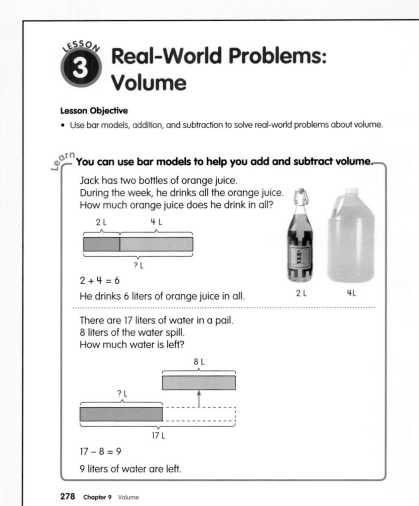

LESSON
3 Real-World Problems: Volume

Lesson Objective
• Use bar models, addition, and subtraction to solve real-world problems about volume.

Learn You can use bar models to help you add and subtract volume.

Jack has two bottles of orange juice.
During the week, he drinks all the orange juice.
How much orange juice does he drink in all?

2 L   4 L

? L

2 + 4 = 6

He drinks 6 liters of orange juice in all.   2 L   4L

There are 17 liters of water in a pail.
8 liters of the water spill.
How much water is left?

8 L

? L

17 L

17 − 8 = 9

9 liters of water are left.

278   Chapter 9   Volume

Student Book A p. 278

DAY 1 Teach

Learn

Use Bar Models to Help You Add and Subtract Volume (page 278)

Children use bar models to help them solve real-world addition and subtraction problems involving volume.

• Have children read and understand the problems.

• Have children draw the models with all the necessary information filled in and write the sentences to solve the problem.

Best Practices You may want to have children work in pairs. Give each pair several strips of construction paper in two colors to use as bar models to replicate the problems.

Guided Practice

Solve.
Use the bar models to help you.

1 A tank has 34 liters of water.
George pours 17 more liters of water into the tank.
How much water does the tank have now?

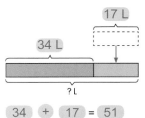

34 + 17 = 51

The tank has 51 liters of water now.

2 On Saturday, the Stevens family uses 32 liters of water.
The Martin family uses 28 liters of water on the same day.
How much more water does the Stevens family use than
the Martin family?

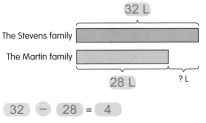

32 − 28 = 4

The Stevens family uses 4 liters more water than the Martin family.

Lesson 3   Real-World Problems: Volume   **279**

Student Book A p. 279

Check for Understanding

Guided Practice (pages 279 and 280)

This practice reinforces children's ability to use bar models
when solving real-world addition and subtraction problems.

1 This exercise checks children's understanding of addition
concepts to solve a one-step real-world problem.

2 This exercise checks children's ability to compare and apply
the correct operation to compare and solve the problem.

3 and **4** These exercises check children's ability to apply
both addition and subtraction concepts when solving two-step
real-world problems.

Problem of the Lesson

Container A has 27 liters of water.
Container B has 38 liters more water than
Container A.
Container C has 16 liters less water than
Container B.
(a) Find the volume of water in Containers B and C.
(b) Find the volume of water to be poured from
Container C to A so that they both have the same
volume of water.

Solutions:
(a) Container B = 38 + 27 = 65
Container C = 65 − 16 = 49

(b) Difference in volume of water in Containers A and C
= 49 − 27 = 22

Volume of water to be poured
= 22 ÷ 2 = 11

Answers:
(a) Volume of water in Container B: 65 liters
Volume of water in Container C: 49 liters
(b) Volume of water to be poured from Container
C to A: 11 liters

Differentiated Instruction

English Language Learners

Read aloud each word problem and discuss which operation(s)
will be used to solve the problem. Have small groups work
together to draw pictures or write number sentences to solve
each word problem.

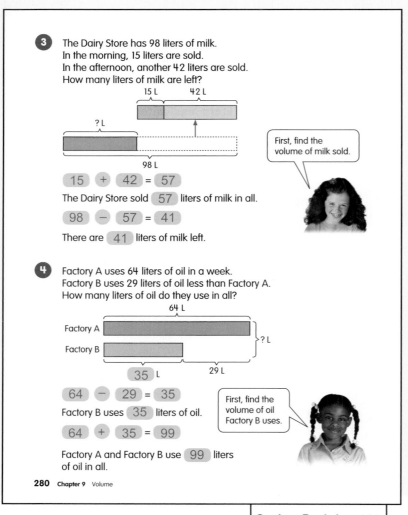

3 The Dairy Store has 98 liters of milk.
In the morning, 15 liters are sold.
In the afternoon, another 42 liters are sold.
How many liters of milk are left?

First, find the volume of milk sold.

$15 + 42 = 57$

The Dairy Store sold 57 liters of milk in all.

$98 - 57 = 41$

There are 41 liters of milk left.

4 Factory A uses 64 liters of oil in a week.
Factory B uses 29 liters of oil less than Factory A.
How many liters of oil do they use in all?

First, find the volume of oil Factory B uses.

$64 - 29 = 35$

Factory B uses 35 liters of oil.

$64 + 35 = 99$

Factory A and Factory B use 99 liters of oil in all.

280 **Chapter 9** Volume

Student Book A p. 280

Let's Practice See Additional Answers.

Solve. Draw bar models to help you.

1 There are 55 liters of orange juice for a party. 37 L
After the party, 18 liters of orange juice are left.
How many liters of orange juice were served?

2 A medium tank can hold 76 liters of water. 88 L
It can hold 12 liters of water less than a large tank.
How many liters of water can a large tank hold?

3 Factory A uses 45 liters of oil in a week. 119 L
Factory B uses 29 more liters of oil in a week than Factory A.
How many liters of oil do both factories use altogether?

4 Pail A contains 15 liters of water. 16 L
It contains 3 liters more water than Pail B.
Betsy pours another 4 liters of water into Pail B.
What is the volume of water in Pail B now?

ON YOUR OWN
Go to Workbook A:
Practice 4, pages 227–230

CRITICAL THINKING SKILLS
Put On Your Thinking Cap!

PROBLEM SOLVING

Tank X has 8 liters of water in it.
Tank Y is the same size.
It has 6 liters of water in it.
Jason pours more water into Tank Y until it has
1 more liter of water than Tank X.
How many liters of water did he pour into Tank Y?

$8 + 1 = 9$

Tank Y is filled with 9 liters of water.

$9 - 6 = 3$

He poured 3 liters of water into Tank Y.

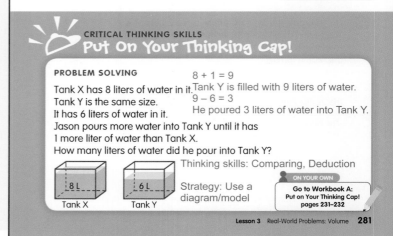

Tank X   Tank Y

Thinking skills: Comparing, Deduction

Strategy: Use a diagram/model

ON YOUR OWN
Go to Workbook A:
Put on Your Thinking Cap!
pages 231–232

Lesson 3 Real-World Problems: Volume **281**

Student Book A p. 281

Let's Practice (page 281)

Exercises **1** to **4** provide more practice in solving real-world problems related to volume by using the addition and subtraction concepts and bar models as visual representation. Encourage children to draw bar models to help them solve each problem. See Additional Answers, page T66.

Common Error Some children may choose the wrong operation to solve the word problem. Make sure children understand what is being asked.

ON YOUR OWN

Children practice solving real-world problems related to volume in Practice 4, pages 227 to 230 of **Workbook 2A**. These pages (with the answers) are shown on page 281A. The Math Journal on **Workbook 2A**, page 231, consolidates Lessons 1 to 3. This page (with the answers) is shown on page 281A.

Differentiation Options Depending on children's success with the Workbook pages, use these materials as needed.
Struggling: Reteach 2A, pp. 183–186
On Level: Extra Practice 2A, pp. 137–138

CRITICAL THINKING AND PROBLEM SOLVING
Put on Your Thinking Cap! (pages 281)

This problem solving exercise involves addition and subtraction concepts related to volume. Children work individually or in groups to answer the questions and present the solutions to the class. Have children draw bar models to help them solve the problem. See Additional Answers, page T66.

Thinking Skills

• Comparing
• Deduction

Problem Solving Strategy

• Use a diagram/model

ON YOUR OWN

Because all children should be challenged, have all children try the Challenging Practice and Problem Solving pages in **Workbook 2A**, pages 231 and 232. These pages (with the answers) are shown on page 281B.

Differentiation Options Depending on children's success with the Workbook pages, use these materials as needed.
On Level: Extra Practice 2A, pp. 139–140
Advanced: Enrichment 2A, pp. 76–81

Practice and Apply
Workbook pages for Chapter 9, Lesson 3

Name: _____ Date: _____

Practice 4 Real-World Problems: Volume
Solve.
Use bar models to help you.

1. Mrs. White brings 70 liters of juice to the school picnic.
After the picnic, 12 liters of juice are left.
How many liters of juice does everyone drink at the picnic?

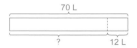

$$70 - 12 = 58$$

They drink ___58___ liters of juice at the picnic.

2. A fish tank contains 12 liters of water.
Another fish tank contains 7 liters of water.
What is the total volume of water in the two fish tanks?

$$12 + 7 = 19$$

The total volume of water in the two tanks is ___19___ liters.

Workbook A p. 227

Name: _____ Date: _____

Solve.
Use bar models to help you.

5. Container A has 18 liters of water.
Container B has 5 liters of water more than Container A.
Container C has 16 liters of water less than Container B.
What is the volume of water in Container C?

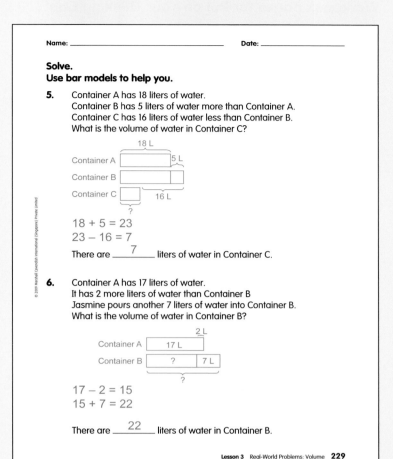

$$18 + 5 = 23$$
$$23 - 16 = 7$$

There are ___7___ liters of water in Container C.

6. Container A has 17 liters of water.
It has 2 more liters of water than Container B.
Jasmine pours another 7 liters of water into Container B.
What is the volume of water in Container B?

$$17 - 2 = 15$$
$$15 + 7 = 22$$

There are ___22___ liters of water in Container B.

Workbook A p. 229

Solve.
Use bar models to help you.

3. Sylvia fills two containers of the same size with water.
She fills Container A with 5 liters of water.
Then she fills Container B with 3 more liters of water
than Container A.
What is the total volume of water in both containers?

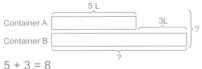

$$5 + 3 = 8$$
$$8 + 5 = 13$$

There are ___13___ liters of water in both containers.

4. A barrel has 60 liters of rainwater.
Jan uses 17 liters to water her flower garden.
She uses another 15 liters to water her vegetable garden.
How much rainwater is left in the barrel?

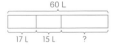

$$60 - 17 - 15 = 28$$

There are ___28___ liters of rainwater left in the barrel.

Workbook A p. 228

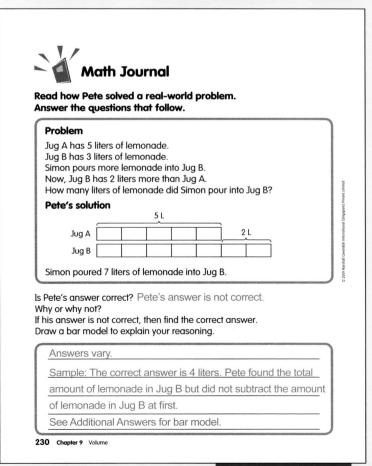

Math Journal

Read how Pete solved a real-world problem.
Answer the questions that follow.

> **Problem**
> Jug A has 5 liters of lemonade.
> Jug B has 3 liters of lemonade.
> Simon pours more lemonade into Jug B.
> Now, Jug B has 2 liters more than Jug A.
> How many liters of lemonade did Simon pour into Jug B?
>
> **Pete's solution**
>
> Simon poured 7 liters of lemonade into Jug B.

Is Pete's answer correct? Pete's answer is not correct.
Why or why not?
If his answer is not correct, then find the correct answer.
Draw a bar model to explain your reasoning.

> Answers vary.
>
> Sample: The correct answer is 4 liters. Pete found the total
>
> amount of lemonade in Jug B but did not subtract the amount
>
> of lemonade in Jug B at first.
>
> See Additional Answers for bar model.

See Additional Answers, page T66.

Workbook A p. 230

Practice and Apply
Workbook pages for Put on Your Thinking Cap!

Name: _____   Date: _____

Put On Your Thinking Cap!
♟♟ Challenging Practice

Look at the pictures.

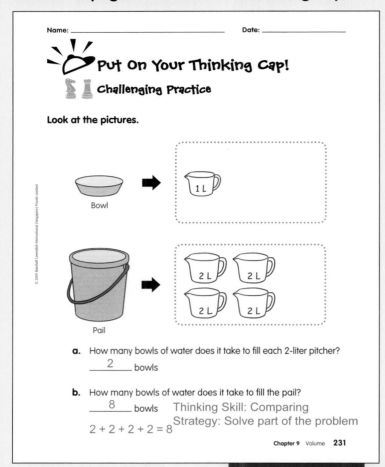

Bowl

Pail

a. How many bowls of water does it take to fill each 2-liter pitcher?
_____2_____ bowls

b. How many bowls of water does it take to fill the pail?
_____8_____ bowls   Thinking Skill: Comparing
Strategy: Solve part of the problem
$2 + 2 + 2 + 2 = 8$

Chapter 9 Volume **231**

Workbook A p. 231

Put On Your Thinking Cap!
Problem Solving

Jasmine is a scientist.
She found a new liquid called Liquid X.
On the first day, she made 2 liters of Liquid X.
On the second day, she made 1 liter more of Liquid X than on the first day.
Every day, she made 1 liter more than the day before.

What was the volume of Liquid X she made on Day 5?

First day	2
Second day	$2 + 1 = 3$
Third day	$3 + 1 = 4$
Fourth day	$4 + 1 = 5$
Fifth day	$5 + 1 = 6$

Try **making a list**.

The volume of Liquid X she made on Day 5 was 6 liters.

Thinking Skill: Deduction
Strategy: Make a list

232 Chapter 9 Volume

Workbook A p. 232

Notes

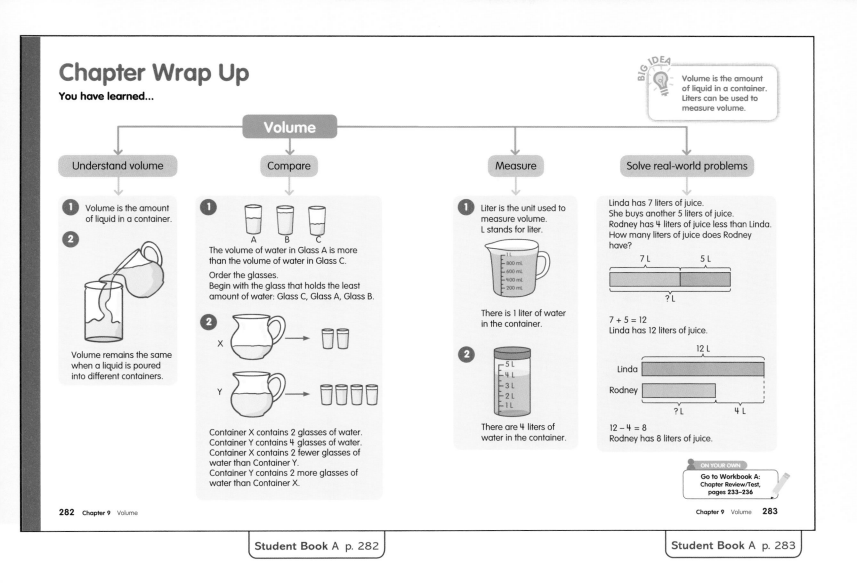

Chapter Wrap Up

You have learned...

Volume

Understand volume

1 Volume is the amount of liquid in a container.

2

Volume remains the same when a liquid is poured into different containers.

Compare

1

A   B   C

The volume of water in Glass A is more than the volume of water in Glass C.

Order the glasses.
Begin with the glass that holds the least amount of water: Glass C, Glass A, Glass B.

2

X →

Y →

Container X contains 2 glasses of water.
Container Y contains 4 glasses of water.
Container X contains 2 fewer glasses of water than Container Y.
Container Y contains 2 more glasses of water than Container X.

Measure

1 Liter is the unit used to measure volume. L stands for liter.

1L
800 mL
600 mL
400 mL
200 mL

There is 1 liter of water in the container.

2

5 L
4 L
3 L
2 L
1 L

There are 4 liters of water in the container.

Solve real-world problems

Linda has 7 liters of juice.
She buys another 5 liters of juice.
Rodney has 4 liters of juice less than Linda.
How many liters of juice does Rodney have?

7 L   5 L

? L

$7 + 5 = 12$
Linda has 12 liters of juice.

12 L

Linda

Rodney

? L   4 L

$12 - 4 = 8$
Rodney has 8 liters of juice.

ON YOUR OWN
Go to Workbook A:
Chapter Review/Test,
pages 233–236

Student Book A p. 282

Student Book A p. 283

Chapter Wrap Up (pages 282 and 283)

Use the examples in the Student Book to review understanding, comparing, and measuring volume as well as solving real-world volume problems. Encourage children to use the chapter vocabulary:

- volume
- less than
- most
- liter (L)
- more than
- as much as
- least
- measuring cup

ON YOUR OWN

Have children review the vocabulary, concepts, and skills from Chapter 9 with the Chapter Review/Test in **Workbook 2A**, pages 233 to 236. These pages (with the answers) are shown on page 283A.

You may want to use the Cumulative Review for Chapters 7 to 9 from **Workbook 2A**, pages 237 to 244 and the Mid-Year Review from **Workbook 2A**, pages 245 to 256. These pages (with the answers) are shown on pages 283C to 283G.

Assessment

Use the Chapter 9 Test Prep on pages 63 to 67 of **Assessments 2** to assess how well children have learned the material of this chapter. This assessment is appropriate for reporting results to adults at home and administrators. This test is shown on page 283B.

You may also wish to use the Mid-Year Test on pages 68 to 82 of **Assessments 2**. This test is shown on pages 283H to 283J.

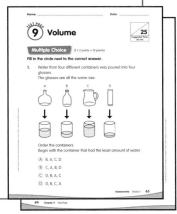

Assessments 2 pp. 63–67

Workbook pages for Chapter Review/Test

Name: _____ Date: _____

Chapter Review/Test
Vocabulary
Fill in the blanks using these words.

| volume | less | liters | more |

1. The ___volume___ is the amount of liquid in a container.

2. The volume of a liquid can be measured in ___liters___.

3.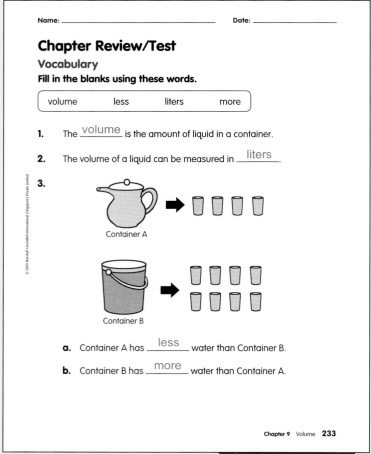

Container A

Container B

a. Container A has ___less___ water than Container B.

b. Container B has ___more___ water than Container A.

Workbook A p. 233

Concepts and Skills
Fill in the blanks.

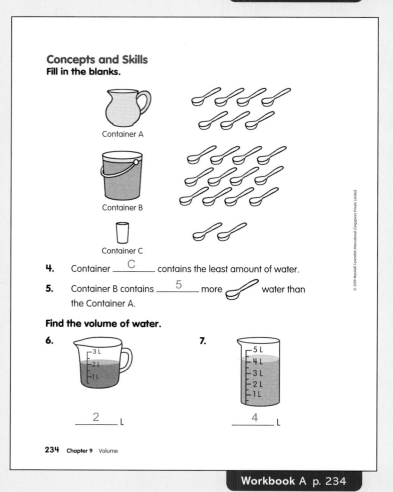

Container A

Container B

Container C

4. Container ___C___ contains the least amount of water.

5. Container B contains ___5___ more 🥄 water than the Container A.

Find the volume of water.

6. ___2___ L

7. ___4___ L

Workbook A p. 234

Name: _____ Date: _____

Find the volume of water.

8. ___7___ L

9. ___8___ L

Problem Solving
Solve.
Use bar models to help you.

10. Mr. Gomez makes 7 liters of apple juice for a party.
He also makes 4 liters of orange juice.
How much juice does he make for the party?

$7 + 4 = 11$

| 7 L | 4 L |
?

He makes ___11___ liters of juice for the party.

11. A tank has 13 liters of water.
Lila uses 5 liters of water from the tank.
How much water is left in the tank?

$13 - 5 = 8$

13 L
5 L | ?

___8___ liters of water are left in the tank.

Workbook A p. 235

---

12. 12 liters of water are in a barrel.
Mr. Lopez pours 3 more liters of water into the barrel.
Then he uses 7 liters of water from the barrel to water trees.
How much water is left in the barrel?

12 L | 3 L
?

$12 + 3 = 15$

15 L
7 L | ?

$15 - 7 = 8$

___8___ liters of water are left in the barrel.

13. A tub can hold 15 liters of water.
2 pails with 6 liters of water in each pail are poured into the tub.
How much more water is needed to fill the tub?

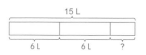

15 L
6 L | 6 L | ?

$6 + 6 = 12$
$15 - 12 = 3$

___3___ more liters of water are needed to fill the tub.

Workbook A p. 236

Assessments Book pages for Chapter 9 Test Prep
Answer key appears in Assessments Book.

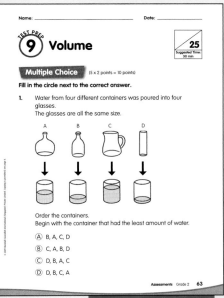

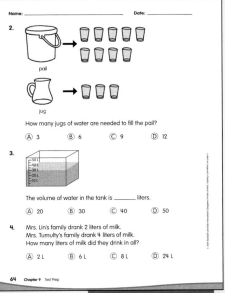

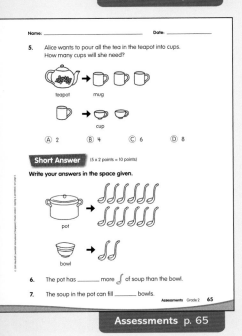

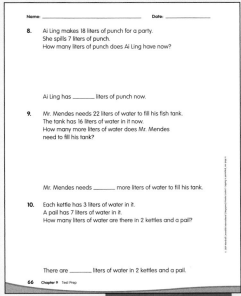

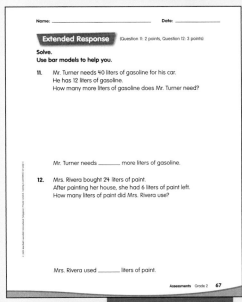

Cumulative Review for Chapters 7 to 9

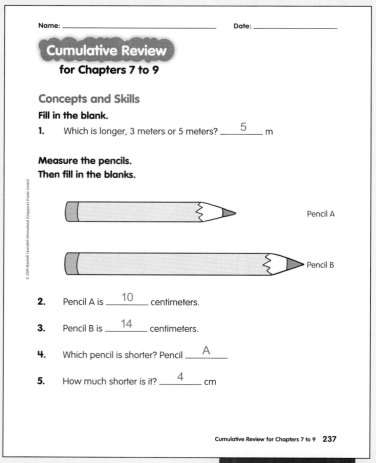

Name: _____ Date: _____

Cumulative Review
for Chapters 7 to 9

Concepts and Skills

Fill in the blank.

1. Which is longer, 3 meters or 5 meters? ___5___ m

Measure the pencils.
Then fill in the blanks.

Pencil A

Pencil B

2. Pencil A is ___10___ centimeters.

3. Pencil B is ___14___ centimeters.

4. Which pencil is shorter? Pencil ___A___

5. How much shorter is it? ___4___ cm

Cumulative Review for Chapters 7 to 9   **237**

Workbook A p. 237

Name: _____ Date: _____

Fill in the blanks.

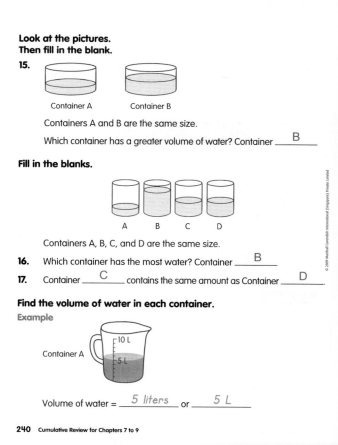

10. The chicken has a mass of ___540___ grams.

11. The duck has a mass of ___710___ grams.

12. Which is lighter? ___chicken___

13. How much lighter is it? ___170___ g

Fill in the blank.

14.

What is the mass of the bag of rice? ___7___ kg

Cumulative Review for Chapters 7 to 9   **239**

Workbook A p. 239

Draw. Then label.

6. Draw a line 7 centimeters long.
   Label it Line X.

   Accept a line 7 cm long; labeled Line X

7. Draw a line 4 centimeters longer than Line X.
   Label it Line Y.

   Accept a line 11 cm long; labeled Line Y

Fill in the blanks.

8.

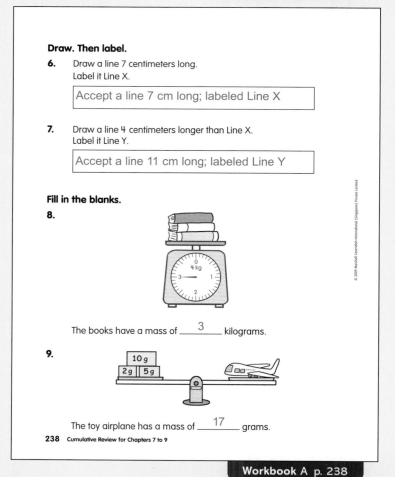

The books have a mass of ___3___ kilograms.

9.

The toy airplane has a mass of ___17___ grams.

238 Cumulative Review for Chapters 7 to 9

Workbook A p. 238

Look at the pictures.
Then fill in the blank.

15.

Container A   Container B

Containers A and B are the same size.

Which container has a greater volume of water? Container ___B___

Fill in the blanks.

A   B   C   D

Containers A, B, C, and D are the same size.

16. Which container has the most water? Container ___B___

17. Container ___C___ contains the same amount as Container ___D___

Find the volume of water in each container.

Example

Container A

Volume of water = ___5 liters___ or ___5 L___

240 Cumulative Review for Chapters 7 to 9

Workbook A p. 240

18.

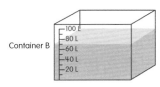

Container B

Volume of water = __70 liters__ or __70 L__

19.

Container C

Volume of water = __40 liters__ or __40 L__

20.

Container D

Volume of water = __2 liters__ or __2 L__

Fill in the blanks.
Use your answers for Exercises 18 to 20.

21. Which container has the greatest volume of water?

Container __B__

22. Which container has the least volume of water?

Container __D__

Look at the pictures.
The containers are filled with water.
Which containers contain less than 1 liter of water each?
Circle each answer.

23.   1 L   Total volume = 1 L   Total volume = 1 L

Problem Solving

Solve.
Draw bar models to help you.

24. Mrs. Kim's empty suitcase has a mass of 5 kilograms.
After she packs some books into the suitcase, her suitcase has
a mass of 21 kilograms.
What is the mass of the books?

21 kg $21 - 5 = 16$

5 kg   ?

The mass of the books is __16__ kilograms.

---

25. Seth has a ball of string.
He uses 35 centimeters of string to decorate his scrapbook.
He uses another 78 centimeters of string to decorate a gift.
a. How much string does he use in all?
b. If he had 200 centimeters of string at first, how much string
does he have now?

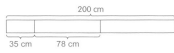

200 cm

35 cm   78 cm

$35 + 78 = 113$

a. He uses __113__ centimeters of string in all.

$200 - 113 = 87$

b. He has __87__ centimeters of string now.

26. Tania's hand puppet has a mass of 440 grams.
It is 120 grams heavier than Hector's hand puppet.
What is the total mass of the two hand puppets?

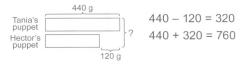

440 g

Tania's puppet
Hector's puppet   ?

120 g

$440 - 120 = 320$

$440 + 320 = 760$

The total mass of the two hand puppets is __760__ grams.

---

27. A tank contains 65 liters of oil.
Another 15 liters of oil are added.
Later, 40 liters are poured out.
What is the volume of oil in the tank in the end?

65 L   15 L

40 L   ?

$65 + 15 = 80$
$80 - 40 = 40$

The volume of oil in the tank in the end is __40__ liters.

28. Sarah sells 27 liters of milk in the morning.
She sells another 8 liters of milk in the afternoon.
Ray sells 48 liters of milk.
a. Who sells more milk?
b. How much more?

27 L   8 L

Sarah   ?

?

Ray

48 L

$27 + 8 = 35$

a. __Ray__ sells more milk.

$48 - 35 = 13$

b. __Ray__ sells __13__ more liters of milk.

Mid-Year Review
Test Prep

Name: _____ Date: _____

Multiple Choice

Fill in the circle next to the correct answer.

1. Which shows three hundred four?

Ⓐ 34 ⊗ 304 Ⓒ 340 Ⓓ 344

2. Which number is shown in the chart?

Hundreds	Tens	Ones

⊗ 450 Ⓑ 405 Ⓒ 350 Ⓓ 315

3. Continue the pattern.

540, 650, 760, 870, _____

Ⓐ 890 Ⓑ 950 ⊗ 980 Ⓓ 1000

4. Add the two numbers shown on the chart.

Hundreds	Tens	Ones

⊗ 879 Ⓑ 560 Ⓒ 319 Ⓓ 241

5. 275 + 16 = _____

Ⓐ 281 ⊗ 291 Ⓒ 381 Ⓓ 415

6. Subtract the two numbers shown on the chart.

Hundreds	Tens	Ones

Ⓐ 488 Ⓑ 367 ⊗ 246 Ⓓ 121

Name: _____ Date: _____

7. Subtract.

```
  5 4 7
- 2 5 4
```

Ⓐ 801 Ⓑ 393 Ⓒ 313 ⊗ 293

8. Use these digits.

[2] [7] [5]

Make the greatest 3-digit number.
Then make the least 3-digit number.
Then subtract the two numbers.

Ⓐ 587 Ⓑ 505 ⊗ 495 Ⓓ 477

9. Darren has 86 marbles.
Max has 74 marbles.
How many marbles do they have in all?

Ⓐ 12 Ⓑ 86 Ⓒ 150 ⊗ 160

10. Felix has $125.
He uses $70 to buy a pair of shoes.
How much does he have left?

Ⓐ $195 Ⓑ $87 Ⓒ $75 ⊗ $55

11. Look at the picture.

How many flowers are there?

Ⓐ 7 + 5 ⊗ 7 × 5 Ⓒ 5 × 2 Ⓓ 5 × 10

12. The length of a placemat is about _____.

⊗ 40 cm Ⓑ 40 m Ⓒ 1 cm Ⓓ 1 m

13. Rosa has a ribbon 100 centimeters long.
She uses 45 centimeters of it.
What is the length of ribbon left?

Ⓐ 155 cm Ⓑ 100 cm ⊗ 55 cm Ⓓ 65 cm

14. Letoya buys 35 books on Monday.
She buys 21 books on Tuesday.
She sells 40 of these books.
How many books does she have left?

Ⓐ 14 ⊗ 16 Ⓒ 56 Ⓓ 96

15. A carton of milk has a mass of 450 grams.
Two cartons are put into a box with a mass of 37 grams.
What is the total mass of the cartons and the box?

Ⓐ 413 g Ⓑ 863 g ⊗ 937 g Ⓓ 974 g

Short Answer

Read the questions carefully.
Write your answers in the space provided.

16. Write 386 in words.

Three hundred eighty-six

17. Write 520 in expanded form.

500 + 20

18. Order the numbers from greatest to least.

[609] [712] [699] [543]

712   699   609   543
greatest

19. Add 438 and 156. ___594___

```
    4 3 8
  + 1 5 6
    5 9 4
```

20. Subtract 17 from 831. ___814___

Workbook A p. 249

---

25. Fill in the blank with *more than* or *less than*.

The container has ___more than___ 1 liter of water.

26. The Recycling Committee has $746.
They raise $198 more.
How much do they have now?

$ ___944___

27. In a game, the Green Team scored 270 points.
The Yellow Team scored 363 points.
How many more points did the Yellow Team score
than the Green Team?

___93___ points

Workbook A p. 251

---

21. Subtract 284 from 861. ___577___

22. Fill in the blanks.

$7 \times 2 =$ ___14___ $2 \times 7 =$ ___14___

___14___ $\div 2 = 7$ ___14___ $\div 7 =$ ___2___

23. What is the length of Drawing A? ___12___ cm

_____ Drawing A

24. What is the mass of the vegetables?

___250___ g

Workbook A p. 250

---

28. Gina has 200 beads.
94 of the beads are red.
The rest are yellow.
How many yellow beads does Gina have?
Complete the bar model.
Then find the answer.

(94)

| Red | Yellow |

(200)   ? $200 - 94 = 106$

Gina has ___106___ yellow beads.

29. 138 cars and 27 vans are in a parking lot.
How many vehicles are there in all?
Draw a bar model.
Then find the answer.

138 cars   27 vans

$138 + 27 = 165$

?

There are ___165___ vehicles in all.

Workbook A p. 252

30. The mass of a bottle of oil is 2 kilograms.
What is the mass of 9 such bottles?

$9 \times 2 = 18$

The mass is ___18___ kilograms.

31. Eva has 40 crayons.
She gives them to her friends to be shared equally.
Each friend receives 5 crayons.
How many friends are there?

$40 \div 5 = 8$

There are ___8___ friends.

Workbook A p. 253

---

34. Mikayla has 5 strings of beads.
Each string has 4 beads on it.
Mikayla divides her beads into 2 strings of beads.
  a. How many beads does Mikayla have in all?
  b. How many beads are there on each string in the end?

$5 \times 4 = 20$

  a. Mikayla has ___20___ beads in all.

$20 \div 2 = 10$

  b. There are ___10___ beads on each string in the end.

35. The height of Kory's desk is 58 centimeters.
The height of Kory's door is 239 centimeters.
  a. What is the total height of Kory's desk and door?
  b. What is the difference in height between Kory's desk
     and door?

$239 + 58 = 297$

  a. The total height of Kory's desk and door is
    ___297___ centimeters.

$239 - 58 = 181$

  b. The difference in height between Kory's desk and door is
    ___181___ centimeters.

Workbook A p. 255

Extended Response

Solve.
Show your work.

32. The Finch family drives 352 miles on vacation.
The Perez family drives 168 miles more than the Finch family.
  a. How far does the Perez family drive?
  b. How many miles do they drive in all?

$352 + 168 = 520$

  a. The Perez family drives ___520___ miles.

$352 + 520 = 872$

  b. They drive ___872___ miles in all.

33. Tasha has 249 cards.
Tim has 53 fewer cards than Tasha.
Lee has 79 more cards than Tim.
How many cards does Lee have?

$249 - 53 = 196$

Tim has 196 cards.

$196 + 79 = 275$

Lee has ___275___ cards.

Workbook A p. 254

---

36. A barrel contains 60 liters of rainwater.
Mrs. Potts uses 14 liters of rainwater to water her
vegetable garden.
She uses another 13 liters of rainwater to wash her car.
How much rainwater is left in the barrel?

$14 + 13 = 27$
$60 - 27 = 33$

___33___ liters of rainwater are left in the barrel.

37. Ling mixes 120 cups of lemonade in the morning.
She mixes 93 cups of lemonade in the afternoon.
  a. How many cups of lemonade does she mix in all?
  b. She sells 207 cups of lemonade.
    How many cups of lemonade does she have left?

$120 + 93 = 213$

  a. She mixes ___213___ cups of lemonade in all.

$213 - 207 = 6$

  b. She has ___6___ cups of lemonade left.

Workbook A p. 256

Assessments Book pages for Mid-Year Test

Answer key appears in Assessments Book.

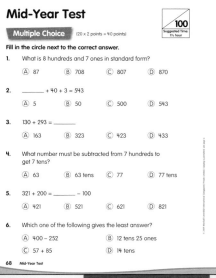

Name: _____ Date: _____

Mid-Year Test

Multiple Choice (20 × 2 points = 40 points)

[100 / Suggested Time: 1½ hour]

Fill in the circle next to the correct answer.

1. What is 8 hundreds and 7 ones in standard form?
   - Ⓐ 87
   - Ⓑ 708
   - Ⓒ 807
   - Ⓓ 870

2. _____ + 40 + 3 = 543
   - Ⓐ 5
   - Ⓑ 50
   - Ⓒ 500
   - Ⓓ 543

3. 130 + 293 = _____
   - Ⓐ 163
   - Ⓑ 323
   - Ⓒ 423
   - Ⓓ 433

4. What number must be subtracted from 7 hundreds to get 7 tens?
   - Ⓐ 63
   - Ⓑ 63 tens
   - Ⓒ 77
   - Ⓓ 77 tens

5. 321 + 200 = _____ − 100
   - Ⓐ 421
   - Ⓑ 521
   - Ⓒ 621
   - Ⓓ 821

6. Which one of the following gives the least answer?
   - Ⓐ 400 − 252
   - Ⓑ 12 tens 25 ones
   - Ⓒ 57 + 85
   - Ⓓ 14 tens

68 Mid-Year Test

Assessments p. 68

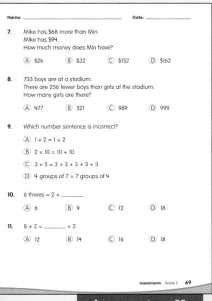

Name: _____ Date: _____

7. Mike has $68 more than Min.
   Mike has $94.
   How much money does Min have?
   - Ⓐ $26
   - Ⓑ $32
   - Ⓒ $152
   - Ⓓ $162

8. 733 boys are at a stadium.
   There are 256 fewer boys than girls at the stadium.
   How many girls are there?
   - Ⓐ 477
   - Ⓑ 521
   - Ⓒ 989
   - Ⓓ 999

9. Which number sentence is incorrect?
   - Ⓐ 1 × 2 = 1 + 2
   - Ⓑ 2 × 10 = 10 + 10
   - Ⓒ 3 × 5 = 3 + 3 + 3 + 3 + 3
   - Ⓓ 4 groups of 7 = 7 groups of 4

10. 6 threes = 2 × _____
    - Ⓐ 6
    - Ⓑ 9
    - Ⓒ 12
    - Ⓓ 18

11. 8 × 2 = _____ + 2
    - Ⓐ 12
    - Ⓑ 14
    - Ⓒ 16
    - Ⓓ 18

Assessments Grade 2 69

Assessments p. 69

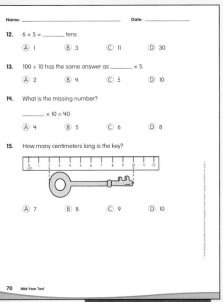

Name: _____ Date: _____

12. 6 × 5 = _____ tens
    - Ⓐ 1
    - Ⓑ 3
    - Ⓒ 11
    - Ⓓ 30

13. 100 ÷ 10 has the same answer as _____ × 5.
    - Ⓐ 2
    - Ⓑ 4
    - Ⓒ 5
    - Ⓓ 10

14. What is the missing number?
    _____ × 10 = 40
    - Ⓐ 4
    - Ⓑ 5
    - Ⓒ 6
    - Ⓓ 8

15. How many centimeters long is the key?
    - Ⓐ 7
    - Ⓑ 8
    - Ⓒ 9
    - Ⓓ 10

70 Mid-Year Test

Assessments p. 70

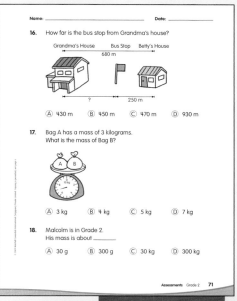

Name: _____ Date: _____

16. How far is the bus stop from Grandma's house?

    Grandma's House   Bus Stop   Betty's House
    680 m
    ?   250 m

    - Ⓐ 430 m
    - Ⓑ 450 m
    - Ⓒ 470 m
    - Ⓓ 930 m

17. Bag A has a mass of 3 kilograms.
    What is the mass of Bag B?
    - Ⓐ 3 kg
    - Ⓑ 4 kg
    - Ⓒ 5 kg
    - Ⓓ 7 kg

18. Malcolm is in Grade 2.
    His mass is about _____.
    - Ⓐ 30 g
    - Ⓑ 300 g
    - Ⓒ 30 kg
    - Ⓓ 300 kg

Assessments Grade 2 71

Assessments p. 71

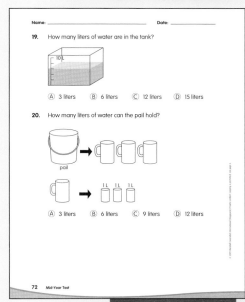

Name: _____ Date: _____

19. How many liters of water are in the tank?
    - Ⓐ 3 liters
    - Ⓑ 6 liters
    - Ⓒ 12 liters
    - Ⓓ 15 liters

20. How many liters of water can the pail hold?

    pail

    1 L 1 L 1 L

    - Ⓐ 3 liters
    - Ⓑ 6 liters
    - Ⓒ 9 liters
    - Ⓓ 12 liters

72 Mid-Year Test

Assessments p. 72

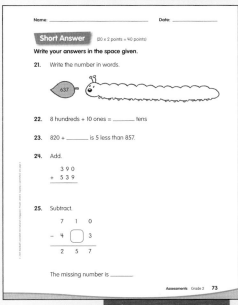

Name: _____ Date: _____

Short Answer (20 × 2 points = 40 points)

Write your answers in the space given.

21. Write the number in words.

    637

22. 8 hundreds + 10 ones = _____ tens

23. 820 + _____ is 5 less than 857.

24. Add.
    ```
      3 9 0
    + 5 3 9
    ```

25. Subtract.
    ```
      7 1 0
    - 4 ▢ 3
    _____
      2 5 7
    ```

    The missing number is _____.

Assessments Grade 2 73

Assessments p. 73

---

26. There are 550 marbles in Box A and Box B altogether.
Box A has 327 marbles.
How many marbles are in Box B?

Box B has _____ marbles.

27. Mr. Thomas bought 5 kilograms of rice in March.
He bought 2 kilograms more rice in April than in March.
How many kilograms of rice did he buy in April?

Mr. Thomas bought _____ kilograms of rice in April.

28. Lucy has a 250-piece jigsaw puzzle.
She puts together 56 pieces on the first day.
She puts together 48 pieces on the second day.
How many pieces are left?

_____ pieces are left.

29. Multiply 7 by 5. The answer is _____

30. 3 × 6 is _____ more than 10.

Assessments p. 74

---

31. 20 ÷ 2 = 2 × _____

32. ☆ × 3 = 15

☆ × ☆ = _____

33. A group of children borrow 45 books from a library.
Each child borrows 5 books.
How many children were in the group?

_____ children were in the group.

34. Joshua packed 60 balloons equally into 10 bags.
How many balloons did Joshua pack in each bag?

Joshua packed _____ balloons in each bag.

35. Measure the length of the pen.

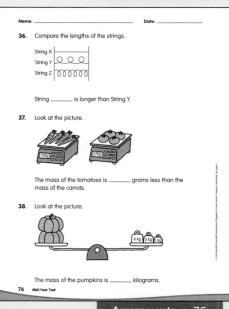

The length of the pen is about _____ centimeters.

Assessments p. 75

---

36. Compare the lengths of the strings.

String X
String Y
String Z

String _____ is longer than String Y.

37. Look at the picture.

The mass of the tomatoes is _____ grams less than the mass of the carrots.

38. Look at the picture.

The mass of the pumpkins is _____ kilograms.

Assessments p. 76

---

39. Look at the picture.

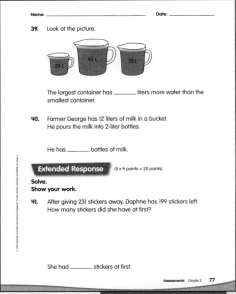

The largest container has _____ liters more water than the smallest container.

40. Farmer George has 12 liters of milk in a bucket.
He pours the milk into 2-liter bottles.

He has _____ bottles of milk.

Extended Response   (5 x 4 points = 20 points)

Solve.
Show your work.

41. After giving 231 stickers away, Daphne has 199 stickers left.
How many stickers did she have at first?

She had _____ stickers at first.

Assessments p. 77

---

42. A bag of sugar and a bag of flour have
a mass of 786 grams in all.
The bag of sugar has a mass of 350 grams.
Find the mass of the bag of flour.

The bag of flour has a mass of _____ grams.

43. Tim is putting wheels onto 10 tricycles at his shop.
A tricycle has 3 wheels.
How many wheels does Tim need for the tricycles?

Tim needs _____ wheels for the tricycles.

Assessments p. 78

---

44. Cristina has 100 beads.
She shares them equally among 10 girls.
How many beads does each girl get?

Each girl gets _____ beads.

45. A tank has 20 liters of water in it.
Jack pours 2 buckets of water into the tank.
Each bucket contains 5 liters of water.
How much water is in the tank now?

There are _____ liters of water in the tank now.

Assessments p. 79

Bonus Questions

1.   Each cactus stands for a number less than 5.
     The sum across each row is shown on the right of the row.
     The sum down each column is shown below the column.
     What number does each cactus stand for?

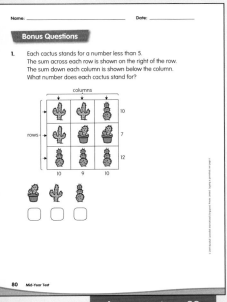

Assessments p. 80

---

2.   How many rabbits have to get onto the third see-saw to balance it?

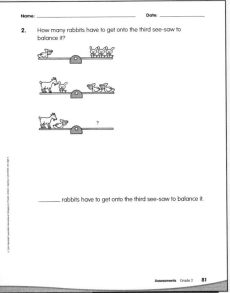

_____ rabbits have to get onto the third see-saw to balance it.

Assessments p. 81

---

3.   Uncle Pat builds three bird houses.
     Bird House A is 25 centimeters taller than Bird House B.
     Bird House B is 12 centimeters shorter than Bird House C.
     Bird House C is 126 centimeters tall.
     What is the height of Bird House A?

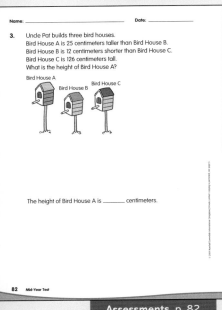

The height of Bird House A is _____ centimeters.

Assessments p. 82

Notes

ossary

Glossary

A

- **add**
  Put together two or more parts to make a whole.

$$5 + 3 = 8$$
part part whole

- **as heavy as**

The pear is as heavy as 7 marbles.

- **as much as**

Container A   Container B

Container A has 4 liters of water.
Container B has 4 liters of water.

Container A contains as much water as Container B.

B

- **bar models**

This is an example of a bar model.
Use bar models to help you add and subtract.

C

- **centimeter (cm)**
  Centimeter is a metric unit of length.
  Write cm for centimeter.

The crayon is 8 centimeters long.

- **compare**
  When you compare, you find out which set has more or fewer things.

I have 4 strawberries.   I have 6 pears.

Compare the number of pears and strawberries.

There are 2 more pears than strawberries.
There are 2 fewer strawberries than pears.

D

- **divide**
  Put into equal groups or share equally.

$$15 \div 3 = 5$$

Divide 15 dog biscuits into 3 equal groups of 5 dog biscuits.

- **division sentence**
  $6 \div 2 = 3$ is a division sentence.

- **dot paper**

This is dot paper.
It shows 3 rows of 2.

E

- **equal**
  Having the same amount or number.

3 is the same as 2 + 1.
$3 = 2 + 1$
equal sign

- **equal groups**
  Having the same amount in each group.
  You add equal groups to multiply.
  You subtract equal groups to divide.

$2 \times 2 = 4$
$4 \div 2 = 2$
There are 2 toy cars in each group.

- **expanded form**
  $400 + 30 + 2$ is the expanded form of 432.

F

- **fact family**
  $2 + 4 = 6$ $4 + 2 = 6$
  $6 - 2 = 4$ $6 - 4 = 2$

  This is a fact family.

G

- **gram**
  Gram is a metric unit of mass.
  Write g for gram.

The grapes have a mass of 880 grams.

- **greater than (>)**

$5 > 4$

5 is greater than 4.

- **greatest**

2   6   20

20 is the greatest number.

- **group**
  See **equal groups**.

H

- **heavier than**

The hen is heavier than the chick.

- **heaviest**

Flour   Sugar

Rice

The bag of rice is the heaviest.

- **height**

The height of the fence is 2 meters.

- **hundred**

10 tens = 100

hundreds

Hundreds	Tens	Ones
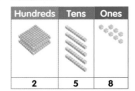		
2	5	8

258 = 2 hundreds 5 tens 8 ones

J

join

When you join sets, you add the number of objects in one set to the number of objects in another set to find the total.

I have 4 apples.

I have 3 apples.

4 + 3 = 7
They have 7 apples in all.
See **add**.

K

kilogram

Kilogram is a metric unit of mass. Write kg for kilogram.

The mass of the bag of oranges is 5 kilograms.

L

least

2   6   20

2 is the least number.

length

Describes how long something is.

A   B

To find the length of the drawing, measure from Point A to Point B.

See **meter** and **centimeter**.

less than (<)

2 < 5

2 is less than 5.

lighter than

The hen is lighter than the cat.

lightest

The bag of sugar is the lightest.

liter

Liter is a metric unit of volume.
Write L for liter.

This carton contains 1 liter of milk.

longer

Longer

Glossary p. 288

Glossary p. 289

longest

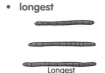
Longest

M

mass

How heavy an object or a set of objects is.

The mass of the potatoes is 3 kilograms.

See **kilogram** and **gram**.

measuring cup

This is a 1-liter measuring cup. It contains 1 liter of water.

measuring scale

This tool measures the mass of an object.

meter (m)

Meter is a metric unit of length.
Write m for meter.

The car is 3 meters long.

meterstick

A meterstick is used to measure length.

more than

There are more ☆ than ♥.

There is 1 more ☆ than ♥.

most

Joe   Luis   Pepe

Pepe has the most marbles.

multiplication sentence

3 × 3 = 9 is a multiplication sentence.

multiplication story

There are 2 children.
Each child has 3 oranges.

2 × 3 = 6
They have 6 oranges in all.

multiply

Put all the equal groups together.

There are 5 groups.
There are 2 muffins in each group.

5 × 2 = 10
There are 10 muffins in all.

Glossary p. 290

Glossary p. 291

- **place-value chart**

Hundreds	Tens	Ones

R————

- **regroup**
  Sometimes you need to regroup numbers when adding and subtracting.
  When you regroup numbers, you change:
  - 10 ones to 1 ten or 1 ten to 10 ones
  - 10 tens to 1 hundred or 1 hundred to 10 tens

  Example

  $$\begin{array}{r} \overset{1}{4}\,5 \\ +\ 3\,8 \\ \hline 8\,3 \end{array} \qquad \begin{array}{r} \overset{5}{6}\,{}^{1}5 \\ -\ 2\,7 \\ \hline 3\,8 \end{array}$$

- **related addition and subtraction facts**
  See **fact family**.

- **related multiplication facts**
  $5 \times 2 = 10$
  $2 \times 5 = 10$
  These are related multiplication facts.

- **related multiplication and division facts**
  $5 \times 2 = 10$
  $10 \div 5 = 2$
  $2 \times 5 = 10$
  $10 \div 2 = 5$
  These are related multiplication and division facts.

- **repeated addition**

  You can use repeated addition to find the number of turtles.

  $3 + 3 + 3 + 3 = 12$
  Groups of 3 are added 4 times.

  See **equal groups**.

- **repeated subtraction**

  You can use repeated subtraction to find the number of groups.

  $6 - 2 - 2 - 2 = 0$
  Groups of 2 are subtracted 3 times.

  See **equal groups**.

S————

- **set**
  A collection of items.

  There are 2 sets of toy airplanes.

- **share**
  Divide into equal groups.

- **shorter**

shorter

- **shortest**

shortest

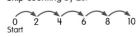

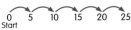

- **skip-count**
  Skip-counting by 2s:

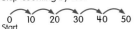
0 2 4 6 8 10
Start

  Skip-counting by 5s:

0 5 10 15 20 25
Start

  Skip-counting by 10s:

0 10 20 30 40 50
Start

- **standard form**
  657 is the standard form of 657.

- **subtract**
  Take away one part from the whole to find the other part.

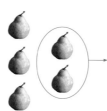

  $5 - 2 = 3$
  whole part part

T————

- **take away**
  See **subtract**.

- **taller**

taller

- **tallest**

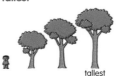
tallest

- **times**
  See **multiply**.

- **thousand**

  10 hundreds = 1,000

U————

- **unit**
  Units are used to measure objects.

 can be used to measure. It represents 1 unit.

  The bracelet is about 5 units long.

V————

- **volume**

  The amount of liquid a container has.
  See **liter**.

W

- **width**
  How wide an object is.

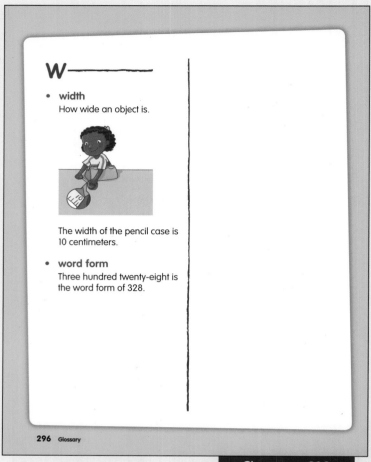

  The width of the pencil case is 10 centimeters.

- **word form**
  Three hundred twenty-eight is the word form of 328.

Glossary p. 296

Professional Resources Bibliography

erican Institutes for Research.® *What the United States*
Learn from Singapore's World-Class Mathematics
em. U. S. Department of Education Policy and Program
lies Services, 2005.

pin, Susan and Art Johnson. *Math Matters:*
erstanding the Math You Teach. Math Solutions
lications, 2000.

pin, Susan, Catherine. O'Connor, and Nancy Canavan
erson. *Classroom Discussions: Using Math Talk to*
Students Learn. Math Solutions Publications, 2003.

rles, Randall. *Teaching and Assessing of Mathematical*
lem Solving. Lawrence Earlbaum, 1989.

ley, Juanita. *Mathematics in the Early Years,* National
ncil of Teachers of Mathematics, 1999.

ley, Juanita. *The Young Child and Mathematics,*
onal Council of Teachers of Mathematics, 2000.

zales, Patrick, Juan Carlos Guzmán, Lisette Partelow,
Pahlke, Leslie Jocelyn, David Kastberg, and Trevor
ams. *Highlights From the Trends in International*
hematics and Science Study: TIMSS 2003.
Department of Education, National Center for
cation Statistics, 2004.

ert, J., T. Carpenter, E. Fennema, K. Fuson, D. Wearne,
urray, A. Olivier, and P. Human. *Making Sense:*
ching and Learning Mathematics with Understanding.
emann, 1997.

g, Dr. Ho Kheong. *The Essential Parents' Guide to*
ary Maths. Marshall Cavendish International, 2002.

Peng Yee, ed. *Teaching Primary School*
hematics: A Resource Guide. Singapore Math
cation Series, McGraw Hill Education, 2007.

Peng Yee, ed. *Teaching Secondary School*
hematics: A Resource Book. Singapore Math Education
es, McGraw Hill Education, 2008

Liping. *Knowing and Teaching Elementary*
hematics. Lawrence Earlbaum Associates, Inc., 1999.
rtin et al. *TIMSS 2003 International Mathematics Report:*
lings from IEA's Trends in International Mathematics
Science Study at the Eighth and Fourth-Grades.
itute of Education Sciences, 2004.

National Council of Teachers of Mathematics.
Curriculum Focal Points for Prekindergarten through Grade
8 Mathematics, 2006.

National Council of Teachers of Mathematics.
Principals and Standards for School Mathematics, 2000.

National Mathematics Advisory Panel. *Foundations for*
Success. U.S. Department of Education, 2008.

National Research Council. *Adding It Up: Helping Children*
Learn Mathematics. Washington, D.C., National Academy
Press, 2001

Ng Chye Huat, Juliana (Mrs.) and Mrs. Lim Kian Huat. *A*
Handbook for Mathematics Teachers in Primary Schools.
Marshall Cavendish International, 2003.

Polya, George. *How to Solve It.* Princeton University Press,
1945.

Richardson, Kathy. *Developing Number Concepts Books*
(Grades K-3): *Counting, Comparing, and Pattern Book 1;*
Addition and Subtraction, Book 2; Place Value,
Multiplication, and Division. Dale Seymour Publications,
1998.

Stigler, James W. and James Hiebert. *The Teaching Gap:*
Best Ideas from the World's Teachers for Improving
Education in the Classroom. The Free Press, 1999.

Sullivan, Peter, and Pat Lilburn. *Good Questions for Math*
Teaching: Why Ask Them and What to Ask. Math Solutions
Publications, 1997.

Van de Walle, John A. *Elementary and Middle School*
Mathematics: Teaching Developmentally. Allyn and Bacon,
2003.

Additional Answers

Student Book

Chapter 4

Lesson 1, Let's Practice (page 102)

1.
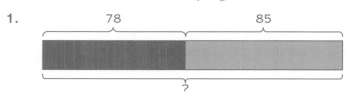

2.
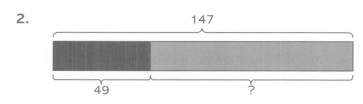

3.
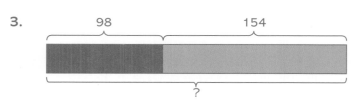

4.
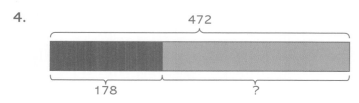

5.
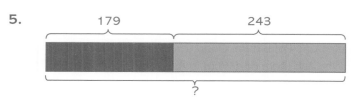

6.
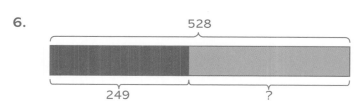

Lesson 2, Let's Practice (page 108)

1.
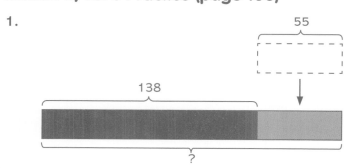

2.
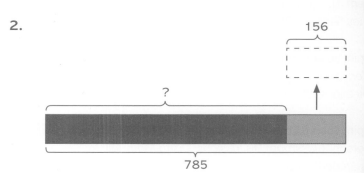

3.
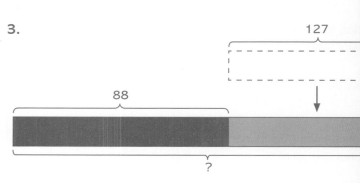

4.
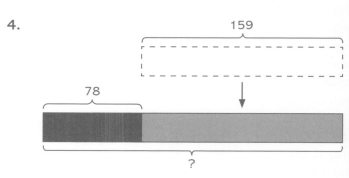

5.
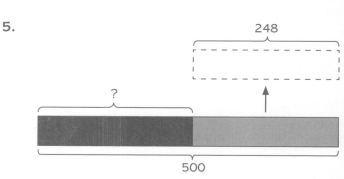

6.
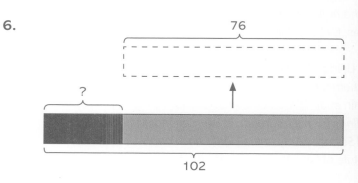

Lesson 3, Guided Practice (page 113)

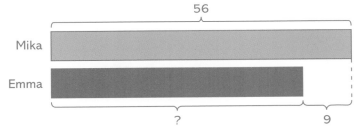

56

Mika

Emma

?   9

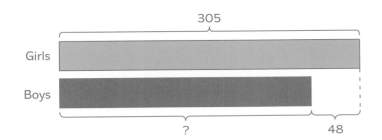

305

Girls

Boys

?   48

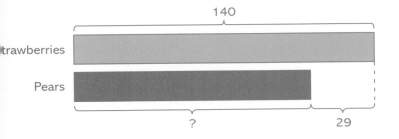

140

Strawberries

Pears

?   29

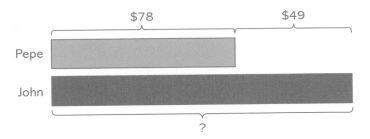

$78 $49

Pepe

John

?

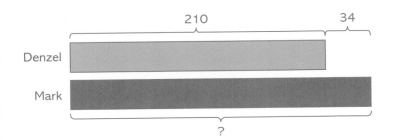

210   34

Denzel

Mark

?

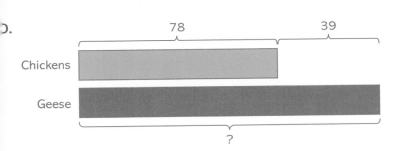

78   39

Chickens

Geese

?

Lesson 3, Let's Practice (page 114)

1.

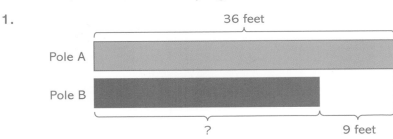

36 feet

Pole A

Pole B

?   9 feet

2.

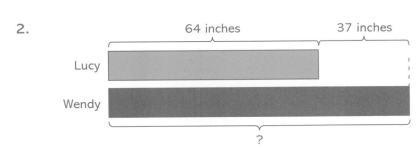

64 inches   37 inches

Lucy

Wendy

?

3.

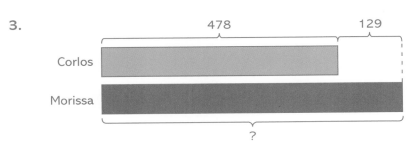

478   129

Corlos

Morissa

?

4.

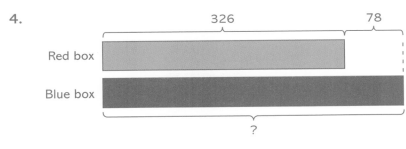

326   78

Red box

Blue box

?

5.

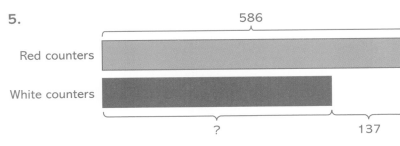

586

Red counters

White counters

?   137

6.

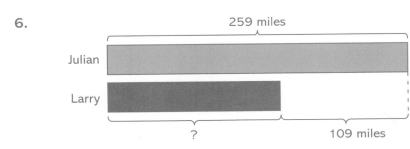

259 miles

Julian

Larry

?   109 miles

Chapter 8

Lesson 5, Let's Practice (page 258)

1.

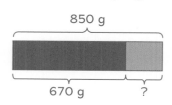

2.

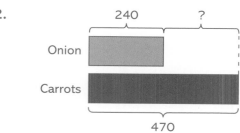

3.

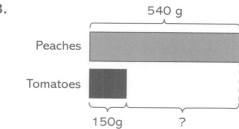

4.

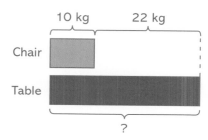

5.

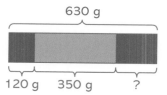

Chapter 9

Lesson 3, Let's Practice (page 281)

1.

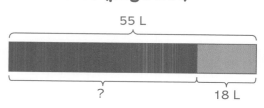

2.

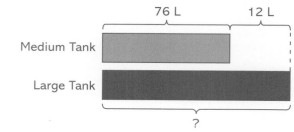

3.

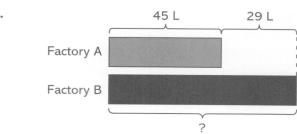

4.

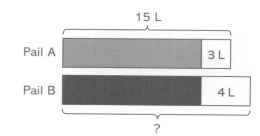

Put on Your Thinking Cap! (page 281)

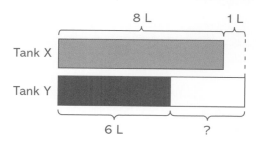

Workbook
Chapter 9

Math Journal (page 230)

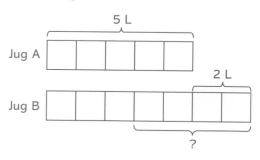

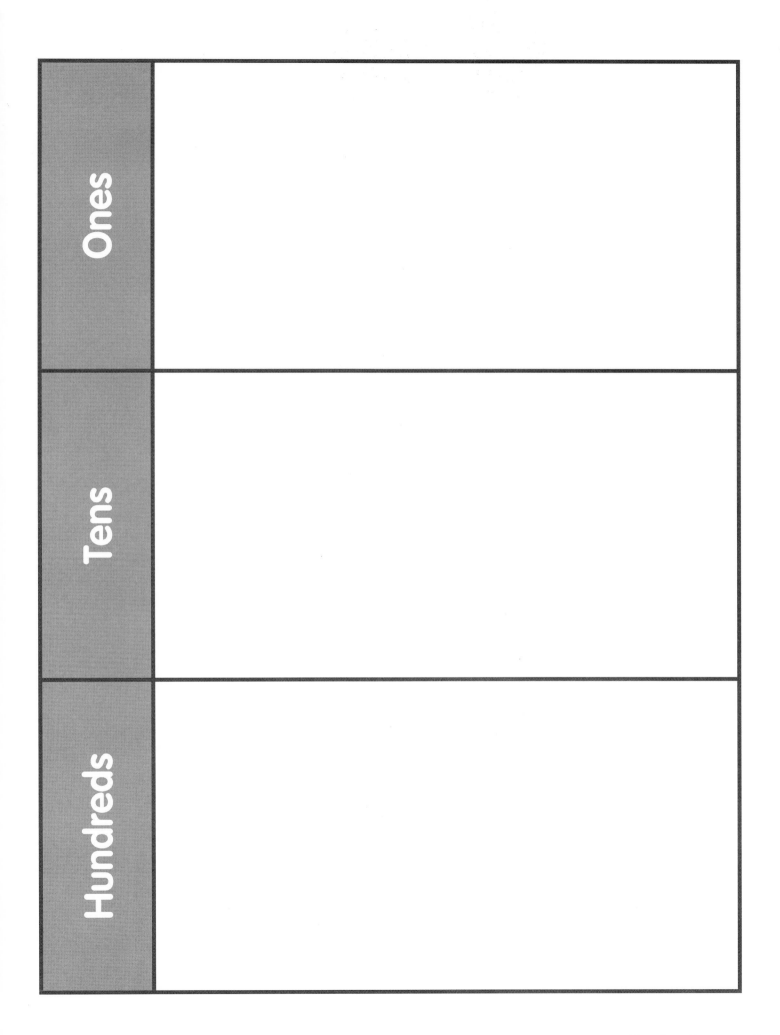

Hundreds	Tens	Ones

Hundreds	Tens	Ones

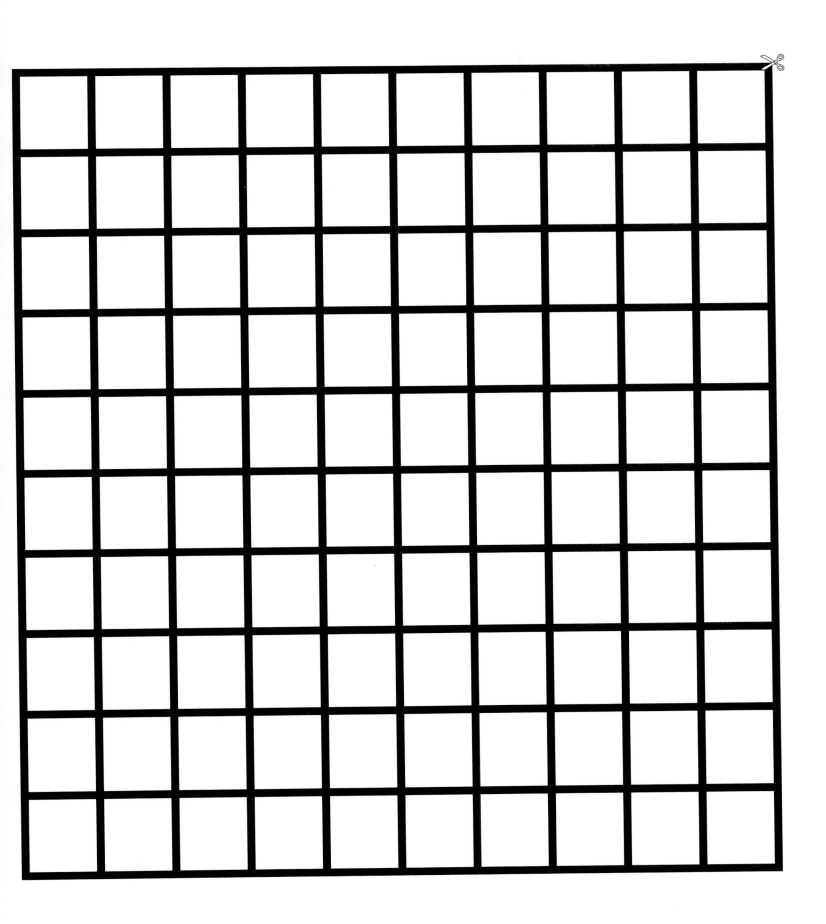

ase-Ten Cut-Outs   TR03
se with Student Book pp. 15, 44

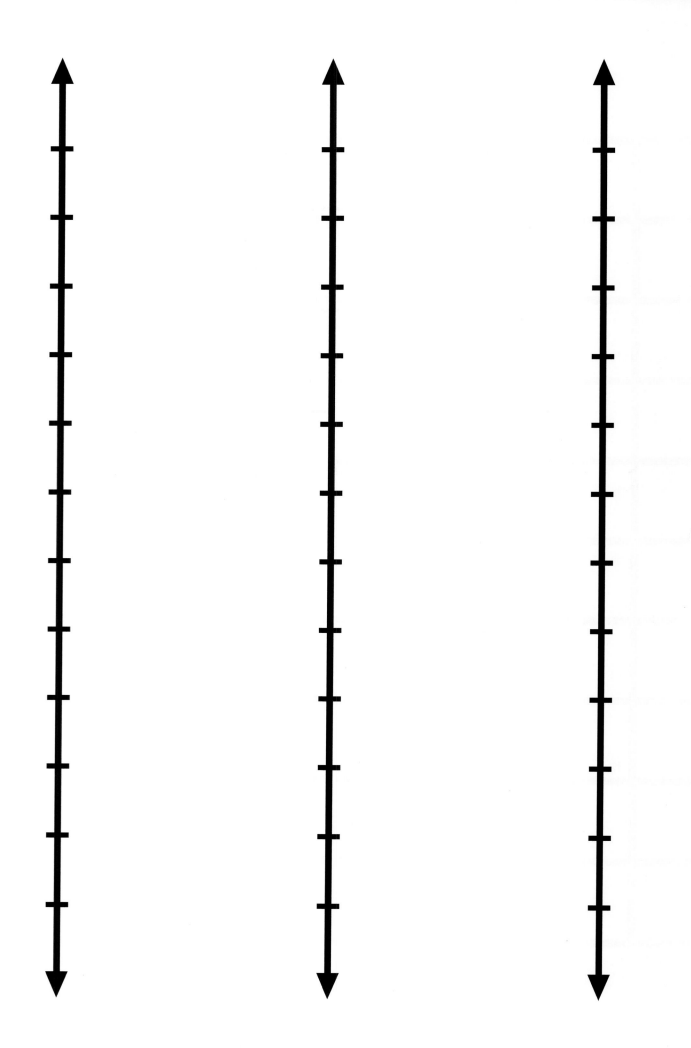

Blank Number Lines TR
Use with Student Book pp. 24, 27, 30,

Number	
1 more than the number	
1 less than the number	
10 more than the number	
10 less than the number	
100 more than the number	
100 less than the number	

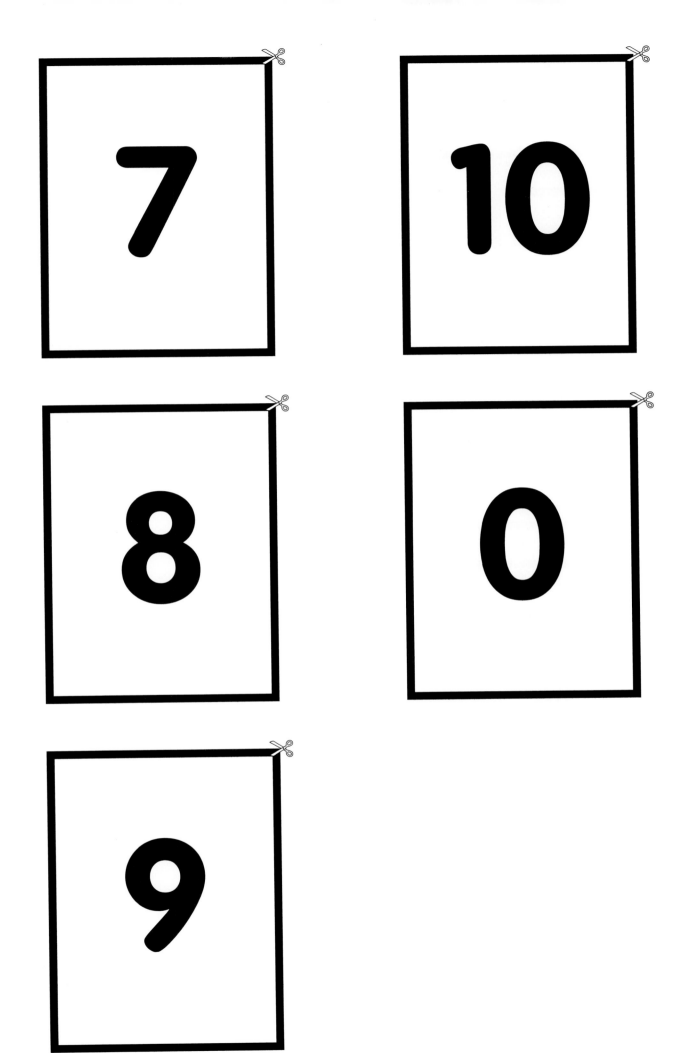

Number Cards   TR06
se with Student Book pp. 52, 166

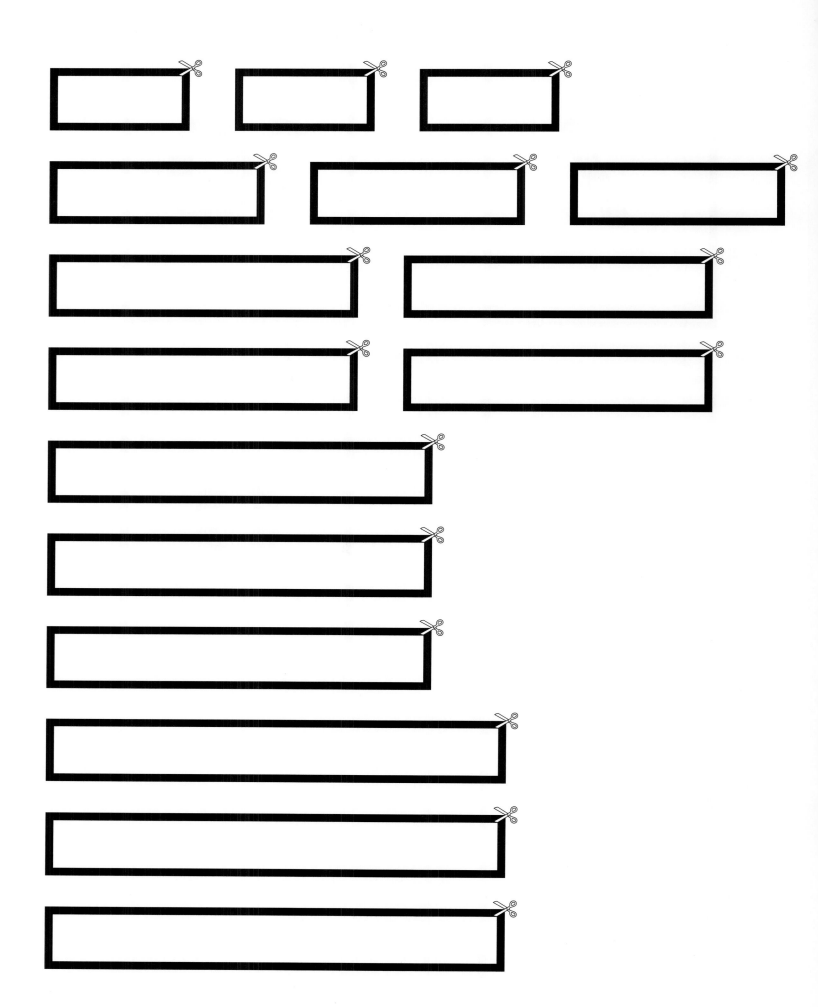

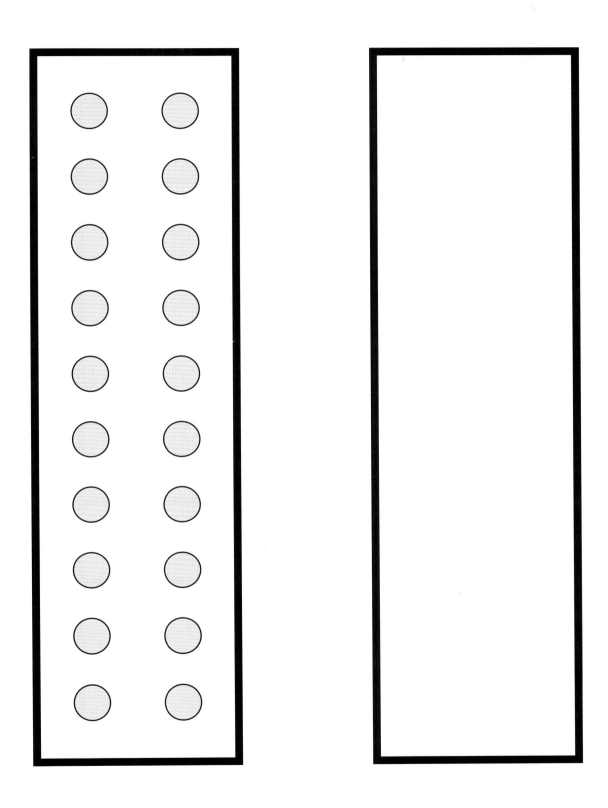

1	2	3	4	5	6	7	8	9	10
11	12	13	14	15	16	17	18	19	20
21	22	23	24	25	26	27	28	29	30
31	32	33	34	35	36	37	38	39	40
41	42	43	44	45	46	47	48	49	50
51	52	53	54	55	56	57	58	59	60
61	62	63	64	65	66	67	68	69	70
71	72	73	74	75	76	77	78	79	80
81	82	83	84	85	86	87	88	89	90
91	92	93	94	95	96	97	98	99	100

×	1	2	3	4	5	6	7	8	9	10
2										
5										

Dot Paper of 5 T
Use with Student Book p.

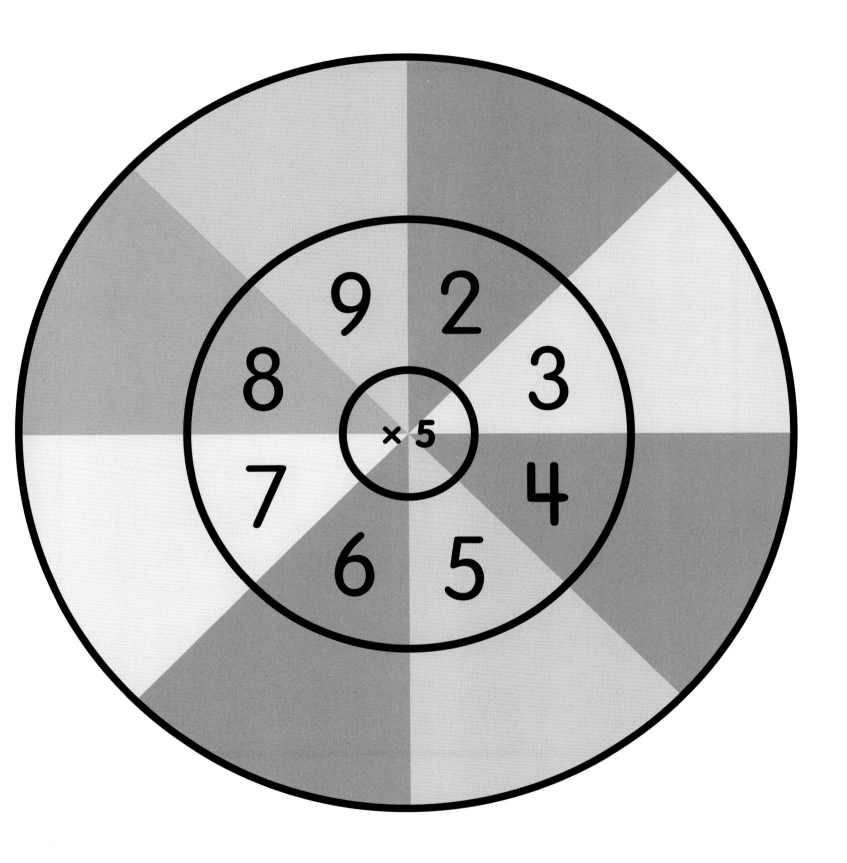

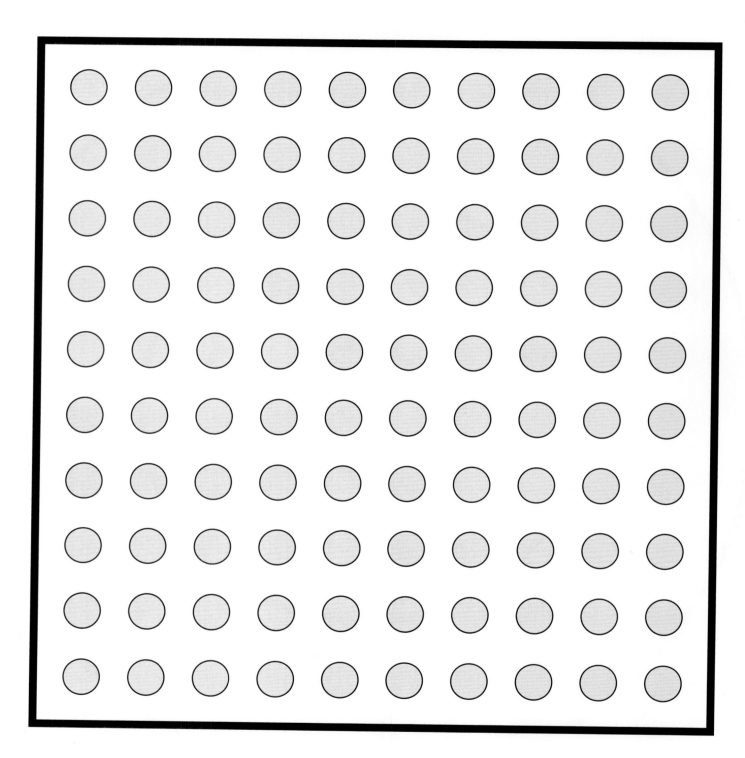

Dot Paper of 10 TR
Use with Student Book pp. 176, 1

Dot Paper of 10   TR13
Use with Student Book pp. 176, 177

	My guess	The length is between
The height of your classroom door	About 2 meters	2 meters and 3 meters
The width of your classroom door		
The width of a classroom window		
The length of your friend's arm span		
The length of your teacher's desk		
The width of your teacher's desk		
The length of the gym floor		
The width of the gym floor		

Object	Less than 1 meter	1 meter	More than 1 meter
Shoe	✓		

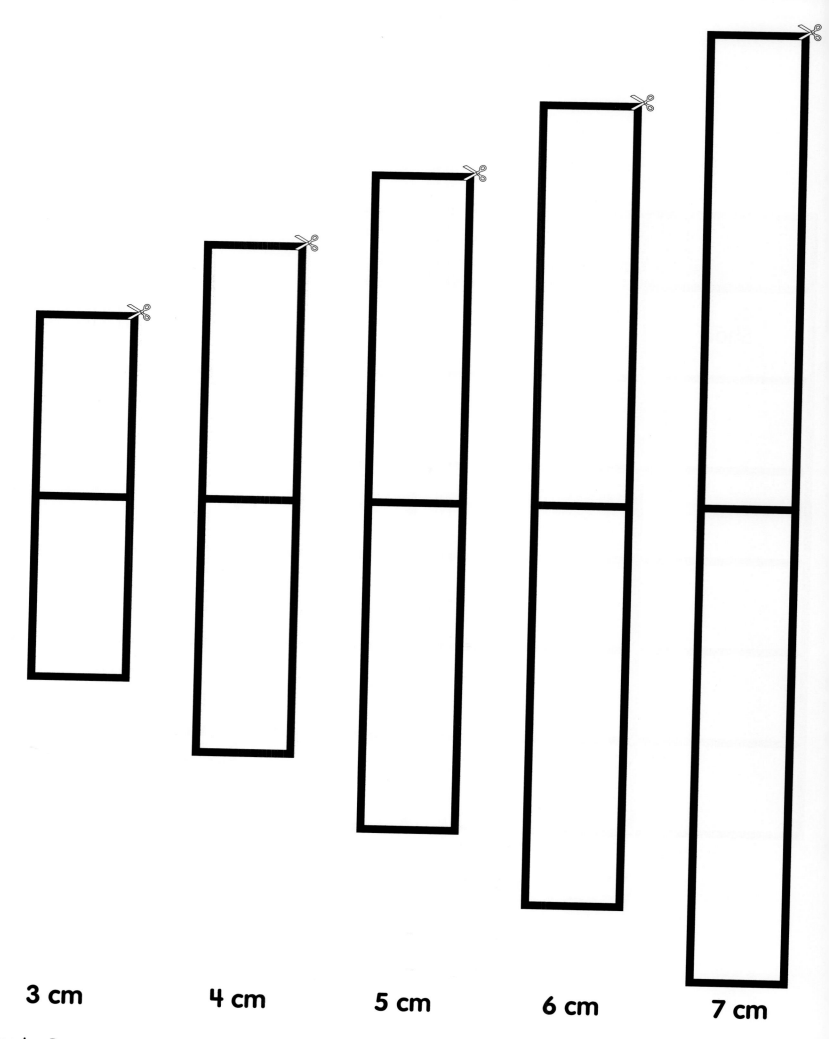

3 cm   4 cm   5 cm   6 cm   7 cm

Paper Strips of Varying Lengths TR15
Use with Student Book p. 20

Name of Object	My Guess			Actual Guess		
Name of Object	Less than 1 kg	1 kg	More than 1 kg	Less than 1 kg	1 kg	More than 1 kg
A bag of sugar						

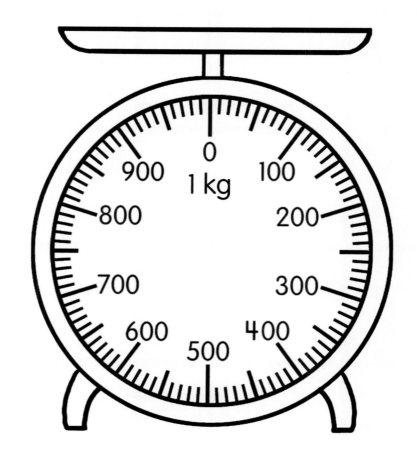

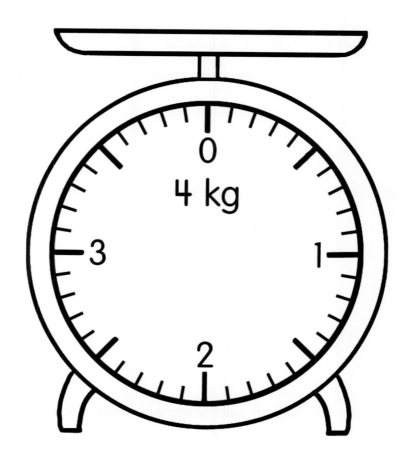

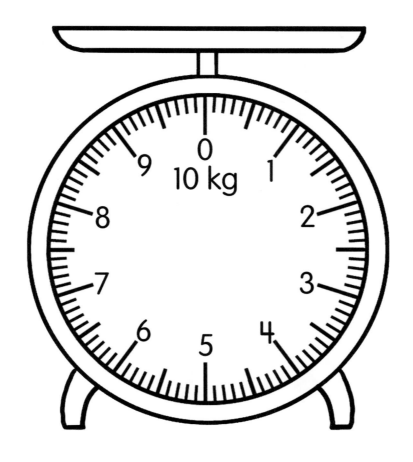

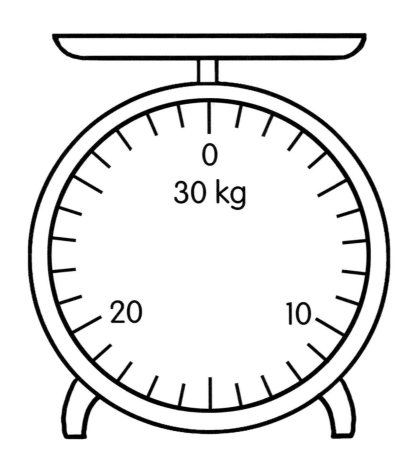

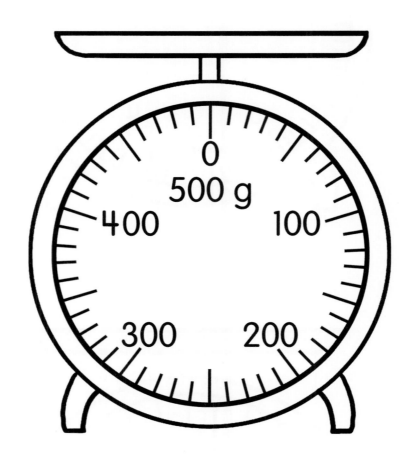

	My Guess	Actual Mass
Bag X		
Bag Y		
Bag Z		

Index for Book A and Book B

O

Odd numbers, 170–171, 172

Ones, *See* Place value

On-Going Diagnostic Assessment, *See* Assessment

On Level Learners, *See* Differentiated Instruction

On Your Own, 10, 17, 23, 31, 32, 33, 41, 45, 48A, 53, 54, 55, 66, 71, 77, 83, 87, 89, 90, 102, 108, 114, 121, 122, 129, 133, 141, 146, 147, 148, 155, 161, 167, 172, 178, 185, 186, 187, 195, 200, 210, 215, 220, 221, 223, 234, 239, 244, 252, 258, 259A, 260, 272, 277, 280, 281, 282; 7, 15, 19, 26, 37, 40, 61, 65, 69, 70, 82, 89, 96, 97A, 106, 110, 117, 121, 126, 127, 128, 136, 141, 149, 156, 157, 158, 169, 174, 178, 183, 189, 190, 191, 200, 205, 216, 217, 218, 231, 237, 241, 244, 246, 257, 264, 265, 266, 286, 291, 302, 303, 304

Operations, *See* Addition, Division, Multiplication, *and* Subtraction

Ordering, *See* Fractions, Length, Mass, Numbers, Time *and* Volume

P

Pacing, *Found in* Chapter Planning Guide *for each chapter in TE. See for example,* 1D, 42D, 73D, 100D, 130D

Part-part-whole, **96,** 97–102, 102A, 121A–121B, 123A, 123C, 216–218, 220, 256–258, 258A, 261, 261A, 278, 280–281, 281A, 283, 283D, 283F

Patterns, **26**
    in the Hundred Chart, 162–163, 167A, 173, 178A
    missing terms in table patterns (functions), **88–89,** 186
    multiplication chart, 159
    number
        creating, 29–30, 31A, 32A, 33A
        completing, 26–28, 31, 31A, 32, 32A, 33A, 89, 123C, 123D, 155, 178A, 188C
        describing 26, 29, 31A, 32, 89
        extending, 32
    skip-counting, *See* Multiplication
    shapes
        completing, 294, 299, 301–302, 302A
        creating, 292–293, 305
        describing, 294, 296, 302A
        repeating, 292–295, 298, 300, 302A
    picture graphs, **220**
        making, 232–234; 237A–237B
        reading, 224–231, 231A
        tally chart, 232, 234, 237A, 237B, 247A

Place value, **11**
    chart, 11, 15, 17A, 31A, 33A, 38–40, 42
    comparing numbers, **18,** 19–23, 23A, 33A
    expanded form, **12,** 13–17, 17A, 33, 33A, 123C, 283E
    hundreds, **9,** 11–17, 17A–17B, 18–31, 31A, 33A, 38–41, 41A, 42–43, 45A, 48A, 54A, 55A, 61–65, 66A, 68–69, 71, 71A, 72–75, 77, 77A, 79–82, 84–87, 88, 90–91, 91A, 123C, 283E
    identifying, 11–17, 17A–17B, 18–23, 23A, 24–31, 31A, 32A, 33A

ones, 11–17, 17A–17B, 18–31, 31A, 33A, 38–41, 41A, 42–43, 45, 45A, 48A, 54A, 55A, 61–65, 66A, 67–69, 71, 71A, 72–75, 77, 77A, 78–79, 81–82, 84–87, 88, 90–91, 91A, 283E
standard form, **12,** 13–17, 17A, 33, 33A, 123A
tens, 11–17, 17A–17B, 18–31, 31A, 33A, 38–41, 41A, 42–43, 45, 45A, 48A, 54A, 55A, 61–65, 66A, 67–69, 71, 71A, 72–75, 77, 77A, 78–82, 84–87, 88, 90–91, 91A, 123C, 283E
thousand, **7,** 10, 33A
word form, **12,** 13–17, 17A, 33, 33A, 283E
zeros in, 12–14, 16–17, 17A–17B, 21–23, 23A, 24, 27, 31A, 32A, 33A

Plane shapes, *See* Geometry

Practice
    Guided Practice, *throughout. See for example,* 7–9, 12–15, 21, 25, 27, 39–41, 43
    Let's Practice, *throughout. See for example,* 10, 16–17, 23, 30–31, 41, 45

Practice and Apply, Workbook pages, *Found in every lesson. See for example,* 7, 15A, 19A, 26A, 37A

Prerequisite skills
    Pretest, *see* Assessment: Prior Knowledge
    Quick Check, 4–5, 37, 59–60, 95, 126, 151–152, 191, 226–227, 265; 5, 44, 74, 102, 132, 163–165, 197, 223, 251–252, 269–270
    Recall Prior Knowledge, 2–4, 35–37, 57–59, 93–94, 125, 150, 190, 225–226, 263–264; 2–4, 43–44, 74, 101, 131, 160–162, 195–196, 221–222, 249–250, 268–269

Pretest, *see* Assessment: Prior Knowledge

Prior Knowledge, *see* Assessment

Problem of the Lesson, *Found in every lesson in TE. See for example,* 6, 9, 17, 20, 29

Problem Solving
    building mathematical knowledge, *See* Hands-On Activities *and* Let's Explore
    Put on Your Thinking Cap!, 32, 32A, 54, 54B, 88–89, 121C, 147, 147A, 186, 186A, 221, 221A, 259, 259A, 281, 281B; 39, 70, 70A, 97A, 127A, 128, 157, 158, 190, 190A, 193, 217, 217A, 240, 245, 265, 266, 303
    real-world problem solving, *See* real-world problems
    strategies
        act it out, 32A, 121C, 147A, 186A, 221A; 97, 265
        before-after, 121, 121C
        draw a diagram, 32A, 89, 121, 121C, 137, 147A, 186A, 259, 259A, 281; 97, 190
        guess and check, 54B, 89, 147A, 221; 70, 70A, 127, 190A
        look for patterns and relationships, 32, 32A, 147A, 186; 38, 158, 190, 190A, 245, 265, 303
        make a list, 54B, 89, 281B; 70, 70A
        make a systematic list, 54B, 89, 281B; 243
        make a table, 245
        make suppositions, 221A; 157, 158
        mental math (addition and subtraction), 8, 10–15, 15A, 19A, 26A

S

Notes

Notes